RITES OF PASSAGE
at $100,000 to $1 Million+

YOUR INSIDER'S STRATEGIC GUIDE TO
EXECUTIVE JOB-CHANGING
AND FASTER CAREER PROGRESS

JOHN LUCHT

THE VICEROY PRESS
NEW YORK, NY & RALEIGH, NC

Also by John Lucht

INSIGHTS FOR THE JOURNEY...
Navigating to Thrive, Enjoy, and Prosper in Senior Management

And EXECUTIVE JOB-CHANGING WORKBOOK

Senior Editor: Geri Sherriff
Editors: Pam Deutmeyer, Amanda Hawker

Library of Congress Cataloging-in-Publication Data is available upon request

ISBN 0-942785-33-9

“This is what I tell my friends.”

John Lucht

CONTENTS

RITES OF PASSAGE

at $100,000 to $1 Million+

CRITICAL ACCLAIM FOR *Rites of Passage . . .*

**Rites* has been reviewed and/or excerpted in scores of publications (several times in many), including: Business Week, Wall Street Journal, Forbes, USA Today, New York Times, Working Woman, Self, Boston Globe, Denver Post, Chicago Tribune, The Philadelphia Inquirer, Los Angeles Times, Chief Executive, Seattle Times, American Way, Financial World, Portland Telegram, Dallas Morning News, Omaha World-Herald, New York Daily News, Savvy, Salt Lake City Tribune, American Banker, Women's Wear Daily, Psychology Today, Minneapolis Star & Tribune, Industry Week, Newsday, Investor's Business Daily, St. Louis Post-Dispatch, Training, Publishers Weekly, San Antonio Express News, National Business Employment Weekly, Harper's Bazaar, Chicago Sun-Times, Board Room Reports, Newark Star-Ledger, Cleveland Plain Dealer, Baltimore Sun, El Paso Times, Wichita Eagle, Across the Board (The Conference Board), Men's Health, Personnel Executive, Training & Development Journal, Atlanta Journal / Constitution, Indianapolis Star & News, Executive Female, Manchester Union Leader, Personnel Administrator, Worcester Telegram, Akron Beacon Journal, Brandweek, Human Resource Executive, Madison State Journal & Capitol Times, Success, Albany Times Union, Career News (Harvard Business School Alumni Career Services), Corpus Christi Caller-Times, The Bricker Bulletin, Canadian Industrial Relations & Personnel Development, World Executive's Digest (serving Asia from Singapore), China Technology Market News (mainland China), and many more.

Chapter 1

Let's Proceed Together Toward Your Next Highly Paid Executive Position

For more than three decades I've recruited upper echelon executives for many of America's leading corporations. Now, I'd like to share with you what I've learned.

If you'll accept my help, together we'll move you into the highest and most satisfying position of your career, whether \$100,000+, \$300,000+, \$400,000+ or \$1 million+.

Very few executives ever figure out all that you're about to master. You'll have a career-building advantage from now until you retire.

***(See partial listing on prior page.)**

Who's in charge of your career? Obviously, you are.

Does that fact change with the changing economy? With the changing fortunes of your employer? Your field?

With attitudes toward your: Experience? Education? Age? Gender? Race? Sexuality? Appearance? Physical challenges? Family life? Employment status? Achievements? Mistakes?

No, not at all. Countless factors may influence *how* you manage your career. But who *cares* enough about you to take on that responsibility never changes.

And most assuredly, who's responsible does not change when you're the subject of a commercial transaction...in the hands of an executive recruiter of any kind, or a career or outplacement counselor.

Also just as surely not, when you're a Human Resource...in the hands of a company and its managers from the Chief Executive on down, whose interest is mainly in the corporation's wants and needs, not yours.

You know the bottom line. If you don't pay attention and make sure you're getting what you really deserve and want from your career, you have no one else to blame.

Which brings us to the "Rites of Passage." Those so called "primitive societies" had a great idea when they took their young men and women off to the side for a few days or weeks and gave them knowledge that otherwise would have taken years to acquire.

As the saying goes, "We get too soon old and too late smart." With respect to career matters, let's fix that. And since we can't start yesterday, let's start now.

Rites of Passage

For over 35 years, I've been filling high-level executive positions for some of America's leading corporations. Day after day, in good times and bad, I've observed...and brokered...those pivotal company-to-company transitions that launch a fast-rising career into higher orbit, and that restore momentum when an executive is underutilized or let go.

And whether the scenario is doing-better-elsewhere...moving-up-in-the-company...or seizing-victory-from-a-setback, what I've observed is that a very few exceptionally aware and self-secure executives...maybe the top 1/2 of 1%...seem to have a virtuoso's mastery of the job-changing process. Exceptionally able in doing their job, they're just as able when it comes to changing jobs.

They deliberately attract the attention of the top executive recruiters...something I want you to do, too. As a result, they're periodically told about attractive opportunities, many of which they may turn down. That is, until there's something really worth moving for...or unemployment and an immediate need for a new position. Then they snap into action, and win out over tough competition. They don't move too often. But when they do, their careers are strengthened.

Even when they refuse to look at something a recruiter proposes, they build up future career momentum. The recruiter who called them realizes how well situated and fast rising they are with their current employer, so he or she resolves to offer something much better next time.

These people also take advantage of web technology to speed and improve their career management. They're wised up to the fact that headhunters—from the sleaziest to the most prestigious—now use the web in ways that *look* similar, but must be treated differently.

Yet, successful as these executives are in handling recruiters, they also know when it serves their self-interest to ignore them entirely and go straight to the potential employer...something you too should do under the proper circumstances.

And when contacting a company directly, they shrewdly choose between two clearly differentiated routes. One, classic and low-tech, approaches the decision-maker. The other, more web-based, usually enters through the HR department.

Indeed, it's knowing all of today's techniques and how differently they should be used under similar-appearing circumstances, that makes the most successful executives as impressive in advancing their careers as they are in doing their work.

These able and observant men and women have mastered the art of executive job-changing, whether at $100,000+, $300,000+ or $1 million plus. At the executive level, the rules and methods change. There are more initiatives to take, more contacts and opportunities to explore. But also more pitfalls and misinformation.

So you and I are about to do something we saw years ago in Sociology class. Remember how those "primitive societies" took their "initiates" aside and gave them a cram course in what they ought to know for future well-being? They got life's practical knowledge once-and-for-all-in-a-hurry, instead of painfully by trial-and-error over the next 20 years. And of course, they also learned secrets they'd never have found out, unless an insider told them.

"Rites of Passage" is what the professor called that process, and you and I are beginning a modern version of the same thing.

Here in *RITES*, I'll hand you all the advanced-level job-changing wisdom I've picked up from the executives who do it best. To that I'll add behind-the-scenes information on the executive search industry which even they haven't had access to. And, to complete the package, I'll help you get the good—and not the bad—from the current technology.

The result is a comprehensive cram course in accelerating your career. It's "Rites of Passage," updated and upscaled for you...an old idea in a new time and place.

But before we go any further, let's look at one of the most important benefits of knowing how to change jobs advantageously.

It's the self-confidence to push for faster advancement right where you are.

Realizing that you are building powerful job-changing skills and contacts, you'll feel a lot freer to have periodic frank discussions with your current superiors, letting them know that you feel ready to step ahead, and drawing out their unvarnished reactions to your self-appraisal.

There's truth in the old saying, "The squeaking wheel gets the grease." The person who's doing an excellent job and has the self-confidence to ask about the company's tentative timetable for his own promotion is much more likely to get the next higher-echelon position that opens up than his equally-fine-but-silent co-worker. The reason:

> "We felt we had to do something for Jason pretty soon, or we might lose him."

And the person whose career is marked by a *series* of fully deserved but sooner-than-her-superiors-might-have-preferred promotions is the one who winds up "way ahead of her age level" in the corner office. By that time her equally able, hardworking, and loyal co-workers have stopped asking, "What's Kate got that I haven't?" It's obvious:

> "She's just got more on the ball. Why, she's moving up through the organization like a shot! She knows where she wants to go and she isn't wasting any time getting there. Mark my words, someday she'll be running this company!"

Momentum is its own reward. Momentum is also a self-fulfilling prophecy.

Kate's superiors don't want to be faulted by top management for not recognizing an exceptional talent when they see one...nor for petty jealousy. So they cheer her along, either as ready now to take their job so they can move up or, if that's not possible, as an ideal candidate for a higher-level position somewhere else in the company:

> "She's ready for more responsibility right now. Unfortunately, I just don't have it for her, unless you want to give her my job. She could handle it!"

Kate's current supervisor, Steve Steady, is being shrewd, not stupid, when he talks like that. The reply he gets proves it:

> "Certainly not, Steve. You're doing great right where you are. In fact, one of your many fine talents is your ability to recognize and help groom the future leaders of this company. You stand out like a beacon in contrast to some of the other old guys around here who'd feel threatened by a young superstar like Kate. That's why we like to put our up-and-comers through your department...to get your solid knowledge of the business, without holding them back and dampening their enthusiasm."
>
> "Incidentally, Kate speaks well of you too, Steve. She'll probably be giving you some promotions as the years go by!"

That's the way it works. When career momentum takes hold, it builds. Ironically, having the self-confidence that comes from knowing you can change jobs efficiently, even when others cannot, *will strengthen your resolve to press for maximum progress where you are.*

But please...no blackmail!

Don't misunderstand. I'm not talking about actually interviewing for an outside job, getting an offer, confronting your employer, and eliciting a counteroffer. That's a bad idea. Even if you get by with it once or twice... "three strikes and you're out." Nobody likes a blackmailer. And no one earmarks him for the future presidency of the company.

In fact, after a pivotal executive is "saved" by a counteroffer, he's usually not looked upon in quite the same favorable way. Instead of being slated for important future positions, he tends to be left out of organizational planning. Or he's categorized as an *alternate*:

"Well, *if Ron's still with us*, we could *also* consider him for that job."

No, don't come in with an outside offer you hope your company will meet or beat. It serves you right if they just wave goodbye, and you're headed for a job and a company you don't really want.

Instead, take this approach. Tell your boss:

> YOU: "Got a call today from a recruiter looking for a Vice President of Marketing for a $5 billion specialty foods company. I told him I wasn't interested, but I'd call back with some suggestions. He didn't name the company. Who do you think it might be?"
>
> HE: "Maybe NutriCroft. They're about that size and they just put in a new President. Maybe she's reorganizing. Who called you?"
>
> YOU: "A guy I know, Hunter Probe, at Randolph Ripley Associates. I like it here, and I haven't personally been interested in anything he's had so far. But I've pointed him toward other people, so he keeps calling. Remember my friend Carol Stevens? Hunter put her into Clarendon Foods as Marketing VP...a big jump for her."
>
> HE: "I didn't know you knew anyone at Randolph Ripley Associates. How'd you meet Hunter Probe?"
>
> YOU: "Oh, he just called one day last fall. He was looking for a head of Brand Management at Modern Consumer Foods, and some people mentioned my name. I told him I like this company, and he'd have to come up with a lot bigger job than that to attract me away. However, they were offering a bushel of money...about $80,000 more than I'm making now, even after that big raise you pushed through for me in January."
>
> HE: "You never told *me* any of this!"
>
> YOU: "I didn't see any need to, Bill. I knew you were doing everything you could to fix the salary situation. No point in trying to put pressure on you. What I'm really hoping, is for you to get Sally's job when she retires next summer, so maybe I can have your job."
>
> HE: "*You and three other people!* And they've all been here a lot longer than you have. But I must admit, Randi, you're doing *excellent* work. You've got our attention. We're planning a great future for you. In fact, when Alex approved your raise, he said..."

Now you've got it right. You can't whack a relationship into place with a sledge hammer. You're likely to shatter it. A gentle tap on the shoulder will do far more good...and less harm...than a big dramatic hit.

It's almost never too late for the right move.

And it's possible to look outside, without risking the job you have.

Let's go back to Kate's boss, Steve Steady, the older fellow whose department the company likes to put its "young superstars" through...to get his "solid knowledge of the business, without holding them back and dampening their enthusiasm." Obviously the company likes him a lot better than it does "some of the other old guys around here who'd feel threatened by a young superstar like Kate."

But is Steve happy? Is he enjoying enough status, and making enough money, to justify relegating himself to "unsung hero"? He appears to have some job security. But does he have job satisfaction?

Maybe not. Maybe somewhere under Steve's 25-years-with-the-company recognition pin beats the heart of a striver, who still craves challenge, status, and rewards. Actually, he's in quite a good position to pursue them. True, he's 56. But he's also more comfortably established and more mobile than a younger person. His pension is vested. His home is nearly paid for. And his youngest child is almost out of college.

Steve can afford to take risks. Since he's no longer on the "fast track," his compensation isn't particularly high. Even if Steve has bad luck in the first outside job he takes, he can probably duplicate his earnings in *some* subsequent position. And knowing Steve's ability and commitment, *he won't fail!*

Moreover, the outside world may be receptive. Steve has a consummate knowledge of his industry, gained in one of its most respected companies. Chances are, a hot young growth company could greatly profit from his experience...and possibly even from his mature image, which will lend credibility to sales and/or investor presentations led by an under-30 CEO. Also, a dynamic, youthful company may provide an exciting equity opportunity that Steve could never hope for where he is.

Steve's problem is to identify his best outside opportunities *without letting his employer know he's looking*. How to do so by using both traditional and web methods is something else you and I will cover before we part company at the end of this book.

For some executives, even a lateral move can be attractive...

and sometimes a counteroffer should be accepted.

Let's look in on Steve Steady's 54-year-old sister Sandra, who runs a large out-of-the-mainstream department in an altogether different company. Unlike Steve, Sandra is a specialist. Aided by a leading search firm, the Chief Operating Officer of a competitor is asking her to join Next-Co in the very same job she's always handled brilliantly at Current Corp.

The incentive to switch: Considerably higher compensation...about 15% more than industry-average pay for her job, whereas Sandra's now making 25% less than industry-average. That's actually a 53% improvement in cash, plus a company car, which she doesn't have now.

Should she accept? She'd be a fool not to. In fact, Sandra resigned yesterday.

But her boss, shocked and upset, asked her "not to say anything about this to anyone else for 24 hours, and until you and I have talked again." Obviously, there's a counteroffer in the wind.

Usually it's a big mistake to forego a leap-ahead opportunity and stay in response to a counteroffer.

But Sandra may be an exception.

As a specialist, she now heads her function in one of the largest corporations. She's gone about as far as she can reasonably expect to go. Unfortunately, for that reason and because her superiors have assumed that no outside company would identify and grab her, Current Corp. has been neglecting her compensation. Now that she's resigned to join Next-Co, Sandra's superiors are suddenly waking up:

> "Face it, Adam, we've been getting by with murder. We knew Sandra loved her job, and loved that department she's built. We figured she'd never try to leave, and we never imagined that anyone would swoop in here looking for her. So we haven't been paying what she's worth. She'll be getting $345,000, including first year's bonus *guaranteed*, plus a car, plus options. You know what we're paying her? Assuming she earns full bonus, $232,500!"
>
> "If we have to replace Sandra, we'll probably have to come up with about the same money they're offering which, with the car,

> comes to more than $370,000. And it'll cost us at least an extra $100,000 just to hire a recruiter to look for somebody."
>
> "Therefore, I say let's hit Sandra with $400,000, including bonus, and no car, since we have a policy against cars. But let's also throw in an EVP title, which will qualify her for Class A stock options. And let's include a new office for her when we remodel the East Wing. Let's give Sandra the recognition she deserves. We've got the best person in the industry! Let's at least try to keep her."

Well, Sandra, under your unusual circumstances, maybe they're coming up with a counteroffer you should seriously consider. It's too bad your bosses didn't "get religion" sooner. But now that they realize you're visible to the outside world, they're not going to be so casual about your "care-and-feeding" again. You love the department you've built. Maybe you should stay.

Obviously, Sandra, your superiors don't even suspect that *you drew yourself* to the attention of the executive recruiting community.

And we won't tell them. Congratulations. Mission accomplished!

Out of a job?

That's when you can take full advantage of all the "Rites of Passage" right away.

Nearly all of the most successful senior executives I know have been out of work at least once in their careers...and many, several times. The difference between these "winners" and others less successful, is in how creatively and aggressively they've handled their unemployment. Much of the help in this book comes from observing them. Read on, and you'll soak up their knowledge and experience.

On the other hand, by far the most misunderstood job-changing resource... at all points of an executive's career...and *especially when he or she is out of work*...is the executive search industry, including its widely misunderstood role in the online job sites. You can't get past the myth and misinformation, until you have an insider's perspective on upper-level recruiting. And that's what you'll have when you're halfway through this book.

Later, when the remainder of this book has prepared you for it, you can take a postgraduate course. It's in Appendix I. See a search through the recruiter's eyes. When you've finished *Rites,* you'll know as much about recruiting as if you've actually been a recruiter yourself.

"Power User" of the Web? Or Web Shy?

Probably you're somewhere in between...fully adept, but not quite a savant. As we cover all the main issues in managing an executive career—most of which are *not* high-tech—I'll suggest web-based ways to improve the process. I'll also show you the best for your purposes of the many—currently estimated at over 80,000—job sites on the web covering, in general, their usefulness and pitfalls. Also, I'll show you *RITE*Site, the minimally-commercial Executive Information Exchange I've set up to assist *RITES* readers and recruiters.

To Investigate: Access an infinite fund of information on companies, industries, people, professions, salaries, geographic data...the resources are endless. Also turbocharge your networking. Use the web to locate key contacts you've known but lost touch with, and also to figure out whom you know that knows—and hence might introduce you to—someone you should meet.

To Deliver: Use the web as an alternative to the Postal Service in making yourself known. Participate wisely in the online employment sites. These days, they're infinitely numerous. Informed, you can achieve the right balance of safety, dignity and confidentiality vs. all-out hazard-ignoring haste.

So now you know what we'll be doing together.

Let's just glance at a bit more of what's to come, and then we'll get down to business.

By the time you complete these "Rites of Passage," you'll clearly know the motives and methods of every sector of the "people business." Everyone from the headhunting firm that got you your first couple jobs after college (who today call themselves a "management consulting" or "executive search" firm)...right through the most prestigious recruiters...to the job websites which—if you can discriminate among them—merit your participation...to the "outplacement" and "executive marketing" segments of the industry.

As a mobility-seeking executive, you're likely to be involved with all of the "professions" that move executives around. Therefore, it's worthwhile to take this once-and-for-all-in-a-hurry opportunity to see how you should deal with each to best serve *your self-interest*, which often does not match theirs. For example, one of many practical suggestions is as simple as this:

"Watch the money change hands!"

That's a good rule in general. And especially helpful, when you're the subject of a commercial transaction.

Of course, dealing with "professionals" in the "people business" isn't the only way to proceed.

We'll polish every facet of your game...from handling your own personal contacts...to "networking" among helpful strangers...to telephone technique with recruiters to smoke out whether what they're calling about is in your best interest...to researching and contacting potential employers on the web... to creating a really persuasive resume...to interviewing with both employers and recruiters for your maximum advantage...to conducting a direct mail campaign or its paperless on-line alternative...to negotiating your employment agreement. And lots more.

Whatever could put you a thought or a step ahead in the advancement of your career we'll cover. And wherever a "professional" in the "people business" may be a step ahead of you, we'll even the odds. Fully prepared, you can overcome your inevitable challenges—and challengers—on your very personal route to maximum career success.

Chapter 2

Five Main Ways to Go

I can't know your situation at this moment.

Your degree of job satisfaction may range anywhere from totally delighted to utterly disgusted. You may even be unemployed and in the midst of an all-out search for your next position.

You may be so pleased with your current employer and your progress that you don't want to hear about any opportunity unless it can advance your career at least three to five years. At the other extreme, you may be delighted to hear about anything even remotely close to your latest job.

Over the years, your circumstances will vary. And you'll probably come back to this book at different stages of your career. Therefore, we'll proceed on the broadest possible assumption...that you're interested in everything you can possibly know about changing jobs. This is a complex and fascinating subject, but it centers on just a few fundamentals.

The Five Methods
Four are classics. One is newer.

Until nearly the end of the '90s there were only four basic routes to an executive-level job outside your current company. Anything else was a minor variation.

1. Personal Contacts...getting in touch with people you already know.
2. Networking...getting in touch with a series of people others refer you to.
3. Executive Recruiters...dealing with the various species of "headhunters."
4. Direct Mail...letting the Postal Service take your message more places than you can visit and phone.

And then came a fifth way.

5. The web...taking advantage of technology in job-hunting and career management.

With No. 5—the Web—a modern medium crowds out older ones, as technology is applied to Nos. 3 and 4.

Look at Monster.com and the others. They're incredibly cost-efficient. Newspapers have huge costs—reporters, editors, paper, printing, delivery, etc. Websites have none of those expenses. They're highly profitable and these days gross hundreds of millions of dollars and run TV ads on the Super Bowl. With low overhead as their competitive advantage, the websites have nearly driven most newspapers out of the executive employment advertising business.

First, No. 3 - the Executive Recruiter Dimension: Who's advertising job openings on the employment websites? The same people who formerly used newspaper ads...headhunters (No. 3) and corporations. Later, we'll discuss headhunters in detail. We'll observe the various games they play, and determine how you can protect and advance yourself, regardless of what they're up to. Just remember that almost all of the headhunters on nearly all of the job sites are the very same type of firm—one of only two types—and perhaps *not* the type that best fits your needs.

And Secondly, No. 4 - the Direct Mail Dimension: What are you doing when you post your resume on a Monster.com-type website? Basically, the same thing you're doing when you mail an unsolicited resume to a search firm or a company. You're *sending out* your information in the hope of reaching someone who'll have or get an opening you fit. Now, however, you're using wires instead of paper and stamps. And, of course, zapping is a lot quicker, easier, and cheaper than mailing.

But who are your recipients?

Are they the same firms you'd address your envelopes to in a well-thought-out direct mail campaign? No! Nearly all of the headhunters paying the modest fees required to post their openings on an employment site and to view its resume database are *not* the ones you would intentionally mail to.

Why not? Well, just hang on. We'll cover that...and much more.

Structuring Our Time Together

Before we're finished, we'll not only cover the essentials, we'll also sweep up a number of minor related possibilities...such as answering on-paper advertisements which now are mostly in trade publications, not newspapers. We'll also examine an intriguing alternative that doesn't aim for a corporate payroll but may put you there anyway...becoming an independent consultant. Plus many other matters, such as resumes, interviews, "outplacement," the implications of e-mailing vs. "snail-mailing" your paperwork, and all the issues involved in negotiating your compensation. But let's format our discussion around the five most basic and powerful job-changing methods.

Each of those five will get enough attention to exploit all of its possibilities and avoid its pitfalls: one chapter each, for Personal Contacts and Networking; plus six for Executive Recruiters and three for Direct Mail (and a sophisticated alternative to it). We'll point out web implications everywhere they're an option throughout those eleven chapters. Then we'll bow to the web with its own chapter. Those matters will take up over half of our time together...12 of 19 chapters...so I've organized with them. But there's lots more to know, and we'll deal with it all.

The End Game

You've played video games. They're usually pretty vicious. And often the objective is to be the last person standing. Somewhat the same thing happens when a very desirable job is filled. There are hundreds of candidates to begin with, and your goal is (1) to get into the game and (2) to survive all other contenders.

Does that mean you should play tough and nasty?

Not at all! But bear this in mind: you will almost never be the sole prospect for any promotion or new job. So get ready to reach out for whatever you desire *and deserve*, recognizing that others will be desirous and deserving too. The outcome will depend to some extent on your skills as a player. Please play fair. Be a person you can fully respect at all times. But don't hesitate to become skillful...and play *to win*.

WHAT'S GOING ON HERE?

RITES is not quite what it appears to be.

It looks like a reference book...and it will be when you come back to it later.

But right now it's more of a novel.

So kick off your shoes, relax, and go straight through. That's the only way to get what's really in *RITES*.

If you read 100% by skipping around, you'll see about 50% of what's going on...and not even the better half, because the real story is sequential and beneath the surface.

Chapter 3

Personal Contacts: Pursuing the People You Know

As you soar above $100,000 and far beyond, you acquire something you didn't have early in your career...*valuable personal contacts*.

Pick up the phone. Senior officers at most of your competitors will accept your call or call you back.

So will lots of other high-level people who do business in your industry... from direct customers, wholesalers, and distributors...to suppliers of raw materials, components, sub-assemblies, and packaging...to providers of services such as engineering, contract manufacturing, accounting, banking, advertising, management consulting, market research, and PR.

A few of these people have hire-and-fire power over jobs that could be excellent next steps in your career. And nearly all are in a position to hear about openings that might interest you, and possibly even to make an appropriate introduction.

Personal contacts are the resource you'll turn to first, when you think of changing jobs.

People you already know are your #1 asset.

If you can get your ideal job just by talking to them, why do anything more?

There's a big difference between talking to someone you've known awhile... possibly very well, and maybe for years...and talking to a stranger whose name you've just been given. In the next chapter, we'll discuss "networking" the strangers you meet at the suggestion of someone else. But let's start right now by getting in touch with people you already know.

True personal contact has advantages over Networking, Executive Recruiters, Direct Mail, and even your usual interface with the web.

Greater Impact. Talking with friends and associates is easier and more effective than with strangers.

Better Confidentiality. Long before you're ready to "go public," you can speak to the people you trust.

Less Need to Persuade and Sell. People who already know your professional skills and like you personally don't have to be convinced.

Maximum Efficiency. Why bother writing a resume? And why deal with letters, emails, job boards, phone calls, and appointments...if you don't have to?

No question about it. If you can get the career-advancing job you want through Personal Contact, it's the quickest, easiest, and most pleasant way to go.

Unfortunately, *LUCK* plays a starring role in what you accomplish through personal contacts. *Who* do you know? And does your inquiry come at the *opportune time* when someone you know happens to have, or know of, the right position? If so, great! If not, you'll have to proceed to other job-changing methods we'll discuss later on.

But now let's look at my all-time favorite "case history" of successful job-changing through a Personal Contact. We'll see one of America's most gifted marketing-oriented general managers get into the position of needing a job change...and then actually achieving one. And he does both in what I believe to be the prevailing world-record time. These events happened. Only the identities have been changed to protect the guilty:

> Several years ago Matt Marketczar, a suave, marketing-oriented general manager from New York City, became President of SpecialFlavor Foods Co. in a smallish city we'll call Elmdale. SFC markets nationwide under a famous brand name, just like any other big corporation. However, it's actually a cooperative owned by growers of the main ingredient of the company's products.
>
> Unfortunately, at the time Matt arrived, America's appetite for foods containing the key ingredient was declining, and supply was increasing...trends that threatened the financial health of the farmers who owned the company.
>
> Happily, within just a few years Matt accomplished a management miracle. He brought out hugely successful new products based on the special ingredient, and producer prices rose 300%, while costs declined slightly. The growers were delighted.
>
> Matt was assisted by his brilliant secretary, Lucy Local, wife of Larry Local, a lifetime Elmdale resident. Besides accompanying Matt to his frequent business meetings in the nearby town of Midday, which were usually held at the Midday Motel, Lucy also took care of his expense reports, which she documented by saving his American Express bills and vouchers from Midday Motel.
>
> On Monday of the eventful week that interests us, Matt determined that Lucy's services were no longer required...strictly a management decision, and one in which Lucy did not concur.
>
> So, resourceful to the very end, Lucy filled an envelope with expense account documentation, and mailed it to Matt's clever wife, Sylvia Fox Marketczar. Lucy didn't bother to include a note, figuring that Sylvia would know what to do.

Mrs. Marketczar indeed required no explanation, and added none herself, as she merely transferred the data to a fresh envelope, which she then forwarded to` Lucy's husband, Larry Local, at his business address.

That's why, early Saturday morning, when Larry might otherwise have gone squirrel hunting, he arrived on the front lawn of the Marketczar residence, with his trusty rifle, and opened fire on the front windows. Matt grabbed a pistol and returned the fire, while Sylvia hurriedly summoned the sheriff.

That afternoon, with Larry safely in custody, a hastily convened meeting of the Board of Directors of SpecialFlavor Foods accepted Matt's resignation.

Early that same Saturday evening, Matt made just one phone call which proves, more graphically than any other example I know of, the advantages of Personal Contact over all other job-changing methods.

Matt called Bernie Bigdeals, who'd been Matt's boss several years earlier. Bernie, now Chief Executive of a huge diversified corporation, picked up the phone at his home, halfway across the U.S., and received an unvarnished account of the circumstances under which Matt was now offering his services.

Result? Monday morning...approximately 38 hours after a single Personal Contact phone call...Matt reported to work as President of the Foods Division of Bernie's corporation.

Before Larry was even out on bail, Matt was already at his desk in a stylish office more than a thousand miles from Saturday's unpleasantness, holding meetings and making decisions as the much-more-highly-paid President of a corporate subsidiary several times the size of SpecialFlavor Foods in Elmdale.

How's that for an eventful weekend? As they say, "Truth is stranger than fiction."

In over 30 years of executive recruiting, plus a prior decade as an executive myself, I've never come across a more perfect example of job-changing by Personal Contact. Absolutely every aspect was at its optimum, including the accident of *timing*. Not only did Bernie Bigdeals have hire-and-fire *control* of an attractive job, the job happened to be *open*. And not only did he *know* Matt, he'd *directly supervised* Matt, and had firsthand knowledge of his ability and personality. Moreover, there was *no possibility that Matt's performance had declined since they worked together*, because his success at SpecialFlavor Foods had been widely publicized in the trade press. And of course Matt's *reason-for-leaving* couldn't have been clearer.

The moral of this story, if there is any, certainly isn't that crime pays. In the long run, it doesn't...for marketing geniuses, or anyone else. But we can all have a lucky, or an unlucky, day. And apparently it's possible to have notable amounts of both kinds of luck on the same day.

The point is that luck is fully as important...and often more so...as skill in determining what you'll achieve through your personal contacts on any given day, or in any four to nine month period that you happen to be interested in a job change.

Fortunately, however, there are techniques that will polish your proficiency and improve your odds. Let's look at them.

Take inventory of all your personal contacts.

Arrange them in priority order, and focus on the ones who can be most helpful.

Personal contacts can be time-consuming.

True, just one out-of-the-blue phone call to a former boss that lengthened into a three-hour employment interview solved Matt Marketczar's problems with possibly-world-record speed. But everything just happened to work perfectly. Matt enjoyed a moratorium on Murphy's Law on that one day in his life when he needed it most. Unfortunately, Murphy keeps pretty close watch on you and me. Personal Contact, for us, involves a long series of lunch and breakfast dates, other appointments, and countless phone calls and emails which, added together, take up lots of time.

Therefore, it's extremely important to plan your personal contact campaign carefully. Before you reach for the phone, try to think of everyone you know who might be worth contacting. Only when you've identified all the people you might call, can you determine whom you should call, and in what order.

Matt Marketczar obviously chose to make his first call to his most likely contact. And if Bernie Bigdeals hadn't solved Matt's problem, you can bet Matt's *second* call would have gone to his second-most-likely contact, not to his thirteenth. Moreover, if a more subtle across-the-lunch-table approach would have been more likely to succeed, Matt would surely have employed it.

Determining Priority:
Who to contact earlier...and spend more time with...
is a trade-off between two issues:

1. Relevance: how likely to control, or at least know of, appropriate jobs, and

2. Knowledgeable Enthusiasm: how likely to react favorably to your availability.

Obviously, if you know her well, the Chief Executive of the company in your industry you'd most like to work for should be number-one priority. She controls at least one job you'd want...maybe several. But if you merely shook hands at a convention four years ago, and she's unlikely to remember, then you'd better get a new introduction. Or write her a letter, as you would any other important stranger.

On the other hand, a first-class former subordinate who's always considered you a genius, and who now runs a small but respected supply, distribution, or service company in your industry, might also be a high-priority contact. There's no spot for you in his organization. But he knows what's happening in your field; he's enthusiastic about you and eager to help; and he's intelligent and discreet...not an oaf who might smudge your image while trying to polish it. His eyes and ears could be very beneficial.

Above all, beware of the perverse natural tendency we all have to get in touch with the people we know best and are most comfortable with, rather than the ones who can do us the most good. Remember:

> You can make a relevant contact more enthusiastic, but you can't make an enthusiastic one more relevant.

Allocate your time accordingly.

Here's a hierarchy for ranking the twin trade-offs:

Relevance

1. Control of Jobs. These top-priority people have hire/fire power, or at least influence, over a job you'd want. Think of CEOs, outside

Directors, and heads of functions such as Human Resources, Finance, Marketing, Manufacturing, R&D, etc.

2. Vantage Point. Lower-priority, but still valuable, these contacts are extra eyes and ears. Consider middle managers in companies that interest you, and other people in your field...suppliers, customers, and consultants.

3. Neither Control nor Vantage Point. Lowest in relevance are the people outside your field altogether. Some may be widely connected, and you may be interested in off-the-wall suggestions. So there's no harm in an occasional try for serendipity. But give it low priority.

And now the opposite trade-off. How well and how favorably does the contact know your achievements, and how well does she like you personally?

Knowledgeable Enthusiasm

1. Co-Workers. First-priority goes to your former supervisors, subordinates, and peers. No need to convince. Just update them on your latest exploits, and they're automatically enthusiastic. On the other hand, if you suspect their opinion from the past is negative, don't bother. Nothing you say now will overcome what they believe they saw with their own eyes.

2. Closely Dealt-With Outsiders. Suppliers, customers, consultants, and others you've dealt with also have enthusiasm...or lack of it...based on prior direct experience. Moreover, they've probably heard about you from your superiors and subordinates. They can't be quite as sure as if they'd seen you from inside your company, but they're capable of justified enthusiasm. If it exists, take advantage.

3. By-Reputation-Only Contacts. You've met these people and know them slightly. And, although they've never done business with you, they've surely heard others speak about you. Consider trade press editors, trade association executives, competitors you've met at industry functions, suppliers who've solicited you and customers you've solicited where no business ensued, etc. There's a little more going for you than with a stranger, but not much.

4. Non-Business Connections. These are the very same people listed as number-3 under "Relevance." You may know them very well indeed, but they're not part of your business milieu. Hence, they're "long shots" as job-advancement contacts.

Scoring Your Contacts

The purpose of these lists is merely to encourage you to think about all your possible contacts and emphasize the ones most likely to be helpful, rather than the ones you'd most enjoy getting in touch with.

However, you can use the lists for a combine-the-numbers game, if you temper it with judgment. The lowest total number using both lists, 2, is obviously best, as Matt Marketczar showed us. The highest, 7, is least likely to be helpful. The numbers in between provide roughly comparative rankings.

Now the most valuable suggestion I know on how to handle personal contacts:

Ask for a reference instead of a job.

This technique was pointed out to me many years ago by the President of a New York advertising agency. And the logic behind it is so compelling that... to this day...it's still my most helpful tip on personal contacts.

Imagine the following conversation. You're not out of a job. However, you could be, and all the same logic would apply. But for our example, let's just say you're definitely fed up and want to make a change. Today you've asked a former boss to lunch. You admire each other and enjoy working together, and you've both made outstanding progress since leaving the company where he supervised you. So you pop the question:

> YOU: "FlamingTiger.com has been a great learning experience. The venture capitalists made sure that I got a ton of stock when they brought me in as CEO, in order to dress up the management prior to the IPO. They believed I could take our existing consumer brands, build an e-business around them, and actually make a profit from that mix if anyone could. And they promised they'd raise as much cash as we needed for as long as we had to keep burning it. So I signed on. At the peak of the pop after the IPO, my shares were worth—on paper—nearly $70 million.
>
> "But that was then and now is now. We've actually got a good little business going. We'd even turn a small profit if we didn't have to keep on with more advertising support than we ever dreamed we'd need, in order to fend off all those copycat competitors that have come out of the woodwork. If the VCs would only keep their word on funding, I believe we could make a go of it. The VCs

admit that I've got the business going as well as anyone could reasonably expect. But now that we really *are* a business, they're beginning to talk as if the size of the opportunity is too small in comparison to a couple of other irons they have in the fire.

"Those bastards!

"If I leave, the stock will totally tank. We're on the brink. But I don't give a damn. My stock is $10 under water. We're at $1.02 and struggling to stay above the dollar mark. My $70 million that I never really had is gone in a puff of smoke. I feel sorry for the staff. We've all worked so hard. But they're a bunch of great young people, and what they've learned is priceless. They'll do just fine. In fact, they're beginning to get raided out.

"So frankly, Jim, my reason for wanting this lunch with you is to see if you might have anything for me over there at SolidGrowth Corp. I tremendously enjoyed working for you at Early Corp. What do you think? Is there something I can do for you?"

JIM: "Gosh, Bill, I'd love to have you on my team again. In fact, you're one of the best people I've ever had the pleasure of working with.

(Long pause)

"But, unfortunately, no. I just don't have anything for an outstanding financially-oriented general manager right now. In fact, I just went outside a couple months ago to fill a Divisional slot that would have been perfect. Got a good person. But I'd rather have you...especially with your e-commerce experience. I wish you'd called me then. I'll definitely give you a ring next time a job like that opens up."

That's it. You asked. He answered. Matter closed. You both order coffee, split the check, and get on with the remainder of a busy day.

But now let's go back and change your script. Let's have you ask for a reference instead of a job:

YOU: "So frankly, Jim, my reason for wanting this lunch with you is to ask a favor. I've decided to leave FlamingTiger within the next six to nine months...as soon as I can line up something worth moving for. I'm already putting out feelers. And at some point I'll need some confidential references. Would you be willing to talk to a few people about what I did for you at Early Corp.?"

JIM: "Yes. Absolutely! I'd be delighted. You're one of the very best people who ever worked for me. In fact, as you recall, I was the one who persuaded you to get out of finance and go into marketing, working for me. I told you you'd get into general management faster that way. And of course you did, because a year and a half later I gave you that sick little division in North Carolina, where you not only had your own finance and marketing, but also your own manufacturing as well. You turned out to be a 'natural' as a General Manager."

YOU: "What made you think I'd do well as a GM?"

JIM: "Well, you were such a practical finance person...not just a 'green-eye-shade' type. You had so much curiosity and creativity. In short, you were a problem-solver. I was particularly impressed when you went down to Savannah and worked out that inventory-control system that we later installed in all locations worldwide.

"Of course the rest is history. I moved you up to Division Manager in the shortest time of anyone who ever worked for me. The skeptics fought me tooth and nail. But I said, 'What can we lose? We've been trying for years to sell that operation, and nobody will touch it. We'll probably have to shut it down anyway, so why not give the kid a chance?'

"Frankly, I was as surprised as everyone else with the turnaround you accomplished. And your strong financial and systems background had a lot to do with it.

"Bill, I'd be delighted to be a reference. I just wish I had a spot for you at SolidGrowth. That opening a couple of months ago would have been perfect! Damn! I'd much rather be getting you myself, than just recommending you to someone else!"

See the difference?

In both instances you told Jim you've decided to leave FlamingTiger. And in both he told you he's sorry, but he doesn't have anything for you at Solid-Growth.

However, something very different happened when you asked for a reference than when you asked for a job.

Answer to a reference: "Yes. Absolutely!"

Answer to a job: "Unfortunately, no."

So you could say that the answers are as different as *Yes* and *No*. That's true. But, in fact, they're even more different. When you asked about a job, you got *one* answer: No. But when you asked about a reference, you got two answers: the job answer, No, plus a resounding Yes on serving as a reference. *The reference inquiry achieved everything the job inquiry did, and more, too.*

Moreover, the reference question served as a *springboard for further conversation about you*. Jim did what all newly recruited references do: discussed the background of the "referencee." If we'd listened longer, we'd have heard him probing for even more information...further recollections of what you did for him, and news of how you've "kept up the good work" since he lost track of you.

Above all, the biggest advantage of your asking for a reference, rather than a job, is the *positive and open-ended frame of mind* Jim takes away with him as he leaves this thoroughly enjoyable lunch with you.

Ordinarily, under similar circumstances, Jim is directly asked for a job. The accident of timing almost always guarantees that he won't have an opening. And it's always awkward to have to say so...especially to a colleague who, unlike you, may be out of work, and whom Jim might want to think about for several days (and possibly meet alternative candidates) before offering to rehire.

So when Jim is asked if he has an appropriate job, he normally hastens to say No...*and then piles on convincing reasons why not*. That way the asker won't suspect that Jim has any hesitancy about *him*. Your requesting a reference rather than a job was a refreshing change. It allowed Jim to reassure you by talking about your merits, rather than why he has no job. You let him say:

> "Bill, you're great! *And here's how great I think you are*."

You didn't force him to say:

> "Bill, you're great! *And here's proof that I have no job for you*."

Therefore, Jim's commitment to you is far more open-ended...both in outward promise, and psychologically as well. If you'd asked for a job, Jim would have coped with your query right on the spot by explaining that there wasn't one, and why not. The matter would have been finished.

But you asked for a reference. *Jim accepted an assignment*. Follow-up is forthcoming. Jim leaves the lunch table recalling what it was like working with you, and preparing to tell others.

> *Too bad,* Jim muses, *that I don't have something for Bill. Everything I said was true. He really is one of the best people who ever worked for me. So versatile! And a real problem-solver. Wish I could be hiring him, instead of just recommending him.*

A month goes by. You've almost forgotten your lunch with Jim. And then out-of-the-blue, your assistant says he's on the line:

> JIM: "Bill, I've just had an idea. You wouldn't consider going back to Finance, would you?"
>
> YOU: "It's certainly nothing I've had in mind. I love general management for the same reasons you do. And besides, it was you who took me away from Finance way back in 2013. Are you admitting you gave me a bum steer?"
>
> JIM: "Well, hear me out. I've kept thinking about you off-and-on since our lunch, and frankly I couldn't quite figure out why. But then the light clicked on. It's because I'm bucking for President and Chief Operating Officer of the entire corporation over here in about four years, when Caroline retires, and Ken moves up to Chairman.
>
> "So I've got to groom a successor. My General Managers are doing okay with their own relatively small units. But they're all up from Marketing or Operations. None is really strong in Finance. And I have a hard time believing that any of them will ever be able to monitor and supervise several businesses.
>
> "Now, what brought all this thinking to a head is that Friday Ken, our President, asked me if I might consider giving up my Financial Officer, Sue Stacy, to our Energy Industries Group. They've got problems—and they haven't even started in B-to-B e-commerce. I'd like to cooperate. You don't score points for being selfish. But up to now, Sue's been my ace in the hole. I've been bringing her into monitoring the businesses, and in a couple years I planned to have one or two of them report to her...sort of gradually building her into my successor.
>
> "But Bill, with your e-commerce experience, you've got even more to offer than she does in terms of my agenda. So here's what I propose: Come to my Group as CFO. Since you're already a proven General Manager, I'll announce that the two large businesses we have 'on probation' for possible divestiture will report directly to you...I'll remove them from our regular divisional structure. And I'll also announce that you're our key person in looking

for acquisitions for the Group...something we'll get active on if we can dress up and sell off something we already have.

"Clearly you'll come in with Group Officer overtones. As CFO and basically my chief lieutenant, you'll be in on the Management Reviews of all the operating units. Plus you'll have two good-sized businesses of your own. They're sick ones, but that's not so bad, because if they stay sick it's not your fault, and if they get better, you're a hero. So you're line, as well as staff. You'll update your credentials at a higher level as a Financial Officer. You'll get experience in acquisitions and divestitures. And you'll have one foot in the door as Group Officer and my successor, if we both play our cards right and you help me look good.

"What do you say, Bill? Can we have lunch and talk about it?"

Wow! Sounds like a great opportunity. Aren't you glad you didn't get to Jim until after he filled that Division Manager job that "would have been perfect"?

And aren't you also glad you asked him for a reference, rather than a job? That was a good tactical move. You left Jim with a refreshed memory of your skills and achievements, and what it's like to work with you. When you and he shook hands outside that restaurant, he walked away with an open-ended assignment to think about you and to tell others about you. As it turned out, the person he convinced was himself.

What about purely social contacts?

Generally they're low-priority in advancing your career. But the rare exceptions can be wonderful!

So far, we've only concerned ourselves with your business contacts.

Indeed, our priority-list "numbers game" ranked purely social contacts at the bottom...3 on Relevance and 4 on Knowledgeable Enthusiasm. They don't control or influence jobs in your industry...or even know about them. And, not having worked with you in business, they probably haven't observed your professional abilities closely enough to be knowledgeably enthusiastic about them, even though their unbounded personal enthusiasm for you may have them convinced...rightly or wrongly...that you're outstanding in your work.

Moreover, your close friends may subscribe to the generally wise policy against hiring friends as business subordinates. Trying to nudge them in that direction may prove both embarrassing and frustrating. Certainly it puts your friendship at risk.

And when a purely social acquaintance recommends you to someone else, the potential employer may be wise enough to realize that the recommendation isn't backed by any firsthand knowledge of your professional competence. You'd be better off, if possible, coming in under more knowledgeable and less biased sponsorship.

And if you take a job-changing campaign with you into the recreational parameters of your tennis, golf, or athletic club, there's the very real danger of becoming thought of as "Poor old Joe, down on his luck and bending everyone's ear"...a hapless aura that will lower your self-esteem, further depress your spirits, and probably rub off on your family members in the same social orbit.

Now, having duly pointed out the downside, I must also tell you that there are marvelous exceptions to the generally wise policy of not trying to use purely social contacts to advance your career.

Time and time again I've seen marginally appropriate...and even marginally competent...executives catapulted into prominent positions they would never even have been considered for on any objective basis. On rare occasions I've seen these appointments occur even when the employer had a slate of ideally qualified internal candidates, several of whom he or she would actually have preferred to hire. An opportune personal contact tipped the scale!

Nowhere is it written that you have to be the best obtainable candidate for a job in order to turn in an acceptable performance. Therefore, I cannot report to you that less-than-optimum choices inevitably fail and are thrown out. It's just not so. Indeed, some have become my clients, and I've watched them succeed brilliantly...largely because they're very intelligent and have lots of common sense. But in part, too, because together we quickly recruited outstanding subordinates for them, who really *do* know the fundamentals of the businesses involved. And of course, within a year or two, the competent "surprise" choice will have filled in any significant gaps in background.

Moreover, serendipity knows no bounds. A widely connected social friend just might introduce you to an employer who needs precisely what you offer. Stranger things than that happen every day.

The Bottom Line: Diminishing Returns

After you've depleted your ideal business contacts, you may indeed want to try a few of your likeliest social contacts. Only your own good judgment can tell you what you should and shouldn't ask of someone you know.

However, here's a suggestion that applies to every job-changing activity, including every variation of Personal Contact: *Don't do too much of it!*

There are several techniques to advance your career, and we'll look at all of them. Since the total amount of time you can devote to career development may be limited, it's important not to spend so much time on any one activity that you neglect the others. Take advantage of the most obvious opportunities that all the techniques offer, and don't pursue any to the point that your time could more productively be spent on something else.

You see what to do. But, sadly, you've lost contact with some of the former colleagues you should be talking to.

Let the web come to your rescue!

What to do is clear. Ask for a reference, rather than a job. It's an amazingly helpful and versatile technique...absolutely the best way to approach the people you know from all your years in business who may be in a position to hire you into—or recommend you for—the ideal next step in your career.

Unfortunately you—like me and just about everyone I know—haven't kept in touch with all of your former bosses, subordinates, peers, customers, fellow board members of civic and charitable organizations, etc. whom you'd now like to phone.

Make that *doubly* unfortunate. Not only do these folks merit recontacting because of the warm mutual respect you vividly recall, some of them—since you last talked—have risen to far higher and more powerful positions. Today their opinion of you is just as favorable as ever. But now they're much more able to help...a pleasant surprise that awaits, if and when you can reconnect.

But your Roll-O-Dex has been comatose for many years, and your smart phone still hasn't yet been introduced to some of these people. How do you find them?

Fortunately, the PeopleFinder websites have cleaned up their act. Now you'll find almost anyone fast ... and for free as promised.

Nearly all PeopleFnder sites are based only on listed phone numbers. And until a few years ago, virtually every one was operated as a "bait-and-switch" scam. They promised you could "search free." But after you ran your unpaid search, they merely told you that they'd found your person. They did not reveal phone number or address. To get those, you had to pay a fee or buy a membership or give up your own personal information.

Today, most sites that offer "free search" actually deliver it—accompanied by advertising. "Free" now really means free.

Interestingly, when you now find a truly free site, chances are it's powered by a highly commercial older site that continues to operate separately under its original name and payment method. So pay or don't pay. You now have a choice.

Here is my personal favorite of the "new breed" of PeopleFinders. It delivers ... and it doesn't charge:

WhoWhere.com ... (powered by WhitePages.com)

If WhoWhere keeps growing as I expect, you may never need to try any other PeopleFinder.

However, in case you need or want to look further, here's a sampling of similar sites, paid and unpaid. Switchboard.com, BigFoot.com, InfoSpace.com, and AnyWho.com, among many others. Moreover, always input the city and/or state if you know them. If you don't have a location, performance will vary. Some sites will do better than others on the same inquiry. Try several!

Also, a bit of poking around may help. For example, let's say I input the name of my high school classmate Dick Vanner, plus WI, our state in those days. Nothing. Then I try *Richard* Vanner. Bingo!

But when I input Ralph Lauren and NY...nothing. Why? Unlisted residential phone. But then I try the business listings. Bingo! Of course. His name's included in the name of his firm. Might your lost person now be in business as an independent consultant?

Your "Wild Card"

The more specific your information input is the better. However, there's even a way—called "wild card"—to use *fragments* of information. Put in as many letters as you're sure of...and then an asterisk. Say you're looking for Richie Delgado. You don't know if he's Richard or Ricardo. Maybe he's even switched to Rick, which he once mentioned wanting to do. Try Ric* or Ri* Delgado. Or could it have been Delga ***t*** o? Try Ric* Delga*. With a name as distinctive as RD's you're likely to find him if you specify the right city or even the right state. Try several possibilities. Cinci* serves as well as the perfect spelling of the Ohio city, whereas a wrong spelling of Cincinnati may *defeat* your search.

What about unlisted phones?

So far, so easy. But the game will get far more challenging. Many of the contacts you and I will want to locate have *unlisted* phones. Creativity must come to the rescue. Think up questions to ask yourself.

Does the person have children who would now be 10 to 19 years old? Do you remember their names? They may have a phone and it probably *will* be listed. "*Is your dad there?*" Or an older child, as you recall, became a lawyer or an MD or a DDS and is likely to be living and practicing...where? Professionals will have listed office numbers.

Do you remember a close friend of your lost contact, whom he or she may have kept in touch with? The friend's phone may be listed.

Or you might try for an e-mail address.

But be prepared for disappointment! Most white- and yellow-page phone lookups do email lookup also. However, inputting the same facts that instantly yield a phone number and address ***usually fail*** to yield an email address. Moreover, the site ***may not tell you*** it could have delivered your person—if only you'd asked for phone rather than email info.

Worse, if you go to a typical email-only site, chances are it'll force you to ***reveal your own email address*** before spilling any beans it has (often none) on the person you're inquiring about. You're left feeling manipulated—and awaiting spam.

Try http://People.Yahoo.com. It does email lookup that ***doesn't*** demand your email address. Unfortunately, it seems to supply only @Yahoo addresses.

Or become Sherlock Holmes

In seeking the person/friend/child, become Sherlock Holmes. Ask yourself wider-ranging questions. Are there any special interests, hobbies, college alumni or professional rosters, church or temple affiliations, etc. that could be accessed online or phoned at headquarters or locally for (1) published information or (2) a conversation with a "Good Samaritan," whom you might be able to chat into helping you by bending non-disclosure rules.

Maybe you'll wind up with a "Samaritan" who *knows* but won't *tell*. If so, try to strike a deal to send Ms. or Mr. S a letter to forward to your target person, asking him/her to contact you. If you do, I suggest you leave the stamped forwarding envelope unsealed, so that your brief note inside can be perused. "I've left the envelope open," you'll say, "so if you want to, you can enclose a note before you seal and send it." That way, your merciful helper can see that he or she isn't forwarding a blackmail demand or a dunning letter. Your note (on your stationery with address and phone numbers) will be very brief:

> Bill —
> I've lost track of your address since we were together at Acme Corp. Ms. Samaritan is protecting your privacy, but has been kind enough to forward this to you. Please give me a call.
> Regards, Aaron

Search the Web for a Name Then Narrow by searching for a Name Plus a Clue

Okay, "Sherlock." Let's say you've struck out with phone listing and e-mail address searches. Now we'll use the search engines/directories and forget about the specialized "people-finding" sites. Google is my favorite search engine and probably yours too. Like most, it has its own proprietary set of "advanced search" features you should try, including an ability to limit the pages found according to how recently they appeared...a handy feature, when you're sleuthing.

But let's just do the basic search. If you're lucky, the person you seek will have a distinctive first or last name. Is she Takishia Radicchio-Questria? If so, nothing but the lettuce sandwiched in the center is generic. Just put in her first and last names and you'll probably find any page that mentions her.

These sites give you a choice of how they'll match your words: "*any*," "*and*," and usually also "*as a phrase*." With Takishia Questria, you're probably best off choosing "***any***." That way, if you've got either name spelled right you're likely to find whatever's available on her. Had you chosen "and," your search would have failed if you misspelled first or last name. Of course, when doubtful about spelling you'd also play the asterisk "wild card" game.

But now let's suppose you're looking for David Jones. Choose "as a phrase," because lots of pages will have both of those words in them and you want to be sure that they're coupled together.

Now, however, you're probably getting far too many references. Here's a screening trick to try. Put quote marks around the name. That will cause most search engines to search for the words as a phrase while still leaving you free to ask for an "and" search. Put the multi-word name in quotes and also add to the search another word that's a clue as to which of the many David Joneses is the right one. Choose a word that characterizes a field in which David might be prominent enough to be mentioned...perhaps his industry, profession, civic involvement, interest or hobby. For example, maybe he's active in parachuting. He might have been elected an officer of a club or perhaps he's just listed as a member on a published roster. You get the idea. With a reasonable amount of luck, the concept really does work!

So much for general techniques that will help you use not only PeopleFinders but, indeed, any type of search engine.

During well over two decades, I've used many different websites to locate people. What impresses me most is how many sites that were obscure and feeble a decade ago have survived and become impressively powerful.

Also, many new PeopleFinders have been started from scratch in recent years, become known, and developed a following. Here are my three best observations and suggestions:

1. Experiment. Try lots of these sites. Find the ones you like best. You'll be surprised how many there are and how differently they'll perform on different searches.

2. Don't pay for information. If a site claiming to be "free" teases you with a fact that shows they've found your person, but then they hold back the phone number and/or address until you pay a fee, buy a "membership," or surrender personal data, **move on**. Don't reward "bait and switch." Punish it! Use the "teaser fact" as an added clue to help get your desired information free from a different site.

3. Persist. Using the web, you can find virtually anyone. Just poke around until you do.

Be sure to try the Generalist search engines, Metasearch engines, and Specialist engines.

Beyond the telephone and email lookup sites specifically designed to find people there are, of course, many generalist search engines not narrowly focused on finding people but surprisingly helpful (think Google.com and Ask.com). Also, try the Metasites, which search a number of sites simultaneously to deliver a combined result (think Dogpile.com, which searches Google, Yahoo Search, LiveSearch, Ask, and others). And finally, consider the many specialist search sites (for example, Google's BlogSearch tool and Technorati.com).

Here's an array of sites that might prove helpful. Of course, there are far, far more than I can list here. We'll begin by repeating my favorite phone listing site ...

WhoWhere.com ... (powered by WhitePages.com)

USA-People-Search.com Dogpile.com Ask.com

ZABAsearch.com Pipl.com YoName.com Wink.com

ZoomInfo.com 123People.com Google.com PeekYou.com

Zillow.com Spokeo.com Facebook.com LinkedIn.com

Flickr.com YahooPeopleSearch.com ZoomInfo.com

About.com Intelius.com Jigsaw.com NationalPhoneBook.

com WikiWorldbookPeopleSearch.com SpockPeopleSearch.com

PeopleSmart.com ... and more, as you'll discover when using these.

Many sites of various types might yield your person, but the above sampling should be more than enough to get the job done.

LinkedIn.com ... It Merits Your Serious Attention

LinkedIn.com has the world's largest database of primarily business and professional members. Indeed, you're probably already among them. If not, sign up. You'll be able to search among hundreds of millions of executives in the U.S. and abroad who are already members, plus several thousand more joining every day.

Moreover, LinkedIn aggressively markets use of its database to recruiters It sells thousands of single-user "seats" for thousands of dollars per recruiter per year. So you can see that being in the LinkedIn.com database gives you exposure to lots of recruiters. And it does so, without your making any obvious job-hunting moves that could alert and offend your current employer.

The Bottom Line

When you're networking, the people who already know you and think well of your ability, personality, and accomplishments are pure gold. Don't lose them. Find them if they're lost!

Chapter 4

Networking
There Are Two Types...and We'll Look at Both.

The First Is Classic, Local and Face-to-Face.
The Second Is Online "Social Networking."

CLASSIC NETWORKING
It's Local, and Face-to-Face

Networking is a form of Personal Contact. But much less personal than getting in touch with people you already know.

Networking is contacting people your contacts know...and people their contacts know...and people their contacts' contacts know.

Because it's done face-to-face, networking is "Personal Contact" in that sense. And since someone you've met introduces you to...or lets you use his or her name with...the next person you see, it's also "personal contact" in that sense.

Unfortunately, there' a big difference between asking people you already know for help and suggestions, and making the same request of strangers you're sent to.

That's why we're looking separately at working with your Personal Contacts and Networking among strangers, even though lots of people prefer not to make that distinction. Above all, we'll concentrate on getting the good out of Networking and avoiding its pitfalls.

Networking in all its forms is the single most powerful job-changing tool, so you must learn to use it effectively. Whether you give it heavy emphasis, or just let it happen spontaneously, networking is inevitable every time you seek a new or better job.

First let's look at the advantages and disadvantages of Networking, including its most famous advantage:

"Networking increases your contacts geometrically."

For people who are actually out of work, Networking may well be the most effective method of finding another job. Certainly it's the most widely recommended way...particularly among the "outplacement" consultants that employers hire to help terminated employees find new jobs.

As those experts point out:

"Networking increases your contacts geometrically."

The concept is that everyone you approach, while probably not personally in control of a job that would interest you, can at least refer you to several additional people. And each of those can send you to several more. If each person only passed you along to one further person, your progress would be *linear*. But each Networking visit leads to multiple further visits, so your progress is said to be *geometric*.

Everyone has at least a few contacts. Through Networking, those few can mushroom. Consider the following advantages:

More people meet and know about you. Your finite circle of acquaintances expands infinitely.

People who want to help can help. Only one hard-to-find person will provide your ideal job, but everyone can suggest additional people to see.

There's high impact in a face-to-face visit. Particularly in comparison to a printed resume arriving in the mail or by email or posted on a job board.

Here's a process you can initiate. Rather than passively waiting for a recruiter's call, you can be as active as your time and energy permit.

The job you find probably won't require relocation. Local visits lead you toward local jobs.

Appealing as its advantages are, classic local networking also has some disadvantages:

It's time-consuming. Making and keeping Networking appointments is slow, arduous work.

There's no confidentiality. You can't network without making your intentions public.

You reach relatively few people. You're doing well if you make and keep 2 or 3 Networking appointments per day...not enough to survey the overall employment marketplace very quickly.

Requesting favors from strangers isn't easy. Asking help from friends is hard enough; pursuing other people's friends is tougher still.

Focus is random and local. If you want to scour the nation for jobs in a particular field, a series of random local visits isn't the way to do it.

At its best, Networking is Personal Contacts. The big difference is that you're not limited to the few people you already know. At its worst, Networking is like dealing with Personal Contacts on a mass-production basis, with much of the "personal" removed. Where on the spectrum you position your own version of this highly individualistic medium is entirely up to you.

Now let's look at Networking in practice.

Some of its implications are obvious, but others are not.

Let's go back to Jim, who wanted you to consider becoming his CFO and potential successor, and let's change the situation. Now let's say that he's *not* "bucking for President and Chief Operating Officer in about four years, when Caroline retires, and Ken moves up to Chairman." Let's say, instead, that Jim just got to SolidGrowth nine months ago. He's still consolidating his own position, and the Caroline/Ken scenario is at least 8 years away.

We'll also change the facts to make your problem immediate. Flaming-Tiger.com is one of four startups...all financed and controlled by the same family-dominated venture capital operation. The four were showcased together in a *Wall Street Journal* campaign for the VC firm, which dubbed them "*4 Fast Starts*." "Tiger"—under your leadership—is the only one of the four that has built a reasonably strong and growing business. All four had dramatically successful IPOs. But today, at $1.02 a share, Tiger is the only one still reported as a Nasdaq stock in the daily papers. The others are virtually worthless. Now the family patriarch, who controls the VC operation *and* these startups, has decided to merge the other three into "Tiger" and put his stepson, who's headed the failed three from their inception, in charge of the merged company. You and virtually everone in all of the companies but Tiger are suddenly out of work. Confidentiality is no longer a factor in your job-changing efforts.

However, Jim feels exactly as he told you. He's sorry he didn't know of your availability when he had that "perfect spot a couple months ago." Unfortunately, he doesn't foresee having another opening for a General Manager in his Group for at least the next couple years, and by then you'll already be somewhere else.

But Jim *does* want to help. Let's listen as he calls his friend and favorite customer, Norma Nice, Co-Founder and CEO of a young fast-growing multi-divisional marketing company that sells mainly business-to-business:

> JIM: "Norma, last week I had lunch with one of the best young General Managers who ever worked for me, Bill Versatile. In fact, I promoted him into his first general management job several years ago, when I was at Early Corp. Gave him a division that had been a loser for years...one we'd tried to sell and couldn't *give* away. We were almost ready to shut it down. Well, he pulled off

an amazing turnaround...improved efficiency, lowered costs, modified the product line, and brought in some new customers. He got the thing very respectably into the black and kept it there for two years. In fact, he put it on a good growth trend, so that we had no trouble unloading it at a favorable price.

"Bill's done a lot of equally fine work since then, most recently an amazing job at FlamingTiger.com., the only success in that stable of four startups you saw advertised in *The Wall Street Journal* as '4 Fast Starts.' Well, it's a sordid tale with some not-too-nice people in it, but they're merging the other three essentially defunct companies into Tiger and the Chairman of the VC outfit that controls the whole mess is putting his step-son, who fell flat on his face heading the three losers, in charge of the surviving company, which will really be nothing but Tiger. So Bill, who's done another extraordinary job, is out of work!

"As you know, I've filled my Division Manager opening. If I'd had any idea I could have got Bill, he'd be here right now. I'd even fire a couple people to fit him in, but I can't make another change so soon after getting here myself. That's why I thought of you, because you're looking for a President of that B-to-B e-commerce company you just bought. Of course I say that selfishly, because with someone like Bill in charge, that business would take off, and you'd be buying a lot more of our stuff to sell through it."

NORMA: "You really think he's that good?"

JIM: "Darn right. I only wish I could have him myself!"

NORMA: "Well, on a recommendation like that from you, Jim, I think I've got to at least meet him. But, unfortunately, I'm in about the same position you are. I finally found a candidate I like for that job, and he's agreed to take it. In fact, I sent him an offer letter last night by Federal Express. Unless they come up with a big counteroffer, my job is filled. But have Bill call me and come over. There's always the chance my deal may fall through."

JIM: "And even if it doesn't, maybe you can refer him to some other people. He's really great, and I'd appreciate any help you can give him."

NORMA: "I'll certainly try. Thanks for thinking of me, Jim."

There you have an ideal example of Networking. Everything is operating entirely in your best interests. You can only gain from Jim's effort to be helpful.

Jim:
1. knows you well,
2. enthusiastically recommends you, and
3. unequivocally asks help for you.

Norma:
1. knows Jim well,
2. respects his judgment, believes his recommendation, feels a friendly obligation to him, and
3. is very likely either to have a job for you, or to be able to refer you to someone else who can be helpful.

When you meet Norma, you've got almost as much going for you as when you met with Jim. At least Jim has tried to set it up that way. Indeed, given Jim's top-notch credibility with Norma, she may even be hoping that her deal with the other candidate falls through.

But alas, your cookie crumbles. The signed-and-returned employment contract from Norma's new Division President is on her desk by the time you arrive for an interview tomorrow morning. Norma likes you on a personal basis and wants to oblige Jim. So she treats you to an early lunch. And afterward, she makes several phone calls in your behalf. One is to Sam Supplier, from whom Norma buys a lot of what she sells:

> NORMA: "Sam, I don't know whether you need a Division Manager over there or not, but I just had a very impressive young man in my office that you ought to take a look at. He's one of the casualties at that mess that was advertised as '4 Fast Starts.' Well they're cutting back now. But he's a *very* able guy, according to a friend of mine, who thought he'd be good for President of that e-commerce company I just bought. But it's too late. I just hired somebody else. Could you meet him and see if you can use someone like him? And if you can't, could you maybe introduce him to some other people who might need a really good executive?"
>
> SAM: "Sure, Norma. I'd be happy to help. I really don't think I need anyone at quite that high level. But let me meet him and see what I can do to refer him to others who might."
>
> NORMA: "Thanks, Sam. I knew I could count on you."

No question about it. Sam Supplier will cheerfully see you to oblige Norma, who's one of Sam's biggest customers. He'll also set up further appointments for you. He almost has to. But this time there's no specific job in mind. And Norma can only relay Jim's endorsement. She doesn't speak from firsthand knowledge. So Sam doesn't hear quite the same glowing words Norma did.

And by the time Sam sees you and begins passing you along to people who owe him a favor, the transaction may be on quite a different footing. There may even be a disclaimer thrown in:

> SAM: "Say, Phil, would you do me a favor and see a guy who's looking for a job? He was sent to me by my biggest customer, Norma Nice at Buyathonics, and I've got to show I've tried to help. His name's Bill Versatile. I don't personally know how good he is, since I've never worked with him. But he seems like a reasonably intelligent guy. He's one of the crew they dumped out of that disaster that used to be called the '4 Fast Starts.' And Phil, if you possibly can, please try to pass him along. I did almost 15% of my total volume with Buyathonics last year."
>
> PHIL: "Okay, I'll help...even though you've hit me at a really busy time. But, *I* did pretty good business with *you* last year. And I appreciate it. You can count on me, Sam, anytime."

And so it may go. As you get farther away from the people who know you and believe in you, there may be less interest in you as a potential employee and in helping you find employment. And as that phenomenon sets in, Networking, which is basically your most useful job-changing technique, becomes less worthwhile. You spend lots of time on appointments, and yet the value of that time may be considerably less than outward appearances suggest.

We've just looked at classic "please-help-him-as-a-favor-to-me" Networking.

But Beware! There's also a more aggressive form: Networking-as-a-contact-sport.

Know about it. But use good judgment in practicing it.

I call it *NFL Networking*.

Consider it Networking-as-the-ultimate-scrimmage. What used to be a rather prim and polite pastime, not too far removed from lawn bowling and croquet, has been transformed into a rough contact sport.

Unemployment is a nasty thing...especially for the executive well above $100,000. Cutting off his income is like trying to choke off his air supply.

He'll fight for life just as fiercely as any other wounded and cornered animal. Motivation he's got. Give him a strategy and he'll execute.

So, long before it became a huge national sport, the stage was set for NFL Networking. There were plenty of players available...all of them adequately motivated without resort to Pro Football's megabucks. The only things needed to get a good rough game going were aggressive coaching and a recognizable set of rules.

Enter the "Outplacement Counselors." The outplacement industry, which is paid by employers to help terminated executives find jobs, provided the missing factors: an aggressive and creative coaching staff which, in turn, has provided appropriately revised rules. Networking is the number-one favorite job-changing technique among these professionals, and they have contributed greatly to the advancement of the game.

The basic problem with the classically polite lawn-bowling-and-croquet form of Networking...the please-help-him-as-a-favor-to-me version...is its passivity, its lack of vigorous combat. The job seeker is put into play by someone else, who wishes to be helpful and therefore opens doors and makes appointments that the executive might otherwise have difficulty achieving on his own. Merely capitalizing on these thoughtfully provided opportunities, the unemployed executive keeps these dates, presents himself and his achievements as pleasantly and persuasively as he can, and graciously accepts whatever is offered at the conclusion of each appointment...employment, offers of further help, or merely good wishes. Regardless of the outcome, he expresses genuine appreciation for the time he's been given, and he may attempt to kick an extra point with a "thank you" note.

How bland and wimpish! In these days when there's more mayhem in love songs on TV than there used to be in shoot-'em-up shows, the game of Networking was obviously long overdue for an update. That modernization has been brilliantly accomplished in NFL Networking.

The breakthrough change has been to free the job-seeking executive from prior restrictions on his actions in the game. Indeed, he's now encouraged to seize and retain, if possible, total initiative for every aspect of play. No longer does he passively wait to capitalize on play-making opportunities created for him by others. Under professionally-coached NFL rules, the job-seeker initiates every phase of play, and fiercely defends his prerogative not to surrender the initiative to any other player. Let's first scan the usual rules, and then I'll interview Axel Bludgeon, reigning world champion NFL Networker.

Rules of NFL Networking

1. Never fail to get into the office of anyone whose name is mentioned to you.

2. Never depart with less than 3 new names.

3. Never leave follow-up solely in the hands of the person you just saw.

Now let's talk to Axel Bludgeon, who's emerged victorious (continuously unemployed) for the past three years as the most aggressive job-seeking executive in the U.S. under NFL Networking rules.

JOHN: "Congratulations, Axel. You've won again! When you first got into NFL Networking, did you ever imagine that you'd become champion and hold the title three years in a row?"

AXEL: "Thank you, John. But before I answer your question, I also want to thank all those executives who helped me win. A big annual victory like mine is just a series of daily skirmishes. And if those guys and gals hadn't let me beat them down to get an appointment and come in, then I couldn't have forced them to give up the three names so I would leave. So thanks, fellas...and ladies...I owe it all to you!

"Okay, now I'll answer your question. No, when I first started Networking in NFL competition, I had no idea I could stay unemployed for three years, despite meeting close to 1,000 executives *in their offices*. Surely, I thought, somebody would want to hire me, and then I'd be out of contention. But early on, I met some of my competition...like in corporate reception rooms, where we were both waiting to see different executives. And when I saw what wimps they were, I was pretty confident. Did you ever meet Pete Polite, or Carl Courteous, or Cathy Considerate? I think the longest any of them stayed unemployed was five or six months!"

JOHN: "Axel, NFL Networking as a contact sport is something some of our readers may not be familiar with. Would you please explain how it works?"

AXEL: "Sure, gladly. First, somebody has to give you a name to get started. And then you go right ahead as if it were standard old-fashioned *pre*-NFL Networking. You call up the person at their office and say:

'Hello, I was talking to so-and-so, and she told me to call you. I'm in the process of a career change, and I'd like to come in and see you for just 15 minutes to get the benefit of your thoughts and suggestions. Now, I'm *not* going to ask you for a job. It's just that so-and-so speaks so highly of you, and she feels your advice could really be helpful. When would you like me to come in?'"

JOHN: "What if this person is too busy to see you, or maybe doesn't believe you're going to be out of there in 15 minutes? What if he'd rather just tell you what you want to know on the telephone? Then he or she can hang up when your 15 minutes are over."

AXEL: "NOBODY is too busy to see me. That's NFL Rule #1, *Never fail to get into the office of anyone whose name is mentioned to you.* I can't let them cop out on 'busy,' or I'd never get to see anyone important. And I sure can't go ahead on the phone. That's clearly against the rules, precisely because they can hang up on me in 15 minutes. Of course, *nobody*, even Cathy Considerate, would be in-and-out of an *office* in 15 minutes. Who ever heard of a 15-minute meeting on any subject? It's impossible. Once I'm in there, I'm good for a half-hour at least. And pretty often 45 minutes. How do you think I got to be National Champion? Under-promising and over-staying is an important technique."

JOHN: "Another question on your basic spiel. If so-and-so really wants this person to see you, why doesn't he call the person himself?"

AXEL: "Good question. Look at NFL Rule #3, *Never leave follow-up solely in the hands of the person you just saw.* I never leave anybody without finding out who they have in mind for me to talk to. That's NFL Rule #2, *Never depart with less than 3 new names.* If they say they'll call a few people and try to set up some appointments, I demand to know *who* they intend to call. That way, I'm no longer at their mercy. If they don't bother to follow up, I can go right around them, call the people they mentioned, and say they wanted me to meet those people, which of course they did. That was one of the first things my coach taught me."

JOHN: "Speaking of your coach..."

AXEL: "Excuse me, John. But let me just go back to your other question about why not have the person call for my appointment instead of calling myself. That question shows that you just don't grasp the fundamental change in Networking from the old sissy way to the new NFL tactics. Under the old rules, I *could* leave it up to the person I just saw to call and arrange my meeting with the next person. Because, under the old way, the person I just saw would know and like me enough to really *want* the next person to see me. Or at least he'd have a good dollars-and-cents *business* reason to pass me along. Under those circumstances he really would follow up. And I could walk out of his office without forcing him to tell me the names of the people he was thinking of calling in my behalf. Under the old style, people would be seeing me because *he wanted them to*. The fundamental motivation of the game would be *him* saying:

'Help Axel as a favor to me.'

"But today, under NFL rules, I've got to see lots more people and get lots more referrals. And many of those referrals have got to come from stone-cold strangers, who don't know me from a hole-in-the-wall, except that I'm in their office and I won't leave until they give me names. If I simply walk out, do you think they're going to call their friends and business contacts and tell them they've got to see me? Don't be naive! Under the new rules, it's up to *me* to keep the game going. Since the guy I just saw isn't likely to put much pressure on, *I* apply the pressure, and say he told me to do it. Instead of trying to get him to say, 'Help Axel as a favor to me,' I say...or at least I imply:

'Help me, or I'll see to it that you're in trouble with him.'

"Now of course I can't *really* get the guy I'm calling in trouble with the one who told me about him. But *he* doesn't know that! Get my drift? The guy whose name I'm using doesn't care much one way or another whether I get my next appointments...certainly not enough to call for them himself. In fact, he'd be too embarrassed to call and be as pushy in getting me an appointment as I can be when I use his name to get my own appointment. So you see the NFL rules put *me* in charge of the game and don't depend nearly so much on how other people feel about me."

JOHN: "Very interesting, Axel. I see you've really given a lot of thought to your game."

AXEL: "I've had to. You see, the intimidation of NFL Networking is psychological, not physical. So the entire game is mental strategy. It's not easy to get a no-agenda meeting with a really busy person. And the ones who aren't really busy aren't important enough to want meetings with. And besides, I'm not the only job-changer who's calling them. Some senior executives get several calls a week just like mine. So I've got to be the one who gets in when the others are turned away. I've done a lot of thinking about the psychological handles I can use to manipulate these people... first to get an appointment, and then to get the names I came for, so I can leave. Do you want to hear what I've come up with?"

JOHN: "Why yes, if you feel you want to give away such strategic information."

AXEL: "No problem. Just because other people know what the levers are doesn't mean they'll be able to pull them as hard as I do. Here are the psychological weaknesses I can appeal to in getting what I want, and I try to go for as many as possible in each case:

Friendship. Personal friends want to help if they can.

Altruism. The desire to help another human being in need. There's a streak of 'Good Samaritan' in everybody.

Greed. The desire to do business with the person whose name I mention...in the present and the future.

Fear. Concern that if they don't do what I want, it will prejudice business and personal relationships with the person I name.

Guilt. The feeling that if they don't do what I ask, they'll be letting down the person I mention, who probably *would* do what I want for somebody they sent to him.

Charm. The idea here is that if I'm face-to-face with people for a half hour, I can get them to do anything I want...from hiring me to spilling all the names they know. I always go in counting on charm as my main leverage, and then I wind up using anything else that works better."

"Now, John, there are two other possibilities I've thought about but never used, because they're against the rules...even the rougher, more realistic rules of the NFL. They're *Sex* and *Bribery*. The closest I've come to those is that I've sometimes used a CEO's ***really*** *significant other* as the name that referred me. Since, technically, that's just using one name to get another, it's perfectly within the rules. And it *does* get attention!"

JOHN: "Well, Axel, you've certainly been generous in sharing your expertise with us. One final question...and I'm almost embarrassed to ask it so late in our interview...but what is the exact connection between the National Football League and the NFL Networking title you hold?"

AXEL: "Don't be embarrassed, John. We're now a well-established sport, but just about everyone still asks that question. There's no connection. My sport is purely an individual one-on-one activity...not a team sport, and nothing to do with the National Football League. It's the *Networking by Force League*."

JOHN: "Thank you, Axel Bludgeon. And best wishes for another year of unemployment through obnoxious Networking by Force."

There you have it: up-to-date, truly aggressive Networking, as practiced by a master. Axel Bludgeon is managing to get into the offices of a great many executives...and to walk out with the names of plenty of additional executives, whose offices he'll also penetrate. He has a virtuoso's mastery of the techniques of modern high-pressure Networking. It's the objective he's lost sight of. *Axel is not getting hired.*

There's a "catch 22" in basing a job campaign on the brutally aggressive style of Networking.

Using force to generate appointments offends the people you're trying to impress.

Let's look at this problem...and ways to overcome it.

If you're in a high-profile position...in control of attractive jobs, or likely to know about them...chances are you're up against a lot of Axel Bludgeons. Either you're *seeing them and resenting them*, or you're *fighting them off and feeling guilty*. "After all," you think, "just a slight turn of the corporate-wheel-of-fortune could throw *me* into Networking. And then how would I want people to react to me?"

But your work week is more than filled with your job. And if anyone's going to get an extra half or three-quarters of an hour from you, it ought to be a family member or a friend...not some stranger who drops a name and insists on an *appointment* for a "15-minute" matter, instead of straightforwardly handling it by phone.

On the other hand, if you're currently out-of-a-job, you're in an even worse position. What are you supposed to do...ignore the most widely recommended job-seeking method? Walk away from advice your former employer may have paid $5,000 to $50,000 for? Possibly delay restoring proper income to your household? And all because you're too prissy or sissy to do what others are doing every day?

If you're the appointment-giver, you're weighing the "clout" of the name that's dropped. How much do you revere or fear it? What's it worth in business gained or lost? Would the "name" see someone you sent her? *Would* you send her anyone? Is your caller *really* close to the "name" he's using? How busy are you? Do you *like* the caller's manner? Do you *want* to help him? Does he sound willing to accept your best efforts right now on the phone, or must you flatly say "No"? Or are you willing...*or forced*...to say "Yes"? Only you can decide. And only on a call-by-call basis.

In this situation one thing is clear. If you're the appointment-seeker, you've got the more difficult decision to make. Pressure or no-pressure? And how much pressure? If you push too hard, you can alienate the person you're approaching...even if she feels obliged to see you and even if she gives you further names.

Moreover, you could easily lose the respect and sponsorship of the "name" you're using. Regardless of what you imply, you only have a slight and probationary acquaintance. If you wield the "name" like a war club, there's a good chance the person you're approaching will ask the "name" about you. He'll find out your relationship is tenuous at best, and he'll feel obligated to let the "name" know about your foolhardy use of his most precious asset. Then you'll be on two you-know-what lists.

Overaggressive Networking can backfire into "mop-up" calls disclaiming connection with you. I make such calls. And I always inform my friends and contacts when their name is inappropriately used with me. My loyalty is to them...not to the strangers they've mistakenly tried to help.

Obviously you don't want to portray yourself negatively, while seeking appointments to present yourself positively. Here are some ways to get around that dilemma:

Emphasize close, rather than distant, contacts. The nearer along the networking chain you are to the people who know, respect, and genuinely want to help you, or have a business reason for doing so, the less pressure you'll have to use in getting appointments. Consider shifting to widely connected purely social contacts before relentlessly pursuing reluctant strangers.

Consider leaving appointment-solicitation in the hands of the person you've

just seen. If someone says she'd rather call her contacts than have you call them, back off...even though this violates NFL rule #3. If she does set up dates, you're way ahead. You walk in with no prior record of bullying. If she doesn't follow up, you can probably make one discreet reminder call and offer to save her bother by calling the contacts yourself. If she fails to proceed on either basis, you've probably lost the right to use her name with those people. But you never really had it anyway. Maybe someone else will introduce you. Or you can write letters and introduce yourself.

Listen carefully during your self-introductory phone call. Tune to the "vibes," as well as the words. Whether you're being obnoxiously pushy is subjectively up to this listener, at this moment, of this call. It's not up to you, nor to any "Counselor" who has instructed you. If you've only met your sponsoring "name" during a brief networking visit, no matter how cordial, she's not *your* friend. She's the friend of the person you're calling. The only interpretation of this phone call she'll ever receive and believe will come from her long-standing contact...the person you're talking to. Don't sacrifice a successful prior networking contact through insensitive handling of a later one.

Also, reactions to your networking calls will differ with each person you phone, and even with the day and moment your call happens to come in. Be alert and flexible.

Consider accepting immediate help on the phone, rather than holding out for a visit. There's inherent weakness in your logic when you insist that you must have a face-to-face appointment, and yet you'll "only take 15 minutes" and "not ask for a job." If it's true that you only want "the benefit of your thoughts and suggestions," and only 15 minutes of them, then why not accept them right now on the phone?

Of course, what you *really* want is to *display your personality and charm*, which you expect will expand the 15 minutes into a pre-employment interview, or at least a "we-forgot-all-about-the-clock" brainstorming session. After dozens, and even hundreds, of calls like yours, and plenty of appointments like you're asking for, the person you're calling knows exactly what you want. If he's refusing it, and offering a valuable substitute, be smart. Accept and benefit. Make the most of what you *can* get. Otherwise, you may exhaust the time your respondent is willing to give you and wind up with neither on-the-phone help, nor an appointment.

Realize this. Calls like yours are frequent. And everyone's delivering the same high-pressure get-an-appointment script. When the person you call tries to get you to deal with him in the efficient and logical way he prefers, you have two choices: (1) Do so, and stand out from the crowd; you may so impress him with your alertness, common sense, and flexibility that he may decide to see you after all. Or (2) stick to the script and increase the pressure; prove your ability to follow instructions, while disproving your flexibility and resourcefulness.

One further point: Armed with the kind of resume you should be using (which we'll thoroughly discuss later on), you'll feel more confident than you do right now, to speak by phone and follow up by sending your resume by email, mail or messenger.

Make lots of polite contacts, keep records, and use time as your ally. Rather than besiege and bully a few key contacts, deal lightly-and-politely with lots of them. And be sure to keep careful records. That way, you can graciously leave follow-up in the hands of others, if they prefer. You won't forget to inquire about loose ends. And with lots of contacting underway, you won't be tempted to push anyone too soon or too stridently.

Concentrate on your current industry, where talking to you will seem most relevant. Except for your own purely social contacts, the people likeliest to grant you appointments will be in your industry, not unrelated fields. They'll expect an interesting conversation, which may even include new competitive scuttlebutt gained in your job-searching travels. So besides helping you, they'll figure there may also be some benefit for them.

Try to have something other than just your employment interests to talk about. The most irksome aspect of a networking appointment is its one-sidedness. Unlike almost every other business meeting, this one has nothing in it for your host...that is, unless he might want to hire you. And 99% of the time, he knows in advance he won't. He spends time, possibly risks valuable contacts, and maybe takes on a follow-up assignment. Yet he personally has nothing to gain. No wonder he's unenthusiastic!

Try to think of a topic that may interest your host, and offer it as part of the agenda:

> "I'd really appreciate your thoughts and suggestions. And maybe, since you're planning to build your own plant in Brazil, you'd be interested in some of the things we found out."

Who knows? Besides melting your host's resistance, you may get scheduled for more than 15 minutes. Incidentally, Chapter 18 is devoted to consulting which, if it matches your career objectives, enables you to conduct a meeting of genuine interest to your host, while still doing the same self-selling you'd do in an ordinary Networking session.

Trust your own good instincts, good manners, and good taste, whenever they conflict with what "experts" are telling you to do. You're just as able to judge what behavior will and won't turn people off, as any "expert" urging a commando raid. And unlike Axel Bludgeon, you want to get hired. Most people don't hire foot-in-the-door vacuum cleaner salesmen...or subtle extortionists...into high-level executive positions. And they're not comfortable entrusting their valuable contacts to them either. Through Axel's type of manipulation, someone may have to see you. But she doesn't have to like you. And you'll be a lot better off if she can do both.

Above all, don't fall for the "informational interview" strategy naively advised by many outplacement counselors. The concept is to present yourself as a sponge eager to soak up knowledge. Convey this idea: "You're so smart and I'm so dumb (or at least weak and needy at this moment); let me come in and drink from the font of your wisdom. Here we need Joan Rivers to shout, "*Oh, come on!*" A fresh young college grad can plead ignorance and ask for charity. An experienced executive cannot. Before the merger, you were a brilliant competitor. Today, downsized, you're no less able. Otherwise, who'd want you? The only time this flattery-plus-obsequious-modesty approach could possibly work would be in trying to switch to an entirely new industry or function. But even then you have far better approaches, and this chapter has shown them to you.

Use all the various job-changing techniques for what each can do best. Many "outplacement" advisors urge Networking almost to the exclusion of everything else. By the time we've examined all the "Rites of Passage," you'll see Networking in clear perspective among all the various job-changing methods, and you'll have the skill to use each when it's most appropriate.

If you're ever out of work, Networking will be your #1 most powerful technique...and the one you turn to most frequently. It's always available as a productive, open-ended outlet for your time and energy. After you've done about all you can with your Personal Contacts and Executive Recruiters, and perhaps you've even conducted a Direct Mail Campaign and also used the Internet productively, Networking will still beckon to you:

"Make another contact, and get several more to make."

That's Networking. Used sensitively, it can be richly rewarding.

Now let's Network in reverse.

Let's go beyond meeting everyone your contacts send you to. Let's also pick someone you especially want to meet and find a contact who may introduce you.

We'll call this technique "Targeted Networking." and you'll benefit from it even if you never change jobs.

Is there a Chief Executive you should meet?

Maybe he's a CEO whose head of a division, or a corporate function, is nearing retirement with no replacement in sight. Or possibly a CEO with a division or a function so mismanaged that he *should* be looking for a new executive, whether he is or not. Or maybe she's a CEO who's searching for candidates, but using a recruiting firm that's ignoring you because your employer also gives it business. Or perhaps a CEO with a corporate asset that's well-managed, but falling far short of its potential because nobody in his organization sees that potential as you do.

Who else do you want a personal introduction to? A specific senior business or financial executive? Or perhaps the head of a university, a scientific association, a philanthropic foundation, an art museum, a professional sports league, a labor union, a charity, or an opera/symphony/ballet company? The possibilities are endless. But traditional methods of identifying someone you already know who also knows the high-level person you want to meet are the same.

Maybe you can score an "end run" using a Social Networking web site. Most Likely Prospect: LinkedIn.com

Today there are lots of sites that assist their members in discovering "who do you know that knows" a target person who also happens to be a member. In this particular function, the sites are are based on the famous "Six Degrees of Separation." Each member is encouraged to input a list of his/her contacts. That way, the computer can check to see who knows someone who knows someone who knows the target person.

Of all those sites, one—**LinkedIn.com**—is the most strongly oriented to promoting business contacts. It may provide your answer. Hundreds of millions of executives—many of them quite prominent—in the U.S. and around the world are members. Probably you are too. If so, the persons you know who directly or indirectly know your target person are instantly revealed to you by LinkedIn's computer. Most other social networking sites provide similar services.

With luck, a simple search will disclose the intermediary you need—someone who knows both you and your target person and is willing to introduce and recommend you. That's the ideal outcome.

Unfortunately, as you may have already noticed, many of the most prominent and powerful people have not joined LinkedIn (or any other social site you're trying to use).

The Power of Small Groups

Suppose LinkedIn or another social networking site has your target person as a member. Good. Unfortunately, however, it may not have any third party who (1) knows your target and (2) also knows you well enough to introduce and warmly recommend you. Are you stymied?

No. Studying the biography of your target person on the social site reveals his/her membership in a number of groups, some of which are small enough that your target is certain to know every member. Check out that group's membership list. Know anyone on it? If so, you've found your introducer.

Don't overlook Marquis *Who's Who in America* as a source of information. True, they'll put just about anybody who'll buy their book into it as one of their many thousands of "Honorees." How big an honor is that? However, you don't care how flimsy their basis for "honoring" is. You're just glad that the "honoree" fills out the Marquis questionnaire with precisely the information you're seeking..

We'll say you want to meet...

> ARNOLD P. ACCESSIBLE
> CHAIRMAN AND CHIEF EXECUTIVE OFFICER
> ADVANTAGEOUS CORPORATION

Here's Mr Accessible as profiled in *Who's Who in America*:

> **ACCESSIBLE, ARNOLD P.** corp. exec.; b Petersburg, Va., July 7, 1955; s. Franklin and Julia (Keys); m. Sally Slade, 1988 (div. 1996); children: Nancy L. (Mrs. Thomas Morse), Paul D., Stephen K.; m. Lacey Tracey Parker Aug. 12, 1996; Children: Ralph T., Adam N. B.B.A. U. Mich., 1990; M.B.A. Amos Tuck

> Sch., Dartmouth Coll.; LL.D. (Hon.) Pepperdine U., 2004; asst. sls. mgr., reg. sls. mgr., Entry Corp., 1992-94; sls. & mktg. mgr., v.p. mktg., Advancing Corp., 1994-96; v.p. mktg., sr. v.p. mktg. & sls., Larger Corp., 1996-2000; pres. consumer products group, 2000-2001, exec. v.p., 2001-04, pres. & chief operating officer, 2004-2008, chmn. bd. & chief exec, officer, Advantageous Corp., 2008, also dir.; dir., Diversified and Amalgamated Corp., Global Triumph Corp., Consolidated and Conglomerated Corp.; bd. dirs., Center for Enlightened Thinking; bd. dirs., Foundation for Fostering Progress; chmn. bd. dirs., Fashionable Ballet Theatre Foundation; chmn. exec. com., dir., Drug Rehabilitation Outreach Services; mem. Sigma Alpha Epsilon, Phi Beta Kappa. Presbyterian. Clubs: Metropolitan, Century, Sleepy Hollow. Home: 641 Fifth Avenue, New York, N.Y. 10022. Office: 345 Park Avenue, New York, N.Y. 10022.

This entry is typical. You'll usually find a business history, plus varying amounts of personal and outside-activity/interest information, depending on how expansively the "honoree" filled out the *Who's Who* questionnaire. On the Internet, of course, the information may be scattered among various sites and publications. But however you choose to get it, you'll have plenty of information to proceed.

Let's see who Mr. Accessible is sure to know. Anyone you know too? The possibilities are obvious:

> **Former Companies.** He worked at Entry Corp., Advancing Corp. and Larger Corp., before joining Advantageous Corp. Scan your memory for prominent people you know, who were at those places when he was, and might have stayed in touch. Chances are 3 or 4 possibilities come to mind.
>
> **Present Company.** Look at the senior officers (8) and particularly the outside directors (11) listed for Advantageous Corp. Know any?
>
> **Services to Present Company.** Directories and web research will tell you who Advantageous Corp. uses for accounting, investment and commercial banking, advertising, and law. From perhaps 6 to 10 such firms, you probably know 3 or 4 people who might be working closely with Accessible.
>
> **Fellow Corporate Board Members.** Now we really hit pay

dirt! Accessible is on the boards of Diversified Amalgamated, Global Triumph, and Consolidated & Conglomerated. These average about 14 members each, and insiders can introduce you just as well as outsiders; so here are 42 people (14x3) to consider.

Fellow Nonprofit Board Members. Another treasure trove! And each of the nonprofits has an Internet site you can visit to see who's on their board. Mr. Accessible is on these boards: Center for Enlightened Thinking, Foundation for Fostering Progress, Prestige Ballet Theatre Foundation, and Drug Rehabilitation Outreach Services. A couple are very large boards. Figure an average of 17 members (not counting Accessible), so four boards yield 68 people who could introduce you to Mr. A. Know any of them?

So far, then, here are your potential "introducers":

People at Former Companies	3
Senior Officers at Present Company	8
Outside Directors at Present Company	11
Suppliers to Present Company	3
Fellow Corporate Board Members	42
Fellow Nonprofit Board Members	68
Total potential contacts so far:	135

Plus Purely Social Contacts. All 135 people we've identified so far are working with Mr. Accessible in a business context... or at least serving with him on the board of a nonprofit organization. If none of the 135 contacts is a "natural," his memberships in the Metropolitan Club, the Century Club, and the Sleepy Hollow Country Club may provide a link. Ask your closest friends in those clubs if they happen to know Mr. A well enough to make a friendly introduction. It's a long shot, but worth a try.

A Few Parting Comments About Targeted Networking

Targeted Networking is a lot of work. You won't do it, unless there's a very compelling reason...probably to meet someone who controls an ideal job for you. And that job either is open...or looks from your vantage point as if it should be.

Then an all-out effort to reach your "target" may be justified. But when you get your introduction and make your pitch, be sure you're easy to say "Yes" to. Use the strategy we discussed in asking for a reference, rather than a job. Don't frontally attack. Instead, do lots of listening and subtle questioning. Maybe toss in one or two of your best ideas as possible approaches you might explore if, on closer inspection, things are as they appear.

The strongest response you can hope to get at the end of your meeting is:

> "This has all been very interesting. I'll be thinking about our discussion, and we probably ought to get together again."

If the best way the person you've reached can use you is to fire whoever has the job you're aiming for, he or she may ultimately decide to do so. On the other hand, he or she may come up with a different way of using your talents that appeals to you even more. But one thing is almost certain: If you go in with guns blazing, naming names and suggesting tough action, you'll get the fast, easy answer..."No"...rather than the one you want..."To be continued."

Classic face-to-face Networking is your #1 tool.
But use it carefully.

Networking—"targeted" and otherwise—is your single most valuable job-hunting tool. But always bear in mind that the further Networking takes you away from people who actually know you and can vouch for you, the weaker your referrals will be. And if you push too hard to get appointments with reluctant strangers, your behavior may become stridently self-defeating. In asking for your appointment, try to imply that you're inclined—and able—to *give*, not just take:

> "There is *one* good thing about job-hunting. And that's getting up-to-date on the really important things going on in the industry. I couldn't do that when I was chained to my desk. For exam-

> ple, those new wholesaler incentives that Acme has put in, trying to get the industry to adopt their Plan-O-Gram as a standard... At least four companies I've talked to are saying they're not interested and won't implement..."

You get the idea. In attempting to set up a networking appointment, try to subtly covey that you don't just seek information. You're different. You may have valuable information to share.

Social Networking

. . . Online Strategies for the Career-Minded Executive

These days whether you like it or not, any company considering you for a job above, say $200,000, will probably do a comprehensive search of the web to compile a report displaying virtually everything they can find about you online. The work may be done by the HR Department or by outside sleuths hired to use the web to vet anyone the company is thinking of hiring into an executive position.

It will be interesting to see what the general news media and professional publications have reported. But potentially far more interesting—and damaging—will be the words and pictures you have put out about yourself.

Does the entire web mosaic of comments, facts, and photos that you've ever posted anywhere (and not yet mopped up) portray you as a solid citizen and a respected corporate executive? If not, you've got some serious scrubbing to do.

Look! There's a bleary-eyed bare-chested photo of you taken at a sleazy party years ago "Surely, you think, that old pic won't get into a report compiled on me at this late date." Don't count on it!

Clean Up Your Mess!

Think this way: Even if one would-be employer has a sense of humor and gives you a pass, not everyone else will. And even if many hiring decision makers might be able to see beyond the social networking trivia to recognize and appreciate your fine accomplishments, there are lots of far less hip individuals (think HR screeners and outside recruiters) who may cover their you-know-whats by leaving you off the slates of candidates they recommend.

Right now, today, is the time to clean up your mess. Now as you prepare for an important job search. Now, while you can still conveniently remember the locations—and the passwords to them—of the damaging material you've posted about yourself on any website anywhere at any time.

Don't Give 'Em a Laugh at Your Expense

Nothing can undermine a sterling executive career as quickly as being laughed at throughout an organization. At this point I can't resist telling you about the most amusing example of malicious career bashing fun I've ever witnessed. It happened decades ago, when I was beginning my career in New York's largest advertising agency.

An extremely tall and handsome young Account Supervisor (think Robert Redford) dated—and then didn't date—an attractive young woman who was a rising star in the creative department. After the romance ended, a couple pairs of his Jockey briefs remained in her laundry hamper. Applying her ample creativity, this young lady deep fried both pairs. She wrapped each in aluminum foil and then, using the agency's internal mail, sent one pair to him and routed the other to every female friend she had in the company.

So why do I tell you this ancient incident?

I purposely chose an example from before there ever was an internet. Technology has advanced. But human nature has not. Imagine our heroine today. Now she can easily vent, not only in the workplace, but also world-wide on the web. Judging by what she was able to do with ordinary kitchen equipment, just think what she could accomplish with a sophisticated global communications network that reaches virtually everywhere at almost no cost. Today, the guy might even get his 15 minutes of fame (or should we say, shame?) in a clip that goes VIRAL... providing entertainment for hundreds of thousands, not just his co-workers.

"But John," you say, "that was a tale of justified malice. I've never given anyone reason to go after me hatefully on the web." Okay. But have you left anything lying around that could be found and used to make fun of you?

Perhaps not in recent years. But ever? Think back. How great you looked in your Speedo!...ripped, relaxed...and totally wasted! Of course, you've allowed that hot sexy you to remain on display. And, if you're a woman, you may have stretched your 20 minutes of fame as a Victoria's Secret model by leaving your hottest pics online. You may say, "Anyone would." Well, not necessarily!

"But," you say, "I've Been Careful. I'm Protected."

I know. You've only gone where you've been promised that access is strictly limited to your list of closest friends...and securely placed behind a firewall. To that I can only reply that many people are very surprised if and when they ever get to see the embarrassing material flushed out during a corporate-sponsored web check. The professionals who do that work are very resourceful.

Show Me The Money!

Virtually every very large social networking site now "monetizes its asset" by selling headhunters and corporate recruiters the right to search its membership database.

Is this added income just a minor sideline? Hardly. In a recent quarter, one of the largest social sites reportedly took in over $138 million—roughly half its income—from recruiters of all types. Typical purchase: $8,000 annually to license a "desk" (up to 2 users).

And how is this method working for employers? Bloomberg BusinessWeek provides an example: Adobe is getting "more than half it's new hires" using social sites. Job boards reportedly fill only about five percent of its openings. Note that Facebook, Twitter and about a dozen newer sites also sell the use of their databases to recruiters.

"When you come to a fork in the road, take it."

Yogi Berra's famous advice applies here. When you originally signed up for the social sites you now use, you may have been quite concerned about privacy. But have your circumstances changed? With the the database now being aggressively mined for job candidates, you now have two exposure strategies: (1) wide open to maximize recruiter attention and (2) shut tight to preserve your privacy.

Check Your Privacy Settings.

If you are attempting to stay in the shadows, check to make sure the privacy pattern you chose when you entered has not been altered. The social sites selling access to their database are now eager to make it as exposed as possible (at least to the headhunters paying to use it). The site may have altered wordings to make you and many others slightly more visible (as their "fine print" may allow). If you don't investigate, you may now be permitting somewhat more exposure than originally stipulated. On the other hand, you may now be preventing recruiter inquiries that you're eager to receive.

Putting Yourself "Out There"

Let's say that you've thoroughly cleaned up everything on all social networking sites that could make you look bad. Now let's float out information on the social sites that will make you look good...information you *want* the sleuths to find.

Emphasize your highest, best, and most noteworthy professional achievements. And realize that when you post your resume on LinkedIn.com and similar sites, they will almost always scream, **"Include more...INCLUDE MORE!"**

Not a bad idea. But also, not one to implement without some thought..

The "more" had better be virtually all about impressive achievements that have occurred since you entered your chosen professional field. Just to get "more" into your online resume, do not go back to trivial college triumphs or even—God forbid—high school highlights.

And don't brag about achieving early career milestones that are routinely accomplished on roughly the same schedule by just about everyone pursuing a career path like yours. You don't want the decision maker to think ...

"So what. I did all that too. Everyone does!".

Keep in mind what you are trying to accomplish. It is not to prove that you are a good solid average player. No, you want to prove that you are special. Figure out *what's special* about you and put it on display. That's the whole point of the "personal branding" craze that swept career coaching and outplacement a few years ago. "Branding" is a tired cliche. But "what's special" always has been—and always will be—the main issue in all hiring.

Announcements of Promotions, Recognition and New Jobs

Don't miss any opportunity to tell your business-oriented social networking contacts of your exciting new assignments as they come along.

If your boss or a new employer writes nice things about you in the announcement, be sure to include those kudos. That will conveniently save them for your potential future use. More important, it will sprinkle them in the path of corporate sleuths who later check up on you.

Shoot the Black Swan!

On the other hand, after a few years hindsight, a program enthusiastically announced with you at its helm, may become widely recognized as a flop. If so, do whatever you can to remove the early hype. As John F. Kennedy said (quoting an earlier sage), "Victory has a thousand fathers and defeat is an orphan." Indeed. And you'll keep it that way.

Above all, recognize that your footprints in online social networking can—and in the future may—be tracked. Plant good impressions as you go along. And double back to clean up when necessary

Rock Solid Family Life

Disclose all the personal information and pictures you want, as long as they paint a wholesome overall picture of you. Anything showing your happy home life and generous public service is probably a plus. Certainly it can't hurt. Religious and social activities within any mainstream organization may be okay too. But don't bring up your participation in any group that many people might consider unusual or "extreme."

That advice—obvious though it is—may have raised the hair on the back of your neck. You don't want to cower before the thought police. I don't either. But try to think of it this way: You actually take away their power when you manipulate them, rather than letting them manipulate you!

A Pitfall to Avoid

One area you'll keep largely on the down low is Politics. If you reveal a fervent preference for one party or candidate, Murphy's Law virtually guarantees that it may not be the decision maker's favorite. Frankly you're smart to find out before accepting any job if your potential boss—

or the entire organization—has views that differ sharply from yours. How much tongue-biting can you do on a daily basis?

But don't put your political leanings on display. You don't want suppositions about you formed before you and the decision maker have met.

The Bottom Line

Check everything anyone else can find out about you on the web. Then, polish and refine!

Chapter 5

Executive Recruiters: Two Types, Depending on How They're Paid

You couldn't be above—or far, *far* above—$100,000+ and not already know a lot about executive recruiters.

Probably you've been placed in one or more jobs yourself by a "head-hunter." And chances are, you've also used professional help in identifying people to work for you.

So, what can you possibly find out that you don't already know?

Plenty! Because we're going to look at recruiters from an entirely new angle...*your self-interest*. And that's *not* the way they've been presented to you up to now.

There are, of course, two kinds: contingency and retainer. The difference is in how they're paid. The contingency firms get paid only if and when someone they submit is actually hired. And the retainer firms are paid for their professional skill and effort, *regardless of whether anyone they provide is hired.*

Even though the employer pays both types...and you never do...your self-interest is very different, depending on which type you're dealing with. And often that's not easy to determine. These days, both look the same and call themselves by the same names. Even more confusing, both types may switch their compensation method, when it suits their self-interest... not yours...to do so.

Moreover, it's not a matter of "good guys" and "bad guys." Your self-interest very seldom lines up with either type. So in this and later chapters, you and I will figure out:

1. **What's best for you with both types, and**
2. **How to tell them apart...in person, on the phone, and on the web.**

Even when a recruiter you've known for years shifts opportunistically from one mode to the other, you'll recognize that shift, and react accordingly.

But we won't stop at polishing your reactions. You're going to reach out to these people, and get them to do more for you.

When we're finished, you'll know as much about recruiters as if you'd spent a decade of your life working in their industry.

WARNING

You are approaching Dullsville...the only speed trap in this book. Before you exit this chapter you'll say: "Why is John slowing me down with the history and business methods of the recruiting industry? I just want to be a candidate; I don't want to run a firm!"

Bear with me. Obey the speed limit. Master every concept. In the following chapters, when we're whizzing along the beltline, you'll see why we took this tour of the downtown business district.

Understanding their hidden financial arrangements is the first step toward understanding all headhunters who come your way.

On the surface, contingency and retainer recruiters are far more alike than different. Both:

Fill executive positions. Recruiting is the same function, regardless of payment method.

Are paid by the employer. You won't pay either type.

Range in size from small, intimate firms to multi-city giants. You can't tell them apart by the number and size of their offices.

Have handsome quarters. Neither type has a monopoly on ambience.

Call themselves by the same names. "Executive Recruiters," "Management Consultants," "Executive Search Consultants." Both types use all the same words. And the public calls both kinds "headhunters."

Keep vast numbers of resumes. Both will accept your unsolicited resume and both may keep it in their database, along with the resumes of people they've interviewed.

Fill jobs from resumes in their databases and on-paper files. That's why they both maintain extensive records.

Telephone employed executives. When your phone rings, either type may be calling.

The fundamental distinction between the two kinds of firms is in how they're paid.

Contingency Payment

Contingency recruiters are paid by employers only if and when someone they submit is actually hired. They may just go through their information and send over a few resumes. Or they may do telephone investigation and persuasion to develop candidates, and then interview them, to screen a highly appropriate group for the "client" to see. Either way, these recruiters are operating strictly "on contingency"...on the *chance* that someone they submit will actually get hired. Otherwise, there's no fee. If the employer hires his or her in-law, a next-door neighbor, somebody who mailed or emailed in a resume, someone submitted by a different contingency recruiter, or nobody at all, the contingency recruiter gets nothing for his efforts.

Retainer Payment

Retainer recruiters, on the other hand, ***are paid by the employer regardless of whether anyone they submit is actually hired***. They're compensated for their professional skill and effort. Like the doctor, who's paid whether the patient lives or dies, and most lawyers, who're paid whether their case is won or lost, the retainer recruiter is paid merely to *attempt* a solution. He or she is not required to achieve one. In-laws, neighbors, contingency-recruiter-submissions, mailed-in resumes, internal promotions, and positions left unfilled don't keep the retainer recruiter from being paid.

Does it sound like the retainer recruiter has the better deal?

Why doesn't every recruiter operate on retainer, rather than contingency?

Everyone always asks these logical questions.

Approximately half of the executive recruiting organizations in America today operate "on contingency," and the other half work "on retainer." With equal numbers on each side of the compensation issue, the answer certainly isn't that the contingency firms don't know what the retainer firms are doing. Indeed, many contingency firms also accept retainer assignments, and retainer firms sometimes glide opportunistically into the contingency mode.

Percentage fees are about equal for both types.

Clearly, which method of payment a firm chooses is not explained by the amounts involved, because fees for both are very similar. The leading retainer firms usually charge one-third...33.3%...of estimated first-year's compensation of the executive sought.

Most bill their "1/3 fee" in monthly thirds or fourths during the three or four months the search requires. If the search takes longer, there's no further fee. If, when the search is over, the recruited executive earns more than the early estimate, a final bill adjusts the fee upward. A few price-competitive retainer firms charge 30% and fewer yet charge 25%, but 33.3% is typical among top-ranking firms. A very rare few charge a fixed negotiated fee which may come to more or less than 33.3%. Of course, during a recession all of those proud firms price-compete aggressively. All retainer firms allow cancellation of the project, which cuts off the billing. If termination occurs after the three or four months of billing, the recruiter keeps the full fee.

On the other hand, the traditional fee for a contingency firm is "1% per thousand, up to a maximum of 35%." This formula yields 35% of estimated first-year's income on $100,000 jobs and 26% on a $26,000 job. Retainer recruiters hardly ever work on positions under $100,000, whereas many contingency recruiters do. During recessions, of course, fee-cutting abounds.

During the pre-2000 "bubble," recruiters were eager to take all or part of their fee in stock. Not today!

Recruiters can be just as prone to gamble on a surging stock market as everyone else. They never used to be. For decades, search fees were paid only in cash. But then came the internet and its "dot com" mega-million-dollar deals in the late '90s.

Recruiters saw venture capitalists and investment bankers making gigantic on-paper fortunes by getting hold of founders' or very-early-stage stock in hot new start-up companies. So—in a chorus—they said, "Let us in on the action!" Needless to say, they got burned!

All recruiters—retainer and contingency—were willing, and even eager, to help a fledgling company conserve its cash by taking all or a part of their fee in stock, warrants, or options...negotiating a separate and different deal for each young company based on its circumstances and perceived potential.

Indeed the very largest retainer-compensated firms acquired vast reams of paper in lieu of cash. Some even added venture capital activity as another part of their ongoing business. Those attitudes and activities tended to fizzle in the dot com meltdown.

Suffice it to say that "approximately one-third of annual compensation" is still the jumping-off point for negotiating a search fee with a top firm. Cash, not stock, is the preferred medium of exchange.

Recruiters choose retainer or contingency status, depending on whether or not they want to be obligated.

The reason a recruiting organization chooses one payment method over the other is the *degree of commitment it's willing to undertake*. The retainer recruiter promises to search diligently—even exhaustively—for qualified candidates. The contingency recruiter does not.

A retainer recruiter accepts full payment for doing a successful search as his three- or four-month billing cycle elapses. Having taken the money, he's under a heavy obligation. He's been paid for success. So he'd better come up with it. Otherwise his reputation and the future of his business will suffer. Even if the client is capricious in rejecting candidates, or makes unrealistically low offers, or in any other way fails to recognize good candidates or drives them away, the retainer recruiter must try to deliver the desired result to someone who's already paid for it.

The contingency recruiter, on the other hand, has no such problem. His or her "client" pays absolutely nothing for effort, nothing for candidates...unless and until someone the recruiter submits is actually hired. If what the employer wants proves difficult to find, or hard to deliver at the intended salary, the contingency recruiter shifts her attention to an easier target.

Here's the contingency recruiter's philosophy, as summarized to me by one of the finest people in that field:

> "I don't mind if I don't get paid for every speck of work I do. I can fill three easy ones, John, in the time it takes you to do one hard one on retainer. And at the end of the year, I'll bet I count up as much or more money than you do. And everybody I collect from is somebody who actually got an employee from me. I tried retainer, and I stopped. When you accept a retainer, the employer thinks he *owns* you. I value my freedom!"

Touché! The point is well taken. After 35 years as a retainer recruiter, I agree. "Three easy ones" can be done on contingency as quickly as one "hard one" on retainer. However, retainer assignments tend to be at higher salaries, so fees tend to be higher. What makes the "easy ones" less difficult is that they're usually at a lower level, where both the number of openings and the supply of good candidates are more numerous.

So who knows who's ahead on total fees at the end of the year...retainer or contingency recruiters? Both types have coexisted for 70 years, and the industry today is split about 50 / 50. Chances are, we'll have both types for many years to come.

Now you know the two payment methods, and why a recruiter chooses one or the other.

As we'll see later, your self-interest is different with each type. Therefore, it would be convenient if each would stick to his or her chosen method.

Unfortunately, some recruiters of both types switch back and forth.

You can probably guess why some recruiters sometimes shift gears.

Contingency firms also accept retainers.

Many contingency firms "also accept retainers," or "also do search" (meaning the same thing). The idea is to get the employer to pay a fee for the firm's attention, and thus nail down more time and effort than his or her opening would otherwise merit under the "easiest-first" priorities of contingency operation.

There's also another interesting wrinkle when a contingency firm accepts an optional retainer. Normally the contingency firm is one of many such firms "working on" the employer's "listing," and must race the others to fill it. The retainer arrangement gives the firm an "exclusive" on the job, and a respite from the race. Nonetheless, being accustomed to focusing on openings that are easily filled, the contingency firm may still balk at giving too much time to a resistant project "on retainer."

The solution: accept retainer payments during several months of exclusivity, and afterward, if the job proves hard to fill, merely refund all or most of the retainer...thus pleasing the "retainer" client with the firm's "honesty," while winding up no worse off than if the same work had been devoted to the opening on a non-exclusive contingency basis. Such a refund is *never* made by a true retainer recruiter.

Retainer recruiters sometimes "lob one in" on contingency.

Occasionally, a retainer recruiter may volunteer a candidate without being paid on retainer to look. But not often. *And only under cover of an excuse* (more about this later).

The reason for the retainer recruiter's furtiveness about his or her rare grab for a contingency fee is that, if it becomes known that he's willing to provide candidates without being paid to find them, then clients will ask for more "freebee" candidates, rather than pay the customary retainer.

Since retainer payment is more stringent and prestigious than contingency, the contingency recruiter can accept retainer assignments without jeopardizing his or her contingency status. On the other hand, the retainer recruiter can *not* toy with contingency activity without endangering his or her retainer status.

So much for the two compensation systems...and the fact that their proponents may sometimes switch.

Contingency and retainer recruiting are different businesses: brokerage, and consulting.

They have different "roots"...and methods... which you should know about.

Despite their surface similarity when you deal with them as an executive intent on forwarding your own career, contingency and retainer recruiters are really operating two different kinds of businesses. And that's true, even though each may sometimes resort to the other's payment method.

The contingency recruiter is basically a broker, and the retainer recruiter is fundamentally a consultant. This clear distinction prevails, even though the contingency recruiter often gives the employer valuable advice, and the retainer recruiter has to deliver employees; advice won't suffice.

Contingency recruiters are in the brokerage business.

Contingency compensation...payment only if and when an introduction leads to a sale...is the central characteristic of all brokerage businesses.

The real estate agency is a perfect example. No matter how much work the broker puts in...no matter how many prospects are shown the property... there's no fee until there's a sale or lease. It's a volume business. The more properties "listed," the more chance of having what any buyer wants. It's a competitive business. Lots of other brokers are trying to make matches among the same prospective buyers and sellers. So speed is important. Move fast, or the seller will have sold...or the buyer will have bought...through another broker.

History of the Contingency Recruiting Business

The contingency executive recruiting firm is today's highly evolved version of the "employment agency" and the "personnel agency" of the 1950s, '60s, and '70s. Up until the mid-1960s, the *employee* paid the low fee...6% to 12% of annual compensation. As the demand for good employees heated up in the booming '60s, employers began paying agency fees as a way of competing for the best people. And with employers paying, the agencies raised their fees to the 20%-to-25% range that, by then, had been successfully pioneered by the retainer recruiters.

Contingency firms then adopted the retainer firms' terminology...becoming "management consultants" doing "executive search," and submitting "candidates" rather than "applicants." "Personnel" and "agency" were dropped from company names. Along with upscale prices and terminology came elegant offices, and the solicitation of truly executive-level listings. Forty years ago, contingency firms would never have been "working on" jobs above $100,000. Today some contingency recruiting firms are filling ***very*** high level jobs.

Newspaper, Web, and SmartPhone Advertising and Telephone Solicitation

Contingency firms always have—and still do—run a lot of advertising in newspapers and trade publications. Today, of course, they're doing most of their advertising on web jobsites. Advertising is the fastest way to bring in plenty of candidates to submit on the jobs listed with them...their "searches," under modern terminology. Most truly retainer firms never advertise any particular job they fill. This is true throughout the U.S., although not in Canada and the U.K. So if you see a firm advertising its jobs, it probably does most of its work on contingency. Conversely, *not* advertising strongly suggests...but doesn't prove...that a firm is primarily "retainer."

As percentage fees and salary levels both rose, the contingency firms could afford to put more effort into attempting to fill each of their higher-level openings. When newspaper ads didn't draw enough of the right candidates, they began telephoning employed executives, exactly the same way retainer firms do. Today both types of firms phone-recruit extensively.

Industry Specialization

Historically, most but not all contingency firms have tended to specialize in a single industry, such as consumer products, publishing, retailing, health care, high-tech, banking and brokerage, legal, ecommerce, etc.; and/or a particular function, such as marketing, sales, finance, IT, engineering, law, etc. Not being guaranteed payment for their efforts, they gear up for high-volume cost-efficiency, and that generally means moving around lots of similar people in the same industry.

Today many industry-specific contingency firms have evolved to the point of requesting retainers for almost every job opening presented to them. Yet they still do not accept "searches" that require looking beyond the people their postings and ads are bringing in, plus a not-too-burdensome number of phone calls to contacts they already know. If a firm does any contingency work, chances are it tends to do all of its work in its accustomed contingency-oriented manner.

Interviewing and Screening

Because the contingency recruiter isn't assured payment, he or she usually can't invest large amounts of time in interviewing and screening candidates for any particular opening. The decisive employer who lists frequently, gives clear specifications, and actually hires what's asked for will, of course, get more attention than someone who provides less business and is vague and capricious. However, in a brokerage business like contingency recruiting, the more candidates any employer is shown, the more chance of achieving the placement. So the rule-of-thumb is:

"When in doubt, send 'em out!"

In other words, do not screen restrictively.

Non-exclusivity and the Need for Speed

An employer who uses contingency recruiters likes to list the same job simultaneously with lots of them. After all, she pays nothing for their efforts. And since they're not obligated, she's unsure how much, if anything, any of them will do for her.

Not having an "exclusive" on the job, the contingency recruiter must act quickly...if he decides to act at all. He's in competition with other contingency recruiters, and also with all the executives who may be sending their resumes directly to the employer...not to mention the employer herself, who may promote from within or hire her next-door neighbor.

Financial bias precludes a consulting relationship.

Since the contingency recruiter is paid only if and when one of his candidates is hired, he's financially biased. Therefore, he hardly ever acts as a consultant to the employer. Unless he enjoys extraordinary personal rapport with the employer, he's never asked to evaluate any candidates he doesn't supply, and he never interviews internal candidates.

Where's the price-tag?

In contingency recruiting, the price-tag is ***on the head of each candidate*** submitted by the recruiter. The more candidates, the more chances this broker has to make a sale.

On the other hand, if there are several obviously appropriate candidates in the marketplace that the contingency recruiter *hasn't* contacted and tagged, then each one of them represents a definite risk that he'll lose the sale. Therefore, at levels high enough for candidates to be clearly apparent, and in industries the contingency recruiter is familiar with, he'll certainly get on the phone and attempt to affix his price-tag to the head of *everyone* who's at all likely to be hired into the job that's listed with him. Indeed, he may even try to get his tag on the heads of all the most obvious candidates, even if the opening has *not* yet been listed with him.

At or beyond $100,000+, you're a prime target for the contingency recruiters serving your industry. Sometimes it will be very much in your self-interest to explore what they propose. Other times it will *not* be. Subtle and fascinating issues and tactics are involved, and we'll examine them in the next chapter.

But now let's look at retainer recruiters.

Retainer recruiters are in the consulting business.

Unlike the contingency recruiter, who's presumed to be biased in favor of the candidates he'll make money on, and against all others, the retainer recruiter is in an economic position that allows him to be objective. Moreover, his professional prestige and expertise are usually substantial enough to be considered part of what his client is paying for.

Therefore he's a consultant. But he'd better come up with some very impressive people. Words alone won't justify his fee.

History of the Retainer Recruiting Business

With the exception of one narrowly specialized New York firm, retainer executive recruiting didn't exist until after World War II. But as America returned to a prosperous peacetime economy in the late 1940s and '50s, and boomed in the '60s, many corporations needed more and better managers than they were developing internally.

The solution: Hire an aggressive third party to scout the best managers at competitive companies and persuade them to consider a career-advancing move. No more settling for the ad-answerers and the unemployed as served up by the contingency agencies. And no need to become involved in the tacky matter of directly soliciting a competitor's key employees.

A New Process...with No Advertising

Retainer recruiting was a radical idea in the late 1940s and '50s, when it first took hold. Employers were asked to pay an expert in the identification, evaluation, and persuasion of executives to address time and skill to the filling of a key opening, *without any guarantee, or even a promise, that he or she would succeed.* And the fee was a hefty *20% to 25% of annual salary.*

Tough terms. And during the early years, a tough sale.

But 25% of annual compensation is only three months' salary for the position (even today's 33.3% is only four months). *Not* unreasonable, if it provides a truly different and superior recruiting process.

Obviously, running ads and screening applicants could never have supplied the necessary point-of-difference. Employers were already doing their own advertising and screening. So were the agencies, who didn't charge unless there was a hire.

The retainer recruiter's answer to hesitant employers...from the beginning, and still today:

> "We don't just advertise and hope that somebody good will see the ad and feel like *approaching us*. We research the companies and industries of interest to you, and find out who the *very best people* are. Then *we approach them*. The best people are usually well chal-

> lenged and generously rewarded where they are. They're busy with their fast-rising careers, not answering employment ads. They're the ones you want...and we find and solicit them for you."

After sixty years, the original promise of retainer recruiting still represents its highest expression. Whenever an excellent retainer recruiter is sufficiently unimpeded by entangling client relationships, he or she can study an entire industry and select its finest people as candidates. Then the client can hire the very best person, and thereby shift the competitive balance of management power in the industry. As I tell my clients:

> "Somebody's got to have the best person. Why not you?"

So the pioneers of retainer executive recruiting turned their backs on advertising. Instead, they reached for the *telephone*. Among retainer recruiters, it's been that way ever since. Even in Canada and the U.K., where many prominent retainer recruiters *do* advertise, telephoning is their primary technique.

And Then...the Web!

For 70 years the retainer firms have proudly differentiated themselves from the contingency firms by not getting their candidates through advertising. Newspaper recruitment advertising always existed, but most retainer firms made it a point never to use it.

Suddenly the internet exploded into view, with "job boards" springing up like mushrooms. Rather than ignore this mighty phenomenon, the largest retainer firms launched their own web subsidiaries. Korn/Ferry brought out *FutureStep*, a joint venture with *The Wall Street Journal*. Heidrick and Struggles soon followed with *LeadersOnLine* (since closed).

"Yes we have a site. But it doesn't do what we do!"

Both Korn/Ferry and Heidrick and Struggles stressed that their sites were ***totally separate from the parent firm's traditional retainer search practice***. The internet units, they explained, provide a different, lower-level service...a slate of candidates delivered very fast, by sifting the database of people registered on the site. And, of course, since the internet subsidiary is not the parent company, there's no logical inconsistency in advertising the site and/or its jobs. That service, they said, is ideal for filling middle management jobs, where candidates are numerous and interchangeable. At upper levels, they hastened to add, the firm's traditional no-advertising telephone-based searches are still required. Indeed! When the "bubble" economy burst, K/F's FutureStep survived on a noticeably reduced promotion budget. H&S's LeadersOnLine foundered and disappeared into the parent company's site.

Later on we'll thoroughly cover how you should take advantage of web job-sites. However, the point for now is just that any ads you see for retainer-firm-sponsored sites such as FutureStep or the jobs they're filling does not mean that their prestigious retainer-firm parents have changed their classic telephone-rather-than-advertise way of doing business...even though they may have offspring units that run ads (post job openings).

Specialists in Senior Managers...Not in an Industry

The vast majority of truly retainer firms—the ones that make absolutely no referrals "on contingency"—are "generalists." Typically, they do *not* specialize in any industry, although some of the largest firms have certain recruiters who work mainly in specific fields and a rare few firms *are* narrowly specialized. All retainer recruiters *do* specialize, however, in the *higher levels of management*. Corporations willingly accept pay-regardless-of-hiring when looking for senior managers. And of course, salaries...and therefore fees... are higher at the higher echelons. So the retainer recruiters seek upper-level assignments, while shunning lesser ones.

Moreover, at the senior levels, target people in the target companies are highly visible...even to a non-specialist. Also, any significant degree of industry-specialization tends to severely restrict the number of companies the retainer recruiter can tap, because of "don't-bite-the-hand-that-feeds" considerations. Most retainer recruiters would prefer to serve lots of industries with minimal restriction, rather than serve just one field in a handicapped manner.

Full Participation in the Hiring Process

Paid regardless of who's hired, the retainer recruiter normally *is* used by his clients as a *consultant*.

Unlike the contingency recruiter, who's presumed biased in favor of the candidates who'll earn him or her a fee, the retainer recruiter is often asked to interview and evaluate candidates whom the employer finds on his own, and even internal candidates.

Where's the price-tag?

The retainer recruiter's price-tag is on his ***professional services***, not on your head.

Far from being a broker operating on contingency...and thus owed nothing unless a purchase is made, the retainer recruiter *has a professional relationship* with the employer. He's brought in as an outside expert...fully-paid, fully-involved, and fully-trusted.

Moreover, since he's being paid to look for exactly what's needed, the retainer recruiter's candidates are presumed to have been *found specifically for the client who's paying the bill.* Therefore, if the retainer recruiter follows the time-honored rules, he will *never offer the same person to more than one client at a time.* The contingency recruiter, on the other hand, *always* offers the same person to as many potential employers as possible, as fast as possible.

The professional relationship between the retainer recruiter and his clients...and his firm's clients...creates two severely restrictive "off-limits" barriers against you:

1. He may not be able to touch you, even when you're the best person in the world for his client's position.

2. If he can show you any jobs at all, he can't show you many.

The way a retainer recruiter is paid...for his or her skill and effort, rather than on contingency, creates a professional relationship between the search firm and the employer. And that relationship creates two barriers that prevent you from seeing all but a very few...and perhaps *all*...of the jobs you'd want, which are "searched" by any retainer firm, no matter how large.

Even if the retainer firm handles dozens—or hundreds—of jobs per year that you'd be appropriate for:

1. *You may not hear about ANY*, and
2. If you do hear about some, chances are it *won't be more than two or three within any 12-month period.*

Two different aspects of the retainer recruiter's "don't-bite-the-hand-that-feeds" relationship with clients create these limitations. And there's seldom any way around them, no matter how many of the search firm's offices you visit, nor how many of its recruiters you know personally.

Barrier #1: The You-Work-for-a-Client "Off-Limits" Rule

Let's begin with the barrier that can keep you from seeing any jobs at all.

Because the retainer recruiter is being paid to strengthen the client organization, he or she has a corresponding duty ***not to tear it down***. When the client agrees to pay the recruiter to attempt to fill an empty office, she has a right to expect that the recruiter won't simultaneously...or shortly afterward...try to empty another office.

Indeed, no employer wants to contribute to the financial health of any recruiting organization that currently is...or soon will be...working against the health of the employer's organization.

As a Result: The Industry's Traditional "Off-Limits-for-Two-Years" Rule

How long should a retainer recruiter have to consider a client's employees "off-limits," after being paid for a consulting assignment?

For a while, at least. But certainly not forever. Over the years, most of the retainer recruiting profession has always upheld the industry's traditional "**Two Years Rule**." Its essence:

> ***For two years after accepting a retainer fee to strengthen a client company's management team, the ethical firm will not weaken that team by recruiting away any of the client company's people.***

Traditionally, the rule protects a client from being raided by the retainer firm for 2 years after purchasing its services. In recent years some of the giant firms have squeezed that interval to just one year, and some have even tried to deny protection to clients who provide less than a certain dollar amount of business. Such arrogance paid off during the "bubble economy" of the late '90s, It evaporated in the early 2000s. And today it toggles on and off as the economy reheats and cools. The ethical pendulum swing of the largest firms is perpetual. Meanwhile, for less-than-giant firms, traditional values—two years off-limits among them—are among their major selling points.

Large retainer firms with dozens of recruiters and multiple offices handle hundreds...even thousands...of jobs per year. Therefore, at every moment they may be handling dozens—perhaps even hundreds—of jobs that would be right for you. Unfortunately, they also have hundreds of client companies "off-limits," and there's a strong chance that yours may be among them. If so, you'll hear of ***no*** opportunities from that search firm.

How many clients *are* off-limits at the largest firms? Current information is a deep, ***deep*** secret. However, a 1989 *Forbes* cover story reported these numbers: Korn/Ferry 2,150; Russell Reynolds 1,567; Heidrick & Struggles 1,289; and SpencerStuart 1,250. When Heidrick & Struggles went public in 1999 its S-1/A filing with the S.E.C. stated that the firm "worked for more than 1,800 clients in 1995 and over 3,100 in 1998." Sensitive to off-limits implications, all large search firms try (quite successfully) to avoid ever disclosing how many clients they serve (the stale info here is latest available).

With numbers like those, it's likely that your employer may be "off-limits" to several of the sizable retainer firms...especially if you work for a major company, since big companies are the ones most likely to have used several recruiting firms recently.

Regardless of how outstanding you are, you probably won't hear about any job *suitable for you* from any firm your employer uses. You may, however, be called to suggest people for jobs that obviously *wouldn't* interest you.

Moreover, the barrier isn't removed if you contact the search firm and ask to be considered.

It doesn't solve the "off-limits" problem if you approach the retainer recruiter yourself, instead of waiting for him or her to call you. If she were unethical, she'd approach her client's employees and, with their cooperation, merely claim that they approached her. Therefore, the recruiting firm protects itself from any seeming impropriety by not involving you at all in its projects. The ethical retainer recruiter won't empty offices in any company where she's recently been paid to help fill them...indeed, not for two years, according to traditional industry practice.*

*Up until '96, the "Two Years Rule" was written into the "Code of Ethics" of the AESC, the trade association of retainer recruiters. In '96 the "Code" was stripped of almost all ethical prohibitions. Nonetheless, most fine retainer firms still automatically provide this traditional client protection, and most savvy client companies still demand it in writing when awarding substantial amounts of search business.

Barrier #2: The You're-Allocated-to-Another-RecruiterWithin-the-Firm "Off-Limits" Rule

Under the Allocated-to-Another-Recruiter-in-the-Same-Firm rule, which is traditional among retainer recruiting firms:

> *You'll never hear about more than one-job-at-a-time ...probably no more than two or three per year.*

You may simultaneously be asked to suggest candidates for several jobs that would *not* interest you. But on jobs you'd personally be interested in, most retainer firms will only let you know about one-at-a-time.

The way it works is that only one-recruiter-at-a-time is given permission within the firm to contact you. And he's only allowed to tell you about one-job-at-a-time. Not until you declare yourself uninterested in job #1 do you have any chance of being told about job #2. And unless the very same person you turn down has a second job he wants to ask you about, chances are that weeks or months of inside-the-firm red tape may have to unwind, before another of the firm's recruiters can tempt you with something else.

Searches usually take three to four months, plus a while afterward during which administrative assistants "close out" completed searches and return non-recruited executives to the "pool." Therefore, even if you're given maximum exposure, you probably won't see more than two or three...or conceivably four...of any retainer firm's appropriate-for-you opportunities per year.

Not allowing prospective candidates to know about more than one search at a time is based on two compelling business reasons:

1. *Clients of retainer firms pay handsomely for each candidate.* On a $250,000 position, the recruiter bills upwards of $80,000... more than $16,000 each, if there are five candidates. *Client A* should be furious if any of his $16,000 candidates are simultaneously provided to *Client B*, against whom he then has to compete in the hiring process.*

2. *Filling jobs is the objective; accommodating executives is not.*

---

*With contingency recruiters this consideration doesn't apply, because clients pay nothing for candidates and are billed only when someone is hired. Therefore, contingency firms introduce all candidates to as many employers as possible, but sometimes with sad results for the candidates, as we shall see in the next chapter.

> Therefore, any executive who is shown any job...unless she refuses to consider it...must not be distracted by alternatives. Suppose an executive lives in Greenwich, CT, has two kids in high school, a spouse with a lucrative local job, and a beautiful house the family loves. Even so, she's willing to consider an attractive position in Nome, Alaska.
>
> Needless to say, she'd better not find out about an equally or more attractive situation only twelve miles from her home.

Point (2) above also has an unfortunate corollary for the *unemployed* executive. He's presumed to be "hungrier" for a new position than someone who's happily employed. Therefore, he's more likely to be shown jobs involving unattractive features...relocation, lateral responsibility, modest compensation, unstable and small companies, etc. And he won't hear about anything more attractive until the first project chosen for him has been disposed of.

How These Barriers Operate Within the Recruiting Firm

It's simple. Every recruiter in a traditionally ethical retainer firm is forbidden to phone any executive as a prospect for a job until he or she checks to determine that the executive:

1. *doesn't work for a client*

AND

2. *hasn't been allocated to a different recruiter* doing a different search.

Only if the retainer recruiter is lucky enough to hurdle both barriers, does he have permission within his firm to tell you about a career opportunity. Otherwise, it doesn't matter that you're his closest personal friend, or that he knows you're extremely unhappy with your current circumstances which, if allocation-to-another-recruiter is the problem, *may even include unemployment*.

The recruiter who wants to "use" you as a candidate simply cannot break the "off-limits" rules under which virtually all retainer firms operate. These rules are for the economic benefit of the firm and its individual recruiters.

When one firm member helps himself by breaking the rules, he hurts his company and his colleagues. *Such behavior is not tolerated.*

Isn't there some way around the retainer firm's off-limits rules?

Not if the firm observes traditional ethics and looks out for its own interests, rather than yours.

The you-work-for-a-client barrier prevents you from being called as a potential candidate. However, it usually doesn't prevent your being called as a "*source*" of suggestions of other potential candidates. But only if the job would clearly be inappropriate for you...too junior if it's within your function (a Chief of Financial Planning, if you're a CFO), or in a different function (Marketing, rather than Finance). But even then, the traditionally ethical recruiter will ask you only for executives *not currently working for your off-limits company*. She'll want people who've been there and left, and people at competitive companies.

If the job might appeal to you personally, you will *not* be called, *even for suggestions*, because of the obvious danger that when you express personal interest and are told you're off-limits to the recruiter because of client conflict, you'll merely go straight to the employer. After all, you don't care about the recruiter's "don't-bite-the-hand-that-feeds" problem. It's not your problem... nor that of the recruiter's client, whom you'd like to work for, and who'd be delighted to have a chance to consider you.

If a job represents a fine career opportunity for you, and you'd be an ideal candidate, then both you and the potential employer are hurt—not helped—when the recruiter has to keep you apart. Therefore, the recruiter doesn't want you showing up on his client's doorstep and illustrating what fine candidates he's forced to withhold. And he certainly doesn't want your present employer to find out that he's emptying your office, after just being paid to fill the one down the hall. For both reasons he'll steer clear of you.

Moreover, it wouldn't be any excuse to say that you went ahead on your own after the recruiter specifically told you he couldn't make an introduction because of the You-work-for-a-client "Off-limits" Rule. After all, tempting you with the job, and then telling you that *he* couldn't introduce you is exactly the way he'd manipulate you into the hands of his latest client, if he were a sleazy operator with no ethical policy.

Traditional Ethics Are Challenged!

The time-honored and once universally acknowledged ethical principles of the retainer recruiting industry—unquestioned for decades—are increasingly being debated and eroded.

Ironically, the most vigorous adversaries are the largest firms—now public and pursuing growth—which for at least 30 years were the leaders in establishing the rules and encouraging the industry to follow them.

The reason, as you can imagine from the chapter you just read, is that these off-limits rules—installed to protect client employers—restrict the actions and curb the growth of a search firm.

Nevertheless, the rules remain widely recognized and followed. You need to know them, so you can work within them—and when appropriate *bend* them—to achieve your own personal advantage.

The giant firms feel unfairly hampered by the rules, while the medium and smaller firms proudly adhere to them. And smart clients demand in writing the principles that traditionally could be taken for granted.

To see what industry insiders are loudly talking about, take a look at pages 159 to 164. The issues are clear. The answers are not.

Looking Five Chapters Ahead

That's it. Now you know the ground rules.

All the basic facts that govern your dealings with recruiters—both contingency and retainer—were in the chapter you just finished reading. From here on, we'll look at the *implications* of those facts.

Think of dealing with recruiters as a game. You now know how the game works. But there's still a wide-open opportunity to improve your skills as a *player*.

The stakes are high. If you play expertly, and have a little luck, you may never have to do anything more to achieve career advancement outside your current company than just to handle recruiters effectively. Don't worry about what recruiters *won't* do for you. What they *will* do, if you treat them right, can still be the most favorable of all outside influences on your career.

That's why we'll pay special attention to the subject of executive recruiters. To polish this extremely important part of your career-advancement game, I'm not just going to hand you some written instructions, and walk away.

Far from it. You're going to get the nearest thing to *actual practice* that a book can provide. Rather than just tell you how to hold the bat and how to swing, I'm also going to throw you a systematic series of all the fastballs, curves, sinkers, and spitballs that you're likely to encounter in big league play at $100,000 to $300,000 to well above $1 Million.

What's more, you're going to meet the same concept more than once, and in more than one context. So, as you read on, don't feel that you must take notes or mark pages whenever you hit an intriguing new insight. Just understand it...and zip right along. Chances are, I'll throw you the same pitch again, from a slightly different angle, until it's a permanent part of your business sophistication.

In the next few chapters you're going to develop a whole new set of *reflexes*. From now on, you'll automatically reach for your maximum advantage every time you encounter a recruiter. You'll be thoroughly accustomed to major league pitching. And you'll be batting 1000...or darn close to it.

Here's how we'll proceed. First we'll check out *your self-interest* when you deal with *contingency recruiters* (Chapter 6) and *retainer recruiters* (Chapter 7). And then, knowing what's best for you with both types, we'll make sure you get it when *you call them* (Chapter 8), when *they call you* (Chapter 9), and when you *do business* with them (Chapter 10).

And finally, after you've absorbed this entire book as background, you'll get a postgraduate course in Appendix I. There you'll witness the filling of a high-level executive position through the eyes of a fine retainer recruiter at a large and prestigious firm. After you've seen the process through his eyes, it will never look quite the same to you again.

Of course, I can't absolutely guarantee that this regimen will make you a life-long whiz at dealing with recruiters. But I'll be very surprised if it doesn't.

Chapter 6

Contingency Recruiters: Look Out for Yourself

This chapter...and the entire book...aims relentlessly at one objective: *your self-interest*.

What's best for *YOU*! Not for contingency recruiters. Not for retainer recruiters. And possibly not for your current employer, who'd rather not lose you to a better opportunity.

Early in your career, your self-interest neatly matched the interests of contingency recruiters. Chances are, one or more of them gave you invaluable help in entering the business world, and possibly in climbing the first few levels of the corporate pyramid.

But beyond $100,000 and beyond $1 Million your interests are no longer quite the same as those of *any* recruiter...contingency, or retainer.

Sorry about that!

You're on your own now. And in this chapter we'll focus on your self-interest whenever the recruiter you're dealing with is working "on contingency"...whenever he or she gets paid *only if you're hired.*

Chances are, your career got some of its early momentum with the help of a contingency recruiter.

Forget how special you are now.

Years ago you were a commodity in vast supply: a management trainee; a financial analyst; an assistant account executive or an AE at an advertising agency; a "member of technical staff" in an R&D lab; an engineering manager; a plant superintendent; a computer programmer or analyst; a lending officer in a bank; a field salesman or a zone manager; a copy editor; an assistant or full product manager...I could go on and on, but you get the idea.

Early in your career, you were just another face in the crowd of bright young people striving to get ahead. You needed all the exposure you could get. So you were properly grateful to find a friendly "counselor" at an agency (which today probably calls itself an executive recruiting or search firm), who saw the good qualities in you.

This "counselor" sent your resume...and extolled your "potential"...to HR departments and middle-managers all over town. Finally, you landed the job you wanted. You appreciated your "counselor's" help, and you may have kept in touch with her for years. Maybe you got a subsequent job through her. And perhaps you've used her as a source of junior- and middle-management people reporting to you, as you've moved further up.

Most of us who've climbed the corporate pyramid have warm memories of several fine contingency recruiters who touched our lives in a very positive way. Certainly I do, and I'll bet you do too.

Very helpful earlier, the contingency recruiter no longer serves your self-interest the way he used to.

Now you're at, or within striking distance of, the senior-management level. You're already earning upward of, say $100k or $300k and perhaps *way* upward. You've outdistanced the crowd. You now have an impressively responsible position. You've made a track record. Your resume speaks for itself. Remember the contingency recruiter saying, "Keep it on one page"? That was because you hadn't done enough yet to justify more. And besides, she was your spokesperson in the Human Resources Department.

Today you don't need an advocate trying to break down HR Department doors for you. And when it comes to contacting the CEO or any other senior executive who'll take the initiative in bringing you into a company, you *don't want an advocate*. You can write your own covering letter and submit your own resume. And doing so will be considered more straightforward and dignified than if you're served up on a platter by a headhunter with a financial stake in promoting an introduction.

Avoid having a price-tag on your head.

Whenever a contingency recruiter introduces you to a company, you arrive with a price-tag on your head...usually more than $80,000 if, for example, you're making about $250,000 (see pages 74-75 for fee explanation).

It doesn't matter whether or not the recruiter has been specifically requested to offer candidates for an open position. The price-tag is firmly affixed. Maybe he's just taking a flyer and sending your resume with no prior request for it, and possibly no prior contact at all with the employer he sends it to.

Nevertheless, if it's the recruiter who draws the company's attention to you, you can't be hired without his being owed a fee. Standard industry practice is that such referrals are "solid" for at least six months. All incoming resumes are date-marked—physically or in a database—in the HR Department. And if two contingency recruiters submit the same person, the recruiter whose submission arrives first is the one who gets paid.

Racing You to Your Employment

Anyone paid on contingency has this objective: *to receive a fee when someone is hired*.

Ideally, the recruiter pursues her goal by securing a listing from an employer with a specific job that she and other recruiters are invited to try to fill. She then *races the other contingency recruiters to fill the job*.

But suppose a contingency recruiter—or a retainer recruiter who shifts opportunistically into the contingency mode—encounters an exceptionally desirable *employee*. Then, despite having *no listed job* that this employee fits, the recruiter may nevertheless decide to attach his or her price-tag, and *race to all the companies this employee is likeliest to wind up working for*. After all, new job openings occur every day. There may be one the recruiter doesn't know about.

Let's assume that you're not just good, but outstanding. You're one of those exceptional executives that companies will surely hire if they have an opening. "Seen is as good as sold."

Moreover, the list of companies in your industry that might want you is just as obvious as your excellent record and personal attributes. Those companies, of course, are the ones you'll logically contact first when you're interested in changing jobs. They're also the ones where you may already have your own personal contacts. And they're where, even if you're not already personally acquainted, a letter and resume from you may spark immediate interest.

Therefore, the contingency recruiter has no time to lose. Since you're talking to him, you're probably talking to *other headhunters too*. And soon you'll be in touch with the most obvious *employers* as well.

So he may immediately submit your resume to all the companies most likely to hire you. If he's ethical, he gets your verbal okay first; if not, he doesn't bother. Either way, he moves quickly, to get your resume submitted before any other recruiter does...*and before you do*. After all, if your resume gets there before his submission arrives, he'll be out-of-luck. Therefore, he "covers" you at all the companies you're most likely to join. A copy of your resume, an envelope, and a stamp—or merely an email—just might produce an $80,000+ fee...or at least insure against losing one.

Would a recruiter be so brassy as to write and phone a CEO or another key officer he didn't already know personally?

Absolutely. CEOs and other senior executives I work with on a retainer basis have shown me this kind of mail many, many times. Moreover, their secretaries say it's often followed by persistent phone calls...especially if an opening has been reported in the trade press. Of course the more usual and circumspect submission will be to the HR Department in any company the headhunter normally does business with. There, he can't afford to overreach the people who give out the contingency listings of lower- and middle-management jobs.

The Harm That's Done to You

What's wrong with the above scenario from your point of view? After all, you're not paying. You don't care who does or doesn't collect a fee. You just want to find the right job to advance your career. Isn't it a good idea to be introduced by a professional who'll do everything possible to promote the idea that you ought to be interviewed?

No. The entrée you achieve by personal contact, networking, or an impressive letter and resume you send is likely to be more, rather than less, persuasive than a headhunter's. The recruiter may have saved you some effort, but it's not likely that she's enhanced your image.

Assuming you get interviewed and hired and the headhunter gets paid, it's true that you haven't been economically hurt, since these days the employer always pays employment fees.

But the sad fact of the matter is that you're far less likely to get seen—much less hired—than if you'd arrived under your own steam, with no $80,000+ price-tag attached.

Behind-the-Scenes After an Unsolicited Referral by a Recruiter

Notice I did *not* say "by a *contingency* recruiter." Any referral that is not specifically requested by the employer is "on contingency," even if made by a prestigious retainer firm in a convenient lapse from publicly professed behavior.

Step One:

> Letter and resume (or email) arrive; perhaps followed by phone calls from the recruiter.

Step Two:

> Submission is duly noted in the central HR Department.

Step Three:

> You make contact. Through personal contact, networking, or your own mailing. Or even a fortunate accident.
>
> Maybe you meet Mr. Decisionmaker on an airplane, or on the golf

course, or at a trade show, or at your daughter's swimming meet... whatever kismet the fates send or you can contrive. Impressed, he begins to think about meeting you in his office, with an eye toward potential employment. He doesn't have anything specific right now, and your background may be a little offbeat. But he's intrigued with you and thinks, "Let's have her in here. We can shoot a few ideas around, and I can at least pick her brains. Maybe nothing will come of it; even so, no harm done."

Step Four:

Mr. Decisionmaker follows proper company procedure. He calls the HR department first, as everyone is supposed to before scheduling a meeting that could lead to employment. Let's listen:

DECISIONMAKER: "Have we got anything on a Judy...or more likely it's Judith...(fill in your last name)? She's over at Stodgy Corporation. I met her last evening and she impressed me. I don't exactly have an open slot and maybe I won't be too interested after I know her better. But then again, I've been thinking of several ways I might do some reorganizing."

PERSONNEL ASSISTANT: "Oh, yes, Mr. D. I've found her in our file. Judith A. (you!)...the Stodgy Corporation. Yes, we have her full resume here."

DECISIONMAKER: "How could we? I just met her last night."

PA: "The resume was sent in by a Mr. Ralph Quick of Quick Associates, a headhunter firm...letter dated the 14th and we got it on the 19th. Mr. Quick also phoned us, and I see he also sent a letter to Mr. Big, which Alfred sent down here for us to file."

DECISIONMAKER: "Well, what does all that mean to me? I met her at my daughter's swimming meet. Diane beat her daughter by just one second. They were both awfully nice...congratulated us as we were leaving...and she and I got to talking. No connection at all with Quick Associates, whoever they are."

PA: "They're a pretty decent headhunter firm, and we've listed with them from time to time. I think they hit with a manager for our New England Region a year or so ago. I suppose that if anything *did* develop between you and Ms. (you!), we could call them and tell them about the swim meet and all and maybe they'd..."

DECISIONMAKER: "No, never mind. It's not worth the trouble. I really don't have my thinking squared away yet. 'Bye now. Thanks!"

Sandbagged! And you never knew what hit you. The headhunter didn't know either. Maybe she's very nice...perhaps a personal friend. She might even have backed off, rather than jeopardize an opportunity for you.

Too bad you had a price-tag on your head.

There are three circumstances under which you might be submitted "on contingency."

And in all three, you're better off getting to the employer on your own.

Let's take a close look at your self-interest in every possible situation where you might have the alternative of introducing yourself...or being introduced by a recruiter operating "on contingency," whether he or she is normally "contingency" or "retainer."

Possibility One: The employer has NOT listed the position with the recruiter.

Submitted "on contingency," you arrive with, say an $80,000+ price-tag on your head. Nobody asked for you. And now the company is $80,000 less interested in seeing you than if you'd submitted yourself.

Possibility Two: The employer HAS listed an opening with a fine and highly ethical contingency recruiter.

Now we've got a much closer case. However, I think you'll agree that you're probably better off to reach the employer on your own...having had nothing to do with the contingency recruiter, and not knowing that he had a listing for the same job you hear about and apply for on your own, regardless of whether you find the opening through personal contact, networking, direct mail, a story in a trade journal or a newspaper, or a job listing on the corporation's own online job board...whatever.*

---

*These possibilities for you to discover an opening on your own and "go direct" to the employer *do not*, of course, include responding to a recruiter's Internet or newspaper ad to learn the employer's identity. In fairness you must reach the employer without being involved at all with the contingency recruiter.

On the negative side, you won't have the recruiter advocating your candidacy. But is he primarily in touch with Mr. Decisionmaker or with the Human Resources Department? And of course, if you're ever discussed with the contingency recruiter (not likely, because he's biased), he may "faint-praise" you and plug his people.

But you cost *zero*, and the contingency recruiter's people have all got (in our example) $80,000+ price-tags on their heads. Even without advocacy, you can count on an objective evaluation by the employer.

The situation would have been different several years ago, when you were a recent graduate, or a junior- or middle-manager trying to get a leg up after just a few years' experience. Then you may have needed advocacy, just to be considered. Today you and all the other candidates at your level have track records that can—and will—be objectively compared.

Let's even be a little cynical. Not having to make a capital investment of $80,000+ to acquire you, Mr. Decisionmaker can feel *freer to try you out*. If you don't succeed, he can dump you, without having $80,000 worth of egg on his face. You have a political, as well as an economic, edge.

Possibility Three: The employer has assigned a search to a retainer recruiter. Now another recruiter submits you without a listing from the employer.

This happens much more often than you would think.

Sometimes a contingency recruiter may submit you without knowing that a retainer search has been assigned. You're a nifty candidate, so Mr. Contingency attaches his price-tag, and races to your likeliest employers. Or Mr. C reads in a trade paper about an executive switching companies, thereby creating an opening at the former company. Bang! He's in touch with you, and your resume is on its way.

On the other hand, perhaps the recruiter operating "on contingency" *does* know that a retainer recruiter has been engaged...and chooses to involve himself anyway. Consider the following examples:

Perhaps a contingency recruiter regularly gets lower- and middle-management listings from a company. He "hits" well, but the company assigns its highest-level openings to retainer firms. Knowing of an on-going retainer search, Mr. Contingency "lobs one in from the sidelines."

Or perhaps there's a "shoot-out" in which several *retainer* firms compete for a search assignment. Here are two ways I've personally seen unethical retainer firms "go contingency" in an effort to snatch victory from the jaws of defeat:

1. Write the company expressing regret at not being chosen, and enclosing resumes of "some great candidates we had lined up for you."

2. Call the employer three or four weeks later, ask if the job has been filled (of course it's too early), and offer to do "a computer run, to see if we come up with anyone your other firm isn't showing you."

No retainer arrangement, and no charge unless someone is hired in (1). And in (2), a nominal fee of $3,000 for the "computer run," after which one of the firm's recruiters also spends two weeks on the phone trying to scrape up candidates...something a contingency firm with a non-exclusive "listing" might also do. The "computer run" was just a flimsy excuse for reversion to contingency operation after failure to achieve a retainer.

As a retainer recruiter myself, I can tell you that I and most other retainer firms would never even imagine such unprofessional behavior. Yet, as the "shoot-out" winner, I've personally witnessed both examples (I could never have dreamed them up) as performed by two of America's most famous retainer firms. Incidentally, I'm pleased to report that both failed to make any headway. But they must succeed sometimes, or they wouldn't try such gambits.

Whenever there's an ongoing retainer search, for which the employer is paying the full fee (in both instances above, more than $40,000 per month was being paid over a three-month period), you're at a monumental disadvantage, if you get "lobbed in from the sidelines" on contingency. An $80,000+ (average) price-tag on your head is *in addition* to the $80,000+ (average) being paid to the retainer recruiter. Hiring you will cost over $160,000! You're like a doubly-inflated basketball the headhunter is trying to slap through the hoop.

The only time you gain from an introduction by a contingency recruiter is when

1. there's a legitimate listing, and

2. it's from a company you wouldn't have contacted, if the contingency recruiter hadn't persuaded you.

Obviously, you're better off without a price-tag on your head. So you really should develop direct contact with all the companies of potential interest to you. That requires some effort. But your reward is being an unencumbered prospect for employment with the companies you consider most attractive.

Indeed, why not cultivate good professional rapport with all the major competitive companies in your field? Someday you may be interested in working for one of them. Or you may ask some of their people to work for you.

A Proper Contingency Referral...Helpful to You and to the Client

But now let's suppose that "out of the blue" a contingency recruiter who has a definite listing from a company you admire calls about the position and persuades you to pursue it. You didn't know the opening existed. Or if you did, you previously chose not to follow up.

Having (1) had a true listing and (2) persuaded you to pursue it, the contingency recruiter has done both the employer and you a service, and she deserves to be paid.

You must, in good conscience, *pursue the opportunity only through her*. It's too late to contact the employer directly. Indeed, the employer wouldn't respect you if you tried to go around the contingency recruiter at this point.

Moreover, because the contingency recruiter has a bona fide listing, there's a good chance that the employer may receive several candidates from her and discuss them with her, thus generating valuable feedback that the recruiter will share with you...another benefit to both you and the employer.

A good, ethical contingency recruiter, under these circumstances, is doing what a good retainer recruiter would do. This is particularly true if the contingency recruiter has an *exclusive listing* and there are no candidates from other contingency recruiters, and no "no-price-tag" candidates who reached the employer directly. Under such ideal circumstances the contingency recruiter becomes a full and objective participant. She's not kept in the dark about candidates from other sources, because there aren't any. And she's not presumed to be economically biased. Every candidate came from her, and she'll be paid regardless of which one is hired.

But beware of a different fact situation that would look the same to you as a potential candidate.

Now we'll assume that the contingency recruiter...or a retainer recruiter switching into contingency...has not been in touch with the employer before calling you. He's merely following up on an item in this morning's edition of your industry's trade paper. Let's monitor his phone call to you:

CONTINGENCY RECRUITER: "Have you heard that Bob Smith, the Marketing VP at Acme, has resigned and is going over to Zolo as President?"

YOU: "No, that's interesting news."

CONTINGENCY: "Well, I don't think there's a better person in the industry to replace him than you, and I'd like you to be a candidate for it. What do you say?"

YOU: "Absolutely! I've always admired Acme and the President over there, Hal Clay...brilliant, and a very nice man. Count me in. I'd love to be considered."

CONTINGENCY: "Great. You'd be a perfect fit. I'll get back to you."

Too bad! You just got a price-tag on your head. Unless Clay has set up a barrier to unsolicited referrals, using his assistant and a simple form letter that begins on the next page, you and any other obvious candidates Contingency can line up are about to have your resumes mailed to Mr. Clay with a pushy letter from Contingency, who has not been asked for his assistance.

Unfortunately for you, Clay has assigned Richard Retainer to do a fee-paid search. Moreover, Clay doesn't yet have his secretarial defense system operating.

So Clay is handed Contingency's letter and the enclosed resumes. He calls HR, and Contingency is identified as "a good resource, who hits pretty well for us on sales jobs and some middle-managers too; really knows our industry and where the bodies are." Rather than offend Contingency, Clay sets up his defense system for the future and writes Contingency a note informing him that Retainer has been engaged to do a search, and that no further candidates should be proposed by Contingency, "although these will be considered."

Then, along with a list of names he's personally thought of as prospects, Clay gives a copy of Contingency's letter and its five enclosed resumes to Retainer, saying:

"Check these out, if you wish. I'd be willing to pay the double fee if you find that one of them is the best we can do. I don't know any of these people from Contingency except (you!). He'd have been on my list too, but you've got his full resume in this stuff here. He's young... maybe a little brash...but he appears to have lots of drive and creativity. Also some good common sense, and that's not easy to find. I talked to him at his company's booth at Product Expo last winter. I'd definitely be willing to consider him if you think we should."

Did you ever hear from Retainer?

No? You're not surprised, are you? It's inconceivable that Retainer would want his—(we'll estimate a fee of $120,000)—project "completed" by a candidate from Contingency...thus making Retainer's efforts superfluous, and doubling the employer's cost of filling the job to $240,000.

Of course, all this is happening before you and I have finished our look at the "Rites of Passage." You'll be handling things a lot differently after our guided tour through the land of headhunters...especially Chapter 9 on "How to Handle a Recruiter Who Calls You."

You'll never again bend over and let any recruiter...contingency or retainer... paste a price-tag on your head, unless he passes your rigorous testing to make sure he has an appropriate client relationship.

You have no obligation to serve as a lottery ticket just because a recruiter calls you on the phone. If the company hasn't asked him to submit candidates, you and he are on the same footing. It's up to you whether he sends your resume or you send it yourself. Certainly the straightforward approach is more to your advantage, now that you're a recognizable executive earning a very substantial level of compensation.

Here's the letter executives use to defend against unwanted contingency referrals and maintain their right to see and talk to whomever they wish, without having an uninvited outsider try to interpose fees of 25% to 35% on what would otherwise be *free speech*:

Dear _____________:

I am Mr./Ms. ____________'s Assistant, and I open his/her mail.

I opened your letter recommending a person (or people) to Mr./Ms. ____________. I'm not passing it on to him/her or to anyone else in our organization, because* we have an executive recruiter on paid retainer to handle the project you refer to. We have not listed our opening with agents and are not accepting agent referrals.

```
So I'm returning your letter.  I have not
passed it or its contents to anyone else in
the organization, and have not kept a copy
of it.

Thank you for your interest.

                Sincerely,


        Assistant to ___________

*Omit "because" clause, if inapplicable.
```

Don't fall for the old "let me represent you" line.

There was a time when "headhunters" did represent potential employees, but they no longer do. As we discussed in the previous chapter, prior to the early '60s, the people who today are contingency recruiters and are paid by the employer, used to label themselves "personnel agencies" and were paid (usually 6% to 12%) by the people for whom they found work...just like the Hollywood agent who, for a 10% to 15% fee, represents Brad Pitt or Reese Witherspoon.

A person who represents someone else is called an "agent" and the person represented (called "principal" or "client") is *always the one who pays*. And the fee, of course, has to be affordable. You wouldn't even consider paying 25% to 35% of your first year's compensation to be "represented," and Brad and Reese wouldn't either!

True representation is intended to help get a person hired, not discourage it. Only if you were paying would you be "represented." Otherwise, any "push" you get from a recruiter is more than offset by the drag of the $80,000+ price-tag he applies. Neither the dictionary and legal definition of "representation," nor common sense, allow any recruiter...contingency or retainer...to imply that he "represents" you. Don't you let him imply it either.

So, when a contingency recruiter calls, you must find out unequivocally, that he or she already has a firm agreement to *represent the employer*, who's promised to pay if and when one of the recruiter's candidates is hired. Notice that the agreement must apply to *the specific job being discussed*. Previous deals with the same employer are irrelevant. Remember, *if the recruiter had been able to obtain a legitimate listing before contacting you, he would surely have done so*. "I didn't have time" or, even worse, "I came to you first" is no excuse.

If you learn...and you'll probably have to dig to get a straight answer...that the recruiter does *not* have a specific agreement with the employer about the specific job he calls and asks to "represent" you on, then there is only one answer:

"No, thank you, I'd prefer to represent myself!"

The recruiter you know may give you more trouble than the one you don't.

Just as crime statistics show you're more likely to be murdered by a family member or an acquaintance than by a stranger, you're also more likely to be hurt by a recruiter you know well than by one you don't know.

Opportunistic handling of the people they know tends to become a habit pattern among some of the recruiters who specialize in a certain industry. They watch the trade press with eagle's eyes, and have the ears of a bat when it comes to the rumor mill. And in incestuous industries and job categories with lots of movement from company to company,* it's not surprising that recruiters come to regard almost every "match" as one they should have made.

It's just a short step from reading with disappointment in the trade press about job changes made without any recruiter involvement where the recruiter happened to know the new employees...and by name at least, the employers...to the point where the recruiter feels that:

1. This industry is my domain, where I know the people. They are my inventory...built up through the years.
2. Therefore, whenever people I know move, whatever companies they go to owe me a fee. I'm entitled!
3. I must act aggressively to make sure I don't lose out on any of the fees I'm entitled to.
4. Therefore, whenever an obvious opening occurs, I must line up and "submit" all of the people most likely to wind up in that spot.

Earnestly feeling approximately as described, industry-specific contingency

---

*Exactly the types that tend to be served by contingency recruiters...the retailing, consumer product, advertising, hospitality, transportation, hi-tech, health care, e-commerce, and publishing industries; and the marketing, sales, financial, EDP, engineering, and legal categories, regardless of industry, are typical.

recruiting firms...or more often today hybrid contingency-and-retainer firms... seem almost innocently oblivious to the disadvantageous position in which they put unasked-for "candidates" in relation to others with no price-tags on their heads.

Self-Interest: The Bottom Line on Contingency Recruiters for the Executive Far above...or Even Just Reaching for...$100,000+

When it comes to referrals involving yourself as the candidate, the situation is clear. You're always better off getting to the employer entirely on your own, unless the contingency recruiter has:

1. A *valid listing* from the employer (not obvious),
2. which is *exclusive* (no other recruiters...retainer or contingency...are involved; also not easy to know), and
3. the job is one which you wouldn't have pursued if it weren't for the contingency recruiter's persuasion.

On the other hand, if the contingency recruiter alerts you to a fine opportunity you wouldn't otherwise have found out about...or persuades you to pursue one you were aware of but otherwise would have ignored...then he's done you and the employer a very valuable service. You owe him your full cooperation...and your thanks.

Above all, don't fall for the "let me represent you" line. Unless *you're* paying the more than $80,000 fee on a $250,000 position—and proportionately more on a bigger one—and therefore are not put at a disadvantage relative to the "no-price-tag" candidates, you're in the best possible position when you get to the employer on your own. This is usually true too, although less obvious, with respect to *retainer recruiters*, whom you and I will look at next.

Chapter 7

Retainer Recruiters: Look Out for Yourself

Welcome to the posh and prestigious realm of the retainer executive recruiters.

These are the headhunters whose efforts and expertise are valuable enough that they must be paid regardless of whether anyone they introduce is hired.
These are the recruiters who usually...but not always...get the assignments to find executives at $100k+...$300k+ ...and $1Million+ + + !

And these are the executive search consultants you can almost...but not entirely...be certain will never slap a price-tag on your head and race you to your most likely employers.

Yes, even some of the most prominent retainer recruiters may occasionally shift into the contingency mode...for their benefit, not yours. Then everything I told you in the previous chapter applies. Consider yourself forewarned.

But now let's take a look at your self-interest in dealing with a retainer recruiter who's operating strictly as a retainer recruiter should.

Getting to the employer before she engages the retainer recruiter is very much to your advantage.

With the retainer recruiter, just as with the contingency recruiter, you're way ahead if you get to the employer before he does. Consider these advantages:

> **The employer saves time and lots of money**...$80,000 if the job pays, for example, $240,000, and proportionately more as you move up. No employer will hire you just to avoid a fee. But if you're right for the job, she's glad not to wait three months for somebody to find you. And not spending $80,000 on a retainer recruiter pleases her just as much as not spending $80,000 on a contingency recruiter.
>
> **You're a class of *one*.** The retainer recruiter would present several candidates. You're good. But don't be overconfident. The employer just might hire one of the others.
>
> **There's no risk that the recruiter won't present you.** We'll soon discuss six reasons a retainer recruiter may not present you. By getting to the employer before he does, you've bypassed all six roadblocks.
>
> **The employer is more open-minded and flexible.** You may not have precisely the background the employer insists on getting in return for an $80,000 or a $150,000 search fee. But whatever you have that's not ideal may look quite attractive before firm specifications are written and lots of money is being spent to pursue them.
>
> **The job may be tailored for you.** If you arrive when the employer is only beginning to analyze her business problems that require outside talent, she may include your availability in her thinking.

I can't overemphasize the benefits of reaching an employer *before* he or she is committed to either kind of search...retainer or contingency. By the time a search is assigned, a specific job is being filled. Detailed specifications have been written. Potential employees who show up at that late date tend to be thought of as either *relevant* or *irrelevant*. Try to arrive before you're considered a square peg, merely because the opening has been declared a round hole.

After a retainer search is under way, you're best off meeting the employer as one of the retainer recruiter's "finds."

Unfortunately, that's not easy to accomplish.

With our example of a retainer search in progress, $80,000 is being spent to have a consultant look for you. And with the money already spent, you're best off walking in as living proof that it was well spent. You have these advantages:

You're custom-selected for the job. Meticulous specifications have been drawn up, and you've been found in response to them.

You're expert-recommended. A professional commanding a substantial fee has identified, examined, and proposed you.

You're not challenged by an expert. Despite his or her financial impartiality, the $80,000 expert may still tend to see more merit in candidates he finds than in ones that, being impartial, he evaluates as *"also excellent."* Talk is cheap. It's human nature...and good business...to want the client to feel she got more than an objective discussion for $80,000.

You confirm the employer's wisdom. She decided to hire a consultant. *You prove she was right.*

No question about it. If you can't get to the employer before the retainer recruiter does, then your self-interest is best served if the recruiter "finds" and presents you.

But *will* he?

Not unless you meet a surprisingly restrictive set of six criteria...three of which have nothing to do with your ability to do the job.

When all six of these criteria are present, your self-interest is served by the retainer recruiter.

His introduction is the best possible way to reach the employer in situations that meet the following conditions:

1. When he's searching to fill a job *you could perform exceptionally well*;
2. When he's searching for someone with *exactly your qualifications*;
3. When he's *personally convinced* that you possess those qualifications;
4. When you're *not blocked by the You-work-for-a-client "Off-limits" Rule*;
5. When you're *not blocked by the You're-allocated-to-another-recruiter-within-the-firm "Off-limits" Rule*;
6. When the recruiter *doesn't already have plenty of other fine candidates.*

Don't you wish there were just one criterion? And of course the one you'd cling to would be #1...*a job you could perform exceptionally well.* However, even #1 can be a pain. "Exceptionally well" doesn't mean "competently." Since the retainer recruiter is being paid upwards of $80,000 to "search," what he finds had better be *something special.*

But suppose you are special. And, at least in your opinion, you're absolutely the right choice for a specific position you know is being "searched" by a retainer recruiter. Suppose, too, that you've found out his name and his firm's name. Should you call him? Or should you go directly to the employer instead?

There's a "catch 22" when you know there's a retainer search and you know who's doing it.

You don't want to be overlooked.

But if you go to the recruiter, you're playing "Russian Roulette" with up to 5 bullets in your 6-shooter.

The only one of the six criteria on which you have direct information is #1.

You know that *you could perform exceptionally well.* That's the harmless chamber in your revolver. However, even then you may be wrong...not about your abilities, but about the job content, which may be differently defined for the new person sought than for the former one, and for people with similar-sounding jobs in other companies.

With respect to each of the other five criteria, you don't know if it's "no problem," or possibly a fatal shot.

For you to get to the employer through the retainer recruiter...admittedly the ideal route...you've got to survive all six potentially eliminating criteria. How different from regular "Russian Roulette"! With only one chamber loaded, and only having to pull the trigger once, the traditional game is as safe as badminton when compared with trying to get a retainer recruiter to "present" you on a job you know he's "searching." Then, five of the six chambers *may* be loaded, and you've got to pull the trigger on all six, hoping that *none* of them is.

We've covered #1. Forget about whether or not you can *do the job.* Let's look at the remaining five of these invisible threats to your candidacy. You should have gone directly to the employer, rather than playing with your Retainer-Recruiter-Revolver, if even one of the other five chambers has a hidden surprise for you:

2. *If your qualifications and experience aren't EXACTLY as specified.* For $80,000, the recruiter is expected to hit the target. If others match the specifications more closely, he'll present them, not you. On the other hand, if you get to the employer directly, and he meets and likes you, he may observe special abilities, or experience, or fine personal characteristics that outweigh your deficiencies. Even if he merely forwards your mailed-in resume to the retainer recruiter, he's implicitly *expanding the specs* to include you.

3. *If the recruiter isn't personally convinced* that you've got the right stuff. You may seem more appropriate to the employer than to the recruiter. If so, let's hope you meet them in that order. Meet the employer first and you're in the running. Meet the recruiter first and you're dead.

4. *If you're blocked by the You-work-for-a-client "Off-limits" Rule.* Then you must go to the employer. The recruiter's "don't-bite-the-hand-that-feeds" problems mean nothing to the

employer. He'll ship you to the recruiter...or deal with you himself, if the recruiter refuses to touch you.

5. *If you're blocked by the You're-allocated-to-another-recruiter-within-the-firm "Off limits" Rule.* The only way you'll ever hear about two appropriate-for-you jobs simultaneously within the same retainer firm is if *YOU go to Employer #2.* No recruiter will ever tell Client #2 that you're his at a cost of $80,000, but he may have a hard time hiring you, because the firm is also providing you to Client #1.

6. *If the recruiter already has plenty of other fine candidates.* Whenever you're one of a great many people who'd be appropriate, *ordinary statistical odds* will usually kill you. The recruiter doesn't need you, because he already has a full slate.

Two facts are clear:
1. it's nice to be among the retainer recruiter's "finds,"
2. but that's not going to happen very often.

so

There are two things to do:
1. go directly to employers, and
2. get known to lots of retainer recruiters.

How strong is your interest in changing jobs *right now?*

Would you merely like to hear occasionally about career-advancing alternatives to a job you love and would hate to leave? Or are you eager to move? Are you out of work? Your degree of interest in changing jobs will dictate how much you do.

But what to do is obvious.

Go directly to employers.

As we've just seen, you're better off if you get to the employer before the retainer recruiter is brought in. Even when you find out for sure that a retainer recruiter is working on a specific job you'd love, there's a strong likelihood that she won't "present" you for one or more of the six reasons we just looked at. And of course, 99% of the time you won't know the job exists...nor that the recruiter is working on it...nor that one of the six reasons stands in your way.

So, as a general rule, going directly to employers is your smartest move.

When you're not interested in changing jobs, of course, you won't be contacting any employers. But when you're *very* interested in a change, it's in your self-interest to contact as many employers as possible, as effectively as possible. How to do that will be one of the many "Rites of Passage" we'll cover later on.

Know as many retainer firms as possible.

Since it's clear that each retainer firm...no matter how large...is only going to show you a very few opportunities per year that would interest you, the only way you can know about more recruiter-handled opportunities is to *know more firms*. Certainly your self-interest lies in that direction, and how to achieve that goal—both conventionally and on the web—is something else we'll look into.

Contingency firms, however, are another matter. If a firm offers *any* contingency services—even though it also offers retainer services—consider it a contingency firm and look out for the potential disadvantages we examined in the previous chapter. You're probably already acquainted with some very fine contingency firms which have agreed never to submit you without first identifying both the employer and the job, and getting your advance approval. I suggest limiting your involvement with contingency firms to the ones where you have this high level of personal rapport.

Reach out to firms you don't know only if they're *exclusively* retainer, and hence unlikely to jeopardize their "pay-me-to-look" status by circulating your resume to any company that hasn't paid.

And now a logical question everyone always asks:

Wouldn't getting in touch with lots of retainer recruiting firms make me seem too readily available?

Absolutely not.

Retainer recruiting firms do not call each other up and compare notes on who's been in touch with them. Neither do employers.

And of course no two retainer firms will ever be "searching" the same job simultaneously, since no employer would ever pay two suppliers to do the same work at the same time.

Therefore, no employer...and no retainer recruiter...will ever find out how many other recruiters and employers you've been in touch with.

Limiting the number of retainer recruiters who know about you doesn't increase your value to anyone. Such "exclusivity" merely reduces the number of attractive positions you'll know about, by reducing the number of search firms that know about you.

The only potential problem you could have along these lines would be if you happened to contact both the employer and his retainer recruiter simultaneously. Then the employer might feel that the recruiter didn't have to look very hard to find you. However, the recruiter will also present several other fine candidates who *weren't* obvious, so he's in no trouble for presenting one obvious candidate. Indeed, he might have seemed remiss *not* to identify and check out the obvious one.

Notice that medium-sized and smaller retainer firms are likely to do you just as much good as the largest ones.

Don't neglect medium-sized and smaller firms. After all, no retainer firm—no matter how large, and how many of its jobs would interest you—is likely to show you more than one-at-a-time and two or three a year. Therefore, a firm that annually handles only thirty jobs you'd want may be just as likely to show you three-a-year as a huge company that handles three hundred you'd want.

Incidentally, from the sophisticated employer's point of view, the smaller firms can sometimes be *far more valuable as recruiters* than the largest ones, because they're far less handicapped by the "you-work-for-a-client" and the "allocated-to-another-recruiter-within-the-firm" barriers.

Don't imagine that being well known to a retainer firm will get you exposed to the most attractive opportunity they have in terms of your self-interest.

As you know, a retainer firm that observes traditional ethics will only tell you about one-opportunity-for-you at a time...usually no more than two or three per year. Chances are that "Murphy's Law" will have you allocated to an opportunity in Hog Wallow Bend, when the firm is asked to fill the job you'd love in an ideal company just twelve miles from your home.

If this happens when you're actively "looking," and you fail to reach the nearby employer, don't blame the retainer recruiter handling the Hog Wallow Bend search...nor his colleague doing the Hometown search. And don't blame me. You knew that you should have been in touch with the target employer directly. *You're* the one who failed to watch out for your self-interest.

Contact retainer firms long before you're ready to move. Avoid the "He's-in-trouble-so-we-can-show-him-anything" presumption.

Getting in touch with a recruiter raises an unfortunate presumption. Executives ordinarily do so only when they're out of work, or in trouble and anxious to move. The more recent the contact, the more it looks like the difficulty is *now!*

So if your resume is a recent arrival, you'll probably be earmarked for something relatively unattractive. The firm *won't* feel you have to be lured away from a great situation. And once you're allocated to a recruiter for a search, nobody in her firm can contact you on anything else, until she's finished her project and her administrative assistant has "returned you to the pool." You'll never know if something more attractive is co-pending, or comes along during the weeks and months before you're back in circulation.

Keep in touch as your career progresses.

For all the reasons we've just seen, it's good strategy to have your up-to-date information in the databases of all the exclusively retainer recruiting firms well *before* you actually want to move. Each time you get a major promotion, use that opportunity to send the announcement memo to the firms you've had contact with.

The implication is that you're continuing to move ahead on the fast track. You're the type of person the retainer firms want to show their clients. You're not in trouble. You're not answering the ads placed by the contingency firms in newspapers and on web job boards. So you certainly can't be offered uninteresting, low-salaried, out-of-the-way jobs. Your announcement arrives at a time when you're obviously on a high. And the firm updates its information on you accordingly.

But suppose you're only belatedly contacting retainer firms, and you want to move right now.

Should you try to visit several offices and meet several recruiters in the largest firms?

No. Make contacts that are convenient and time-efficient. But don't waste lots of valuable time that you could devote to other aspects of a well-rounded job search.

Remember that even the largest firms normally allow you to see only one-position-for-you at a time...probably only two or three per year. Once any firm has you in their database and you've met even one of their recruiters, you're about as fully involved as you can possibly be.

Moreover, if any firm is already *actively discussing* any job with you, you know that you probably won't hear about anything else from them until that search is completed, or you've declared yourself a non-candidate...*and* until the recruiter you're talking to has relinquished you in the firm's database.

The only sure way to get strongly involved with any retainer firm, large or small...and with any retainer recruiter, regardless of firm...is to be frank and helpful whenever you're called to solicit your personal interest and/or suggestions. Then *you're* helping the recruiter, not trying to get him to help you. If you sound impressive on the phone...and you genuinely try to help...those facts will be noted and preserved.

Later, when other recruiters in the firm get their hands on your information, the first recruiter's comments will encourage them to call you for suggestions, even when you don't personally look like the solution to their problem. Gradually, over the months and years, you'll meet many of the firm's recruiters by phone, and...when you're appropriate to be interviewed...face-to-face as well.

Just as you can't get a baby in a month by getting nine women pregnant...or if you're a woman, by encouraging nine men to get you pregnant...you also can't become the darling of Korn/Ferry or Russell Reynolds Associates by hustling several of their recruiters simultaneously. Rather than spending lots of time trying to reach more recruiters in the same large firm, you'd be better off contacting additional firms.

Go to the employer *before* you hear about his job from the recruiter ...not afterward.

You must reach the employer before the retainer recruiter tells you about the employer's position. Once you hear about the job from the recruiter, it's too late for the direct approach.

Of course, if the retainer recruiter is free-within-his-firm to deal with you, and he's likely to decide you're an ideal candidate, you don't want to "go direct." Then you bask in the spotlight of his recommendation. You're part of what the employer paid upwards of $80,000 for...a "finalist candidate."

But suppose you're interviewed by the retainer recruiter...in the office, or just on the phone...and he decides you're *not* a "finalist." Maybe you lack something the employer has clearly asked for. You feel, on the other hand, that what's missing is outweighed by special advantages which, when the client's aware of them, will cause him to widen his specifications to include you...and perhaps others like you.

Now, however, it's too late to do what you easily could have done earlier. Now you *can't* go straight to the employer. If you do, it will be an outrageous affront to the recruiter. And remember that the retainer recruiter, unlike the contingency recruiter, is financially unbiased. Therefore, he usually helps the client evaluate *all candidates from all sources*, not just the ones the recruiter supplies. Someone you've slapped in the face will probably be asked his opinion of you.

On the other hand, if you'd gone to the employer *before* the recruiter turned you down, the employer might have pronounced you a worthy candidate. Or asked the recruiter to check you out...indicating that your deficiency wasn't disabling. Then, the recruiter could have "adopted" you. Indeed, you'd have broadened the specifications and *made his work easier*.

Now, however, you're a pain in the neck! Now you've *defied* the recruiter. And you've *called his judgment into question*. Why didn't he at least see you as a close case? Why didn't he at least *ask* if you were worth considering?

Pursuing a recruiter's client after the recruiter rejects you is unforgivable. Your centrally maintained information will be annotated. No other recruiter in the firm will ever risk a similar experience. *You'll never again be a candidate of that firm*. Yes, Virginia, there *is* a death penalty!

Going to the employer before... rather than after...talking to the retainer recruiter not only avoids his wrath; *it may delight him*.

Once you get to an employer and persuade him you're a viable candidate, hidden blockages with the retainer recruiter disappear. Either the employer meets and evaluates you without involving the recruiter; or, more likely, he passes you on to the recruiter, who's forced to follow up.

If you were held back merely because the recruiter had plenty of other fine candidates, he may keep plugging his "finds." But he'll also "adopt" you. And he'll be glad to get the job filled, regardless of who's hired.

If "You-work-for-a-client" was the barrier, the recruiter may reveal it to the employer as his excuse for not "finding" you. Secretly, of course, he'll be delighted that you've innocently helped him complete his search.

If "You're-allocated-to-another-recruiter-in-the-firm" was the problem, the recruiter will never admit it, because this handicap of larger recruiting firms is never publicly exposed. However, he'll be equally pleased to have this road-block removed.

Whatever the barrier may have been, you've broken through by going straight to the employer. *And the retainer recruiter is probably just as happy as you are with the result.*

By now you may be saying: Wait a minute! Aren't you telling me two diametrically opposite things?

1. I'm better off as the recruiter's "find" than just walking in off the street, and yet

2. I should go straight to the companies I want to work for.

Isn't this inconsistent?

No. Most of the time, your *only choice* is to contact the potential employer directly. Because most of the time you won't know:

1. that a suitable position is open, and

2. that a retainer recruiter is filling it, and
3. who the recruiter is.

And unless you know all three facts, you have no choice. Contacting the recruiter is impossible.

Even in the rare instance when you *do* happen to find out all three essentials, you'd better think long and hard before you go to the recruiter instead of the employer.

Whenever you contact a retainer recruiter on a job you know he or she is handling, you're playing Russian Roulette with potential bangs in five barrels.

Play those odds if you want to.

I wouldn't.

An "advanced technique" with retainer recruiters:

There is one terrific way to get around a retainer firm's rules and learn about the position you'd like best among all those the firm is filling.

This "end run" can only be scored if you've already established a close personal friendship with one of the firm's recruiters...a relationship built over a period of years. Your friend probably first called you as a potential candidate. You weren't interested, but you went out of your way to offer excellent suggestions. Several became "finalists" or valuable "sources" of further ideas. You've made money for the recruiter. You've also been trusted with secrets that never leaked out. Maybe you've even met with him or her on several occasions.

Now you want to move. So you call your friend and ask if there's anything at his firm that might meet your objectives.

> YOU: "Jim, I'd really like to get out of this family-owned business and into a big public company where I can develop a track record with full P&L responsibility for a good-sized subsidiary, and I was wondering if there's any way you could possibly let me know what's going on over at your place that might fill the bill."

If your recruiter friend wants to—and he certainly has no obligation other than friendship to "go around the rules"—he can do the following:

1. *Get your information.* He'll pull you up on his computer screen and identify himself as the person currently authorized to deal with you. And if someone "has you," he'll click "next to use," so he can have you when the current person "drops" you. This will pull you away from searches that don't appeal to you.

2. *Look up the firm's assignments that could interest you.* He'll consult his PC, or iPad, or smart phone, or a weekly printout for this information.

3. *Tell you the relevant searches, and help you select the ONE you like best.* Probably there will be 20 to 60 or more such assignments among the various offices and recruiters of a large retainer firm doing thousands of searches per year. The computer will tell your friend the location, name of company and subsidiary, projected salary range, and name of the firm-member doing the search, for every active project. How far out on a limb he'll go to reveal these facts to you will depend on how much he trusts you to keep the discussion *absolutely confidential.*

When you and he agree on the best opportunity for you that his firm is working on, he'll then call up the recruiter handling it:

> YOUR RETAINER RECRUITER FRIEND: "By the way, Dick, I know somebody who'd be terrific for that Ideal Subsidiary project you're working on for Charington Corporation. In fact, he's a personal friend of mine, and he's marked for me on the computer. Not only does he have the perfect background, but I'm sure he'd be interested. Would you like me to turn him over to you?"
>
> DICK: "Is he really good?"
>
> RECRUITER FRIEND: "Outstanding! I've tried several times to get him to be a candidate on general management projects I've been handling. But he works for a family-owned mini-conglomerate and they've kept giving him more money and responsibility, so I've never had anything he was willing to spring for. In fact he's practically running the place now.
>
> "They're about $850 million in everything from consumer products to a grey iron casting company. But he's finally decided that it's time to build his career in a big public company; he's gone about as far as he can where he is.
>
> "Your project makes sense, because his experience is exactly

right...and you've got a high enough salary on that job to be able to afford him. Most public companies don't pay as well as Charington does."

DICK: "Well, if you think he's that good, let's go ahead. I've got three fine candidates right now, and I could use a fourth to round out the slate."

RECRUITER FRIEND: "Fine, I'll turn him over to you in the database. He's on my screen right now. I'll tell him to expect a call from you."

But remember, your retainer recruiter friend can only do that if he's sure you're going to play square with him.

If you later contact the employers on some of the other searches your recruiter friend has told you about, *it'll be obvious that you violated his trust*. Every one of the firm's clients that you reach is likely to involve his or her recruiter from the firm in evaluating you. And every recruiter will check the firm's central computer to get permission to deal with you. Bang! Your deceit is *automatically* exposed! If you cheat, you'll be blacklisted by your friend's firm, and you'll lose one of the most valuable recruiter contacts any executive can ever have.

Networking Your Way Around the Problem

When I first wrote *RITES*, I saw the strong personal relationship shown above as your only hope of gaining insight into the many appropriate searches going on simultaneously in the giant retainer firms and making sure you're involved in the one you consider best for you.

Not so! A reader—in the midst of changing jobs—called me with the following suggestion, which I find absolutely diabolical in its insight and effectiveness:

"John, I'm a pretty hot property at the top search firms. Almost every one of them has me meeting one of their clients. A couple have been naughty and introduced me to two clients at once, trusting me not to spill the beans.

"On the other hand, there's lots of good stuff the top firms have that they're *not* showing me.

"But I've found a way around that. In my networking, I'm making it a point to stay tight with just about everyone who's left my

> company in the past year or so and found a new job. Their backgrounds are just like mine." (This fellow had just left McKinsey.)
>
> "Those folks have all worked hard to become acquainted at the top retainer search firms, and now they're getting lots of calls, either as potential candidates or asking for suggestions. All the jobs fit me perfectly. Immediately, my friends call to let me know what a recruiter has called them about.
>
> "Right now" (one of the very largest firms) "has me as a candidate for a big job at CitiGroup. And yesterday they began looking to fill exactly the same position at Chase. Of course they didn't call me. But by this afternoon, I had six voice mails from people they *had* called...and *those* people called me.
>
> "What I'll do is mail a letter and resume to the person the job reports to. It's a real power resume...I used your tips and spent a lot of time on it. And what'll happen—in fact it already has, several times—is I'll either get a call directly from the client—in this case Chase—or the headhunter on the Chase search will call and explain that his client is asking for me.
>
> "And of course they" (the search firm) "can't be mad at me. I didn't hear about the job from them and then go behind their back. I'm innocent. I'm just sending out letters like anyone else who's looking for a job."

Wow! He's right. The search firm *can't* object. He hasn't used their information and gone behind their backs. In fact, whoever is handling the Chase search at the giant search firm will probably be delighted to have another fine candidate...and one that, by the rules, he could never even have talked to until CitiGroup had either (1) hired or (2) rejected our savvy job-seeker.

When headhunter #2 calls from the same search firm because his client wants our wise young friend to be a candidate on his search, the firm has become involved in what the very large firms now call "parallel processing." Yes, it's against traditional practice but, as discussed earlier, flexibility is increasing. (See page 162-63.)

Chapter 8

How to Handle Executive Recruiters ...When You Contact Them

We've come a long way together in exploring the two types of recruiters ...contingency and retainer...and your self-interest with both. I've also shown you quite a bit about how to handle each type.

But that hasn't been our main thrust. I've raised "how-to-handle" issues only as they came up in the context of the basic "self-interest" concerns.

Now, as we continue our trek through the land of headhunters, let's cover all the remaining "how-to-handle" information. This chapter's on "when-you-call-*them*," and the next two will deal with "when-they-call-*you*."

Soon we'll have seen headhunters from every angle, except the inside of their own offices. And that vantage point, too, is available to you in Appendix I. There you'll observe an executive search from start to finish, through the eyes of the recruiter. That account...fictionalized, of course, to protect everyone, and to make sure it covers everything you should know...is your postgraduate course. Do take it. But only after you've read the whole book as background for it.

Meanwhile, back to the matters at hand.

Sometimes you won't be content to wait for the recruiter's call.

Obviously, you'd love to have the most respected retainer firms phoning every few months to tempt you with leap-ahead opportunities.

Then, if you happen to feel stymied and frustrated when a call comes in, you can say, "Interesting...tell me more." With very little effort...perhaps not even the preparation of an up-to-date resume...you'll be swerving past the obstacles at your present company, and gaining momentum on the fast track.

But suppose that right now you're known to only a few firms...and not well known. You have no close personal friend at any major firm who'll go out on a limb for you as we saw at the end of the last chapter. You're a stranger to most of the firms. And you want them to know you...as favorably and as soon as possible.

Be careful. Don't go "cruisin' for a bruisin'."

Whenever you develop a strong determination to seek out recruiters and spark their interest, you're ripe for trouble.

You're in just the right frame of mind to be delighted when a contingency recruiter proposes to put a price-tag on your head and rush to potential employers before you do. And you're equally vulnerable to having that same price-tag applied by a retainer recruiter, who's so impressed by you that she's tempted to slip momentarily into the contingency mode.

With enough of the right bad luck, you can even wind up with a double price on your head...tagged for $80,000 or more by someone lobbing you in on contingency, with respect to an opening that a retainer firm is already being paid over $80,000 to fill.

The first step in handling an executive recruiter is to figure out which type you're dealing with ...contingency or retainer.

You certainly can't tell from the name on the door, since these days both contingency and retainer recruiters call themselves by exactly the same names ..."executive recruiters," "management consultants," "executive search consultants," etc. And you can't tell from the office decor, since both have posh layouts.

Moreover, both types fill $100k and $200k and $500k positions, although they're far more frequently handled by retainer firms than by contingency firms. Both may have the utmost polish*...and impeccable integrity*. And to make things even more confusing, both types may switch opportunistically to the opposite payment method.

A warm welcome is a hot clue.

It's only natural, when you're presenting yourself to a recruiter, to want a favorable reaction.

Ironically, it's a contingency recruiter inclined toward the broadest possible distribution of unasked-for resumes, who will be most eager to grant you a courtesy interview. After all, his business is attaching price-tags to people and scattering their resumes to the four winds. He *wants* people coming in.

So if your appointment is easy to get, and the visit itself rushes along very favorably, warning bells should go off in your head. You may be "working with" a recruiter who feels you're "highly marketable"...a lottery ticket to be played with a few dollars worth of postage or a list of e-mail addresses.

Beware of the recruiter who tells you what you want to hear.

Imagine someone arriving for a courtesy interview. After the opening pleasantries, he hands the recruiter his resume. As the recruiter scans it quickly, the executive speaks to reinforce the major points, telling about present responsibilities and outstanding accomplishments. The recruiter looks thoughtful... smiles...and renders a verdict:

> "Well, this is a very impressive resume! And you've also impressed me on a personal basis, Bob, as we've been sitting here talking. I'm really glad you came in. You seem like just the kind of executive who'd do well in several companies I'm thinking of that I could present you to."
>
> "Just leave a copy of your resume with me. I'm going to see what I can do to get you some interviews."
>
> *(He stands up and shakes your hand.)*
>
> "I think I can help you."

An executive who didn't know as much as you already do about recruiters might make a serious error in interpreting what we just saw. He might meet his wife for lunch and say:

> "Just had a great meeting! I saw an executive recruiter who was really impressed, and he said he'd be working to help me."
>
> *(Time out for a discreet hug to express the good mood.)*
>
> "Let's pick up a bottle of champagne; I've got a hunch it won't be long now before we're celebrating!"

This guy's interview was certainly no cause for rejoicing. Quite the contrary. *The recruiter just gave his guest fair warning that he intends to begin racing him to the employers most likely to want to hire him.*

It was obvious from a scan of the executive's resume and the fine personal impression he made that he was highly employable, if unemployed...or obviously ready to move up, if currently employed. So the recruiter is about to offer the executive—with price-tag attached, of course—to all the appropriate employers the recruiter can think of.

When a recruiter circulates a resume to various likely employers it's called "*floating*" the resume. I consider it absolutely reprehensible for any recruiter, whether contingency or retainer, to refer the name and background of any individual to any employer without the prior knowledge and consent of the individual.

And *every* recruiter will invariably tell you he would never do such a thing. In fact, however, it seems to happen fairly often...and it may be done by both contingency and retainer people. "*Floating resumes*" is a little like "insider trading." Everyone claims not to do it. And yet it still happens.

What to Tell the Eager Recruiter

Whenever you hear a recruiter say he thinks he can "help," the best thing to do is grab your resume and head for the door. Tell him you don't want to be submitted, unless he contacts you ahead of time and gets your approval to offer you to that particular employer for that particular opening.

Indeed, it wouldn't hurt to write him a letter to the same effect. As we discussed in Chapter 6, you absolutely do not want a recruiter preempting contacts you'd be better off making on your own.

The Old "Tell Him, but Don't Let Him Know You Told Him" Technique

The conversation we've just imagined is, after all, a pretty blatant announcement of the recruiter's intention to "float" his visitor's resume. Some approaches are much more subtle. For example, some recruiters actually *obtain your permission* to send your resume to literally scores of prospective employers. The discussion goes something like this:

> RECRUITER: "Well, Judith, you look like an outstanding consumer products marketing executive. I think you're ready to become overall vice president of marketing for a diversified consumer products company...or maybe it's about time for you to move up to the presidency of your own division of a very large consumer products company."
>
> YOU: "That all sounds great to me."
>
> RECRUITER: "I'd like to test out some of the types of companies you'd be interested in working for. Now I could see you fitting in beautifully at Lever Brothers, or Colgate. Or maybe Clorox or Ocean Spray or Quaker Oats, or Nabisco Brands, or Carnation out on the Coast."
>
> YOU: (assuming that the conversation is purely speculative) "Well, yes, I think I could fit in at any of those places...and I wouldn't mind moving to California."
>
> RECRUITER: "Or I could see you being successful and enjoying yourself in one of the big cosmetics companies, like Revlon or Estee Lauder."
>
> YOU: "I guess that's a possibility, too."

> RECRUITER: "Or you might go all the way to the fashion field with a Michael Kors or a Ralph Lauren."

> YOU: "Well, I hadn't really thought about it, but I guess if the right thing came up..."

> RECRUITER: "Or I could even see you in one of the more advanced and forward-looking industrial companies...they're sometimes interested in grabbing a consumer marketing generalist with an outstanding track record. I'll see if I can come up with any companies like that. And have you ever considered getting into the marketing of financial services, or information products, or..."

The recruiter talks on and on, outlining what seem like nothing more than attractive options for the future development of your career. You think he's merely mentioning some of the types of companies for which he might consider you, if and when they come to him with an appropriate opening to fill.

But he's deliberately taking your nods and smiles as permission to send your resume to all of the companies and industries he's mentioned. If he does a good job of canvassing your interests and mentioning potential employers, you may find that he's outrun you to almost all of the companies you're likely to end up working for.

As times goes on, you may find out by accident that your resume has been submitted to the companies that the contingency recruiter mentioned to you during your courtesy interview. Perhaps you'll see Mr. Decisionmaker at another of your daughter's swim meets. Remember him from Chapter 6? This time he mentions that he happened to notice that your resume is in his company's HR department's files, submitted by Quick Associates.

You call Ralph Quick to protest. His response:

> "Don't you remember when we met in my office? We talked about a number of companies you'd be interested in. So I submitted you to all those companies. As a matter of fact, I kept notes on our visit and jotted down that long *list* of companies we discussed; it's here in your file. I've put in a lot of effort to help you."

What to say when, during a courtesy interview, you run into a recruiter who's preparing to race you to all the employers he mentions, is this:

> "You've talked about a lot of companies. I hope you don't intend to send those companies my resume, when you don't have a specific assignment from them. I've already made contacts myself

> with a number of companies, including many of the ones you've just mentioned. And I'm going to be contacting others."
>
> "Therefore, I'm not authorizing you, or anyone else, to submit me to any company without letting me know first what company you've been engaged to represent, and what job that company has asked you to fill. You *must* check with me first...before you submit my name anywhere. You must get my 'go-ahead' for that particular job at that particular company."

Getting in to see an overly-aggressive recruiter is as easy as slipping on a banana peel.

Getting your foot in the door at the best retainer firms can be difficult. Some clout will help.

Getting into a prominent retainer recruiting firm usually isn't easy. After all, every retainer recruiter needs you only if he personally happens to have a search at the moment that calls for someone with exactly your qualifications.

In *Texas Business*, the chief of the Houston office of one of America's largest retainer firms came out with the most forthright statement I've ever seen in print on this subject.

> "People are always trying to break through to us, but our operators and assistants are very well trained. The only time an unsolicited call will make it through is if a recruiter is searching for someone with that background."

Nonetheless, most retainer firms will, if you persist, arrange for you to receive a courtesy interview...often with one of the most junior members of the firm, who's forced to handle PR duties that the more senior and busier recruiters try to avoid.

If you're a very high-level executive, then just your resume in the mail and a follow-up phone call may get you a courtesy interview. One reason is that you may be someone the firm can use to fill one of its current or future assignments. But a far more likely reason is that the firm wants to get acquainted with you now, so they'll be in a better position to solicit your recruiting business later, when you're building your own team in a new job. And that solicitation will occur, regardless of whether they're involved in your transition.

Even if you're not at quite such a high level, but have a fine track record, well communicated by an impressive resume, you can probably wangle an interview. But if you're just one among many high-potential middle-managers-on-the-way-up, then the *clout of a referral* is essential. And it's always helpful, regardless of how prominent you are.

But whose name should you drop? Whose referral will give you the most clout? I'm continually amazed at how naive many executives are in picking names they think will blast open a reluctant recruiter's door. Here are the people who might refer you...ranked from most to least clout:

> *1. Ideally, someone who spends lots of money with the firm you're trying to meet*...the Chief Executive, or the head of Human Resources, or another senior officer of an important client. The recruiter will always shake a hand that has shook a hand that feeds.
>
> *2. Next-best is someone able to provide future recruiting business*...the Chief Executive, or the head of Human Resources of a non-client company. And that's especially true if there's already been a hint that business could be forthcoming.
>
> *3. People who've helped the recruiter in other important ways...* someone the recruiter placed in a job, even though that person hasn't yet spent money with the recruiter. Or a *very-well-thought-of-candidate* on a past search. Or a *valuable "source,"* who's provided much-needed information. Having befriended and profited from these people, it's hard for the recruiter to deny them the favor of seeing you.
>
> *4. The least clout...even negative clout...comes from the mention of a competitive executive recruiter*, proudly referred to as someone you know well and have done lots of business with. It seems bizarre to me that many executives think that invoking a competitive recruiter's name will force a courtesy interview. Why should it?
>
> Every recruiter wants to think of every candidate as a potential future *client*, not just a possible solution to today's search. If you stress your well-established relationship with another recruiting firm, not only will you *not* obligate the unfamiliar recruiter to give you a get-acquainted interview, you'll make him leery of ever proposing you at all. Why should he jeopardize a solid client rela-

tionship by bringing in someone who's known to favor another recruiter?

The Limited Goal of a Courtesy Interview: "To Be Continued"

Of course, you *hope* to just walk in and find the retainer recruiter hard at work on a search that represents an exciting next step in your career. Or if she isn't, you hope she'll take you right down the hall to meet another recruiter who is.

Don't you wish!

What you're hoping to gain from an interview that *you* ask for sounds far too much like what you'd be lucky to get, even if you were already well known, thoroughly checked out, and eminently respected by the recruiter you're meeting...not just an attractive "walk-in" making your own unsubstantiated assertions of background and achievement.

Moreover, the recruiter handling your courtesy interview has no authority to declare you a candidate on any search except the few she's personally handling at the moment you're in her office...probably no more than eight to ten. So even if you have her totally convinced, and even if she's with a giant firm handling upwards of 3,000 searches per year, the statistical odds are infinitesimally small that what you're selling is what *she's* buying on the day you walk in.

So keep your goal realistic. Expect only to demonstrate these three points:

1. *Valuable experience*...potentially appropriate for some client someday, but probably not for a current search of the person across the desk from you today;

2. *Excellent track record*...consistent and impressive achievements; and

3. The *personal characteristics* that tend to indicate...but don't guarantee...a fine executive.

Once you've successfully registered these points, a warm *to-be-continued but later-and-probably-by-someone-else* assumption will suffuse the conversation.

That's it. That's all for today. Take "yes" for an answer! And, like any other good salesman, leave before your "sold" customer begins to have renewed doubts.

Prove you're an effective business communicator, and your courtesy interview is a success.

Prove you're *not*, and you're finished at the firm.

The courtesy interview will be short and superficial enough that you can easily get through it without revealing that you don't do your job very well. Challenging discussion on that subject won't come until you're brought back as a potential candidate on a search.

But the get-acquainted interview *will* reveal whether or not you're potentially *an attractive candidate*. To prove you are, you'll have to demonstrate one attribute that's important for success on the job, and even more important for success as a candidate:

You must be an effective business communicator.

Prove that you have the common sense to figure out what's important for you to cover, and the poise and confidence to put it across in a limited time.

If you don't show these abilities in your courtesy interview, the recruiter will assume you won't in a client interview...or on the job. And he'll mark you as an unlikely candidate for future searches by his firm.

Do unto the retainer recruiter as he'd like to be done unto:

Thoughtfulness and efficiency will win him over.

When you arrive for a courtesy interview with a retainer recruiter, you're getting—free—his most precious resource, the only inventory he has to sell: *his time*.

Format your visit so you don't waste it:

1. *Express appreciation* for seeing you.

2. *Exchange pleasantries.* Maybe admire something in his office. Probably mention the contact who brought you together. Whatever. A few unhurried but brief pleasantries will make sure that you don't just barge in and take over.

3. *But then, get right down to business.* You'll get plus-points, not demerits, for being organized and efficient. You've asked for this meeting. So it's okay for you to subtly assume some early initiative. Chances are the recruiter aches to say, "Let's get this over with, so I can get back to my search work." By moving along, you give him what he wants, without forcing him to be impolite enough to ask for it.

"How much time do we have?"

As attention turns toward your "sales pitch," try to get a sense of timing:

> "How long do we have? I realize you can't afford to give me the same amount of time you would if this were an interview on one of your searches. So I'll fit my background into the time you have for it."

It won't seem pushy to ask for time parameters, if you do it out of sensitivity to the recruiter's needs. And it'll certainly help you pace yourself. Not overstaying will dazzle and delight the recruiter, because hardly anyone else is ever so considerate and efficient.

The average recruiter spends about one-hour to an-hour-and-a-half interviewing a candidate he's referring on a search. Therefore, you can't expect to get more than one-third as much time...about *thirty minutes maximum*. And, if you can get in and out in 15 or 20 minutes, the recruiter will breathe a sigh of relief, admiration, and gratitude...thinking to himself:

> "Wow! That guy was really on the ball. He knew what he came for, and he got his message across. He was very efficient, yet thoroughly pleasant, attractive, and likable. What an effective executive he must be!"

Bring your resume...and hand it over.

Good business communication is two-fold: written and oral. And the written is indispensable to an effective courtesy interview with a retainer recruiter.

You'd never attempt an important presentation at your company without visual aids, and a persuasive document. If you were presenting a budget review, or requesting money for an acquisition, or proposing a new product introduction, you'd use a screen or a projector and a good "leave-behind"...the tools that help a business audience "track" your message, and refer to it later.

Similarly, at the courtesy interview, you must have your resume. You asked for this meeting. So you're obviously selling. This is no time to play coy and say, "Oh, I don't have a resume." Or "It's not in finished form yet." *Of course* you have a resume. And it wasn't difficult...or vastly time-consuming...for you to prepare it. After all, you *are* a highly competent and well-organized person.

Believe it or not, quite a few executives deliberately employ the irksome tactic of showing up for a courtesy interview without a resume...perhaps because there are several how-to-get-a-job books that recommend it. Don't fall for that advice. The premise is that you'll appear "less eager" by not having a resume. Or that you'll get a second shot of the recruiter's time and attention when your resume and follow-up letter arrive in the mail or by email.

Face it. Your eagerness was out of the bag when you asked for the courtesy interview. And the recruiter's lasting impression will be formed while meeting you face-to-face. It won't be something she reads later. Indeed, she may not bother to read anything you send later. Don't be tempted to play the "withhold your resume" game. It's obvious and obnoxious to every experienced recruiter.

Bring in a polished resume and leave it behind. Then immediately after meeting you, the recruiter can conveniently set up a file on you...to which she'll add her fresh-in-mind favorable comments about what an effective communicator you are.

The recruiter's comments will be far less favorable if you have to "wing" your presentation without a visual aid, and if afterward you tell her to wait for a letter or an e-mail to deliver a clear impression of you.

Four Loathsome Lines...and One Bad Attitude: Retainer-Recruiter "Pet Peeves" About Courtesy Interviews

Retainer recruiters consider courtesy interviews a "necessary evil"... whereas contingency recruiters run ads on web job boards and in newspapers to encourage them.

So you're "swimming upstream" to even get a courtesy interview with a retainer recruiter. He's busy looking for people who fit several narrowly-specific searches and...no matter how polite and cordial he may be...he's more likely to think of you as an interruption than an opportunity. Therefore, you'll want to avoid several amazingly prevalent mistakes that executives make in seeking and handling courtesy interviews:

1. "Let me buy you lunch." Here's the #1 loathsome line, that makes every retainer recruiter cringe. Lunch is too much time, when you're not part of a current search. With only five lunch dates per week, the recruiter can't allocate them to people who... for now at least...aren't the ones he's looking for.

The only situation where you probably *will* have lunch with a retainer recruiter is when you're suggested by somebody who spends lots of money with him. Then *he'll* take *you*, as a display of respect for the person who referred you. Bear in mind, too, that lunch isn't an ideal setting. You may be overheard. Also, it's hard to read and handle papers. They're forbidden at most private clubs, and awkward anywhere, until you're down to the last few minutes over coffee.

"Let me buy you lunch" also has an insulting twang. Is the retainer recruiter so hard up socially and financially that he can be manipulated with a free lunch? Indirectly, of course, the offer also says that the person making it is petty and cheap...vigilantly conscious of who pays at the lunch table.

A truly seductive offer, on the other hand, could be made by changing just one word in the hated "Let me buy you lunch." The retainer recruiter would be thrilled if you could truthfully offer: "Let me buy you *time*." And of course you can, by being considerately well-organized and brief when...at your request...you visit him.

2. "What do you think of my resume?" This question wouldn't be so bad if it were asked right up front to indicate that the executive wants to use the session for free counseling, instead of pushing himself as a potential candidate. But it usually comes after having answered all the recruiter's questions, and used up all the interviewing time. Then it demolishes the visitor's image as a secure, decisive executive. It's a loser's question...a departing plea for further attention, from someone obviously frustrated and frightened because he isn't getting much response to his job-changing efforts.

Polish your resume to your satisfaction. Ask help from anyone knowledgeable. Use the *EXECUTIVE JOB-CHANGING WORKBOOK*. *But don't spoil your courtesy interview!* Winding up with a question about your resume is like winding up a presentation to your CEO with: "What do you think of my *visuals*?"

3. *Don't ask for career counseling.* Just as bad...and usually delivered at the same wrong time...is a request for career advice. Don't say, "With my background, what do you think I ought to be doing next?" Or, "What level do you think I'm ready for?" Surely, if you know anything, you know that. If you need counseling and psychological testing to figure out what kind of job you're suited for, get it before you reach the retainer recruiter. Don't ask for it at the end of a courtesy interview when your time is up.

4. *"How's the job market?"* This question should never be asked. The market is always elusive to almost every executive at the moment he wants to change. But ultimately it turns out to be excellent for the outstanding executive. The other types, of course, have difficulty regardless of the economy. So here's another downer that implies you're a fearful, frustrated loser.

5. *Don't demonstrate a "God's gift" attitude.* Don't be the person who comes in rather pompously, feeling that the retainer recruiter obviously needs grist for her mill, and ought to grovel in gratitude for grist like him. If you take this attitude, you're dead. The underlying assumption, of course, isn't true. There's a *glut* of grist...even in strong job markets. And plenty of the finest executives have a pleasant, straightforward, cooperative attitude. You'd better, too, or you'll be cancelled out.

Don't be misled by what's said at the end of a courtesy interview: the "pseudo review" of searches in progress.

At the end of your courtesy interview with a retainer recruiter, he'll probably look at a screen or a book to check a list of current assignments... information visible from where he's sitting, but *not* from where you are.

If the firm is a large one, it may handle well over 1,000...and even 4,000... searches per year. You know darn well that there must be several—most likely dozens—that would represent excellent next steps in your career.

Since reading this book you also know, of course, that you'll hardly ever hear about more than one at a time. But now that you've been through an exploratory interview, you surely expect to hear about *at least one* that looks like a potential fit.

In fact, however, unless you come very highly recommended, have made an incredibly fine impression, and your interviewer is personally looking for someone exactly like you, that's not what will happen.

Instead, referring to his notebook or iPad, the retainer recruiter will give you a *pseudo-review of current assignments*. He'll summarize several of the firm's searches, in a performance that will seem confusingly like the "ideal relationship" review I showed you at the end of the last chapter. But it will be different in three important ways:

> *1. There will be something unacceptable to you about every job that's mentioned*...industry, function, location, compensation, title and reporting relationship, size of business, or calibre of company, etc. And each "fatal flaw" will be one that would be obvious to anyone knowing what you just told the recruiter.
>
> *2. The identity of the company will not be revealed*...unless the position has already been filled. "Too bad you weren't here a few weeks ago when we recruited the..."
>
> *3. You won't walk away knowing for sure that you'll be a candidate on the job you like best among all those the firm is actually working on.*

Suppose you sense that, in his interview-ending review of current assignments, the retainer recruiter is deliberately overlooking the searches on his list that would be highly attractive to you. Or, if he does read off pertinent searches, you suspect he's ad-libbing into the description of each job a factor that he knows will make it unacceptable to you.

You're probably right!

But don't feel bad. You just received the standard "*pseudo-review of current searches*," which most retainer recruiters almost always use to close a courtesy interview.

Why do they do this?

Because turning to a reference, and appearing to check what the firm has underway in your field and at your level implies that:

1. you passed the recruiter's screening, and

2. you'll be called when the firm receives more-appropriate assignments.

The recruiter doesn't have to declare you a non-candidate; *you do that yourself.* Meanwhile, you're quickly on the way out of his office...happy in the knowledge that there are obviously no prejudices against you and no failure to understand and admire your qualifications.

Chances are the retainer recruiter will close your courtesy interview like this:

> "Well, it's always an accident of timing, whether we have anything that fits or not. I'm sorry these jobs today are either in the wrong place or too low paying. Of course, there's that one job that *would* interest you. Unfortunately, I'm not handling that one, and I think I heard that it was filled last week. But I'll check, and if there's still a chance on it, I'll call you. Meanwhile, I'll put your information into our system and we'll wait to see what new assignments we get. Thanks for coming in. We'll keep in touch."

That's what he says. Here's a smorgasbord of possible meanings; take your pick:

> "You look right for a search one of our other recruiters is handling. But she may already have all the candidates she wants for now. I'll tell her about you. But I'll save her the bother of dealing with you if she doesn't want to, by not telling *you* about her."

OR

> "There's a search here that looks perfect for you. I'll pass your material along to the recruiter handling it. He can check out your

story with someone else he may know in your company before deciding whether or not to talk to you."

OR

"I see that my colleague down the hall is doing a search you'd be perfect for, and it's exactly what you want. But *I'm* likely to get a similar search within the next month or two. I may as well save you for myself."

OR

"Too bad you're such a vague communicator, and so unattractive to boot. You'll *never* be a candidate on one of our searches."

OR

"Mister, I *had* to be nice to you, because you were referred by a client who spent $750,000 with this firm last year. But I don't buy your act. No way."

Don't place a lot of significance on it...one way or the other...if you get the usual "pseudo-review" of current assignments at the conclusion of your courtesy interview with a retainer recruiter. How favorably and how soon you'll hear from his firm...if at all...may have very little to do with what was said as you walked out.

Chapter 9

How to Handle the Recruiter Who Calls You

You're happily employed...doing an outstanding job for a fine company that recognizes and appreciates your contribution, pays you well, and has you on its fast track toward bigger and better things. You're not dissatisfied. You're not thinking about leaving.

Then the phone rings.

Your caller says he's an executive recruiter filling a major position in your industry at a level you realize you'd have to wait at least two, and maybe five to seven, years...or longer...to achieve in your present company. Are you interested?

Perhaps you should be.

But only if the opportunity stands up to some important questions you can raise over the phone, and only if the recruiter himself passes your savvy scrutiny.

Your caller may be working on a retainer search...or on a legitimate contingency listing...to fill a job that could advance your career. On the other hand, he may be "trolling" for resumes by describing an extremely attractive but nonexistent opening...or an actual and widely publicized opening which he has not been requested to fill.

He may be calling because he's heard great things about you through one of his dependable contacts who knows you. But it's equally possible that he's calling you "cold," just because you're at the right level in a company he's "targeted" to explore, in which case he has no idea whether you're terrific...or just two weeks away from being fired for gross incompetence.

He may even be soliciting you and your company as a possible executive search client under the guise of approaching you personally with some non-existent "opportunity."

How you react to a recruiter's call depends entirely on his relationship with the employer.

There are only three possibilities:

1. **a retainer search assignment,**
2. **a valid contingency listing,**
3. **no relationship at all.**

Figure out what he's up to, and you'll know how to handle him.

By now you know where your self-interest lies with respect to all three relationships a recruiter may have with an employer.

And, despite a dizzying dose of doubletalk that may be administered when you try to figure out what the relationship is, there are only three possibilities. Let's review them, and then let's take some phone calls.

1. A Retainer Search

This is the ideal relationship from your point of view. You're too late to reach the employer ahead of the recruiter, and maybe get the job without competition from recruiter-supplied candidates. Now a recruiter is being paid $80,000* to look. Therefore, you're best off as one of his "finds."

If the caller is on a true retainer assignment, you'll want to cooperate.

2. A Valid Contingency Listing

This is a good, but somewhat less-desirable, relationship, as far as you're concerned.

If the caller has a contingency listing directly from the employer on the job he's describing to you, then you may wish to cooperate. Generally speaking, however, you're not obligated to do so.

There is only one narrow set of circumstances in which you're morally obligated to go ahead with a contingency recruiter...or forgo the opportunity. We'll cover that subject later.

3. No Relationship at All

This is a lousy situation from your point of view. The recruiter couldn't get either type of relationship with the employer...retainer or contingency...so now he wants to tie *you* up!

If the caller...whether normally a retainer or a contingency recruiter...has no direct arrangement with the employer on the job he's calling you about, you do not want to cooperate.

So much for the ground rules. Now, paraphrasing the sportscaster on TV, "Let's go to the phones,". First, an easy one.

> YOUR CALLER: "Hello, I'm Joan Chase from the executive recruiting firm of Randall Radley Associates, and I'm calling because I

---

*The fee on a $240,000 position. Your level may be much higher. If so, the fee—typically one-third of annual compensation—is proportionately more.

have a situation that might be of interest to you or perhaps to someone you might wish to recommend."

YOU: "Oh, I know your organization. It's one of the fine retainer firms. I've met a man named Stevens in your company; do you work with him?"

CALLER: "No, Bill's in our Atlanta office, and I'm calling you from Cleveland. But of course we know each other."

Enough already!

You know the firm and its fine reputation as a retainer recruiting organization. This woman is obviously with them, because she knew Stevens and volunteered his correct location. So let her go on, and listen open-mindedly. She appears to be entirely on the up-and-up, and doing exactly what she says she's doing.

"But," you say, "couldn't she be who she is and still be calling about a job on which she hasn't been in touch with the client, intending to 'float' my resume?"

Not likely. She seems to be a rank-and-file recruiter in a well-known retainer firm, just grinding out one of their regular assignments in the regular way. Remember that retainer-only firms hardly ever jeopardize their "pay-me-to-look" status by offering resumes they haven't been paid to find. Let's put your conversation with Ms. Chase "on hold" for a while, so you can answer a more challenging call.

This time we'll listen as you smoke out the intentions of someone who really *is* planning to "float" your resume. Ironically, this caller is someone you've known and been friends with for years...a contingency recruiter specializing in your industry, who helped you find one of your early jobs, and whom you've used occasionally to recruit subordinates during your rise to $100,000+ and beyond.

CARL CONTINGENCY: "I suppose you saw in the trade papers that Andrea Williams left Colonial to become President of TransWestern. That means they'll be needing a new President over at Colonial, and I don't think there's anyone inside who's up to the job. As you know, Blake Stevens, their new VP - Marketing, was just promoted to that level from head of the field sales force a few months ago. He's certainly not ready for the presidency. And they surely won't give it to some finance or manufacturing person in

> such a marketing-driven company. What do you say, Bill? Would you like me to put you in the running for the presidency over there?"

What an easy example!

You're immediately skeptical. You're surprised that Carl would be seeking a President. As far as you know, his mostly contingency practice...while widely and justifiably respected...hasn't been filling positions at quite that high level.

Moreover, Carl is being perfectly straightforward. He isn't saying he's been *requested* to seek candidates for the presidency of Colonial. Indeed, he makes it clear that he's merely reacting to what he's read in the trade papers and drawing his own conclusion. No search has been assigned. Or if one has been, it's obvious that Carl doesn't have it. He hasn't been briefed by the CEO of Colonial. If he had been, he'd have told you so.

Since Carl is referring to an opening publicized in the trade papers, it's a situation that everyone in your industry knows about. Indeed, you've probably already been thinking about writing or calling the Chairman of Colonial. You know her slightly, because you were on a panel she chaired at your industry's trade convention two years ago.

Have you missed your chance to go ahead on your own, just because Carl's phone call reached you before you made your move?

Absolutely not.

Let's see you take it from here:

> YOU: "Thanks for the call, Carl. In fact, I've been thinking along those same lines. I've intended to call up Gloria Wing, the Chairman over there, or send her a letter and a resume...I haven't decided which. I was on a panel she ran at the trade convention in Las Vegas a couple years ago. Now, Carl, I gather that Mrs. Wing hasn't put you on retainer to find her a President, has she?"
>
> CARL: "Well, no she hasn't talked to me specifically about this situation. But I've filled quite a few jobs over there during the past several years. I'm perfectly sure I can present you."
>
> YOU: "Thanks for offering, Carl, but I'd rather not. I'd prefer to be in touch with her on my own. I'd rather handle it myself."

Simple as that! You figured out that Carl has no mandate. So you turned down his offer to interpose himself between you and the employer. He offered. You politely refused. The only explanation you needed to give was:

"I'd rather handle it myself."

Now, you're just as free to get in touch with the Chairman directly as you were before Carl called. If Mrs. Wing hasn't yet engaged a recruiter, she may decide to meet you and perhaps one or two other obvious prospects. Indeed, she may make her choice without ever feeling the need to hire a retainer recruiter, or to put out contingency listings. On the other hand, perhaps she already *has* hired a retainer recruiter. If so, you're still free to be part of that person's project, without the handicap of an extra price-tag applied by your friend Carl.

However, don't become overconfident. Carl wasn't really trying very hard. He helped me help you, by delivering a classic pitch designed to demonstrate the basics.

Now let's take a much more challenging call. This one's from a prominent *retainer* recruiter whom you know and trust. You'll have to be more alert and probing, because Randy's not going to send you the obvious signals Carl and I contrived for you in the previous example. Randy's going to give you the full treatment.

> RANDY RETAINER: "I'm not sure if you're aware of it, but I've done several recruiting projects over the years for Pete Pinnacle, the Chairman over at Acme Consolidated. He's got an opening at the top of his Industrial Products Division, what with Jason Evans leaving to become Chief Executive of Trombley Consolidated. You'd be absolutely perfect for that spot, now that you've got a few years' experience under your belt as number-two in an operation that's almost their size and, if anything, is doing even better than they are. What do you say? Would you like to be a candidate on it?"

> YOU: "Maybe, Randy. I've been thinking it's time for me to take over my own show, and I've been wondering what they'll do to fill Jason's job. I thought maybe they might promote somebody from one of their own divisions. If they stay inside the Industrial Division, I'm afraid I have to agree with you...nobody there would be as good for the top job as I would be. Matter of fact, I was thinking of maybe dropping the Chairman a hint that I might be interested...possibly through one of his outside Directors I know

pretty well, or through another friend of mine, who's one of their biggest distributors.

"Tell me, Randy, has the Chairman definitely made up his mind to go outside to fill that job, and has he put you on retainer to do the search?"

RANDY: "Oh yes; he's got to go outside. It doesn't make any sense at all to take somebody like Nancy Stein...who's doing a great job, by the way...out of their Maritime Division and put her into Industrial Products. And the same goes for Clem Smith, who's Executive Vice President of their Defense Systems Division. He's a great guy and certainly ready to run his own operation. But it ought to be something closer to his field. He's never sold to any customer but the Pentagon. Really they don't have anybody over there who'd be as appropriate as you would, to take charge of Industrial Products.

"Why do you think I called you? Not just because we haven't talked for awhile. Today we're doing business. I want you to be a candidate. In fact, I think you'll be the strongest of all the candidates I'll be presenting. What do you say?"

YOU: "As I said before, I might be interested. But I didn't quite get your answer to the other part of my question. Have you personally got a retainer search assignment to fill this position? Because, if you do, then I'd like you to tell me a lot more about what the Chairman has told you he's looking for. Has he put you on retainer to solve this thing?"

RANDY: "Well, not exactly. Not quite yet. But I'm sure that if I let him see someone as ideally appropriate for his Industrial Division presidency as you are, that'll make it obvious to him that he shouldn't stay inside. What do you say? Would you like to go for it?"

This time you had to work a lot harder. And you were up against a tough adversary...a well-known retainer recruiter, whom you certainly wouldn't have suspected of "floating resumes." Randy knew plenty of detailed information. Moreover, you were well aware that he had previously done high-level recruiting within that company.

But even this retainer recruiter you've known and trusted for years failed to pass your savvy scrutiny, now that you're challenging *every* headhunter who calls you, to find out whether he has a client assignment and what the exact nature of that arrangement is.

Now you're faced with a choice.

Randy has previously worked for the Chairman on retainer. Maybe he'll be asked to do so in this instance, too. If so, he may not be enthusiastic about your candidacy...on this or any future job...if you're uncooperative now. On the other hand, the Chairman doesn't always use a recruiter when he hires a high-profile person from outside. And even if he does assign a retainer search, he may not choose Randy this time.

Indeed, if Randy were confident of getting a retainer search to fill this opening, he'd have waited to get his mandate before contacting you or anyone else. Maybe he suspects the Chairman will promote from within...or "go it alone"... or choose another recruiter. Maybe the Chairman already *has* chosen another recruiter.

(Time out while you decide what to do.)

Congratulations!

You've decided to remain your own person. I thought you would. You didn't get where you are now by allowing people to manipulate you. Now let's see how gracefully and inoffensively...yet firmly...you handle this situation:

> YOU: "Thanks for offering, Randy. But I'd rather not have you bring me up with the Chairman until you've got a firm search assignment from him. Why don't you take the next few days to get in touch with him and see if he wants you to take charge of finding someone on the outside for the presidency of that division?" (You know this won't be easy for Randy...if it were, he'd have done so before calling you; but he can't say that.)
>
> "Please don't tell him that I might be a candidate. I want to keep my options open. If the Chairman does assign a search, there's nobody I'd rather see get that project than you. But if you don't, I want to still be in a position to go after him through informal connections, or to be contacted by the recruiter he does select, or maybe just to drop the whole thing. I'm going to be away on Wednesday and Thursday. Why don't you call me on Friday and let me know how you made out? I won't do anything until I hear from you."

> See...it wasn't all that difficult. You caught Randy proceeding when he didn't have the proper basis to do so. But you didn't make a fuss. You didn't back him into a corner. And you also didn't allow him to corner you, which was the purpose of his call.

Congratulations again. You matched wits with a master...and you came out ahead.

Always qualify the recruiter.

Even if you know him well, you still don't know his connection with the employer.

By now it's easy to see the central truth that you should always keep in mind when answering every headhunter's call: You don't know for sure whether your caller has a definite arrangement with an employer, and you don't know what the exact nature of that arrangement is. Since both points are important, you'd better clear them up before agreeing to anything the recruiter proposes.

And you're *able* to find out...as you've just proved. You caught a prominent retainer recruiter, whom you personally know and respect. He was about to put a price-tag on your head in one of his exceedingly rare departures from his professed way of doing business. Firmly, but gracefully, you stopped him. If you can do that, surely you can figure out what just about everyone else who calls you is up to...and *react strictly according to your own self-interest*.

But before we leave Randy Retainer, let's speculate on his motives. He may have a strong relationship with Pete Pinnacle, the Chairman of Acme Consolidated. Maybe Randy's altruistically concerned that the Chairman will make a less-than-optimum appointment from the inside, if not confronted with unasked-for resumes from outstanding outsiders. It's far more likely, however, that Randy has a weakening, marginal, or defunct connection with Mr. Pinnacle, and suspects or knows that another retainer recruiter will be the one officially looking for the next President of Acme's Industrial Division.

No retainer recruiter will ever attempt to submit you on contingency if he can readily get himself hired on retainer to look for you. And the likeliest reason he can't get hired is that somebody else already has been. If so, you'd better be the other recruiter's "find"...or the employer's. Otherwise, you probably won't be hired.

Ironically, when you're a high-level executive, your resume is much more likely to be "floated" by a recruiter you know well, than by a stranger.

It's no accident that the two people you've caught intending to forward your resume without a proper employer-mandate have both been people who know you well...not strangers. If you're a senior executive, that will usually be so.

And *when a true retainer recruiter is involved*, that will *virtually always* be so. The reason, once again, harks back to his normal fee arrangement...to get paid *for the act of looking*, regardless of whether anyone is hired. Therefore he normally never offers resumes without first being paid to find them. If he did, the employer would think, "Why pay him just to look, when he'll submit candidates without being paid, just like a contingency recruiter does?"

Therefore, a true retainer recruiter breaks his operating pattern...if at all...only on very rare occasions when he has no shot at a fee unless he does something drastic. And even then he won't, unless he knows the potential "candidate" on a personal basis well enough to hide behind this excuse:

> "She's *someone I've known very well for a long time*, and she'd be perfect!"

The retainer recruiter can never admit he *actually looked for new people* that he's sending over on a contingency basis, because to do so would destroy his claim to be strictly a retainer recruiter.

The *contingency* recruiter, on the other hand, has a different problem. He isn't usually asked to fill extremely high-level positions. Therefore, he lacks credibility when he claims to have a high-level executive tied up and accessible only through him. He almost *has* to say:

> "This is *someone I know very, very well*."

If you're a middle- or lower-level executive, my tip that the headhunter likeliest to float your resume is probably someone you know well does not apply.

The further down you are from President, General Manager, or head of function such as Finance, Manufacturing, Marketing, R&D, etc., the more numerous are the positions in which every organization can use your talents, and the more frequently...perhaps even continuously...the organization has an opening at your level that urgently needs to be filled.

Under such circumstances, suggestions of potential candidates tend to be much more welcome, regardless of source. Contingency listings may be handed out to virtually any headhunter who asks. And resumes may be cheerfully accepted and kept on file, even though the headhunters submitting them haven't bothered to secure a listing in advance.

Indeed, as I pointed out in Chapter 6, when you're seeking a foothold at the bottom- and middle-levels of the corporate pyramid, being pushed by an aggressive contingency recruiter may be very helpful. It may get you noticed, when you wouldn't be otherwise. And the contingent price-tag on your head may not matter much, because it's a low fee at your low salary level; and paying agency fees is pretty much standard practice when lots of openings have to be filled and a busy personnel department doesn't have time to pick over hoards of applicants.

Don't fall for the "you should be represented" comeback.

Whenever you respectfully, but firmly, refuse to be introduced by any headhunter who lacks an employer mandate...or by a contingency recruiter who has one...you'll invariably be socked with the usual high-pressure pitch:

"Surely you don't want to be *unrepresented*!"

Just say:

"Yes, thank you, in this particular instance that's what I prefer."

Only if you're a glutton for futility will you try to get the recruiter to admit that being your "representative"—your agent—would require that *you* be the one paying him and not the employer, as you and I discussed in Chapter 6.

Unfinished business with caller #1...

Once you established that Joan Chase was from a well-known retainer recruiting firm, you gave her the benefit of the doubt and let her complete her pitch. Chances are...999 out of 1,000...that she's working on a regular retainer assignment. Since she's a rank-and-file member of the firm, and since she didn't previously know you and have a cordial relationship with you...nothing outside the ordinary character of the firm appears to be involved in her routine call to you.

Nonetheless, it won't hurt to ask:

YOU: "Who's your contact on this assignment? Are you working directly with the Chairman?"

CALLER: "Yes, I had a meeting with him and with their Vice President of HR last Wednesday."

Stop beating a dead horse. Clearly, she's doing a retainer assignment. Feel free to go ahead.

But now let's take another call.

YOUR CALLER: "Hello, this is Mae Findham from Seekim Associates. We're management consultants specializing in the field of executive search, and I'm calling you about a very attractive position that might be of interest to you...or if not to you, to someone you might wish to recommend."

YOU: "I'm sorry, I didn't quite get the name of your firm. Did you say, Seekim Associates? How is that spelled?" (She tells you.) "And you're located here in Chicago? Or where are you calling from?" (She tells you.) "Let me have your phone number, in case we get interrupted, so I'll be able to call you back. I'd like to hear what you have to say, but I may not be able to stay on the phone any longer than just a very few minutes right now. But go ahead."

CALLER: "Well, of course I can't be specific as to the actual identity of the company, because this is a highly confidential assignment, but there's a..."

YOU: (Here's your opening; jump on it.) "Oh, why is that? Are they firing the person who has the job now, and he doesn't yet know about it?"

CALLER: (slipping away) "Well, you might say it's something like that, although not exactly. All I can tell you for right now is simply that I'm not at liberty to disclose the identity of the client."

YOU: (interjecting again) "Well, I certainly don't want to press too hard for the client's name, if you're not in a position to give it. Are you working on retainer? Or is this a contingency assignment?...In which case I can perfectly understand why you aren't comfortable in being specific about the client."

CALLER: "Rather than concern ourselves any further at this point about who the client is and why I can't give you that information, let me just tell you this...it's a client we have served many times

> over the years, and one I personally know very well. But right now let me tell you a little more about the job so we can see whether it's an attractive one for you to consider, or whether you would prefer to recommend someone else."

You now let the recruiter drone on, and you pursue the full line of questioning we'll look at in the next chapter for screening any "opportunity" that's pitched to you over the phone. However, the tone of this conversation so far has been sufficiently mysterious and evasive to let you know that you may well be dealing with a headhunter who, at best, has a nonexclusive job listing, and indeed may not have any direct commitment from any employer. *You will proceed with caution*!

If Ms. Findham had been a retainer recruiter with an assignment conferred directly by the employer, she would have immediately told you so, explaining that her secrecy was not because of a tentative mandate, but rather because of specific reasons why it would hurt the employer if his search became known.

Does a headhunter's calling you about a job force you...legally or morally...to pursue the job only through him?

Have you lost your right to contact the employer directly?

Usually not.

Of course, if he's a retainer recruiter being paid to look for you, you want to be one of his "finds." You hope he will introduce you. If he refuses, you can ignore his "wet blanket" and go directly to the employer. He'll resent your action, and "blackball" you for all future searches by his firm. But he can't stop you.

With the contingency recruiter, the shoe is on the other foot. He'll seldom say no to you. He *wants* to submit you...with his price-tag attached, of course. But you may prefer to go directly to the employer without his tag. Can you?

Usually you can.

If the contingency recruiter *hasn't* identified the employer and job to you, you have no obligation whatever to let him apply his tag and send you onward to an undisclosed recipient. You're just as free after his call as you were before it, to canvass any and all employers you wish and offer your sevices.

Even if he *did* tell you precisely the employer and the job on which he wants you to be his candidate, and even if he has a valid listing, you're still at liberty to contact the employer directly if some other source of information... apart from his phone call...has also made you aware that the job is open and likely to be filled from the outside.

But be forthright; otherwise the recruiter will think you took advantage of his call and sneaked around behind his back. Just tell him that you already know of the opening through other sources, and that you may or may not wish to follow up on your own. The contingency recruiter won't be pleased with your decision, but there's nothing he can do about it. You have every right to refuse his offer to make an introduction that you prefer to make yourself.

Suppose the contingency recruiter just happens to be someone you don't like or respect. You don't want him to know whether you're willing to be a candidate or not, and you don't *ever* want to be submitted to any employer by him. Just say:

> "George, I'm not sure whether I want to be a candidate over there, or that I want to go there through you. Please do not submit me. I think I'll wait a while and read about the situation in the trade papers. Then, if I decide afterward that I want to go ahead on my own, I won't feel I've taken unfair advantage of this phone call from you."

Needless to say, you must *really* dislike the contingency recruiter to take this approach. But it's your prerogative. Any recruiter...contingency or retainer... merely *offers* to introduce you. He doesn't own you.

The only situation in which you're morally obligated ...and possibly legally too...to go ahead with the contingency recruiter, or not at all, is when he:

1. **has a valid listing from the employer and**
2. **has revealed a situation that you wouldn't have known about, or wouldn't have pursued, if he hadn't caused you to do so.**

You know what's fair and what's not. Let your conscience be your guide. When the opening is not public knowledge, and you learn about it only from the recruiter, then you *are* morally obligated...and perhaps legally, too...to pursue the opportunity only through an introduction made by him.

Similarly, if the existence of the job was known to you through other channels, but the recruiter told you about attractive hidden features which caused you to go ahead when you wouldn't have otherwise, then too, fairness demands that you pursue the position only through the recruiter.

When a contingency recruiter has a valid listing, the employer has agreed to pay the recruiter if he hires someone the recruiter places before him. So, if the reason you know enough to contact the employer is because the recruiter has contacted you, then the recruiter has done his job and has earned his fee.

Moreover, in my opinion, that's true even if the recruiter doesn't specifically identify the employer, but drops clues enabling you to *guess* the employer, or presents the job so tantalizingly that you canvass *all* the employers in your industry attempting to hit the job the recruiter has told you about.

It would be highly improper for you to "go around" the contingency recruiter under any of those circumstances, in an attempt to make yourself less expensive for the employer to hire. If you were to do so, any ethical employer would consider your behavior sleazy in the extreme. He should forgo hiring you on the basis of low moral character. And if, by chance, the employer were to be sufficiently devious himself to applaud your actions, his own moral character would be such that you'd be better off not working for him. Or, perhaps, you'd deserve each other.

Here's a question a lot of people ask:

"Is there any sure and easy way to tell whether a headhunter who calls is from a contingency or a retainer firm?"

There's no simple "litmus test."

But the calls you've taken throughout this chapter have all helped sensitize you to "contingency vibes" and "retainer vibes."

An aura of secrecy is one of the strongest clues that your caller may be approaching you from the contingency direction. Often a contingency recruiter will be highly vigilant that you not figure out who her client employer is unless and until you agree to be a candidate...and maybe even then, not until just before you go to see the employer.

That's because your knowing creates several hazards to her earning a fee: You may go directly to the employer. You may start grapevine rumors that send *other candidates* to the employer. And those same rumors may send *competing contingency recruiters* to the employer. Your call from Mae Findham was a classic example of "contingency vibes," telegraphed by a secretive manner.

So, as early as possible in any phone call from a headhunter, you may as well ask the ultimate question:

> "Are you *on retainer* to submit candidates for this job, or are you working *on contingency*?"

The recruiter on the other end of the line may be a bit shaken by your highly aware and direct question. If so, that momentary discomfort may be your answer.

On the other hand, if he's glib and experienced, chances are he'll give you a side-stepping answer:

> "Oh, I *regularly* send this client outstanding people."
>
> OR
>
> "We have a long-term relationship with them, going back to 2012, when we recruited the person who's now General Manager of their Catalog Marketing Division."
>
> OR
>
> "We have a *standing order* to send them people we feel would be right for the businesses they have."

The variations are endless. But the theme is consistent. *Previous* contact is invoked to suggest a definite arrangement to fill the job the recruiter is phoning about. Unfortunately, in the words of the immortal Gershwin tune: "It Ain't Necessarily So."

If in doubt, call "time out."

Another thing you can do to "qualify" the recruiter on the other end of the line is to interrupt your conversation, offering to call back later. Meanwhile you have time to do a little investigating.

One strong indication that a U.S. recruiting firm *doesn't* operate on contingency is membership in the Association of Executive Search Consultants (AESC), the professional association founded and supported by retainer firms.

You can call them at their New York headquarters, (212) 398-9556.

Unfortunately, the AESC has approximately 25k0 members out of the nearly 650 or more qualified U.S. retainer firms. However, many of the largest and best-known firms *do* belong to the association. Not being in AESC says nothing negative about the firm you're trying to check on. But membership can be a favorable indication, because there is a peer review procedure prior to entry.

A more expedient way to check on a larger number of recruiting firms is to see if the firm is shown in Appendix II of this book or listed on *RITE*Site.com as a *RITES*-honored recruiting firm. Both of these resources identify virtually the same list of outstanding search firms.

The most expedient technique you can use to determine whether a recruiting firm operates on contingency...or more often contingency *and* retainer... is simply to call the firm's switchboard and ask what kind of arrangements it offers an employer interested in using that firm to find an employee. Ask the receptionist or secretary who answers:

> "With your firm, is it necessary to pay even if nobody you supply is hired? I know some firms operate that way...'on retainer,' they call it...but that's not the kind of arrangement I have in mind."

The telephone-answerer may conceivably give you a more straightforward response than you'll get from an executive of the firm, who'll be trying to size you up and will speak much more cautiously. The receptionist may say:

> "Well, I know we *prefer* to work on retainer, but we also work the way you have in mind. Let me put you through to someone who can tell you more."

> **Note:** The next several pages discuss relatively arcane wrinkles in the retainer recruiting business. Logically they belong in Chapter 7. They're here because this is where *you* will find them more interesting and relevant.

A trend toward de facto revision of traditional ethics in the search business is getting its momentum from some of the very largest and most prestigious firms.

Know what's happening. Use it to your advantage.

Two main ethical rules have governed retainer-compensated executive search ever since it began, and they're the same common sense principles that apply to every business that has customers.

You already know them: (1) you can't bite the hand that feeds, and (2) you can't sell a single item to two customers simultaneously and charge both of them the full price.

Today, even these verities are being challenged in a battle that you—as a noncombatant—may be able to exploit.

First . . .

The We-won't-take-your-people-for-at-least-2-years Off-Limits Rule (**employer's viewpoint**)

...which is also the

You're Off-Limits for 2 years after the retainer firm has been paid to assist your employer (**potential candidate's viewpoint**)

Don't injure or offend a customer who's just spent money with you. That's the #1 reason for the "Two Years" rule (or similar protection reduced to a year or less).

There's also a second reason. In doing a retained search, the recruiter ***acquires deeply confidential information***. Coming in as a trusted consultant, he or she is told about the strengths and weaknesses of executives currently on staff: Who's excellent and slated for promotion? Who's merely adequate at current level or—although promising—newly proving himself? And who will probably have to be replaced in a future search?

Would a client "tell all" if she thought the recruiter interviewing her about today's search would conduct a well-informed raid on her organization just as soon as the final retainer check hits the bank?

Hardly!

Which is why the "Two Years" rule was born and why, even today, it is proudly and enthusiastically observed by virtually all small and medium—and many large—retainer search firms. However, the very idea of off-limits protection has proved increasingly inconvenient for the giant firms, because it tends to limit their growth. The more companies they've recently worked for, the fewer whose people they can solicit. And with fewer places to look and fewer people to choose from . . .

Well, you get the idea. And so do the Wall Street analysts. Several of the very largest firms are public companies!

Today, the time-honored rule—once religiously evangelized by the giant firms as the ethical leaders of the industry—is no longer merely inconvenient. Now it jeopardizes the business plan! Now it must be made more flexible... and, if possible, *nonexistent*.

That's a tall order. Clients and potential clients are resisting. Competitors—many using off-limits-centered sales pitches—claim to be "holier than thou." Talk about controversy!

Nonetheless, several giant firms are making steady progress in narrowing the precepts they led the industry in establishing. Off-limits protection is no longer standard for all their clients...and no longer featured in their selling literature. Its duration, when granted, may now be 12 months or even less. Sophisticated clients realize that they must specifically negotiate this issue prior to start of a search, and they must get any protection they achieve written into the engagement letter.

Unsophisticated clients fail to raise the issue. Sophisticated ones awarding ***lots*** of business ***can*** and ***do*** insist on the traditional "Two Year" protection. With their economic power, ***they can usually get it***. Other clients—led by their HR professionals—realize they must ask in order to receive. But they may intentionally pursue a "Don't ask; don't tell" policy. Reason: they want to hire the big name search firm. Their CEO expects them to. But their occasional search won't be sufficient volume to force strong off-limits protection. Yet they don't want to be faulted for ***not*** securing protection if the current *recruit-in* is soon followed by a *recruit-out*. So, by not raising an issue they don't have enough economic power to win, they preserve a way to save face later. If and when trouble surfaces, they can say to the CEO...and maybe even to the search firm too: "I had every right to ***assume*** that the traditional protection applied."

Meanwhile, of course, the vast majority of less-than-giant firms aggressively flout their righteous adherence to traditional values. Their brochures, engagement letters, and "shoot out" sales pitches all aggressively promote the "protection" issue.

So what does this conflict mean to you as a potential candidate?

Certainly nothing bad!

For one thing, you'll probably see a few more opportunities from the largest firms your employer uses than you would have seen just a few years ago. That's *great* from your standpoint!

Moreover, knowing about the escalating ambiguity on this issue, you may be emboldened to sketch out your career desires to the recruiters who are now working inside your company to select your subordinates and peers. If you do, you may feel a tap on your shoulder a lot sooner than you'd normally have expected.

Similarly, of course, while you're cautiously talking ***more*** about yourself, you'll ***not talk at all*** about your own best subordinates. You're smart. You know what to do.

And secondly the . . .

You-Paid-for-These-Candidates-/-They're-Yours-Alone Off-Limits Rule (employer's viewpoint)

...which is also the

You're-Allocated-to-Another-Recruiter-in-the-Firm Off-Limits Rule (potential candidate's viewpoint)

The common sense of this rule is that no vendor should be able to sell the same work to two customers simultaneously and get fully paid for it by both. The client pays a stiff fee for candidates. At the traditional one-third of annual compensation, the fee on just a $240,000 job is $80,000. Even if as many as 5 candidates are presented, they each cost over $16,000 for the recruiter's work in finding them. If only 3 are presented, each costs over $26,000.

At that rate, how do you imagine the employer will feel if his or her candidates are simultaneously provided to another client of the same retainer search firm?

Not happy!

Client employer #1 is now under time pressure to hurry up and select the best candidate before client #2 hires him away. Client #1 may also have to overpay, in order to out-bid client #2. And all this difficulty is being created by the recruiter who's being paid to *solve* the problem, not *compound* it!

Not a happy situation!

Since the dawn of retainer recruiting, presenting the same candidates to two retainer-paying clients simultaneously has been unthinkable. Indeed, *not* doing so has been one of the main points of difference and superiority in contrast to the employment agencies (contingency recruiters), who—being paid nothing for their efforts until a transaction occurs—present all the candidates they have to every employer willing to meet them.

Traditionally, it's always been assumed that a consultant fully paid on retainer for finding candidates will deliver them only to the client who has paid for the search. Only after *that* client has chosen one of the candidates to fill the position, is the consultant free to offer his remaining "finds" to another retainer-paying client. In a recession, even the giant firms observe this rule.

But whenever the economy booms and excellent candidates are scarce and hard to move, the rule becomes a serious drag on the publicly owned search firm's ability to be the growth stock Wall Street wants it to be.

So what to do?

The solution is obvious. Dump the rule! In the red hot economy of 1999, all that was needed to facilitate that radical change was a euphemism for doing so. Here's the term that was invented. You'll still sometimes hear it today:

"Parallel Processing"

That's what the recruiter—paid on retainer by client X—will say be's doing when he simultaneously presents the same candidates to clients Y and Z and charges all three the full fee.

In *The Wall Street Journal*, the CEO of one of the two largest publicly owned retainer search firms was quoted in September '99 as saying that his firm:

> "began to permit 'parallel processing' of candidates for as many as four assignments as long as clients and search consultants agree. 'We tell client companies that we are going to parallel-process and even triple-process,'" said the CEO, adding "The approach makes sense, 'given the time limits involved and the fact that there are a lot more openings than there are good candidates."
>
> The article continued, "Rival executive recruiters oppose the shift

> because client companies could end up vying for the same executive. 'Clients would be very distressed that they would be competing with their own search firm for a candidate,'" a spokesman for a competitor was quoted as saying. Then the *Journal* went on to state that the remaining two of the three largest retainer firms—both publicly traded—"also prohibit the practice." But the article wound up saying, "Despite such public pronouncements, search-industry watchers say, parallel processing is widespread."

Yes indeed! But in good economic times only; not in a recession.

What does all this mean to you?

Merely that you—as a presumably hard-to-find "good candidate"—may have a lot more bargaining power than you would imagine...especially if you're dealing with an extremely aggressive giant firm during a booming economic period.

At least you now know the magic words..."parallel processing." ***Use them*** when you want to be presented on a second job you find out is being filled by the same search firm that already has you as a candidate on another position.

However, ***unless the same firm member*** you're already working with is also personally filling the second position, I think you'd be better off pursuing the second job directly with the hiring company which, of course, may gracefully return you for "processing" by *their* recruiter. Here's why. Recruiters tend to support most warmly the candidates they feel sure will actually accept their job if offered. Telling recruiter #1 that you're more interested in another job being filled by recruiter #2 in the same firm may diminish the first recruiter's enthusiasm for you as his preferred candidate, while not necessarily getting you very far with recruiter #2. On the other hand, if the first recruiter is also handling the second job, he'll close one or the other of his two searches using you, no matter which job you take. That, he'll figure, is a "win-win" deal.

There's another new wrinkle in Off-Limits policy. However, its impact is more important when you're hiring than when you're hoping to be hired.

During the "dot com bubble," many of the largest retainer search firms were eager to accept stock warrants or options in return for filling positions with so-called "new economy" startups and promising young companies.

According to *The Wall Street Journal*, in March 2000, America's largest retainer-compensated search firm had warrants or outright stock at "more than

360 companies"...all of it acquired in full or partial payments for searches.

Which brought up in my mind an interesting question: If a firm owns a substantial equity stake in a company for which it has done search work, when is that company ***not*** off limits?

A young company can ill afford to lose a key manager. Will a search firm that has a major financial interest in their success penetrate them in behalf of its other clients? Will it *tell* its other clients if it will not?

These are interesting questions, although far ***less*** interesting now that lots of those "360 companies" from March 2000 have dried up and blown away.

But are there any practical implications that ***you*** can take advantage of?

Yes!

Whenever you hire any recruiter to seek an employee to work for you, you'll supply a ***written list of the companies you want searched***. And you'll demand in return a written list of any and all companies on your "hit list" that the search firm ***will not enter*** in your behalf.

Observers who don't understand the business sometimes report that the leading retainer firms are doing contingency recruiting.

It's not true.

And what they *do* occasionally do has no effect on your self-interest at all.

Recessions hit the retainer search industry with devastating ferocity. That was true in the early '90s, again in 2001 and 2002, and yet again for a distressingly long time, beginning in 2009. A leading trade publication, reported combined U.S. revenues of the 10 largest U.S. retained search firms fell 25% and worldwide revenues of the six largest global firms fell 20%. In times like those, even the largest firms drastically cut staff and closed marginal offices. They also applied survivalist price-cutting as a marketing tool.

"Preferred Supplier" Deals

If an employer will guarantee X number of searches or Y dollars of fees annually, the search firm cheerfully reduces its fee from the traditional 33% to a lesser percentage. This "cheaper-by-the-dozen" approach (1) undercuts competitive firms on price and (2) puts all or most of the client's search budget beyond the reach of competitors.

A True Retainer...With Some Contingency Added

When the climate becomes a buyer's market, some companies that have multiple searches to give out even during those lean times, use their "clout" to drive a hard bargain. After squeezing the fee percentage as much as possible, they apply this coup de grace: "We'll pay the first 3/4, 2/3 or 1/2 of your fee as a retainer regardless of whether we hire any of your candidates, *but we won't pay the remainder unless we hire*."

In a boom economy, the giant retainer firms say "get lost" to any prospective client making such a demand. But when approached by a mega-client with a fist full of searches during a devastating recession those same firms say, "What an interesting and creative idea; let's try it."

Born of necessity, "preferred supplier" lives on and on. These price-cutting deals negotiated corporation-wide at the parent company/headquarters level tie up much of the mega-client's total search budget. In one preemptive blow, that money is cut off from all the smaller, hungrier, or more specialized firms that may have spent years forging tight relationships with the corporation's far flung subsidiaries and business units.

Watch the economic barometer. The cheaper-by-the-dozen idea now survives in good times and bad. In good times the hold-something-back-'til-we-hire feature is disdainfully shunned. In less prosperous times, however, even the most prestigious firms are surprisingly innovative.

Whether those slightly-contingent retainer deals are "in" or "out" at the moment makes no difference to you as a candidate.

So what, if all 100%...or merely 75% or 66% or even 50%...of the traditional fee is paid regardless of whether anyone is hired? Still the employer is paying the retainer recruiter as a consultant, not merely a broker. Any client powerful enough to impose super-onerous terms on a retainer recruiter will certainly continue to enforce the "don't-take-my-people-for-at-least-two-years" and the "don't-present-my-candidates-to-anyone-else" rules. So as far as you as a potential candidate are concerned, the contingency vs. retainer distinction is unaffected by making the last third or quarter of the fee contingent.

Do you want a price-tag on your head? When and why should you go straight to the employer and steer clear of the recruiter? How do you play the recruiter game to win? These are the questions you care about. And they depend on the up-front payment that's nailed down...not the uncertain remainder that's left flapping in the breeze.

Chapter 10

Doing Business with the Recruiter... on the Phone, and in His or Her Office

Okay. When a recruiter calls, your first reaction is to find out exactly who that recruiter is and...even if you know the person well...the exact nature of his or her mandate, if any. How appropriately the recruiter is tied to the employer and the job may be far more important than how attractive the job is.

From here on, we'll assume that you've examined the recruiter and his or her client relationship, both of which are fine indeed.

You've accepted the recruiter. Now let's do business.

Interestingly, whereas your first few minutes of the recruiter's call were somewhat adversarial—you brought up something *not* on the recruiter's agenda—now that you're getting down to business, your interests and the recruiter's are almost identical.

Of course, the recruiter is still trying to sell you something which you may be wise not to buy. That will be true up to the moment you accept the employer's job and resign your present one. But during this initial phone call, you and the recruiter both want to know the same things... although in opposite order of priority:

Recruiter's Priorities	**Your Priorities**
1. Are you qualified?	*1. Are you interested?*
2. Are you interested?	*2. Are you qualified?*

You want to find out whether the *job* is right for you...and whether the recruiter knows enough about it to actually have a proper assignment to fill it. The recruiter, on the other hand, wants to know whether *you're* right for the job. And if not, he or she doesn't care how interested you are.

Let's do it *your* way.

Let's indulge your priorities. First, are you "interested"? And only secondly, are you "qualified"?

If you've got a job and the recruiter's trying to get you to consider a different one, then *you're the buyer* and *he's the seller*. He'll have to follow your agenda, if you just assert it:

> YOUR CALLER: "I'm in the process of filling an exceptionally attractive position for a management information executive in your industry, and I've heard some very good things about you. But I'm not entirely sure that your background is a 'fit.' Tell me, first of all, are you in charge of systems-development throughout the entire corporation, including the subsidiaries in the U.K. and on the Continent?"
>
> YOU: "Yes, I am. But I'm in very good shape here at Outstanding Corporation. Before we go into my background, why don't we just see if the situation you have is something that I ought to think

about. And if it's not for me, I'll try to suggest some other people who'd be more appropriate."

Right at the outset you've got things rolling in the direction that's best for you. You've conveyed a pleasant, receptive, helpful attitude. But you haven't given up your superior bargaining position. You've politely asserted your obvious advantage.

Already the recruiter is sizing you up. On a subliminal level...and probably on a conscious level, too...he's now alert to the fact that, on this call, he's dealing with a highly aware and competent person. Maybe you're the one he's looking for.

Of course, if you were out of work and the recruiter were calling in response to your letter and resume, your buyer/seller roles would be reversed. You'd be willing to answer all his questions about your background and track record prior to hearing the specifics of the job he's filling. He'd be the buyer.

Ask probing questions about the opportunity.

They will:

1. **further qualify the recruiter;**
2. **rule out a no-benefit opportunity;**
3. **at the same time, demonstrate you're the calibre of person the recruiter wants.**

If there's some reason for you not to deal with the recruiter, or not to be interested in the job, you want to find out right away. Then you don't waste your time or hers.

Ask probing questions. Simultaneously you'll find out whether the position is worth considering, and whether the recruiter is well-informed enough to really be on retainer to fill it. Sometimes, *although far less often than most people think*, even a retainer recruiter may not be at liberty to identify the employer. But if she's tied in, she can describe the *job* in detail.

So ask everything that will help you see whether you should spend any time beyond the initial phone call to explore the opportunity:

What are the specific responsibilities?

What's the title?

What position would you report to?

How many subordinates? With what functions?

Is it chief executive, reporting to an outside board? If it's president or general manager of a subsidiary, does it report to the CEO, or to the COO, of the parent? Or is there a group officer in between?

If it's a top marketing job, does the sales force report to it? How large is the sales force? How many product managers? Are manufacturers' reps and distributors used? Which ad agencies? Budget? Media mix?

If it's chief financial officer, does the position have responsibility for administration, management information services, internal auditing, subsidiary controllerships (straight or dotted line), etc.?

If it's a top manufacturing job, does manufacturing engineering report to it? Quality control? Purchasing? Physical distribution? How about off-shore operations and plants? Plants within the subsidiaries?

If it's a top engineering job, does it just include work on new products? What about quality control and manufacturing engineering?

Don't trust the title to describe the job. Whatever your specialty, ask, ask, ask! And then go further:

What's the boss like? What characteristics does he value most in his employees? What's his preferred working style...lots of documentation or very little paperwork...lots of autonomy or close supervision?

What's the location? Would you have to move?

What about compensation? Will it include an incentive program? Stock options?

What's the structure, momentum, and atmosphere of the company or division? Highly centralized, or decentralized? Growing.... plateaued...in trouble? What are the short-term, intermediate, and long-range goals of the business? What's its share-of-market and its reputation for quality and customer satisfaction?

Why is the job open? What specific business problem is supposed to be solved—or opportunity exploited—by going outside to fill this position? What happened to the person who's had it up to now? And the person before?

I could go on and on. And you have every right to do so too. Find out whether it's worthwhile for you and the recruiter to go to the trouble of a face-to-face interview.

Fortunately, the same questions that will convince you to proceed will simultaneously show the recruiter that you're the right calibre of person...an alert, analytical executive, who can quickly ferret out key issues and come to an informed decision.

Indeed, the more your questions show an awareness of the problems and opportunities facing your industry and specific companies in it, the more he'll be sure that you're someone his client wants to meet.

If the opportunity is wrong for you,
it will probably be for one of three reasons:
1. wrong responsibility,
2. wrong location,
3. wrong money.

Save your time...and the recruiter's.
Dispose of all three in the initial phone call.

Chances are you can't be certain, just from the recruiter's call, that the job definitely is for you. That will take in-person, in-depth meetings with the client, not just the recruiter. But you can quickly find out why the situation is *not* for you.

All of the top-three turnoffs can be smoked out in the initial phone call. And they'll eliminate 90% of the "wild goose chases" you might otherwise be subjected to:

1. Wrong Responsibility. Question the recruiter. The job had better be considerably more attractive than the one you have now. A same-echelon job in a much larger and finer company can be an excellent reason to move. So can a higher job in a same-level company. But money alone usually isn't enough. And if you're on the brink of a breakthrough where you are, say so. There's no reason to withhold information at the outset which, in the end, will cause you to say "no thanks."

2. Wrong Location. If the job isn't commutable from your home, you can certainly decide

a. whether you're willing to relocate at all, and
b. if so, whether the proposed location is acceptable.

If either answer is no, or if you have to poll and persuade your family, say so. If your husband's or wife's career isn't portable, or if your children are in special schools, or if you want your daughter to keep that swim coach who has her almost ready for Olympic tryouts, or if you can't desert an ailing parent, then you can immediately...or after an evening or a weekend to think it over...rule out a job that requires relocation.

Don't waste your time, the recruiter's, and possibly even the employer's, on an interview, when your personal life prevents your taking the job. If you do, you'll prove you're a lousy decision-maker. And then the recruiter won't call when he gets another fine opportunity that *doesn't* require relocation.

3. Wrong Money. The recruiter almost certainly will not tell you upfront exactly how much the client prefers to pay. And of course, until the job is filled, nobody knows what will be negotiated.

However, the recruiter has a very good idea what the *upper limits* are. He's undoubtedly found out what peer-level jobs in the client company pay. And a smart recruiter always asks the compensation of the position directly above the one being filled. So even if he doesn't want to "go public" by telling you, the recruiter does know "how much is too much."

So how do you uncover too-low money?

Simple. Just give the recruiter a clear idea of what you're making now, and what improvement you expect within the next year. If the recruiter is someone you already know and trust, or appears to be a first-class professional from a respected firm, you may decide to be forthright:

> "The responsibility is very attractive. I'd certainly like to be running my own show. But I'm not sure this situation would make sense for me *financially*. My base is going up to $250,000 on August 1, and I'll earn about a 40% bonus on top of that. So we've got to be talking close to $450,000 for me to come out with any real improvement in money."

If you're less confident about the recruiter's integrity and confidentiality, just give the bottom line without saying anything specific he can repeat to others about your compensation:

> "I like it here and I'm very well compensated. However, I *would* be willing to listen if you're talking upwards of $450,000. Otherwise, I'm really not interested in changing."

Knowing where you stand on money, and knowing there's a ceiling at $290,000 in base-plus-bonus, the recruiter will immediately pull back and ask you for suggestions of other able people in your field. Best of all, he'll regard you as smart and decisive. You haven't wasted his time. Expect to hear from him again, when there's a higher-paying job.

"Sounds like a lateral move."

Quite a few executives...almost routinely...react to every new situation they're phoned about with an irritatingly common cliché:

"Sounds to me like a *lateral move*."

Using these precise words is a bad idea, because they're a formula response. Hardly ever will any new situation be exactly on a par with what you have.

So skip the cliché. But use the same approach. Latch on to the specifics the recruiter mentions, and point out all the ways the proposed job doesn't appear to be an advancement:

> "Of course I already have my own profit center, and we've been doing well since I took over three years ago. We're already larger in sales...and I'll bet a lot stronger in profits...than the company you're proposing, even though they've been around longer and lots of people probably still think they're bigger than we are."

OR

> "Of course I'd love to have a 150-person sales force, because so far we've had to use manufacturers' representatives, and I'm only just now getting a few of our own people into the field. But here I have total responsibility for all Marketing, reporting to the President. And if I understand you right, in the situation you're describing I'd be reporting to a Vice President of Marketing, who also has a Product Management group that I wouldn't be involved with. I think I'm better off to stay here and keep building this business...

> and wait for you to call me again in a couple years when we've made even more progress. Then you may have a job like his for me to consider."
>
> OR
>
> "They're a big outfit, and I believe you when you say that I can probably make a nice improvement in salary by going with them. But money isn't everything, by any means. Increased responsibility and long-term career progress are what really interest me. Tell me what this opportunity might do for me in those terms."

See what you've done? You've virtually forced the recruiter to give you more information right there on the telephone.

If you're going to say "No," do so as soon as possible.

Move the conversation quickly to your key decision points. These are issues that only you know about, since they have to do with your current situation and your career objectives.

And as soon as you know you'll ultimately say "no," by all means do so. Then offer to suggest more appropriate candidates. You'll not only save time; you'll enhance your image in the eyes of the recruiter. Seeing how efficiently you handle her inquiry, she'll figure you're equally adept at your job. Expect to be called again!

If you don't find any disqualifying negatives, let the recruiter "sell" you by phone ...and then ask for more information by mail.

If your caller does have an attractive opportunity, hear her out. Let her sell you.

Then ask for a little homework. Have the recruiter send you an annual report, a 10K, a proxy statement, a product catalog and price list, a description of the position...whatever will supplement your telephone impressions. If the recruiter doesn't have such materials, chances are she's not on retainer.

Suggest a time when you'll call the recruiter...or she'll call you...to continue the discussion, after you've studied those items. A retainer recruiter...highly paid to serve her clients' interests...will gladly call you in the evening or on the weekend, if that's what you prefer.

Never pretend to be interested if you're really not.

Some executives, unaware of the behind-the-scenes workings of a recruiting firm, will pretend to be interested in a job, just to get to know the recruiter... in the hope of discovering more-appropriate openings than the one being described.

As you can see, this strategy is way off base. If you express interest in the search you're called about, the recruiter's firm *won't show you any other job* until that project is finished and all the prospective candidates on it are returned to the central talent pool...which may take several months. It's a guaranteed method for staying *out* of the action at that firm for a substantial time.

If you say "No," try to offer helpful suggestions ...even hook the recruiter into your network.

If you're not interested, always try to suggest people who'd be more appropriate. Also suggest people the recruiter should talk to as "sources." They wouldn't want the job, but probably can suggest potential candidates.

Indeed, if you're highly impressed with the recruiter, offer to *let him use your name*. Help him get through to the people who know you, but don't know him. He'll be grateful...and will chalk up another reason why you should be one of the first people called when he or someone else in his firm undertakes a search that could interest you.

In closing the phone conversation, also be sure to let the recruiter know what sort of an opportunity *would* excite your interest. Might as well plant a seed for the future. If you've been competent, warm, and helpful, the climate is right.

Beware of the recruiter who wants to meet you after you've said "No."

If you've clearly pointed out mismatches between the recruiter's proposal and your situation, and he still urges you to come in for an interview, you should suspect him of wanting—above all—to apply his tag to your head and see that your resume is widely circulated. Chances are he won't merely be wanting, as he'll say, "to know you better for the future when the right thing *does* come across my desk."

Generally speaking, true retainer recruiters are extremely busy finding the people clients are paying them to look for today, this week, this month. The successful ones have very little time or inclination to interrupt their ongoing searches to meet anyone...no matter how able and attractive...who doesn't fit a current search.

The odds are overwhelmingly against any retainer recruiter...no matter how large the firm he or she works for...ever personally getting the exact project that's right for you at the exact time when it's appropriate for you to move. Expect the recruiter to behave accordingly. *And be wary of one who doesn't.*

How much manipulation are you willing to put up with?

Lots of recruiters...sometimes encouraged by employers who'd like them to operate that way...will try to get you to come in for an interview without telling you the identity of the employer you're being considered to work for.

After you've expressed potential interest in their proposition, they go on to say something like this:

> YOUR CALLER: "Naturally, of course, I can't give you the identity of the employer *on the telephone*. We can talk much more frankly in my office, if you'd like to come in and explore this situation further. And do bring your resume. We can look it over as we talk, and we'll have it in case we decide to go ahead."

What baloney!

Is the recruiter's phone bugged...or yours? Conceivably, a receptionist or a PA might overhear *yours* if you're at work. But *his* shouldn't be a problem. And he raised the point...you didn't. Any legitimate concern—and only you will have it—can be eliminated by continuing this call via your home phone tonight, or on the weekend. And all first-class recruiters—retainer and contingency—will gladly do so.

Re-read what the recruiter said. Did he promise to identify the employer, even if you *do* go to all the trouble of visiting his office, and you hand him your resume, *and* you submit to an interview? No, he didn't! And don't expect him to, if you meekly go ahead as he suggests.

Obviously the recruiter wants the option of knowing everything about you and conveying nothing specific to you about the identity of the employer...if indeed he's actually been engaged by one.

Plenty of recruiters would like to proceed that way. But no employed executive has to accept such ground rules. Indeed, the unemployed executive who objects to them will be considered a lot more formidable than the one who doesn't. Let's hear how you pick up the conversation:

> you: "Oh, I have no problem with the phone; we're perfectly free to go ahead.
>
> "Also, I can't tell you whether I'm interested in interviewing for a job unless I know what the job is, and of course that includes knowing what company I'd be working for. I'm doing very well here, and haven't been thinking at all about making a change. On the other hand, what you're suggesting does sound interesting...at least on the surface. Is there something more you'd like to know about me, in order to see whether you think we should go any further?"

The ball's back in his court. If he wants you for a candidate, he'll just have to be more forthcoming now, while he has you on the phone. You're warmly open and cooperative...offering to address any potential shortcomings.

If the recruiter doesn't come forward now and ask his key questions which might disqualify *you*...and let you ask your key questions that might disqualify the *job*...he knows he'll lose you. Then he'll have to go to the trouble of finding someone else with your qualifications...and with your interest in the opportunity. Someone who, unlike you, is willing to submit to a highly one-sided procedure. That means someone more insecure in his or her job...or as a person...than you are. And unfortunately, the employer probably won't be as interested in that person as he would be in you.

So even if you're sitting at the other end of the wire absolutely quivering with delight at the prospect of having a shot at the position the recruiter has described, *you have clout*. Use it.

What will the recruiter do now? One thing's absolutely certain. He won't think less of you just because you're not a pushover. His next move will depend on the actual motives behind this call to you:

1. If he's trying to tag your head prior to nailing down a proper client assignment, he'll forget that idea...meanwhile telling you, "Too bad; you're missing out on a great opportunity!"

2. If he was going to befriend you, and later pitch for your executive recruiting business, after this nonexistent "search" is...alas... "cancelled," he'll forget that idea.

3. If he has a retainer search, and is merely proceeding with approach #1 of his standard "M.O.," he'll shift very smoothly into

approach #2. In return for your telling him what he needs to know, he'll tell you what you need to know...including employer identity, which he'll request you to "keep confidential." *Expect this result 80% of the time.*

4. If he has a retainer search and also a legitimate mandate for secrecy *from the employer*, he'll come out with a specific and plausible reason for not being able to name the employer:

> YOUR CALLER: "I'm sorry, but I really can't identify the company. The person in the job is going to be fired, and we're lining up a slate of candidates who'll be all set to go when that happens."
>
> YOU: "Well, I guess I won't be standing there all interviewed and waiting, when the other person gets the axe. But do call me when you're in a position to be more specific. I definitely might be interested, depending on who the company is. Meanwhile, I appreciate your thinking of me. Thanks for the call."

Only in possibility #4 was there any legitimate employer-dictated need for confidentiality. And I'm being very generous in estimating that such a need may actually exist in as many as 10% to 20% of the instances when a recruiter calls you. Then, of course, he can't back down.

But what will he do? By holding out, have you lost your shot at the job he called you about?

Probably not. Chances are, you've made yourself more desirable.

In all likelihood, when the recruiter briefs the employer on the executives who were willing to be interviewed without knowing whom they'd be presented to, he'll also describe the two or three *even more impressive ones*...like you... who wouldn't go along with that procedure. He'll explain that he can re-contact these, as soon as the employer lifts the secrecy. Chances are ten-to-one that the employer will immediately say:

> "Don't wait. Open up to them right away, so that we can meet any of those who are willing to talk to us, right along with the candidates you've already interviewed."

So, even in this rare instance where there was an employer-imposed mandate to interview without disclosing company identity, you came out just as well by standing firm as you would have by caving in. In fact, you probably look stronger and will be more sought after than the people who jumped at the chance for a "blind" interview.

Of course, if you'd been out of work when the recruiter called, your reaction might have been different.

If your caller had been from a *retainer* firm where you'd been trying for weeks to get a courtesy interview, you'd instantly have accepted the invitation. However, you'd have known that interviewing on this job would have assigned you to this search, even if you weren't told the employer's identity. Therefore, you probably wouldn't have been returned to the firm's talent pool for consideration on anything else, until after the "mystery" search was completed.

Of course, you'd *never* have submitted to interviewing by a contingency recruiter without being told to whom you were being offered, unless you were sure that the firm is totally ethical. Otherwise, they might have taken your willingness to be offered to one undisclosed employer as permission to covertly submit you to any company that might hire you.

The furthest I'd be willing to compromise, if I were you...

If I were happily employed, I'd never agree to be interviewed for any "opportunity," no matter how attractively described, unless I knew in advance the employer's identity. However, if I were eager to move, I might propose the following:

> YOU: "I'd be pleased to meet you and discuss my background, which seems to be exactly what you're looking for. The only thing I ask is that you not submit me to any employer without telling me whom I'm being offered to.
>
> "You can tell me who it is after the interview, if you decide to present me. Or tell me that you have other candidates that you prefer, and therefore you *won't* submit me. Or tell me you *don't know yet* whether I'll be submitted, and you'll get back to me later if I *am* to be submitted.
>
> "I just don't want my name and information submitted to anyone without knowing who it is. Is that OK with you?"

Even employment agencies for clericals accept the proposition that "applicants" have the right to say in advance what companies they are and are not willing to be presented to. When you state your position in this way, *no legiti-*

mate executive recruiter can refuse. But do so on the phone prior to your interview...when you'll have more clout, and you'll get a clearer answer.

You can push the recruiter toward frankness by being frank yourself.

To encourage a "let's get down to it" telephone discussion, volunteer a thumbnail review of the points...pro and con...that should spell "go" or "no go" to the recruiter:

> YOU: "Look, I'm in charge of all marketing and sales over here, reporting to the President. I moved up to this job three years ago from head of product management. Since then we've been making very strong gains in market share, volume, and profitability. Here are a few things you should also know, however: I'm 54 years old and I don't have an MBA. In fact, I don't quite have my BS. My only college has been at night at NYU, and I've let that program slide since my promotion to this job. I'm about 15 credits shy of a BS in Marketing. Also, you've got to be talking *over $300,000* or you can't reach me on money."

It's all there!

That took you less than a minute to say. Yet it summarizes the key points the recruiter would have tried to draw out in a face-to-face meeting.

If the recruiter knows his client will never accept a non-college graduate (and in my opinion, that's very shortsighted), or won't want somebody in his 50s when the search has already turned up several outstanding candidates in their late 30s, then both you and the recruiter will be spared a useless interview.

On the other hand, if the prejudicial factors you raise are not disabling, then you've undoubtedly "sold" yourself to the recruiter with your 60-second summary...a virtuoso display of cutting through to the heart of a matter. The employer will be identified, and you'll be invited to meet the recruiter.

If the recruiter is uncertain about the employer's attitude toward the factors you've laid on the table, he'll:

1. say that his client is a wonderfully broad-minded person who'd never break the "equal-opportunity" laws, and

2. promise to get back to you with "further information," once he's "ready to go ahead."

Meanwhile he'll find out what his client really does feel about the points you've raised. If and when the recruiter calls back, you'll know you're not wasting your time by exploring a job you'll never, in the end, be hired for.

Special Note for Employers Using Executive Recruiters:

Your first impulse...particularly if you haven't been served and coached by top professionals in the recruiting field...will be to request your recruiter to keep your project "highly confidential," and perhaps not to reveal your identity until after he's interviewed the executive and "confirmed that the person is really a strong candidate."

The less competent your recruiter is...and the less honest, as he competes for your business by telling you what you want to hear...the more likely he'll imply that he can provide such "confidentiality" and still get you the strongest possible candidates. Don't imagine for one minute that this is true.

The executives most willing to go along with such treatment are out of work (which these days doesn't mean they're not good)...or in difficulty...or so marginally qualified for your job that they're thrilled to pursue it, regardless of the overbearing procedure.

Executives who are already at the right level for your job, and are currently employed by companies that think they're excellent and reward them accordingly, will not be clogging their calendars with interviews by recruiters who won't tell them who they're being solicited to work for.

Face-to-Face with a Recruiter: Your Interview for the Job She Called About

You and a recruiter have accomplished about as much as possible over the telephone. You tried to disqualify the opportunity, and you couldn't. You're not "sold." But you *are* interested. So you're going to go see the recruiter...or possibly she's coming to see you. Now what?

Now you prepare for the meeting!

That's right. Even though the recruiter called you; you didn't call her. Even though you agreed to the meeting only after she drowned you in charming persuasion. Still you *prepare*. This meeting is far more important to you than to her. It's just part of one day's work to the recruiter. But it could change...for better or worse...your entire career.

So take some time to figure out what you want to accomplish. What questions do you want answered? And what do you want to communicate, so that the recruiter will rank you among her finalists and will accurately convey your best features to her client?

Your Two-Fold Agenda: Selling and Inquiring ...with Emphasis on Selling

One objective must be virtually in-the-bag by the end of the meeting. The other can be pursued later by phone, if necessary.

If time runs out on your interview and you haven't asked quite all of your questions...or if new ones occur to you afterward...you can always phone for answers. Is there anything wrong with this?

> YOU: "A few important questions occur to me that we didn't get a chance to cover when we were together..."

No, nothing at all out of line. But imagine this call:

> NOT YOU: "Unfortunately, Paula, I was so busy asking questions during my interview, that I got home and realized I hadn't told you some additional...and very impressive...things you should know about me. Make yourself comfortable, and I'll begin reciting my further virtues to you now..."

You get the point. You had plenty of chance to challenge the job during one or more phone calls before your interview. And you can phone with more questions later. The interview is your chance to let the recruiter find out how ideal you'd be for the position. Don't wind up with you convinced that the job's right for you, and the recruiter not convinced that you're right for the job.

Of course you can try to fill in omitted selling points with a follow-up letter. Indeed, that's your only shot. But the recruiter's impression will overwhelmingly be based on your face-to-face interview. It's almost impossible to raise your ranking by anything you mail in afterward.

So ask and sell. But don't fail to sell.

At the outset:
1. determine how much time you have, and
2. reconfirm the ground rules, if necessary.

As in the courtesy interview, you'll be wise to ask:

> "How much time do we have?"

And if you've got to leave within a limited time, let the recruiter know right away:

> "I hope I've scheduled enough time for this, and I'll be glad to come back if you want me to. But I couldn't avoid setting up another meeting at four o'clock. So I'll have to leave here by three-thirty."

Forewarned, both you and the recruiter can modify your agendas to fit the pre-acknowledged time slot. Such a statement isn't discourteous; it's the mark of a thoughtful and efficient executive.

Candidate interviews by recruiters usually range from an hour to an hour and a half. I personally devote far more time to them, but I also pre-screen very restrictively and invite only a few exceptional people to interview. Each recruiter has his or her own personal style. Achieve your objectives by adapting to the recruiter's game plan.

Another point. If you agreed to this meeting without knowing in advance the identity of the employer, you should also reconfirm, right upfront, the ground rules that were negotiated earlier:

> "You know, Paula, you still haven't told me who the employer is. Your feeling was that at the end of this meeting, you'd know whether or not you'll be presenting me. Then you can tell me *who it is*...if we're going ahead...or that I'm *not a finalist* if we won't be going further. That's just fine with me. What I really want to be sure of is that we're agreed that I won't be presented anywhere, unless I know in advance where that will be."

Beginning with a recapitulation of points agreed on earlier over the phone is merely appropriate businesslike procedure. But if you delay them to the end of the interview, the same points will seem nagging and distrustful.

Set up an informal agenda.

Once timing is established, it's not offensive...and can be helpful...to send up another trial balloon:

> YOU: "I don't know where you want to start. I do have some potential reservations about the job...especially since reading the 10K and proxy statement you sent me. Or do you want to start by talking about me? I just know that before I can agree to be a candidate, I'll have to have answers to a few key questions."

Your concerns aren't such "show-stoppers" that you should have phoned and possibly cancelled your interview. But they do have to be addressed. The recruiter can now decide whether to tackle them right away, or to go ahead and talk about your qualifications, with the understanding that she can't sign off until your questions are answered. Indeed, your down-to-business approach may encourage her to proceed just as frankly:

> "Let's take a look at *our main questions* first, and cover whatever else we have time for at the end. My two basic questions about you are: How much experience have you had in acquisitions and divestitures? And what happened at Yesterday Corporation?"

Or the recruiter may even say:

> "Look, I'm already convinced that you're one of the best candidates in America for this position; let's get your questions out of the way first, and then let me tell you some further things I've learned about the job."

The better you and the recruiter know how much time you both have, and the issues of greatest interest to the opposite party, the more useful...and persuasive...the meeting will be.

Do you have a resume? And do you hand it over?

Yes! You never come to a recruiter interview without a resume. And once you're satisfied that you're dealing with a professional you respect, you don't hesitate to hand it to her.

As a successful executive at and far beyond $100,000+, you know about visual aids and leave-behinds. A resume is both. Even if you're more concerned about getting information than communicating it, the resume will still be helpful. It will speed the recruiter's inquiry...and make more time available for *your* questions.

If you're being courted by the recruiter, and the job seems only marginally attractive, just bring in the last resume you made...even if it's ten years old. Update your home address and phone number. Also jot down on a sheet of yellow pad the dates and titles of your more recent jobs. Your early career will be thoroughly covered, and you can talk your way forward from there. First-class recruiters always type up their own version of candidate information. So informality won't count against you, even if you wind up meeting the employer.

On the other hand, if the position could be a major career breakthrough, it's certainly worth the time and effort to prepare a highly persuasive resume stressing your most recent...and presumably your greatest...accomplishments. Not only will it help the recruiter understand and communicate what you've done, the very act of creating it will prepare you to meet the recruiter *and* the employer. You'll be in command of facts-and-figures...not only on what you're doing now, but on what you've done in the past.

If you just bring an old resume, be sure to *read it over*. I'm amazed how many people hand out papers they seem totally unfamiliar with. Time is wasted as the recruiter, who's freshly read your information, seems to know more about your early career than you do. You're a dud as a business communicator when that happens.

Also, be prepared to *talk* your way through your work history. Some recruiters will read your resume carefully, asking questions and making notes. Others will set it aside and ask you what happened. You won't score points with a "tell-me" recruiter if you clam up and say, "It's all there in the resume."

Bring along any supplementary information you may need.

If you don't have an encyclopedic memory, bring a few sheets of statistics, so that you can refer to them when a performance question arises.

A recruiter's interview has two purposes:

1. to obtain information, and

2. to see how well you handle yourself and how thoroughly you seem to understand what you're in charge of.

Short answers are better than long ones. And specifics are far better than vague generalizations. You may not want to hand over confidential charts. But have them handy, to remind you of the numbers you've achieved. Vague, nonspecific communication will count against you.

Be honest about negatives.

Be frank up front about major negatives that referencing will highlight. Expect the recruiter to check you out before he passes you along to his client. If you've been fired, or if profits have evaporated under your management, he's probably going to find out. And it will be a strike against you that you tried to conceal the information. No one has a record of perfect achievement. And many very able people have been fired. Offer a brief explanation that establishes your version of the matter, but don't highlight it, and don't be defensive.

Don't view the retainer recruiter as your "advocate."

Bear in mind that the retainer recruiter is paid to represent the corporation's best interests, not yours. Don't expect him to conspire with you about the best way to present your qualifications. It would be a breach of professional ethics to try to convince the client that you're a strong candidate when you're really not.

Are there any special considerations associated with your candidacy?

If so, bring them up.

Anything that could make you more costly or inconvenient to hire than other candidates should be brought out during—or prior to—your interview. Then the recruiter can forewarn the employer, and you'll be considered from the beginning with your "disadvantages" in full view.

If you're the best person, then simultaneously with his growing interest in you, the employer can think of ways to deal with your special needs. Above all, there won't be "unpleasant surprises" later, to throw cold water on your candidacy and raise doubts about your candor.

For example:

> Selling your current home will be difficult and costly. You don't expect the new employer to compensate you for circumstances he had no part in creating. But you obviously need lucrative basic compensation in the new position to make joining his company worthwhile.
>
> You'll lose $125,000 in profits on stock options which won't vest for another ten months.
>
> You have a child with a costly medical problem, and you can't afford to move unless the illness won't be excluded as a "preexisting condition" under the new company's insurance.
>
> You're in the midst of renovating your house, which could be tough to sell right now at its proper value. You'll have to stay where you are, unless you can have the services of a home relocation company that will price it fairly and take it off your hands.
>
> You have a pension that vests, all-or-nothing, in seven months, and you'll move prior to that only if you can negotiate a settlement

with your present employer or receive special treatment from your new one.

Tell the recruiter about any problem that may require modification of the way his client normally handles a new hire.

Prepare yourself for a later client interview.

If it looks like the recruiter is "sold," and you're going to be a "finalist," ask questions that will get you ready to meet the employer. Take advantage of the recruiter's knowledge of his client's situation...either at the end of the interview if there's time left, or in a later phone call. Find out exactly what the employer is looking for, and get a sense of what to expect at the interview.

The Ideal Result: "To Be Continued"

Just as with the courtesy interview, a positive ending to this session is the sense that exploration of your candidacy is "to be continued." If and when it becomes clear that you're a "finalist," accept "yes" for an answer, and leave. And if there are questions in your mind about whether you should be a candidate, resolve them with the recruiter and either decide to go ahead or withdraw.

Executive recruiters can be frustrating. Grin and bear it.

From the job-changing executive's point of view, retainer recruiting firms seem dismayingly inefficient. When you deal with a large and respected firm, you know that, at that very moment, they're handling hundreds or even thousands of searches...many of them almost certainly an ideal "next step" for your career. Yet you only hear about one at a time. And which one is largely accidental, depending on which recruiter in the firm happens to be in a position to deal with you, what jobs he's trying to fill, and what success he's had with each of them.

For example, he may show you something in Distant Falls, a place that doesn't particularly appeal to you, because that's his most urgent search at the moment. Meanwhile, he says nothing about the job that's even more attractive, and located only twenty minutes from your front door...simply because he already has more candidates than he needs on that one.

There's very little you can do about the haphazard way your involvement with a retainer search firm unfolds. It's simply the way those recruiters work...a method that's not designed to favor *your* interests as a job-changing executive.

Still, a good, ethical retainer recruiter does know of jobs that can advance your career. Under the right conditions, he or she and others in the firm may show you at least one opportunity...possibly even two or three...within the year or so that you may be seriously thinking about a move. And you can know more opportunities handled by retainer firms if more firms know you.

Consider the highly professional retainer recruiters as *one conduit* to career opportunity...and the highly ethical contingency firms as another.

But now that you know how executive recruiters really work, you can clearly see why they shouldn't be the only way you seek to advance your career. At least not when you want to move fairly quickly. And not when you want the widest possible knowledge of what's available in the marketplace.

Read Before Chapters 11, 12, & 13

I CONSIDERED ELIMINATING some of what I'll show you now. But then I decided to fully cover DIRECT MAIL. Why? Because its principles will supercharge your job hunt, even if you do NOT conduct a direct mail campaign.

In Chapters 11, 12, and 13 we'll get into the principles of DIRECT MAIL. Indeed, we'll even use them to improve your resume and cover letter and turn them into a Communications POWER TOOL.

And we'll do that, even though *I'll bet you have already decided that you will NOT use direct mail.*

That's OK. I understand. You favor one or the other of two reasons... both based on a realistic view of today's marketplace. They are:

> **1. NEGATIVE: Higher Costs. Prices are way up on postage, stationery, printing, mailing lists...and labor, if you purchase help.**
>
> **2. POSITIVE: Higher Response. Largely because of the higher costs, today fewer executives are sending on-paper mailings. So the mailings that do show up get more attention and better results.**

Choose between reasons 1 or 2. Either way, I strongly urge you to prepare for a direct mail campaign, even if you don't intend to conduct one. That's because developing a resume and cover letter designed for direct mail provides your world beating multi-purpose....

Communications POWER TOOL

If you are willing to invest the effort to write a resume and cover letter effective enough to succeed in a direct mail campaign, you'll have a POWER TOOL that you can send out one or two at a time to...

1. Breeze past the thousands of job seekers answering an internet job posting.

Those people merely "click to apply." Hopeless! Too many are doing the same thing. Instead, you will figure out (1) the probable company, and then (2) who within it is likely to be the decision maker. Address your letter directly to him or her.

You'll bypass the thousands of "applicants" lined up for the usual processing in the HR department or a search firm. If more than one person in the company might be the decision maker, you'll write to both. And if several companies might have posted the job, you'll send to all of them.

But you will never say, "I saw your posting." Instead your cover letter will say, "Do you need..." just as if it were part of a massive mailing. It will appear that you could not know that you were reaching just the right person at just the right time.

2. Bypass retainer search firm blockages.

Suppose you are already a candidate on one search by a retainer firm. You know you usually will not be shown multiple jobs by such a firm. So you go directly to the employer on other openings being searched.

3. Avoid a contingency firm's price tag on your head.

These firms try hard not to disclose employer identity. They don't want competing firms—or candidates they haven't yet price-tagged—to get in touch with the employer. However, that's exactly what you *do* want to do. And you'll do it with your Direct Mail POWERTOOL.

You know your industry. If more than one employer fits the description in the job posting, write to all.

4. Keep you Innocent.

Because you're using a classic direct mail package, every recipient will conclude you're merely conducting a direct mail campaign. Even when your perfect timing may seem a little too lucky to be accidental, no one can be sure it's not. You won't affront the employer's HR people that you bypass. And you won't offend search firms by using any information they have provided directly to you.

Your generic direct mail paperwork is your Kevlar armor. Wear it whenever you want to arrive innocently via a perfectly timed accident.

5. Be cost efficient.

In a conventional direct mail campaign, you'd send out 1k or 2k or even 5k or 6k letters and resumes. Deploying your communications POWER TOOL, you only mail a few handfuls. The savings are huge because you are not blindly playing random statistical odds. You are distributing only where you have definite knowledge or an informed suspicion that a current opening actually exists. The savings are huge, now that you are powerfully "fishing where the fish are."

6. Make your POWER TOOL as persuasive as you'd make it for a massive mail campaign costing thousands of dollars.

Read on, to enter the sophisticated realm of direct mail and, a few pages later, to begin polishing the resume that is the backbone of any full-scale direct mail campaign you'll ever conduct. It's also the essence of your Communications POWER TOOL.

Direct mail has always been costly and a lot of work. However, it has also rewarded many executives with the job they wanted. It can still do the same for you.

And that's true, even if you only mail a few of your POWERTOOLS to just a few carefully selected recipients.

And now ONWARD to CHAPTER 11

Chapter 11

Being Where You Can't Be ...and Selling When You're Not There

Isn't it too bad that you can't be everywhere at once, and find out about every major career opportunity that might interest you?

Wouldn't it be great to have your own equivalent of a spy-in-the-sky satellite that could survey a forty-mile radius of your house...or the entire USA...or the world...to identify all the situations you'd like to know about, whether current openings, soon-to-be openings, or searches underway at recruiting firms?

Then you'd be sure not to miss any situation that could foster your career.

Of course there's always the likelihood that you'll learn of career-enhancing job possibilities through personal contacts and networking...talking to old business friends and associates, meeting lots of new people, and picking the brains of everyone you reach.

Unfortunately, although face-to-face communication is the most powerful form of contact, your time is limited. No matter how diligent you are, you simply can't be everywhere at once. You'll make your networking contacts one at a time, maybe two or three a day, a dozen or so a week. That's not exactly a speed-of-light aerial reconnaissance. And it's likely to miss *most* of the jobs available "out there somewhere," which your contacts don't happen to know about.

You've also clearly seen that retainer executive recruiting firms aren't going to show you everything they're working on. They'll reveal only one job at a time, and probably no more than two or three per year.

In fact, there is only *one way* by which you can even attempt to find out about *all* the available or soon-to-be-available jobs that may be the right "next step" for you. That's Direct Mail, number four on our list of five main methods. Number 5, the web, although less comprehensive than Direct Mail, can reveal a v

Let's look again at our list:

1. Personal Contacts...getting in touch with people you already know.
2. Networking...getting in touch with a series of people others refer you to.
3. Executive Recruiters...dealing with the various species of "headhunters."
4. Direct Mail...letting the Postal Service take your message more places than you can visit and phone.
5. The Web...taking advantage of modern technology in job-hunting and career management.

What do 4 and 5 have in common? They're ways to get yourself known to far more people than you'll ever be able to meet face to face.

One Message. Two Different Distribution Methods.

Your message, obviously, is:

"Here I am. And here's what I can do for you."

To find out about all the jobs that might interest you, you'd have to get that message to (1) every employer currently needing to hire someone exactly like you, and (2) every recruiter now being paid to search for such a person.

Up until a couple decades ago there was only one way to simultaneously reach such a vast number of employers and search firms that statistical odds would guarantee you'd surely hit a few who were actually seeking you when your message arrived.

Direct Mail was the only way to dispatch your message to more people than you could meet through networking. Indeed, it still is the only way to make a dignified and appropriate—rather than an obnoxious and self-defeating—overture to a CEO or to the head of a division or a department who might right now want to hire someone exactly like you as a subordinate.

The web, however, is now an alternative way to reach many recipients. E-mail is lightning-fast It's also convenient and appropriate in many situations. It defeats "snail mail" in every speed contest, and it also has an appealing informality and even intimacy that can sometimes be very desirable. But it is absolutely *not* the way to send an unsolicited self-introduction and an accompanying resume to any never-heard-of-you chief executive you want to impress favorably.

First of all, you probably can't get his or her personal e-mail address. But even if you had it, would you use it?

Ask yourself: Are you pleased when unexpected e-mails are spammed into your list of incoming messages? Do you read those e-mails? Are you grateful that someone has sent them your way? Does your assistant open them, glance at their content and appearance, and select a rare few that might actually be of interest to you?

Your answers: No, No, No and Probably Not. So don't even dream that someone at the right level to hire you as a subordinate is going to react any more eagerly to your spammed e-mail than you would if you received something similar from someone else.

Forget the web —method #5—when you're trying to contact strangers in the most polite and persuasive possible way. An elegant on-paper letter and resume delivered by mail is still the best way to do that.

Clearly, barging onto the incoming e-mail list of a person you might want to work for is usually far too pushy and obnoxious. If someone *invites* you to send a resume by email, that's a wonderfully fast and efficient way to transmit your information. But when you merely invite yourself to do the same thing, it's often a tragically dumb move. Either you may get deleted and not remembered at all...or you may get noticed as impolite and obnoxious and perhaps shunned when you later arrive in a more polite and appropriate fashion. Heads...you lose. Tails...you lose.

However, there's nothing impolite or too pushy about sending an elegant and persuasive *letter* to someone you don't know and want to reach with a message that might be of interest. That's been a common and effective practice for at least two hundred years. Indeed one of the most prized possessions of a friend of mine is a letter handwritten by Abraham Lincoln, who is graciously responding—albeit in the negative—to a person he's obviously never heard of, who wrote to the President about wanting to become his personal assistant.

But isn't direct mail a weak method?

Many people think direct mail is a weak technique, particularly for a job search. I've had lots of senior executives...even top marketing executives (who should know better)...say to me:

> "John, I don't believe in direct mail. It's not effective. Nearly all the letters you send are either thrown away or relegated to the Personnel Department for a polite 'no-thank-you.' Therefore, you just don't get anywhere with a direct mail campaign. It doesn't have the punch that personal contact does."

Mostly true. But whenever I meet people who criticize direct mail as weak and ineffective, I remind them of their own reactions when they've needed to hire someone they were having a tough time finding:

> "When you had a really difficult hiring problem and you urgently needed someone with a particular background to fill an important spot, didn't you *then* follow up by contacting *everyone* whose resume came to your attention and seemed to show exactly what you were looking for?"

Invariably they reply:

> "Well, of course *then* I did. *Anyone* would."

So I press the point:

> "What if, instead of the Postal Service bringing that resume, it just blew in through the window...all tattered and dirty, along with a bunch of autumn leaves? Wouldn't you still call up the person if he or she looked like the possible solution to your problem?"

You know their answer. It would be yours too.

My firsthand experience as a retainer executive recruiter doing searches at the highest compensation levels for well over 30 years has proven beyond doubt that mailed-in employment inquiries do get attention.

In about one out of every two searches I conduct, the ultimate decision-maker who hires me hands over at least one...and more often several...resumes he or she has collected before calling me. Approximately a third of those have been forwarded by outside directors, employees, customers, suppliers, lawyers, accountants, etc. (the product of personal contact and networking). The majority, however, were merely delivered by mail. And of course I'm not called—and never see the resume—when anyone is so tempting that there's an interview, offer, and acceptance without any need for me.

It's all a matter of timing.

The key advantage of direct mail is not how strong a medium it is, but the fact that it's strong enough, if it reaches a decision-maker *at exactly his or her moment of need.*

Moreover, it doesn't matter what method you use, if you reach the decision-maker when he or she has *no* need. Even you-in-person...with all your persuasive logic, charm, wit, elegant grooming, and both your new shiny shoes... won't achieve a sale if your host isn't seeking what you're selling. That's always the problem...with most networking calls, and with most mailed-in resumes, too.

On the other hand, your resume, dog-eared and folded, that a CEO happens to find protruding from the pocket on the seat ahead of him when he takes a commercial flight to the Coast could net you an exciting phone call. The same lucky break might also occur if you happen to sit next to him on the flight... assuming of course that he talks to seat-mates.

The value of direct mail is not in how it's delivered, but rather in the great number of potential buyers it can reach simultaneously, in order to stimulate one or two of the rare few who happen to have the right need right now.

Use direct mail to reach the whole universe of potential buyers.

That way, you should hit some of the very few who are actually ready to buy.

Consider what corporations do. The President and the Chief Marketing or Sales Officer may personally contact key accounts that provide enormous volumes of business. Customers who buy fairly often will be handled by the direct salespeople...perhaps 150 or 300 professionals spread across the country. And finally, to reach customers in out-of-the-way places or who order only once-in-a-while—customers it isn't feasible to serve with salespeople—companies rely on direct mail, or telephone marketing, or a combination of both.

But even telephone calls have serious limitations. You can only call so many people per day. Your listener will seldom stay on long enough to hear a comprehensive sales pitch for a complex product. And afterward there's nothing left behind on paper to refresh his memory and encourage follow-up.

So the method companies turn to when they want to cover the whole market at once, to get where they can't send a salesperson, and yet deliver their entire selling message and have it remain afterward in writing...is a wide-ranging direct mail campaign.

Indeed, direct mail *is* effective, or it wouldn't be so widely used. The proof is in your mailbox every day. If direct mail weren't effective, the companies who send it would soon be out of business, having thrown their money away on something that doesn't work.

You're surprisingly similar to the other products direct mail sells very effectively.

What kinds of products are sold through direct mail? Not the inexpensive, uncomplicated things that everyone needs every day. Soap, corn flakes, diet cola, floor wax, and nationwide "fast food" chains are best advertised in TV commercials aimed at the entire population. Such products are easily understood. Just about everybody is a potential purchaser. And the whole story can be boiled down to 30 seconds or a minute. Forget the "cents-off" coupons. The long letters in your mailbox are not about canned soup and laundry detergent.

What *are* those long letters about? Seldom-purchased products and services that:

1. only a few people out of the vast population are likely to need and be able to afford at the moment they get the advertisement, and

2. require more explanation and persuasion than can be crammed into a 30-second or one-minute TV spot, or even into a one-page magazine ad.

Examples: professional-development seminars; building lots and time-share condominiums; insurance plans; expensive "limited-edition" books, porcelains, and store-of-value collectibles; tax planning and investment services; special-interest magazines; economic newsletters...those sorts of things.

You see the analogy. An executive is a seldom-acquired item...very costly, unique, and relatively complicated to understand and evaluate. One of the best ways that the marketing geniuses of the 20th and 21st centuries have found to spread the news about such an item was by direct mail advertising. And the fact that—despite the advent of the web —you're still receiving plenty of direct mail in the 21st century, is dollars-and-cents proof that it's still highly effective.

The Networking vs. Direct Mail Trade-Off

If you reach someone when he or she has no need and knows of nobody else who has a need, there's no sale. And it doesn't matter whether you get there in person or in writing.

The advantage of a personal visit—networking—is its human interaction. Your host may not have or know of a job that could advance your career. But seeing and befriending you...and wanting to do a favor for the person who referred you...she can usually be persuaded to pass you along to several others. Your contacts will, indeed, "*increase geometrically*." But "geometrically" *only* until you have more people to see than you have hours to go see them. After that, you've got strictly a linear progression of appointments to make, two or three a day...probably ten to fifteen a week.

The advantage of direct mail, on the other hand, is that you can reach an unlimited number of people simultaneously. Therefore, *you can inflate that number to the point of very high probability* that you'll reach some of the rare few who actually do need what you're selling at the very moment you happen to make your contact. And when you finally do reach someone with an immediate need for what you're offering, that person is likely to be interested... even though no mutual acquaintance made the introduction.

Is there a downside to direct mail? Will reaching the potential decision-makers in lots of companies make you seem:

a. too available?

b. too eager?

c. unwanted and unloved?

d. desperate?

e. none of the above?

The answer, of course is E, "none of the above." And the reasons why, when you think about them, are pretty obvious.

No chief executive nor anyone else in control of a job that might represent a valuable career advancement for you is sitting at his desk wishing a letter and resume from you would arrive...that is, unless he's one of the infinitesimally rare few who right now happens to have that job wide open, urgently needing someone like you to fill it.

The person who doesn't need what you're offering will merely throw away your mailing, or pass it along for filing and a courteous "no thank you." He's *not* going to pick up the phone and ask his peers in other companies and his contacts in the leading executive recruiting firms if they also got your mailing, and what did they think of it, and what are they going to do about it, and weren't you stupid not to have known in advance that he and they didn't need anyone like you right now.

The fact is, either he'll do you *some good*, or he'll do you *no harm*. And in the "some good" department, you may be pleasantly surprised. If a colleague in his own organization, or a friend, or an executive recruiter calling him for suggestions happens to mention a need for someone like you, the person who's just received your resume and doesn't need you himself will probably pass your resume along, just as one of your networking contacts would.

And if your mailing is so impressive that the recipient or his HR department saves a copy for a few weeks or months, he might wind up referring several inquirers to you. When extremely well done, direct mail can, with luck, take on a bit of the same "geometric" dimension networking has.

"But," you ask, "will I diminish my luster and usefulness to the prestigious retainer recruiting firms if I conduct a direct mail campaign?"

No. A lot of people worry needlessly about this possibility, so let's examine it.

Retainer recruiters actually *expect* you to send your mailing to the decision-makers in a wide range of companies, because it's in your best interest to do so. They realize too, that you'll contact other retainer search firms. Since no two retainer firms are ever working simultaneously on the same project, you simply *must* send to additional firms to reach additional searches.

Of course, as we discussed, it's unlikely that you would simultaneously be presented... "sold" at the rate of $15,000 or $30,000 or even far more per candidate...to more than one client of the *same* retainer search firm because of the reasons we looked at earlier. But there's no client PR damage to either firm when two different retainer firms present you to two different companies. If either or both of these companies should find out, they can't blame their own retainer firm for what a different one has done.

Moreover, the idea that you may have written to her client company won't scare away the one-and-only recruiter in a sizable retainer firm who, for the moment, has the right to deal with you. She always expects you to have taken that perfectly logical step. And she has no reason—or method—to reward you if you haven't. Indeed, going directly to companies is the only way you can possibly break through the barrier that confines you to this recruiter and her client company, while putting you "off-limits" to all the other recruiters in her firm and to all their client companies.

Believe it or not, if you're really a good candidate, a retainer recruiter is less worried that his client won't be amazed when he identifies you, than he is that the client will think he's a dope for not finding you when you've already made yourself obvious to the client company.

The bottom line on trying to be more attractive by being less known:

It doesn't work!

Known is like pregnant; you're known or you're not known...by each person individually. The way the relationships we're interested in work, each player in the game either knows of you or he doesn't; they're never going to gang up on you and take a poll to see *how many* know about you.

What will *make you less attractive is being unemployed a long time, and the fewer people who know about your fine background and your availability, the more likely that might happen.*

The only circumstance where being widely known is dangerous to your economic health is when a recruiter *operating on contingency* submits you... price-tag attached...to companies who never specifically engaged him to do so.

Getting around on your own is altogether different. It's great. Circulate!

Enough about the "why" of direct mail; let's take a look at the "how." And in the process, we'll add the persuasiveness of direct mail copywriting to your resume.

You may never need to conduct a full scale direct mail campaign to advance your career, although it is one of the "Rites of Passage" you should thoroughly understand.

You and every other executive should always have a persuasive sales-representative-on-paper standing by, ready to go anywhere...by hand, by mail, or by email... to do the best possible job of communicating your abilities and achievements to people who haven't witnessed them firsthand. That's a resume. And its purpose is *to be where you can't be and sell when you're not there*. Direct mail marketing is the *science* of doing just that...the most thoroughly understood and quantifiably proven of all the marketing techniques.

In Chapter 13, I'll tell you ways to use mailings to advance your own career development.

First, however, I want to show you in Chapter 12 how to employ proven direct mail copy writing techniques to make your "sales representative"—your resume—as compelling as it can possibly be, regardless of how it's delivered.

When polished to maximum effectiveness and coupled with a cover letter, your resume is also your Communications POWER TOOL, highly effective when sent to just one prime prospect you already know controls an ideal job for you.

Chapter 12

Your Personal Sales Representative

As an upwardly-mobile executive, you need a really good personal sales representative...one that can be where you can't be, and sell when you're not there.

You need a resume.

And it should be as persuasive as you can possibly make it. Indeed, it should be compelling enough to take on the hardest selling challenge of all: to make "cold calls" on complete strangers...and get results.

That's what a resume has to do as the core of your Communications POWER TOOL, whether you (1) send it to just one individual, or you (2) send out POWER TOOLS by the thousands in a classic direct mail campaign. Your resume arrives uninvited and unexpected. And usually it's assisted by nothing more than a brief covering letter. If it can convince someone who's never before met or heard about you to call, email or write you a letter, then surely it can do everything else you could ask a resume to do.

You can trust such a resume to be your spokesperson whenever you can't be present. Whether you leave it behind after a successful interview, or send it ahead hoping to get an appointment, it will give every recipient the same persuasive, ungarbled message you'd convey in person. Effective all by itself, your resume will also be an indispensable aid to anybody who wants to "sell" you to someone else...from the recruiter telling his client about you, to your potential boss telling her boss, to the CEO informing his Board.

Before we start creating your optimum "Sales Representative" resume, let's discuss why it's worth the effort, and dispose of your excuses for not making it.

It'$ your most valuable credential.

How long did you spend in undergraduate college...four years? And maybe in grad school after that...two to five years? And besides the time...the money? And for what?

Alphabet soup. Credentials! Stuff on paper that you hoped—and to some extent you've found—could enhance your earning power and career achievement, in addition to culturally enriching your life.

Suppose it takes you a month, at the outside, working every spare moment nights and weekends, to compile a succinct but compellingly information-packed recounting of what you've learned and achieved since college...the only things a potential employer really cares about and pays you big money for. The resume you wind up with is the most valuable credential you can have today. Like your diploma(s), it's merely words on paper, But far more negotiable at the bank!

"I don't need a resume right now, since I'm not considering a change."

Great! Now's the ideal time to examine your career and demonstrate its value. Now...when you have the leisure and the objectivity to do a really thoughtful, comprehensive job.

Tomorrow's paper may bring news of an unexpected opening at a leading company in your industry...one that's likely to be filled from outside, and one where you could easily reach the decision-maker through networking, or maybe just by picking up the phone. He'll probably ask for your resume. Is it ready?

And shouldn't you also have your most persuasive possible resume in the hands of your friends at the top retainer search firms? Even if you're permanently on file electronically, they may be glad to have your "formal" resume handy whenever they're actually presenting you as a candidate.

The "total immersion" study of your career and its accomplishments that's necessary to produce the ultimate "sales representative" resume will help—indeed force—you to size up (1) where you stand now relative to your long-range goals, and (2) how special you really are—or aren't—relative to your peers. Maybe you're already gaining momentum in the passing lane on the fast track. But maybe you're just cruising along an access road. There's no speed limit on your career, so why not step on the gas?

"I don't need a resume because it's classier not to have one."

Well, at least it's less work.

"I don't need a resume because I'm not looking. And when the prestigious retainer recruiter comes after me, he'll create my resume."

That's true; at least so it will seem to his client. Even if you hand him an excellent resume, his assistant will probably word-process it so that it will appear consistent with the papers he presents on his other candidates.

But suppose he's got a really terrific opportunity for you...*and five other people*. Do you want to rest your case on what he'll write from memory after an hour or so of conversation? If you hand him a highly persuasive resume, he won't make it worse to match the rest. And if he has to write it, chances are he can't make it good enough to match the best.

"Fortunately, I don't have to bother writing my own resume; the people who fired me have paid for outplacement services."

Some things are more important to you and to your future than they are to anyone else. The document that positions you in the employment world is one of them.

Incidentally, a "superior-performance" resume trumps a "superior- education" one. Could that fact help you?

Okay, we've got the "whys?" and "why nots?" out of the way. Now let's talk about your ultimate credential, the true "Sales Representative" resume... strong enough for use in direct mail, and therefore best for every other use, too.

Direct mail selling is the hardest test persuasive writing can be put to. By mailing to large numbers of potential purchasers, it's possible to blanket so many that you'll surely hit a few who have a need at the exact moment your envelope arrives. But grabbing attention, engaging interest, and convincing strongly enough to stimulate action...that's still a lot to ask of mere words on paper. You'd better send something persuasive. It must truly be a Communications POWERTOOL. And its core is your resume, which speaks for you when you can't be there. Moreover, that's true regardless of whether your resume:

1. *arrives "cold"* in the mail, or by accident, or

2. *is hand delivered*...by you yourself, or by someone who's met you, and wants another person to know you as fully and favorably as she does.

   Indeed, as we shall see, a resume effective enough to perform in those situations will also be effective when

3. *you offer it as an orientation aid at an interview*.

...And now for the shocker. What's the number-one principle of direct mail copywriting?

In almost every industry, there's a bedrock principle discovered years ago... and reconfirmed again and again through the experience of everyone in the field...until it becomes the rule that all know and follow. In real estate, for example, it's:

"Location is everything."

Or, stated another way...

"The three principles of real estate are:
(1) Location, (2) location, and (3) location."

In direct mail copywriting, as in real estate, success or failure is proven in dollars and cents. Before any company sends a mailing to 5 million or 50 million households, several different versions are tested, ranging from short to long copy, and trying new gimmicks, such as envelopes that look like bank statements, bills, newsletters, etc. Objective: to see which variation pulls most orders per thousand dollars of cost.

Some of the new gimmicks test well and are used. Others are forgotten. But, like real estate, direct mail copywriting has one bedrock principle that everyone respects...proven during seventy years of testing and reconfirmed by test after test today:

"Long copy sells."

Proof of this honored axiom is delivered to your home every day. If shortness worked, brevity would be in your mailbox. And all the companies now using long-copy direct mail could achieve multi-million dollar savings in paper, printing, and postage...everything that makes several pages more expensive than just one. Those companies aren't stupid. They test. They don't spend more money unless the results *more* than justify the extra cost.

However, this proven axiom might, as advertising guru David Ogilvy pointed out, be more accurately stated:

"Factual copy sells."

Famous for his "long-copy" ads, Mr. Ogilvy was also a crusader for very clear and *succinct* writing. He conveyed each fact with arresting clarity and *brev-*

ity, and then piled up a wealth of these impressive facts to prove his client's product superior to competitive brands. Master of the concise well-turned phrase, Ogilvy summed up the principle this way: "*The more you **tell**, the more you **sell**.*"

Incidentally, the experts I've talked to tell me that the only exceptions to the "long copy sells" rule occur with simple products that every recipient is already thoroughly familiar with before the mailing arrives. In such cases, explanation of the *product* is unnecessary, because only the briefly stated *offer* is new.

For example, you can sell someone a cut-price subscription to *Forbes* or *Fortune* with a postcard or a little self-mailer envelope, whereas it will take several pages of facts and pictures to persuade the same person to sign up for a "four-months-free, cancel-and-pay-nothing" offer on a new publication.

When you get in touch with a prospective employer, you're always an unknown new publication. You're not *Business Week*, *National Geographic*, or *The Wall Street Journal*, and don't you forget it!

There are always, of course, a few "celebrity" executives in any field who... at least during their heyday...may be able to get by with brevity instead of a convincing dose of selling copy. For example, Steve Jobs before his untimely passing could have sent out multiple copies of the following brief note...and produced a flood of inquiries:

```
I've pretty much finished what
I set out to do at Apple,
Pixar, and Disney.

If you think I could be help-
ful to your company, please
give me a call.
```

John's Fire-in-the-Forest Analogy

I had a very successful career as a consumer products marketing executive before I got into executive recruiting decades ago, and I've thought many times about the question of *why* long copy—or as I prefer to describe it, *adequately specific* copy—invariably sells complicated, expensive items by direct mail much better than short copy does.

The experts either say:

"People need a certain amount of *convincing* to break down their barriers."

Or they say:

"Who *cares* why? Experience proves that long copy works!"

Well, over the years I've come up with a little analogy which has helped satisfy my need for a "why," and it may strike a chord with you, too.

Hitting people "cold" with a written sales pitch and taking them all the way from no-such-thought-anywhere-in-their-heads to the point of grabbing a phone or an ipad and taking action requires quite a process of change to take place step-by-step in their minds.

Think of the process as a chain reaction analogous to building a fire in the forest when you have just one match. Before you strike that match, you must have the entire makings of your fire all laid out. First you find some tinder... maybe an old Kleenex®, or some dry leaves. Then you add dry twigs and small dry sticks. Then some bigger sticks and branches...as dry as you can find. And on top of everything else some big branches and logs...dry, if possible, but if not, the other stuff burning under them will get them ready to burn. What you've assembled will keep the fire going all night, or at least long enough for you to round up more fuel.

You wouldn't dream of wasting your match by starting the chain reaction with only part of your fuel in place. You'd have everything ready. Otherwise, your fire might get off to a promising start...and then go out.

Something similar, I submit, must happen when a mailing convinces its reader to buy a complicated, expensive, seldom-purchased item. The letter must take him from complete unawareness and indifference...to first spark of interest... to casual but somewhat more interested reading...to avid devouring of all the information provided...to contacting the sender. Since we know for a fact that short, sketchy copy doesn't perform as well as longer, more informative copy, I submit that the reason may be too little fuel.

The reader may have a first flicker of interest...which may grow into casual, and even attentive, reading. He's not yet convinced to phone or email. But he *is* willing to read further.

Suddenly the fuel runs out. The reader would have considered more information...*but it wasn't there!* And not deeply involved, he doesn't bother to send out for more facts.

You've got just one match. Don't waste it!

You have your reader's attention when she first glances at your resume... whether it blows in through the window or it comes in the mail. Your match is lit and burning. It ignites the dried leaves. But if you haven't laid out enough persuasive factors to fuel the chain reaction, your match is wasted. You've sparked attention. But there's no bonfire. And your phone doesn't ring.

Q: What happens when you apply direct mail copywriting to your resume?
A: It goes from 2 pages to 3 or 4 pages... and it contains 3 or 5 times as much of the persuasive information employers are interested in.

"Look, John," I'll bet you're saying, "forgetting for the moment the fact that everyone has always told me resumes should be brief, not long...and maybe conceding that the direct mail people do know about stimulating action through a written sales presentation...still I can't let you get away with saying that *doubling* the pages from two to four will provide *five times* as much persuasive information."

I knew I'd grab you with that idea.

But think about it for a minute. On two pages you're barely able to list your name, address, phone numbers, email address, college degrees, a couple personal facts, and lay out a reverse-chronological listing of all the companies you've worked for and the progression of titles and responsibilities from college to now...all requisites of a good resume (although you'll drastically condense any early history that merely matches what everyone else does early in a similar career). Certainly you'll feel squeezed as you create a nice clean layout with lots of white space separating all the elements, so that where you've been and what you've done is easy to scan...a point we'll get back to later.

So in two pages, you *are* able to list the job titles you've held and give a skimpy description of responsibilities for the more recent and important ones. Unfortunately, you haven't got room to say much, if anything, about what you *achieved* when you held those responsibilities. And achievements proving you're special are what a prospective employer is looking for.

Everyone has been given responsibility. Only a special few—you among them, I hope—have given back anything really substantial in the way of achievement.

Let's say that in a nice, open, quick-to-scan layout, with your chronological units floating in a decent amount of white space, you get 400 to 500 words on a page, 800 to 1,000 on two pages...and 75% of them are devoted to covering the mandatory data. That leaves about 200 to 250 words for accomplishments that could make you stand out as interesting—and hopefully special—in the eyes of a potential employer.

Now go from two pages to four. You've got room for 1,600 to 2,000 words... 800 to 1,000 more than before. And *every additional word* can be devoted to achievements, because the basics were already covered in the two-page version. Add your original 200 to 250 words on achievements, and the box score looks like this:

	Total Words	Basic Data (Words)	Achievements (Words)	How Many Times As Many Achievement Words?
2 Pages	800-1000	600-750	200-250	1
3 Pages	1200-1500	600-750	600-750	3
4 Pages	1600-2000	600-750	1000-1250	5

But now let's go back to the point about everyone telling you to keep your resume brief. Who told you? And when? And why?

Who and When?

Was it your "Counselor" at the contingency firm that helped you get your first job out of college or graduate school? Was it someone who "worked with" you or "headhunted" you as you moved into middle management with your second or third job?

Face it: in those days you hadn't done anything really significant yet. At that stage no one has. Or if they have, nobody is prepared to believe they have.

From entry level up through middle management you're somewhere from a "GI Joe" to a first lieutenant in the army of industry. What an employer wants to know is where you've been...how fast you're moving up...and how closely your experience matches what she wants done. That information fits neatly on one page...certainly no more than two. Indeed, if you're bright, attractive, and ambitious, it won't matter if your entire early career has been spent working on a string of corporate *flops!* You won't be blamed. You didn't commit the corporation to those misadventures. And you weren't so centrally responsible for implementation that anyone will figure you made a good idea fail.

Today, however, you're in an altogether different situation. You're at or far beyond $100,000+. Now you're at least a "field commander." You legitimately *can* claim some victories. And you can be held responsible for some defeats. *Your resume must deliver more factual information.*

Also consider the "why" behind the advice you're given.

If you're now way above $100,000+, and "*when*" you were told to "keep it brief" was yesterday, and "*who*" told you was a prestigious retainer recruiter...then maybe we should consider "*why*" he said that.

The most obvious reason is that you only have a fleeting moment of your reader's time and attention before he'll give up on your resume as too tedious to figure out, and toss it aside. *This reason I totally agree with.* However, I don't agree that the solution to the problem is to strip away your persuasive factual information.

The other reason could be that the retainer recruiter has orally "pre-sold" you to his client, so your resume doesn't have to be persuasive. My reaction to this reason from your standpoint is "OK...*but*." The recruiter is introducing several other candidates besides you, and if you have some impressive achievements, you want them clearly known to the employer as she chooses between you and the others.

Your resume must perform two functions.
Brevity suits one...and defeats the other.

Your resume absolutely must do two things. Unfortunately, while brevity achieves one, it defeats the other. Therefore, unless your exploits were the cover story in Monday's *Fortune*, brevity isn't your answer.

1. Quick Orientation

Your reader will allow your resume only about thirty seconds...no more than a minute...to orient him to who you are, and whether you might be relevant to his needs right now. Certainly that's true if it arrives "cold" in the mail or is blown in through the window; he'll spend *more* time with it, not less, if he's paid a retainer recruiter over $80,000 to look for it.

Most of the time your resume will reach the reader when he doesn't need you. Your "one match" will burn less than a minute. By then, if you've done a poor orientation job, he'll have dumped you for being too tedious and confusing. And even if you've done a good job, he'll almost always have dumped you for not being needed right now.

2. Thorough Convincing

But in the rare, rare instance when you do happen to hit a reader at the moment she has a need you might fill, and you quickly orient her to that fact, then she's willing to extend her attention span a bit further.

She didn't find you irrelevant. Now she's looking to find you ordinary. But, wait a minute; you've been involved in several things that were impressively successful...another "turn off" bypassed. Okay, but probably these programs were conceived, planned, and strategically implemented by others, and you were merely a supporting player. No, wait another minute; your clear, succinct explanation of the reasons underlying the actions that were taken certainly sounds like you were the strategist, not just the "gofer." Your reader decides:

"This guy is *interesting*. I'll read to the end. And then I'll go back over this whole thing again. If he still looks okay, maybe I'll even call him up."

As you see, a very brief resume could have performed the quick orientation and helped your reader turn off. Unfortunately, it probably couldn't have turned her on...and on...and on...to the point of picking up the phone and calling you.

Fortunately, a resume written according to the "long copy sells" principle of direct mail copywriting is capable of walking and chewing gum at the same time.

Right away you're probably saying, "I can see, John, where long copy will be great at 'Thorough Convincing,' but won't it interfere with 'Quick Orientation'?"

No. Not if you're careful to make your resume *visually accessible*. Format and layout become extremely important. Just make your resume:

Scannable!

Your reader will glance at 3, 4, 5, or more pages if it's instantly evident with just one glance what's on each of those pages. If you arrange your resume right, the recipient will probably glance through *all* of the pages before reading *any* of them. That's everyone's normal impulse as a reader anyway. You probably flipped through this book before you began reading it page-by-page. Fortunately, with resumes in particular, it's easy to help that normal human tendency along.

But don't go crazy! A great many people cannot be trusted with the knowledge that they can have a multiple page resume. They somehow jump to the conclusion that more words on more pages is better. They become legends in their own minds. Their accomplishments only merit two or three pages, and they vomit out words far beyond a tight, succinct telling of their story. If you are merely adding words, rather than exciting and very succinctly stated recent accomplishments, you are going WRONG. Please don't say that I made you narcissistic and boring!

Don't you just hate topically-oriented resumes? Don't you wish everyone did?

I have never yet met anyone who likes to receive a topically-oriented resume.

You know the kind...where practically the whole thing is a list of claimed accomplishments, presented entirely out of context of when they happened... who the executive was working for...what his title, responsibilities, reporting relationships, and staff were...and what the size and nature of the businesses were. Finally, if you're lucky...and it's not always there...you find a deliberately sketchy little "Chronology of Employment" buried at the end, from which...if you're not already too turned off...you try to guess when and for whom and from what position of how much authority those previously claimed management miracles were achieved.

You and I are in the overwhelming majority in disliking topically-oriented resumes (also sometimes euphemistically referred to as "achievement-oriented"). When on the receiving end, virtually everybody prefers the good, honest, comfortable, easy-to-read old-fashioned kind, where name, address, email, and business and home phone are at the top, and work history proceeds backwards from current job on the first page to earliest on the last page.

Everyone's recognition of...and preference for... the standard-format resume solves your "scannability" problem, without getting you into the brevity trap.

If you don't go out of your way to confuse your reader, you've got the scannability problem solved...no matter how long you choose to make your resume.

Everyone in a position to hire an executive earning over $100k or 300k or 500k has read hundreds of resumes before. If yours is in standard reverse-chronology format, and each employer/time/position copyblock floats in enough white space to make it clear where one segment ends and the earlier one begins, *your reader will go on automatic pilot*...scanning through any number of pages in just a very few seconds.

One page or five, he quickly sees that you're *not* somebody he can use right now. But if by stroke of lightning you happen to have dropped into his hands at precisely the time he *does* need someone with a background even remotely like yours, he'll read on...and on. Having your entire "fire" laid out, you've got an excellent chance that your reader will proceed all the way from flicker-of-interest to action. Expect a phone call or an email!

Not only does the standard reverse-chronology resume solve the scannability problem; it's also more convincing, because it's more straightforward.

Forget about "long copy sells." Assume that two resumes, one reverse-chronological and the other topical, are *the same length...any length*.

The one that deliberately strips away the employment context from the claimed accomplishments not only frustrates the reader's comprehension, *it also raises the presumption that there must have been some very good reason for doing so*. "This person obviously has something to hide," thinks the reader. "I wonder what it is."

Usually it's too-brief tenure at the latest or two latest jobs...and maybe at lots of jobs along the way. That's what the reader immediately suspects. And readily confirms, if a truthful "chronology" is included anywhere in the resume. And assumes if it's not.

Wanting to de-emphasize their latest job and not put it at the top of a reverse-chronological list is overwhelmingly the reason executives turn to a topically-oriented resume...even though when they're personally hiring, they hate to receive one. That's a mistake. It's better to deal with the problem straightforwardly.

Below I've shown a successful lead-off entry for a reverse-chronological resume. This person wisely stuck to the traditional format.

2015 (9 months)

FLY-BY-NIGHT SCHLOCK ELECTRONICS CORP.

Vice President - Engineering

After seven years of increasing responsibility at Alcatel-Lucent and predecessor, Bell Labs Div. of AT&T, I was recruited as Chief Engineering Officer of this fast-growing five-year-old maker of video games and electronic gambling devices (2014 sales, $332.5 million), by the Founder/CEO, who'd been his own chief engineer.

Six months later, I still hadn't received the equity stake which was a primary incentive to join, and still hadn't been allowed to install any of the operating changes I felt could benefit the company. So I proposed and the Chairman agreed that I should re-distribute my duties to subordinates and seek a situation where I can assume a more assertive role.

2002 - 2015

BELL LABORATORIES DIVISION
(ALCATEL-LUCENT AND PREDECESSOR LUCENT/AT&T)

Group Director - Laser Engineering Department

As you see, by the third paragraph on the top page of his resume, the writer is back to telling the Bell Labs story he loves to tell. Above all, he hasn't been forced into a topical resume...a cure far worse than his mild disease.

If you're right, John, that almost everyone prefers to read standard-format resumes, why do people write the other kind? And do the executives who write them also dislike receiving them?

Questions I've always been curious about, too. So I've checked into them with the people who've handed me topical resumes over the past 35 years.

Invariably, once we got down to talking frankly, these people pointed out problems similar to the one I just dealt with, which made me conclude they felt forced to give up the standard reverse-chronological format. I can't recall a single person maintaining that he went to the topical format because that's the type he prefers to receive.

And now, maestro...an appropriate drum roll and cymbal crash as we unveil a sample resume written according to the "long copy sells" principle of direct mail copywriting.

It's from Sam Sage, one of the many executives you'll meet when you view an executive search through the eyes of a retainer recruiter in Appendix I.

As you look at Sam's resume...begin by doing what everyone always does with a resume. *Scan* it for a few seconds.

What function does Sam perform?

Who's he done it for?

How long has he been at it?

See if Sam's someone you might need right now. Chances are he's not. And you'll see that at a glance.

Next...before you actually read the resume...do me a favor. Ask yourself:

Could a shorter resume have turned you off any faster?

Would Sam be any further ahead if it had?

Having scanned the resume, do me another favor. Change the facts. Pretend that you now have even the slightest...the weakest possible...glimmer of interest in someone even remotely like Sam. For that reason, you're inclined to begin *reading* the resume.

Are you interested enough to continue from page 1 to page 2?

From page 2 to 3? All the way to the end?

Face it. If you're not interested enough to spend the two or three extra minutes it'll take you to finish reading about Sam, you're certainly not interested enough to call him up and kill an hour or two meeting him face-to-face.

Finally, after you *have* read all the way to the end, ask yourself:

Could Sam have "sold" you better with a shorter resume?

Would knowing less about Sam have made you like him more?

What information could he have withheld in order to *really* turn you on?

And is that information anything that even the briefest one-page resume *could* conceal?

Note...

The resume we're developing here is the classic high quality document you should always have ready and up-to-date. It's your best possible representative, whether delivered by mail or email, or handed over at an interview, or passed along by people wanting others to appreciate you.

SAMUEL P. SAGE
219 Waring Drive
Denton, New Jersey 07299

Home: (201) 719-0932
Office: (212) 121-3000
ssage@aota.com

2010 - Present

FARRINGTON LABORATORIES
(Merged into Pan Global Pharmaceuticals Ltd. in October '15)
New York, New York

Vice President - Chief Marketing Officer

Recruited to this privately-owned $1.3 billion maker of prescription drugs as Vice President - Chief Marketing Officer by Blair Farrington, Founder/Owner/CEO in 2010, when sales were $592 million.

Mr. Farrington doubled what I'd been making in the same position at the much larger (then $1.2 billion) Swiss-owned Medica Suisse USA Ltd. But the primary incentive was this 72-year-old gentleman's plan to take the business public with me as his successor, after we worked a few years together to increase volume and improve profitability. Instead, the company has been purchased by...and merged into...Pan Global Pharmaceuticals (October '15'). With their acquiescence, I'm seeking a new challenge...hopefully a Presidency; otherwise Chief Marketing Officer with early transition to general management.

Following (with Mr. Farrington's permission) is a summary of the company's performance since I joined in 2010 and 3 years prior:

	Sales ($millions)	% Change	Pretax Net ($millions)	% Change	% ROI
'15	1,342.6	+31.5	223.0	+62.4	28.1
'14	1,021.0	+24.9	137.3	+52.3	24.6
'13	817.5	+36.1	90.2	+43.1	17.2
'12	600.6	+23.2	62.9	+39.8	12.7
'11	487.5	-17.7	45.0	+81.9	9.4
'10	592.4	-2.4	24.8	-16.8	3.6
'09	606.9	+4.5	29.8	+6.6	4.9
'08	580.8	+7.2	27.9	+8.2	5.7
'07	541.8	+6.1	25.8	-1.1	9.1

The product line was reduced from 618 SKUs in '10 to 309 profitable items in '13 (expanded with new products to 384 by '15). The 109-person sales force was reorganized into 11 regions in '10 and expanded to 225 people by '15.

Nine profitable new drugs were introduced via cross-licensing agreements with other manufacturers ('15 sales, $258 million; $62 million pre-tax net), and $23.4 million pretax was generated by granting licenses to other companies.

SAMUEL P. SAGE - 2

Physicians' top-of-mind brand-name awareness of our three largest-selling drugs was raised from 18% in '10 to 62% in '15 by a massive sampling, detailing, and professional advertising campaign (budget tripled from $18.8 million in '10 to $58.2 million in '15).

As a result of Farrington Labs' excellent growth trend and high profitability, Pan Global paid 30 times estimated '15 earnings in a 50%-cash/50%-stock transaction.

2007 - 2010

MEDICA SUISSE USA LTD.
Marshall Plains, New Jersey

Vice President - Pharmaceutical Marketing

Rejoined this $3.6 billion Zurich-based maker of prescription drugs, veterinary biologicals, and fine chemicals as Director of Pharmaceutical Marketing, reporting to the Managing Director - USA, and heading all marketing and sales for all North American pharmaceutical lines (total '07 sales, $630 million) after a two-year hiatus to aid my family's automobile business in Ohio.

By 2010 sales were nearly double ($1.2 billion) 2007 volume, and ROI had increased from 17% ('07) to 24% ('10). Market share of U.S. prescription tranquilizer market rose from 11.6% in '07 to 19.2% in '10, and veterinary products gained 1.3 share points to 7.2% in '10.

My earlier recommendation (in '05) that the company's consumer pet-health lines be sold to generate cash for acquisition of young growth companies in the higher-margined ethical drug field was implemented while I was away (2006), and I helped identify and purchase in '07 and '08 three small companies...BioTRITON, Radio-Tra-Chem, and Synestial Laboratories...which have all grown and prospered under Medica Suisse ownership. One of these, BioTRITON, was publicly reported as having worldwide sales of $560 million in '14, with the highest ROI of any Medica Suisse business anywhere in the world.

'08 Vice President - Pharmaceutical Marketing. Promotion in title, no change in duties.

'07 Director - Pharmaceutical Marketing. Rejoined Medica Suisse in charge of corporate Marketing, Market Research, Telemarketing, and Sales Promotion departments (total of 41 people); plus two sales forces...Ethical Drug (135-person) and Veterinary (32-person).

2005 - 2007

SAGE CHRYSLER / TOYOTA, INC.
Kensington, Ohio

Upon my father's sudden death (2005), I took charge of the family business ($2.8 million sales in ’05, $4.4 million in ’07), holding it together until my younger brother could finish his MBA at Wharton (’07) and join my mother in running the company.

Increased TV advertising, and diversified by building two Taco Bell fast food franchises (since expanded to seven). Profits nearly doubled in two years.

2003 - 2005

MEDICA SUISSE USA LTD.
Marshall Plains, New Jersey

Group Product Director

Invited to join my client from New World Advertising Agency as Group Product Director (with 4 Product Managers and 5 Assistant PMs), in charge of:

(1) Marketing existing U.S. lines...$68 million consumer (Krueger’s flea-and-tick collars and home remedies for pets) and $96 million professional ($42 million veterinary and $54 million human prescription drugs); and

(2) Introducing new family of prescription tranquilizers (Dopatreem) for Rx sales in the U.S.

Since introduction of a major new Rx drug is impossible without a large field force (and Medica Suisse had only 22 salesmen carrying both Rx and veterinary lines), I cut off advertising on all lines for 10 months; used the cash flow to build a 100-person field force calling only on MDs; and launched a $20 million sampling and ad campaign for the Dopatreem line.

Result: 14 months after introduction, Dopatreem and Dopatreem X were #2 and #5 tranquilizers in the U.S., with $440 million combined annualized rate of sales. Profit from Rx lines was then temporarily diverted to help rebuild other lines to all-time high share levels.

1999 - 2003

NEW WORLD ADVERTISING AGENCY
New York, New York

Vice President - Account Group Supervisor

Joined as Account Executive on $38 million Whiskers cat food account when the AE on my P&G business moved to New World as Account Supervisor and asked me to join him. Through growth of Whiskers and acquiring new accounts, became VP - Account Group Supervisor in charge of $102 million in billings (4 AEs and 3 Assistant AEs) from Megopolitan Foods ($76 million on Whiskers and Arf! brands) and Medica Suisse ($14 million on consumer items and $12 million on veterinary and Rx human drugs).

SAMUEL P. SAGE - 4

As AE in ’99, led the task force that “re-staged” Whiskers brand with CLIO-winning “Caesar-the-Cat” TV commercials and portion-control packaging that doubled Whiskers’ market share from 5% (’99) to 11.2% (’03). Factory sales rose from $106 million (’98) to $298 million (’02); and advertising rose from $18 million to $52 million. Led successful solicitation of $14 million Arf! dog food account (’00), which billed $24 million in ’03 (sales rose from $64 million to $158 million). Personally brought in Krueger’s flea-and-tick collars ($8 million in ’01) from Medica Suisse, which consolidated all their North American business with us in ’03.

2001 Vice President - Account Group Supervisor. A 26% 12-month sales increase in Krueger’s flea collars, etc. from Medica Suisse enabled us to win their veterinary and prescription drug accounts...the first medical advertising handled by New World. Promoted for building of Megopolitan and Medica Suisse accounts.

’00 Account Supervisor. Turnaround on Whiskers enabled us to land $14 million Arf! dog food billings (’00) and Krueger’s consumer pet items (’01).

’99 Account Executive. Entered on the Whiskers account with assignment to stem share decline (averaging 0.9 point per year since ’94).

1996 - 1999

PROMOTE & GAMBOL COMPANY
Cincinnati, Ohio

'98 Assistant Brand Manager. Handled $52 million TV & print media and $16 million sales promotion budget on GLOSS-X floor cleaner. Promoted to head successful test marketing and regional expansion of new GLOSS-O floor wax.

'96 Brand Assistant. Traditional P&G home office and field sales training assignments; handled TV copy testing for Soft-Ah! paper products.

EDUCATION: MBA, Harvard Business School, 1996
BA, University of Michigan, 1993

PERSONAL: Born June 1, 1971
Married, 3 children.
6' 1", 185 lbs.

Editor's Note...

This model resume by John Lucht in RITES OF PASSAGE has raised the prevailing standards for proving one's superiority to other candidates for a desirable position. To master these breakthroughs, use pages 41 to 135 in his EXECUTIVE JOB-CHANGING WORKBOOK, which provide (1) "real life examples" and (2) templates for creating your personal job-winning resume.

Could Sam have made you like him better by omitting something you just read?

And if so, could even the shortest one-page resume have concealed that *particular* "something"?

You scanned Sam's resume in seconds.

You saw at a glance that he's a *marketing* executive. And a very *high-level* one.

Is there any kind of resume, no matter how brief—or any kind of letter, no matter how vague and misleading—that could have hidden Sam's basic information from you? And could he have benefited from the concealment, even if it were possible?

I don't think so.

If you didn't need what Sam was selling, merely limiting your knowledge couldn't have increased your need.

But if you'd had even the slightest interest in anyone even remotely like Sam, then seeing how very special he is would have made you more...not less... interested.

Indeed, Sam even managed to tell you that he believes he's ready to be a president; to imply that he's recently been functioning almost like one; and to demonstrate over and over that he certainly thinks like one.

You saw, too, that Sam's been transplanted several times and has succeeded in each new context...even running the family car dealership. He's versatile. And his sense of loyalty...as extended to his mother and brother...is also admirable.

About the only thing you could imagine Sam wanting to hide is the fact that he's spent the most-recent and highest-level part of his career marketing *drugs*...a fact which, if known, might turn off a CEO looking for someone to market anti-aircraft missiles or panty hose.

But Sam can't even *name* his employers without letting his "drug experience" out of the bag. And no CEO...indeed, no reader...is going to be turned on by self-praise in mere "percentage" terms by someone who refuses to reveal who he's worked for until *after* he's been granted an interview. Straight to the wastebasket with a letter or resume like that!

After reading Sam's resume, you and I suspect that he could market just about anything...missiles and stockings included. Nonetheless, no retainer recruiter being paid, let's say $150,000, to find a "defense" or a "soft goods" person can get by with just offering Sam plus a "he-could-do-it" pitch...even though Sam might make a good "wild card," tucked in among several "on-target" candidates.

On the other hand, if Sam can somehow get the resume we've just read into the hands of the CEO of an armaments or a hosiery company *before* he's paying somebody $150,000+ to find exactly what he wants, the CEO may think:

> "What the hell? It won't cost anything just to meet this Sam Sage. He's done some very impressive things. And frankly, most of the marketing people in our industry don't impress me at all. Marketing is *marketing!* A smart outsider like Sage might just show us a few tricks we never thought of."

Face it. Despite any kooky advice to the contrary, there's no way Sam can "package" himself differently for different employers. So he's being straightforward. And he's right! Just like you and me, others will also admire Sam's achievements...their diversity...and *the thinking behind them.* They too will envision him doing an outstanding job, no matter where he ends up.

No question about it. Sam's taken the best possible approach with his resume. He's told the *truth* openly, voluntarily, and impressively.

David Ogilvy knew what he was talking about when he said:

"The more you tell, the more you sell!"

Notice that Sam used narrative paragraphs, rather than "bullets" to tell his story.

There are two common approaches to presenting a work history. One is to use paragraphs, with each job written up as a mini-essay. The other is to use "bullets"...sentence fragments preceded by a raised dot. Commonly used by advertising copywriters, the "bullet" format attempts to make every single point seem like a highlight.

Either style is acceptable. But, for several reasons, I strongly prefer paragraphs...very tightly and specifically written. Sentences in paragraphs are easier for the reader to comprehend and believe, because they closely resemble what he sees in newspapers, magazines, books, memos, and other informational writing. Bullets, on the other hand, resemble advertising copy... subliminally *not* an aid to believability.

Also, sentences in paragraphs enable you to use transition phrases and conjunctions that *connect* the various statements in ways that serve your purposes better than a series of unrelated exclamations. It helps to be able to say: "In recognition, I was promoted to..." "When my report was accepted by the Board, I was asked to assemble a team..." "After consolidating these three acquisitions..." You get the idea.

Sam also made his resume factual and concrete...something many people have trouble doing. Here are a few tips:

Orient your reader with specifics.

For each management-level job, orient your reader to the size, nature, and trend of (1) the larger unit in which you participated and (2) the part of it you were responsible for. What was the size of your operation in people, sales, and profit? What was its mandate? The general business climate around it? The problems and opportunities you identified? The strategies you came up with? And the results you achieved?

Use numbers wherever possible.

Focus on quantifiable data. Give dollar figures for sales, profits, ROI, costs, inventories, etc. before and after your programs were implemented. When you use percentages, you'll usually want to give the *base*...plus any comparative figures on the rest of the industry or another part of your company that will show your numbers are special.

Avoid empty words and statements.

Omit the self-praising adjectives that losers wallow in..."major," "significant," "substantial," and "outstanding." Wherever such a word is justified, a number will be far more persuasive. And never make meaningless over-generalized statements like this:

> "Responsible for managing the strategic technical issues impacting the company's ongoing core businesses."

What does this person do all day? What's his budget? Whom does he report to and who reports to him? Has his employer gained anything from having him around?

Create a mosaic.

You've seen those pictures made out of lots of little colored stones. Imagine that each promotion to a new job, each numerical improvement, each specific point of analysis and strategy is a stone. When put together in the right order, these fragments will be connected by your reader into an image of you. Don't assert what the shape of it is. Just lay out enough specific facts...stone by stone...so she'll see for herself the favorable patterns they imply. Let her create her own picture in her own mind.

If you'd like to change industries or career fields, consider making a second version of your resume... but even then, don't switch to topical organization.

Maybe you're in a declining field and you'd like to move into a growth industry. Or you're re-entering the commercial sector after a sojourn in the military, government, or academia. If so, make a special version of your resume that drains off industry-specific buzz-words and explains your exploits in terms everyone can appreciate. But resist the temptation to "go topical" and try to hide "where" while emphasizing "what."

Your reader will never quite be able to believe your claimed achievements unless he has a mental picture of you located at some specific place and time in the real world actually doing them. Withdraw orientation, and he drops belief...and probably attention, too.

Rather than resort to a topical resume, you should:

1. Write a covering letter that says what *specific need* your reader may have that you from another field can fill for him in his field. Don't say, "Here I am; guess what I can do for you."

2. And be realistic. If you're stumped when you try to write a persuasive covering letter explaining how you can fill a specific need of an employer in an unrelated field, then stop. Think of someone else in a different field for whom you *do* have a persuasive message. Don't pursue a hopeless mismatch. If *you're* not persuaded, you can be absolutely certain that no one else will be either.

Should you include a "Career Objective"?

Many resumes begin with a statement of what-kind-of-job-I-want labeled "*Career Objective*," or simply "*Objective*."

This is a good idea when you're fresh out of college or grad school and you want to orient the "Counselor" at an employment agency, or the personnel department of a corporation, to what you're looking for. But it's seldom necessary after your career is well underway. By then, what you're prepared to do next should be pretty evident from what you've already done.

If you're retiring from the military or the diplomatic corps, or leaving academia or the priesthood, then maybe your resume should begin with a statement of what you seek in the business world. Otherwise, let your resume be a clear and self-confident statement of where you've been and what you've achieved. Say what you're looking for in your covering letter and through personal contact.

Instead of an "Objective," a very brief summary can be effective. But don't label it "Summary." ***Don't label it at all!***

If you want a *very few* words of orientation at the top of your resume, make them a strong and succinct statement of what you've proven you can do. Now you're *not* talking about what *you want*—a job, of course—but what you deliver that an *employer* wants. However, if you use a strong assertion as, in effect, the headline of your resume, the rest of your resume had damned well better prove you deliver what you've so boldly claimed on top.

Examples: (All are preceded by Name, Address and Contact Info)

1 CEO with a Track Record of Turn Arounds

2 Chief Financial Officer or Chief Operating Officer
Successful in Improving, Building and Restructuring Companies

3 Chief Marketing Officer - Consumer Products Company

4 Senior Human Resources Executive
Comprehensive Policy and Operational Leadership...Domestic and International

5 Operations Executive or Chief Information Officer
...Successful at Improving Business Operations

6 Chief Exeutive / Chief Technology Officer
Performance. Economy. Solving Problems. Making Profit.
From "Fortune 50" to IPO, I've made technology pay.

I get results: 7
As General Manager, I've just finished saving a failing business.
Net worth is up from zero in 2011 to more than $200 million today

As Chief of Corporate Planning, I brought strategic planning 8
to one of the world's largest manufacturing companies...
helping many of its businesses in many ways.

As Manager of Engineering Departments, 9
I've always delivered on time and on budget.

Those are not hypothetical examples. Each headed the resume of an executive I personally assisted. The prior employer (not the individual) paid 15% of annual compensation ranging from a minimum fee of $50,000 to a maximum (cap) of $75,000. As you can imagine, at those rates I put in lots of effort—often 20 to 30 hours at my computer—helping create a resume that's (1) 100% true and (2) fully supportive of its bold thematic summary.

Results? Every one of these people got a more attractive job than the one he or she had just left. Number 6, for example, got $175,000 higher base salary than in his prior job and made close to $1.5 million in option profits in his first year. Number 4 went from #2 in HR in a very large company to #1 in an even bigger one. Number 7 sent out 500 letters to CEOs of Fortune 500 companies and, just from that mailing, was immediately hired as Chief Technology Officer of one of them. And Number 5 met his goal of moving from consulting to line management at equal or better income without relocating from his medium-sized midwestern city.

The Most Important Ingredients of a Resume: Time and Thought

Above all, you must devote plenty of time and thought to (1) deciding which facts will prove you get great results...and (2) stating those facts in a distilled, clear way. You'll face competing candidates. To defeat them, you must appear on paper and in interviews to be the one person who can be counted on to turn in the #1 best performance of everyone being considered.

When I provide assistance, the person spends two days one-on-one with me in New York (plus another day with a psychologist if they're willing). At least 4 hours are my taped interview probing accomplishments, which my staff transcribes. The person then goes home and, using the transcript, works hard on the resume (ideal preparation for future interviews). We continue by phone, and e-mail. Finally the person has done his or her best. Depending on the result, I may still spend further hours polishing to remove excess words and sharpen meaning (see page 69 of my *EXECUTIVE JOB-CHANGING WORKBOOK* for a before-and-after example). Usually I can cut at least one full page without dropping a single fact. So can you. But only if you work hard to edit what you've written. The tightened result is quicker and easier to read...and far more convincing.

Lots of people will tell you that resumes don't really matter. True! The generic *this-could-be-said-about-everyone-in-the-industry* resumes those folks would have you write *do not matter*. But a resume that truthfully shows by past performance that you're likely to outperform everyone else being considered *does* matter. If you have the right stuff, be sure to put in sufficient time and effort to display it well.

Reasons for Moving

Your resume may look like you've had too many recent jobs to really be a star performer. Yet the opposite may be true. If you joined Company X, made a great impression, and were soon asked to follow your boss to Co. Y, ***say so!*** Don't let having been a star make you look like a dog. And if you were one of 2,000 sluffed off in a merger—or one of 6-out-of-8 senior officers dumped by a new CEO who brought in a team from his former company—why not say so? Don't be defensive. And don't give a reason for *every* move. Then, says Shakespeare, "Me thinks thou doth protest too much!" But if at a few pivotal times you'd otherwise take a bum rap, set the record straight.

Creative Use of Avocational Interests in Your Resume

In general, never mention your hobbies and other outside interests.

If you had time to be assistant pastor of your church, chair the United Fund drive, coach a Little League team, do petit point, build an extension on your home, train for and run a marathon, and groom and show poodles in the U.S. and three foreign countries last year, when did you have time to work?

But if you're 58 years old, it might be good to mention your marathon running, and the fact that you're an avid scuba diver and an instructor for Outward Bound. Your stamp collection, of course, will remain in the closet.

And if you're a paraplegic, your competitive sports car driving and skeet shooting might just be a worthwhile inclusion. So might building that wing on your house, if you're only missing one arm or one leg.

If you just have a high school diploma, the fact that you're an amateur writer who's published stories in *Harper's* and *The New Yorker*...or even a trade journal or the business section of your daily newspaper...could help show you have a mature, cultivated mind others respect. So might your appointment to the Mayor's Commission for the Arts, your being on the board of the Inner City Improvement District, or your playing duplicate bridge.

And if you're in a racial or ethnic minority and have the stomach for such a gambit, you may feel like listing your memberships in exclusive social and athletic clubs that haven't always had people with names or faces like yours. Everyone else should maintain a discreet silence on all clubs.

Now, as we wind up on resumes, let's look at several other items of purely personal information and how to handle them.

Age

If your age is likely to be viewed favorably, don't go out of your way to hide it. Don't, for example, feel you must omit the years of your college degrees so your age can't be estimated. True, employers can't ask. But voluntarily including common statistics subliminally shouts "forthright and self-confident," whereas concealing age just because the law permits you to do so sends out the opposite "vibes"...and might even suggest that *you* think you may be over the hill.

Incidentally, employers who, in the 1970s, considered 30 to 35 the ideal age now seem to feel that way regarding mid-to-late-40s, and have virtually no qualms about dynamic people in their 50s. They still find a young hotshot attractive. But they no longer—and legally they'd better not— insist on one. I absolutely refuse to discriminate on the basis of age, and have recently had candidates in their ***late*** 50s win out over excellent candidates ten and twenty years younger.

Education

List college degrees, *with years*...highest and latest degree first. Forget about Class President, and Varsity Letters. You've moved on to more recent and bigger achievements.

If you have several years but no sheepskin, say: "Completed three years toward B.A. at Syracuse University." And if you flunked out of several fine schools, say: "Two years of college, intermittently at Carleton, Dartmouth, and the University of Virginia." With no college, you may want to say, "Self-educated during an uninterrupted career," and then bail yourself out under the heading "Other Interests," with some suitably cerebral and cultural avocations.

Marital Status

Say nothing. Or say "Married," "Divorced," or "Single," whichever applies and, if you wish, number of children (not names, ages, or with how many and which mates).

Gender

If you're a woman with a name like Lindsay or Leslie, or a man with a name like Carroll or Kelley, use a middle name to be more specific...or just let your reader be surprised when he or she meets you.

Height and Weight

Nice to put in, men, if it's favorable. If not, be silent. Women, of course, will omit height and weight, because it seems inappropriate to raise the subject. If you're a man, don't let anyone convince you that ***voluntarily*** including favorable height and weight will ("because it facilitates discrimination") automatically prevent you from being considered for employment. It won't!

Religion, Politics, and National Origin

Silence! If the reader has a prejudice, you may stimulate it.

Health

Don't mention. It's fine, or you should be writing a will instead of a resume.

Picture

Never, *NEVER, NEVER!* Nobody could possibly be attractive enough to justify the narcissism implied by attaching a picture.

Read Before Chapter 13

"CHERRY PICK"

As we proceed to Chapter 13, you'll see techniques for a typical Direct Mail Campaign that will apply equally well to using your Communications POWER TOOL in a limited distribution of just one—or a few—or a moderate number of—mailings.

I needn't point out specific opportunities. You'll recognize them. "Cherry pick" which you'll use. Indeed, your personal circumstances will prompt you to think of more uses for some of the ideas in this chapter than I could possibly think of for you.

Nothing will please me more than to see you get the results of a massive Direct Mail Campaign (the type we'll now cover) while—if possible—sending only a few tightly crafted and targeted letters.

Chapter 13

The Classic Direct Mail Campaign

...still the #1 way to reach the many decision-makers who might want to hire you

When I first wrote *Rites of Passage* there was only one way to get your resume into the hands—and hopefully the minds—of people who were too distant or too numerous for you to reach face-to-face.

The only alternative was to distribute your resume and cover letter by direct mail. And of course there were two types of recipients:

(1) decision makers who might want to hire you for their own organization, and
(2) recruiters who help them search for executives.

For reasons we've already discussed, classic direct mail is *still* the only polite and practical way to reach employer decision makers.

Even if you could smoke out their e-mail addresses at the office and at home, you probably wouldn't spam them with your resume at either place. You're smart enough to realize how irked they'd be by that treatment...as you'd be too, if you were in their position.

Recruiters are a different matter. They make their livings by finding out about executives who might fit the openings they're attempting to fill. They have channels specifically designed to receive and sort electronically submitted resumes. Using those channels—as we'll discuss in the chapter after this one—is something you should sometimes do.

But for now, let's cover the skillful use of direct mail to reach and persuade the decision makers who directly have the power (1) to hire you themselves...or (2) to instruct others—subordinates and recruiters—to give you very serious consideration.

Orbiting Your Spy-in-the-Sky Satellite

Now that your resume has been strengthened by direct mail copywriting, let's use it to launch a full-scale direct mail campaign...the nearest thing to scanning the globe via spy-in-the-sky satellite to find the opportunities you should know about.

Delivered by mail, a powerful resume can truly "be where you can't be and sell when you're not there."

And unlike every other method, direct mail can be almost limitlessly increased in power, when you're eager to change jobs. It can also be targeted toward exactly what you want in terms of industry, size of company, location, or any other set of criteria.

Moreover, a direct mail campaign can be modified to perform its unique functions *secretly*. Believe it or not, you can use this powerful medium without letting your current employer discover you're "looking."

This chapter will tell you everything you need to know to make sophisticated use of direct mail: how many letters to send, whom to send them to, what to say in your covering note...and how to keep your current employer from finding out, if you want to look for a better job with minimum risk to the one you have.

The Accident of Timing

Timing is the problem.

Don't you wish we could crack open every job that might advance your career...and do so at precisely the time you're considering a move? We'd schedule all the retirements, firings, and additions-to-staff just when they'd create ideal options for you. Then, with just a few calls to your personal contacts, a few networking visits, and a handful of letters, you'd be exploring plenty of exciting opportunities.

Regrettably, Murphy's Law of Career Opportunity works the opposite way. Virtually all the jobs you'd be most interested in will be *filled* at the moment you decide to make a change.

Every company needs you at least once in several years.

Unfortunately, the overwhelming odds are that they won't need you within the four to fourteen weeks that your inquiry will be considered current.

Face it. No matter how appropriate you are for a particular company, how much you'd like to work for them, and whom you're able to talk to inside that company...when they don't need you, they won't hire you. Appropriateness and desire don't count, if timing is off.

In the rare instance when the right need does exist, a compelling resume and covering letter sent to just the right person at just the right time will usually get you considered.

Unfortunately, the concepts of using direct mail to reach corporate decision-makers in a well-thought out executive job-changing campaign have become widely known and understood. *RITES OF PASSAGE* has been a major contributor to that fact. As a result, the standards by which executive resumes and cover letters are judged have risen very high. Today a mediocre career presented in a mediocre resume-and-letter—*indeed, even a superb one in a mediocre resume-and-letter*—won't even get you a nibble! Don't waste time and money on direct mail when it's hopeless (beginning on page 269 we'll discuss when that is).

But for now let's assume your career *and* writing skills are strong enough for direct mail. Even so, timing is critical. What you send must arrive at *exactly* the right time. For three or four months your inquiry may be considered current. After that, you'll be presumed to have found your job, if you're really good. Otherwise, you'll be presumed *not* to be as good as you seemed. And if you've relocated, but are still willing to "talk," you'll seem unstable, unethical, or both.

Harsh and ***unfair*** presumptions! But they're almost universal. Might as well face them...and work around them.

Now for the bad...and good...news:

"Playing the numbers game" with direct mail can be lots of work.

However, if you're willing and able to do it right, you're very likely to succeed.

The beauty of direct mail is that, depending on how hard you're willing to work, you can infinitely increase the number of contacts you make until you reach enough decision makers to be virtually certain that at least a few will actually need someone like you ***at the time you write***.

Everyone's odds are different, of course. Some folks at some times shouldn't even play. But typical odds these days are about *3 to 1 in favor* of an aggressive direct mail campaign generating a few attractive job leads for the very able person who makes an unstinting effort.

On the other hand, the odds are at least *199 to 1 against* the possibility that any one *letter* in a massive mailing will arrive at the moment someone like the sender is actually needed. And the way the laws of probability work, you can't be sure that by sending only 200 letters you'll actually hit one recipient who has a need. To have a statistical shot at hitting on 1 out of 200 letters, *you must send at least 1,000 letters*. A few years ago, that number should have yielded 5 or 6 interested replies...an average of about 1 for each 200 letters sent out. Today, many companies have downsized. Management pyramids are flatter. And most CEOs and high-level executives are far less impulsive about hiring. Therefore, you may need several times as many letters to hit even fewer decision-makers at an opportune time.

Here's the classic formula. This effort...and more...will be needed:

Send at least 1,000 letters...not less.

Expect to receive 3 to 5 affirmative replies...not more.

But *if you do it right*, those 3 to 5 meaningful replies should lead to 2 or 3 interviews and 1 or 2 offers of almost exactly what you want.

When I lay out these numbers, most people say:

> "But, John, can't I get by with *less than* 1,000 letters?"

And my answer is always the same:

> "Absolutely! You only need five letters. But *which five?*"

You could be very lucky and have your first four or five letters bring encouragement. On the other hand, the last five might be the ones that pay off. And if you get less than five interested responses, you might get the two or three that lead to offers...or you might get the two or three where you interview but *don't* receive an offer.

Success is likely...if you enter the realm of *statistics*. But if you insist on merely *gambling*, then just send one letter. Or five, or 600, or 900. Only at (or much better at *twice*) 1,000 do you begin to play the odds. Don't complain if you get disappointing results from fewer letters. You haven't bypassed mere chance and grabbed statistical probability.

And of course the odds I'm quoting assume you're seeking a position for which you'll seem obviously relevant. If you're attempting a drastic switch of career fields, or if you're trying to overcome an apparent deficiency in your background or a glaring failure in your track record, you should probably triple the threshold number of 1,000 letters, in order to be realistic about the response you're likely to get. Or maybe you should ignore direct mail at *this* unfortunate juncture.

"John, I hate the idea of 1,000 letters just to get in the game."

"On the other hand, I love the idea of 2 or 3 interviews and 1 or 2 offers out of just 5 affirmative replies."

"Why such good odds after such poor ones?"

The reason you do so well after having done so poorly is that, although only a very few decision makers will need what you're offering at the time you write, those few who *respond* will be the ones who *do* have a need. The only reason they reply is that they feel they may want to hire you.

And if you've done a good job on your mailing, the openings you'll be called about will be ones you prefer and are qualified for. And, of course, those are precisely the jobs you're likely to interview successfully for and wind up getting.

Also, since you're taking the initiative, rather than waiting for a recruiter to contact you, there's a good chance that your mailing may arrive before a search has been assigned. If so, you won't face the usual stiff competition from five or six additional recruiter-supplied candidates. Not only do you find out about the job; you're early enough to have a better-than-usual shot at getting it.

Building a Mailing List for a Conventional Direct Mail Campaign

There are many suppliers of direct marketing lists. Unfortunately, nearly all the lists merely offer traditional sales leads. They do not penetrate the hierarchy of management all the way up to the CEO and the senior management team. Forget about those lists. They're useless in compiling your list.

To my mind, the best—and really the only—viable source of management information for completing your list is ***Lead Builders*** from Dun & Bradstreet and Hoover's. Until D&B acquired Hoovers several years ago both companies maintained enormous separate databases of American companies and their managements. Now merged, both data-sellers share a single vast database, which D&B says has 90,000 U.S. businesses in it.

Both sell minimum annual deals of two users for roughly $2000. Check both.

D&B - (800) 590-0065　　　Hoovers - (888) 611-5295

Or avoid both ! Most large public libraries are members and will let you in on their membership for FREE.

If you wish to purchase and enjoy the convenience of home use, perhaps you should line up one or two co-purchasers who will split the cost of an annual membership with you. Each user in a group of two or three should expect to pay about $1,000 for his/her share of the membership fee. If you purchase alone, you'll pay at least $1,800 to $2,600. When using your membership, you may sign on from your PC, tablet, smartphone—wired or wireless.

Yes, that's pricey! But I know of no other resource that will identify virtually every U.S. company you might might ever want to work for...and list its entire management team. Sort by location, industry, sales volume, number of employees, and virtually every other criterion you can think of.

You will be fascinated as you totally immerse yourself in identifying all the companies where you might make a needed contribution. There will be far more than you ever dreamed there could be . What's more, if you specify a location, a surprising number may be within commuting distance.

But make no mistake.

You are only looking at employers that *might* need you.

You do NOT know which—if any—now do.

To find out which—if any—have a need ***now*** and will be sufficiently impressed by your mailing to contact you, you must send letters to all the decision makers you have identified. That's direct mail. You have to send lots of it to hit on the handful out of thousands who, by accident of timing, happen to have an open spot in their organization that you should fill.

"Well," you say, "that accident of timing makes for lots of work. Can't I figure out the timing issue and just send letters to decision makers who ***do*** have an opening for someone to fill the job I'd fit in their organization?"

Sadly, no. Not if you decide to conduct a full scale direct mail campaign to learn at which of the companies your self-introductory letter will (if you do it well and address it personally to the decision maker) get you considered.

Once you've lined up your information resources, start making your mailing list. Begin with the most obvious companies you should contact.

Keep broadening until you have 1,000 or more that really interest you. Once you get rolling, they're not hard to find.

Most people begin their mailing list with companies in their current industry. The top ten or twenty leap to mind. But, using a comprehensive resource like the D&B/Hoover's list, you may be surprised to discover several hundred additional firms, perhaps including quite a few that are commutable from your home. Most, of course, will be smaller than the famous giants. Although probably offering less prestige and perhaps lower compensation, these companies may also offer advantages, such as less bureaucratic red tape, and even a major equity opportunity...things you may not get from the giants.

Also, you'll undoubtedly want to send *several* letters to each of the largest corporations. Those near the top of *Fortune*'s 1,000 list have many subsidiaries that are larger than entire companies lower on the list. And each has its own CEO, CFO, head of manufacturing, head of R&D, head of marketing and sales, etc. Indeed, you'll probably wind up sending letters to five or ten separate business units in each of *Fortune*'s top 100 corporations.

Moreover, don't feel that you must arrive at your minimum of 1,000—or better yet 2000—letters by staying within your current field. If you're a financial or an MIS manager, your skills can be used in almost any industry. Might as well write to every one of the *Fortune* 1,000 and most of their subsidiaries. As head of manufacturing you're more specialized, but the processes you know are used for many other products than the ones you're making right now. If you're in marketing and sales, look for industries selling to the same customers, or through the same channels of distribution. Whatever your job, you have relevance to many industries including those from which your current company buys its components, raw materials, and supplies...and to which it sells its goods and services.

Don't worry, you'll soon have your list of 1,000 companies...and, if you're really aggressive, 2,000 or more.

One of the great advantages of direct mail is that it can be concentrated on a very specific target, in order to achieve objectives you might not accomplish any other way.

If, for example, you want to move to a different location...for later retirement in a warmer climate, or for putting your children through college, or for aiding your aging parents...you can make geography a key criterion (and there may be a state or a "metro" website or even an on-paper directory to help). If you want to move from a technologically obsolescent industry into one that you feel will be on the leading edge of technical and market growth for the next decade, you can look up the companies in your favorite fields and mail only to them.

If you're sick of dealing with products you find boring and of little real value to society, you can write only to companies which provide products or services you find interesting and intrinsically beneficial. And if it's big-company bureaucracy and politics you'd like to leave behind, you can mail only to companies with no more than 500 employees...or 100, for that matter, because you can readily identify companies that small and smaller.

You get the idea. The beauty of direct mail is that the choice of each corporate mailbox is entirely up to you. The industries, companies, and locations that recruiters present to you will be chosen at random, *except for a strong bias toward offering you more of exactly what you have right now*. On the other hand, the companies (and nonprofit organizations) you decide to mail to will be the ones you really want to explore.

"Making a list of more than 1,000 companies seems like so much work! Can't I have someone else do it?"

It's true that selecting a massive mailing list of potential employers is a time-consuming project. So you may be tempted to delegate it to someone else...a secretary, a professional researcher, or an outplacement firm which, to save itself effort, may try to discourage you from conducting an extensive tailored-for-you direct mail campaign. *Resist the temptation!*

There's no substitute for your own decision-making. Only *you* can decide how you feel about various companies: products that interest you vs. ones that don't; large vs. small company; high vs. low prestige; preferred vs. unattractive location; entrepreneurial and fast-growing vs. stable and well-established organization; regional vs. national or global operation; risk-taking vs. conservative environment; etc.

Would you be willing to work for a casket company if it were in your preferred location...or if you could be its president? Would you work for a struggling company in real danger of going under if you could have the number-one or number-two spot? Would you leave your industry in order to stay in your present location? Which seemingly unlikely companies might actually appeal to you? No one else can answer these questions. This research...tedious though it may seem...must be done by you.

Moreover, the process of considering and deciding these potential trade-offs is a valid, creative exercise which will help you come to grips with your own talents, desires, and goals. No two people viewing the same information resources—even people with similar backgrounds—will come up with the same list. Each person makes his or her own subjective judgments...and gains new self-knowledge.

One thing I can assure you. I have never seen a dynamic, creative executive set out to develop a mailing list of 1,000...or even 2,000 or 3,000...companies and fail to do so. And never has such a person failed to comment enthusiastically afterward about what a valuable self-assessment process compiling his or her list turned out to be.

Write to the CEO ...or a person two levels above your target job.

At the same time you're investigating to determine what companies you'll write to, you must also decide *what position* on their organization chart is your ideal point of contact. When you're writing about a top-level executive position, you certainly can't send out letters addressed "Dear Sir/Madam" or "To Whom It May Concern."

Whom should you write to?

If you're expecting to be president and chief operating officer of an entire company, of course you'll direct your letter to the chairman/CEO; or if it's a subsidiary of a holding company, you'll address the HC's group officer responsible for that subsidiary or, better yet, the chief operating officer of the overall corporation.

My general suggestion is to address your letter *two levels above the job you want*...to the person who supervises the boss of the job you're aiming at. Since titles can be misleading and lines of responsibility aren't always clear, it's much better to aim too high than too low.

There are several advantages of aiming high:

> First, the person just one level above your target job...your potential boss...may be in trouble. If so, he's certainly not going to invite you in and show you around...only to become his future competition. If you'd written to his boss or his boss's boss, you might even have been considered for *his* job, a level higher than you'd have guessed.

Moreover, your letter gains ''clout'' by being passed downward. If your potential boss merely gets your letter in the mail, she can dispose of it casually. If it comes from a superior, she's far more likely to follow up.

And the higher the person who receives your letter, the more likely he or she is to know of potentially appropriate positions in additional business units, subsidiaries and affiliates.

Indeed, your letter may even spur a CEO or division-leader into taking action to replace a shaky manager...and you may be a candidate to fill the opening. Or the senior executive may want to talk to you because he knows that a whole department will be restaffed as soon as the head of it (as yet unaware) is let go.

Therefore, write to a real, living person—addressed by accurate name and title—who has the function you think appropriate to control the boss of the job you've got your eye on.

Data sources—even the vaunted D&B / Hoover's list—

are continually about 35% out-of-date whenever you look at them.

Believe it or not, even corporations' own Web sites are surprisingly obsolete.

Someone should phone to check each name, title, and address. Fortunately, this is a job you can delegate.

Publishers, both on-paper and web-based, do make an effort to update, by sending out questionnaires and computer-accessing published announcements. But an incomplete effort at best. Worse yet, if a book is involved, it goes to the printer several months prior to the date on the cover. And chances are, you won't use it until several months—or even years—after publication. Meanwhile, corporations continually reorganize. The average senior executive remains in any specific position only about one to three years (a few more if CEO), so you can see why roughly a third of all published information is inaccurate.

Surprisingly, many corporations—including even some of the very largest—are sometimes several months behind in updating the senior executive rosters displayed on their websites. News releases of staff changes appear on the site at the same moment they're sent to the press. But bios and pics of the top brass are not tended to as promptly. Glance at a year of press releases (the topic headings scan quickly), before you accept the website roster as gospel.

Sending your mailing to the wrong person in the organization...or to someone no longer there...won't achieve your purpose. Therefore, someone should check by phone to see that each person an information source has indicated for your mailing actually has the title, function, and name-spelling listed. Unless you phone to confirm, about 350 of your 1,000 mailings will be wrongly addressed and probably worthless. In effect, you'll only be sending 650...not enough to escape chance and launch into statistical orbit.

Enlist any competent help you can get...secretary, temp, college student, spouse, mother, father, teenage daughter or son. Whoever calls should ask for the decision maker's personal assistant...bypassing the operator/receptionist...and follow approximately this script:

> "I'm sending a letter and want to be sure I have the right information. He's Chief Executive?" (or some other title you seek). "And the exact spelling of his name...and the office address?"

Then probe for reassurance on other key points:

> "Executive Vice President...is that for the entire corporation, or for a specific subsidiary or division?"
>
> "Vice President of Operations...does that include responsibility for the Management Information Systems function?"
>
> "You say she's gone? Who took over her duties?"
>
> "Oh, *he's* not? Then who *would* be in charge?"

Unfortunately, the public's increasing familiarity with the use of direct mail has altered forever what you must do, and how effective you can be.

Recognize today's facts of life ...and work around them.

Fifteen years ago, you could have written to the Chief Executive of a "*Fortune* 500" company, and a secretary might have brought in your letter and resume along with the rest of the opened mail. And that might have happened even if your letterhead, letter, resume, and envelope were all obviously mass-produced...automatically run off using identical styling, type face and pale-ivory paper.

But today that same CEO routinely receives dozens of such letters per week. Indeed some high-profile CEOs get that many per *day*. Not surprising, when you realize that these people are programmed into the word-processing equipment of scores of outplacement and "executive marketing" firms "counseling" thousands of executives. Here's what the personal assistant to one of those CEOs told me:

> "We get executive job-hunting letters every day. Usually they're the assembly-line kind, where everything matches. But sometimes they're disguised as personal letters with no resume enclosed. Those are easy to spot too, because a real personal letter doesn't begin 'Dear Mr.,' and the applicant wouldn't dare write 'Dear Harry.'
>
> "So on every employment letter, my assistant who opens the mail runs off a form response and sends the letter down to Human Resources for filing. Mr. _______ can't spend his time reading that stuff or he'd never get any work done. However, sometimes, if an extremely impressive letter and resume come along, and I know he might be looking for that kind of person, I put it into a folder he does glance at. 'Cream-of-the-crop,' we call it."

You see the problem.

Automatic mailings have virtually destroyed the receptivity of all their standard targets...the CEOs of America's leading companies. We'll design a letter for you that will stand out from the crowd. Even so, it may not escape the standardized handling of such letters in the offices that get lots of them.

The only solution is to write at least 1,000 of your letters to senior executives who are ***not*** likely to be on the mechanized lists. Send to Presidents of the appropriate *subsidiaries* of the largest companies. Send to heads of functional departments. Send to the CEOs of *smaller* companies that, although interesting to you, are not at the top of everyone else's list. And in "*Fortune* 500" companies, be especially careful to restrict yourself to the person *only two or three levels above* the job you want...probably not the CEO.

Don't feel you must ignore the most obvious targets. Do let your outplacement firm send your mailing to them...or send to them on your own. But supplement any mailing to these high-profile executives with at least 1,000 letter to others who aren't being deluged. That way you won't be counting on a normal reaction to your mailing among people whose circumstances are not at all normal.

Shssss! We can seize the "Accident of Timing"

... and Game the System!

Ordinary Direct Mail requires your sending letters to a thousand or several thousand decision makers.

Why thousands?

Because the "accident of timing" virtually guarantees that only a rare few letters will hit when there's an opening. Virtually all others (probably 98%) will arrive at the wrong time—and thus are wasted. If we could have known which recipients actually had a need, of course, we'd have sent only to them. We'd have saved the cost and effort of sending to all recipients with no need.

Is there a way to identify employers who actually have a current need?

Absolutely!

Go after the ones who are currently advertising (posting) their job opening(s) in an attempt to fill the position you seek, or who have engaged contingency recruiters who may now be advertising (posting) those job openings.

...but Hang on!

We need to perfect your command of Direct Mail with a few fundamentals and some very important hidden tricks before you're equipped to take full advantage of the one big trick on conquering some of the randomness and need-for-thousands-of-letters problems of Direct Mail.

We'll look at that in our next chapter. It's on using the web in executive job-changing.

But first, some essentials ***you will use, even if you never conduct a regular direct mail campaign.***

Now let's design a covering letter that will do the best possible job of making whoever receives it want to look at your resume.

To get any attention at all for your resume, your covering letter absolutely must convey two essential messages regarding you as a human being, and you as the potential solution to an immediate business problem:

1. This is a ***fine person***, obviously desirable as an employee.
2. He or she might be ***for me***, possibly the executive I need right now.

If your papers in the reader's hand don't shout "fine person," then there's no point in reading them to see if your background might be what's needed right now.

So first of all we'll make sure your covering letter conveys the right personal impression. Then we'll perfect the story it tells.

Right away and above all, your covering note must—at a glance—label you as a first-class individual, regardless of background.

You must instantly be perceived as an intelligent, well-educated, socially poised, tasteful person...dynamic not passive, self-confident and cordial but not obnoxiously pushy, oriented toward delivering what others are interested in, an effective communicator, basically competent and commonsensical, and maybe even *interesting!*

Now I'm not saying that you, I, or anyone else can instantly prove for sure that we have all those fine characteristics in 300 words or less. But we'd better not give off even the slightest subliminal hint that we *don't* have them. Your reader won't even consider the contribution you could make to the organization, if you don't seem like the right sort of person to bring into it.

There's a double standard. Employers will tolerate employees with less than ideal human characteristics if they're outstanding performers on the job. But they won't go out of their way to bring in anyone who doesn't "feel" right to begin with. And face it...perusing your resume is going out of the way. The easiest reaction is just to throw it in the wastebasket. *Your covering note must not give off any negative "vibes."* And in that regard I submit the following:

Don't seem insensitive, bumbling, and not customer-oriented.

You've already avoided the biggest pitfall in this direction by having someone phone ahead to make sure you've got your reader's name-spelling, function, and title right. Your letter has come to the right person, and has approached him or her with impeccable courtesy.

Avoid looking tasteless and cheap.

Recent college graduates can get by with plain copy paper for their covering letter. You can't. Good quality stationery with your name, home address, and phone numbers, steel-engraved at the top, is ideal. Monarch size ($7^{1/4}$" x $10^{1/2}$") looks especially nice clipped to a standard-size ($8^{1/2}$" x 11") resume, and if you boil your message down to attention-grabbing brevity, it'll fit on a Monarch page. Paper should be crisp, with rag/cotton fiber, in classic white or a *very* pale tint of grey or ivory. Letterhead ink should be black.

Get both Monarch and standard-size stationery...mostly Monarch, because you'll use it for the "cover letter" that accompanies your resume (also for "thank yous," etc.). Envelopes, on the other hand, should be mostly #10 (business-size), because they will hold your resume, in addition to your Monarch letter. Put your return address on the envelope-flap, rather than the front (on both sizes), because that looks more like truly "personal" stationery. And before you buy, check the web and Yellow Pages for "Engravers"...not "Stationery, Retail." Buy proper quantities for a direct mail campaign, and you'll get the same low prices accountants, lawyers, and businesses enjoy.

Unfortunately about eight weeks' lead time may be required for true steel engraving. If you're rushed, or short on cash, substitute ordinary printing. *Or use plain but nice paper and your laser printer, applying a letterhead in contrasting type as you print the text of your cover letters.* Keep the design understated...three or four lines, each no more than $2^{1/4}$" long...with your phone and web address smaller but legible on the bottom line. Avoid all suggestions to use decorative lines or flourishes. Plain is better! Unless your covering letter describes unusual circumstances that make it appropriate, never use your current employer's stationery.

Don't appear pretentious.

Display modesty and matter-of-factness in name, address...and stationery. Imagine a letterhead from "Cottsworth O.M. Kensington-Smithers IV," who lives at ''Nine Chimneys,'' followed by street number, etc. What fun it would be to throw *his* resume into the waste basket! Moreover, since you're sending a business letter, avoid all gimmicks on the stationery... family crest, house-picture, yachting flags, crossed polo mallets, colored or shaggy borders, etc.

Avoid looking like the passively-packaged product of an outplacement firm.

Today so many terminated executives are being processed by outplacement firms, that every retainer recruiter and almost every senior executive knows the #1 tell-tale sign: perfectly matching paper and computer typography used for stationery, covering-letter, resume, and envelope.

Following the theory that ''colored papers stand out on an executive's desk,'' most of these firms eschew classic white and turn instead to a distinctive shade I call *''Outplacement Ivory.''* And of course everything matches, because it's all produced at the same time on the same paper by the same equipment.

''What's wrong,'' someone might say, ''if my mailing openly proclaims that the people who let me go nonetheless cared enough to buy me outplacement services?"

Only this, in my opinion: Your reader will be more interested in what you have to say if he or she feels it's been written and sent solely by you, rather than by someone else who's been paid to get you out of one office and into another. There's absolutely nothing wrong with accepting outplacement help. But you'll seem much more confident and creative...far less hapless and passive...if you appear to be preparing and sending your own correspondence.

Therefore, make sure your covering note and resume *don't* match. A Monarch-size note is especially helpful. The smaller paper forces impressive brevity; reveals at a glance that your resume *doesn't* match; is consistent with genuine personal stationery (*never* 8 1/2" x 11"); and is inconsistent with outplacement cover letters, (*always* 8 1/2" x 11"). Your note can be run on a quality laser-printer, and your resume can be done the same way. However, if you're printing a large quantity of resumes—say 500 or more—it probably won't cost you much more to have them done by true offset printing, rather than laser printing. That way, your resume, when mailed, will arrive looking sharp and clean. If you laser print your resume and mail it rubbing against another laser printed surface, chances are it will arrive badly smudged, If you doubt me on this, run a test. Mail four copies to yourself with laser printed pages against each other. You'll be shocked at how bad they look when they reach your mailbox! Use classic white paper for your resume, and a different texture or shade of white, or else *pale* ivory or grey, for your cover letter.

So much for appearances.
Now let's get to the content of your covering letter.

This is your "free sample."
It demonstrates that you're a "fine person"
in terms of thinking and communication skills.

Only after evaluating "how you say it"
will your reader weigh "what you say."

To succeed, your covering letter must be pleasantly businesslike in tone, and conjure up the image of a competent, self-confident executive who's letting a colleague know that he or she is available to help, if there's a need. Somehow, a letter from such a person is never a jarring intrusion, whereas a letter from the typical "job applicant" always is.

The difference is dramatic. So few people are able to write a really good covering letter that, when one arrives, it stands out like a beacon. Its author is immediately given "plus points" for outstanding executive communication skills, and the resume is almost always scanned, in the hope that it offers something the recipient...corporate officer or recruiter...can take advantage of.

Fortunately, creating such an impressive covering letter isn't difficult, if you incorporate the four central attributes that outstanding ones have and poor ones don't. Be sure your covering letter:

1. **is not too long.** Brevity is essential! Get right to the point, and leave out all the useless and obnoxious things that "job applicants" put in their letters.

2. **has a central theme.** Your message must be arrestingly clear...not diffuse and blurred.

3. **offers benefit to the reader,** rather than merely harping on what *you* want.

4. **deals with compensation.**

Later on I'll cover point 1 by giving you a list of stuff to get rid of, so your letter won't be cluttered with the unproductive statements "job applicants" put in theirs. And after that, I'll show you in detail how to handle compensation to your advantage. But first let me deal with points 2 and 3 by showing you a cover letter that has a clear central theme (point 2) of benefit to the reader (point 3).

The cover letter on the next page is from Sam Sage, whose resume we've already reviewed. Sam's an exceptionally competent executive. And from the minute we first glance at his covering letter, we begin to see how very special he is. No nonsense. No wasted words. And no claims that aren't fully backed up by his accompanying resume.

Samuel P. Sage
219 Waring Drive
Denton, New Jersey 07299
Phone (201) 719-0932 Cell (201) 633-0964
spsage@aota.com

(Date)

Mr. Sherman J. Summit
Chairman and Chief Executive
Integrated Standard Corporation
4225 Scenic Parkway
Lovelytown, New York 10591

Dear Mr. Summit:

Could I help you as a divisional president...or corporate chief marketing officer?

The $1.3 billion company I've helped build over the past five years as Chief Marketing Officer has more than doubled sales, increased profits nine-fold, and raised ROI from 3.6% in '10 to over 28% in '15.

We've done so well, in fact, that we've just been bought out at 30 times our estimated '15 earnings by a company that's absorbing us into their own operations.

Although I'm far more interested in a fine company and an intriguing challenge than merely in money, you should know that in recent years my total compensation has been in the range of $460,000 to $590,000.

May we talk?

Sincerely,

Sam Sage

Samuel P. Sage

SPS:mj

Editor's Note...

For John Lucht's in-depth help with your own personal job-winning cover letter use pages 136 to 163 of **Executive Job-Changing Workbook**. Available at all booksellers.

Sam rang all the bells!

Sam's central theme is sure to dilate the pupils and speed the pulse of any red-blooded CEO...impressive advances in sales, profit, and ROI.

For many letter-writers those claims would be too bold. They'd be mom-pie-'n-flag *clichés* that the accompanying resume couldn't possibly live up to. But Sam's got the stuff. So he flaunts it.

Notice too, that Sam didn't waste words on anything that's obvious. His resume *is* enclosed...no need to say so. And *of course* Sam would like Mr. Summit to get in touch with him...or Sam may call Mr. S. No need to talk about that either.

Moreover, Sam didn't invoke self-praising adjectives and adverbs. Rather, by making numerical claims, he directed attention to his resume, which is packed with specific facts and figures that *demonstrate* what he can do. Sam also treated compensation in an advantageous way that we'll discuss later.

Above all, the sparseness and directness of Sam's letter tell us a lot about him. He's an exceptionally dynamic, clear-thinking person. On the rare occasions when a letter from someone like Sam comes in, the reader will always glance at the attached resume. Indeed Mr. Summit became quite interested, as you'll see later in Appendix I.

Changing Your Letter for Recruiters

These examples are addressed to employers. For recruiters, merely change your opening question from "Do *you* need...?" to "Does *a client* need...?" or "Are you looking for...?" Replacing just a few words in the first one or two sentences will neatly reposition any letter, without destroying the brevity and directness that are just as attractive to recruiters as they are to employers.

Later on, I'll show you a website (RiteSite.com) I've set up to enable you to email your resume to your selection among all of the purely retainer-compensated search firms with utmost ease. Your resume comes from your personal email address, not RiteSite, and bypasses all the restrictions your internet service provider normally imposes on your sending of emails.

Even with RiteSite available, you will still send a few elegant on-paper mailings to prominent retainer recruiters and search firms (1) you're especially interested in and/or (2) you know personally.

Karen S. Kash
12 Countinghouse Road
Pittsburgh, Pennsylvania 15213
Phone (412) 999-1814 Cell (412) 888-4619
kskash@apremidia.com

(Date)

Mr. Peter R. Pinnacle
Chairman
Acme Consolidated Corporation
6902 Postal Turnpike
Pittsburgh, Pennsylvania 15224

Dear Mr. Pinnacle:

Could Acme Consolidated...or one of your largest divisions... benefit from a strong chief financial officer?

Having been continually challenged and rapidly promoted at U.S. Heavy Industries—last year I became our youngest CFO since USHI was founded in 1869—I've never before thought about joining any other employer.

But now we're shutting down our steel mills and home office here in Pittsburgh, and headquartering at our insurance company in Hartford. Relocation would be a hardship for my family. So I'm contacting a few outstanding Pittsburgh area companies before committing to a move.

If you have a need, I could do an excellent job for you.

Sincerely,

Karen Kash

Karen Kash

P.S. Money is <u>not</u> my main consideration, but in recent years my total compensation has been in the range of $280,000 to $450,000.

> Editor's Note...
>
> For John Lucht's in-depth help with your own personal job-winning cover letter use pages 136 to 163 of **Executive Job-Changing Workbook**. Available at all booksellers.

Matt Ginyus
146 College Point Drive
Skilton, Massachusetts 01128
Phone (413) 112-2465 Cell (413) 397-5985
mattgin@trionet.com

(Date)

Mr. Gerrard Global, Chairman
International Interchemicals, Inc.
1202 Industrial Beltline
Wilmington, Delaware 19808

Dear Mr. Global:

Could any of your laboratories...corporate or divisional...be more innovative?

If so, perhaps I can help.

Within the spending limits of a young fast-growing $196 million company, and with only a 26-person laboratory, my staff and I during the past five years have produced 14 commercially exploitable new compounds...6 of which are already on the market, providing 72% of current revenue. During that time I've personally received 8 patents, and my staff has received 46.

Having proven what I can produce for a small company, I'd like to do a lot more for a much larger organization.

An exciting challenge will be the main reason, if and when I move. But you should know that in recent years my total compensation has been in the range of $260,000 to $450,000.

Please keep my inquiry confidential, Mr. Global. The published rumors that we may be acquired have prompted me to think about the world outside DrexelChem. Nevertheless, I don't want to disturb either my staff or the rest of the company just by considering alternatives.

Thank you.

Sincerely,

Matt Ginyus

Matt Ginyus

Different Pokes from Different Folks!

Different as they were, all three of the letters you just read would have stimulated the interest of any reader who needed what they offered.

Why? Because each:

1. was **not too long,** and
2. had a **central theme**
3. of **benefit to the reader.**

Sam Sage presented his outstanding track record as a marketing virtuoso-cum-general-manager. Matt Ginyus amply demonstrated his ability to get results in the laboratory. And Karen Kash showed that she was an outstanding employee, who'd never have been available, if not for exceptional circumstances. Her letter said, ''Help yourself to someone else's superstar.''

Of course, the very best thing about each of these letters is that only one person in all the world could have written it. Each person came to life through mere words on paper, because those words were clear and specific, and *applied only to him or her*. There were none of the vague generalities that give most such letters a boring fill-in-any-job-applicant similarity.

So before we move on to point **4, dealing with compensation,** let's list some things you'll make sure to *leave out*, which litter the letters of ''job applicants.''

OMIT...OMIT...OMIT!

Everything obvious, and all clichés. Letters from ''job applicants'' always state the obvious, and lean heavily on clichés: ''Enclosed please find...'' ''I would like to take this opportunity to...'' ''This letter will serve to...'' ''Here is a copy of my resume for your review and consideration.'' ''If my background and accomplishments are of interest, I would appreciate hearing from you.'' ''Thank you in advance for your interest.''

Self-evaluations. Don't bother describing your personality or your performance. You're biased, so we can't take your word for it. And if you enclose or quote something from a psychologist, we'll *know* you're on the defensive. Don't say, ''I'm a results-oriented executive with a proven track record,'' or that you're ''intelligent,'' ''analytical,'' ''profit-minded,'' ''honest,'' ''hardworking,'' ''loyal,'' ''reliable,'' or any of that stuff. ''Job applicants'' use those words.

Willingness to relocate. "Ho hum," if you're willing to move for a great opportunity. So is everyone else. Don't bring up relocation unless the fact that you won't relocate is the reason a lucky local employer has received your letter. If your employer...or your specific job...is leaving town and you don't want to, you've got a good believable reason for writing your letter. Exploit it. Otherwise say nothing about relocation. And don't give personal hardship details. Just say, "My family and I prefer to stay in Indianapolis." The fact that your spouse's real estate practice brings in twice what you do, or that your mother has a health problem doesn't make you any more attractive as a potential employee.

"Further information and references." Every "job applicant" is "pleased to supply further information and a list of references." But you're smart enough not to say so, and thus you further differentiate your letter from theirs. Besides, your "sales representative" resume...unlike theirs...has "further information" built right in. The next thing your reader will need or want is to see you.

The Mafia approach. Don't end your letter with a warning that you intend to make a follow-up phone call. "Job applicants," salespeople, and Cosa Nostra do that. If your reader is a prospective "buyer," he or she will probably take the next step. The "foot-in-the-door" approach needlessly makes you look pushy, because without the warning you are just as free to call as with it. Indeed, including it may prompt the reader to give orders to block your call.

And now "point 4"...current compensation. Rightly or wrongly, it's the #1 screening criterion.

Every employer wants to know that "money is right" before "wasting time" on any candidate.

The ideal covering letter gives that assurance ...and rushes the reader right into your resume.

One of the most important factors in establishing the "this-person-might-be-***for-me***" reaction on the part of your reader...and indeed any employer... is your level of compensation.

Yet most executives omit any mention of money...either current or desired. They worry that some employers may be frightened off because the figure is too high, and others may lose interest because it's too low. And any employer who winds up making an offer, they fear, may propose less than he otherwise would, if he knows what they're accustomed to.

What these wary executives don't realize is that by *not* mentioning salary, they've created a situation that's even *more* limiting. Compensation is the *single most important factor* in categorizing people as appropriate or inappropriate for a particular job. For employers...and executive recruiters as well...it provides a quick and easy way to figure out whether a candidate is "the right size." Titles can be misleading, and the importance of a given position can vary considerably from one organization to the next. Salary remains the most reliable index, since it's determined by the marketplace.

So the challenge is to mention compensation in a way that encourages consideration. You want every potential employer to look at your money and think:

"Well, that's in the ballpark. He might be ***for me***."

Obviously, if your money is above what the position pays, she'll figure she can't attract or hold you. And if you're earning far less, that's a pretty good indication that you're not yet ready for the responsibility the position entails.

So how do you handle compensation?

Here's a magic sentence that will do the best possible job of getting you considered:

> **"Although other factors such as (fill in your own non-financial 'turn-ons') are of primary importance to me, you should know that in recent years, my total compensation has been in the range of ________ to ________."**

To appreciate what that disclosure accomplishes, you must first:

Meet the weasels.

In consumer-products marketing, there's a term for wordings that state the truth precisely enough to wiggle through the narrow openings defined by company attorneys and government regulators. They're called "*weasels*," after the squirmy little animals that are almost impossible to catch.

The three key phrases..."weasels"...in your compensation statement are: "*in recent years*," "*total compensation*," and "*in the range of*." Used together, they open the way for you to state, *perfectly truthfully*, a broad range that will make you seem "right ***for me***" in the mind of every reader who controls a position you could possibly be interested in and qualified for.

The "*low-end*" figure will be the least take-home pay you'd consider, assuming the job offers major advantages beyond immediate compensation. After all, the preface to your "three-weasel" sentence said, in effect, "money isn't everything to me." For this bottom figure, use a round number that approximates your tax-return "income-from-employment" for a recent lean year.

For the "*high-end*" figure, start with your top base salary within the past few years. Then add everything else you're getting:

> performance bonuses (use the figures that...combined with base... represent your best year);
>
> the amount of your employer's contribution to FICA;
>
> the value of medical, dental, and life insurance provided by your employer;
>
> money paid by the firm into pension and profit-sharing accounts in your name (whether or not fully vested);
>
> any other tax-deferred compensation, such as annualized incremental value of your stock options, and your employer's matching contribution to thrift and stock-purchase plans;
>
> and the pre-tax value of miscellaneous perks, such as a company car (less your pay-back for personal use), city and country club memberships, the right to use the company condo in Nassau for two weeks vacation per year, and the college scholarship your child receives under a competitive company-wide program.

You can even estimate this year's raise, and include that in the base of your "high-end" figure.

Thus, using the three "weasels," you can truthfully state a wide range. You'll probably end up with numbers that are $50,000 to $90,000 or $150,000 apart...maybe even more. *It's perfectly reasonable for the second figure to be 50% larger than the first:* $150,000 to $230,000 for example, or $390,000 to $520,000.

Let's imagine that you've specified a range of $180,000 to $250,000.

First we'll picture your letter reaching the CEO of a young growth company with great prospects, but with venture capitalists on its Board who don't want Management draining its life blood with high salaries. This CEO looks at your low number, $180,000, and figures she can realistically reach *up* to you. She can't offer more than $115,000 in cash compensation. But you'll have the opportunity to purchase at 50 cents per share 50,000 shares of treasury stock the company expects to take public at about $20 per share within 18 to 24 months; and as an officer, you'll have a company car. She's pretty sure she can grab your attention. So she calls to suggest a get-acquainted lunch.

Now picture the CEO of a large multi-national corporation who must fill a job he thinks is worth a little over $300,000. He sees your top figure of $250,000...assumes it represents your most recent year...and reaches *down* to you. After all, you're probably expecting an increase of at least 10% or 20% for making a move. Obviously, your next job should be in the neighborhood of $300,000...just what he expects to pay. So he asks his assistant to give you a call.

As you see, your "three-weasel" range of $180,000 to $250,000 has actually triggered a "***for me***" response in the minds of two very differently situated employers. You're being considered for jobs paying anywhere from about $125,000 (with car—plus stock) to a bit over $300,000 a year. Cash compensation on one job is more than 100% above the other.

Moreover, you haven't given up any negotiating flexibility. You've got a shot at a job that pays even more than the top figure you mentioned. And of course you can always settle for less, depending on the job's advantages that extend beyond immediate in-pocket cash.

Mentioning money...and having it "right" for your reader...encourages him or her to consider your resume. And using a "three-weaseled" range lets you be "right" for every reader whose job could possibly be right for you.

And now a word of warning...

Don't fritter away the #1 advantage of direct mail. Avoid the hill-beyond-the-hill-beyond-the-hill dilemma.

Just about everybody refuses to believe they can be as good as they are, send out lots of letters describing how good that is, and not be swamped with phone calls, appointments, and interviews. Worrying that they can't cope with too many responses, they hold back on their mailing, sending only a portion of their ultimate total per day or per week.

Don't make their mistake!

Don't drop your spy-in-the-sky satellite back to earth. Don't forgo the instant reconnaissance that only direct mail can give you. Instead, send your letters everywhere at once, so you'll look everywhere at once. Do an *aerial scan of the entire desert*. Survey every oasis. See all three, four, or five of them... simultaneously. Then you'll be able to pick the greenest.

Sending only a few letters, when you could have sent them all, puts you back on the ground, where you can only see as far as the horizon.

You're still looking for water in the desert. But now you're riding a camel. Suddenly you spot a brackish little watering hole in the valley below. Should you head for it? Or should you keep to the high ground and peer into the valley beyond the next hill? Maybe that's where you'll find the main outflow of the underground stream this little trickle merely foretells. If so, the water will be cool, sweet, and abundant. There'll be plants, fruit trees, and maybe even a comfortable bed for the night. And if not beyond the next hill...then surely beyond the one after that. But what if there's only sand? Then you'll fervently wish you hadn't passed up the meager security of this little spot.

You see my point.

Believe me when I say that 1,000 letters won't bring more than 3 to 5 interested responses...2 or 3 interviews...and 1 or 2 offers. *And that's* ***not*** *too much "action" to handle all at once.*

No matter how good you are, *timing* will be wrong at almost every company you contact. So send all your letters at once and get all your offers simultaneously. Then you can choose the best the market has for you at any moment in time. What's more, you'll *know* it's the best, and not a compromise you feel forced into, because you can't risk waiting to see what's behind the hill behind the hill.

Another mistake is to neglect direct mail until very late in an all-out job-changing campaign.

Ideally, it comes right up front.

For some reason many people think direct mail should only come *after* personal contact, networking, and reaching out to executive recruiters, in an aggressive job search. There's only one logical reason I can think of to justify that view, and it's because direct mail is a lot of work. So most people don't bother with it, until after the other methods are tried and seem to be failing.

That's really shortsighted. The *first* things needed in a powerful executive job hunting effort are an outstanding resume and cover letter—strong and clear enough to be effective in a direct mail campaign, yet always handy to be sent out whenever else written communication is needed. They're your communications POWERTOOL You'll make them persuasive enough to succeed in direct mail and find them endlessly useful for other purposes as well.

Moreover, just as preparing your "sales representative'' resume forces you to study your achievements and what to say about them, preparing your mailing list forces you to survey prospective employers and determine where you're most likely to do well and gain satisfaction. Shouldn't this strategic analysis come at the beginning, rather than the end, of your job-changing efforts?

Bear in mind that:

1. Your personal and networking contacts will only know a very few of the possibilities that exist for you in the world of work, and

2. The retainer recruiters will only show you a very few of the opportunities they're working to fill.

So hurry up and get the five or six leads your 1,000-letter direct mail campaign can generate. Meanwhile, don't neglect tempting opportunities to "Game the System" (see page 298 and onward).

Also take advantage of the 200 or 300 rejection letters you'll get. Sift them carefully to find the unusually cordial ones...perhaps 10 or 20...from people who were so impressed by your mailing that they really *did* wish they had a place for you. Since they're at high levels in industries and companies that appeal to you, they're ideal early contacts for your networking campaign, which would otherwise be narrowly based on the people you already know.

Begin your ''search'' by skimming your best personal contacts and alerting the retainer recruiters you're already acquainted with..and also by alerting the executive search community in a quick and easy way we'll discuss. If you haven't solved your problem within the first month you're ''looking,'' then chances are you're in for a full-scale effort. If so, you may save many months in the long run, by devoting two or three weeks to vigorous direct mail right at the outset.

We've looked at the sunny side of direct mail. Now let's examine its dark side.

Some products can be sold by direct mail and some can't. Same with people. It works for some and not for others.

Moreover, the requirements for direct mail success are exactly the same for both people and products. So let's talk only products for a moment, and bypass the ego and emotion that make it nearly impossible to talk about ourselves as people. Here are the make-or-break questions:

1. **Is the product special?** Exceptionally high quality? Uniquely useful? Then we're interested. But if it's ordinary...something we see in every store all over town...we'll pay no attention at all when we get a letter about it.

2. **How many potential purchasers?** Is this something nobody has and everyone wants? Something everyone has and nobody needs two of? Something nobody has and nobody wants? There are things a letter can't *fail* to sell; and others it can *never* sell.

3. **Is the description enticing?** Maybe the product is truly wonderful...surpassing everything else. But if the description makes it seem like something we see in every store all over town, we yawn, and throw the letter into the wastebasket.

You, I, and everyone else have no difficulty accepting and dealing with such tough, obvious facts about products. But seeing ourselves....our own backgrounds, achievements, and persuasive writing skills...with such merciless objectivity is an entirely different matter.

That's why I'm glad we're not face-to-face right now. I can deliver some harsh facts and—even if your gun is loaded—you can't shoot the messenger.

For most people during most of their career, direct mail is one of the five components of an all-out job search. But for some of us at certain times, direct mail cannot possibly work Even most of the online activity we'll discuss in Chapter 14—although worth doing when approached strategically because it's so easy—is likely to fail when a person's employment facts are unappealing or poorly presented.

Then methods 1 and 2...skillful handling of personal contacts and unrelenting networking among strangers...are the only really good bets. At such an unfortunate moment, whatever the Postal Service delivers cannot be both truthful and persuasive. And the respectable retainer recruiters will not risk their credibility by pleading the job seeker's currently weakened case.

Direct mail plays the odds.

And for some people at some times, those odds are almost unplayable.

Here are five surprisingly prevalent situations in which sending out your letter and resume probably won't pay back your mailing expense:

1. Too many too-brief jobs. It's very difficult to seem special...exceptionally high quality, or uniquely useful...when you haven't been in place long enough to generate impressive recent accomplishments to include in your letter and resume.

Sometimes, of course, brief jobs *can* be favorably written up. For example, the boss who recruited you to a new company may have been so impressed with your first six months' achievements (describe them!) that he took you with him to a more exciting company. But then a takeover swept you both into a third company, where you were both forced out. Written up as a three-year segment of great work for the same superior, those three short jobs may look very good.

Remember, however, that employers all realize that it takes the better part of a year for you to dig in and get established. During that time you're more pain and drain, than gain. So even if you do wonderful things for a few months afterward, but then walk out, it's right back to pain and drain with someone new. Your former employers are *not* thrilled. And readers of your mailing probably won't be either.

Face-to-face...preferably with supportive friends and acquaintances..is the only effective way to convince a potential employer that "this time it will be different." For direct mail to work, the premise has to be "more of the same."

2. Not special enough. What if you've been a good, honest, kind, congenial, competent, zestfully healthy employee, with an engaging sense of humor, a great home life, outstanding kids, a wide and devoted coterie of friends, and lots of commendable civic involvement? And what if, at work, you were never absent, never late, never given a poor performance review, and never unwilling to sacrifice an evening or a weekend to cope with a crisis?

But now you're looking for a new job.

Can even the finest direct mail copywriter make you as tantalizing as that dastardly, driven, and devious workaholic with the string of remarkable accomplishments that even those of us who detest him are forced to applaud?

No. I like you a lot better than I like him. And I'd much rather have you as a friend, a neighbor, or an in-law. But in job-hunting, you'll do far better face-to-face with the many people you already know and the strangers they'll enthusiastically introduce you to, than you will if you go to the Postal Service or even the web to do your communicating.

And besides, with your fine connections in your community, you're likely to find a fulfilling job right where you are. One of the great advantages of direct mail is that it can extend your search to unfamiliar companies in far-off places. But are they where you want to go?

And what do the nay-sayers mean, ''Not special enough''? You're plenty special...among the people you're special to. So make absolutely the best resume you can. Develop it into a ''sales representative'' on paper. And then put it into circulation *in person*. Don't dump it in the mail box!

3. Changing field or function. Suppose you've toiled for years in a certain field or performing a specific function. You're exceedingly proficient. You've racked up enviable accomplishments, and in the process you've become quite well paid.

But now you've had it. You're *bored, BORED, BORED!*

Or the handwriting is on the wall. Your field or function is a downer. And you want to get into something more promising.

Or maybe you're retiring from the military or the diplomatic corps, leaving the clergy or teaching, walking out on your family's business, or ending an ill-fated entrepreneurial venture.

I could go on and on. But you get the idea. You've been something significant for quite a while, and you're very good at it. You have an expert's accomplishments and, hopefully, you're earning an expert's pay. If you decide to continue, you can probably write a great ''sales representative'' resume and get a similar or better job for the same or better money.

But no! You want to do something different. Something in which you're *not* yet an expert, something other people know a lot more about than you do. And you'd like to keep right on making your usual or better money, while somebody gives you on-the-job training, or patiently waits for you to bring yourself up to speed...somebody who could just as easily hire an already-established expert with lots of experience and a string of achievements that are just as impressive in the matching field or function as yours are in a foreign one.

Isn't that too much to expect from just a letter and a resume—no matter how elegant—merely dropped into the mail by a complete stranger interested only in his or her preferences, and not the recipient's needs? Usually it is.

Generally speaking, when you're trying to stretch-fit yourself into an entirely new situation, direct mail is ***not*** a realistic option. Nor is the executive recruiter who, to earn his pay, is earnestly working to "fulfill the specifications."

When a "leap of faith" is required, you're much more likely to achieve it face-to-face through your already-supportive personal contacts and the open-minded strangers you meet and impress through networking.

4. Special, but you can't, or refuse to, communicate. You may be very special indeed. But if you can't look shrewdly into your career and choose as the theme of your letter and the show-pieces of your resume the things you've done that will best recommend you to a new employer...and if, having chosen, you can't distill them into a very few clear, simple, straightforward, and non-self-praising words...then you'd better not waste your time and money on a direct mail campaign.

Direct mail is merely another form of advertising. And with all advertising, success or failure depends on whether or not it identifies the most strongly-felt consumer need the product can satisfy, and then persuades the consumer that the product *will* meet that need.

If you insist on writing a cover letter centered on what you want, rather than what the employer wants that you provide (based strictly on specific past accomplishments that are likely to be repeated, rather than self-praising adjectives and evaluations)...and if your resume is nothing but the usual recitation of times, titles, and responsibilities...then don't mail it. It won't do you any good at all, unless you hand it over in person, concealing the self-centeredness and insensitivity your cover letter would otherwise have revealed, and unless you're right there extolling the achievements your resume leaves out.

If you can't, or refuse to, create a direct mail resume...then by all means, don't undertake a direct mail campaign.

5. Not very good and your mailing proves it. Remember, whatever you send in the mail is a free sample of your intellect and your performance. If it's obviously inferior, nobody will respond. Nobody will invite you in for an interview. And you'll never know why.

Just one example will illustrate:

> A few years ago, I heard of a man who sent out 5,000 letters and resumes and didn't receive a single affirmative response. Intrigued, I invited him to come in and bring me a sample of his mailing. He sounded great on the phone. And in person he was a perfect "10" in executive looks, tailoring, and personality.
>
> The resume was on two pages in reverse chrono format with latest jobs on page one, dwindling to personal data at the bottom of two. I noticed right away that his four latest jobs were within the past 5 years. And virtually no accomplishments were stated (not surprising, since there was no *room* for any, and probably little *time* for any in such brief jobs).
>
> Why, I wondered, would a top marketing executive spend his own money on such an unpersuasive advertisement? But then I *glanced again*. "*Forget the brief jobs,*" I thought. "*Look at the* ***words!***" Condensed, here's his first page...the most important 50% of his resume:

Name/Address/Phones/Email

<u>Objective</u>
(lengthy)

To do great marketing for a marketing-oriented company.

<u>Summary</u>
(lengthy)

A Marketing executive experienced in all phases of marketing.

<u>Work History</u>

Company A	Vice President, Marketing and Sales
Company Y	Senior Vice President, Marketing
Company X	Vice President, Marketing and Sales
Company W	Vice President, Marketing

What's wrong with it?

This fellow spent lots of his own money on an ad campaign with *no advertising!* Over and over he said, "I am a marketing person looking for a marketing job"...not "I am a *good* marketing person, as these accomplishments prove." Just the four titles on page one tell us he does marketing. And mailing his resume says he's job-hunting. The "Objective" and "Summary" take up the top half of page one, 50% of his best space...25% of his total space...and yet they tell us absolutely nothing that isn't obvious!

Should we hire this Senior VP to make sure our corporation gets maximum effectiveness from every dollar it spends on advertising? No way! Forget the dark cloud of four jobs in five years. Here's a total eclipse of marketing judgment, as *demonstrated* by his resume. He has sent you, me, and 4,998 other people a free sample of his work. And not one of us has liked it enough to want more!

The same thing happens when an educator's resume displays poor grammar (hazardous to the rest of us too); a lawyer's isn't logical; a CFO's leaves us wondering whether some of his figures are pre- or post-tax; a President's or General Manager's speaks only of sales and not profits, and confuses ROI. You get the idea.

Your resume is always scrutinized as a sample of your work, whether you mail it, or walk in with it. But the risk is greater when you mail, because you're not there to distract attention. If you're not very good and your resume proves it, don't go near the Post Office!

A bit more, before we leave this fellow. You're probably thinking, "Yes, John, but doesn't he also represent fault #4, 'Can't, or refuses to, communicate'"? Yes, that too. His merely saying "Marketing, marketing" rather than "Good marketing" is also a #4 failing. But since communication is the very *essence* of marketing, he proves he's no good at his *job*. Failure or refusal to communicate under #4 could be accomplished by someone who told us "Manufacturing, manufacturing" rather than "Good manufacturing," but we wouldn't know from just his resume that he can't do his job. Obviously too, the resume displays fault #1, "too many, too short jobs." Recommendation: Non-stop networking (ultimately successful for this fellow).

How Many vs. How Good?

Just 20 outstanding letters and resumes...or even one or two...are far more likely to get you an interview than tons of mediocre ones. Statistical odds are overwhelmingly against a few succeeding. But tons of unimpressive...or as we've seen, *negatively* impressive...letters and resumes won't do any good at all. And mailing them does a lot of harm, because it wastes precious time and money.

So I warn you against this very real danger: If and when you're ever unemployed, you'll be under lots of stress, and you'll tend to become the panicky soldier in the old cliché:

"Ready...fire...aim!"

Please be careful. Try to get back into the same objective frame of mind I insisted on as we began this section by talking about *products*, rather than people. Your letter and resume are a small free sample of *you*. The sample had better be good...or don't send it.

Knowing the terrible statistics of direct mail...only three to five out of 1,000 companies having the right job open right now...lots of people panic and think only "How many?" They forget that success is even more dependent on "How good?"

Hiding Behind the Post Office

Most of us are shy.

Probably you're like me. You love a big party, if you know everyone there. But you hate going to the same affair if you only know the host or hostess. Because after a couple minutes with them, you'll be on your own...an embarrassed wallflower, or a pushy nerd, accosting unintrigued strangers.

And if you have to make phone calls for your church, temple, or trade association, you don't mind rescheduling a picnic. But like me, you're a lot less comfortable asking for money.

Unfortunately, networking by its very nature demands we do both unpleasant things...plunge in among strangers, and request help. No wonder most of us would rather avoid it if we can.

But sadly, we can't. Reaching out to our personal contacts and networking among strangers are the most powerful of all job-hunting techniques. Face-to-face communication *does* have more oomph than a letter. But what direct mail does—and very effectively—is to lengthen our reach beyond the relatively few and nearby people we can visit face-to-face. Direct mail *expands* networking; it doesn't replace it.

So here's the single biggest danger and downside of direct mail:

Hiding behind the Post Office.

Lots of basically shy folks like you and me are tempted to avoid massaging our personal contacts and networking strangers, merely because we don't enjoy that sort of activity. If we did, we'd be VP of Sales, instead of CFO. So quite understandably, we'd rather stay home and do nothing but send out letters. That's dumb...cowardly...and lazy! If it becomes your idea of an all-out job campaign, don't say I suggested it.

The Trade-Off: Follow-Up vs. Get-'Em-Out

Obviously, there's potential benefit in calling up the people you write to, and trying to see them for a networking visit. Or perhaps phoning them long-distance to network.

Some people I know have even succeeded in making friends with the PAs of their direct mail targets. They call to ask if their letter arrived; what's being done with it; whether it's realistic to try for a few moments of the boss's time in person or on an aptly-timed phone call; who else might be more appropriate to receive such an approach; and so on.

Unfortunately, aggressive follow-up takes lots of time. If that's your strategy, you can't handle more than 50 or 100 per week. At that rate, it will take you 10 or 20 weeks...two and a half to five months...to send out 1,000 letters (and preferably today a lot more) in the hope of hitting just three to five recipients who, according to statistical odds, ought to have the right job for you *open* or soon-to-open.

Of course, if your letter and resume do a fine job of selling your impressive accomplishments (and they'd better *be* impressive), then just the mild stimulus of your mailing without follow-up should trigger a call from those few recipients who have a screaming need for someone like you right now. Wouldn't it be sad if a delay-for-follow-up strategy made your mailing too late for the one or two most attractive jobs that will open up while you're unemployed?

I can't tell you how to balance this trade off. Should you risk under-exploiting your mailing? Or should you risk missing current opportunities? And, of course, also missing the looked-everywhere-before-I-had-to-decide benefit of a direct mail spy-in-the-sky satellite.

Maybe you should divide your mailing into two categories:

1. Highest-priority are the most attractive employers, and the ones where you're already so well-connected that they merit maximum follow-up.

2. Lesser-priority are the far larger number that are less attractive, or where you're less well acquainted.

How long can you afford to stretch out the release of your highest-priority letters? A month? Two months? How many letters can be aggressively followed-up in that time? Skim that number and schedule them accordingly.

The remainder might as well go into the mailbox right away, because even the best mailing will generate only about three to five interested replies...certainly not enough to disrupt your high-priority activities. Moreover, any unusually warm "no thank yous" will arrive in time to be "networked" when you finish processing your high-priority letters.

There's no pat answer to the follow-up vs. send-'em-out dilemma. But at least there's an organized way to deal with it.

The Proof is in the Proofing

Here's a tip from the exceptionally sharp-eyed woman who opens and sorts my mail:

"Tell them not to trust their own proofreading."

She spies a typo in "about a third" of the letters and resumes she looks over. And quite often it's in a spot Murphy himself would have chosen... like an early paragraph of the letter or the first title in the resume. Her theory on why:

> "I'll bet these people work so hard on *thoughts* that they almost stop seeing *words*. Give 'em a week to cool off, and they'll spot their flubs just like I do."

Be forewarned. Show your mailing to two or three completely fresh-eyed people before you push the mass-production button.

Also, don't count on the computer's "spell check" function. It's no substitute for careful human proofreading. If you typed "or" instead of "of" or left out the word "not"—the sort of thing I do all the time—the computer won't catch your goof.

So much for the basics. Now let's take direct mail to its ultimate extreme.

Let's mount a wide-ranging campaign right under your current employer's nose, and never let him suspect you're "looking."

First of all, you'll need an anonymous version of your "sales representative" resume. And secondly you'll need a "sponsor" to send it out for you... and to receive the three to six interested responses you're likely to get from a 1,000-letter mailing.

Your Anonymous Resume

It's easy to omit your name, address, phone, and email from your "sales representative" resume. And it's not hard to describe your current and recent employers "generically," rather than identify them by name. Employers that are "ancient history" can be left "as is."

Please thoughtfully consider this resume transformation. Doing so will help prepare you for Chapter 14, where we'll look closely at the web and the safety issues that arise.

Assume, for example, that your "regular" resume has headings like the ones shown on the next page.

As you see, it's possible to substitute information about the corporation and what it does, for the name of the company. In effect, you're merely moving facts you'd otherwise provide in the first sentence of the following paragraph up into the line that normally identifies your employer.

Try to give concrete orientation to your reader, even though you can't "name names." Leave out specific trademarks. But state all the same numerical comparisons you'd include in an "open" version of your resume. Also, give your actual college degrees (with dates), and your marital status. After all, you're not the only married person who graduated from Stanford in 1999.

2012 - Present

DIAMOND/ACME COMPANY
(Subsidiary of Multi-Continent Industries)
Bucolic, Vermont

Vice President & General Manager

2006 - 2012

NEW-MOTION CONTROLS LTD.
Sunbelt, Arizona

'09 Vice President - Marketing

'06 Director - Product Management

Restate your headings like this:

2012 - Present

$190 Million Manufacturer of Flow-Control Devices
(Subsidiary of Conglomerate)

Vice President & General Manager

2006 - 2012

$450 Million Manufacturer of OEM Control Assemblies
(Privately owned)

'09 Vice President - Marketing

'06 Director - Product Management

> Editor's Note...
>
> For John Lucht's in-depth help with your resume and cover letter use pages 40 to 135 and 136 to 163 of the **Executive Job-Changing Workbook**.

Your Sponsor

You're doing something difficult. And this time you can't do it without help. You must have a "sponsor" who's willing to "front" for you...distributing the anonymous version of your resume and accepting replies from employers who are interested in meeting you.

Of course, you might instead try to be a "Lone Ranger." You *could* send out your own identity-concealed resume. And you could ask that responses be addressed to a post office box, explaining your need for secrecy, and hoping that mystery and novelty might make up for your lack of straightforwardness.

Unfortunately, this approach has already been tried many times. And as far as I know, it has always failed. Considering candidates for management positions is no joke. And people in a position to do so are too busy to fool around. Your resume won't be taken seriously unless it comes from an obviously credible source.

Therefore, since *you* can't send the resume—and you certainly don't want it circulated by some headhunter who's attached a price-tag—you need someone else who can submit it almost as straightforwardly as if it came directly from you.

You need a *"sponsor"*...a real live respectable person who'll openly send your name-omitted resume, say why she's doing so, and forward to you any interested responses she receives. Moreover, it will be a big help if the person is rather prominent in the business world...someone obviously capable of knowing a fine executive when she sees one. Then her mailing out your resume will more than make up for your anonymity. Indeed, *it will enhance your image*.

"Sounds great, John," you say, "but who am I going to get to do that for me?"

Well, it can't be Leonardo DiCaprio, Pope Francis, or Dr. Ruth Westheimer. Prominent they are. But experts on who would make an ideal chief manufacturing officer for a large metal-bending business they're not. Better for your purposes—and easier to enlist—would be someone who could begin this letter knowledgeably:

> "As president of a $550 million division of Innovative All-Steel Products Corporation, I know the importance of having a Vice President of Manufacturing who can really be depended on."

That was a person you and I never heard of...yet a perfect "sponsor." Lining up someone like that probably isn't beyond your reach.

Since your spokesperson should claim to have firsthand knowledge of your outstanding on-the-job performance, chances are he or she is a former boss or subordinate. She's probably *not* just a prominent businessperson you know socially or as a fellow board-member of a nonprofit institution...although "any port in a storm," as they say.

However, you don't want a sponsor who's *too* high on the corporate totem pole relative to the position you should occupy, because one essential element of his letter must be a believable statement of why—despite your being so special—he can't use you himself. If your sponsor is Chief Executive of IBM, it's hard to believe he can't fit you in somewhere. Therefore, the reader will suspect he doesn't want to.

Here are the essential elements of a "sponsor's" letter sending out your identity-concealed resume:

1. His ***credentials*** that make him a valid judge of executives like you;
2. His ***vantage point*** that enables him to endorse your on-the-job effectiveness;
3. His ***recommendation***;
4. His ***reason for not employing you himself***;
5. His ***explanation of your need for secrecy***; and
6. His ***offer*** to put the interested reader in touch with you.

Now let's look at a "sponsoring" letter that meets all these criteria.

TRILOVANCE ELECTRONICS CORPORATION
1010 Solder Circle, Verdant Valley, California 95014 (510) 962-1000

Monique Micreaux
President

(Date)

Mr. Donald Drive
President
Peripheron Corporation
18 Silver Saddle Road
Diva Del Sol, California 95038

Dear Mr. Drive:

As Founder/CEO of a publicly-held young high-tech growth company—we started four years ago and will hit $390 million this year—I know the importance of a Chief Financial Officer who can provide absolutely reliable information without needlessly cumbersome procedures that stifle momentum.

Those people are rare and difficult to identify. Which is why I'm writing to you.

Last week I learned that the financial executive I respect most after 12 years with IBM and North American Dauntless Corporation—and tried hardest to recruit as CFO when I founded this company—is now willing to explore outside opportunities.

However, since he's very solidly employed, he can't afford to "go public" with his intentions. And, since I can't capitalize on his availability without doing an injustice to the person who took the plunge with me four years ago, I'm sending his identity-omitted resume to you and several other CEOs of high-tech growth companies.

If there's any chance that you may have a need, just let me know, and I'll put you in touch with one of the very best financial executives you could possibly consider.

Sincerely,

Monique Micreaux

Monique Micreaux

MM:gr
Enclosure

P.S. Although growth environment and equity opportunity will be primary concerns, you should know that his total compensation in recent years has been in the $275,000 to $360,000 range.

What an endorsement!

The ''sponsored'' mailing not only provides ''cover,'' it also heightens impact.

Someone introducing a colleague can say things that modesty prevents the individual from saying about himself.

And such a plug is far more believable coming from a senior executive with no economic axe to grind than from a headhunter filing for $80,000 or $120,000 or more. Moreover, a ''no-price-tag'' introduction is much more likely to be followed-up.

''Sponsored'' direct mail is often ''the only alternative'' in a ticklishly sensitive situation. Fortunately, when handled well, it also becomes a highly persuasive marketing campaign.

The Dual Standard on Stationery

Notice that the ''sponsor'' used her corporate stationery when recommending someone else, whereas she normally would *not* do so when proposing herself.

The reason for this dual standard is purely psychological. Corporate stationery is virtually essential to prove that the sponsor is indeed a substantial, knowledgeable person in the business world. And fortunately, the reader has no negative reaction to the use of office paper to help a colleague.

But the ''vibes'' are totally different when the writer offers himself. Then using his employer's paper triggers a negative reaction. His reader thinks, ''Wow, at the same time he's trying to get me to hire him, he's ripping off his current company's stationery and postage meter.''

''I know a couple people, John, who'd be ideal to send out a mailing like that, and they respect me enough to do it.''

''But they're extremely busy. I could never ask them to take on so much work.''

Absolutely right! You couldn't. And you *won't*.

You're requesting a huge favor, just to have them lend you their name, mailing address, and phone number. So you've got to get virtually all the work done without burdening either your sponsor or his personal assistant.

Here's what *you* do:

1. Get your sponsor's general agreement to help.

2. Show him a letter you've drafted (to save him work), stressing that he may change it as he sees fit, since it's his letter.

3. Establish agreed-upon wording for the letter, and walk away with at least two reams of office stationery and 1,000 #10 envelopes (enough for 1,000 letters).

4. Create your mailing list, check it by phone, and have "his" letter word-processed. But first, show him a sample to make doubly sure he's satisfied. Also offer to let him see your mailing list, in case he wants to make sure you haven't accidentally hit anyone he'd rather not be "writing" to.

5. Sign, stuff, stamp, and mail the letters yourself. That's right, I said sign them...with *his* signature. Unless he feels like signing 1,000 letters, he'll gladly leave this chore up to you. But ask before you barge ahead; this point is inconsequential to some people and an emotional issue with others.

Here's what your sponsor and his assistant do:

1. Almost nothing else. After he approves your letter and list, he's just about finished. *Remember, an excellent 1,000-letter mailing will produce only 3 to 5 interested replies*...hardly enough to create a traffic problem.

2. Letter replies will be opened by your sponsor's assistant with the rest of his mail, and merely forwarded to you every couple days in a large envelope. These could be a slight nuisance for a week or two, because 200 to 300 recipients will send polite "no thank yous."

3. The 3 to 5 phone callers who inquire about you will be cordially dealt with by your sponsor. He'll say he doesn't know the exact status of your explorations at the moment, but will gladly forward their name and number to you. Then, if you're not already in your new job, you'll call their office, giving your spon

sor's name as well as your own, so they'll know you're the person they inquired about.

That's it. Nothing more.

But look what you've accomplished. While keeping yourself completely hidden, you've probed 1,000 (or more) companies to find the *rare* 3 to 5 who right now are interested in what you have to offer. And you've done so without tipping-off your current employer!

True, you've put a lot of work into the project. But, except for checking a few times with your sponsor, *no more work than sending the same mailing under your own name*. Your sponsor has also contributed some time. But not much. You've done everything, except sat in his office and been him when three to five people called to ask about you.

"Sponsored" direct mail can do more than keep a secret.

It's also a problem-solver.

Joyce is in a tough spot.

She needn't be secretive. But she does face a high hurdle. Someone almost has to "speak the unspeakable," and it's a matter Joyce can't very well bring up for herself.

See how a "sponsored" mailing can come to the rescue.

MONOLITHIC FOODS CORPORATION
White Plains, New York 11618 (914) 992-1000

MAURICE MARKETIER
Vice President - Marketing

(Date)

Mr. Cabot Carson
President
Family-Owned Candies, Inc.
10 Ginger Road
Scottsdale, Arizona 09099

Dear Mr. Carson:

As Vice President - Marketing of Monolithic Foods, I've seen hundreds of fine marketing executives over the years, and one of the very best is my former boss at MegaFoods, Joyce McKee, who taught me most of what I know.

Recently the company where she's been Vice President - Marketing, Yumm Foods, was acquired through an unfriendly tender offer. And now at an amazingly youthful age 59—Joyce ran the New York Marathon again this year—she's available for another assignment.

Although company and opportunity will be Joyce's main concerns, you should know that in recent years her total compensation has been in the range of $290,000 to $420,000.

Joyce is the calibre of person there's hardly ever a shot at hiring, and nothing would please me more than to bring her in here. Unfortunately, I can't do that without dealing an undeserved blow to one of the two executives who head my Marketing Department...or by giving up my own job.

So, on the chance that you may have need for an exceptionally dynamic, creative, and versatile marketing executive, I thought I'd bring Joyce to your attention.

Sincerely,

Maurice Marketier

Maurice Marketier

MM:jc
Enclosure

P.S. With Joyce's exceptional knack for training and recruiting, you can count on her building a strong department, with excellent people to take over whenever it's time for Joyce to retire.

Think of "sponsored" direct mail as your "SWAT team," to be called in when the going gets really tough!

You catch the concept. The more tendency to discriminate against an executive, the more helpful "sponsored" direct mail becomes.

With direct mail, the number of employers contacted can be infinitely expanded. Maybe 2,000 or 3,000 will have to be reached in order to find 5 to 8 with an immediate need, because only one-in-three or one-in-five will consider a disadvantaged candidate. Fortunately, a "sponsor's" letter can deal with the prejudicial factor far more frankly and successfully than one from the candidate herself...or from a headhunter or an outplacement firm with a fee on the line.

Whenever there's a severe problem, consider sponsored direct mail. A successful business executive who's a retired military officer can make a strong case for a former subordinate now mustering out. A former top-echelon businessperson who's become an ambassador or a college president can knowledgeably extol a current subordinate who wants to enter business from the diplomatic corps or academia. And any high-level executive can sponsor a former subordinate or boss with an attribute most employers will shun—lawfully or not—such as age, physical handicap, obesity...even, perhaps, return to work after a jail sentence for "white-collar-crime."

Direct mail, with or without a "boost" from a sponsor, may turn out to be the only viable "Rite of Passage" when you're looking for the exceptionally rare employer who must have—in addition to need, which is always rare anyway—broadmindedness, compassion, or firsthand knowledge that an apparent disadvantage isn't disabling.

Try it. For yourself...or for a friend.

And there you have direct mail ...the ultimate career-development weapon.

Results are limited only by how hard you're willing to work.

I used to say exactly what you've just read. Direct Mail ***is*** a lot of work.

But, because of advancements in web technology with respect to certain job-hunting sites, it has become possible to Game the System and remove much of the effort involved while conducting a campaign so active and far reaching that it almost resembles Direct Mail.

Move on with me to the next chapter.

We'll clear up some of the fog about the value—or lack of it—contributed by the web to an all-out executive job search and we'll cover my two main tips on using the web in executive job changing.

If you're fully challenged and well rewarded where you are—and you're also fairly often being tempted by retainer recruiters—you won't bother reaching for the unlimited power of Direct Mail and my "Game-the-System" version, which I call "Faux Direct Mail."

Direct mail and its "faux" cousin are extremely high-powered. As job-changing methods, they're rather like the police, the fire department, and the hospital. Drastic! But great to have around when needed.

Read Before Chapter 14

Online Executive job-hunting has a...BUM RAP!

We're headed for Chapter 14 on using websites in executive job changing and career building. But first...some ***debunking:***

What about the stories in the media that very few people are getting their jobs online?

The stories are true. More people are posting their resumes on job sites. More are answering job board postings. Yet only a few are actually ***finding*** their jobs online. And, as you'd expect, that's especially true at the highly paid executive levels.

But look at the other side. More and more ***jobs are being filled*** with the help of web sites. And that, too, is increasingly true at the highly paid executive levels.

Any inconsistency? No, just common sense.

Depending on the job and the site(s) used, there may be many—perhaps even thousands of—replies. Suppose the process of finding some worthy candidates and hiring one of them works perfectly.

What are the bottom line STATISTICS?

Even when the process works perfectly only three people are happy.

1. **One boss has found a needed subordinate.**
2. **One recruiter has completed a search and earned a large fee.**
3. **One individual has moved into an attractive new position.**

For those three, the process has been 100% satisfactory!

Sadly, however...
Hundreds—perhaps thousands—are disappointed. They were not hired. Indeed, they probably didn't even get an acknowledgement. They report that, based on their experience, the process is hopelessly flawed.

So what's the truth?

The fact is that more recruiters—in search firms and in corporations hiring directly—are using the web as one of several valid candidate-finding tools. Moreover, they're applying it to higher and higher level jobs. And they're doing so because, from their point of view, the technique is useful.

Don't expect them to give it up.

Instead, unless you want to seriously handicap your job-finding and career-advancing progress, figure out how you can personally take advantage of online job-hunting. It's here to stay!

Chapter 14

Using the Web in Executive Job Changing: We'll steer past the obvious and concentrate on two major issues. One is a constant and unavoidable hidden hazard. The other is a constant and sparkling opportunity.

We're entering territory you already know a lot about.

There are many job boards and you've probably used quite a few. There are also lots of social networking sites. You've used those too, including LinkedIn.com—always the most business-oriented of the social sites and and now also making hundreds of millions of dollars annually by marketing its database to employers and recruiters.

Moreover, new social sites continue to spring up like mushrooms after a spring rain. Some succeed and go public, and their founders become billionaires.

All of that is fun to observe and discuss. But we're not going to "go there." Instead, we'll examine two phenomena—one bad and one good—that have the potential to affect your search for a new or better executive job.

#1, we'll consider the...

BIG HONKING PROBLEM.

Unfortunately, it **DOESN'T HONK!**

That's right.

Whenever you're about to do anything involving your career on the web, you're normally in the dark, standing on the edge of an abyss. Chances are that you have no idea that the chasm even exists. Nor that, with one step forward, you are about to enter and become an uninformed participant.

Moreover, the chasm spans farther and will endure longer than you ever would have imagined.

Click that "Apply" or "Post" button—either one—and, chances are, you're entering an entirely new realm that we'll now examine together.

Contingency Recruiting Firm Fee-Splitting ...and the Huge Unseen Database It Creates

For many decades, contingency search firms have have arranged to share the resumes of attractive potential candidates. Let's listen: "I've got no use for him/her right now. But he/she is potentially a winner. I'll send you the resume. And if you or someone you know can bank a fee, we'll split it." That's the deal.

Traditionally, the split is anywhere from 35/65% to 50/50%, always in favor of the headhunter who winds up collecting money from the hiring employer. Sometimes the headhunter who contributes the resume may have to split with yet another headhunter who originally collected the resume from the individual it describes.

Today, with the power of the web, fee-splitting is on steroids

Building shareable databases now is easy. It's no problem to create a pool of resumes, mark who contributed each, and arrange to share a portion of the placement money, if the resume ever generates any.

I can't tell you how many such resume/revenue sharing arrangements there are. But let's say we accept the common estimate that there are about 12,000 contingency search firms and independent recruiters in the U.S. And then let's speculate that each of those 12,000 have sharing hookups with at least 2 additional entities and contribute about 50 resumes per year to each database they share. Well, I won't labor the point. You get the idea. Once a resume enters the big hidden "Black Hole" full of resumes, it is likely to be widely distributed by the headhunters who maintain the pool!

The largest individual database of resumes shared by U.S. contingency firms that I'm aware of has about 200 participating headhunter firms. From this fact alone, you can see that, once your resume enters the pool serving 200 firms—some very sizeable—it is blowing in a fast wind, totally out of your control.

Do the executives ask to have their Resumes circulated this way?

No, certainly not. It is just common practice in the field to deposit every resume for a potentially "good candidate" into such a database. The process is silent and virtually automatic.

Sadly, the "Big Honking Problem ***doesn't honk***. You get no warning until something goes wrong. And very soon I'll give you real life examples of how that has occurred.

Is this phenomenon necessarily bad for you?

No, not necessarily. At the beginning of your career when you are struggling to get any recognition at all, as we discussed earlier, you may very much appreciate headhunter publicity. But once you become a successful and highly paid executive, you normally will prefer to control all information being distributed about you. As you're well aware, usually you're much better off ***without a price tag on your head.***

Promises of Safety

True, many websites will promise you confidentiality. And many, perhaps even most, will keep their word. But once your resume becomes part of the vague, foggy environment I am describing, you have lost control. Surprises lie ahead.

Here are examples I've personally observed.
Note the wide range of players. Meet...

1 the Nervous EVP / COO
2. the Specialty Lady, and
3. the Business School Prince

Two of those three examples stemmed from the shared database thought to be serving over 200 contingency firms and independent headhunters. Note that, in each case, it took some sleuthing to discover a shared database as a source of the problem. And in the case of the specialty lady, I don't think she ever fully accepted the fact, which I knew from first-hand conversations with the decision maker, that a headhunter she'd given lots of business to over several years successfully squelched one of the best career opportunities she would ever get so relatively late in her career.

The Nervous EVP / COO

As a retained-executive recruiter I'd tried eight or so years earlier to recruit this individual to one of my clients. We'd kept in touch afterward. One day he called to invite me to lunch, wanting my opinion about a "headhunter problem" he was having. .

He was visibly on edge when we met. Did I have any idea why he was getting two or three calls a week from various contingency headhunters he'd never heard of. His and his boss's secretaries sat at adjoining desks. They answered and overheard each other's phone calls. Now, he was concerned that his boss, "who owns the company and is a paranoid loyalty freak," might suspect he was "shopping for another job."

I recognized some of the large contingency firms who had called. So, my advice was to cordially welcome the next caller, explain the time wasn't right for a move, offer to help, and say, "By the way, is your firm tied into the" (200 firm) "network, or how did you happen to get my name? Was it from" (the 200 firm database)?

Bingo! We hit with our first lucky guess. However, I understand it took several angry phone calls before my friend was finally able to get the resume removed from the network's database.

The Specialty Lady

A senior management resume sat in a multi-firm shared database for several years. Then a contingency recruiter used it (without permission) to submit a woman we'll call Specialty Lady for a position he knew was being filled by a retainer firm. The stored resume isn't the only reason for a sad outcome, but it contributed in a big way.

One of my long time clients was setting up a new products lab to take her company into a highly specialized product category.

She assigned me to find a VP-R&D to head the new lab. Simultaneously, she assigned the leading contingency recruiter specializing in the target field to find several product managers for the startup.

When I presented candidates for VP-R&D, the client already was familiar with my #1 recommendation (Specialty Lady). Reason: 24 hours earlier, my client had received a resume on Specialty Lady among the handful of Product Manager resumes submitted by Contingency Recruiter.

Obviously, CR planned to talk up Specialty Lady and try to get her hired into the top job, and earn a fee despite his having no legitimate standing to submit candidates for the VP position.

Well, it didn't work out that way.

I reported the situation to Specialty Lady, who had loyally hired Product Managers from Contingency Recruiter over the years and had paid him several fees. She was livid! "How dare you present me without my permission and without my knowledge?," she asked him. "And how did you get my resume? You didn't ask me for it!"

"It's the same one you used 4 years ago, when you were looking for your current gig. It's in a database a lot of firms contribute to, and we all use. I just updated it to show your current job."

Contingency Recruiter immediately shifted gears. Now he viciously tore down Specialty Lady to the decision maker (his and my client). Pointing to SL's chronic cough, CR convinced the decision maker that SL was in dire physical condition. But she wasn't! References who'd worked with SL for many years confirmed to me that "she's always had that cough, and yet she has boundless energy and enthusiasm for her job." SL even offered to submit medical records and take a physical.

All to no avail! Specialty Lady had the #1 best track record in her narrow field. Yet she lost the best opportunity she'll ever see in the late years of her outstanding career. To this day, I regret that I couldn't overcome the untruths told about SL by CR.

As I originally said, the stored resume wasn't solely responsible for the bad scenario. But it did enable Contingency Recruiter to enter the game, as he might not have been able to do otherwise.

Moral of the story? If possible, do not have your information lying around where it can be picked up by anyone who wants to use it.

The Business School Prince

For over 20 years, a small "mom-and-pop boutique recruiting concern enjoyed a fine national reputation for their 100%-retained executive search practice. They were "generalists," working in just about any industry at the highest executive levels. Based on their excellent reputation, I included them as "Rites-Honored Recruiters" in the very first (and every subsequent) edition of *Rites of Passage at $100,000 to $1Million+*.

They must have been making good money, because they sent their son to a top Ivy League university, followed by one of America's most celebrated business schools. After graduation, the young scion assumed his predestined role in the family business.

One of the B-school discussions our young prince clearly did not sleep through was "Monetize Your Assets," as the B-schoolers are wont to say. He saw an opportunity. The family business would continue to be 100% retainer compensated. But what to do with the many incoming unsolicited resumes that didn't happen to match any of the firm's current searches?

Let's "think out of the box," reasoned our young graduate. He signed up with the 200+ contingency firm database. The family company would maintain its retainer-only reputation by not doing any contingency searches. But whenever a job-hunting executive sent them an unsolicited resume (and some arrived daily), it would go into the fee-splitting contingency headhunter database.

I learned of this bizarre scheme when I was told by a RiteSite.com member that a resume he had intended to be seen only by "Rites-Honored Recruiters" had ended up in the hands of a contingency firm. This was a serious breech.

The member and I went into intensive "Sleuth Mode." In a couple hours we determined what had happened. Within five more minutes, the previously impeccable family boutique search firm was no longer Rites-Honored on RiteSite.com.

The rest of the world may still accord the firm the respect they earned over the years. But knowing we can no longer trust them, we do not.

We've looked at a few unexpected results of resumes existing outside of their owner's control.

What are the two main ways you're most likely to send your resume into widespread availability?

1. By submitting your resume in response to any *headhunter's* job posting you see on the web. If you must answer by providing your resume or filling out a detailed form, be forewarned that all of your information may go into one—or maybe several—databases that headhunters and employers can pay to look into.

These days, selling access to their database is often the #1 source of income for some of the well known job sites. Payment to post jobs used to be #1, but at many job boards it's now slipped to #2

EXCEPTION: True 100% retainer compensated search firms. They only do custom searches and never sell the ability to search their databases. You just saw what happened to the search firm of "Business School Prince." Scroll the list of fine firms on the "Who is Rites-Honored" page of RiteSite.com. It's the list from which "Prince's" family firm was dropped. There is no charge to check the list...and only a very modest one-time charge to use the site's full services, which include automatic emailing of your resume to your choices among the retained firms. No matter how many years you use RiteSite's full set of services you will never be charged a renewal fee. (More about RiteSite beginning on page 304.)

2. By submitting your resume in response to any *employer's* job posting on the employer's own website. These days, some companies—including several of the largest—have delegated management of their employment website to one or another of the largest commercial job sites.

Whenever that happens, incoming resumes are likely to go into the delegated site's main database just as if submitted there directly. I can't list for you which corporations today do and do not outsource management of their job openings database. But I can say with certainty that, if you knew, you'd be surprised. Shocked might be a better word! Chances are, employment sites you'd never intentionally provide your resume to may already be displaying it in their commercially available databases.

One other practical fact to bear in mind:
Some jobs you'll see posted do not exist.
They've been posted merely to suck in resumes for the firm's own—and for shared fee-splitting—databases.

Obviously, you'd better not bite on one of these baited hooks. Moreover, there's no sure way to recognize and avoid them. The best clue that I can suggest is one you've heard before in many other contexts:

"If it sounds too good to be true, it probably isn't true."

So why do I tell you all this?

Certainly I do NOT want to make you scared to venture forth into digital job hunting.

You want to go forward. You're willing to take ***some*** chances. You must live and work in the digital universe. But don't be reckless.

My only goal is to sensitize you to the fact that there's a lot going on under the surface. Activity you can't see. Factors you'd never normally think about.

In ***Rites of Passage***, I'm merely trying to alert you to hidden potential problems and opportunities. I'm arming you with a wider awareness—a sharpened intuition—and not a bunch of cookie cutter rules. You can't go on autopilot. Yet you must be prepared to take off.

But Wait!

Even though the web has become—in fact always has been—innately hazardous, it has also steadily become more helpful.

Now we'll turn to what I consider the #1 most exciting online development which has finally matured to the point that you can use it to help land your next executive position.

#2. And now onward to

my favorite increasingly helpful online phenomenon...

Meet the CONSOLIDATORS

For years several websites have worked to report the job postings that appear on any and all websites anywhere on the web. I like to call these sites the "Consolidators," because their goal is to gather together on their site a description of—and a link to—every posted job opening shown on the web.

That's a tall order. but now one of those ambitious competitors has come close enough to the goal to merit your attention.

Meet the WINNER INDEED.COM!

For years there was a wide open race. Then two sites moved to the front—Indeed.com and SimplyHired.com.

Now the issue is no longer in doubt. Indeed is the clear winner. Indeed may not be finding and cataloging all the job openings posted on the web. But it comes close enough for us to use them as our #1 defining example of the Consolidators.

From here onward, consider that every suggestion and comment applies to all the Consolidators, but most especially to Indeed.com.

Go to Indeed.com.

Poke around and look at the kind and the amount of information available to you.

If this is your first visit, I know what your reaction will be:

1. First, you'll think...

WOW! So many jobs!

2. And secondly...

WOW! Several are near my target location!

From there on, I believe you'll be hooked.

But this is, after all, the web.
Everything we've observed so far applies.

It's certainly nice that Indeed's software has been able to look in so many places for job openings, find them, and report them back to us. But are these jobs any different from the ones we'd have found at their original sites on the web if we'd taken the time and effort to look for them?

No. They're the very same, and every observation that we've made up to now about how to proceed applies to them.

Most importantly, the "Go Direct" principle still applies.

Every job you see will attract the usual excessive number of online applicants who follow instructions and click "Apply." Those job-seekers wind up lumped in with hundreds or even thousands of others also applying for the position. Do you want to join them? If not, then...

Do your homework.

Maybe the job was posted directly by the hiring company, which clearly identified who they are. Or the job may have been posted by a contingency headhunting firm that's gone out of its way to disguise the identity of the hiring company.

Either way, you won't merely comply with the instructions in the job description and dump your application onto the pile of hundreds or thousands of replies the web posting generates.

Instead, you'll send your on-paper POWERTOOL combo of resume-and-cover-letter by ordinary mail. You will NOT use FedEx or UPS, because (1) that looks too panicky and (2) it reveals you probably ***do*** know there's an advertised opening and you are just evading the proper bureaucratic procedure specified in the job posting.

Don't worry that, by using ordinary mail, you'll arrive too late to be considered. It takes at least a couple weeks (or should we say months) to fully process the replies generated by any web-posted job. You'll arrive in plenty of time. And most importantly, you will arrive on the decision maker's desk separately, and not in the irksome glut of too many applications.

Advantages of an On-Paper Ordinary Mail Response

1. You achieve the most attractive and persuasive presentation possible—far better than everyone in the heap of emails who followed instructions.

2. You get through to the decision maker. That's not likely to happen, if your submission has to be selected from among hundreds and even thousands.

The Illusion of Innocence

Please note that your letter begins, "Do you need...? Or, "Could I be helpful in your...? Your letter absolutely does NOT begin, "I see you're advertising for a..." Or even worse, "I've heard you need..."

The arrival of your POWERTOOL at just the right time must merely be a happy accident. It's not an in-your-face affront to the HR Department. You want them to ease your way into the company and to work closely and productively with you all the time you're there.

Guessing the Company and Decision Maker

1. Sometimes you won't have to guess. If the company is publicizing its own opening, they will usually describe themselves openly and accurately. Even so, you won't apply as instructed in the posting. Don't let the company's openness lull you to sleep. If you merely press "Apply," you've joined 600 or 1,000 others who've done the same thing. Is that what you want?

2. But sometimes you'll be up against a really shrewd contingency recruiter who has handed you a cipher. He/she has described the opportunity (1) accurately and temptingly enough to bring in qualified candidates and yet (2) vaguely and misleadingly enough to make it almost impossible for would-be candidates to "go direct" to the decision maker...and for other contingency recruiters to submit competing candidates.

Omissions and False Clues to Mislead You

When a contingency recruiter posts a job, here are some of the ways he/she tries to conceal the hiring company.

1. Omit specific location. No information. Could be anywhere.

2. Misstate location. Name the wrong suburb of the right city, or even name a different regional city.

3. Wrong product line. Name a different product manufactured by similar processes or sold by similar methods through the same channels.

4. Wrong size company. Why give you an accurate clue if it doesn't affect what you'll do to apply?

5. Imply a separate free-standing company, when the employer is actually a subsidiary of a multi-business giant (or the opposite).

Either way, you—and competing contingency recruiters—are thrown off-track by the way the job description is worded.

Just be aware that misinformation may have been inserted to defend against savvy job hunters and competitive headhunters.

Moreover, your sleuthing efforts may point you toward, say, four employers, not just one. If so, you'll check each and write to all. How ironic! Thanks to a shrewd contingency headhunter trying to throw you off-track, you're now approaching three additional potential employers you hadn't thought of before!

And finally, consider this important Moral Issue.

This is an issue I don't want you on the wrong side of.

Obviously, the headhunter who posts a job knows the identity of the hiring company and the decision maker. So do clerical members of his/her organization. In your sleuthing efforts you may feel tempted to call the headhunter's office, hoping to persuade a naive staff member to give up the name of—or clues about—the hiring organization. Don't do it!

After all, if you proceed knowledgeably, you are already in competition with the headhunter and already using information he/she has tossed into the public domain.

If you try to ferret out further information under false pretenses, you are behaving unethically...and possibly illegally too. I hope that offends your sense of fairness and, for that reason, you won't do it.

Countless times over the years, recruiters have complimented me on the people who read *Rites of Passage* and use RiteSite.com. They are informed, able and "a class act." Please, let's carry on.

As we've seen, Indeed.com does a great job of tracking jobs posted by contingency recruiters. Can we also use the web to help with retainer recruiters?

That's a different and much more complex issue. It's also one I have been working on for several years. To tell you about it, I must introduce you to...

RiteSite.com

Note that RiteSite.com is a modestly commercial service I provide at or below cost to help *Rites of Passage* readers identify and deal with always hard-to-reach Retainer Recruiters.

If you wish to avoid reading about this and another commercial service, skip to Page 309, where Chapter 15 Begins.

RiteSite costs only a one-time payment of $94 which, despite numerous enhancements, has never been raised since the site's introduction in 1994. Moreover, there is not—and never has been—any renewal fee. Today we have members who've been with us more than ten years, after only once paying $94.

Here are the main benefits, which all aim at helping you identify and interact with retainer recruiters:

1. Rigorous Identification To be listed as a Rites-Honored Recruiter on RiteSite.com, the search firm (ranging in size from world leader to respected boutique) must do all work paid on retainer...no contingency. Nearly every contingency recruiter will, if possible, try to get retainer assignments whenever they can. If that were good enough to qualify, there would be thousands of retainer recruiters on RiteSite.com.

Unfortunately, everything you know about contingency recruiters applies to firms that do part of their work on contingency and part on retainer. Those firms have no incentive to impose a strict retainer fee structure and operating method on themselves. Even the prominent Kennedy Information "Red Book" directory only requires a would-be "retainer" firm to state that it does "no more than 15%" of it's work on contingency. Merely making that statement is no safeguard to you as a job seeking executive. and it does not pass muster on RiteSite.

2. Automated Emailing of Your Resume to Your Choice of Retainer Search Firms. RiteSite lists nearly 600 Rites-Honored firms, all operating entirely "on retainer." You'll find some have specialties in fields that don't apply to you. Others you may already be working with and you don't want to duplicate that coverage. Omit those firms when you send. Overall, you'll save many hours of effort in making your basic distribution to retainer recruiters with the help of RiteSite.com. Some firms may respond by asking you to fill out a special form presented by their computer. This is valuable knowledge and you'll, of course, cooperate.

A very special benefit of this emailing service is that (1) emails ***appear to come directly from you,*** not from RiteSite, and (2) you totally ***avoid the limits on too many emails*** that your service vendor would otherwise impose on you.

3. Post Your Resume Where Only Retainer Recruiters Can See It. RiteSite has a resume database visible only to Rites-Honored Recruiters. When emailing your resume to recruiters, you have no control over whether the recipient does or does not put it in the firm's database...nor how long they keep it there. On RiteSite, you have exposure that's limited to a key segment (retainer recruiters), and you can insert, maintain, modify, or remove your resume at any time.

4. Post Your Identity-Concealed Resume Where Anyone Can See It. RiteSite has a separate resume database that can be searched by anyone who's interested. However, to contact you, the person must go through RiteSite's computer. You'll respond only if you're interested in what they propose. Contingency recruiters, employers, and others can reach you in this way. With rare good luck, you may even show up on a Google search.

Realize, however, that if you choose to post an ID-Concealed resume, it is entirely up to you to change the resume's wording to hide who you are. For example, you'll replace specific company names with a clear, brief description of what the company does.

5. Weekly *Memos from John*. I write these emails separately. They deal with career and job-hunting strategy, but are not drawn from *Rites of Passage*.

6. Weekly *Insights*. These emails contain tips for succeeding and moving up when you are already in or are entering a senior management position.

7. Concerned Customer Service. Attentive help on the phone from a member of our customer service team. We cannot do your work for you. But we will try to help if you have any difficulty using the various computerized aids on RiteSite.com.

As you see, a lot of effort has gone into programming and continually improving RiteSite.com. Take advantage of it!

Are There Other Sites Devoted Exclusively to Retainer Search Firms? Yes , There Is One...BlueSteps.com from AESC, the Global Trade Association of Retainer Firms

BlueSteps.com (nearly 300 U.S. retainer firms) costs a one-time basic fee of $329, plus partial annual renewal fees for "premium services." Ritesite (nearly 600 U.S. Retainer firms) costs a one-time fee of $94 (no renewal fee). Notice that the two sites have comparable core features, plus unique additional features, with very little overlap.

On the most important factor both sites are consistent. Both consider as "Retainer Firms" only those that profess to do 100% of their searches on retainer, For many years my own firm held the longest uninterrupted membership in the AESC. As you would expect, I recommend both RiteSite.com and BlueSteps.com for your consideration.

Quick help from RiteSite.com . . .

After our mop up in Chapter 15, you'll still have questions. Or someday you'll want a quick review on a topic. If you're a RiteSite. com member, go to** RITESITE UNIVERSITY (virtual, of course)**. Pushbuttons will flash you to what you want in concise "college notes."

Chapter 15

References, Newspaper Ads, Barbed Wire, Busy Signals, Trick-or-Treat Letters, Getting Personal, Franchises, & "The Hidden Job Market"

This chapter picks up loose ends.

We've got five remaining topics that require separate chapters. But now let's take a break, and cover a few matters that also merit discussion...but not a lot of it.

References

For most people most of the time, references are no problem.

Indeed, bosses, subordinates, and peers are your greatest source of career opportunity. Your current boss may promote you. Coworkers' comments may help move you ahead. And former associates may lead you to outside opportunities.

It's nice to be well spoken of. And I'll bet you are...almost all of the time, by almost everyone. But when you're being "referenced," you want to make doubly sure the right impression is given. Here are some suggestions:

Your first step in job-changing is to get in touch with your references.

Begin any job campaign by reaching out to your work-related personal contacts, past and present. Ask for a reference rather than a job, and achieve all the advantages we discussed in Chapter 3.

With a little effort you'll soon have plenty of pertinent people whose enthusiasm you've tested—and re-stimulated—either face-to-face, or by long-distance phone. Interviewing potential references advertises your availability. It also lets you know who's enthusiastic, and who's lukewarm.

Don't "wear out" your references.

Even though you know from the start precisely whom you want potential employers to talk to, do *not* accompany your resume with a list of references. Neither recruiters nor employers expect such information until you're about to get a job offer. And you're better off not providing it.

Your references feel most enthusiastic and least imposed upon the first time they're asked about you. If they have to respond several times, fatigue and boredom set in. Their answers become perfunctory. And after a while they begin to wonder why lots of people have investigated you, and nobody has hired you.

Whose names do you give?

Since you're being considered for employment, almost all of your references must be *work-related*. Moreover, your potential employer wants to know how good you are today...not how special you were a long time ago.

So if you're employed, you must open a window on your current reputation in your present company. And if you're "between jobs," you've got to show how you were regarded in the job you've just left. The number-one person your potential employer wants to talk to is your current boss, if you're employed. Or your most recent boss if you're not.

Normally, of course, you can't deliver your present boss as a reference on an outside job. And no one will expect you to. But do try to come up with two or three people whose confidentiality you can rely on, and who know first-hand how well you're doing *now*. Perhaps a trusted subordinate. Maybe a peer. Possibly the head of a department or function who works closely with you...and ideally, with your superiors and subordinates too.

Anyone discreet who's recently left your company is a good bet to maintain confidentiality. She doesn't care whether you leave or stay, and chances are she won't be in touch with the people who do. An outside supplier or customer who works closely with your organization is another possibility. He, too, observes your situation. He isn't quite as knowledgeable, but can be helpful nonetheless.

If you're employed you can, of course, refuse to allow contacting of anyone in your current company. But "stonewalling" will raise doubts. Every competent and commendable human being makes at least a few friends among the people he or she works with. If there's *nobody* you can trust, your potential employer will surely wonder why.

On the other hand, when you're out of work, there's no logical reason why your would-be employer can't talk to your most recent boss. So even if you parted on the worst of terms, you'd better prepare for the inevitable. Much as you'd like to, you probably can't substitute your favorite boss for your most recent one.

There's safety in numbers.

The more open and helpful you are in allowing yourself to be checked out, the stronger you look right from the start...even before a single person is contacted.

So when you're about to be hired and the time for serious referencing has finally arrived, either hand over, or volunteer to prepare, a comprehensive list. Say something like this:

> "When I'm hiring, I like to learn as much as possible about the person I'm considering. I'll put together a list of names and phone numbers, and you can call anyone you want to."

Then, taking the confident "my-life's-an-open-book" approach, supply a list that covers all of your recent jobs and includes a generous sampling of bosses, subordinates, peers, and maybe even customers and suppliers, if appropriate. Provide home as well as office phone numbers, if your references are willing to receive calls at home.

Since your list is fairly extensive, you can *edit*. You must include the person for whom you've done most of your most recent work, even if the parting was unfriendly and the evaluation is likely to be negative. Omitting him or her would sound a warning. But you can make sure that person's opinion is in context of others who will be objective.

Maybe, if you're lucky, the person you're worried about won't be called. Or won't be available. "Negative" references tend to avoid returning calls. Moreover, today most companies have policies restricting commentaries to nothing more than dates of employment. Potentially "negative" references tend to cite the policy and clam up, whereas "positive" references often ignore it and enthuse at length.

With a "safety-in-numbers" long list of references, even if the worst occurs... your nemesis is called *and* treats you unfairly...your potential employer has right at his or her fingertips the names and numbers of additional people who will balance the bad words with a far more fair and favorable account.

Consistency is the key.

When an employer or a recruiter talks to a reference, he wants to hear the same story he heard from you. Suppose you say:

> "I've always got along well with all my bosses, and Sharon was no exception."

But when Sharon's called about you, she says:

> "Frankly, the chemistry wasn't good, and the constant bickering got to be a drag after a while."

Now you've got a problem. Much better to have provided a safety-in-numbers list of references and *forewarned*:

> "I've always got along well with all my bosses, and all my co-workers too. Sharon was the only exception."

Don't go overboard anticipating problems and raising negatives that may not come up. Most people like to be gracious and upbeat when called as references. Indeed they're often fearful of being otherwise. Even the boss who just fired you will probably feel guilty and want you to find a new job quickly and to think and speak well of him in the future.

But don't fail to lay a little groundwork, if there's a negative you're *absolutely sure* is coming. Above all, referencing probes the consistency of your story. Are things really the way you presented them?

But suppose you were fired for cause. There *was* a problem. Then control damage by using the "reference statement."

If you've been fired and the pertinent people have good reason to take a dim view of you, then the outplacement firms urge you to move in quickly with a *reference statement*.

Within the first day or two after you're fired, they say you should draft a concise statement...no more than one page...stating your tenure and performance in terms as favorable as possible to your future employment. Present it to your former boss. Will he or she go along with it? If not, negotiate until you have a written statement you can both live with. Then line up two or three additional references who are pertinent and hopefully more favorable to you. Negotiate written statements they, too, can live with. And make sure a consistent theme links all versions.

These statements become the "party line" when anyone inquires about your departure...former co-workers, customers, suppliers, *and potential employers*. The actual written statement is never handed to anyone; it merely becomes the agreed-on script for conversations about you. Here's an example:

> "Dale Jones was with us eleven years, and rose from Plant Superintendent, to head of Quality Control, to chief of Plant Engineering, to Vice President of Manufacturing, his job for the past three years. As Vice President, he was responsible for three plants employing 1,800 people, and he reported directly to me as President. He left because he saw the company pursuing one course and we saw a different one, and he felt his career would be better fulfilled elsewhere."

That's not a terrific reference. But at least it leaves out the fact that your employers were scared to death that the bigoted and boorish behavior they continually warned you about would eventually provoke a law suit charging the company with discrimination and/or sexual harassment.

You can survive this reference and find another job. The main thing is to have a consistent and not *too* damaging story told by all three or four of your current-company references. If what we've just seen is what the person who fired you will say, and you've managed to line up some other observers who will be more expansive and generous, you'll probably do fine.

If you're in enough trouble to need a "reference statement"—and most people never are—the important tactic is to move quickly and take personal charge of the story that will be told about you. Don't wait passively until weeks later, when a prospective employer is about to phone your references. By then the situation will be out of control. The rumor mill will have filled the vacuum. And the word on you may be a lot worse than the consistent and only-slightly-negative story you could have negotiated earlier.

Frankly, as an experienced recruiter, I'd smell fish immediately, if I called even a couple references and got nothing beyond strategically brief, consistent remarks. But this *is* the prescribed method for damage control. I'd be very surprised—and disappointed—if you should ever need such a strategy. But if you do, at least you know the defensive steps to take.

What about purely personal references?

If some of your most admiring friends are also friends of your prospective employer, you may want to drop their names into your interviewing conversations. But don't list non-business acquaintances as business references.

And don't suggest your pastor, priest, or rabbi. He doesn't observe you in the office. Moreover, people who are truly moral or religious feel no compulsion to prove their virtue. And experience teaches us to suspect anyone who does.

Also, don't bring up that college or military friend you've kept in touch with for 25 years. He or she is not an on-the-job observer. Moreover, friendship has destroyed any objectivity.

Who else should I talk to?

Before we drop the subject of references, here's my best tip for checking someone *else's* references. After you finish talking to each person whose name you've been given, ask if there's anyone else who would also know about the person you're checking. Who would have an even closer vantage point on his or her work? Who might know his/her personality even better?

Unless you're on the phone with the person's direct boss for the past several years, you'll surely get additional names that are even more pertinent. If the candidate has already provided those same names, you know that she's open and self-confident. The unflinching relevance of her list is, in itself, an excellent reference.

If, on the other hand, the names you've been given are rather off-target, call them anyway, to compile a list of bull's-eyes. Don't phone the more-relevant people you've identified...especially if you've agreed not to go beyond a specific list. Instead, go back to the candidate and ask permission to contact the further people you've found. Now the whole story will spill out:

> "As a matter of fact, I *purposely* didn't list Herb and Paula because there was a situation I felt they might not be completely objective about."

There's your thread. Pull on it!

Should you reply to newspaper and web ads?

This is a more interesting question than it might seem at first glance. And the answer is:

It depends on who placed the ad.

If it's *signed by a corporate employer* attempting to fill its own opening, go right ahead. Employer-signed ads are always authentic. And the attractiveness of the opportunity often stems from the prestige of the company that's asking you to consider working for it.

But be careful if the ad is *signed by a recruiting firm*. Retainer firms almost never advertise. On the other hand, contingency firms always do. Indeed, advertising attractive jobs that may or may not exist is the main way they get new people for their database. If you're an entry-level or middle manager seeking a toehold, the contingency firms are very helpful. And these days, they may have surprisingly high-level listings. You will, however, be self-interestedly vigilant.

The recruiter-signed ad to really steer clear of is the one with *only a newspaper or post office box number* for replies. No address. No phone number. A relatively few corporate personnel departments sometimes place ads under phony names designed to look like executive recruiter partnerships, in newspapers and on employment websites. The purpose is "to find out what's available in the marketplace," without revealing that the company has openings. Answer one of these little beauties, and you may be communicating with your own employer. They're just one more reason why, if you're well beyond $100,000, you should approach newspaper ads and web postings with extreme caution, *unless they're straightforwardly signed by corporate employers, or by reputable recruiting firms that include their address and/or phone number*.

What to submit in response to a *straightforwardly signed* ad is easy. Use your POWERTOOL resume-and-cover letter combo... the same thing you'd use for a direct mail campaign or after posting yourself online. But *who* you send it to may be a different story...

In answering newspaper and web ads, never do as you're told!

When Mega-Merger Corp. advertises that they are looking for an executive to take charge of their XYZ function, that's a solid gold job lead.

Found gold, as a matter of fact, because the nugget is right out in plain sight. You don't have to network for it, or cultivate recruiters, or mail letters. Just open the paper...or click a button!

However, if you're going to be successful in pursuing the opportunity, you'd better *not* bend over as instructed in the ad. Do *not* send "a complete resume and salary history" to "Box 2996" or to the "Corporate Director of Recruitment and Staffing."

Instead, find out where the job is and who it reports to. Suppose it's Director of Laser Engineering. By networking and phoning directly into Mega-Merger, you can readily determine that all of their laser development activity is handled in their West Coast R&D lab in Sunnyvale, California, which is headed by Shirley Steele, VP - Electronic Technologies.

Now your task is simple. Is there anyone who knows both you and your professional abilities *and* Shirley Steele well enough to introduce you? If so, great!

If not, merely address your standard mailing to Ms. Steele, and bypass the entire screening procedure in the HR Department. Now they get no chance to decide you don't meet specifications...and, even if they think you're right-on-target, to shuffle your papers into a big stack of "qualified applicants."

You've reached the decision-maker days and perhaps weeks ahead of the deluge through proper channels. If you're excellent, as demonstrated by a "sales representative" resume, yours will be the achievements that later arrivals are measured against. Maybe you'll even be met and hired before the responses to the advertisement have been culled and forwarded.

"But," you ask, "don't I risk offending the HR Department by going over their heads?"

Not if you don't refer to the ad in your letter. And of course, you'll never *volunteer* that you've seen it. Let it be a happy accident that what you appear to be sending to ***all*** the likeliest companies happened to hit Shirley Steele at just the right moment.

A Case that Proves the Point

I give lots of speeches and seminars. And during Q&As at one of them, a young woman told us:

> "You're right! That's how I got the job I have now. For weeks, I answered ads, including the blind ones. And, of course, I networked my head off, and I also waged a direct mail campaign.
>
> "My current boss called me up right after he got my mailing—he was desperate to find somebody—and we had a great interview. At the end of it, he hired me. And then he showed me a huge blind ad the Personnel Department had been running. Hadn't I seen it? And if so, why didn't I answer?
>
> "Seen it! I'd answered weeks before, with exactly what I mailed him. So he grabbed the phone and called Personnel. Why hadn't they sent him my reply?
>
> "They *hadn't wanted to bother him*. He was insisting on an MBA, and I didn't have one. I had a PhD!
>
> "Incidentally," she added, "my resume clearly showed that, besides heading market research for a competitive company, I was also an Adjunct Professor in a Business School."

Sound familiar? Whether the position is advertised or "headhunted," the winning strategy is usually to go straight to the decision maker.

Bending the Barbed Wire to Get Beyond What's Published

Suppose you know that a company is looking for someone like you. Perhaps they're running an ad. Or you've heard on TV that they've won a major contract, or taken over a poorly managed company, or announced an expansion into your area of the country.

Whatever. You know they might have a new position you could fill. But where would that position be? Who would it report to? And how do you find out?

Let's retrace your steps through the corporate barbed wire to Shirley Steele, VP-Electronic Technologies, in Sunnyvale, California. You reached her with no map beyond an ad for a Director of Laser Engineering signed by "Mega-Merger Corp., P.O. Box 2996, Rye, New York, 10914, an equal-opportunity employer."

First, you got on the web and found Mega-Merger's corporate site. It described the various businesses they own and indicated the headquarters address of each. There were at least four divisions at various locations that could require "Advanced Laser Engineering." The site also had pictures and personal profiles of its top officers, including the corporation's Senior VP-Research & Development, Selwyn Circuit.

When you called headquarters you were told Dr. Circuit is at a 201 area code number in New Jersey. But when you asked his administrative assistant whether laser engineering is handled corporately or divisionally, at what location, and who it reports to, you were asked why you wanted to know:

> "I'm writing a letter and want to direct it to the proper person."

You gave the right answer. It was truthful and should have elicited the information, if the assistant were inclined or permitted to cooperate. Unfortunately he said:

> "I'm sorry, but we don't give out that information on the telephone. If your letter concerns employment, I can give you the name of the Director of Recruitment. If you're selling something, I can refer you to our Purchasing Director. And if it's anything else, just send your letter to Dr. Circuit and he or I will direct it to the proper person."

Stonewalled! Here's a senior executive's assistant who does his job. Fortunately, however, the citadel has less alert sentries. Here are seven techniques, any of which might have led you from Dr. Circuit to Ms. Steele:

1. Call again. Try at lunch time, when a pinch hitter who doesn't know Dr. Circuit's "Don'ts" but does know the organization may help you.

2. Call the switchboard. Phone company information (or Google) will yield your target company's number in the location you're probing. Ask the switchboard operator for "someone a bit lower than Dr. Circuit, but in his area." Let the operator select a person who's also inside the barbed wire, but whose assistant may be more forthcoming.

3. Call unrelated departments. Phone and ask for the #2 or #3 people in other areas (assistants to #1 might be as guarded as Dr. Circuit's was). Try Accounting, Manufacturing, Quality Control, the Computer Center (often a font of organizational information), Marketing, PR, etc. Explain to the answerer that you've obviously reached the wrong person, but could they refer you to someone at such-and-such level in the target department. Chances are, they will.

4. Call sister subsidiaries. To identify your person in Subsidiary X, call Subsidiary Y. Choose one with related products, markets, suppliers, etc. The person you reach will probably know and name his counterpart.

5. Call "Customer Service." Don't ask for the people who deal with the public. Get to the ones who expedite orders for major customers. They usually know who does what to whom and cheerfully share their knowledge.

6. Call the working people. To find a biggie in headquarters marketing or sales, ask a product manager. Or the Assistant West Coast Sales Manager 1000 miles from headquarters. Or call a Plant Manager to find out the hierarchy in Manufacturing.

7. Call after hours. If all else fails, call one, two, and three hours after quitting time. Use the same numbers that yielded no cooperation during the day. Less wary workaholics may pick up at night. Also try the switchboard. Probably you'll get a recording. But if you're lucky, you may reach a night receptionist or even a watchman, who'll dial several numbers "up there" trying to find one that will *answer*.

Trick-or-Treat Letters... the Direct Mail You Can Do Without

I wouldn't use our limited time together to discuss these odd concepts, if it weren't for the fact that successful books have been written about them, and they're always handicapping a considerable number of people. Hence, this digression.

The "Tease-'Em-and-Spoof-'Em" Method ...a Short Letter, and No Resume Until Later

This direct mail technique was the subject of a very successful book about executive job hunting that flourished in the '60s and early '70s, then went out of print for many years, and now has been reintroduced...helped along by a strong plug in a popular lower level job-hunting book.

What it says, basically, is:

1. Send out a very brief letter that makes *one or two exciting claims*, which will surely get you an interview. *Do not enclose a resume.*

2. Go to your interview. *Do not bring a resume.* Find out what sort of person and what background the employer wants.

3. Go home and *write a special resume* proving you have exactly the right stuff. Mail it with your "thank you" note.

4. Enjoy your new job, for which only you—among all the people the employer has seen and talked to—seem pre-eminently qualified.

This method has a nice clear logic to it. If you accept *three* very doubtful premises, then the scenario will unfold exactly as promised. Otherwise, maybe you should forget this ploy. Let's consider each assumption separately.

Premise #1:

> That anyone less famous and currently admired than, for example, Warren Buffet, who included *no claim whatsoever* in the hypothetical note that we saw earlier, can create a short letter with *one or two claims so compelling that he or she will be granted an interview* on the strength of it.

You've undoubtedly received one- or two-claim "teaser" letters from people trying this method. And, like me, you probably questioned their sanity or at least their business sophistication. This will refresh your memory:

Dear ________:

As Director of Marketing, I increased sales 30% per year during each of the past three years.

If that's the kind of performance you'd like to see in one of your divisions, perhaps we should meet.

Sincerely,

Sidney Surface

Maybe this guy did a terrific job...and maybe he did a rotten one...we can't tell. However, since he's obviously looking for work, we suspect it was the latter and not the former. How fast were sales of competitive products in his market rising...50% or 200% per year? What happened to profits? Did they plummet as he hyped sales with too-rich deals; filled the pipeline with unsuccessful new products now being returned for credit; and failed to weed unprofitable low-volume items from the line which, streamlined by his successor, is now highly profitable and poised for solid growth?

The fact that this guy obviously thought we'd be jumping up and down to meet him after reading his "teaser" letter confirms that either he thinks in a very unsophisticated manner, or he figures we do. Too bad. Heads...he loses. Tails...he loses.

Premise #2:

> That anyone can go through an interview with either you or me and not have us make her say what she's done in her career so far...even if she does claim not to have a resume, or to have left it home.

Maybe she can keep us talking and answering her questions during most of the interview, and thereby keep us from figuring her out while she's in our office...although I doubt it.

But afterward, will our impression be so favorable that we'll eagerly await her resume—whether e-mailed or snail mailed—proving she's exactly what we're looking for? Of course, maybe she'll have been so wonderfully glib that we're left with an oral preview of her "perfect-for-us" resume. If so, and we don't hire her, she'll probably land a starring role in the Second City improvisational theatre group.

Premise #3:

> That it's fundamentally possible, even after hearing what we want, for anyone to write a "custom" resume proving they have what we seek, when a more straightforward version would have revealed they don't.

Here we have the fatal flaw of every "withhold-your-resume-so-you-can-doctor-it" scheme. This concept doesn't have to be tied to a "teaser" letter mailing, just because a widely read book links these two ideas. If it worked, the same thing could be done in every interview, regardless of how the interview is obtained. Unfortunately, it doesn't work.

Frankly, my advice is to check out a great many potential employers until you find one...or hopefully a choice among several...where you're right for the job and the job is right for you. Then your straightforward "sales representative" resume will be your ideal aid in getting the job.

You'll be a lot better off trying to *find a fit* than, through distortion and misrepresentation, trying to *fit a find*.

The "Spoof-'Em-Only Method" ...a Long Letter and Never a Resume

Here's another deviant form of direct mail, which you've undoubtedly received and may even have considered sending. This one omits the "tease-'em" lead-in and skips all the way to the "spoof-'em" ending. The trick here is to avoid having a resume altogether, by writing a long letter, which will say just what you want to about your career...*and no more*.

Like the topically organized resume, this long letter lets you escape from the revealing contours of a chronological work history, so you can spotlight whatever you wish, and leave out whatever you want to conceal. Indeed, because it isn't labeled "Resume" at all, you're not even obliged to make a bow in the direction of chronology somewhere near the end, as most people feel they must in a topically organized resume.

If you're really desperate to bury your work history...which includes short jobs, bad references, and maybe a jail sentence...this is undoubtedly the best way to do it. Your reader will surely hanker for a revealing straightforward resume, and will presume that there must be a good reason why you've gone out of your way not to provide one. Nonetheless, you may get a long way into your "sale" before the demand for a specific chronology of prior employment comes up...especially if you send the long letter prior to your interview and handle yourself very smoothly during your visit.

An astute employer should very pointedly ask for your resume during the interview and...failing to get it...should ask you to take home and fill out one of those "Application for Employment" forms normally required only from lower-echelon people, which will smoke out your chronology. But if she doesn't, "Caveat emptor," as they say. "Let the buyer beware."

But now let's assume you have nothing to hide. Let's look at the long letter as a communication device, in comparison to a brief covering note and a "sales representative" resume. There's no contest. The two-, three-, or four-page-long letter lacks the crisp introduction a brief covering letter provides, and is *not* scannable the way a traditionally blocked-out resume would be. Because the long letter lacks visual organization and isn't broken up into familiar segments, it's more bothersome to the reader. It's less inviting to enter, harder to plow through, and raises naggingly negative presumptions as well. If you don't need it, don't use it.

"Personal and Confidential"

Puh-leeeez!

Don't put "Personal and Confidential" on any envelope you mail to a stranger when you're job-hunting. People often try to attract attention that way, and it's always a dumb idea. (On the other hand, "Personal and Confidential" on your blackmail and extortion notes may be appreciated.)

If there's anything an assistant is trusted to do, it's open the mail. So, regardless of how your envelope is marked, it will be handled in the usual way. That's what happens in *your* office, isn't it? Attempting to bypass an assistant with such a warning just makes you look naive, even silly. And that's *not* what you had in mind.

There's only one way to get your mailing looked at when others are not. Make it more impressive. Write a shorter, clearer, more elegant cover note. Enclose a very succinctly worded, yet logical and factually persuasive, resume. And don't let whatever you send merely be the 50th of a common thing and no better than the 49 that preceded it.

Signing Letters

Remember when you and the other kids used to write your signatures every which way, trying to make them impressive? Girls dotted *i*'s with circles. Boys swooped up to cross *t*'s. Swiss bankers, I'm told, are *required* to have an illegible signature. U.S. physicians too?

How you sign does make a difference.

Surely there's no harm in a confident, legible signature. (In Europe handwriting is often analyzed; here it's not.) But even more important than *how* you write is *what* you write. And judging by the mail I get, at least a third of all executives give no thought to the impression their signature makes.

They write, hoping for a friendly reaction...ideally a phone call. Indeed, they may even imply friendship or at least warmth by starting out,"Dear John." But look at their signature! It's "Wendleton P. Wellington III." Or "W. P. Wellington." Or "WPW." And maybe even with their secretary's initials added, to further stress that the reader is utterly insignificant.

Maybe these folks are not as arrogant as they appear. But it's obvious who they think is the lesser party in an as-yet-unformed relationship. Is that because I'm a headhunter? No, they probably write to CEOs the same way.

Please don't make their mistake. You're too nice a person to behave like that.

The One Best Way to Sign

Here's a simple rule for signing job-hunting letters to strangers: Sign informally, using the first name you'd like the recipient to call you.

If you sign Richard P. Smith, how can anyone know whether you go by Richard, Dick, Rich, Richie, Rick, RP, Bud, or Pete? Same with Katherine, Kathy, Kate, or Kay. Signing your preferred conversational name lets your reader become friendly and informal at the slightest impulse. And isn't that what you want?

But go back up to the top of the letter. What about the salutation when you write a stranger? This is strictly "feel" and judgment, and yours is as good as mine. But I veer toward caution. I hesitate to use a stranger's conversational name, even if I know it. Many folks aren't offended. I'm not. You're probably not. But what's the harm in extending a respectful Ms. or Mr. at the top of the letter, and then signing an unpretentious and friendly Jim Jones or Shirley Smith at the bottom?

There's No Harm in Asking

When you're phoning to check name-spellings, title, address, etc., there's absolutely no harm in asking what the person likes to be called:

> "Does she prefer Suzannah, or Sue, or what *does* she prefer?"
>
> "I notice his name is William. Does he go by Bill or Will, or something else?"
>
> The answer you get may surprise you.
>
> "He's the finest dearest person you can imagine, and we all love him. But he's from the old school. People who don't know better will sometimes call him Bill. He's so polite, he just doesn't say a word. But inside you know he's seething. Nobody here ever calls him anything but Mr. Kennedy...to his face or behind his back."

Now you know something important that others will not know.

Try To Get Up Close and Personal

...as Soon as You Can, but *Not Too Soon*

Your objective every time you reach out to a potentially helpful stranger is to establish communication, congeniality, respect, trust...perhaps even a relationship as customer, mentor, employer, friend.

But be careful. Don't go too fast. Everyone is surrounded by zones of privacy...their own space, ringed by invisible barriers at inner distances known only to them.

As they gradually accept you, they drop one barrier after another, *inviting* you each time to come a bit closer. Unfortunately they relax—and stiffen—those barriers *subconsciously*. And even more unfortunately, they expect (again subconsciously) that you'll recognize each new freedom to come closer without offending. *And if you don't proceed, you seem like a wimp!*

But beware. There's another barrier right inside the one that just went down. If you barge through the next one prematurely, *you're an insensitive, pushy boor!*

Become a wimp *or* a boor, and your progress with this person—potential customer, mentor, employer, friend—is set back, maybe ended. I'd love to write a whole book about that. But for now, these tips:

Get on a First Name Basis Right Away

Be alert. Go "first name" as soon as you politely can. Suppose you're entering Mr. or Ms. Big's office. He or she is very prominent and powerful...and perhaps the key to a major new job or customer relationship. With warm handshake and sparkling eye-contact, the Great One says:

"Hi, Bill, I'm delighted to meet you. Sit down."

Surprise! You expected formality, standoffishness. You expected you'd always have to call him *Mr*. Big. Instead, here's your chance to go right onto a first-name basis. Seize it:

"Thank you. I'm delighted to meet you, Mr. Big; may I call you Ken?"

If he hadn't been so spontaneous and warm, you couldn't have done this. But at this moment, it's hard for him *not* to grant you first-name permission, after so buoyantly using *your* first name. Awkwardness and ambiguity are ended. To you he's "Ken," today and forever.

Notice how much weaker your position becomes with the passage of time. Suppose Mr. Big *never again* uses your first name during the entire meeting. Now try to look him in the eyes and ask, "May I call you Ken?" How pushy...and even weird!

Suppose on the other hand that he goes on to use your first name several more times, and you continue calling him "Mr. Big." Your subservient role becomes etched in stone. Now you can only hope he'll voluntarily pull you up off your knees, saying "Please, call me Ken." Will he?

Suppose instead that he keeps using your name, and you self-consciously avoid calling him anything. *Now* you pipe up and ask for equality. It'd be a devastating put-down to refuse, and Big's not a sadist. But surely he'll think, "What a Milktoast! I never gave any indication that he couldn't treat me as an equal, and *now* he asks permission. I doubt he's got the guts to take over that division."

Who Are You Dealing With?

Mr. Big was a convenient example, because he's clearly more powerful and prestigious than you are. But don't get me wrong. Just because someone has the power to hire you or to sponsor your progress does *not* mean you must ask permission to use his or her first name.

With someone anywhere nearly equivalent to you, use their nickname without asking. Indeed, you'll look like a wimp if you don't. On the other hand, if you want to do a subtly flattering and respectful genuflect, just leave out the preliminary "Mr." or "Ms." and still ask permission:

"I'm very pleased to meet you; may I call you Ellen?"

First-Naming on the Phone

Never is it easier...nor more important...to get onto a first-name basis than when your initial conversation with a stranger occurs on the phone.

Why? Because, there'll be follow-up. Whether it's your new-business proposal or a letter-and-resume, chances are you'll be sending an e-mail or a snail mail almost as soon as you hang up. Handle yourself right, and your letter begins, "Dear Lisa" or "Dear Adam." Fumble, and you wind up feeling and looking far less confident as you write to "Ms." or "Mr."

Actually, first-naming is easy over the phone. If there's no need to be deferential, you just start using the person's preferred name if you know it, and inquire if you don't. If that feels awkward, you'll get another chance when you wind up the call and offer to mail something:

> "Now, your address is"...(get it or confirm it). "And may I call you Fred...or what do you prefer?"...(ANSWER). "Thanks, Fred, I'll get that to you by overnight mail."

Find Out and Remember Names...and More

Before you head off to any important business or social event...and especially to any series of job interviews...always find out and commit to memory the names and backgrounds of the key participants.

Names, above all, you must nail down. Personally I'm no good at those "have-an-amazing-memory" courses that tell you to sear the letters of "George" into your brain by picturing a ***G***iraffe ***E***ating an ***OR***an***GE***. But whatever works for you, do it. Nothing else so simple is so pleasing to people as knowing their names.

But Please Don't OD on First-Naming

Have you had formal sales training? If so, you're in danger of becoming one of the many people who've overdosed on the instructor's exhortation to repeatedly say the other person's first name. That gambit is now so common—and so obviously phony—that it's deeply offensive to almost everyone. You know the script:

> "Well, John, that's another achievement I'm very proud of. You see, John, folks have always told me that I have great people skills. And beyond that, John, I was fortunate enough to have been sent to this sales training course—you know the type, John—the kind that not only makes you a great persuader, John, but also a truly wonderful warm, caring person. And that, John, is another reason I've been so successful."

Ugh! Bring in the next candidate, *please!*

Hang Up "Sir" & "Ma'am" with Your Uniform

Here's some advice I've had to give again and again to men and women who've spent a long while in military service...or who grew up attending one of those superb military prep schools. Please, PLEASE, *PLEASE* stop calling people Sir and Ma'am. Affirming with every utterance that "you're-above-me" is not necessary in the outside world. Until you break that ingrained habit, you'll never be accepted at the executive level in business.

Turn Off Your Cell Phone!

This urgent reminder comes from the proprietor of a prestigious boutique retainer search firm that's "Rites-Honored" on Ritesite.com.

What could be more irritating—and even down right insulting—to a recruiter you want to impress favorably than to interrupt your interview to answer a phone call. Or even just to render a not-as-cute-as-you-think version of *The Yellow Rose of Texas* as a ring tone.

Is the recruiter's time and expertise unworthy of your courteous fully engaged attention? Can you possibly be as arrogant and insensitive as this most prevalent of all interviewing blunders will make you appear?

No! We both know you're not.

Should you consider buying a franchise?

Here's an idea that many outplacement firms will bring to your attention by holding franchise fairs, inviting in franchise salespeople, and distributing sales brochures for franchises.

Frankly, I'm not keen on that tactic. There's nothing inherently wrong in telling you franchises exist, or in suggesting you think about buying one. But is that helping you find a job? Is that what your employer paid to have done for you? How is that better than the newspaper ads the franchisers are always running to lure you to the same spiel they'll give you in the outplacement office? As one national sales manager told me:

> "Whenever we get into an outplacement office full of panicky unemployed executives with severance money in their pockets, it's like shooting fish in a barrel."

Of course. Far easier than corralling and pressuring the idly curious who stroll the franchise fair at the Coliseum on Sunday afternoon.

Maybe a franchise is life's perfect fulfillment for you. Maybe. But please, always be careful with your life's savings. And especially when you're uniquely vulnerable...out of work and bracketed between an outplacer emptying an office and a salesperson filling a quota.

Here are two rules for when folks yell, "Invest in yourself!" and then suggest franchises:

> 1. *Don't risk your savings* when you're unemployed, on something you wouldn't even look at if you had a good job.
>
> 2. *Do work at least one week* in a unit of the franchise without anyone knowing you might be a purchaser. Put on old clothes... drive 200 miles...stay in a motel...do anything necessary...to wiggle your way into a $9.90 an hour job behind the counter or desk of the very same outfit you're about to risk your savings and sanity on.

In at least one local office of one national outplacement firm, about one third of the executives who "found their jobs" during a recent year bought franchises. That is *not* a statistic to be proud of. Nor is the follow-up survey, which revealed that two years after buying their franchises, two-thirds of all the outplaced purchasers were unhappy with their businesses, or had gone belly-up, or had unloaded them (usually at severe losses).

"The Hidden Job Market"

This is a book of plain talk.

I can't close this miscellaneous chapter without mentioning a term you'll often hear in the context of executive job-hunting. It's often used by various people—some of them quite unscrupulous—to mean different things.

The most prevalent and legitimate meaning is the shadowy world of job openings not yet referred to recruiters or advertised in newspapers or on the web. However, some users expand the expression to include jobs-that-aren't-jobs-yet...situations where there's nagging dissatisfaction with the incumbent, but not yet a firm decision to fire. Also, where a need to add a new position is felt, but not yet formalized as an empty box on the organization chart.

Obviously, it's a good idea to discover such situations before others have beaten a path to them. And as long as "The Hidden Job Market" is merely a sexy way of saying "go-straight-to-the-employer-and-quickly" through direct mail and networking, it's certainly a valid concept, even if overly hyped.

The problem comes when "executive-marketing" companies try to extract big money from you or your employer because they propose to "Introduce You to the Hidden Job Market." The clear implication is that there's an undisclosed supply of real jobs which they know about and you don't. And you'll never find those jobs unless they tell you. And they won't tell you unless they're paid a stiff fee.

After all that build-up, "The Hidden Job Market," being such a little idea with such a big bold name, becomes deceptive...or at least very disappointing. You feel "ripped off," when your "introduction" inevitably turns out to be nothing more than a description of networking and direct mail techniques.

So watch out. Hang onto your wallet whenever this term is mentioned!

Chapter 16

The Interview... Making a Sales Call and Demonstrating the Product

Face it. When you go to an interview, a purchase decision is being made. The employer is seeing you and others to determine who she'll acquire and who she won't.

Chances are she's read your resume, which you or a recruiter sent her. Now a salesman is coming over with the actual product. Get ready. She won't just look at the paint job and kick the tires. She'll take a test drive!

You're the salesman. And you're also the product.

Moreover, because it's an interview...not just a social call...your host has permission to probe deeply. She can ask tougher and more personal questions than she'd ask at any other time. And she can examine your

analysis and strategy in solving business problems...yours and hers...far more frankly than she would under any other circumstances.

You've got to be prepared for a really penetrating inquiry, if your interviewer takes that approach. If she doesn't, you've got to reveal yourself to her. And if the interview fails to display your merits, that's your problem, not hers.

Ideally, your potential employer will wind up wanting to buy the car... or at least to drive it again, after she's seen and tried some others. If so, you'll be offered the job...or at least invited back for another round of interviews.

In the end, you may decide that this employer and her opportunity are not for you. But what you and I will work on in this chapter is making sure that she doesn't conclude you're not for her.

Bear in mind that you're proving yourself on two levels:

1. **as a fine person, and**
2. **as someone obviously able to do the job.**

Your behavior and appearance will be scrutinized far more critically when you show up for an interview than on any ordinary work day in the next ten years.

The person who's thinking of hiring you wants to be sure that you're someone he'll enjoy working with. And also someone who can walk around inside and outside the organization as a favorable reflection on the company and on him. Only if he's satisfied on these "***fine person***" points, will he concern himself with whether he thinks you can handle the job, as indicated by your experience and track record. He's hoping to find you:

Intelligent, and also "street smart," with abundant common sense;

Analytical, logical, goal-oriented, and a planner;

A skilled communicator...good at listening, speaking, and writing;

Unmistakably a leader...but also a "team player," cooperative, and congenial;

Healthful, attractive, and well-groomed;

Tasteful in dress and decorum;

Poised, courteous, and cultured;

Sensitive to the feelings of others...not pushy, pigheaded, or obnoxious;

Honest, loyal, and straightforward;

Politically aware, but not a political operator;

Committed, responsible, and diligent;

Cheerful and optimistic, with a "can-do" attitude;

And overall, an *interesting person*, with curiosity, enthusiasm...and maybe even a sense of humor!

Virtually all of the attributes listed above will help you to do the job, once you land it. But in interviewing to get the job, don't underestimate the seemingly superficial aspects that are more "image" than "essence." Appearance and behavior are first to be noticed. And if they're deficient, you may flunk the "***fine person***" test, even though you score plenty of "but-he-could-probably-do-the-job" points.

Interviewing is a time of maximum scrutiny. Make sure you arrive feeling and looking your very best. Get a good night's sleep. Have a fresh haircut or hairdo. Get your shoes shined. Tend to your grooming in every way. Don't wear a noticeable amount of fragrance. Dress as you would for any other daytime matter that you take very seriously. Even if you've heard from the grapevine that you're arriving on a "casual Friday," wear your first-class business attire. That is, of course, unless you've been specifically instructed otherwise by the person who invited you.

So much for "good-impression." You've been making one or we wouldn't be discussing a $100,000+ or $400,000+ interview. The bottom line is that you'll never get "points taken off" because you show respect for someone by polishing your appearance to meet him or her. Any danger that you'll be perceived as a "stuffed shirt" (or blouse), if that worries you, is easily dispelled by a warm, open, unpretentious manner...which I hope you always have anyway.

So let's forget "image" and go straight to "essence." You're about to make a sales call. And, like any other salesperson, you've got to deliver *enough persuasive information to convince the prospect that your product can* ***do the job***.

Interviewing is a difficult form of selling for two reasons:

1. **It's a "package deal," where the salesperson comes with the product; and**
2. **The customer, not the salesperson, controls the unfolding of the sales presentation.**

Ordinarily a customer can take the product...and leave the salesperson. Unfortunately, you're a "package deal." Therefore you must sell with great finesse. Much as you'd like to, you can't just make a well-organized presentation and afterward deal with questions and objections.

The interview is a unique ritual drama, in which a sales call is played as if it's a social call.

Which it's not. One of the two parties is totally in command. He's the buyer. He's the decision-maker at the end. And he's in charge all along the way. By controlling the use of time and the choice of topic in a Q-and-A format, he determines which features are brought up, and in what order, and how thoroughly or superficially each one is discussed.

And the fact that *your* sociability is part of what's being sold prevents you from saying what a regular salesperson would say:

> "That's a very good question. But *let's hold it* until I've finished explaining how the machine works."

> "No, that's really not a problem with this machine. *Ours is the only one* which doesn't have that disadvantage."

Politeness, modesty, loyalty, confidentiality. You must display these and many other attributes, because you're "the product." Unfortunately, having to do so handicaps your sales presentation.

The first principle of interview salesmanship: forgo the monologue ...at the outset, and all the way to the end.

Because the format of the interview is ritualistically conversational, you can't give a too-long answer to any question. You can't sell yourself as socially-polished, if you monopolize the conversation.

So don't use any question...no matter how broad...as a springboard for a monologue. Instead, give a concise answer that hits the highlights in clear and specific terms, including numbers ("a little under $15 million in sales and about 150 employees") and approximate dates ("as I recall, that was in late '98").

Don't ever talk longer than one or two minutes. Finished or not, wind up your sentence, shut your mouth, and look at your interviewer to see if she wants more on the same topic...or would rather switch to something else. If she wants elaboration, she'll say so. What's more, she'll point you in the right direction:

> "Interesting, and I certainly agree with your strategy. But when we tried something along those lines, we ran into trouble with the unions. How'd you make out on that score?"

Now you've got her eating out of your hand! How much better than if you'd bored her with a full explanation before "coming up for air."

Learn "newspaper style." Written and oral, it will make you an outstanding communicator.

...And it's a lifesaver in the interview format.

Do me a favor. Next time you pick up a newspaper, notice the way every item is written:

1. The headline sums up the article.

2. The first paragraph lays out the entire story.

3. The first sentence of every paragraph tells what the whole paragraph is about.

4. And the major facts of every story always come earliest. Lesser, more detailed points come later, and the most trivial are at the end.

There's good reason for this "big-picture"-first format. It allows you, the reader, to get what you want out of the paper very quickly and efficiently. You can stop reading any article after a paragraph or two and still know the gist of the story. And when an article really interests you, you can dig deeper and deeper into the details, by reading further.

See the analogy to what you're trying to achieve in an interview? Just like you reading the paper, your interviewer always has the prerogative to dig deeper, or switch to a different topic. You can drop any article after just a headline or a paragraph. And he can divert you to a different subject, just by asking another question.

Therefore, all of your answers must be organized in "newspaper style." You've got to state your main point in the first sentence or two of each answer. You can't wallow in detail, "setting the stage" for your main point. Because if you do, a new question may cut you off before you *get* to your main point. Then you'll appear petty, illogical, and detail-oriented...even if you're not.

Surprisingly few people—even senior executives—have learned what their newspapers show them every day. Study and master newspaper style. Use it orally and in writing. Every bit of your business communication will improve...not just interviews, but memos and presentations, too.

Just because you can't deliver a salesman's monologue is no reason not to prepare one.

Analyze your product and your customer's needs, and develop the sales message you *wish* you could deliver in a 15-minute monologue.

Then divide it into brief topical capsules. Believe it or not, almost every interviewer... no matter how inept...will ask questions that allow you to present everything you have clearly in mind.

That's right. The questions you receive *will* relate to what you want to say, if you *know* what you want to say. That's because your interviewer really does want to find out how your background and achievements fit his needs, and how they guarantee you'll perform as well for him as you have for others.

Fundamentally, he wants to hear what you want to communicate. Not necessarily, however, in the order you'd like to present it. And, of course, with more attention devoted to your failures and gaps in background than you'd prefer.

So prepare as if you could deliver a salesperson's monologue. If you've figured out what you should present, then you'll hear it asked for. And when each "appropriate" query comes along, you can drop in the right one- or two-minute capsule. Unprepared, you'd have found those same questions "irrelevant," and "not leading anywhere." But knowing where the conversation *should* be going, you'll more readily see the interviewer's questions as a path to get there.

How often have you been asked a question in an important meeting and given a "so-so" answer, only to realize afterward that you had a perfect opening to say something really favorable? That's an experience we all have almost every day. Prepare yourself. Don't let it happen in a potentially career-making job interview.

What about questions specifically designed to give you trouble?

The possibilities are endless...too many to discuss. But almost all such zingers aim for a relatively few slips and wrong answers. Those I can identify for you.

As I said before, your interviewer is on your side. She wants to find out that you are the person she's looking for. If so, her staffing problem is solved. But if you're not as good as you appear to be, hiring you could cause far more difficulty than it resolves.

Therefore, she'll ask lots of questions aimed at revealing your flaws. Even your answers to the most bland and casual queries will be scrutinized for damaging admissions. And chances are, those revelations won't have much to do with your resume-stated background. Instead, they'll relate to your personality and your management techniques...the kinds of shortcomings behavioral psychologists probe. So here are some wrong answers to watch out for...both with the employer, and with the company's psychologist, if you consent to meet him:

WRONG ANSWER: No, I haven't got around to visiting your Web site yet.

This answer is so wrong that you should kick yourself *really hard* if you're ever asked any question that could possibly lead to such an answer. Maybe the site is so innovative that the interviewer is merely proud and wants to brag. More likely, she's thinking something like this:

> "You seem so pitifully uninformed about us that you must have made absolutely no effort whatsoever to prepare for this interview. I wonder if you've even gone to our website?"

Never *ever* go to an interview with an employer or a recruiter without knowing everything a competent and intellectually curious executive should have wanted to find out in preparation for such a meeting. What kind of person are you if you haven't done this? Clearly not the sort the company wants to hire.

Today's corporate websites make it easier than ever before in the history of the world to find out about a company. There are descriptions of all their businesses, profiles of their senior officers, annual and quarterly reports and proxy statements (most recent and prior years), stock performance tables and charts...and more. Plus a treasure trove of news releases neatly filed from latest to earlier. Those will prompt you to look on the Web for related articles in the media. Today, at the executive level, ignorance has no excuse.

WRONG ANSWER: There's more bad than good.

Of all the "wrong answers," this one fits more questions than any other. So many, in fact, that I can't even begin to think up enough examples to suggest its vast possibilities. However, the minute you're about to list attributes of anyone, anything, or any situation, be sure to ask yourself:

> "How many good ones should I mention and how many bad ones?"

Decide shrewdly. Sometimes there should be lots of bad ones and hardly any good ones, as in the list of probable results you mention when your interviewer gets your reaction to an operating policy that verges on the unethical and illegal.

But suppose he asks how you feel about your current job. Obviously, it fails to utilize your prodigious talents and energy level. But don't slip. There's more good than bad; otherwise, the interviewer will expect you to be malcontent in his job, too. And in describing your current boss, there's probably a lot that's admirable, not just shortcomings; otherwise your interviewer envisions you talking negatively about him. Same with your reaction to the overall management of your current company. Some policies and approaches (which you will list) make lots of sense. However, certain *key* ones have serious disadvantages (obvious to any thinking person, including your interviewer).

Needless to say, you also see far more advantages relative to disadvantages when asked how the job you're interviewing for fits your talents and aspirations, and how you fit the job. Same, too, when it comes to balancing the opportunities in contrast to the obvious problems facing the industry and company you're being interviewed for. Same goes for the U.S. and its industrial and other institutions, and on and on.

You're no Pollyanna. You can see defects and problems, analyze them accurately, and conceive and execute realistic and creative strategies for dealing with them. However, you're absolutely ***not*** one of those "nattering nabobs of negativism" a tarnished Vice President of the United States famously warned us about several decades ago.

WRONG ANSWER: You'd live your life differently if you could.

This is the wrong answer to all those "if" questions. If you could be anyone other than yourself, who would you be? If you could go back and change an earlier career decision, what would you be doing today? Don't accept any offer to rewrite your personal history. You're basically a happy and highly functional person, who has high self-esteem and is busy producing and enjoying...not fretting and regretting.

Also bear this "wrong answer" in mind when faced with "if" questions about the future. If you can be anything you wish five years from now, it will be something that represents fine progress along the path you're on right now.

With respect to your current and past marriages, outstanding or difficult children, and other highly personal facets of your life, probably the less said the better...at least until you're sure that your values and circumstances clearly correspond to those of your interviewer. You can't possibly gain anything by being either ahead of, or behind, him on these points.

And of course if you're asked whether you "consider yourself successful," the answer is "Yes" and briefly why...not, "Well, sort of, and I'd have been more so, if it weren't for..."

WRONG ANSWERS: Illustrations of your greatest talents and achievements that:

1. **don't relate to the job you're interviewing for, and/or**
2. **happened long ago.**

Not surprisingly, your strongest attributes and the achievements you're proudest of are work-related and correlate amazingly well with the requirements of the job you're interviewing for. The fact that, after eighteen years of avid competition, you recently bred, trained, and groomed a Dalmatian that won Best-In-Show at the Grand National Competition of the American Kennel Club is hardly worth mentioning. Especially when compared with the fact that last month your Division's hemorrhoid remedy scored the highest market share in the 64-year history of the brand.

Don't be confused. When asked for your "best" achievements, always give your latest ones. Only when specifically asked about early phases of your career will you trot out the corresponding long-ago achievements...thus demonstrating that you've always been an over-achiever. The greatest days of your career are now and in the future, not in the past.

A variation on this theme has to do with what you like most and least in your current job or the one under discussion. Your preferences will match the job you're interviewing for just as neatly as your talents do.

WRONG ANSWERS: You've failed to develop nonbusiness interests.
AND
You spend time on nonbusiness interests.

These wrong answers are bookends; they come as a matched pair. You're apt to be asked what your avocational interests are. Better have some ready to mention. Active sports are always good. Intellectual and artistic interests begin to look respectable when you get comfortably over $300,000 or $500,000...and they take on great luster when you get above $1 million. Charitable and "cause" interests also gain respectability and ultimately cache, as you soar into the corporate stratosphere.

However, until you're being considered for a position high enough to be corporately ornamental as well as useful, don't let on that your wide-ranging interests take any significant amount of time away from work. Chances are your potential boss wants you "hungrier" for performance bonuses than for intellectual and humanitarian nourishment.

By the way, there's a chance you may be asked what interesting books you've read lately. Anyone who asks won't worry about your time, since reading is usually done when and where you can't work. Don't bring up the subject. But do prepare. If you seldom read, you should pick up a critically praised *non*business volume...perhaps a biography or a spy novel... from the current bestseller list. Comment knowledgeably. And if pressed further, mention a couple other books you'd like to read but haven't had time for. That's enough. You're joining a business, not a literary society.

WRONG ANSWER: Your aspirations for the future don't springboard from the job you're discussing.

"What-would-you-like-to-be-when-you-grow-up?" questions are just a variation of the "if" questions we discussed earlier. Make sure your stated objectives are consistent with getting the job you're interviewing for and pursuing it as wholeheartedly as the company could wish.

WRONG ANSWER: Anything but the frank truth about when and why you're leaving.

If you were FIRED, say so. Reference checking will surely reveal the fact, even if you still have an office and phone message service at your former company. Any attempt at cover-up will seem dishonest, unintelligent, and emotionally immature. Give a short, simple explanation, objectively avoiding bitterness and complaint. Show you can rise above temporary setbacks. Your forthrightness and maturity in comparison with most people, who fidget, fiddle, and fume, will come off favorably. More about this later.

WRONG ANSWER: The too-vague answer.

For every job you've held, know and be able to state without hesitation your title, whom you reported to, what size and type unit you commanded (in people, facilities, budgets, sales, profit, market share, etc). Know too in approximate numbers the size and situation of the overall organization of which your unit was a part. You absolutely must know what you're doing now...and you should also know what you've done in the past.

Remember JFK? Most of the nation became convinced he could cope with our problems...in large part because he could speak about them so succinctly, and yet so specifically in facts and figures. It takes no more time to say "a $55 million division in Akron" than it does to say "a medium-sized division located in the Midwest." Yet the former avoids raising several unnecessary questions in the interviewer's mind:

> "I wonder what she means by 'medium-sized.' "
>
> "*Where* in the Midwest?"
>
> "Why didn't she just give me the specifics? Maybe she's afraid I'll know somebody who was there when she was."

WRONG ANSWER: "Confidentiality prevents me..."

Use common sense when it comes to confidentiality. Don't be a blabbermouth. But if the competitor who's interviewing you frankly discusses his business with you, then reciprocate. Knowing the other person's figures won't make them your figures, and vice versa. If you've been responsible for something very brilliant and very recent, which must be screened from your competitor, just give a definite but nonspecific comparison he's undoubtedly already guessed:

> "With the new line included, sales for the first quarter are more than double what they were in the same period last year. *Much* more than double."

The sparkle in your eyes and your smile of pride and achievement will communicate your accomplishment just as well as if you'd stated the exact figure for the new line standing alone.

Remember: A lot of people who've done a poor job use confidentiality as a cover-up, which is what you'll be suspected of if you "take the Fifth Amendment." People who've done a great job are eager to tell about it.

WRONG ANSWER: More than was asked for.

One rather tricky question is to ask for your "four greatest achievements"...or your "three strongest talents"...or some other number of something favorable. Give exactly the number asked for, *and no more*. The test is to see if you'll plunge right past the requested number, piling on achievement after achievement, in a binge of self-praise. If so, you'll be revealed as a braggart, psychologically suffering from low self-esteem. At the very minimum, you'll seem to be someone who doesn't listen and follow instructions alertly.

WRONG ANSWER: A too-long answer.

This wrong answer is asked for by every agonizingly open-ended question... one of the commonest headaches of the interviewing process. Here the remedy is one of those *capsules* that I suggested you create out of the fifteen-minute salesperson's monologue you're not being allowed to deliver. That highly refined quarter-hour of mandatory product description and product advantages nicely fills anywhere from seven to ten 1½- to 2-minute capsules, which can be administered as requested throughout the interview.

Suppose you're zapped with this frequently thrown open-ender:

"Tell me about yourself."

Don't be wimpy and grasp for help:

"Well, what particular aspect would you like to know about?"

Instead, just plunge in and *cope!* Take no more than one to two minutes and hit the highlights, covering everything from childhood to now. Include a few words about where you grew up, because this question is usually asked to evoke a broad-brush personal portrait. To prove it can be done, I'll give you my own:

> "I was born and grew up in Reedsburg, Wisconsin, a small town of 5,000 people, where my father was a partner in the Ford car and tractor business. Worked my way through the University of Wisconsin and the University of Wisconsin Law School as a radio announcer and taught Legal Writing at the Law School for a year. Came to New York City in 1960 as Radio-TV Contract Administrator at J. Walter Thompson Advertising Agency and later became an Account Executive on various consumer products. Joined Bristol-Myers Products in '65 as a Product Manager and ultimately became Director of New Product Marketing. Next I was Director of Marketing for the Sheaffer Pen Company, and then General Manager of the Tetley Tea Division of Squibb-BeechNut. In '71 I got into executive recruiting with Heidrick & Struggles, where I became a Vice President and one of the firm's top producers of fee income. And in 1977 I started The John Lucht Consultancy Inc., specializing in the selection of high-level executives for major corporations...the same firm I operate today. I also continually update *RITES OF PASSAGE*, take on about three high-level outplacement cases per year, do some executive coaching, am an expert legal witness on lost earnings in major personal injury cases, and these days devote much of my effort to *RITE*Site.com ... a membership career website for executives.

That's under two minutes, and yet it certainly covers "Tell me about yourself." If this were an interview, anything else of interest could be asked about

Capsules: The Interview Pain-Reliever

Gapingly *open-ended questions* are one of the worst headaches of the interviewing process. They're painful as you grope for an answer that's appropriate, clear, and succinct. And if not handled well, they can lead to the serious complication of bogged-down monologuing, which can demonstrate that you're innately a poor communicator, disorganized, less-than-candid... and more. Indeed, open-ended questions are asked, in part, because they *are* troublesome to insecure, fuzzy-thinking people, who don't communicate well under pressure...people the interviewer wants to weed out.

I just administered a capsule for "Tell me about yourself." You may not need yours, but be sure you take it with you to your interview. Indeed, take along plenty of capsules. Like the Lomotil®, Dramamine®, Tetracycline®, Alka-Seltzer®, and Pepto-Bismol® you take on your foreign travels, you'll feel better knowing they're on hand, whether you wind up using them or not.

Your interview pharmacopoeia should include:

A "Tell-Me-About-Yourself" Orientation (CAPSULE)

Already prescribed.

Key Segments of Experience and Achievement (CAPSULE)

These are the topically organized segments of the fifteen-minute "salesperson's monologue" you'd love to deliver but can't in the conversational format of an interview. Have your selling points of experience and achievement clearly in mind, with specific figures stapled into your memory. Nothing minimizes an achievement more than failing to remember precisely what it was.

Achievements in Rank Order (CAPSULE)

This one prepares you for any "Top Three" or "Top Five" question. Since your greatest achievements should also tend to be your most recent, you'll ponder the importance/time trade-offs in preparing this list. If there's nothing major to report from your most recent briefly held job, don't feel you have to make something up, just to "represent" the ill-fated career move.

Maybe you have one monumentally large achievement sure to command awe and respect...and clearly attributable to your being there as the instigator and not merely one soldier in the platoon; but it happened too long ago to be one of your "latest-and-greatest." Prepare it succinctly, and deliver it *last*...third out of three, or fifth out of five, depending on how many you're asked for.

Strengths and Weaknesses (CAPSULE)

Give this one some real thought. Your strengths are at the heart of your sales pitch, and they ought to be the right ones for this job...or you'll be better off not getting it. Be ready to name and—if asked—illustrate several. Include your high energy level.

Come up with a proper "more-good-ones-than-bad-ones" answer; the ratio should be overwhelming...maybe 4 to 1. But, within the boundaries of enlightened self-interest, also try to be honest. The standard formula for an interview-confessed "weakness" is "*A strength carried to a fault*."

Examples:

> "Sometimes I may drive my people a little *too* hard. Since I'm a bit of a workaholic, I tend to expect others are, too."
>
> "Sometimes I can be *too* supportive of my people...hanging on to them, still trying to train and coach, when perhaps I should just pull the plug a few months sooner."

And how's this for a reverse-spin on a weakness?

> "I'm the broad overall conceptualist...the strategist, the planner, the schemer...and also the enthusiastic motivator of the team. But I'm not the down-to-the-nitty-gritty implementer. I always make sure to have an operations officer I can absolutely depend on to see that things don't slip between the cracks...and also a meticulous controller, to make sure that there are no financial surprises. Without both of those people doing their jobs, I couldn't do mine."

Obviously, this approach will work only if you're discussing a big job in a big company. But you get the idea and can adapt it to many situations.

Reason for Leaving (CAPSULE)

It's not enough just to avoid the "wrong answer" of saying you quit—or worse yet that you're still doing your job—when everyone who's likely to be asked knows you've been fired. Prepare an accurate capsule on what happened and what your current status is. And *keep it brief and simple!*

If the new CEO brought along his own person for your job, no harm in saying so. Add, if true, that you too might have brought along someone you knew and trusted if you were in the CEO's shoes and had such a limited time to effect such a major turnaround. Indeed, you went out of your way to cooperate with the woman who's now your successor, during those first awkward weeks when you were both on the payroll and she hadn't yet been named to your job. As you see it, what she has to do to be successful is to finish installing this-and-this program which you were putting into place when the upheaval occurred, and she seems to be taking basically that approach (if true).

There wouldn't be room in this entire book for the enormous smorgasbord of familiar firing scenarios...one of which may one day happen to you. A great many, like the one above and all sorts of consolidation and staff-cutting measures, can be frankly stated and endorsed. "Personality clash" with your boss, however, normally should *not* be the diagnosis. Say instead, "Fundamental policy differences," and cite some concrete examples. You simply can't afford to be categorized as someone who can't get along with people.

The trick in discussing firing is to take an open-minded dispassionate, managerial stance. Observe, comment, and react as an informed, objective observer, who's also a very skilled manager...not as someone subjectively involved, wronged, and wounded. You're willing to stand and be judged on the wisdom of your programs and the next administration may have to continue them. On the other hand, if you tried something that failed and you were in the process of changing course, say so. You'll be judged far more on the calibre and comprehension you demonstrate, than on the fact that you were fired. Chances are, your interviewer has also been fired at least once in his career.

Your Management Style (CAPSULE)

For your answer to ring the bells on this issue, you'd better know what style the company feels *it* has. When you visited the company's website you may have noticed a few words about "our corporate values" or "our culture." Above all, be sensitive to clues dropped by your interviewer. The "participative" style is usually in vogue, whereby your door is open to your subordinates and their ideas, and you get results through motivation and delegation.

But for some companies you should hedge your bet..."On the other hand, nobody wonders who the boss is or where the buck stops." Other possibilities include: "Problem solving"..."I enjoy analyzing what's wrong, figuring out a solution, and implementing it." And "results-oriented"..."My decisions are highly concerned with how the result will impact the bottom line." You might add, "On the other hand, I also care a lot about my people; training and developing them and seeing they're fairly treated is extremely important." A pragmatic pastiche, plus taking the pulse of your interviewer, will you get you safely past this issue.

What Appeals to You About Our Job and Our Company? (CAPSULE)

Capsule or no capsule, you will have thoroughly studied the company prior to your interview. When you devour the company's Internet site, be sure to make notes with this question in mind. Nothing warms the heart of a tough, hard-to-convince interviewer quite like an immediate, enthusiastic, and well-informed answer to this question.

Current Status and Long-Range Trends of Your Speciality and the Overall Industry (CAPSULE)

If you know anything at all about your present field, you certainly have some good ideas on where the action is now and where the future may lead. Marshal them. Don't just pull them together on the way *home* from an interview where the CEO of a diversified corporation had more thought-provoking insights into your specialty than you did.

What Would You Like To Know About Us? (CAPSULE)

The easiest or the hardest of questions. Ironically, the more you want the job, the tougher the question is. If you're skeptical about whether the job will advance your career, you're loaded with questions that have to be resolved to your satisfaction.

But suppose you're thrilled to be considered for the job. It's with an impeccable company, and represents a career breakthrough in responsibility. Then what do you ask? Certainly not about benefits and retirement. Maybe about what they see as the key problems and opportunities to be addressed by the person who gets the job, willingness to invest in the business, and whether it's central to the company's future growth or a candidate for "harvest" and possible divestment. But be careful. Shouldn't you *know* what the problems and opportunities are? Check for a *common view* of such issues; but don't imply you can't see without being told what some of the key ones probably are.

The invitation to ask questions is inevitable. Be prepared for it.

Reading...and Writing...Between the Lines

You know darn well that your interviewer will be trying to "read between the lines" of your answers...looking for accidental unspoken nuances that may be even more revealing than your statements.

So, since he's *reading*, you may as well make sure you're *writing*.

For example, when you're asked about your creativity, give some instances where you thought up a great idea that worked out well. But also give some samples of outstanding creativity within the unit you're responsible for, but which you personally did *not* think up. Give credit to the lower-echelon research subordinate whose "far-out" idea you backed with some money from your "Venture Fund," and to your CEO whose unpopular idea worked out sensationally well after you and your subordinates removed the kinks from it, and to the advertising agency that came up with the winning campaign after you asked them to give it "just one last try."

Incidentally, that until-recently junior scientist now has her own sizable section of the laboratory to run. And, far from their being fired, you were able to work successfully with that ad agency and they've now won a client relationship with another division of the company you work for.

We see, of course, that you're creative. But we also read what you've written between the lines. You care about, and listen to, what others around you are thinking...*even your boss*! With you in charge, the company isn't limited to your own personal creativity. You recognize anyone's good idea when you see it. Moreover, you probably get along well with others, commanding their respect and loyalty, because you reward them for a job well done.

You get the idea. When answering questions about talents and triumphs, you have a perfect opportunity to write between-the-lines messages about your other fine characteristics and management techniques.

The "Pregnant Pause"...and How to Deal with It

The "pregnant pause" is a gimmick some interviewers use to unnerve candidates, and to force them to reveal personal insecurity, and hopefully to voice unguarded statements.

Here's how it works. After you've finished answering his question, the interviewer says absolutely nothing to move his side of the conversation forward. Dead silence. No question, no comment. He just looks you in the eye, waiting for you to panic and rush in to fill the awkward pause.

This startling stoppage may come at random...or possibly when the interviewer suspects, or wants you to *worry* that he suspects, that you're not telling the truth, or at least not the whole story. One recruiter I know loves this gimmick so much, he tries to use it on his co-workers at lunch.

The only way to deal with this behavior is to nip it in the bud. The first time your interviewer breaks the rhythm of the conversation this way, pause with him long enough to make absolutely sure he's "pregnant pausing" and to make sure he knows that *you* know that's what he's doing...maybe 20 seconds or more. Then say, kindly and helpfully, as if perhaps he seems to have lost track of the rather complex discussion you've been having:

> "Is there anything else you'd like to know about...(the question you just finished answering)?"

Treating the pregnant pause as a lapse of attention by the interviewer is the only way to deal with it. If you knuckle under to even one "cross-examination by silence," you'll signify that you're the insecure sort of person who submits to interrogation in this arch, smug fashion. If so, you're in for a tense, defensive interview. On the other hand, by kindly and inoffensively calling the interviewer's bluff, you create unspoken recognition and respect. If, by chance, your interviewer decides to try again, repeat the treatment.

Coping with the "Stress Interview"

Let's hope you never run into it, but there is a really bad idea in interviewing that still hasn't completely died out...the "stress interview." Pioneered long ago by an executive recruiter who'd been a prisoner in one of the Nazi death camps, the idea was to discover what he called the "counterfeit executive"... the one who can't take pressure...by applying great pressure and tension during the interview. Seat the candidate with the sun in his eyes; put him in a very low or soft-cushioned chair so that he realizes he is obviously beneath you; quickly interrupt his answers, telling him he obviously didn't understand the question; "pregnant pause;" imply knowledge of information contrary to his statements. The possibilities for rude, challenging, inhospitable behavior are endless.

You'll almost certainly never get the full treatment. Even the guy who invented the process quit operating that way after achieving a few years of notoriety. But you may run into someone who kicks off the interview by throwing down the gauntlet:

"I can't see how you're qualified for this job!"

He goes on from there with argumentative, demeaning, and perhaps embarrassingly personal questions. Maybe he deliberately misinterprets your answers. And probably he avoids looking at you...gazing over your head, thumbing through his calendar, and shuffling papers. You're getting an updated version of the stress interview.

What to do? You have to call his bluff. That may be all he wants. Say:

> "I'd appreciate it if you'd look at me when we're talking. If we can get this conversation on a more cordial basis, we'll communicate much better."

Maybe just saying something like that will pass his "test." If not, I suggest you get up to leave, turning back as you get to the door:

> "I'd still be willing to have a good conversation with you, but this session doesn't really seem worthwhile."

Chances are, he'll call you back, say you passed his "test," and continue the interview on a new and more cordial footing. By then, however, you wonder whether you should even consider working for this guy or the company he represents. So do I.

Who's in Charge of the Interview ...You or the Interviewer?

No question who's responsible for the outcome of the interview. You are. You've got to get your message across. If your appropriateness, your ability, and what a fine person you are fail to register, it's your loss. And it's your fault, not the interviewer's.

But who's *in charge*? Now that's a different question. Believe it or not, some people think that you should take charge. Go in, say "Hello," and see if the interviewer asks the questions that draw out the information you want to convey. If not, begin answering different questions from the ones she asks, and twist and lengthen your answers to make sure you cover all the important points that support your candidacy. Be poised and pleasant, but don't be afraid to demonstrate aggressiveness and leadership...crucial qualities in an executive.

If you're interviewing for Vice President - Marketing of a company that sells vacuum cleaners door-to-door, that's probably good advice. Barge in and take over. But for any other job, in my opinion, a much more polite and sensitive approach is absolutely mandatory.

First of all, you're selling yourself as a ***"fine person"***...polite, socially poised, and someone who, if hired, will wear well as a co-worker over the years. Somehow, the pushy vacuum cleaner salesman doesn't fit that description.

Secondly, and equally important, if you try to take charge and control what information is covered, you may not convey what your interviewer wants to know. You may bore him with a persuasive pitch on points he was willing to concede...meanwhile, failing to address the doubts and concerns you would have discovered if you'd sensitively followed his lead.

Moreover, since the interview is a *demonstration* of how you think and operate, there's a good chance your interviewer may conclude that you're a "hip-shooter"...a superficial thinker, who plunges ahead before gathering information, and checking preconceived assumptions. After all, that's the way you behaved in your interview.

Therefore, all things considered, *don't try to grab control.* In terms of personal image, you can't afford to dominate the interview. And in terms of accomplishing your objectives, you don't really want to.

Steering the Interview with Questions and "Red-Flagged" Answers

Only your own good judgment during the actual interview can determine to what extent you can and should try to influence the direction it takes.

If you're willing to become overtly pushy and aggressive, you can cover whatever you wish. But if you want to stay within the ritual boundaries of a social conversation in which the employer has the prerogative of asking most of the questions, there are really only two techniques by which you can gently guide him toward matters you'd like covered.

Questions

You can always ask a question to see if he's interested in a subject you want to talk about:

> "Is the development and marketing of internally generated new products a major factor in your growth plans? That's an area where I've had a lot of successful experience."

Nothing impolite or too pushy about that approach.

He may say:

> "Absolutely! Tell me about it."

Or he may say:

> "We're not entirely opposed to internally-generated new products. But over the years we've become skeptical. We find we get a lot more for our money by acquiring underdeveloped products someone else has pioneered. Have you ever tried that approach?"

Well, now you know where he stands. Maybe you've also got success stories of the type he's more interested in. In any event, you didn't waste time and suggest future philosophical differences by giving a long recitation of exploits he's not looking for.

Red-Flagged Answers

Sometimes you can wave a red flag at the bull and he'll run for it... sometimes not. Even professional TV interviewers are often unbelievably nearsighted. The famous actress winds up her answer:

> "Of course, that was back when I was stealing cars for a living..."

And the oblivious interviewer moves right along with:

> "Tell me...looking back on all the films you've made...which hairdresser has influenced you most?"

Nonetheless, a valuable technique for attempting to steer an interview along more promising lines is to wind up an answer with a provocative statement that cries out for a follow-up question, if the interviewer is interested:

> "...which is why, of course, I then completely changed our approach to incentive compensation."

Your interviewer ought to be tempted to ask what kinds of changes you made and what resulted. But if he's not, at least you haven't been rude or boring, and you haven't wasted time on a topic he's apparently not interested in. The bull doesn't always run after the red flag.

And that's it. Questions and flagged answers are the two polite ways you can attempt to steer an interview toward topics you'd like to discuss. The advantage of both is that they merely suggest...they don't force...a change of direction. They both leave control of the interview in the hands of the interviewer, which is what you will normally want anyway.

Out of Town Tryouts

Most people find that, in interviewing, "practice makes perfect." By the time they're in their third or fourth interview, they're very effective. But what if you haven't interviewed for quite awhile and you suddenly face an unexpected "biggie"? Or if you look forward to a series of interviews and don't want to waste the first one or two? Then try your show in Philadelphia and Boston prior to opening night on Broadway.

"Role playing," of course, is the answer. A social friend or your spouse can sit in for the interviewer, perhaps asking questions from a random list you've prepared. Better yet, try to set up a real grilling by a business friend from the right industry. Choose someone who can come up with her own tough questions, and who will give you a clear-eyed critique afterward.

The Danger of Being Prepared

There's no such thing as being over-prepared. There always is, however, the danger of being over-eager to play back what you've worked on. And by recommending "capsules," I certainly don't mean to encourage that tendency.

Occasionally I come across people so anxious to deliver the thinking they've developed that they don't listen carefully to the question and conform their answer to it. These people are extremely rare...only one of them for every 50 or 75 who fail to come up with clearly focused, brief, and factually explicit answers to questions they certainly should have anticipated.

You're too alert to make either mistake.

Engines Ready...Contact!

Prepared as you are, you have absolutely nothing to fear as you take off into the sunrise. If you've got anything close to the right stuff, your interview will demonstrate it.

However, let's run through a preflight checklist of practical tips:

Check the forecast. If your interview has been arranged by a recruiter, call her in the morning or the afternoon before. She may have new information since you saw her last, regarding job content, what's looked for, how long other interviews have lasted, what line of questioning was pursued, and what mistakes other candidates made. Don't betray nervousness by asking about all these items. Just say: "Anything I should know before I go over there tomorrow morning?"

Pack your flight case. Into your elegant attaché go extra copies of your resume (just in case your host has misplaced his or wants to pass some along), a yellow pad and a *quality* pen, any charts of figures you may need to refresh your memory if questioning gets detailed, and a *Wall Street Journal* to pull out and read if your host is interrupted or you have to wait a few minutes.

Arrive early and check the equipment. Get there five minutes ahead of time and ask to use the lavatory before being announced. That way you can check for lint on your collar and parsley on your teeth. You'll perform best knowing you feel and look perfect.

Return your salute from the crew. The interview begins in the corridor as your host's PA greets you and maybe offers to shake hands (be alert for this). He, and through him possibly the receptionist too, will probably be consulted for a report on your poise and personality. Your down-the-corridor conversation with him...cordial but not presumptuous...is the start of your interview.

Don't land prematurely. After your *firm* handshake, I hope your host doesn't feign a landing and then pull up, leaving you discourteously plopped for an awkward minute or two. But he might. It's a fairly common maneuver. Circle gracefully until you get landing instructions, or you clearly see where he's landing.

Warning. There's advice going around...maybe via a book or a psychologically oriented outplacement firm...not to sit where the interviewer first suggests and, wherever you land, to *move your chair*. This odd behavior is supposed to connote an aggressive personality. I merely find it obnoxious. Unless you've got a bad back, or the sun's in your eyes, why not just sit down where indicated, and relax?

Five-minute warning. Don't go all-business all at once. Get off to a positive, upbeat start on a relatively personal note. Admire something in the office, or the company's convenient location, or the fine weather. Do *not* start off with the lousy weather, a bad commute, or any other "downer."

Hazardous terrain. Enter the Bermuda Triangle with extreme caution, if at all. Avoid such obviously hazardous topics as politics, religion, and sexually- and racially-oriented issues. Beware of trick questions aimed at exposing your negative attitudes on these matters by implying in advance that the interviewer has such feelings. Even sports can be a hazardous topic until you know your host's opinions. Believe it or not, some interviewers will see your failure to share their views on player trades as an indication that you're probably not a very shrewd analyst in the world of business either.

Keep an eye on the radar. Read the interviewer's body language. Leaning back signals a smooth leisurely ride; tapping fingers, fidgeting, and checking the clock call for crisper answers. "Closed position" (tightly crossed arms and legs) says you're meeting resistance, whereas open, loose limbs say "all clear." And hand-to-face says he...and you...are uncertain, possibly untruthful. Body language can be overrated, but shouldn't be ignored. If you haven't read a book on the subject, you ought to.

Don't go on autopilot. No matter how well things seem to be going, don't let your guard down. The most skilled and subtle interviewer is never the one who treats you roughly. The one who puts you totally at ease is the one who'll find out even more than you'd prefer to tell him.

Debrief promptly. If a recruiter is involved, call soon afterward to debrief. The client will also call, and if the recruiter can play back your favorable comments, they will reinforce the client's good feelings about you. Don't be a sappy sycophant. But don't be coy, either. People tend to like people who obviously like them. And recruiters are more inclined to support candidates who probably will accept, than those who might not.

File your flight report. Why not send a brief "thank you"...two to four paragraphs, using "Monarch" (7 1/4" x 10 1/2") personal stationery if you have it, otherwise "regular size." While you may refer in some way to what was discussed, this note is *not* a parting salvo of hard sell. Instead, it's a courtesy that says ***fine person***...and differentiates you from the vast majority of candidates, who don't bother with amenities. Even more importantly, write down for future reference everything you found out at your interview. Most candidates won't do this either. Therefore, you'll be more on the employer's wave length than they will, at "second round" interviews three or four weeks later.

Answering the Unasked Questions

No interviewer these days is going to invite legal action by asking:

> "Do you really think a woman can handle this job?"
>
> "Aren't you a little too old for a grueling position like this?"
>
> "Do people respond to you just like everyone else, even though you only have one eye?"
>
> "With that brace on your leg, I don't suppose you get out to visit the companies in your group very often, do you?"

In an ideal world, these questions would not only be unasked, they would also be unthought. But our present world is far from ideal. If you vary much from the norm...if you're an ethnic or racial minority, physically handicapped, noticeably younger or older than most executives, considerably heavier or shorter...there may be unspoken questions in the mind of the interviewer about your ability to handle the job because of your "difference." The best course is to rebut these objections, even though they're not voiced.

But you must communicate *indirectly*. You can't simply pipe up and say, "Don't worry about my age; I'm more effective at 59 than I ever was at 30 or 40." If by chance the interviewer *wasn't* thinking of your age as a problem, he'll wonder why you're being so defensive. And if he *was* thinking about it: (1) he'll be offended that you caught him, (2) he'll be unconvinced by your self-serving assertion, and (3) he'll worry that you may already be hinting at legal action if he doesn't give you the job.

Just as in writing your resume, you can answer such unspoken questions with offsetting information. If you're probably a lot older than the other candidates, casually mention spending your vacation as an instructor for Outward Bound...or that you're leaving in August for two weeks of mountain climbing in Nepal. Or maybe just mention your interest in finding a challenging partner for a few good sets of tennis while you're in town. Make the interviewer think of you as healthy, vigorous, and in your prime. Don't talk about something you watched on television, or how hard you were hit by the flu that's going around. Everyone watches TV and gets sick occasionally, but you can't afford to raise image problems with someone who doesn't know you.

Shatter your stereotype.

Offset *youth* with civic and business responsibilities normally reserved for someone more mature...president of a stodgy country club, trustee of a college, outside director of a bank. (For this purpose, forget "when-do-you-have-time-for-it?" concerns.) Fight the *age* problem with evidence of vigorous physical activity and a fast-paced schedule. And if you're a *woman*, stress the fact that you're accustomed to extensive travel, to making difficult decisions, to operating independently. And throw in an anecdote that makes it clear that your household is organized accordingly.

If you belong to a racial or ethnic *minority*, be warm, self-confident, friendly and informal...thus demonstrating (1) that you'll fit right in, and (2) that you don't have any doubt or insecurity about fitting in. And if you're *physically handicapped*, stress your ability to function effectively in the mainstream of everyday life; mention a party you went to recently, grumble about a speeding ticket, talk about your participation in active sports. And if you're *overweight*, stress the fact that you lead a highly disciplined and energetic life... that you adhere to demanding self-imposed schedules...that you work for long-term goals.

What the Interview *Can't* Do for You

For years one of the leading literary agents has been trying to get me to write a book which ought to be called *How to Package and Pretend Your Way Into a Big Job You're Not Qualified For*. Naturally that's not the title he proposes, but it perfectly describes his premise.

Such a concept is not only dishonest, it's ridiculous. No combination of slick resume and glib interviewing can enable you to defeat an array of really excellent candidates and win a job you're not qualified for.

And you shouldn't want such a job. Get it, and your life will be miserable until you lose it...and even more miserable afterward

However, armed with the information in this book, and the willingness to work as hard as necessary to obtain the position you do deserve, you should be able to fight off the other fine candidates competing against you for any job you fully deserve and can perform.

Good luck. I hope you do.

Chapter 17

Negotiating Your Employment Contract... Getting Plenty, and Making Sure

So you're giving up a fine job where you're comfortably settled, well respected, generously paid, and on a fast track toward bigger and better things. You're seizing an even greater opportunity.

Or maybe you're just winding up an agonizing period of unemployment you feared might never end. You're grasping a lifeline.

Either way, the question now is: What are you going to *get*?

The single most important...and the easiest...way to win a very good deal from a new employer is to make him or her fully aware of what a good deal you have where you are. Then the initial offer should be something

you can graciously accept. Bargaining can be minimized or avoided altogether.

Protection is another problem. Probably you're thinking:

> ***"I'd like to have an employment contract.***
> ***But most companies refuse to give them."***

You're right, of course. Most companies don't want to hand you a document marked "Contract." Nevertheless, these days more and more corporations are putting more and more in writing.

And believe it or not, every time you start a new job, you *can* have an *employment contract*...even if you *don't* receive a paper with that title on it. You and I will make sure that your terms-of-employment are solidly nailed down...and as favorable as they can possibly be.

We'll also define the jargon you may be confronted with. And we'll review how you can pleasantly and reasonably speak up for what you want.

Before we talk about anything else, let's pause for a few words about the nature of compensation.

Just a few years ago—it seems only yesterday—we began reading about scores of twenty-somethings getting an idea, writing a business plan, getting "angel" and/or venture funding, working outrageous hours to spark an operation, doing an IPO, and—after a 1-year SEC curb on selling restricted shares and a 6-month lockup imposed by the underwriter—cashing in for millions or even billions of dollars.

And weren't we envious!

These kids had—*still* have—youth, good looks, and boundless energy. Plus, now they also have astonishing wealth. True, they worked unbelievably hard day and night to get it. But for how long? A year, two, maybe three. Max!

I hope you didn't buy *Rites of Passage* expecting I could lead you to a similar result. I can't. For that kind of lightning to strike, you have to be standing in the just the right place at the just the right time with just the right people who are all willing to risk all the traditional wealth and status they have, which—conveniently for a beginner—is almost none.

The Nature and Stages of Compensation in Young Companies

At startup, the only employees of a business may be just an entrepreneur with a dream and a circle of pitch-in-and-do-whatever-is-needed associates. The entrepreneur can't pay much to these people. Even if the business has some income, it's not enough for market-level salaries.

Cash pay is subsistence at best. The real pay is the highly uncertain chance of a huge windfall through stock options, plus far more responsible and interesting work and a higher title than an inexperienced person could command elsewhere.

At intermediate stage, the business is up, operating, and generating sales. Maybe there's even a slightly positive cash flow. Or venture capitalists may have injected funding and there's lots of positive publicity. The potential of the business is more apparent. Risk seems lower. Therefore, less equity is now needed as bait. And more experience is demanded. Indeed, the company now *needs* some sophistication in its key managers. Newcomers are still sacrificing current cash. But less so than the earliest employees. By now we clearly see the nature of compensation...in a young *or* a mature company. There are three components:

1. ***Cash***,
2. ***Career opportunity***...a more interesting and challenging job with a higher title than one could obtain in a larger, more mature and stable company, and
3. ***Equity opportunity***...options or warrants that *might* create great wealth.

At IPO stage, experienced professional managers are needed to impress Wall Street analysts and the investing public. The company needs credentialed "been-there-and-done-that" people. Cash compensation for these people is still lower than they'd make in an established company, and options are still the main reward. Maybe a $500,000-a-year person will accept $200,000, plus options. But by now cash is at least credible.

My point in all of this is that there's no free lunch. If you want to go for the *MegaMoney*, you've got to be willing to be grossly underpaid in cash at every stage of a company's development. In fact, you're really *purchasing* your stock participation...and paying for it in cash! In the earliest stages, you're also being paid to a high degree in career opportunity. Maybe you're just a Financial Analyst in a large company. Now you leap to CFO of a risky startup. If you can mature to the point that your title is merited by your performance, you'll have been paid handsomely for your time, even though not in dollars.

Yes, lots of people have made killings that make us envious. More folks will in the future. But there are trade-offs and enormous risks. Wherever you choose to position yourself on the risk/reward continuum, I wish you good fortune.

Now let's look at the difference between employment negotiations and every other kind.

When you negotiate to buy a house, or a boat, or a car, the object itself stays the same in your eyes, while you haggle over price. Your liking and respect for the seller can drop to zero. But what you're trying to buy remains just as enticing as it was the first moment you saw it.

Unfortunately, when you negotiate for your own employment...and even if someone else "fronts" for you (which I don't recommend)...you're not just selling yourself. You're *being* yourself. You were a "class act" during your interviews. Don't figure it's now safe to turn into a ruthless...or a petty... sleaze, just because the employer has chosen you and begun discussing your terms of employment. As my Granny used to say:

"There's many a slip, twixt the cup and the lip."

If you demonstrate any undesirable characteristics at this point, the whole deal may be off. Anything that seems overreaching or underhanded will be held against you.

So stand by everything you promised, stated, or implied. If you described your current compensation as X, don't suddenly claim it's X plus 35%, just because four friends tell you that's what they're getting for almost exactly the same job you have. And if you initially implied that it would be easy for you to relocate, don't later raise all sorts of costly problems you want your potential employer to throw money at.

He just may decide that you've been less than forthright...or at the very minimum that you're a drag to deal with. And on either basis, you could still lose out to another candidate.

The trick in negotiations is to indicate what a good deal you have where you are.

In the end, you won't move unless you score a significant improvement.

And nobody's going to ask you to. At least *not if they fully appreciate your current circumstances and compensation.*

Responsibility, growth opportunity, and possibly a chance to build long-term net worth...not just a boost in current income...will be the main reasons for you to consider any move. But you *do* expect financial improvement, both immediate and long-term. And the only way your prospective employer can know the full extent of what you're getting now is if you tell him.

As an executive recruiter, I always make sure to find out every facet of current compensation, plus any expected changes within the next 12 months. And I communicate all of this information to my client in a detailed written summary *before he meets the candidate*. That way he realizes right from the start that Candidate X will have to get upwards of $490,000, whereas Candidate Y can probably be hired for $370,000 and possibly less.

Face it. Cost/value assessment works exactly the same in hiring executives as in buying merchandise. There will be no reluctance to pay what you obviously cost...a reasonable incentive over what you're making now...if you're evaluated and proven "the one we want" during realistic shopping for alternatives.

But if you allow yourself to be thought of as a $250,000 candidate, when it will really take more than $360,000 to move you, then don't be surprised to receive an "underwhelming" offer. And don't be surprised either, if subsequent disclosure and bargaining can never quite build the financial platform you should have stood on from day one.

Prepare a written summary of current compensation. It's as helpful as your resume in orienting recruiters and employers.

Take a look at the financial summary I prepare on the candidates I present. I've laid out the information as if you were preparing the chart for yourself.

Unfortunately, many recruiters don't bother to dig into current compensation. Moreover, you may be on your own, with no recruiter involved. So, unless you work up a financial review, chances are your proper figures won't be registered in the early stages when they'll do you the most good.

Indeed, you've probably got to do some figuring, just to find out for yourself where you stand. Nine out of ten executives I meet don't fully appreciate their current compensation until I prompt them to think about it in detail. In the end, of course, everyone always figures out to-the-penny what he or she is now making, in order to weigh the financial offer that accompanies an enticing opportunity. But by then it may be far too late to get the employer to think of you in the right price range.

The summary is *informal* (though precise), so you won't put a title on it.

	X Year (Current fiscal/ ends in 4 mos.)	Y Year (Next fiscal)
Base Salary	$302,250	$385,000 [a]
Bonus	93,000 [b]	155,000 [c]
Short-Term Incentive (Cash)	62,000 [d]	84,000 [e]
Long-Term Incentive (Deferred)	77,500 [f]	103,500 [g]
Company Car Allowance	24,640	24,640
County & City Club Dues	7,130	7,130
Approximate Annualized Value of Stock Options	65,800 [h]	65,800 [h]
Daughter's Tuition Scholarship	18,600 [i]	18,600 [i]
	$650,920	$843,670 [j]

[a] Assumes promotion to EVP/COO in June, and mid-point of $350m to $420m salary bracket for that job. If not promoted, my base will probably rise 8% to $326,430.
[b] Assured; could go to ceiling of $110,000.
[c] Estimate assumes promotion; otherwise $110,000 to $125,000.
[d] Based on achieving personal goals (100% earned in past five years).
[e] Assumes promotion; otherwise approximately $72,000.
[f] Based on Corporation achieving four-year profit goal. Paid past three years, currently on-target.
[g] Assumes promotion; otherwise $84,000.
[h] Difficult to predict; however, this is the actual average of the past three years.
[i] Linda is one of five winners of a company-wide academic high school scholarship competition. Next year is the second-last year of her scholarship.
[j] Assumes promotion; if no promotion, I expect $716,100, based on these figures in Y year: $326,430[a], $117,500[c], $72,000[e], and $84,000[g].

Keep your summary as simple and objective as possible. Only discuss cash. With respect to benefits, don't bring up FICA, insurance, medical, dental and other items. Instead, provide your current company's "Benefit Statement" as reported specifically to you. If you get $328,000 straight salary and nothing else, say so.

But if you've got money coming at you from several directions, point out and add up *everything*. If you expect a raise or a promotion within the next several months, be sure the recruiter and the employer know what's coming. Your incentive to move must be figured on top of what you'll soon get where you are...not just on top of what you have at this very minute.

Even if you're unemployed, you want your prospective employer to realize what you're *accustomed* to getting. If she's sensitive and smart, she won't want you to feel that your duress has been taken advantage of. And, since you'll be nervous about asking more than she offers, you'll want to make doubly sure that her initial offer is as high as possible.

When do you hand over your compensation summary?

Maybe never.

The recruiter or the employer will surely ask, "What's your current compensation?" Answer with an approximate figure justified by your summary. At that point he may say:

> "Well, that's in our ballpark. We can certainly come up with an attractive incentive."

If so, don't go further. Keep your summary in your attache. Obviously you're going to get a tempting offer.

On the other hand, your current compensation may spark a reaction like this:

> "Wow! That's certainly more than I would have thought. How do you come up with that number?"

If so, you're prepared to handle compensation in the strongest, yet least disruptive, possible way:

> "Well, I did a little figuring before I came over here. I didn't want to waste your time, if what I already have is close to what you'll be

offering. When you have a few minutes, you can look this over and see if it's something you can see fit to improve upon."

(Hand over your paper.)

"By the way, are you having any problem with the new emission standards?"

See what your paper does? It lets you register...without being at all boastful, obnoxious, or tedious...all facets of the good deal you already have. And you do so without skipping a beat in the central conversation that is convincing your host that you're the person who best understands his business and can do the most to build it...the person he needs, regardless of cost.

Today executive compensation packages are hardly ever simple and straightforward. They have to be studied to be understood. How anyone will fare in years one, two, three, and beyond in leaving X Company to join Y Corp., which has different programs, requires careful analysis.

Chances are, the person you hand your "summary" to won't even attempt to evaluate it himself. He'll have it looked at by his compensation expert, who can authoritatively analyze what you have, compared to various proposals he might make.

The result will be an offer your prospective employer is comfortably sure will be attractive to you. Moreover, it will probably be accompanied by a visual aid that clearly showed him...and now proves to you...what the advantages of his offer are.

The best way to negotiate is to avoid having to do much negotiating at all. Do your homework right away. And let your would-be employer know as quickly and clearly as possible what you're already getting. He's a lot more likely to make you an offer you can't refuse if he's thoroughly aware of what you *can* refuse

Now let's discuss contracts.

Can you get one?

Yes!

Play your cards right and you can almost certainly put your new employer under a written obligation. And if you're smart, you'll surely try to do so.

As you may recall from your Business Law course in college, a verbal contract is just as enforceable as a written one. *But only if, by its terms, it's to be performed within one year*. This, of course, becomes important if you are looking for a firm agreement of employment to last more than a year.

Indeed, if you only have an oral agreement, it had better not promise anything that can't be performed in a year. Otherwise, the *whole agreement can't be enforced*...even the parts that can be performed within a year.

And of course "time protection" for more than a year is usually the main thing an employee tries to negotiate. When she tells her would-be employer, "I want a contract," she's saying:

"I want to be sure, before I give up the secure job I have, that you can't casually dump me on the street in no time at all, and for no good reason."

And in his traditional reluctance to provide a written "contract," the employer is saying:

"That's exactly what I want to be sure I *can* do. I can't *manage* my business unless I'm completely free to pick and change my team at any time and for any reason."

How do these seemingly irreconcilable views get resolved?

By compromise. The executive asks for a four- or five-year "contract," and the employer comes up with two-years, or less. Seldom will a company commit itself for five years to an executive who isn't already on its payroll.

Consider the "Termination Agreement."
It's better than an X-year "Contract"...and easier to get.

The employee wants firing to be permissible only for criminal acts...and maybe also insanity, wanton negligence, or gross incompetence. The employer, on the other hand, wants just about any reason to suffice, as long as time parameters are respected. In the end, the employer will usually get plenty of leeway as to *cause* for firing. The employee will hold out for...and achieve...*time* protection, which is basically all he ever hoped for anyway.

Which brings us to the advantages of a "termination agreement" over a straight X-year "contract." Employers who are unwilling to grant two- and three-year contracts will usually be more amenable to an 18-month...or if you can't do better a 12-month...termination agreement which says, in effect:

"You can fire me at any time for any reason. But you must give me 18-months' notice, or at least keep me on the payroll for 18 months afterward."

This arrangement doesn't tie the employer's hands, and it doesn't box him in for an exceedingly long time. So he's more willing to go along with it.

And for all practical purposes, you receive even better protection than under a two- or three-year "contract." Security under those deals soon elapses to zero. But with an 18-month termination agreement, there's always a year-and-a-half of future paychecks. Even if you become CEO at $1.4 million per year, you can still whip out the termination agreement you got when you joined the company as a zone manager at $102,000 ten years earlier. You'll collect $2.1 million during the next 18 months...thanks very much!

There are contracts...
and there are C·O·N·T·R·A·C·T·S!

On the one hand, there are handshake agreements,
written into an "offer letter."

And then there are "employment contracts,"
hammered out by opposing lawyers.

If you can get ideal protection from something simple
and friendly, don't hold out for "big deal" paperwork.

I've known lots of prominent and highly paid New York lawyers...business-controlling partners in the famous law firms, and General Counsels of America's largest corporations.

Standing head-and-shoulders above them all is the smartest human I've ever met...about 5' 2" and hardly 100 lbs. (mostly brain)...who attended law school over 60 years ago and since then has been doing post-graduate work in common sense. He's always practiced independently of the huge law firms. Many corporations use them for routine matters...but bring him in on very important and difficult issues. Moreover, the CEOs of those corporations insist on getting his slant on their personal legal matters.

Interestingly, this legal ninja has a devastating secret weapon that many of the other "super-lawyers" seem almost unaware of:

Simplicity!

Phil (not his real name...but close) would much rather have an agreement embodied in a plainly worded letter or an exchange of letters than in a 27-page document full of convoluted clauses.

It's not at all unusual to go to Phil asking that a contract be drawn up to formalize an agreement along the lines of a simple letter or an exchange of letters you show him, only to be told:

"No way! You've got 'em flat-footed on the basis of this *letter*. If they don't perform, we can sue them and get everything you're looking for, plus punitive damages as well. But if we go in and try to negotiate a formal contract with their legal department involved, there's no way in the world we can get language like this.

"Just write them a friendly reply, saying you're pleased to go ahead as they've suggested, except for that one little change in the schedule that you've both agreed to.

"And for heaven's sake, don't misplace the letters. They prove what your agreement is, and you could be mighty thankful to have them later on."

You get the idea.

It may be comforting to have a long and explicit document spelling out every conceivable facet and contingency of your arrangement with your employer. But it's not necessary. She and her company are just as bound by what she writes in her offer letter...assuming you accept her offer and go to work relying on it...as if there's a fancy paper marked "contract," which you both sign. And she's equally bound whether she asks you to countersign her "offer letter" or not.

Today almost every company provides offer letters.

So don't quit your job until you have something in writing.

You have clout.

You may not have enough leverage to get all the money or all the protection you want. But whatever you do get, you certainly have the power to get into writing.

Just say:

> "Well, Herb, I guess we're agreed on all the really important points. The title will be Senior Vice President - Manufacturing. I'll report directly to you as President, and I'll be on the Management Committee. Besides all factories in the U.S. and abroad, I'll have responsibility for Purchasing, Manufacturing Engineering, and Quality Control...but not New-Product Engineering.
>
> "My base salary will be $450,000, and I'll participate in the officer-level short- and long-term management incentive programs—and receive options—as you outlined them to me. I'll also get that $160,000 upfront to make up for not coming under your bonus plan this year, and to help with any moving expenses not covered by your most comprehensive moving package, as described in this booklet. And I'll receive a $1,700 monthly car allowance.
>
> "In terms of job security, I'll be getting 18 months' termination protection. You can discharge me at any time for any reason. But unless I've done something criminal against the company, you must either give me 18 months' notice, or pay me for 18 months after you let me go. And if you give me some notice but less than 18 months, you'll continue to pay me up to a total of 18 months from the time you give me notice.
>
> *"As soon as I have your offer letter putting all of this in writing, I'll go in and resign."*

That's the way.

Just *assume* Herb will be putting what you and he have agreed on into an offer letter. When he does, you'll resign. And, of course, not before.

How can he refuse? He'd have to say:

> "Well, you've accurately summarized what I'm going to do for you if you join us. But I'm certainly not willing to confirm in writing what I've just been telling you. Why, that would help you hold me and the company to it later on!"

No, he can't say that. And when you have your "offer letter," you have your "contract." The essence of your agreement with him is in writing.

About the only resistance he could put up would have to go something like this:

> "We do things here on a handshake. There's mutual trust. It's almost like a family. You have my word. That ought to be good enough. And if it isn't, then maybe you and I don't have the right relationship to go ahead on anyway."

Your obvious rejoinder would be:

> "Herb, there's no question that *you and I* have exactly the right relationship. I know you'd never break your word to me. But, God forbid, something might happen to you...or me...on the way home tonight, or next month, or a year from now. I know of an instance where that's exactly what did happen. So before I resign, I'd really appreciate a note from you."

If Herb refuses, no matter what reason he gives, you're better off not going to work for him.

Virtually no employer will refuse you an "offer letter."

But many will deny you a "contract."

Yet the two papers amount to the same thing!

Ironic...but true. Ask for an "offer letter" and you'll almost never be refused.

But ask for a "contract," and you'll be refused more than half the time:

> "No way, George. We just don't *have* written contracts here.

> Why, I don't have one myself. I can't...and I won't...do for you what nobody's ever done for me. We're not one of those shifty outfits where that sort of thing is necessary. I trust my boss completely to do what he promises me. And he's never let me down. If you can't think of me the same way, then maybe I'm not right for you...or maybe our company isn't right for you."

Now you've confronted yourself with a tough argument to overcome. You've asked for a "contract." You haven't merely *assumed* you'll get an "offer letter"...something virtually every company gives, and something your prospective boss *did* get when he came aboard.

Lots of luck!

Why should your would-be boss try to achieve for you, an unproven newcomer, something he's never received during nine years of loyal service and outstanding performance?

Seen through his eyes, your asking for a "contract" seems presumptuous, if not downright unreasonable. Fortunately, there are several rejoinders you can make, and I'll lay them out for you.

But don't blunder into arguing for a "contract," when an "offer letter" will work equally well, and be vastly easier to get. The trick is to find out in one of your earliest discussions...long before you begin "negotiations"...whether the company uses "employment contracts," and whether they're willing to give you one. If not, don't even bring up the subject later on. Just *assume* your way into an "offer letter" that covers the same ground.

But suppose...for whatever reason...you want to get a mutually signed document labeled "Employment Contract" out of a company that traditionally refuses to give them. Here are the arguments you can use:

1. "It's a logical, businesslike approach to a business matter. People die and move on, and memories fade. A written agreement is the obvious safeguard."

2. "More and more companies *are* writing 'employment contracts' for senior managers these days." Some estimates and surveys suggest that over 50% of America's largest corporations now enter into formal written agreements with a substantial number of their executives.

3. "I have an 'employment contract' at my current company, and

I appreciate the security it provides. It's just one of many advantages, and I don't feel like moving to another company and getting *less* on any score than I've got now."

4. "With today's business uncertainties, all executives are more reluctant to move than ever before. I believe that it's important for your company to rethink its policy against giving contracts. Not only do I want one. But I'll also be trying to recruit other outstanding and well-situated executives to work for me here. Being able to give them the reassurance of a contract will be very helpful."

5. "Moreover the company can extract some important concessions from the executives it has under contract. We can put reasonable restrictions on their ability to walk out and leave us in the lurch...to join our direct competitors...to reveal our trade secrets... to be paid for work other than ours in their spare time...and so forth. Besides helping us get people, our contracts can help us get *what we want out of them*."

There you have your strongest pro-contract arguments. Use them as you see fit.

If you do wind up negotiating a formal employment contract, lawyers will be involved on both sides.

Don't underestimate their prodigious ability to destroy a good deal for you.

I've seen it over and over. An executive gets a once-in-a-lifetime opportunity. In a love-feast of seeing eye-to-eye on absolutely everything, the prospective employer and employee "let the lawyers take over from here." Far from merely "getting things down on paper" or "tying up loose ends," as the happily mated principals expect, the result is total destruction of the deal.

Here are a couple of examples. Names, of course, are changed to protect the foolish.

Len was President of a $550 million group of companies owned by a $18 billion conglomerate. I recruited him to join a far more prestigious $8 billion corporation as President of its $1.2 billion group of similar companies. He wasn't and never would be a corporate officer of the $18 billion company, because his businesses were insignificant to its volume. At the $8 billion company, on the other hand, he'd head one of just four "Groups," and he'd be a corporate officer and a Director.

Len and the CEO readily agreed on everything...salary, duties, directorship, generous participation in incentive programs, and a fistful of stock options. So the CEO supplied a contract, which Len had a week to check out with his lawyer.

On the second-last day, Len phoned me. He was at the office of a prominent attorney used by his sister, a world-famous entertainer. "I don't know what to do, John. I'm getting way more than at X corporation, but this guy points out that it's quite a bit less than the other three Group Officers make. He wants me to ask for more."

I told Len it was too late. The CEO would tear up the contract, if Len went back on his word. And besides, Len was becoming one of five top officers and a board member. Any inequity would be corrected as Len proved himself through performance, and increased the relative size of his group through internal growth and acquisitions. "Attack any other wording of the contract on advice of counsel, but don't let him make you look sleazy and indecisive," I told Len.

"You're right, of course," said Len. "But would you mind coming over here and saying the same thing? This fellow is a close friend of our family. He's an expert, and he's charging me far less than he normally gets. So I don't want to just casually dump on the advice he's giving me."

Shocked...and concerned that the CEO and I had both made a mistake in selecting this otherwise brilliant and successful executive...I walked four blocks and took an elevator 38 stories to the intimidating opulence of the great lawyer's office. The guy was a sleaze! And he was encouraging Len to be one, too. Nevertheless, I spoke diplomatically.

Len did not return his contract as he should have the following day. Nor did he call. After the weekend and two days of the next week rolled by, the CEO and I agreed that I should call Len...hear a good excuse if he had one...and if not, tell him the deal was off. Len may have been advised to await a panicky call from us offering more money. That did not happen. And the deal was off.

Less than a year later, Len's conglomerate divested his unit to a company that didn't need his services. He's had other jobs in the several years since. But none as good as the one he was forced out of. And none even remotely as good as the chance-of-a-lifetime job on which he gave his hand-shake acceptance...and then asked his lawyer to check his contract.

Another example is equally pathetic.

I recruited an executive we'll call Bill, who had built the fastest-growing business in its field for Conglomerate X. The CEO of Conglomerate Y wanted him to take over an operation of equal size and much greater potential.

The attraction...besides an exciting challenge...was a contract, which gave Bill a percentage of increased-profit. Moreover, Bill couldn't be fired except "for cause." Salary was well above Bill's current base-plus-bonus, and the deal was designed to more-than-double his pay after a couple years of his dependably excellent management. Within five years Bill...who was enthusiastic about the opportunity...should have earned about $1.2 million per year, three times his current compensation.

This time the employer's and the candidate's lawyers both helped queer the deal. The CEO of Conglomerate Y wanted Bill's contract signed within 72 hours, to provide extra news at a previously scheduled Monday afternoon meeting of securities analysts. A contract was hastily prepared by company lawyers who, unfortunately, included a clause they use with executives who don't get Bill's deal.

The flawed document was zapped to Bill by facsimile late Friday afternoon. His lawyer pointed out the offending phrase as "bad faith" by the over-eager CEO, who could legitimately be accused of "applying time pressure" toward hasty acceptance. Bill had been invited to call the CEO at home over the weekend with any questions. He didn't. And meanwhile, Bill's current CEO called Bill and pressured him to stay.

Result: Instead of calling his new employer on Monday morning, as agreed, to confirm he'd signed the contract, Bill called to say he was backing out. Shocked, the CEO offered to let Bill's lawyer revise the wording as he saw fit. He also offered to forgo the announcement in favor of any more leisurely schedule Bill preferred. Too late. Bill had been wrongly convinced that his prospective employer was looking forward to breaking the contract.

> Percent-of-profit deals with no cap and no time limit are exceedingly rare. Bill will almost certainly never be offered another one. Indeed, almost no executive ever gets such an opportunity.
>
> But there's a bit more to this story. Although Bill was thrilled with the opportunity, he and his family disliked moving from the "Sun Belt" to the residential suburb of New York, where the business is located. So his lawyer's advice reinforced other qualms. Ironically, Bill's current company soon promoted him to their Manhattan headquarters. Now he lives in a town very near to where his once-in-a-lifetime opportunity is located. But instead of a five-minute drive to the office, he has an arduous daily train ride.
>
> Meanwhile, a more junior executive has completed his first year in the job Bill could have had. Sales are up nearly 50% and profits are up about 70%. This young man receives only ordinary compensation. Bill, on the other hand, would be earning twice what he does with his current company, even after a big raise that accompanied his promotion and relocation.

In both incidents, lawyers served as "sounding boards" and "counsiglieri," when excellent executives were emotionally vulnerable. It's one thing to be coldly analytical and decisive when dealing with business problems...and quite another when weighing an irreversible change in your personal circumstances. Then you reach out for...and cling to...the advice of your lawyer. More than at any other time, you're likely to let someone else *help* you decide, rather than merely provide further input for your *own* objective decision.

Interestingly, the lawyers engaged by both executives were personal friends... supposedly eminent attorneys, and supposedly working for far less than their customary fees. How easy it is to give undue weight to the comments of a lawyer who's your friend, and confirms that friendship through a low fee.

I bring all of this to your attention for a reason. *If and when you negotiate an employment contract, chances are you'll turn to a personal friend who's a lawyer for advice.* From experience I know that's what almost every executive does.

Please be careful.

You've experienced the universal tendency of lawyers to screw up every kind of deal. Know right here and now that they...your friends included... will have just as much tendency to screw up your break-through employment opportunity.

So much for general advice on negotiating your employment contract.

Now let's quickly look at the topics to cover, and how to handle them.

Re-read this section for ideas, whenever you're hammering out a formal contract.

Despite its seeming complexity and its importance to you, your "Employment Contract" will cover only a relatively few matters:

1. Duration of the Contract
2. Your Duties
3. Getting Rid of You
4. Tying You Down
5. Your Compensation, Including Salary, Bonus, Various Stock Options and Grants, Golden Handcuffs, and Golden Parachute.

We'll look at all of these in relation to your self-interest. What would *you* prefer? And what is the employer trying to accomplish?

As you negotiate a formal employment contract, bear this happy thought in mind: Virtually all experts agree that such contracts benefit employees more than employers. You gain more in job security, compensation, and bargaining clout if and when the relationship goes sour, than the employer does in terms of actually preventing you from leaving at an inopportune time and taking your competitively-significant skills elsewhere.

Duration of the Contract

When a new employee is brought in under contract, the agreement is likely to run only two or three years. Key employees already on payroll...and sought-after superstars from outside...are usually tied down for three to five years. The more sure the employer is that he wants you, the longer the commitment he proposes.

Automatic renewal can extend the contract indefinitely:

"This contract shall be extended for additional three-year periods,

> unless either party notifies the other in writing prior to one year from the end of any such three-year renewal."

Very nice protection if you can get it. A more common provision would be an automatic one-year renewal. Consider, however, how favorably an 18-month termination provision may compare with whatever automatic renewal you're offered.

Your Duties

The statement of duties is extremely important, because it opens the door to the two main ways employers try to get out of their commitment. They either:

1. force you to leave by changing your duties, or
2. fire you, claiming you haven't performed them.

It's tough to defend against these twin assaults. But you've got to try. Can you accept a drastic demotion or an onerous relocation? Can you perform to the full extent of a vague and arbitrary standard? If not, keep a sharp eye on the language that goes into your contract.

Nail down specifics. Title? Location? Reporting to whom? With what operations reporting to you? Are you a member of the Management Committee? The Board of Directors? Try to get a statement that you can't be given a lesser title, lower-level reporting relationship, less responsibility, or relocation away from corporate headquarters.

Watch out for these phrases: "*such duties as may be assigned*," and "*full time and best efforts*." If you agree to perform whatever duties you're assigned, stand by for some pretty demeaning ones when your boss wants to get rid of you. Try for a modifying phrase such as "of comparable or higher responsibility and status." And if you pledge your "full time and best efforts," look for an attempt to break your contract if you try to do any outside consulting, writing, or speaking in the evening or on weekends. A better promise would be not to do any consulting or other work for any competitor of your employer during nonbusiness hours while on the employer's payroll.

Getting Rid of You

You'd like to tie up your employer so he can only fire you "*for cause*," as the lawyers say. And very good cause, such as committing a felony against the company. Otherwise, you'd like to force him to employ you to the end of your contract, or at least pay whatever severance is specified.

Your boss, on the other hand, would rather employ you "*at will*," so he can dispense with you at any time, without a reason, and with no financial consequences, just as he could if there were no contract (although these days age-discrimination legislation and sympathetic courts may provide some protection, even without a written contract).

In the end, you'll get a provision that says you can only be fired "*for cause*." But you'll have a tough time getting the statement of what constitutes adequate "cause" worded narrowly enough to give you any real protection. You'll want a lawyer to ponder the exact language. But here are a couple particularly troublesome "cause" statements that you should beware of:

> "*Violations of law and company policy*." Will traffic violations suffice? Taking home pencils and pads to do office work at night and on weekends? Failure to get your expense report in on time? Failing to prevent your teenage son from taking the company car for a spin? Failing to obey any order of a superior officer, no matter how frivolous or demeaning?

> "*Failure to perform duties as assigned from time to time by the employer*." Which duties? Newly-assigned, frivolous and demeaning? Requiring relocation to the island of Elba? Failure to meet unrealistic goals, budgets, and forecasts?

Obviously you should try to get permissible firing "for cause" as clearly worded and as limited in scope as possible. "Illegality" might be tagged "except for misdemeanors not directed toward the employer." And, if possible, try to require "*prior written warning*" before you can be fired for "violation of company policy" or "poor performance." Might as well get a shot at correcting your deficiency.

And try to insist that your firing "for cause" be done in writing, and accompanied by a "*written statement of the reasons*" for firing. If the reasons are flimsy, the company may hate to put them in writing, and may either be less quick to fire, or more willing to pay reasonable severance.

Also insist on an "*arbitration clause*" providing that conflicts under the contract shall be settled by binding arbitration. Court calendars are backlogged for years and trials are prohibitively expensive...at least from your point of view. Quicker, cheaper justice helps you a lot more than it helps your employer.

And finally, try to get a clause continuing your company-provided *medical and life insurance* until you're employed full-time by your next employer. If you fail, federal law [COBRA] may give you some right to continue your medical insurance for awhile. But this area is currently more confusing and faster changing than ever. Check with an expert!

Tying You Down

Obviously one of the main advantages the employer receives is your agreement to work for her during the contractual time period. Since she has you signed up for X years, you'll presumably turn a deaf ear to executive recruiters. And certainly none of the time she's paying you for will go into looking for a better job.

Right up front the contract will say that "the Company employs" and that "the Employee agrees to be employed" from X until Y.

Does that mean you can't possibly leave?

No. As court decisions on these matters often point out, "slavery" ended generations ago. No matter what the paper says, you can't be chained to your desk. The contract gives you various compensation guarantees and some measure of security. But it can't *force* you to work for the employer.

About the best the contract can do for the employer is to try to discourage you from working for any of his competitors. However, that can hurt you. After all, they're more likely than anyone else to want you, and to pay big money to get you. If you're performing brilliantly for your employer, you're able to do the same thing just as well for them.

Two clauses..."*noncompete*" and "*confidentiality*"...will try to keep you away from your most likely alternative employers. Fortunately, both clauses are hard to enforce by suing you for breach of contract, because the employer must *prove damages* in order to get money from you. And most of the time that's not easy. If you leave and take major customers or clients with you, she probably can prove she's lost profits. But if you merely withdraw your management brilliance and the operation doesn't fall apart the minute you walk out, she's got a very weak case.

The "*noncompete*" clause pledging you not to join a competitor during the term of the contract...and possibly for several years afterward...is particularly interesting because there's a logical "Catch 22," which you can use in bargaining with your employer. If you're so valuable that he has to isolate you from all his competitors, then he should be paying you plenty for your work... *and* for your vow of competitive celibacy. Conversely, if your agreement to stay away from your likeliest future employers isn't costing your employer very much, then it shouldn't be very stringent.

Hard as it may be for your employer to recover damages if you join a competitor when prohibited by your contract, the noncompete clause still has some nasty implications. The employer can sue you. And legal costs and time-consuming aggravation will cause you real pain. To your corporate employer they're not burdensome. Moreover, your appeal to other employers may fade if they know you're being sued by your former employer. Indeed, *they* may even be sued...rightly or wrongly doesn't matter...for "inducing" you to breach your contract.

Even though your employer may not be able to win a cent of damages from you in the long run, he can certainly give you trouble when you try to walk out. And in the end he may make you buy your freedom. He may offer to give up his "rights" under the contract if, in return, you give up some of your deferred compensation, a retirement benefit, or your latest earned-but-not-yet-paid bonus.

On the other hand, if you're a really hot property, you may be able to get protection from the company that's trying to hire you. They may be willing to provide the legal defense necessitated by breaking your contract, and to pay any judgment (unlikely) that's entered against you. Now your former employer has to pick on someone his own size. Chances are, he'll drop his sure-to-fail law suit.

So the bottom line is that you can walk out. But you may not be whistling.

In writing the noncompete clause, the employer will try to make the prohibition as broad and long-term as possible...perhaps shielding you from "any company or organization having any activities or interests competitive to the Employer, during this contract, and for X years afterward." You, of course, will want to minimize the prohibition. Try to:

1. *Eliminate the clause.* Say you aren't being paid enough to curtail your most likely employment opportunities.

2. *Void the clause if you're fired*, or if your contract *isn't renewed.* Why should your employer be able to tell you what to do after they stop paying you? Moreover, if discarding you is correct and fair, you'll handicap the competitor. Your current company should cheer you on!

3. *Limit the clause to* ***full-time*** *work for a competitor.* Try to

preserve your chance to do consulting in your industry after retirement or firing.

4. *Narrow the coverage to business units that are directly competitive*. When only one subsidiary of a conglomerate competes with your employer, the rest of it shouldn't be off-limits. Try to get your company to name the two or three competitors it's most concerned about, leaving you a chance to make a future living with the rest of the industry.

The "*confidentiality*" clause pledging you not to reveal your employer's trade secrets is the Siamese twin of your promise not to work for competitors.

Every business has some information it doesn't want outsiders to know... product formulae or diagrams; R&D, manufacturing, marketing, advertising, and e-commerce plans, methods, and breakthroughs; customer identities and buying patterns; incentive compensation schemes; acquisition and divestiture strategy and plans. The list could go further.

The need for confidentiality is legitimate. Unfortunately, the wording of the clause probably *won't* be. It may prohibit you from revealing anything at all about the company while you work there and perhaps long afterward. Indeed, the clause may be so broad that you virtually can't help but run afoul of it. Then whenever the company wants to get rid of you, breach of confidentiality will come in handy as one among several trumped-up reasons.

The employer's strategy is strictly legal harassment. Damages could never be proven for divulging unimportant information that was probably already widely known. But the lawyers could try to claim a "cause" for your firing, as they chip away at your protection under the contract.

Your strategy, on the other hand, is to whittle down the outrageously broad language. Try to *eliminate* the clause. And, failing that, try to have it cover only:

1. intentional (not accidental) disclosures that

2. could be harmful to the company.

In the long run you needn't fear this clause much. But you know why the employer wants it worded to take in the whole blue sky. So do your best to get it worded sensibly

Your Compensation

You'll try to get everything you possibly can, and you'll make sure it's all written into your contract: substantial base salary, maximum bonus opportunity, and maximum participation in all of the company's most lucrative stock-related and deferred-compensation programs.

Go for it!

If you'll report just one or two layers below the Chief Executive, be sure to study the company's 10-K and its Notice of Annual Meeting/Proxy Statement, listing compensation arrangements at the top of the pyramid. And do it *before* your compensation is discussed. The best indication of what you can try for now...and work toward in the future...is to find out what your boss is making, or failing that, what her boss is making.

Chances are, the biggest biggies are covered by programs that don't extend much lower. But you might as well ask whether you're in on a lesser share of the same deals they get. If not, the deal just below theirs? Or a third-level deal? How many people qualify for the highest-echelon incentive compensation program you will participate in? The top 15...or 50? Or the top 5,000?

Despite all the glowing words about how important you'll be, nothing is a clearer indication of where you *really* rank than the echelon of the compensation programs you do-and-don't qualify for. Moreover, some polite pre-employment curiosity may get you included in higher programs, if the goodies your prospective employer is planning for you don't quite match the flattery he's handing out.

When it finally comes to writing your compensation into your formal "Employment Contract," there are virtually no pitfalls. *Without your having to argue and push, the document will fully and firmly state what you're getting.*

Why not? After all, the spotlight is on your compensation. It's the star of the show! It's your inducement to sign the rest of the document. It's what the magician *wants* you to see; whereas up to now we've been on the lookout for what he might be doing with his *other* hand...possibly tying a slip-knot on the contractual straightjacket you're lacing him into.

Since your compensation will slide effortlessly into the contract, the best I can do at this point is to give you a hand with the jargon you may encounter. Plus a few comments, wherever I think they might be helpful:

Base Salary. You want it to be upwardly open-ended..."at least X" and "to be reviewed annually," if escalations aren't included.

Bonus. In general, you'd like any bonuses to depend to a reasonable extent on your performance, or on a smaller unit you'll influence in a major way... not just a huge entity you won't make much difference to.

First-Year Guarantee. Make sure that—at least during the first year—you're assured of making 25% to 30% more than if you stay where you are. Maybe your new salary alone will cover the incentive to move. If not, you can probably get the first-year's bonus "guaranteed" by pointing out that, after years of experience, you know almost-to-the-penny what your bonus will be where you are. Obviously, you're far less certain of the new situation. In the second year, of course, you're happy to be treated just like everyone else.

"Signing," "One-Time," or "Special" Bonus. To make up for not immediately coming under intermediate- and long-range compensation programs and to make your relocation more painless than under standard policy—while still not putting your base-and-bonus out of line with other executives at your level—you may be given a "signing bonus," which occurs only "one-time." It's a sensible solution that's used to take care of a variety of problems, and these days very substantial amounts of money may be involved.

Short-Term Bonus Plan. This is the traditional annual bonus, and it is the most universally used incentive compensation device. You may have to meet goals to get paid, and the amount may vary with performance. But normally, whatever you get is paid in cash and subject to income tax.

Long-Term Bonus Plan. This bonus is paid years after it is earned as if it were deferred compensation and usually depends on your individual performance, rather than the success of the overall company. Payment may even await the time you exit the company, retire, or die.

Stock Option Plans. These differ from company to company, and the same company may have more than one plan in operation.

Incentive Stock Options. Often referred to as "ISOs," these options are highly attractive to employees because the profit they generate may be treated as a capital gain, rather than ordinary income. (Please check current status with your financial advisor.)

Non-Statutory Stock Options. These options are called "non-statutory," because there are essentially no legal requirements as to their issuance other than those resulting from state and security laws. (Here, too, please check with your financial advisor.)

Stock Grants. You don't buy the stock. The company gives it to you...usually as a reward for having been with them awhile and/or for having done outstanding work. The purpose is to give you an immediate sense of owning a stake in the company. Normally grants are ***not*** made to attract a new unproven person, but rather to reward and encourage a valued employee.

Restricted Stock Grants. Here the company "gives" you stock, but you have to stay a certain period and/or meet certain performance goals; otherwise, you won't actually *get* it. Tax implications are continually changing. Check with your personal advisor.

Company Stock with Non-Lapse Restrictions. The company can also grant you stock with a restriction that states that it never lapses, and that you or your estate have to sell the stock back to the company whenever you leave at a price calculated according to a formula established when the stock is granted to you. The formula for the repurchase price must be reasonable...perhaps, for example, book value, plus a multiple of earnings. Here again we have an arrangement that can be used to attract a new employee, who hasn't yet proven how valuable he or she may turn out to be. We also have an arrangement—often used by privately owned companies—that will assure that the current owners of the company will remain forever in control. However, this can be an excellent way to make you legitimately feel—for the time you're there—a "part owner" of what is and may always be a family company.

Phantom Stock Options. This is another device nonpublic companies may use as incentive compensation. Unlike restricted stock with restrictions that never lapse (stock which the company can "buy back" from you), phantom stock options technically aren't stock and aren't options. They are merely the grant of a promise to pay you money in the future according to a formula based on the increasing value of the underlying stock, which you do not and never will own. Although the amount of money you may get is defined by growth in the value of the underlying stock, you personally may have to meet time and performance criteria to get it. This is an unfunded and unsecured obligation, which does not escape creditors if the company goes bankrupt.

Stock Appreciation Rights (SARs). The SAR is a hypothetical unit linked in value to the rising value of the company's stock (if public) or a formula (if the company is privately owned). Value can decrease with the declining value of the stock, but not below the value of the stock (or formula) at the time of grant. Here again, only your personal financial advisor can counsel you on current implications.

Phantom Stock Plan. The stock is hypothetical "shares," not actual shares, and the actual value of the dollar amount originally granted goes up and down with the value of the underlying stock. If the underlying stock splits or dividends are paid, the dollar account is credited with any incremental value, and the actual total value is paid when the individual is terminated, retires or dies. .

Performance Units / Performance Shares. Here a program is devised to encourage the meeting of long-term performance goals by the overall company. Measurements can be in *units* (a dollar amount) or tied to the value of a *share* of stock. Programs can be whatever the company designs them to be, but to earn 100% of the amount targeted to be paid at the end of the program the compounded growth performance during the period has to be X%. Performance at 90% of goal might earn a lesser amount at the end of the period. Lower performance might earn correspondingly even less at the end...or perhaps nothing, depending on the plan's terms.

Performance Cash Plan. Similar to Performance Unit and Performance Share plans, but often with a shorter duration until the proceeds are paid.

Deferred Compensation. Many highly paid executives have historically preferred to defer some of their current pretax income for payment after retirement...or on some other agreed-upon date. These arrangements, called "nonqualified deferred compensation plans," allow you to defer payment of taxes until the income is actually received, when you may be in a lower bracket. (Who are we kidding here?) Income tax rates fluctuate. Recognize that, if you participate in your new employer's deferral plan, you may actually be moving income into a higher future tax bracket than the one you're deferring it out of now.

Also, if you're participating *now* in your *current* employer's plan, be careful to find out what happens to your deferred compensation accounts when you quit. These plans almost invariably change the payout rules upon termination, and the amount of interest you receive often changes, too.

Interest-Free or Low-Interest Loans. If you get a loan from your employer at a considerably lower rate than any other lender would provide, the IRS will want to tax you on what you're saving. And your employer may insist that the loan becomes due if you try to leave...a form of "Golden Handcuff." You're probably better off getting her to strong-arm a bank into loaning you the money.

"Golden Handcuffs." This term covers any compensation program that makes it costly for you to leave the company. Various options, stock appreciation, and incentive compensation schemes make you stick around in future years to get the benefit of what's "granted" now. Click go the handcuffs!

"Golden Parachute." Any compensation arrangement that generously takes care of you, if you're thrown out or demoted because of a corporate merger or takeover is covered by this broad and colorful term. You have to be a very senior corporate officer to get a "parachute." But you'll probably land ever so softly in the lap of luxury, with one to five years of your highest-ever base-plus-bonus annual compensation (your choice of lump-sum or continuation payments), immediate vesting of all "granted" stock, immediate exercisability of all options, immediate payment of all performance-contingent sums under incentive programs, immediate vesting of your pension benefits, and continuation of your company-paid medical and life insurance for the same duration as your compensation, or until you join another corporation full-time.

Notice that you immediately get your hands on lots of stock. Letting the jackals have it at their inflated takeover price will be sweet

> revenge. And even if you're not high enough on the pyramid to enjoy a "parachute," you'll probably get control of a lot of your "granted" and "optioned" stock, when the corporation that promised it to you goes out of existence. You, too, will probably enjoy immediate payment at what will surely be a near-term, and maybe an all-time, high price.

And there you have the jargon of compensation, as it relates to your employment contract. Please understand that the above definitions and suggestions are not intended to provide legal or tax advice. For that, you must engage a competent professional and make him or her aware of all the specifics of your documents and situation.

Unless you're headed for the very apex of the corporate pyramid, you'll have to content yourself with the compensation programs that serve you among many other executives. But make it a point to find out what programs the company *has*, and try to get yourself included in the highest-level ones you can possibly qualify for.

At this point, I've done all I can to help you reach for a wide slice of the corporate pie. Knowing the terms and techniques we've discussed will help you press for the best possible deal...and to document that deal as firmly and cordially as possible.

We've wound up by talking about what you may encounter in negotiating and drafting a formal "Employment Contract." But don't forget that you can also get good written evidence of your employer's commitments in your "offer letter," and in various other letters and memos that will pop up over the years. Save everything in writing that makes a promise to you.

Corporations forget.

To protect your interests, it's up to you to remember.

Chapter 18

Consulting...

You may find your ideal job by not looking for one.

Believe it or not, one good way to find an excellent job working for someone else has always been to try as effectively as you can to become a self-employed consultant.

Ironic? Indeed, but true.

The prospective clients you must solicit to establish a consulting practice, are some of the same people you'd reach through job-hunting involvement with your personal contacts and networking among strangers.

Moreover, these influential people are likely to react far more favorably when called about a meeting to discuss an intriguing consulting proposal, than when hit for the 500th time with the dreary "I'm in the

process of making a career change and would like to have the benefit of your thoughts and advice."

As a consultant, you meet and interact with people who have an ideal opportunity to evaluate you, your thinking, and your work. Eventually there's a good chance that one of your clients will decide that he or she would rather "own the cow than keep on buying the milk." You'll be offered an on-payroll position.

However, by the time that happens you may be doing so well that you value your independence far too much to give it up.

Who knows which option—in the end—you'll prefer? Fortunately, it's "heads you win...tails you win."

Should you try to be a consultant?

Let's be very clear on what we're talking about. We're not discussing the common resume cover-up of a gap between jobs with an entry that says "Self-employed Consultant," even though the writer didn't aggressively seek assignments, and didn't handle any worth mentioning. We're talking about actually trying to sell consulting engagements, with the intention of doing a fine job and, hopefully, building a lucrative practice.

Only if you really *want* to become a consultant, will your solicitations have any credibility. If you ask for an appointment to discuss consulting and then come in and try to wheedle your way onto the payroll, you'll have zero credibility...both as a consultant and as a potential employee.

So don't even consider the consulting option unless you:

1. have *expertise* that would benefit clients;

2. have the *skills and personal characteristics* to be a consultant; and

3. are willing to *accept the advantages and disadvantages* of a consulting career.

We'll consider these three issues separately. Then if "all systems are go," we'll take a look at how trying to become a consultant not only won't encumber your search for a salaried position, but may in the end lead to the happy dilemma of self-employment *and* tempting on-payroll offers.

What expertise do you have that can lead to successful consulting engagements?

Almost every $100,000+...or $400,000+...executive has knowledge that could be valuable to clients. Analyzing problems and opportunities, and figuring out what actions to take, are what every executive does. Consulting merely applies those processes to someone else's problems.

However, the most successful consultants...especially *individuals*, in contrast to the huge generalist outfits like Bain, McKinsey, A. T. Kearney, Cresap McCormick & Paget, and Booz Allen & Hamilton...generally have a *personal specialty*, which they obviously know more about than a crew of MBAs from one of the giants.

To illustrate, here are four enormously successful individuals who now consult for a living, after leaving the payrolls of large corporations:

1. Mr. W headed Marketing for one of America's leading magazine-publishing and direct-marketing companies. Deposed along with his boss, the Chief Operating Officer, in a political upheaval more than 25 years ago, Mr. W immediately offered himself as a consultant to all the other major print media and direct marketing companies. Then only in his 30s and already making an impressive mid-six-figure salary, he immediately

earned more money consulting than he ever made on payroll... and his earnings have more than kept up with inflation Today he still works out of his home with no secretary and only voice mail to take his calls. Over all the years—and still today—many of his former competitors have been the consulting clients who support his handsome lifestyle.

2. Mr. X was Chief Executive of a medium-sized public company (10-figure sales), which he led through a very successful decade of growth, both by internally generated new products and through acquisitions. Deposed by his Board, not for poor performance but allegedly for a drinking problem, Mr. X became a consultant to a competitive corporation with the sole mission of scouting small companies for acquisition. Operating on an annual retainer discountable against brokerage fees on the deals he arranged, for several later years he earned "double what I did as CEO."

3. Ms. Y, a brilliant and widely traveled international marketing executive with one of America's largest corporations lost her job when the unit she worked for was divested and the acquirer already had someone in her role. Her global networking to find employment uncovered an opportunity to barter huge quantities of two basic commodities. "I knew lots of people all over the world," she says, "but nothing about bartering or about those products." She put her first deal together, "with wall-to-wall help from my friends." Now she makes her living (and what a living!) as "an international finder and trader."

4. Mr. Z retired as a senior scientist with a major chemical company while still too youthful to become inactive. Today he helps foreign chemical companies avoid transgressing U.S. patents, and advises them on whether technology they have developed may be patentable in the U.S. He does no work that requires an expensive laboratory or a research staff. He merely draws on his personal expertise and the resources of a public patent library.

Notice that each of these successful consultants offers a personalized specialty. None is a jack-of-all-trades in competition with the large national consulting firms. What comparably special contribution could you make... and to whom? Only you can say. But here are some possibilities:

1. CEOs and Division heads of companies in your field might value a "second opinion" on basic issues. Or they might welcome "take charge" handling of special projects.

2. Perhaps there are companies in fields *related* to yours, that should consider diversification into categories you know more about than they do.

3. If you're from a large company, you may have sophistication that smaller firms can't afford to keep on payroll. Offer project assistance. Or perhaps several days per month on a continuing retainer.

4. Foreign companies wanting to penetrate the U.S. market might need your help.

5. Conversely, domestic companies might benefit from your international experience.

6. If you're on the leading edge of any specialty, there are always "trailing" edge companies, who are potential clients.

7. And all around us are web-related startups of all sorts that need experienced counsel and do not yet have enough capitalization to fill every key slot on the organization chart.

Do you have the skills and personal traits to be an independent consultant?

Okay, let's assume you've figured out how your expertise *could* help corporate clients. There's still the question of whether you have the right *personal attributes*. Working for Bain, Cresap, Booz, McKinsey, or A. T. Kearney is another major-company job. To succeed independently you need everything "large-firm" consultants have...and more:

Salesmanship. Except for "repeats" and referrals from current clients...and starting out you won't have any...every assignment will be one you've had to sell. If you can't approach new people, and can't tolerate rejection, don't go into consulting.

Analytical, Bright, Logical Mind. Clear, insightful thinking is...along with your special expertise...what you're selling.

Written and Oral Communication. Sometimes you'll present informally. But expect to deliver written reports and projected presentations. If your pen and platform skills aren't good, don't enter consulting.

Self-Start and Self-Discipline. Performing *what* you promise *when* you promise is mandatory. And no supervisor will check your progress toward deadlines.

Creativity, Open-Mindedness, Resourcefulness, Versatility, and Adaptability. Being able to invent, improvise, ad lib, and generally deal with the unexpected and unfamiliar is essential. "By-the-book" people have little to offer as consultants.

Common Sense, Practicality, and Pragmatism. Down-to-earth, easy-to-implement recommendations are the best kind.

Service Attitude. Unfortunately, consulting is a service business. If you'd much rather be accommodated than accommodate, consulting is not for you.

Ability to Cope with Financial Insecurity. There's feast and famine...no regular payday.

Fortunately, traits that may handicap you in large organizations are tolerated...and even desired...in an independent consultant.

Do you have these characteristics? If so, you may be more welcome on retainer than on payroll.

Obvious Personal Brilliance. The same superior who feels threatened by a subordinate with an off-the-chart IQ is delighted to find such brain-power in an outside consultant.

Strong Self-Assurance and Matching Ego. Same goes for a strong, sure touch and lack of self-doubt...scary in a subordinate or a peer, but excellent in a consultant who can be summoned and dismissed at will.

Task Orientation and Political Aloofness. A consultant must be politically sensitive. But he or she can concentrate on the work, safely ignoring the day-to-day skirmishes that can undermine the too-task-oriented corporate employee.

If you're not average, not a team player, don't care about petty politics, don't suffer fools (other than paying clients) gladly, and tend to challenge authority and to be outspoken...then perhaps you can do the corporation, and yourself, more good as a paid observer than as a salaried participant.

Indeed, even if you have patently undesirable characteristics from a corporate point of view, you may be able to get by with them as an outside consultant. Maybe you like to work three 18-hour days and take a week off. Maybe you have a drinking problem but can discipline yourself to keep critically important commitments. Maybe you're brilliant, but have a loathsome personality and are insufferable as both a boss and a subordinate; yet you're capable of exquisite charm when you choose to display it. Show your clients only the good side of your Jekyll & Hyde personality, and you can succeed as a consultant.

Don't get into consulting unless you can endure some very negative aspects.

The withdrawal pangs are excruciating!

As a $100,000+ or a $600,000+ executive, you're used to having power. People at your beck and call. The prerogative to decide. Even when you have to seek higher endorsement, *you* determine what is or isn't considered.

Every executive who's had power and suddenly becomes a consultant is shocked by the role reversal. Nothing I say can adequately prepare you.

As an executive, you can call meetings to which any number of people must come...some of them perhaps far more prominent and wealthy than you are. And you preside. One by one the participants tell what they've done to further your objectives since the last meeting, and what they propose to do in the future. Finally, you assess their contributions, and you assign further work in preparation for the next meeting.

How different when you become a consultant.

You can still call a meeting. But this time it's probably a fact-finding session, at which *you* take notes. And if a report has to be written, *you* write it.

Maybe, on the other hand, your meeting is a "progress report" to your client. Elapsed-time-pressure was building up, and you called her before she called you. But now you're the supplier. What have *you* accomplished since the last meeting? And what will *you* do prior to the next one? The shoe's on the other foot. And until you get used to it, it *pinches!*

Moreover, what you produce will be analysis and recommendations. You don't control whether...nor how well...your advice will be carried out. And you may become very frustrated that lots of your time and hard work produces minimal benefit. *Welcome to the world of consulting*. You merely study and suggest. You no longer decide.

Another pain will be the lack of big-company support services. Your computer and laser printer, plus online informational resources, will substitute for personal assistants at the outset. But you'll miss the research department, and the reproduction and mailing people...not to mention all your other capable subordinates. Indeed, you'll even miss the social interaction and the sounding board for ideas that were afforded by the sheer numbers of people around you.

And of course there's the fundamental insecurity of not having a predictable paycheck. Every dollar you get is for a consulting engagement you've sold, and for work you've done...or as general contractor farmed out to others, verified, and submitted to your client. No selling? Then no engagement... no money. Poor performance? Then no repeat business...no referrals...no money. The marketplace is a stern and objective judge. Submitting yourself to it is a gutsy move that shouldn't be taken lightly and, indeed, shouldn't be taken at all by some people.

On the other hand, there are very real advantages to being a self-employed consultant.

True, you don't have a scheduled paycheck. But then you can't be fired. You can lose clients and you can go broke. But through lush and lean, you have a job. There's some security and self-confidence in having even that much control over your life.

And when you make money, only you and the IRS decide what to do with it. Moreover, since you and your accountant will set up an advantageous corporate vehicle and tax-planning program, you'll build net worth faster on your own than on a corporate payroll, if your gross profit matches your former salary.

You will, of course, be wallowing in trivia as you set up your office and begin to generate paperwork. On the other hand, your contacts as a consultant will tend to be at *very high levels*, probably CEOs and heads of divisions and functions. And you'll mainly be dealing with major issues.

Also, for some unfathomable reason, outside consultants seem to be treated with more courtesy and respect than subordinates and peers on the corporate payroll. If you're successful and can revel in prestige-without-power, you won't feel you've gone down in the world.

The freedom and flexibility of a consulting lifestyle is another "plus." You can probably do much of your work at home, or at your place in the country or at the shore. And working hours are entirely up to you.

Moreover, consulting is the one form of self-employment that won't risk your life savings. Your first office will probably be at home, and you can equip it with a first-class computer, word-processing and other software, a printer, copy/fax equipment, a simple brochure, elegant stationery, and cards, for $12,000...maybe less.

If you've ever wanted to be a consultant, the time to "go for it" is immediately after you become unemployed.

To the $100,000+ or $500,000+ executive, loss of job—regardless of reason—is a crushing blow. He feels worse if his boss simply wants to replace him, than if his company is acquired and there's no need for *two* Chief Financial Officers. But not much worse. Either way he's devastated.

Even if he's protected by a generous severance, the worst of the situation is the uncertainty. What next? He does everything possible as fast as possible. Yet he still worries, "How long until my next job?"

But suppose that our former CFO has thought about services he might offer as an independent consultant, if he ever gets an opportunity to become one. He has some intriguing ideas that should appeal to CEOs and CFOs of mega-companies at the top of *Fortune*'s list. And he also has some concepts that might interest the CEOs of relatively unsophisticated companies in the $50 to $75 million range...maybe even the entrepreneurs of promising pre-IPO "early stage companies."

In walks the grim reaper, just as before. But this time our hero is ready. Even before negotiating his final severance arrangement, he visits the printer to order stationery, cards, and a simple but elegant, triple-folded 8 1/2" x 11" brochure. Day one of his "unemployment" becomes the first day of his consulting practice.

"Death, where is thy sting? Grave, where is thy victory?" Far from being traumatized and immobilized, our new consultant is *busy*. He may still be receiving money from various sources as a result of his "unemployment." But he's also developing a new income stream. Today he's his own boss... hard at work for a sensible, pragmatic taskmaster. Yes, he feels pain, disappointment, and self-doubt. But far less of it than most other people in his circumstances, because *he hasn't taken time out to be unemployed!*

If you're going to try consulting, don't waste your "personal contact" and "networking" opportunities on ordinary job-hunting.

Some people solicit consulting assignments only as a desperate "stop gap" measure *after* they've tried several weeks of personal contact and networking in an effort to get another job. This is entirely the wrong sequence for two reasons:

1. Their approach has been *unnecessarily weak and vague*.

2. Having labeled themselves job-seekers, they have *destroyed their credibility* as consultants.

Let's look at the "job-applicant-first" scenario. Here's what's said to the *personal contact* by the applicant who *hasn't* read Chapter 4:

> "Have you got a job for me, Barbara? I'm leaving X Corp."

If the applicant *has* read Chapter 4:

> "Barbara, I'm leaving X Corp., and I wonder if you might be a reference for me on our years together at Y Corp."

And to the *networking contact*, following the classic script:

> "Mr. Kindly, I'm in the process of considering a career move, and I wonder if I might have just a few minutes of your time to

get the benefit of your thoughts and suggestions."

Now imagine going back to these same people weeks or months later and professing to be a consultant. Whether they'll bluntly state it or not, people you've previously contacted as a job-seeker will think:

"So nobody would hire you. And now you're down to seeking part-time work!"

Failure to find full-time employment doesn't enhance anyone's credentials. Why even *consider* someone who's a consultant only because she couldn't get a regular job?

A timely consulting proposal shows you off as a potential employee.

Generally speaking, a sales call as a consultant is a much better "show-case" for your abilities, experience, and achievements than an ordinary "personal contact" or "networking" call as a job-seeker. Consider these advantages:

High level contact. Your consulting targets will be CEO, Division President, Group Officer, or VP-Chief-of-Function. Networking, unfortunately, takes you randomly to whomever your preceding contacts happen to know...maybe the ideal people to evaluate and "sponsor" you, and maybe far from ideal.

Something meaningful to talk about. The most pathetic aspect of a networking appointment from the job-seeker's point of view... and the most irritating from his host's...is the flimsiness of purpose: "a chance to get your insights and suggestions." People worth seeing are busy. Probably your half-hour no-agenda meeting—if you can get it—will cause your host an extra half-hour of homework. How much better to discuss a consulting proposal geared to his needs. He'll feel more interested and receptive...less manipulated and imposed upon.

You MUST show your credentials. When offering to do consulting, you have to hand out and discuss something on paper that states your services and qualifications. Your expertise is what's being sold. And after presenting your consultant's "puff" piece, you can also provide your chronological "sales representative" resume, as a more forthright disclosure than most consultants are willing to make. But be sure there's no "Position Desired" or "Descriptive Summary" that implies ordinary job hunting.

You operate in a "selling" format. Moreover, on a sales call you're *much more in charge* of your presentation than you are in the "social conversation" of an interview, and the "brain picking" of a networking call.

You have greater opportunity to "sample" yourself. Provide a specific proposal that's written as well as oral. If well done, it's a persuasive *free sample* of your work. You submit it as a consultant. But it also demonstrates what a good conceptualist you'd be as an employee.

You don't have to be said "no" to. "Personal contact" and "networking" visits cry out for a disclaimer from your host:

> "I wish, Sandra, that we had a position for you here. Unfortunately, there isn't anything right now."

On the other hand, your consulting presentation tends to get the standard reaction we always give to salespeople...a courteous hearing and a noncommittal answer:

> "Well, I don't know. *Let me think about it.*"

The psychology is just like asking a personal contact for a reference instead of a job. He's left with a matter that's still *somewhat open in his mind*. And you have *an opportunity to come back* with another proposal, based on what you learned at your meeting.

You're easy to say "yes" to. Hiring you as a consultant is low-risk, compared with putting you on payroll. Your assignment is like a "*budget-priced trial size*" of a consumer product. There's enough to measure performance, but no big investment to lose if the product is disappointing.

Without disrupting his current organization, your client can evaluate your performance, and how he enjoys working with you. He may "make you an offer you can't refuse." Or he may pay for your project—which has probably been worthwhile in any event—and say goodbye.

Pitch, Performance, and Payment ...Getting Started as a Consultant.

In all earlier editions of *Rites* I mentioned briefly how consultants—from individuals to giant firms—traditionally solicit and bill clients.

The Usual Way

Regardless of whether the client company or the consultant thinks up the project, it's usually done in segments, with a separate fee or estimate for each "phase." Phase I may be a preliminary study of the issues. Phase II, if warranted by I, expands the investigation or begins to implement the findings of I. And Phase III (plus perhaps others) completes the project. This is the way you will probably be structuring your consulting proposals.

The Selling vs. Doing Dilemma

However, there's a classic problem when any individual tries to function alone as a consultant: "When you're selling, you can't be doing, and when you're doing, you can't be selling." To thrive you must do superb work. Unfortunately, that may leave too little time to go out seeking new clients and projects to keep you busy after your current projects are finished.

Crandall's Way

The first of the four consultants I described earlier was one of my executive recruiting clients until he and his boss were suddenly ousted in a corporate political war. The next day my client and good friend, whom we'll call Crandall, had a phone line for his consulting practice hooked up in his den. Soon, with no support beyond his personal computer, he was advising almost every competitive company in his industry. Right from the start, he said he was making more money on his own than he'd made on payroll. Today, years later, he's still going strong, even though he's so financially secure that he surely doesn't *need* to work.

A few years ago, I asked "Crandall's" permission to tell you the secret of his success and he agreed. Notice how radically he departs from the traditional formula:

> "I never quote on a 'per-project' or a 'per-phase' basis. Instead I negotiate a low monthly billing rate...one the client is extremely comfortable with and will never consider excessive or wasteful. And for that I gladly do whatever they want. If they demand too much, I can ask for a higher monthly rate. And if I'm no longer useful, they can fire me. My low price and flexibility make for an easy sale.
>
> "But notice the advantages: Once a client is signed up, I never have to resell them or convince them to proceed. The 'can't-sell-while-you're-doing' problem disappears. And my monthly bill becomes a fixed part of their overhead. It's always in the budget.
>
> "Also, because my bill arrives every month whether they use me or not, the young people in the company feel free to call for my advice. There's no bill to defend. Senior management people are usually too busy to call; so if I were uppity and only dealt with them, they'd cut me off because of infrequent use. But they like to have me training their young folks. The young people know that. So they cite me in their proposals and reports to senior management. That keeps my name alive in the company. And pretty soon senior management is asking the more junior people, 'Have you checked this out with Crandall?' I become part of the team. As you know, I've got clients who've been with me for 25 years."

How's that for a different and absolutely brilliant approach! Thank you, "Crandall," for sharing it.

When do you get your job offer... when you "pitch" your consulting proposal or after you've performed?

Obviously, an offer could come at either time.

However, I can't caution you strongly enough not to go in with a phony offer of consulting services, which is really a thinly disguised request for employment. If that becomes your game, it's dishonest; it's transparently obvious; it deserves to fail; and it almost certainly will fail.

Frankly, if a prospective client is going to offer you a job, you're better off if the marriage comes *after* a successful consulting engagement, not before. By then your prospective boss knows you and your work. There's less chance that he or she will preempt your independence, only to become disillusioned and discard you later.

Meanwhile, you've also found out some beneficial information. You know lots more about the client company. You know whether you enjoy consulting. And, after your "firm's" pension and profit-sharing plans are in place, you know how much more you're salting away when working for yourself, rather than a large corporation. This is probably your one-and-only shot at independence. Don't toss it away casually.

On the other hand, your earnest pitch for a consulting assignment will show you off to advantage. Therefore, it very possibly may lead to an excellent employment offer, instead of a consulting contract. If so...and if you accept... congratulations and best wishes! You've found a job by not looking for one.

But suppose you don't get an employment offer. You just keep on working for several employers.

Is that so bad...if you make good money and enjoy your work?

Consider two statistical facts:

1. America's largest corporations are cutting the number of executives they employ (and other employees too).

2. America's small- and medium-sized companies are still creating most of the new jobs at all levels.

That's right. More jobs—at all levels—are ending than are being created by our biggest corporations. Fortunately for the nation, and for you if you're seeking employment, our smaller companies are creating more new jobs at every level, including executive, than the largest corporations are ending. Unfortunately, smaller companies struggling to grow can't afford—at their stage of development—to pay high salaries.

So the good news is that smaller companies may have employment for you when the bigger ones don't. The bad news is that, being smaller, they can't afford to pay you as much as you'd make with MegaCorp.

However, with luck, you may get equity participation in a smaller company that can make you far, far richer than if you'd stayed at MegaCorp earning three times the salary for a few more years, while watching your MC options sink under water.

Which brings me to the wise words of my friend Paul, 59 years old, who was tossed out of his Senior VP - Marketing & Sales job after 29 years with the same company:

> "I discovered two things, John: It's true that there aren't always that many *jobs*. But there's always plenty of *work!*"

Acting on this insight, Paul, who'd led a hundred people at headquarters and a thousand in the field sales force, immediately got in touch with the presidents of smaller companies marketing to the same types of customers he'd dealt with for 29 years. He also contacted the presidents of customer companies he'd sold to. And several of those CEOs realized that Paul had a great deal of knowledge they could use.

As a result, Paul got "Crandall-type" continuing relationships with three smaller companies, working the scattered-day equivalent of one-week-per-month for each. He also secured exclusive distribution rights to a couple product lines within his tri-state area.

The bottom line for Paul is *employment*. The three consulting activities generate about the same money he was making in his corporate job. But now he has much more economic security. He can lose any one of his part-time deals and still have a good solid income. Meanwhile, his personal distributorship business continues to grow, entirely separate from his three relationships with other companies. Paul has found the best of all worlds...a chance to become entrepreneur of his own young business, while retaining an income from other people's established businesses.

Chapter 19

The Rites of Passage: What, When, and Whether

We've come a long way in examining *Rites of Passage* within the executive subculture.

We've studied the tribal rites of the headhunters. And we've looked beyond those classic rituals, to every other method by which senior executives move from company to company, including the web...today's tribal drum of the Global Village.

You know *what* to do.

Now let's consider *when* and *whether* you should take advantage of the techniques we've discussed.

You'll use different methods at different times, depending on your circumstances. And if you're willing to invest some effort when you're not about to change jobs, you can put yourself in an exceptionally favorable position to hear of attractive opportunities throughout all the rest of your career.

You know the saying:

"An ounce of prevention is worth a pound of cure."

No question about it. Consider this corollary:

"An ounce of preparation is worth a pound of panic."

And this one:

"An ounce of promotion is worth a pound of patience."

Most people can agree with the logic of statements like these. Yet few can bring themselves to act on them. If you're one of the exceptional few, you'll gain a lot from this chapter.

Knowing the available techniques, let's apply them to the three degrees of job-changing interest you may have throughout the rest of your career:

1. **Happy where you are,**
2. **Unhappy...but you can't show it,**
3. **Unemployed.**

There's no free lunch. Some of the most helpful techniques are also the most work. And the best time for some of them is when you don't have to do them at all.

Sorry about that!

But you're no stranger to hard work. The trouble is you're doing 100% of it for your employer. Divert some to building a career investment in yourself.

If now's the time to move, do everything you can to make the best possible move. Every subsequent job—by promotion or by stepping outside—will build on your next one.

On the other hand, if everything's going great, now's the time to make yourself known. You won't be called and tempted with leap-ahead opportunities, if the most relevant people in the world outside your company don't even know you exist.

1. What to Do Now, When You're Happy and Not Looking

Your objective now, when your current job is extremely satisfying and you're on a fast upward track, is to make yourself and your excellent record known.

You won't leave for another position unless it accelerates your career by at least two to five years in both responsibility and earnings. Otherwise, stay where you are...avoid the risk and hassle of moving...and wait for another opportunity that ***does*** provide a really major leap ahead.

So how do you get offered opportunities which are much better than the excellent situation you already have?

You're Happy: Make Yourself VISIBLE! to the Finest Search Firms

Consider both the traditional labor-intensive way...and also the easy web-facilitated way.

Visibility to the Finest Retainer Executive Recruiters

The traditional way to make yourself known to the top search firms has long been to mail them an on-paper resume for their files. If it's impressive and you're in a field they serve, a few firms might even scan it into their database. A *very* few firms—if you seem outstanding—might also transfer your papers to a folder on a shelf.

The vast majority, however, will merely check to see if you match a current search. If so, you'll go into a pile for consideration. And if not, into the trash. That's the harsh reality. More fresh new resumes will arrive tomorrow morning!

Online submission can make you continually and easily findable by the top search firms. Also, it fits your current favorable circumstances.

Years ago the fate of unsolicited on-paper resumes wasn't so harsh. But today recruiting is fast-paced and computer-aided. Fortunately, increasing automation at even the most prestigious firms can work to your advantage.

Identifying Target Firms for Career-Long Relationships

These days, you have *Rite*Site.com, which—among its other objectives—is specifically designed to help you become known to the finest recruiters. It's the only executive membership site—indeed, the ***only site***—that identifies the nearly 600 search firms (out of 12,000) that do 100% of their searches "***on retainer***" (paid, even if no one is hired). These firms are "Rites-Honored" on *Rite*Site.com and in Appendix II of this book.

Because they work only on retainer, these elite firms submit candidates or resumes ***only when they're paid to do so***. Therefore, you can be reasonably confident that they will ***not*** (1) "float" your resume to lots of companies (possibly including your own employer) and (2) share it with other headhunters for further "floating," as a great many contingency recruiters routinely do.

Two Easy and "Risk-Reduced" Ways to Put Yourself Where the Best Recruiters Can Find You

Not only does *Rite*Site.com eliminate the need for you to research the leading firms, it also provides two unique tools. In ***less than 30 minutes*** you can start your career-long cultivation of a few great recruiter contacts.

1. Use "Email My Resume." This automated tool, is unique. Invest ***just 15 minutes***. E-mail your resume to your choice of several hundred out of the nearly 600 "Rites-Honored" firms. You'll send individual messages that will come from your email address (not *Rite*Site's). You'll send in the format each firm demands (attached document or body-of-the-email). And you'll completely avoid your web service provider's ban on sending too many emails.

I hope you'll send to 400 or 500 of these firms. Only a very few—if any will have an immediate reason to reply to you. And only a few will wind up putting you into their firm's permanent database. But, over the coming months and years, you ***will*** hear from a few members of those few firms. Be cordial and helpful. Become respected and favorably remembered. Today's 15-minute investment may return hundreds of thousands of added dollars as your career evolves and accelerates in the future.

2. Post Your Identity-Revealed Resume in RiteSite's "Rites-Honored Database." Here, too, you'll start to become known to the top recruiters while hiding your interest in outside opportunity from your current employer. This database can only be entered by Rites-Honored recruiters, who pay nothing to do so. Employers and ordinary recruiters, on the other hand, ***cannot buy their way in at any price***. Other job sites, including "Big 4" paid executive membership sites, ***do*** sell resume access to everyone willing to buy.

So invest 10 more minutes. Post where only the "Rites-Honoreds" can find you. This is the perfect supplement to your EMAIL MY RESUME campaign. You cannot know which of the firms—if any—will put your e-mailed resume into their own database, nor how long they may keep it there.

Here, however, you're in control. You're ***absolutely sure*** your resume will always be available to the recruiters you most want to find it. Also, you can edit it whenever you wish. Moreover, if you're qualified for more than one type of position, you can post up to 3 different resumes. Emphasize different experience and achievements. No search firm allows multiple resumes. On *RITE*Site.com, you ***will*** be found when different categories are searched.

Building Equity

Over the years you will occasionally hear from recruiters in the firms you reach now. If you're impressively helpful—and you always mention the type and level of job that ***would*** turn your head, there's a good chance that the miniscule amount of time you'll spend cultivating prestigious recruiters will pay off someday with an extraordinary opportunity you'd never have seen otherwise. Or, your circumstances may change. Then, your cultivated recruiter relationships may yield several good job opportunities when you unexpectedly ***need*** a new position. (See pp. 121-123).

Under this strategy, you invest a very small amount of effort now. Afterward, you just relax and "go with the flow." The trick, of course, is to get the flow started.

A sign in the garden supply store my Dad used to go to said:

The best time to plant a tree is 20 years ago.
The second-best time is now.

Notice the identical verb in both sentences. The horticultural situation *was* no better 20 years ago than it *is* today. Don't fail to take at least some small action for the future right now. Someday you'll be glad you did!

You're Happy: Make Yourself Visible to the WORLD!

Today the web makes it possible to publicize yourself and your achievements to everyone everywhere. Review Chapter 14. Consider to what extent you'd like to be "findable." Invest another very modest effort. Create a truthful and impressive ***identity-concealed*** resume. Post it on *RITE*Site.com and/ or on any other sites that reliably facilitate anonymous posting (something I believe more may begin to do in the future).

Become findable by everyone on the planet...recruiters, corporate employment departments, entrepreneurs staffing startups and—unavoidably—also the many scoundrels plying the web. On *RITE*Site, ***all*** can discover your background and achievements. Indeed, your ID-Concealed Resume may even—with exceedingly rare luck—turn up on a Google search. However, people who find your resume ***still can't find you***. You've concealed your identity. They must ***reveal themselves*** to you. Respond if you like what they propose. Stay hidden if not.

Why, you ask, should you post your Identity Concealed Resume for all the world to see when you're happily employed? And especially why, when *RITE*Site's "Rites-Honored Database" provides immediate availability of your identity-***revealed*** resume to the recruiters of nearly 600 *RITES*-Honored search firms?

The answer is that your career breakthrough may not come from an elite retainer-compensated search firm. You may hear from a respected contingency recruiter with an attractive opening or an entrepreneur with an exciting startup that doesn't yet pay search fees. Or you may hear from fast-growth companies that do their recruiting in-house. For example, the Vice President - HR and Administration of a small but growing consumer products company with sales of over $500 million, whom I know personally, checks for needed management talent on *RITE*Site. When that happens, I'm the recruiter who misses out on a search fee!

Another reason for posting your identity-concealed resume when you're happily employed and don't *need* another job is that you can be entirely frank—and even downright greedy—in stating right at the top of the resume your minimum requirements to even consider a move. Make them stiff and forthright. You can't do *that* if you wait until you're unhappy and need another job. In essence say, "Don't bother me unless you've got at least this to offer." Your identity-concealed resume begins:

> CHIEF FINANCIAL OFFICER / VICE PRESIDENT - FINANCE
>
> Now Controller of Fortune 100 Company. In line for CFO. Prior blue chip Investment Bank / VC experience. Deep M&A experience.
>
> EQUITY STAKE IN EXCITING YOUNG COMPANY ESSENTIAL. WILL NOT CONSIDER ANYTHING ELSE.

That certainly lays it on the line! But why not? You're happily employed and will not consider anything less than ideal. Say so!

Note that you can comfortably say something quite blunt in an identity-concealed resume posted on the web, when you'd never even think of doing so in an identity-***revealed*** resume e-mailed into the database of a prestigious retainer search firm. There, you'd be more concerned about image...and want to set a more gracious and appealing tone.

The point is: Seize the day when you're strong! Don't lie. Don't exaggerate. If a recruiter contacts you because of your identity-concealed resume and finds you in any way less than you implied, you will be permanently branded untrustworthy on the firm's computer and you'll ***never*** be presented by that firm...even for jobs you're clearly qualified to do. But—within the boundaries of truth—be bold, when bold is easy and might pay off handsomely.

You're Happy: Test the market for potential career and lifestyle changes you might want to make.

When you urgently need a new position or face any kind of employment problem—from an obnoxious boss to the rumored sale of your division—it's no time to try to be creative and seek the position you'd love instead of the one you're likeliest to get.

Now, when you're employed and happy, is the time to experiment and see how far you can push the boundaries. Call your personal contacts who could hire you to work for them in the field you desire. Say, as I suggest in Chapter 3, that you're thinking of a career change into something closer to their field than yours. They know ***your ability*** and ***their field***. Would they be willing to be a reference for you...indicating to others their knowledge of you that suggests you can succeed in their field?

The online equivalent of this strategy is to marshall the best resume you can truthfully create using your experience and successes in unrelated fields to support your stated objective. Post it as *one* of your four *identity-concealed* resumes on *RITE*Site. Retainer search firms normally will ***not*** endorse your outreach in a new direction. But creative, self-confident employers—and especially entrepreneurs—seeking subordinates might.

The point is: When you're securely and happily employed, you have the time, optimism, and creativity to pursue self fulfillment, rather than mere survival.

You're Happy: Prepare a "sales representative" resume.

Every executive should take time out to develop an outstanding on-paper resume. It's the core of your communications POWERTOOL. You never know when you'll have an opportunity to use it. Break-through opportunities pop up unexpectedly. And then there usually isn't enough time to create a resume that accurately conveys your far-above-ordinary performance.

Follow all the suggestions in Chapter 12. Try 2 to 4 pages which, because of crisp formatting with plenty of white space, can be scanned in 20 or 30 seconds and then—in the rare instance when interest develops—can be devoured by the newly-intrigued "reader," who wants to know more.

You'll probably spend several weekends and evenings developing this compelling ***credential***. Figure at least 30 to 60 hours to create those very few pages which—with irreducible succinctness—factually demonstrate how very special you are. Consider the effort a "dirt cheap" investment, in comparison to any other self-advancement program you can undertake. Prepared to perfection, your resume can be used immediately for distribution—either online or by mail—to the retainer recruiting industry. Do the hard preparatory work now. Updating in the future will be quick and easy.

Even if you have no intention to submit this resume directly to search firms or to post it on *RITE*Site, you should create this most important of all career weapons and keep it tucked safely away in a drawer

You're Happy: Take your once-in-a-career risk of publicizing yourself *now*, while it's minimal and you can afford it.

The risk of disclosure when you submit your background to the top retainer firms—whether by e-mail or snail mail—is very small. And the earlier in your career you distribute your information, the less risk there is.

Even if several recruiters in the retainer firms are close friends of your boss, your nastiest rival, or your company's president, it would be highly unethical for them to call and say, "Guess who just submitted her resume?" Or guess who we just contacted because he has his very impressive resume on *Rite*Site?

Loose talk like that is just as verboten as "floating resumes" among the finest search firms. And it's even less likely, because there's no money in it. Presenting your resume to a potential employer during a search might net $50,000 or $100,000 or more. Disclosing mere *receipt* of it to your current employer would earn no fee. All that would produce is a reputation as a gossip...deadly in the search business. (See the exception to this rule on pp. 425-426.)

Several years ago a contingency recruiter serving the advertising industry offered, for an annual fee, to inform subscribing employers whenever she received a resume from one of their employees. Public outcry forced her to withdraw the new "service" a few days later. Employers, interestingly, expressed as much outrage as employees.

Face it. You *do* want to start career-long "awareness" relationships with a wide cross-section of retainer search firms. Sooner is better than later. Even if word should accidentally leak out of one firm, wouldn't you rather deal with that now, when you're "riding high," than in the future when you might be in jeopardy? Wouldn't you rather "explain" to your current boss who's just promoted you, than to his replacement who may be looking for an excuse to fire you?

You're Happy: Get the unattractive job suggestions out of the way now.

Regardless of what you say in your covering note, every retainer firm that directly receives your resume will assume you're either out of work, or afraid you soon will be. That's when—and why—people submit resumes.

Inevitably, therefore, the first opportunity you hear about from each retainer firm you've contacted will probably be no better than lateral in responsibility...and possibly unattractive in other ways, too, such as compensation, location, and/or the prestige and stability of the company involved.

Indeed, whenever a particularly unattractive assignment comes in, the recruiter handling it always alerts the research staff to *"comb the new submissions"* looking for someone unemployed who might want the position, since nobody happy and secure in a comparable job at higher compensation, in a nicer location, or with a better company would even consider it.

Time and refusal are the only rebuttals to the "out-of-work-or-in-trouble" presumption that dogs every submission. If the firm doesn't call you until a year or two after getting your resume, and you're still at the same company with the same title or better, they'll know you're secure. Your letter stated the truth. Similarly if, on their initial call, you refuse a position comparable to your current one, that too will confirm you're "solid."

The recruiter's phone conversation with you will be duly noted in your computerized file. And even though you "submitted" instead of waiting to be "discovered," you'll henceforth be regarded as a secure executive who can't be tempted with anything that isn't a substantial advancement. Let's see what a recruiter types into your information after such a "first conversation":

> "Called him" (date) "to propose VP - R&D of Tacky Technology Corp. Not interested, since he already heads 150-person section of the corporate lab, and is moving up fast, at Blue Chip Corp. *Very impressive* on the phone. Sent in his resume 'just to get acquainted.' So he's ambitious and probably will move for the right thing—*but it better be good!*"

The next suggestion you receive from this search firm will be far more interesting.

You're Happy: Help the impressive recruiter.

At the same time the recruiter was sizing you up, you were evaluating him. He quickly understood that you're secure and won't move laterally. Then he agreed with your realistic assessment of the job he presented, and asked you for recommendations. He wasn't dense. He didn't try "high pressure." Indeed, he seemed professional, pleasant, straightforward, and down-to-earth.

As a result, you went out of your way to be helpful. You listened carefully and came up with several potential candidates, plus another person who wouldn't be interested personally, but might identify candidates. Accordingly, the recruiter made an additional notation that becomes a permanent part of the firm's information on you in their database:

"Helpful source" WP

Congratulations! You're well on the way to becoming what they call in the business a "hot file"...someone every recruiter in the firm tries to get access to the minute he or she undertakes something relevant. You'd be a great candidate...and if not, a great help.

Do not, however, help all recruiters equally. If the person sounds like a dope—and some may, even from the most prestigious firms—don't open up to him or her. Any firm may have new and/or inadequate recruiters on payroll, who will ultimately flunk out. No point in going out of your way to help them.

Be most helpful to the most impressive. In each firm, they're the ones you want to have knowing how good you are, and fighting for the right to call you up. They'll be the most discreet with the information you give them. They'll appreciate it most. And they're the most likely to be handling the bigger and better jobs that will interest you in the future.

You're Happy: How much help is too much? Should you identify people in your own company?

First let's consider prospects who are above you. If you're in a relatively small firm which might be hurt by the loss of a potential candidate, keep quiet. The company would be hurt, and you would also be hurt.

But if the company has several layers of good management, it probably won't be hurt, and a promotion to fill a vacancy above you may "domino" into a promotion for you, too. Figure that a really good recruiter will dig to find out what he needs to know. If you won't tell him, he'll just keep asking until someone else does.

Even when the recruiter's opportunity could be a career breakthrough for one of your subordinates, you may decide to identify your person and let him know that you're his benefactor. One of the most senior and respected executives at General Electric (now retired) always recommended his best subordinates to me. Several became candidates. But every single one that wound up getting an offer from one of my clients ultimately refused to leave GE. They just couldn't walk out on a boss—and because of him a company, too—with such obvious concern for their welfare.

Of course, the best way to shield your subordinates and others in your organization is to suggest lots of ideal candidates from other companies. That way, the recruiter has less need to probe your place. If you're extremely helpful and she likes you, she'd rather not cause you grief, even though circumstances will sometimes force her to do so.

You're Happy: Keep records on recruiters.

The recruiter isn't the only one with a computer. You've got several too!

Start your own file on every retainer recruiter—and his or her firm—that you have any contact with. Begin by noting any submissions you make. Then update each firm's information whenever one of its recruiters calls. And, of course, start a new file whenever someone calls from a firm you haven't contacted.

Years go by and memory fades. Computers don't forget. You want to know who called from each firm, when, what position was discussed, who you recommended if you weren't interested, and *your evaluation of the caller*. Armed with this information, you'll always know who is at least vaguely aware of you at each firm. If more than one person from the firm has called, you know who sounded the most competent and with whom you had the best rapport. And if you suggested people who filled the recruiter's jobs, you can later remind him who they were.

Let's see your notation after the conversation on Tacky Technology. It's the first entry in your file marked "Gordon, Rossi & Boodles":

> Will Pickham, VP, called to suggest VP - Engineering job at Tacky Technology. Shaky-sounding company. Only 55 engineers. Seemed to think I was in trouble. But then became interested in how well I'm doing, and what it would take to move me.
>
> Told him "*no way*" on Tacky, and recommended Dan Daring and Renata Ready at Intel and Fred Fearless at Xerox. Also Sally Smart and Peter Plunge. Loved the idea of Sally—said, "Mr

Tacky would flip for someone from Microsoft." Will was fascinated that 5 years after leaving, I'm keeping current with their people to staff my department here, and could name a young risk-taker over there. Also surprised I'd name one of my own best subordinates, and he let *me* tell Pete to call him about Tacky, so I could stress having Pete's interests at heart. I also told Will to use my name and call Erna Entrepreneur for ideas, because Erna's company is in the same field as Tacky.

Liked Will! Very professional, yet down-to-earth. Restoring a Model A roadster. *Excellent GR&B contact.*

Your conversation with Will Pickham has been well documented on both sides. Before we move on, let's look again at the last couple words in Will's notation about you:

"Helpful source" WP

That modest description hardly conveys Will's full enthusiasm for you. In one phone call, you've gone from "just a submission" to someone Will won't forget when he has another search in your field. Meanwhile, of course, you may be hearing from other recruiters at Gordon, Rossi & Boodles...some of whom you'll like, and help, as much as you did Will. But until someone else comes along that you like even better, Will's your key to GR&B.

You're Happy: Update the records that recruiters are keeping on you.

Switch to on-paper and voice mail contact with recruiters you know.

From now on, whenever you receive a promotion or change companies, send a brief personal note to the recruiter with whom you have the best relationship at each retainer recruiting firm.

Or maybe just write something like you'll see on the following page across the top of a copy of the official announcement:

Will —
An exciting challenge
Is the roadster finished?
Regards
Paul

Will's assistant will probably see that your improved title and duties get into the firm's information on you. However, you won't rely on perfect staff work inside Will's firm. If it's large enough to have several recruiters besides Will—and it does, as you'll see in Appendix I—you'll also submit your news via an impersonal "Dear Recruiters" e-mail to the overall firm at the same time you send your personal on-paper note to Will. Indeed, if you're a member of ***RITE***Site.com, its EMAIL MY RESUME feature enables you to effortlessly zap your announcement note and revised resume to any firms you select from the Rites-Honored Recruiter list. With almost no effort on your part, these firms are updated on you without your ever reassuming the "out-of-work-or-in-trouble" presumption.

Chances are, by the time you're announcing your next promotion two or three years after doing your initial submissions—or posting your ***identity-revealed*** resume on *RITE*Site.com for only "Rites-Honored" recruiters to see—you still won't have heard anything from three-fifths of the firms who've had access to your information. They:

1. Haven't yet needed anyone with your background;

2. Didn't get around to calling you when they did have a need;

3. Or they automatically purged your resume from their database because there had been no contact for X years or months after submission.

If you're dealing directly with these firms, "update" the nonresponding ones with a brief "Dear Recruiters" note announcing your promotion—or your move to a new company—just as you do Will at his firm.

Sure, these outfits have probably thrown your resume out of their computer or weren't equipped to gobble it into their database when you first submitted it to them. ***But that's no reason why you should go back to zero with them and reaccept the "out-or-in-trouble" presumption***. Instead, refer to your original submission and include a copy of your current resume updated to show the happy new development. Say something similar to the example on the following page.

The vast majority, but not all, of the fine retainer-compensated search firms will be set up to receive resumes by email. Prior to a broad-ranging distribution like this, check to see how each firm currently prefers to receive resumes. A majority require that you submit your resume as a separate Microsoft Word document sent as an attachment to your e- mail. A minority have the opposite requirement. They refuse to open attachments and insist that emailed resumes arrive in the body of the email.

Obviously, if you send in the unwanted format, you're no better off than not sending at all. If you don't feel like phoning or visiting the websites of recipient search firms to determine their current format preference, an easy solution—indeed the only solution I know—is to use the EMAIL MY RESUME tool on RiteSite.com. It automatically sends in the firm's preferred receiving format. The only other popular resume-submission tool widely used by executives is offered as a separate purchase by a leading directory company. Just one emailing by them costs about the same as a no-renewal-fee membership on RiteSite with no charge for additional emailings to Rites-Honored recruiters, even years later. Also, the other service is far less stringent in its definition of retainer operation (85% vs. RiteSite's 100%). Moreover, it makes no effort to identify and comply with search firm format preferences. All resumes in its one-time distribution are sent as attachments.

Note that a very few Rites-Honored search firms refuse to receive resumes by either email method and insist, instead, on submission only via an input form on their website. These firms are identified on RiteSite, where a convenient alphabetical list of links makes it easy to visit the websites of these few—and all other—Rites-Honored firms

Sample Promotion Announcement via E-mail

(Use current date.)

RITA R. READER
638 North Wingra Avenue
Milwaukee, WI 53959
Home: (524) 302-3093
Office: (524) 302-9800
Cell: (069) 830-1995

RE: PROMOTION TO SR. V.P. - GLOBAL MARKETING & CORPORATE STRATEGY

Dear Recruiters:

This is to update my information submitted January 7, 2015.

I was then V.P. - U.S. Marketing of Sterling Steel U.S.A., the central domestic business unit of Sterling Steel Industries Inc., and also chair of our Global Expansion Task Force.

On April 7, 2015 I was promoted to Sr. V.P. Global Marketing, Sales & Strategic Partnerships, reporting to the CEO, in other words, corporate Chief Marketing Officer. In part, this promotion rewards my work as strategist and lead negotiator on nine major international acquisitions and/or joint ventures during the past 27 months.

Sterling Steel is a $14 Billion diversified basic industries company with mining, smelting, fabrication and power generation operations in 18 countries.

For your convenience, my updated resume completes this e-mail.

Sincerely,

Rita Reader

CHIEF MARKETING OFFICER OF FORTUNE 500 CORPORATION

QUALIFIED FOR CHIEF EXECUTIVE OR CHIEF OPERATING OFFICER

As Vice President - Chief Marketing Officer of this $14 Billion diversified basic industries company I supervise the Marketing, Sales, and Strategic Planning functions in 35 autonomous

(Continue to finish complete resume.)

If you're doing an on-paper distribution, here's a promotion announcement letter that also encloses an updated resume:

(Date)

Mr. Powers Prominent
President
Prominent Associates, Inc.
925 Park Avenue
New York, New York 10025

Dear Mr. Prominent:

Since I originally submitted my confidential resume for your records in November 2015, I've continued to receive additional responsibility at Blue Chip Corporation, which last month promoted me to Vice President - Engineering.

Paul

Paul Crane

Enclosures: Announcement
Resume

And there you have it...a program designed to bring you maximum personal advantage from the retainer executive recruiting industry, throughout the rest of your career.

Rejoice! If you've fully taken advantage of today's computer technology, you have a better chance than ever before of not being overlooked—although not necessarily *called*—when your ideal opportunity pops up, whether inside a leading search firm or in the vast employment universe beyond.

A modest investment of effort now, while you're happy, may pay an incredible dividend in future years. It could be as valuable as a lottery win, if it lets you know about a breakthrough career opportunity you wouldn't have had a shot at otherwise. Even if it only reveals a sporadic series of lateral moves you might make, it could be as good as a lottery win...if it comes at the right time to spare you the unforeseeable future pain of job-hunting while unemployed

One more thing to do right now if you can *easily* afford to: Buy some elegant personal stationery.

Every executive should have *engraved* (not thermographed) stationery listing home address, and (despite "high society" tradition) phone numbers and email address in *discretely tiny type* (for future job-hunting). In the office and at home, personal stationery enhances congratulations, condolences, gift enclosures, RSVPs, and correspondence in support of charitable and cultural causes. Bringing traditional personal stationery into the 21st century isn't easy, so here's an example for your consideration:

Rhett A. Butler
1175 Tara Plantation Drive
Charleston, SC 29041
Phone: 803.977.1357 Cell: 803.977.3827
rhettb@southern.net

Order now, and get the 8-week production period out of the way. Ignore stationery and jewelry stores, and shop the "Yellow Pages" or the web under "Engravers." Get the prices commercial users enjoy. You may not want to store enough for an emergency job campaign...at least 1,000 Monarch ($7^{1/4}$" x $10^{1/2}$") and 500 standard ($8^{1/2}$" x 11") letterheads; plus 500 Monarch and 2,000 standard (#10) envelopes. If so, just buy the "minimum"...probably 1,000 Monarch sheets and #10 envelopes. Your "die" will be cut and on file, and additional quantities will only take two or three weeks.

For less than $1000 (including die) your minimum order should provide enough stationery to be a "class act" for the next ten years. And with your die on-file, you'll have an insurance policy against the "production-line look" for as long as you have your current home, email, and phone, and the engraver remains in business. (To get a *really* good price, ask your lawyer and your accountant what engravers their firms use.)

Fine stationery lends a classy executive tone to your correspondence, which more and more these days is likely to be just a quick handwritten Monarch note...alone in its matching envelope or attached to an interesting clipping or announcement. Nice personal stationery is also terrific for lending credibility to your resume's cover letter in your Communications POWERTOOL that you use in a future on-paper direct mail campaign to corporate CEOs. Recruiters, except for the ones you've met or talked to on the phone, can best be handled online these days.

But look again at the prior headline. It says, ***"If you can easily afford to..."*** Don't delay a school tuition payment or even a family vacation just to indulge in luxury stationery. For most people most of the time it may not be worth what it costs.

2. What to do when you're unhappy... but you can't show it.

Too bad you didn't submit your resume—or at least make yourself available on *RITE*Site—to the recruiters of the nearly 600 *RITES*-Honored firms two or three years ago, when you were well situated. There's no better remedy for "unhappy-but-I-can't-show-it" than an opportune call from a recruiter. Taking action two years ago would ***not*** be bringing a flood of calls now. But a few welcome calls would be trickling in...maybe one or two a month...and that might be enough to solve your problem.

But let's drop the "I-told-you-so's." Now we'll swing into action...***but cautiously***.

Secretly Unhappy: You can still contact retainer recruiters. But now you must be far more careful to avoid the ones your employer uses.

If you think your employer may be as unhappy with you as you are with him, then you've got to be especially careful not to send your resume to the retainer recruiters he uses. Ordinarily you could accidentally contact those recruiters and there'd be no problem. Professional ethics would prevent their calling your employer and saying, "Guess who we just got a resume from."

Now, however, circumstances are different. Your employer may have confided his concerns about you to one or more of the firms he uses. Clients usually *do* discuss key managers' strengths, weaknesses, and probable destinies with trusted retainer recruiters. And after that happens, recruiters *will* disclose receipt of a resume from an employee previously described as questionable:

> "You mentioned last week that after we finish the Director of Engineering search, you want us to work on the VP - Manufacturing slot. And maybe early next year, if she doesn't get on the team, you may want to think about a replacement for your head of R&D.

> Well, I feel a little awkward telling you this, but under the circumstances I feel I must. Today we got a resume from your VP - R&D. Maybe we should proceed immediately on that search, too. What do you think?"

Of course you can't be forewarned if your employer is having secret discussions with a recruiter the company hasn't used before. But stay away from any that he and the rest of the company are known to use.

How can you determine which to avoid? Probably only three or four should concern you, and you may already know them. However, before you proceed, make some discreet inquiries. And if your personal assistant is tight-lipped, subtle, and loyal, send her on reconnaissance, too. Provided with a good "cover story," she may get better information than you will.

Also, if you haven't already done so, consider putting your information at the disposal of leading search firms by posting your identity-revealed resume in *RITESITE*.com's hidden database that only "Rites-Honoreds" can see. Merely allowing yourself to be found and contacted on *RITE*Site has a far better chance of not causing notice or repercussion at a dangerously connected search firm than hitting that same firm's researchers with an on-paper submission as a current client's employee. That scenario *always* sets off a loud alarm, which is *always* relayed to the person heading the firm's relationship with the client. Whether his or her lips stay sealed may depend on what will generate the highest billings...not on your preferences or safety.

Secretly Unhappy: Talk to your best personal contacts.

Obviously, your personal contacts can be trusted. Explain that everything is "hush, hush," but you're beginning to look around. Will they serve as a *confidential reference*? As we discussed in Chapter 3, this request will announce your availability just as clearly as asking for a job or job leads. Yet it avoids the up-front final negative, "Sorry-I-don't-have-anything-and-don't-know-of-anything."

Approaching personal contacts is your #1 most obvious and potentially productive step to take when you're secretly unhappy and beginning to look around.

This technique is also extremely versatile. Are you ready for a Board membership? Try saying to a CEO whose Board you'd love to be on, "I'm expecting a couple Board inquiries...although nothing's underway so far that I'd really be interested in. But you know me and how I'd behave and be helpful. Would you mind being a reference if and when the time comes?" This strategy has put quite a few of my friends and clients on their first corporate Board. Additional memberships are infinitely easier to achieve than the first...and, of course, involve different tactics.

Secretly Unhappy: Consider "targeted networking."

Ordinary networking is obviously out of the question when you're trying to maintain confidentiality. However, if there's a specific target person you want to reach—perhaps a CEO who has a key executive nearing retirement with no obvious successor—you may be able to do so as suggested in Chapter 4.

A word of warning, however. CEOs and other executives aren't as sensitive to your need for confidentiality as most first-class recruiters are. These executives aren't malicious...just less accustomed to professional caution. Try to reach your "target" with *no more than one trusted intermediary* who knows your "target" personally and will be sure to stress your need for secrecy.

Secretly Unhappy: Log onto the Web

Visit the sites of all of the *companies in your field that you'd most like to work for*. Are they posting any jobs that interest you? If so, do some investigation. That shouldn't be too difficult, since it's your industry. Find out who the posted job apparently *reports to*. If you already have even the slightest acquaintance with that person, pick up the phone. Accept voice mail if that's all that's offered. Explain you're employed and need utmost confidentiality. Say you've ***heard***—not read—that she ***may*** be looking for someone like you. May you send her your resume? If you don't know her, try for a confidential introduction through a trusted mutual acquaintance. Do *not* meekly apply as instructed through the HR department when you have a more personalized and confidential route.

Spend a couple evenings or a weekend online, checking to see what jobs at your level have been posted on the commercial employment sites. ***Indeed.com*** is your most obvious starting point for a wide ranging review of openings posted on the web.

If you have not yet joined *RITE*Site.com, now would be an ideal time to sign up. Quite apart from posting your *identity-revealed* resume to be seen only by *RITES*-Honored Recruiters, you also have the ability to post up to four different *identity-concealed* resumes. *Identity-concealed*, you can still—even now as the dark clouds gather—present yourself in ways that feature different truthful aspects of your background in addition to just "more of the same." Yes, post three of your four RiteSite.com *identity-concealed* resumes in pursuit of the position you realistically are most likely to get. But also devote one to an equally truthful resume that pursues your dream.

Secretly Unhappy: Do a secretive direct mail campaign.

When you absolutely must get into action in a hurry—and do it secretly—you should always consider direct mail, with a "sponsor" signing the letters and getting the replies. The method described in Chapter 13 can reach upwards of 1,000 or 2,000 potential employers within 2 to 4 weeks and locate the approximately 3 to 6 among them who, according to realistic odds, currently may need you. If luck and odds are with you, about 1 to 3 of the 3 to 6 will be sufficiently impressed when they meet you to extend an offer.

But please don't ignore the warnings on pages 269 through 275. If what you have to offer—or what you write—won't be persuasive, then you're not going to be any more successful having someone else send it than if you'd sent it yourself.

3. Unemployed!

A rough time. But at least there's no need for secrecy; all options are open to you.

And knowing what you do now, you'll find a new job far more efficiently than you would have before.

The reason many executives have agonizing difficulty finding another job that fits their talents, background, and compensation requirements is that they don't know what you do.

They're able. And not lazy. Indeed, they work desperately hard.

But they misallocate their efforts, spending huge amounts of time on activities where they've long since passed the point of diminishing returns. Meanwhile they mistakenly neglect other techniques that could be highly productive, because they consider them of little value or even counterproductive.

Unemployed: Approach executive recruiters realistically.

Executive recruiters are the most misunderstood and misused job-hunting resource. Be sure you use them wisely.

Many unemployed executives spend lots of time early in their search hoping to find a recruiter who'll offer to "help." If they're attractive and readily employable, these executives eventually find the harmful "help" they seek... widespread emailing—and perhaps mailing, too—of their resumes to their likeliest employers with a price-tag attached.

You'll deal knowledgeably with contingency recruiters, restricting yourself to the fine ethical firms you're confident will never send your resume or refer your name to *anyone* without contacting you first and getting your authorization for that specific referral. You'll also keep a knowing eye peeled for suspiciously "helpful" behavior by retainer recruiters. And, above all, you'll avoid the unfamiliar—and uninvestigatable—recruiters who abound on the web.

On the other hand, the commonest and saddest of all errors made by senior executives is wasting precious time by haunting the halls of the largest retainer firms, trying through networking and other cajolery to meet yet another of the firm's recruiters in yet another office. Vainly they hope to find out about more than one-job-at-a-time, among the dozens and even hundreds of appropriate openings a firm of that size is always in the midst of filling. You know that this strategy is impossible, and you know why.

Sadly too, many unemployed executives fail to submit their resume to many reputable retainer recruiters, hoping by such misguided "selectivity" to enhance their appeal and usefulness to the small number of firms they choose.

You're aware of the "selectivity" pitfall. So when you're unemployed, you'll routinely submit your resume to the widest appropriate array of retainer firms...knowing that no two such firms will ever be working simultaneously to fill the same opening, nor will they ever ask or care which other *retainer* recruiters you've provided your resume to.

If any retainer firm is already showing you an opportunity, you realize that they're about as involved with you as they ethically can be. You won't try to pressure them further, except perhaps, to inquire if they do ***"parallel processing"*** after you discover a second search that you'd like to be a candidate on *being done by the same person in the firm.* If the second search is being done by *another* of the firm's recruiters, chances are you're better off pursuing the job on your own, never letting on that you know the firm is involved in search #2. If you do that and the employer on search #2 submits you to his recruiter at the firm, you may *automatically* get parallel processing!

Needless to say, you will call up the one or two most impressive people you already know at each retainer firm where you seem to be dormant. You'll tell them your current circumstances and mail them an updated on-paper resume.

And when you want to push aggressively into the consciousness of retainer firms that don't already know you, you may *encourage an appointment* by using the clout of someone who spends money with them or who's been a candidate or a helpful source. You won't invoke the name of a competitive recruiter. You also won't waste time on more than one "door-busting" visit per firm, and you won't storm multiple offices of the same firm.

Above all, you won't devote the overwhelming preponderance of your time to recruiters, as so many ill-informed executives do. As you fully appreciate, your main mission is to break through to the vast number of jobs the retainer firms are withholding from you, not merely to pursue the one-job-in-3-or-4-months that each firm may actually show you. Even in the less-than-a-handful of the largest firms that now publicly admit to doing some "parallel processing" you're not going to see more than twice that number.

Unemployed: Sign up for *RITE*Site if you haven't already.

When you're unemployed, you have plenty of free time to take full advantage of all of *RITES*Site's recruiter contacting services. Use *RITE*Site.com to make yourself findable by the entire world, while *withholding* your identity and all of your contact information. Here's instant publicity, with maximum safety. Also, of course, post your *identity-revealed* resume for viewing only by members of the nearly 600 *RITES*-Honored retainer search firms.

Notice, too, the list of links to the websites of all the Rites-Honored firms. If a site has a form for direct insertion of your resume into the firm's database, ***use it!*** Simultaneously, of course, you'll also use the EMAIL MY RESUME tool. There's no harm in reaching the same firm twice using two different channels.

Don't worry. You will not suffer any penalty for redundancy. Yes, it may seem that you are currently in an all-out job search. But why not? When true, that's the only impression you can or should convey. Make your communications truthful and impressive and they will be considered. Would you rather be overlooked?

Unemployed: Use personal contacts effectively.

Needless to say, you'll call your closest contacts immediately...and perhaps get together with the best-situated ones (see Chapter 3). They'll be surprised and pleased when you merely ask them to serve as a reference. Relieved that you haven't asked them for a job, as most unemployed executives do, their long-standing esteem for you will rise even further.

Reminded of what they already know you've done, and apprised of your latest accomplishments, your contacts will think about how they or someone else in their company may be able to use you. Here, too, you've avoided the serious mistake most executives make, by not forcing a closed-issue "unfortunately-we-don't-have-anything" answer.

Unemployed: Use networking. But keep it in perspective.

Now that you're out of work, you can openly indulge in networking. But don't over-emphasize it to the total exclusion of other useful techniques. Lots of executives have that tendency...especially when pointed that way by "single-method" outplacement counselors. For example, there's a psychologist in a fine firm that offers outplacement among its many other services and endorses networking as the only worthwhile method. When he and I discussed the plight of unemployed executives, he cited one of his close personal friends as a successful example. A very high-level executive of a top company in a huge industry, the psychologist's friend lost his job when two giants in that field merged:

> "Fortunately, networking saved him. After being 'out' for more than a year, he finally found a job as executive director of a trade association in a totally different field. He makes a lot less money than he used to. And I don't think he likes his new work very much. At least I know he's unhappy not to be in his regular field. But without networking, he wouldn't even have the job he's got. Networking saved his life!"

Did this man launch a direct mail campaign?

> "No, I advised him not to bother. You get very limited response from that."

Did he try to launch a consulting practice in his specialty? As former head of a large portion of one of America's leading companies, he'd be considered an authority.

"I don't know."

What a classic result of networking-and-nothing-else! This person got the kind of job you'd expect him to get eventually, if he continued long enough meeting and questioning kindly people in the large city where he lives...a job uncovered virtually at random, which has nothing to do with his prior background and current preferences.

Take a more balanced and realistic approach ...even when you don't want to relocate!

If the fellow had spent "more than a year" marketing himself to his regular industry nationwide, chances are that's where he'd be working today. Random local networking is ideal for lower- and middle-managers, whose non-specific skills and moderate compensation fit a broad spectrum of jobs. It's far less adequate for the $100,000+ or $400,000+ executive who wants to capitalize on years of experience in his specialty.

If you're ever unemployed, you'll certainly use networking. Often it will serve your purposes better than any other technique. For example, *if you strongly want to avoid relocation, and your skills fit well into a wide variety of companies, and your compensation isn't unusually high, then networking may be the only method you'll ever need to look for a hometown job.*

Let's say you're a financial officer who's been CFO, controller, and chief of internal audit in various size companies at various stages of your career, and you need to stay in Cleveland. Obviously, you can be useful to a wide range of companies and nonprofit organizations. Meeting prominent people all over town and getting each of them to refer you to two or three others is a good way to find out about potential local opportunities.

But also do what you can to speed up the process. Visit your main public library. Make friends with the Reference Librarian. Ask about resources—online and print—that will identify the companies, financial institutions and nonprofits large enough to potentially be your employer. If you're a *RITE*Site.com member, check the Direct Mail section on the left menu. Go to a public, corporate or university library that will allow you to use their subscription to ***LeadBuilders.com***, the most comprehensive of all resources for your purposes. Within commuting distance of your home, you'll probably discover dozens—and perhaps even hundreds—of potential employers you'd never have thought of otherwise.

No matter how you identify your "targets," be especially careful to phone-check published data before sending a local area mailing. You've got fewer potential employers nearby than nationwide. They're precious! Don't waste any by overlooking them ... or by seeming careless in the way you address their decision makers.

Doing a meticulous job, you can send the appropriate person in one to two or three hundred local organizations—as many as you can identify—your letter and resume (yes, your POWERTOOL) in just two or three weeks. Afterward, you can settle down to the leisurely pace of networking. Two- or three-a-day networking appointments don't seem so creakingly inefficient *after* you've used your spy-in-the-sky satellite to scan the terrain. Now a ground-level search for clues on foot and by car is the perfectly logical next step.

Indeed, your fast preliminary direct mail scan may help target your follow-up networking. Chief executives who take the time to send you a cordial letter saying they have nothing for you—and a few will reply—can be phoned for the usual "a-few-minutes-to-get-your-thoughts-and-suggestions" appointment. Occupying high-level positions, and having demonstrated kindness and courtesy, these CEOs will be ideal networking contacts to augment the list of people you already know.

The CEO who doesn't need you as her CFO or controller may suddenly realize that you'd be the perfect business manager for the symphony...and as a member of its Board, she can propose you. Or she may send you to her multi-millionaire tennis partner who owns 28 McDonald's franchises in Ohio... someone who can use and pay appropriately for your talents, but whom you'd never have identified by looking through directories or on the web for large Cleveland businesses.

However, if you're a \$100,000+ or a \$500,000+ executive with specific background to exploit and a nationwide or global scene to scan, classic networking visits around town aren't quite enough for you.

Targeted networking, on the other hand, may provide a breakthrough. Want to meet a local CEO who has lost a divisional president and, in your opinion, has no internal replacement? Now that you're unemployed and have no fear of disclosure, you can freely forge a chain of personal introductions leading to your "target," according to the suggestions in Chapter 4.

Unemployed: Don't be afraid to use direct mail.

Unemployed...or at least out from under any secrecy restraints...you're free to orbit your spy-in-the-sky satellite. Moreover, it can be as blatantly identified as the Goodyear blimp. Scour the whole country, or the world. No need to hide behind a "sponsor." No danger that you'll lose your bird-in-the-hand job as you check out the bush.

When you think in terms of your ability to work full-time openly seeking the best possible job for the next stage of your career, unemployment almost seems desirable. And indeed it can be, if you use it knowledgeably and creatively. Unfortunately, many people don't.

I often run into excellent executives who've been out of work six months or longer and remain totally frustrated in their search for another job. They've long since given up hope of finding a better job. I ask them if they've conducted a direct mail campaign:

> "Oh, certainly not. I didn't want to cheapen myself in the marketplace."

These very words come back to me again and again from executives who should know better. I remember a phone call from a former VP - Corporate Controller of a merged-and-purged Fortune 500 company, who'd already been "out" seven months. He answered my question about direct mail with—word-for-word—the #1 cliché on the subject (above). And before I could utter even a syllable of rebuttal, he plunged right ahead with cliché #2:

> "I didn't want to meet myself coming around the corner."

This guy would be unbeatable on the old time TV show, *Family Feud*. "The #1 and #2 most popular answers," as the MC used to say. And...bang...bang... in that order! Both of these classic "reasons" for an unemployed executive not to include direct mail in his job campaign are not only erroneous, they both seem subtly related to a common practice most maturing young adult males and females engage in: going to college.

"I-didn't-want-to-cheapen-myself-in-the-marketplace" clearly relates to Econ IA, and its "Law of Supply and Demand." After they become leaders of American Capitalism, formerly proletarian college students confuse increasing potential *demand* (more would-be purchasers who are aware of the product) with increasing supply (multiple clones of the VP in question).

Erroneously they figure that increasing demand will drive the price down. What the professor actually told them, of course, was that increasing *supply* would do that. Indeed, the professor suggested advertising as a means of making more potential buyers aware of the product (increasing demand) and thus (or so she claimed) driving the price up.

For years I've wondered how so many American executives arrive at the identical misunderstanding of the "Law of Supply and Demand" when applied to the sale of their own services. After all, these are the same people who spend millions of dollars on advertising to increase demand for commercial products.

Moreover, I suspect that in other personal economic matters these same people would not make the same mistake. Suppose they owned a house or a boat and decided to sell it at auction. Would they try to restrict the number of people aware of their property's advantages and availability, so as "not-to-cheapen-it-in-the-marketplace"? Would they try to suppress news of the auction in order to assure a small crowd and thus higher prices? I don't think so.

Why then do these executives get "Supply and Demand" confused only as it relates to *themselves*...and not with respect to goods and services, both commercial and personal?

My latest theory is still predicated on the pernicious effects of the years in college. However, I've stopped looking for ineffective pedagogy in the Economics Department. The faulty curriculum, I'm now convinced, is not Professor Greybeard's text on "Supply and Demand." It's *Mom's* advice on dating. She's repeatedly quoted as saying, "*If you seem easy to get, they won't want you so much*."

Mom's advice clearly presages and parallels the "I-didn't-want-to-cheapen-myself-in-the-marketplace" rationale for not getting in touch with any companies, and likewise being careful to reach only a selective few retainer recruiting firms. Moreover, Mom's principle is adhered to even though the executive knows that no two retainer firms will ever be working on the same job; hence, every firm shunned is potentially a job shunned.

Incidentally, Mom's corollary concern about not getting a "too-available-reputation" can readily be seen as the root logic behind the more colorful, yet enigmatic: "I-didn't-want-to-meet-myself-coming-around-the-corner." Admittedly, that spectre is most disturbing. However, like "cheapening-in-the-marketplace," it's impossible. If you have any lingering concern, check the last half of Chapter 11.

Unemployed: Consider the "Underutilized Asset Discussion" ...an ideal door-opener, if you're seriously interested in becoming an independent consultant in your field.

Absolutely the best way to get an appointment with a chief executive or with any other corporate decision-maker is to have something specific and highly interesting to discuss. Virtually nothing fits that description better than an underutilized asset...a business or other resource he or she has, that could be put to new, better, or additional use, or could be advantageously sold off.

During the years that you've worked in your industry, you've undoubtedly noticed competitors who aren't making the most of something they have. You've probably even noticed similar examples within your own company, but for political reasons, you haven't been able to pipe up.

As an independent consultant—and perhaps a respected former competitor—viewing the matter from outside, you have no such inhibitions. You can go straight to the CEO of any company with a letter and follow-up phone call outlining your thoughts. If you make sense, he or she will probably be interested enough to invite you in for a hearing.

Typical languishing assets you might identify:

Division or product line underperforming for reasons you'll explain. Or appropriate for divestiture or contribution to a joint venture you can visualize.

Opportunities to distribute through different and/or additional channels.

Trademarks that could be used for quick penetration of new markets, or licensed to other users.

Products of overseas subsidiaries that should be imported. Even as America drowns in imports, U.S. multinationals fail to bring in their own unique overseas lines.

Sales forces and distributor networks that could handle related lines.

Patents, technology, and know-how that could be licensed to users in other industries or spawn advantageous entry into other fields. Or possibly even be shared profitably with competitors.

Under-exploited **real estate, air rights, timberland, mineral rights, etc.** Also unused **manufacturing** and/or **computer processing capacity** that other companies might need.

Before you blurt out your analysis which, after all, lacks inside knowledge that only the company itself has, make sure you're on firm ground. Ask questions. Confirm your assumptions, and modify your presentation accordingly. Then show that you've thought more deeply and creatively about the asset than the CEO's own people. Perhaps no one has devoted proper time to it. Or maybe it hasn't had the priority you now demonstrate that it merits.

Propose a consulting engagement. Phase I will study the issues you've pointed out. Phase II, if warranted by Phase I, will implement the recommendations of Phase I. You're prepared to handle implementation totally on the outside, or drawing on inside personnel. Or...*stand by for a job offer*. The CEO may prefer implementation by internal personnel...with you leading the team.

I can't even begin to count the number of executives I've known over the years who've moved from one corporate payroll to the next, by doing a consulting project so impressively that their client hired them as a permanent employee.

On the other hand, if the CEO is *not* interested in more aggressive use of the asset you point out...and if that asset is severable and salable...maybe he or she will entertain an offer from you to purchase it.

If so, you have something tangible to discuss with investment bankers and venture capitalists. Start making appointments with them!

Rites of Passage

Well, that's it. That's everything I wanted to impart on the subject of changing jobs at $100,000 to $1 million+.

We've looked at the employment process from every angle. If you really want to accelerate your career, you've got several important steps you can take right now, while you're happy and challenged in your current job. You can even get extremely aggressive while staying under cover.

And if you should ever find yourself out of work, you know everything you can possibly throw into an all-out campaign.

Someday you may face difficult times. Most of us do at least once or twice in a career. But you'll never have to make the pathetic statement we've all heard so often from previously dynamic executives after months of unemployment, with no leads in sight:

"I feel so helpless. I just don't know what to do."

You know what to do. And at a time like that, you'll be busy doing it, not sitting around wishfully waiting for the phone to ring with news that someone else has done it for you.

You also know what not to do. You'll never make the rounds of recruiters until you find one who says:

"Let me see what I can do to help you."

Nobody will price-tag your head and get to your most likely employers before you do, blocking those casual exploratory sessions your own straightforward contact might otherwise have brought about.

Moreover, you won't waste an undue amount of time on naively ardent courtship of retainer recruiters. You'll get to the most jobs you possibly can through them. And you'll also get past them to far more jobs than they're permitted to show you.

From now on, whenever any headhunter calls, you'll deal with him or her in precisely the way that best serves your self-interest. And over the years, you'll build mutually-trusting relationships with the best retainer recruiters... perhaps even to the point that they'll be willing to suspend their rules to assist you when you urgently need help.

How many and which "Rites of Passage" await you in the years ahead? Almost certainly *interviewing*. Definitely *writing a resume*, and probably a *covering letter* to go with it. Very likely *negotiating an employment contract*. And without a doubt plenty of *personal contacts*, *networking*, and *dealing with recruiters*.

Moreover, modern technology now influences every aspect of executive career development activity. You know how to take advantage of all its aspects, including *RITE*Site.com, which is my effort to help you advance your career with an absolute minimum expenditure of time and money

Come what may, there'll be more method—and less mystery—in your approach to the potential passages that are always open to you in the world of employment outside your current company.

As a result, I hope you'll feel free to pursue what's best for you...not just what's handed to you.

A Parting Word

Here's where I leave you.

For now at least, I've conveyed everything I can think of that could possibly help you negotiate the inevitable "Passages" of a successful executive career at "$100,000 to $1 million+"...and, let's hope, even beyond.

Over the years I've had the pleasure of knowing and observing many of America's leading executives. You and I both owe them a "thank you," because much of what we've covered has come from them. The rest has come from long experience on the opposite side of the recruiter's desk from the one you face...a perspective it's my pleasure to share with you.

But now we part company. You go back to being an executive, and I go back to identifying and attracting the most appropriate ones to meet the needs of my clients.

Let's hope that someday I may have reason to call you as one of the four or five best candidates in America for a specific CEO position that I've been engaged to fill. Or that you rise so far above $100,000 or $500,000 or even $1 million that you have very senior executives reporting to you, and I can help in their selection as a means of further helping you.

Until then, thank you for the time we've spent together. And very best wishes for an outstandingly successful career.

Sincerely,

John

Before you read on...

What about the novella that begins on the next page?

Is it authentic?

Absolutely!

The story is fictional. Yet the issues are the ones that concern everyone who comes in contact with the search industry.

The actions of the retainer recruiters you'll meet—loyal to the time-honored values—are typical of the finest professionals. They really do want to do the right thing.

But what ***is*** the right thing to do?

The ***difficulty*** of fully observing the traditional rules—especially in a major growth-oriented firm—will become obvious. And you will gain two sets of insights: (1) how to obtain maximum advantage for yourself in dealing with all retainer recruiters and (2) the problems they themselves face in adhering to traditional values as their firms grow beyond a certain size.

It's easy to lament and criticize the departures from classic retained search behavior that you will inevitably witness from time to time in the "real world" as you deal with some of the giant firms. However, after reading the novella, you'll understand the pressures that drive them to narrow, bend, and sometimes even drop the rules they previously held sacrosanct... rules that boutique, medium- and large-but-not-giant firms still staunchly observe.

As we come to the end of our time together, my goal is to leave you not only aware of—but also coping with—what's happening in the world of retained search. It's a realm you'll traverse throughout the rest of your career.

Bon Voyage!

APPENDIX I

Behind the Scenes with the Retainer Executive Recruiter

Up until now, your side of the executive recruiter's desk has never been the one with the drawers on it.

Too bad. Because changing jobs through a search handled by one of the retainer firms is perhaps the single most important "Rite of Passage" for the executive at "$100,000 to $1 million+." And how the process really works will never be entirely clear to you until you've seen it from the recruiter's perspective.

Which is why you and I are now going to take a look at what happens inside a retainer recruiting firm during a search...and also what happens to all the executives who are involved, whether they realize they're involved or not.

The Drama Begins

And now for your amusement and amazement, here's your initiation into the victories and defeats, the passion and pathos, of retainer executive recruiting. Silently and secretly we penetrate the posh New York offices of Gordon, Rossi & Boodles, one of America's very large retainer firms. The nameplate on the mahogany door we're entering says "Will Pickham." As we slip inside, the phone emits a quiet buzz.

Our hero answers promptly. He's a genuinely nice guy...a boyishly handsome former preppie and former executive, with a quick smile. Tanned, and trim, he's aging elegantly into his late forties, and he's pleased with executive recruiting as his second career.

"Will Pickham here."

"Hello, Will, this is Sherm Summit at Integrated Standard Corporation."

Wow! thinks Will to himself, *it's the CEO in person. I've never dealt with him before. I wonder what's up.*

"We've got a great opportunity out here. It's proprietary drugs and includes a small e-commerce element. I think you can help us," says Summit.

As he and Summit exchange pleasantries, Will quickly recalls his dealings with ISC, a $9.4 billion corporation. About 18 months ago, Will was retained by the then-President of the Food Division, Bill Beane, to find a replacement for his Marketing VP. Bill hired another food person, Graham Rusk. And since then, Will has stayed close to both Bill and Graham. But so far there's been no new business for Gordon, Rossi & Boodles.

Bill Beane has since been promoted to EVP of the holding company, in charge of five of its eight divisions, including its large and thriving Food Division and its much smaller—and languishing—Proprietary Drug Division. He's thought to have the best shot of anyone in the company at becoming President and COO fairly soon, and CEO when Summit reaches mandatory retirement in five years. Recently, Rusk moved up to replace Beane as head of the Food Division. There've been a couple management openings recently, but they've been filled from inside. So it'll soon be two years with no searches.

This history is fresh in Will's mind. With time running out, and over 1,200 other client companies off-limits to GR&B recruiters, *We'd soon have had to enter ISC*, thinks Will. *I'm glad they've called. If we'd gone in there, my relationship would have been ruined.*

And now the Chairman's on the phone. Fantastic!

"Bill Beane has told me about you," says Mr. Summit, "and your great work in finding Graham Rusk. In fact, Bill partly owes his promotion to you, since Graham did a fine job in marketing, and was ready to take over from Bill as President of Food. This year we're up 40% in that Division, and I give Bill and Graham the credit."

Will murmurs something modest about how it doesn't take a genius to recognize real talent when you see it. And Summit continues as if Will hadn't spoken.

"Now I've got another project I think you can help us with. I'm taking care of this one personally. Partly because Bill's tied up with our tender offer to the KornerKoffee people. And partly because I've lined up an exciting new e-commerce opportunity through some personal contacts. Call that one 'my baby,' and I want it to get underway in that division. So Bill says, "Sherm, since I'm swamped on KornerKoffee, and the new person's going to have to interact with your contacts on the e-commerce deal, why don't you take the lead in picking him or her. That's what I love about Bill. He doesn't protect his turf. I feel like we're almost partners in running this place."

"Well, Bill," thinks Will, *"You've come a long way in these last few months. Congratulations!"*

"And our Senior VP of HR, Al Umans, won't be around much either. He and his number two are coping with a union-organizing drive, which looks like it'll come to a vote in all nine of our Western plants within the next three months. So this is going to be basically you and me."

There's a pause, while Summit swigs Diet Pepsi from a deeply-cut Baccarat glass.

"Now what we want is a new President for our Proprietary Drug Division... the products that sell over-the-counter without a doctor's prescription. I want someone who can walk right in and take charge."

"So it's got to be a fairly senior executive, with strong experience in proprietary drugs, plus—if possible—some successful involvement in e-commerce," muses Will.

"That's right. We need real strength in marketing...and especially the newest trends. We have a great R&D person, and our manufacturing and distribution are the most efficient in the industry. What we need is somebody who can sell the hell out of our stuff. Today that division has fallen behind on the web. Now I've personally gone out and made us a terrific alliance with some young e-commerce types who want to use *MaturiTeen*, one of our geriatric product trademarks, to build an online community of older folks. In fact, I've agreed to contribute the use of our brand name plus $2 million... Well, I'll tell you about it when you come out here to start up the search," says Summit.

"What do you feel the job should pay?" asks Will nonchalantly. He holds his breath as he waits for the answer...which of course determines what Gordon, Rossi & Boodles' 33% fee will be.

"I'd like to pay $590,000, plus our very lucrative incentive programs and stock options. I want to peg it just under what we're now paying Graham. That means our first year's guarantee will be somewhere over $750,000."

An exultant voice in Will's head begins to shout, *Ohhhkayyy! That's a fee of about $250,000. Not bad at all. In fact, it's damned good!* Without noticing it, Will has jumped to his feet and...phone in hand...is happily pacing back and forth.

Will's thrilled. But there's a cloud forming on his horizon. Summit continues.

"Now I hope you've had some experience in the proprietary drug field." Obviously he expects a positive reply.

"Oh, yes. Less than a year ago, we put in the new President of CompuMedic. You've probably noticed it's been one of the industry's most exciting turnarounds." No false modesty for Will at this point.

"Yes, I know. They've become tough competitors. Your firm did that?" Summit sounds almost accusing.

"I personally handled the search, and recruited the top executive of Better & Best. Another search I handled was the President of Orchid."

Summit replies, "Well, there was a lot of talk about that one." His tone suggests that the talk wasn't entirely favorable. "I hear she came from Alphanetics...not exactly a major force in the drug field! Is it true that she was only a Marketing VP in one of their smallest divisions?" There's an obviously critical note in his voice. "You did that?"

Yes, thinks Will, *and not necessarily by choice. We have so many client relationships that most of the big and successful drug companies were off-limits to me. So when I found this really extraordinary person, even though she was relatively inexperienced and came from a place like Alphanetics... But she is a sensational talent and will surely be a major player in the industry someday.*

Will answers calmly. "You can't really associate her with Alphanetics' record, because she was only there for about eighteen months. She's been moving up like a rocket in the industry, and she went to Alphanetics after four years of heading the Prestige Panacea account at PanGlobal advertising agency. Of course, the jury's still out, but she's already got a lot of things moving over at Orchid. Did you notice the introduction of their new pain reliever aimed specifically at lower-back pain?"

"Oh, that was her?" says Summit, almost admiringly. "Now I see your reasoning in putting her in at Orchid. Those ads on TV are obnoxious. But the product's already got almost a 4% market share of the entire headache-and-pain-relief category. I have to admit I'd much rather have their new product for backs than our 30-year-old remedy for menstrual discomfort. It's been mired at a 2-1/2% share for the past seven years. The thing is, their product's nothing new. It's the ad campaign that's moving it."

"That's right. Her ad background is what Orchid really needed," says Will confidently. "And she headed all the marketing and sales at that division of Alphanetics." *And if she hadn't come from a place like Alphanetics, I'd have had a lot more trouble reaching her, with most of the biggies off-limits to Gordon, Rossi & Boodles*, thinks Will.

"Well, it sounds like you've done some good work in the drug field," concludes Summit more genially. "By the way, any other success stories I should know about?"

Will thinks fast. He's learned to be wary of all questions introduced with a casual "By the way." He must find the right balance. On the one hand, Summit wants the reassurance of prior experience. On the other hand, wily old fox that he is, Summit may also be probing the extent of GR&B's client conflicts. The more drug companies they've worked for recently, the fewer they can go into now to look for candidates.

So Will adds carefully, "Yes, we did a job recently for Biopharm" [a small firm on the fringe of the market]. "And we found the Chairman over at Gastrix...you know, the company that makes nothing but that very successful line of indigestion remedies."

Will does well. He gives Summit the additional assurance he seems to want, without identifying any other major companies as "off-limits." And Summit arranges an appointment the following Wednesday for Will to come to the home offices of ISC in Lustretown, N.Y., thirty miles outside of New York City, to get further details about the position and the type of person ISC is looking for.

Will hangs up and conveys the good news to his personal assistant, Wilma. On a high, he heads down the corridor to tell his buddy, Buddy Young. For months, Buddy has been urging Will to go into ISC himself, and open it up to Buddy and the rest of GR&B. So Will can't wait to let Buddy know how well things have turned out because of his patience. What are friends for, if not to suffer a few "I told you so's"?

Will arrives just as Buddy is saying goodbye to a man he's been interviewing.

"Hi, Will, how're ya doin'? Meet Sam Sage, who's here to talk to me about that Expodex job. Go on into my office and sit down, Will. I'm just seeing Sam out to the elevator."

When Buddy returns, he's duly impressed with Will's news, and suggests a drink after work at the Four Seasons to celebrate.

So Will's day ends on a high note.

We Live in an Imperfect World

Early the following week, Will makes time to start the groundwork for his upcoming meeting with Summit. He asks Gordon, Rossi & Boodles' chief researcher in the New York office, Gloria Monday, to check out the top ten companies in the proprietary drug field. He might as well find out how many will be off-limits for the ISC search.

Gloria walks into Will's office at quitting time on Wednesday afternoon. Unfortunately, her report is just about what Will expected. Here's what he has to contend with:

Top Ten Firms

(* indicates "off-limits")

***CompuMedic**: Off-limits, as Will has already told Summit.

***Parker Laboratories**: Off-limits, a fact unknown to Summit.

Better & Best: Open. But after Will took a key person out for the Compu-Medic job, a highly-disliked successor was promoted; other execs have also departed, and now there's no one left that Summit is likely to favor.

***Orchid**: Off-Limits, as Summit knows.

Maxi-Medi-Marketing: Open.

***National Anodyne**: Off-Limits, which Summit doesn't know.

Right Remedies: Open.

***Prestige Panacea**: Off-limits, unbeknownst to Summit.

***Cosa Nostrums**: Off-Limits, also unbeknownst to Summit.

BioDynamics: Open.

In other words, six out of the top ten firms are off-limits to all Gordon, Rossi & Boodles recruiters...although Summit has learned about only two of those six. Of the remaining four companies, Will knows that one is extremely unlikely to have anyone that Summit would consider presidential material. So there are really only three of the "top-ten" proprietary drug companies where Will can find ISC's new division head.

Damn! thinks Will. *On top of everything else, the Chairman is probably going to want e-commerce experience. Now who's going to have that in the consumer pharmaceutical industry?* Will hates to think of the sweat and blood this assignment will require.

Still, as an experienced executive recruiter, Will's faced worse before... and he'll cope again this time. He's good at his job.

Nonetheless, Will is pleased to look up and see Buddy...briefcase in hand... poised in the doorway, beckoning.

"Knock it off, Will. If I don't catch the 6:12 tonight, Linda will have a fit. So let's slip over to the Four Seasons while we can still get a seat, and celebrate. You got a new assignment from ISC, and this afternoon I finally completed my PhantaSee! Fashions search, which has really been the pits!"

Two friends...co-workers in a demanding, but also an intellectually stimulating and financially rewarding, business...unwind together at the end of a tough day. They nab two well-placed seats...and inhale the top third of their drinks. Then, they settle down and slowly savor the rest until train time for Buddy. Soon Will brings up a familiar subject. And although Will and

Buddy, their searches, and their employer are fictitious, the information they discuss about recruiting firms in the real world is from published sources and authoritative estimates.

"Darn it," says Will, "even though I'm thrilled to get the ISC search, it looks like it's going to be a bitch. Gloria came in this morning with the run-down. Six of the top ten proprietary drug companies are off-limits. It's a presidency, for heaven's sake! Why, every VP - Marketing would be willing to consider a presidency. In the end he or she might not move, but they'd certainly be happy to meet the client and talk. *But I can only go into four of the top ten companies*. And a lot of the smaller ones will be off-limits too. I can't remember the last time I was able to go everywhere in my client's industry and look for the *best person*. All I can do is try to find some good people who don't work for one of our other clients. *And we've now got nearly 1,200 clients!*"

"Know how you feel, my lad," says Buddy, who's had eleven years in the business... only two more than Will. "Part of why I came over from Randall Radley Associates eight years ago is that GR&B was only half their size then. So with GR&B I could search in more places for my candidates...and do it much more easily...because there weren't so many companies off-limits. But we've been growing almost every year, and we're now just as big as they were then."

"The real problem," says Will, "is the number of recruiters on staff. Not only do I have to protect my clients...that wouldn't be too bad, because I've only worked for 20 or so clients within the past two years. But I've also got to protect yours too, Buddy. And the clients of 93 other recruiters! *That's* why we've got about 1,200 companies or subsidiaries we can't go into...at GR&B."

"Yeah, but think of the industry giants like Korn/Ferry and Heidrick and Struggles. They have ***more than twice as many*** search consultants in the U.S. as we do." Buddy interjects.

Digging into the "Off-Limits" Issue

"Right!," Will replies, reaching into his briefcase. "Gloria got me some figures for a business review article I'm thinking of writing. There's always been this constant problem, but it's very seldom studied or written about."

"Gloria did her usual thorough job. She tracked everything that's been published over the years about the numbers of recruiters working in the U.S. for the largest search firms. Those numbers, of course, help us gauge how many client companies and non-profits must be marked "off-limits" to protect the number of clients served.

"Way back in October '78," says Will," *Fortune* did a cover story. Heidrick & Struggles had 75 recruiters, and admitted having 2,000 client companies off-limits. *Forbes,* in July '89, found these off-limits numbers at the four largest firms: Korn/Ferry 2,150; Russell Reynolds 1,567; Heidrick and Struggles 1,289; and SpencerStuart 1,250." That article caused a lot of negative comment and, from then on, the search firms became very reluctant to disclose their number of clients."

Going Public ...and Boasting about What's Usually Hidden

"But in early '99, as Korn/Ferry went public they ***proudly disclosed their number of clients***...something the giant search firms ***normally never do***. They reported having done 5,870 searches for 3,750 clients worldwide in fiscal '98, including roughly 43% of the *Fortune 500* companies, according to *Executive Recruiter News*. *Executive Search Review* reported that Korn/Ferry had 392 recruiters worldwide...174 in the U.S. We don't know their number of U.S. clients, but dividing global clients in '99 by global recruiters in '99 is about 10 clients per recruiter—and nearly 1,700 client companies off-limits in the U.S.—with each recruiter having to do about 15 searches per year.

"Heidrick & Struggles also went public in '99, and their S-1A filing with the S.E.C. was reported in *Executive Recruiter News* as having stated that they 'worked for more than 1,800 clients in 1995 and over 3,100 in 1998.' That's really impressive growth. *ERN* reported that H&S wound up '99 with about 391 recruiters worldwide, with about 200 doing searches in the U.S."

In 2007, *Executive Search Review* reported that Korn/Ferry had 236 recruiters in the U.S, and Heidrick and Struggles had 196. That seems to indicate that K/F then had about 3,000 U.S. clients and H&S had about 2,600."

"Those old Korn/Ferry figures are close to our ratios here at GR&B... 12 clients per recruiter and 14 searches per year. So I agree with you, Buddy. We're certainly not alone in off-limits problems and a heavy work load."

Silent Again...but Pictures Don't Lie

In 2013, Korn/Ferry's website listed all of their U.S. professionals and included titles and small pictures of each. Gloria simply went through the list and counted about 250 doing searches in the U.S. Incidentally, the Heidrick and Struggles website had no similar illustrated list. However, Gloria believes that H&S has staffing that is roughly comparable to K/F's.

"Whatever," groans Buddy. "Anyway, Will, you've put your finger on the off-limits problem. Not only have we got our own personal clients to protect, we've also got to protect all the clients of GR&B. And on top of that, we also have to stay away from every executive any of the other 93 GR&B recruiters has gotten permission to talk to."

"Exactly," says Will. "I have to stay away from every executive who works for any of our nearly 1,200 client companies. And I also have to stay away from any of the half-million or so executives we track unless I've checked in advance to make sure that I—and not one of our 93 other recruiters—have exclusive permission to call him or her."

"It's tough," Buddy agrees, distracted momentarily by the thought that he forgot to write and mail two college tuition checks totalling almost $65,000. *Can't afford to loaf these days!*

"And, Buddy," Will continues, "all firms track lots of executives. Way back in that old *Fortune* article, Heidrick & Struggles and Boyden said their database had 100,000 executives, and Korn/Ferry said they had 145,000. Today even the smallest firms are computerized—far better than the giants were back then—and the largest firms now track millions of executives worldwide. In our business the right hand *does* know what the left is doing. And if you're in a retainer search firm, you've damned well got to keep out of its way. Sometimes I feel like I've got both hands tied behind my back."

"Now wait a minute, Will," says Buddy. "I can't let you get away with knocking the database like that. Sure, it's the way we keep track of the people you can and can't call. But it's also the way we keep tabs on people we can use to fill assignments. You love the database when you're looking for a top-flight Controller or a VP - Manufacturing, and Gloria walks in and hands you a couple dozen likely candidates or sources all neatly printed out."

"You're right," says Will. Most of the time I'm damn glad to have it."

"And you're glad, too, says Buddy, that 93 other recruiters have been meeting executives and contributing notes about them to the database for the past umpteen years. Quite a few of the profiles Gloria hands you will be on executives that you, or I, or someone else has interviewed and submitted as a candidate...or worked with as a client. Ten percent, and maybe more aren't just unsolicited resumes from people you have to investigate. They're known quantities...all checked out and, if they're interested in your opportunity, all ready to present."

"You're right on that too, Buddy. There's no way in the world that I could handle my heavy load of assignments, if we didn't have our database. It's the beginning-and-the-end on a lot of my searches. In fact, I had lunch Tuesday with Bill Maverick and Allan Shane, who left us last year to start their own firm. They say that the extra speed and freedom they get from being able to call up practically anyone they want to is partly offset by the extra grunting and grinding they have to do because they haven't yet built up a database of already-met executives as large as ours.

"However, they told me about something else that's pretty interesting. Because of their fine personal reputations when they were with us, their firm has been named one of the *Rites*-honored search firms—just like GR&B is—on that *Rite*Site.com website. That means they can post their positions on the site *without identifying themselves,* and yet executives will know that each position is a search by one of nearly 600 top-drawer retainer-only search firms honored in *Rites of Passage*. On the other hand, the executives who respond don't know *which recruiter* posted *which job*. So Bill and Allan don't have to deal with anyone who replies if they don't want to. The site is attracting lots of visitors. Bill says its technology sorts its resumes even better than we sort ours. He says he and Allan have already filled several of their searches with candidates they got on *Rite*Site.com.

"Lots of times, Bill says, they don't post their search. If the job is pretty standard and easy to fill, they just look into the database for candidates... same as we do with our GR&B database. But there's an interesting wrinkle to that. Executives can enter themselves two ways. One way is anonymously—*identity-concealed*—they call it, so the recruiter or employer doesn't know their name or address or e-mail, and can only contact them through the *Rite*Site computer. If the executive likes what's passed on, he or she responds. Otherwise, the person stays concealed. Or if they're intrigued but doubtful, they ask for more information before deciding whether or not to reveal their identity."

"The other way the executive can post on *RITE*Site is to choose what's called the *RITES*-Honored Option. That means they post their *identity-revealed* resume in an entirely separate database that only the Rites-Honored Recruiters can look into. As members of GR&B, you and I can register and see these resumes and it costs us absolutely nothing to do so. But recruiters who are not *RITES*-Honored—and employers—cannot see into that database. Even if they were willing to *pay*, they couldn't. That way, the executive doesn't worry that his or her employer will see they've posted their resume. That's about the exact *opposite* of all those commercial sites, where whoever is willing to pay can see the resumes...including, very possibly, the person's own employer. So, on the *RITES*-Honored Option, what most executives do is post the same resume they'd otherwise send to the 600 or so top firms in a direct mail campaign. That's the feature Bill and Allan really love. It's almost like the people are in Maverick & Shane's own database."

"So what," says Buddy. "That's nothing on us. We're just as *RITES*-honored as they are. You and I can post jobs and not reveal our identity just like they can."

"Yeah," says Will. We talked about that a couple weeks ago, when you got that letter telling you GR&B is a *RITES*-Honored firm and you're one of the firm members mentioned in the book. Did you ever try out the site?"

"Damn right. Will, I'm way ahead of you on that. In fact I've been meaning to tell you. I posted one of my toughest searches on *RITE*Site.com just to see if I'd get anyone we didn't already have. Well, I did. I got a lot of responses, including a really great guy we'd never heard of. Plus, I also dipped into the *RITE*Site.com database and got a woman whose resume we'd scanned into our system before we began accepting unsolicited resumes by e-mail and by job-seekers pasting them in on our website. Apparently our scanning fouled up her name-spelling and her phone number. On *RITE*Site she'd chosen the *RITES*-Honored Option. So, as a *RITES*-Honored recruiter, I was able to see her *identity-revealed* resume. I called her. She was interested, so I put her into our database *assigned to me*, even though Connie Lyon and someone else had already requested the Research Department to try to locate her and mark her for them in our computer.

"So the point is, Will, I'd never spend any money to post jobs and view resumes on a commercial site like Monster and the others. And certainly

GR&B never would! Why should we? With Gloria's research people and our huge database, we're spending plenty on our own information. We've got over 520,000 of the million people in our database that we have already actually met. We already know them, and we can call them for leads on plenty of others. But this *RITE*Site.com is *neat*. And it's free of charge to recruiters from *RITES*-Honored firms. It hasn't cost me a penny, and it's already about to fill two of my searches. So I agree with Bill and Allan."

"Okay," says Will. "But there's something else going on at that *RITE*Site that may help Bill and Allan catch up closer to where we are in the long run. They take in unsolicited resumes by email just like we do. Now, when an executive buys a membership on *RITE*Site.com, one of the features they get is called EMAIL MY RESUME. It takes the effort out of sending their resume to any and all the retainer search firms—the "Rites-Honoreds" they're called—from the sizeable firms like GR&B to the fancy boutiques like Bill and Allan. *RITE*Site.com also has shortcuts for direct mail, plus links to each firm's website for direct submission. Before, the average executive might never have known or submitted to more than five or six firms—us included. Now, with almost no effort, they also cover Bill and Allan and nearly 600 other quality firms right along with us. That gives Bill and Allan current information on lots of career-conscious people willing to consider a new or better job...people who'd never have been in touch with them otherwise. Bill and Allan feel that *RITE*Site is a real benefit to their business. It shores up their weaker side—not yet being widely known—without taking anything away from their strong side, which is their short off-limits list."

"Well, let me put it this way," Buddy replies with a note of finality, "I'm telling *you* that I'm using this *RITE*Site thing, because we're always helping each other out. But I'm certainly not mentioning it to everyone else around here. Let them figure it out for themselves. The way I see it, if I can fill a few more searches a little quicker using some outside help, that's great. I'll bump up my earnings and maybe free up some time."

"But Will, getting back to the off-limits issue that you brought up, you say that those 93 other recruiters make your life more difficult by ballooning up our client list. You've got to admit that some of them—especially our good friends in the firm—often make it a hell of a lot easier too. You've probably done favors for them...given them candidate ideas when they were stumped... and most of them will try to give you suggestions when the going gets rough. I certainly do. And it was your suggestion of Joan Flannel—thank you very much—that finally wound up my PhantaSee! Fashions search."

"True, ole Buddy," says Will. "I sure as hell wouldn't help everyone the way I do you...and vice versa, as we've discussed many times. But I do have many friends in the firm to exchange ideas with, and that's a great help. Take Bill and Allan. I used to swap suggestions with them all the time. But I probably won't be doing as much of that, now that they've started their own company."

"Yeah, and what about our offices in seven U.S. cities and five overseas? They come in pretty darn handy when you're traveling. No need to interview in a hotel room staring at a bed," says Buddy.

"Or to rent a suite that you've got to bill your client for, if it's a high-level search and you want to make a really good impression," adds Will.

"And speaking of impressions, Will," says Buddy. "I think you're more likely to get a busy executive to return your phone call right away if you're calling from Gordon, Rossi & Boodles, than if you're calling from an unheard-of little firm like Kermit, Piggy & Fudd."

"Certainly potential clients are more likely to call you," says Will. "Name value is very helpful to the Human Resources people. Their jobs are on the line when they recommend a search firm to their CEO or to another top officer. Not every search will run smoothly, no matter *who* does it. But when they recommend one of the largest and most famous firms and there's a poor result, it's because the giant firm screwed up. It's not because they recommended a small outfit that obviously wasn't qualified. The same goes for almost anyone else who chooses a search firm, whether it's a board hiring a CEO, or a division manager going outside for a head of R&D. The decision maker can always claim 'due diligence,' when he or she turns the matter over to a very well-known entity."

"When you get right down to it, Will, the 'off-limits' restrictions...both client and co-worker...are nothing more than a nuisance for you and me on most searches. Normally, we're just looking for a really good person to fill an opening. He or she can come from almost any company...not just a few leading firms in a certain industry. Only in a situation like the one you've got with Summit, where he's trying to shift the competitive balance of power in his field, does it really matter where you can and can't look. And even then, conscientious firms like GR&B can always get someone good, regardless of the obstacles. Three months from now we'll be back here celebrating your completion of the ISC search."

"Just like we're now toasting your new President of PhantaSee! Fashions," adds Will. "Drink up, Buddy, and let's hit the road."

"And all in all, it's a good life, Will. You have to admit that," says Buddy, whose wife will be meeting him at the station in their new Mercedes, which she just picked up from the dealer this afternoon. "They're not holding any benefits these days for Will Pickham, are they?"

That's Buddy's exit line, as he takes off for Grand Central, and Will heads for a pre-theater dinner with his wife, a successful pediatrician.

"That's Exactly the Sort of Person You Need."

The show was a hit. Will and Karen are in a great mood the next morning, as they walk out of their elegant condominium on upper Fifth Avenue. Will may be late this evening. He's driving out to see Mr. Summit.

The interview takes place in Summit's luxurious suite of offices at ISC's headquarters near Lustretown, New York, with every window framing a breathtaking view of the Hudson River. As Summit predicted, no Bill Beane or Al Umans. From Will's perspective, things go very well. He easily skirts the issue of off-limits companies without ever having to say anything that isn't literally true.

Summit begins by stressing two points. First that he's not insisting on prior experience as President or General Manager. "Just get me another Graham Rusk," he says. "A brilliant marketing-oriented business generalist will fit my strategy perfectly. And the opportunity to step up to a presidency will make them hungry as hell to come. With that on the table, you should be able to bring me every one of the best marketeers in our industry. And I *do* mean *in our industry*. I want deep experience in proprietary drugs...drugs sold to the consumer, rather than prescribed by doctors.

"Of course, I know that anyone from the consumer products field could learn proprietary drugs. But even someone very sharp might take a year or more to get up to speed, and I just can't wait that long. The truth of the matter is, I waited far too long to get rid of the guy I had in there."

Summit emphasizes his point by flicking an imaginary piece of lint from the sleeve of his navy pinstripe.

"Now it's essential that I have quick results. So the new person absolutely must be experienced in our product lines, and all set to go. That would be true just on the basis of our regular lines and our current R&D. But there's also an exciting e-commerce angle that, ironically, requires that the President be strong in the basic old fashioned fundamentals...especially the federal regulatory issues on what products we can put out and what we can say in our labeling and advertising. That's subtle—and dangerous—stuff.

"Here's what's happening. My daughter's an editor in New York for one of the biggest international publishing companies. Some hot shot young web developers she knows have acquired the rights to a lot of material on the health and lifestyle issues of people over 60 and they're setting up an online "community" for those folks. My daughter says these kids in their 20s are very creative in writing and design, and they've got some terrific technical experts who've built amazing sites for others. She's convinced that group that they should use one of our trademarks—*MaturiTeen*—which we use on geriatric vitamins, for the name of the site and for a new line of herbal-based food supplements which we will develop for marketing on the site. I've agreed that ISC will provide $2 million seed money for the venture and, of course, we'll supply the products which, after a year's exclusivity on the site, we'll then be free to sell through drug stores and supermarkets.

"So, for no more money than we'd spend to run three or four network TV spots, we'll wind up owning 20% of *MaturiTeen.com*. We'll also get a lot of publicity for our existing vitamin products among computer-savvy "mature individuals"—a hipper, more upscale segment of the 60-plus set than we have now—and we'll be putting out a whole line of new products on which the margins are quite, *quite* good.

"But the problem in all this is that we have to make sure that a bunch of enthusiastic amateurs don't get us into trouble. For that I need the rare combination of a seasoned pro in the proprietary drug field who is also upbeat, aggressive, and optimistic enough to work with bright young people like these kids and not kill their enthusiasm.

"That's a tall order, I know," says Summit, leveling an appraising gaze at Will. "But it's also a fantastic opportunity for the industry's best marketing person to move up in the world. Here's the perfect turnaround. Our regular product lines have been undermarketed for the past several years. I intend to free up plenty of extra promotional funds for the division. And, if this e-project is successful, it will turn every head in the industry our way. Nobody's ever done anything like it...and I think it has a lot of potential. What do you say, Will? Think you can find our person?"

Will smiles broadly and nods...registering his optimism without making any specific commitment. He realizes that Summit isn't going to be willing to look at anyone who doesn't have the background he's asking for. *Too bad... that makes it even more limiting.*

"Now I understand that you can't go into CompuMedic," Summit continues, "because you found their new superstar. But maybe that isn't such a big loss as it seems. Right now that company is so profitable that they'll probably offer whatever it takes to tie down their management team for the foreseeable future. And I suppose you can't go to Orchid either. But I understand your woman brought in a lot of new people, and to tell you the truth, I'd prefer to wait and see if they can really turn that thing around. They're still untested, as I see it, and not a place we're interested in yet.

"However, while we're on the subject of women, Will, let me toss in something that you might wonder about if I didn't bring it up. We have eight divisions in this company, and not a single one of them has a woman President. Is that because I don't *want* any? No way. But is it my *fault*? Damn right. Our COO who retired last year was a male chauvinist of the first order. And his attitudes just kind of permeated all through the organization. I knew it, and yet I didn't do anything about it. As a result, we lost two or three young women to other companies, who would soon have been ready to move up to a job like this. But they're gone, and that's our loss. We've got some terrific young women on their way up, particularly in Bill Beane's part of the company. But they're just Group Product Managers and Regional Sales Managers...several years away from running their own show.

"Will, this is *not* an affirmative action assignment. Just go out and get us the best person you can. If it's a woman, I'd be delighted. But if I think a man is 10% better, he'll get the job. And I think Bill Beane will vote with me on whomever we choose.

"So where do you plan to look?" says Summit.

Will can recognize a hot potato when it's handed to him.

"Well, you tell me. Which companies in the proprietary drug field do you respect? Which ones have the kind of managers you feel would fit what you're trying to accomplish at ISC?"

Will's candid blue eyes look straight at Summit.

"Let's see. Well, of course, Prestige Panacea is probably the best-managed of the big firms in the field...you couldn't go wrong with the Marketing VP from Prestige. And I think National Anodyne does a consistently good job of marketing. Maxi-Medi-Marketing has one of the hottest growth records in the industry, although I believe part of their success is due to their excellent R&D work. Still, one of their people should know what it takes to get the fast growth we want. Now, let me think...Well, of course, there's Parker Labs. They're an outstanding firm. They've built their brands very solidly, and they have an excellent reputation in the business."

Summit pauses for a moment, steepling his fingers as he gazes fearlessly into the middle distance.

"If I were you, I might take an especially close look at BioDynamics. They're moving into some very promising new areas, and that suggests an alert management with good long-range planning, which I'd like to see more of here at ISC. Oh, yes, and Cosa Nostrums. I've heard their management can be a bit ruthless, but they know how to get cooperation from the retailers. They always wind up with more than their share of shelf space. Perhaps a bit of their promotional aggressiveness would serve us well.

"As I think about it now, I really do like the idea of getting someone from BioDynamics. And of course, Parker or Prestige are very likely possibilities..."

As Summit drones on...repeating again the very limited number of obvious companies on his executive shopping list, Will's spirits are sinking. Four of the six companies Summit has mentioned are off-limits to GR&B...unbeknownst, of course, to Summit. *Where am I going to find my candidates?*

But Will copes with his concern as he answers Summit.

"You've listed some outstanding companies. And there are others too. I'm sure we can find a number of able people. Now at BioDynamics," continues Will, selecting one of the companies open to him, "lately I've been hearing from our West Coast office that they've got some excellent marketing-oriented general managers in those decentralized proprietary drug divisions they've set up. In fact, I noticed last week in an investor's newsletter I subscribe to that their stock was being highly recommended because the analyst was impressed by their top management and the entrepreneurship those separate profit centers are supposed to encourage."

"Yes, BioDynamics should be on your list. And I've always liked the sort of people you see at places like Parker and Prestige and National Anodyne."

"Yes," Will replies. "That's exactly the sort of person you need."

Summit is satisfied. He pictures Will searching in those companies. Will is relieved. He knows he hasn't committed himself to anything but an expression of blanket approval of the quality of the executives those corporations employ. So both men are in a very good mood as they head for Summit's private dining room and an elegant luncheon whipped up by ISC's corporate chef: grilled sole with a fresh tomato and basil sauce, asparagus puree, and sauteed wild mushrooms that the chef personally collected that morning in the woods at the edge of ISC's property. It's not until they finish the chef's special strawberry sorbet that they go back to talking business.

"By the way," says Summit, reaching into his breast pocket, "I wanted to give you these." Summit hands Will two envelopes, each containing a resume accompanied by a brief cover letter. "I got these in the mail a couple days ago. I never heard of these people, but they both seem to have the sort of experience we're interested in. And, if true, their accomplishments are very impressive. Might as well check them out."

Will's initial response is thankfulness. It will be extremely hard to find good candidates for ISC, so he's glad to get a couple, even from the client. But his feelings change when he scans the first letter. It's from Sam Sage...the very same person that Will recently met coming out of Buddy's office...the same Sam Sage who's currently assigned within Gordon, Rossi & Boodles to Buddy for his Expodex search.

Damn!, muses Will.

Clearly Will can't tell Summit the real reason he's less than enthusiastic about Sam. But, he quickly glances again at the resume...and sees something else. "I'm not sure," says Will, "that this background is really what you want. If you notice, practically all of his work has been in *prescription* drugs, not proprietaries. He's been marketing to doctors...not consumers."

Summit takes a quick look at the resume again.

"I see what you mean. But I'm impressed by the depth of his experience in drugs... and by the apparent success he's had. And, after all, he began his career as a brand manager at Promote & Gambol. You can't get much better consumer marketing experience than P&G. Why don't you just check him out?"

Faced with Summit's instruction, Will has no choice but to comply.

"Sure, I'll see about this guy," he agrees, as he puts the resume into the breast pocket of his grey pinstripe. *Maybe I'll be able to discourage Summit from asking any further about Buddy's star candidate,* muses Will. *And, of course, if Summit does bring up Sam Sage again, and gets really pushy, that'll be my clout to make Buddy let me also have him. Now that the industry has a bland-sounding name for it—**Parallel Processing**—it's easier to get by with presenting the same person to two clients simultaneously. GR&B always used to consider that hopelessly unethical. Now I can at least ask our management for permission to do it, whenever I'm as blocked for candidates as it looks like I will be on this search.*

The second envelope Summit handed Will is from Wynot Shoitdahl, who apparently has just returned to the U.S. from Prague where he spent three years running all of the Eastern European consumer products subsidiaries of Nestor Corp., a global conglomerate headquartered in Minneapolis. A native of Oklahoma City, Shoitdahl has a master's degree in international marketing from Thunderbird and began his career at Block Drug Company. *"I can certainly see why he caught Summit's eye,"* thinks Will, who calmly says, "I'll check out both of these guys.'

Summit then goes back to the subject of ISC's needs.

"We've talked about a lot of the big companies in the field. But I don't want you just to pursue the most obvious solutions. I hope you'll look in a few other directions. There are some aggressive young companies coming into the market these days. Some of those little biotech ethical drug companies are doing a good job of marketing straight to the consumer, now that the FDA has relaxed its rules on advertising Rx products on TV and on selling previously Rx products over-the-counter. Also, there are one or two fast growing firms in the health-food field that are expanding into mass-market proprietaries...the converse of what we'll be doing with *MaturiTeen*. You might find somebody at one of those smaller companies."

That may be my answer. It's a darn good idea!

"Yes," says Will, "I'll cover the smaller companies, too. Sometimes they've got a really outstanding manager who'd love to get into a major corporation."

Will smiles inwardly. He enjoys it when a client indicates some flexibility and leaves him room for creativity. *"Hmmmm... That may be a life-saver,"* thinks Will.

"Of course, I recognize we're probably not as attractive as one of the top ten firms," says Summit frankly. "Still, it's a $840 million division. And with the right person at the helm using all the resources of a corporation like ISC, growth could be very rapid. We hope that within five years we'll be in the top ten ourselves. I'm willing to spring for acquisitions, if they're brought to me by a credible management team that's doing a good job with our current businesses.

"And obviously I know we'll have to make some major changes in what we're doing now," Summit continues. For example, in an effort to make the division profitable, we've done very little advertising in the past few years. That was the policy of the last division head, and I let him get away with it. But I expect us to be much more aggressive in the future. If need be, I'll pour lots of money into that division for the next couple of years, to enable them to do all the marketing that's required. We've got a great opportunity for the new President. I hope you find us the person we really need."

The meeting concludes with reassurances from Will that he'll get right to work, and optimism from Summit that he'll soon see a slate of several appropriate candidates. In Summit's mind, Will can search almost everywhere in the proprietary drug industry. Whereas, in fact, as Will realizes all too clearly, he's severely limited.

Here are the companies that, following his discussion with Will, Summit visualizes being searched:	***Here is where Will actually can search:***
Prestige Panacea	
National Anodyne	
Maxi-Medi-Marketing	**Maxi-Medi-Marketing**
Parker Laboratories	
BioDynamics	**BioDynamics**
Cosa Nostrums	
"Small up-and-coming companies"	**"Small up-and-coming companies"**

Plus Two Inconveniently Convenient Candidates

There's also the matter of the resumes Summit handed to Will after lunch. As he drives back to Manhattan, Will's mind keeps returning to them. *"Maybe I'll be best off if I treat the two of them differently,"* he muses. *"On Buddy's candidate, Sam Sage, I'll drag my feet and hope Summit forgets about him, at least until about five weeks from now when I submit my finalists. By then, Buddy may have finished his search and released Sage to me. Or if not, I may have satisfied Summit with my regular candidates. Or I may have gotten permission to 'parallel process' Sage, sharing him with Buddy. Procrastination might work."*

"That Wynot Shoitdahl, on the other hand, calls for different handling. "I've never heard of him, and I'll bet no one else at GR&B has either. But maybe I can get some information about him—even if incomplete—and report it to Summit in the next couple days. That'll show I'm quick to follow up, even though I'll take a long time to get back to him on Sage."

Will returns to his office by 3:30. He called Wilma, from the highway, and she greets him with good news: (1) GR&B has never had contact with Shoitdahl and (2) Shoitdahl is now secured for Will on GR&B's computer.

But Shoitdahl did not come to Will by the usual investigation and recommendation route. Will hasn't spoken to anyone about him and, of course, hasn't contacted him for permission to check his references...and certainly not to review his social networking accounts.

But that may happen. On a hunch, Will stops by Takisha Farley's office. Two years ago, she was just a summer intern with an amazing knack for computers and social networking. Now she's #2 to Gloria in New York Research and works on exceptionally confidential projects that can only be assigned by Gloria and certain senior members of the firm (Will qualifies).

"Takisha," says Will, "Check this guy out. If there's anything negative on him, I need to see it now." Will knows that any long ago social networking that was originally in the public domain probably still exists today. If so, Takisha will find it. And if old material suggests an embarrassing interest that may still exist today, Takisha will find what's going on now. "Don't ask how I do it," Takisha tells Will. "Just be glad I do."

Next morning, Will revisits Takisha. She hands him a colored picture of a toga party of business school students. Most have shed their togas. "That hot naked guy in the center that they're all applauding is your Wynot Showitdahl."

"But it says, that picture was posted nine years ago," says Will.

"I'm ahead of you on that," says Takisha. "Mr. Showitdahl posted the same pic three weeks ago. Don't ask how I know. But you can take it to the bank. No question."

"May I show the pic to my client?" "No problem. you can let him keep it. But try not to say the guy used it again three weeks ago."

"Thank you Takisha"

Wilma "overnights" the pic to Summit with a note from Will requesting Summit call at his convenience to discuss it. Which Summit promptly does mid-morning the following day.

"You don't waste any time," says Summit. "I'm impressed!"

"So am I," says Will. "Our research group amazes me almost every day. Notice that the party was nine years ago. What's your reaction?"

"Well", says Summit, "Clearly, it's ancient history. But the guy was in Business School. He was at least 23 years old. Overall not a good sign. We shouldn't be having this conversation. I'd give him a pass if he turns out to be our best candidate when the search ends. However, don't even ask me to consider him unless you've done thorough research that proves he's left all the kinky stuff behind."

"I hear you," says Will. "We'll have several outstanding candidates and, frankly, I can't imagine that Showitdahl will be among them."

"Thanks Will," says Summit, who exits the conversation abruptly by hanging up.

The Struggle Begins

The next morning, as soon as he gets to the office, Will plunges into the ISC search. Better get things moving before his other assignments make new demands on his time.

The first item on Will's agenda is another meeting with Gloria Monday, chief researcher in GR&B's New York office. Since they last talked about the ISC position, she's gone through online industry directories and GR&B's computerized files. Today she brings Will print-outs on the four top drug companies that he's able to look into for candidates. Two of these—Maxi-Medi-Marketing and BioDynamics—are on Mr. Summit's mental list. And two others...Better & Best and Right Remedies...while not on that list, are at least sizable enough to rank among the top ten in the U.S.

Through dedicated digging, Gloria has also come up with a list of second-tier companies not currently off-limits to Gordon, Rossi & Boodles recruiters. Will knows that his success rate at these smaller firms may not turn out to be very high. Their top managers usually have substantial equity stakes. So, if the companies are fast-growing and profitable, their managers are unreachable. And if the companies aren't doing well, their executives won't have track records that will impress Summit. Still, Will's thankful at least to have somewhere else to look. Maybe in one of those companies he'll find Ms. or Mr. Right...or anyway, Right-Enough-To-Present.

Gloria also brings Will printouts of the computerized files on some proprietary drug company executives known to Gordon, Rossi & Boodles who aren't currently involved in any other recruiter's search...all of whom she has marked for Will's exclusive use on GR&B's central computer. Perhaps one of these people will actually become a candidate for the ISC job. And even the ones who are working for off-limits companies may still be useful as sources of information about good people somewhere else in the field.

Will thanks Gloria for all her help and settles down to do his reading. As he leafs through the resume printouts on his desk, he spots the name of Andrea Applewhite.

Andrea! Of course, I know Andrea Applewhite...she's PERFECT! Will shouts under his breath, whacking his desk so hard that his Cross pen bounces onto his interviewing chair four feet away. *(Expletive deleted.) Andrea's the perfect person for Summit! (Expletive deleted.) The first thought he came up with was to get the Marketing VP of Prestige Panacea...and that's Andrea! (Another expletive.) I'd forgotten that Andrea got promoted to VP - Marketing four years ago when Dan Dawson moved up to Senior VP - Marketing & Sales. Why, Andrea thinks exactly like Bill Beane, only she has a consumer drug background instead of food. The chemistry's perfect! Summit would FLIP...and so would Bill. Andrea's always wanted a shot at running an entire business. And an $840 million proprietary drug company, with strong backing for growth...why Andrea would love the ISC job. It's a gimme! (One last expletive, but less strident, more resigned.) And my hands are tied...*

Unfortunately, as Will's silent tantrum reminds us, Gordon, Rossi & Boodles has a strong client relationship with Prestige Panacea. In fact, Applewhite herself was recruited to Prestige by GR&B several years ago. All

Prestige executives are off-limits. And, recruited by GR&B, Andrea is doubly off-limits.

But Andrea is so perfect for the ISC position that Will even briefly considers going to Mr. Rossi and asking if something can be done to release Andrea. Then he remembers that one of the reasons GR&B got Prestige as a client was that Rossi plays golf every Saturday with Prestige's CEO. Will knows he doesn't have a prayer of getting Andrea freed up for ISC.

In fact, if he even so much as called Andrea to ask for suggestions, Will could be in trouble. It wouldn't do for her to learn about the open position... one she'd be as eager to get as ISC would be to get her...because Andrea might then try to go directly after the job herself. The CEO of Prestige certainly wouldn't take it well if his head of Marketing & Sales ended up with a job that GR&B was searching, however it came about. He'd surely complain to Rossi, and Will knows what Rossi would then say to him. And of course the spontaneous appearance of Applewhite on the scene would also create big problems with Summit, who'd either think Will was inept for not identifying Applewhite or less than candid for not stating upfront that he couldn't go into Prestige. No, Will doesn't dare even breathe in Andrea's direction.

Well, so much for Andrea Applewhite. Put her in the "No" pile.

And here's Karol Klasner, over at National Anodyne. Damn, damn, damn!, fumes Will. *Another great person Summit and Beane would love. She's also dying for a shot at general management. But I can't touch National Anodyne. And I'd damn well better not call her for suggestions either. She's a real go-getter. Don't know how she'd manage it, but Karol would be in Summit's office by noon tomorrow. Not quite 31 years old, and she's already had three years as Marketing VP of the sixth largest proprietary drug company. And just look at those new products she's coming out with,* muses Will. *If she doesn't get somebody else's company to run by the time she's 35, she'll probably start her own! A nice person, too. She recycles and develops people; she doesn't just dump them on the street. Well, too bad Will, old boy. On the street is where you'll be if you touch Klasner. Anodyne is Sylvia Gordon's client.*

Next, however, Will discovers the file of the financial vice president at Prestige. Will decides it's safe to call him, even though he can't call Andrea Applewhite, since a finance person is obviously not going to be a candidate for the marketing-oriented division head Will will be inquiring about. This guy's been in the proprietary drug business for a long time, so he might conceivably know of some promising marketing executives who've been at Prestige over the years and then moved on to other companies. Will immediately marks him to be a "Source."

Painstakingly, Will goes through all the profiles, and he downloads onto his iPad the contact and background information on each person he intends to phone. There are no obvious candidates, but Will does succeed in compiling a list of possible sources. Next he tries to build a list of prospects. He turns to the laser-printed pages Gloria and her assistants have gleaned by consulting on-line information services, Indeed.com, and by visiting corporate Websites and the sites of the few relevant trade associations, looking for marketing people in the three big firms he *can* go into: Maxi-Medi-Marketing, Right Remedies, and BioDynamics. Will also checks out the top managements of some of the smaller companies. Today, these people are totally unfamiliar to Will. But as he calls his sources to ask for recommendations, he can also inquire about the people on his list.

After a few days of making calls, Will begins to feel quite anxious about his ability to put together a decent slate of candidates for Mr. Summit. According to the sources Will's talked to, he'll never be able to put his hands on any but the most junior of the people at Right Remedies, a top-ten firm that's open to him although it wasn't mentioned by Summit as one of his favorites. All of its upper management are beneficiaries of an incredibly generous stock option plan that was set up during a period of crisis four or five years ago. Although the program has since been discontinued, all of the key people will be multi-millionaires...as long as they stay on a few more years. So Right Remedies is unlikely to yield any candidate.

Another disappointment is the fact that Will has heard very little about good marketing-oriented presidents, general managers, and VPs of Marketing in the smaller companies. If those smaller firms do contain a wealth of talent, the people are unknown to Will's informants. Will and Gloria's researchers will simply have to phone into those companies and ask for their key executives by title, without knowing anything about them in advance...tedious and often unproductive work, but necessary in a tough situation like this.

Meanwhile, it's beginning to look like Will's entire list of candidates will have to be drawn from just two places: BioDynamics and Maxi-Medi-Marketing. It's been quite a while since he faced a prospect so bleak.

One Step Forward

Will becomes so concerned about the ISC search that he decides to go see Herbert ("Red") Tapecutter. Red is a senior member of the firm...and the person charged with working out knotty problems of client conflict. Will recites his tale of woe, and Red is properly sympathetic.

"Can't you find a way to get just one of those companies on the off-limits list unlocked for me? I know I can't go into Prestige, or Orchid, or CompuMedic...our relationships with them are much too close. But what about the others? Maybe Parker Labs or Cosa Nostrums? I tell you, Red, I need help on this one."

Red promises to look into the situation. Will knows that really means he'll talk to Hamilton Rossi, who usually adjudicates such matters...and get back to Will. In fact, the very next day, Red drops by Will's office with good news.

"Will," says Red, smoothing down the hair that long ago lost the color that conferred Tapecutter's nickname, "It's okay to go into Cosa Nostrums. Our relationship with them on the search we just did was really not very satisfactory. They struck us as extremely unrealistic and demanding, and they certainly acted like they weren't satisfied with our work. I doubt that they'll use us again...and even if they did come back, I'm not sure Mr. Rossi would agree to take any assignment from them. Also, they didn't inquire about off-limits protection. So we didn't promise them any...neither two years, nor any other period. And, of course, the 'Code of Ethics' of the AESC" (leading search firm trade association with about 130 U.S. member firms) "is no longer the bother it once was. So, even though the time limit isn't up, you can go into Cosa Nostrums if you need to."

If I need to. That's a laugh!

"Thanks, Red, I really appreciate the help."

"Any time," waves Red as he departs.

That afternoon, Will at last can look with some satisfaction on his developing list of prospects. As he'd suspected, Better & Best yields no possibilities; there was virtually a complete turnover following the departure of the key executive Will recruited, because his replacement has turned out to be an insecure egomaniac. But Will's heard of a couple people at BioDynamics, and a couple more at Maxi-Medi-Marketing, who sound like good possibilities. He's also going to try some names at Right Remedies, although he's rather doubtful about whether or not they can be lured away. Plus, his research has turned up a couple possibilities at Cosa Nostrums, now happily unlocked. All in all, it's not such a bad starting point.

The next morning, things look even better for the ISC search. Will is able to get through to one of his most carefully cultivated contacts, a senior partner in a major public accounting firm. His contact remembers being impressed with the performance of an aggressive little drug company in Phoenix, called Adam Laboratories. Adam was acquired by a foreign concern, which has since switched Adam to a different CPA firm...the same one it uses for the rest of its U.S. subsidiaries. According to Will's informant, a lot of the credit for Adam Labs' performance goes to their Marketing VP, Charlie Comstock. Will's contact hasn't actually met Charlie, but he thinks there's good reason to believe he might be an excellent prospect.

Will rushes to do a little background research on Charlie, and is delighted to discover that Charlie went to Adam from Parker Labs, where for several years he'd been a senior product manager. It looks like the perfect profile of a young man on his way to the top in the proprietary drug industry. Elated, Will asks his secretary to get Charlie on the phone. Yes, Charlie might be interested in making a move...for the right job and salary... doesn't mind living in the New York area...will send his resume immediately...and can fly in for an interview in the next week or so.

All in all, Will chalks up a good day's work on the ISC job. *I wish I were making as much headway on some of the other things I'm handling,* he says to himself.

But the next day is one that for several weeks hence Will will call "Black Thursday." As soon as he returns from a leisurely lunch with a client, Gloria pops into Will's office. She's bearing news...good for Gordon, Rossi & Boodles, bad for Will and ISC.

BioDynamics is now officially off-limits.

"Off-limits!" Will groans. "But we haven't worked for them in years!"

"That was yesterday," says Gloria firmly. Gloria is a practical woman who refuses to cry over spilled milk. "One of the recruiters in our San Francisco office, Doris DeWitt, has been on a suburban school board with the CEO. And at last night's meeting, he offered her the assignment to fill the job of head of marketing for their consumer healthcare products group."

"Oh, no," says Will. "That's even worse. Not only does it mean I can't go into BioDynamics to look for my person; it also means that Doris and I are going to be chasing the same candidates."

Will gets up and starts to pace as he thinks about how he's going to defend his territory against this new incursion.

"Bad luck," says Gloria sympathetically. "But since I realized this new search was going to put you in a hole, I immediately went through the computer and nailed *everyone* I could find who might be of the slightest use to you on your ISC project...before Randy, the researcher in the West Coast office, requested them all for Doris."

Will swivels around and watches in awe as Gloria drops a thick pile of printouts of GR&B executive profiles on his desk.

"There are 26 in all," she announces, "and all are marked for you in the computer."

"Good work, Gloria!" says Will. There is real warmth in his smile. *Thank God for Gloria! Am I glad I remembered to get her that Hermes scarf last Christmas; it's the best investment I ever made. If I didn't have her on my side...*

Gloria leaves Will's office, her ears still ringing with his words of praise for her foresight. Will immediately reaches for the phone and dials Doris out in San Francisco.

"Doris, darn it, what are you trying to do to me?"

"Just trying to earn a living, Will. Them's the breaks."

"That's easy for you to say," rejoins Will. "BioDynamics was my best hope for the ISC search, a real bug of an assignment, and now you've snatched the company away from me."

"If you want to talk about snatching, my friend, I've got a few complaints of my own. What about the files? Randy here tells me you've got most of the people who might be of any use to me on the BioDynamics search."

"So you noticed that." chuckles Will. "Serves you right, you know."

After a few more minutes of jocular complaining, Doris becomes more serious, and reminds Will she's gone out of her way to help him in the past.

"So Will, the truth of the matter is that I don't even have a place to start on this search... especially since you've got all those files tied up. Can't you at least let me call some of the people you're holding and ask them for suggestions?"

"I don't think I can do that, Doris. Let's face it. You and I are going to be looking for exactly the same person. It's bad enough that I'm going to have to race you to the best prospects, but I simply can't give you a head start."

"How about letting me have just one of those guys Gloria scooped up for you? You've got the file on Walter Alston, and that guy's a personal friend of mine, for god's sake."

"I hate to play hardball with you, Doris, but I need every one of the people I've got. I'm nearly a month into the search already, and right now I have no candidates, and very few solid leads. I've just got to hang on to everything I have."

Doris's sigh is audible on Will's phone.

"You think you've got problems. What about me?" says Doris. "I've got exactly the same problem you have, and on top of it, I've lost the few leads open to Gordon, Rossi & Boodles, because of your quick work in getting there first. Come on, Will, let's see you play on the team."

"I know, it's tough," answers Will sympathetically. *I don't want to cause Doris grief,* he thinks to himself. *In fact I'd like to help her...but I can't give her my people.*

"How about this?" suggests Doris. "If you run across any good people that you can't land because they don't want to move to New York, will you let me have a crack at them? I can pitch them on the climate and the other advantages of San Diego for the BioDynamics job, and maybe I can get them for my search, even if they turn you down for ISC."

"Absolutely. You've got a deal!" Will genuinely likes and respects Doris. She has been helpful to him in the past. And Will may need her cooperation in the future. He's happy to agree.

"Depend on it. Anyone who turns me down, Wilma will assign to you at the same time she releases them from me. That way, nobody else can get their hands on them."

"Thanks, Will, I appreciate your help. I'd like to do a really good job with this search, because I think I can get a lot more business from BioDynamics. They're doing some reorganizing, and they have an ambitious acquisition program, so a lot of positions could open up in the next few years."

"What happened to the guy who used to have the job you're filling?" asks Will, who thinks, *Maybe his going somewhere else will stir up the industry in a way that could possibly be helpful to me*.

"They haven't fired him, and they haven't promoted him either. They've moved him into a staff job at the corporate level, something in corporate planning. My guess is that he just wasn't action-oriented and decisive enough for a company that's becoming very aggressive these days. In describing what they want they've kept harping on ability to make timely, independent decisions. Of course, the kick upstairs may just be a graceful way of giving him plenty of time to look around for something else. I think he's been there a long while."

"Hhhhmmmmhh," says Will thoughtfully. "Maybe there's something there for me. Do you think they'd really like to see him go? Maybe they wouldn't mind if I approached him about the ISC job. What do you think?"

"I can't say for sure, but it might be worth a try. I could check it out with the CEO. If it's true that they want to get rid of him, they might even be grateful if we called him up and got him thinking about the outside world."

"It would sure be great for me," says Will eagerly. "It means I'd be able to present someone from BioDynamics, which is one of my CEO's favorite targets for his search. Not that I'd actually put him in if he's a stiff. But at least I could show that I looked into BioDynamics. And you know, it might even work. If your guy's smart and has a deep background in drugs, he'll appeal to ISC. Maybe it won't matter so much to them that he's a little slow to make a decision, since he'll be reporting to Bill Beane, one of the most action-oriented executives I've ever seen...a guy who's also done some great work in developing people. I know of a couple of dead-assed old farts that he's really got up and running. The guy at BioDynamics is probably a hell of a lot better than they were when Bill started working with them."

"I'll check out the situation with the BioDynamics people," promises Doris.

Losing BioDynamics is a real blow to Will. He'd counted on finding one or two good candidates there...and he knows Summit has been counting on the same thing. Of course, if Doris can swing it, Will may yet present someone from BioDynamics...but he fears it will be largely a matter of window dressing. He still needs to find a really strong candidate to head his slate.

Suddenly, Will remembers the resume of Sam Sage that Summit asked him to check out. More than three weeks have gone by; maybe there's a chance that Buddy can now give him up. *I'd better look into that before Summit raises the issue again*, thinks Will, as he strolls down the hall and walks nonchalantly into Buddy's office.

"Hey, Buddy, you know that guy I met in here a while ago? What was his name... Sam Sage? Is he still a hot candidate for your Expodex search?"

"You bet he is. He's got just the right marketing background, and I think he's going to be one of my strongest runners."

"I was afraid of that," says Will glumly.

He explains that Sam has sent his resume to Sherm Summit at ISC, with the result that Summit has expressed interest in checking Sam out.

"Well, you've got to head that one off," mutters Buddy. "He's mine, and I need him."

"I will if I can, but you know it's not always easy. I already tried to point out that his background is wrong...mainly in ethical drugs aimed at the medical profession...but Summit didn't back off an inch."

"So why don't you tell him you know something...without getting specific ...that makes you think he should pass Sam by? You know, say you've got 'mixed reviews' on him, or something like that, and while he might be great in the slower-moving *ethical* drug industry, he wouldn't be the rockem-sockem guy they're looking for to build their consumer business."

"Buddy, that's not the way I operate," Will replies with strong conviction. "Besides, Summit might hear that Sam got the Expodex job, and was recruited there by Gordon, Rossi & Boodles. Then I'd really look like a jerk!" Will shakes his head in concern. "I'm just hoping that if I keep quiet about it, Summit will forget the whole thing."

"By the way, Buddy, Red Tapecutter freed me to go into Cosa Nostrums. But you'll be glad to know that I didn't ask for ***parallel processing*** on Sam."

"Will, you're not threatening your old pal, are you? Just to be on the safe side," concludes Buddy with a wink and a smile, "I'm going to set up an appointment for Sam to see the guys at Expodex right away...before I have my complete slate lined up. I'm counting on you, Will, to protect me with my clients. They aren't going to like it if we're selling the same guy to two clients... which is the way they'll interpret it."

"I'll do my best, Buddy," promises Will as he heads back to his own office. But the thought of BioDynamics' new status, plus having to try to keep Sam Sage away from Summit, cause Will to say "Yes" when a favorite client calls with a wild idea. It's a beautiful day. Why don't they use his company's tickets for that afternoon at the U.S. Open Tennis Tournament? Why not indeed!

The First Sketchy Slate

Before the week is over, lucky Will adds not one but two candidates to his ISC slate. He hears from Doris on the West Coast, who tells him it's okay to go after the exec who was kicked upstairs. As they had surmised, BioDynamics is pleased at the possibility that Ethan Evans might find other employment. And it comes as no surprise, when Will finally gets Ethan on the phone, that he's equally interested. In fact, on paper he's an excellent candidate: good education, deep experience in the proprietary drug field, long-tenured employment at highly respected companies. Whatever his flaws may be, they're not readily apparent, and Will is sure Summit will be impressed at seeing a candidate of the caliber of Ethan Evans. And of course he'd damn well better see a candidate from one of the three companies that seem to be of greatest interest to him...Prestige, Parker Labs, and BioDynamics.

And then comes a stroke of luck right out of the blue. Will discovers another candidate from the original group Gloria brought him on Black Thursday...an e-mailed letter and resume that had accidentally got shoved under Will's desk calendar.

Terrific! exclaims Will to himself...but this time out loud, and Wilma steps in to see what's up.

"Did you win the New York Lotto?" she says.

"Dan Dawson's been fired!" says Will. "Of course his letter says 'disagreed on policy'...whatever. The point is that he was Andrea Applewhite's boss at Prestige Panacea...Senior VP of both Marketing and Sales. Andrea just has Marketing. Now I'll bet Andrea moves up to head both. Wilma, this is just the break I've needed. Now I can present someone from Summit's favorite company. And Dawson can't be bad...unless something radical has gone wrong lately...because Andrea has always spoken well of him. Of course I can easily get the inside story from her. You know, Wilma, I never wish any executive bad luck, because I've been in the corporate world and I know how tough it is. But this guy's problem is a real break for me. And thank goodness for Gloria. If she hadn't signed me up for him, Doris DeWitt would have him."

Will calls Dan right away, and confirms that he was in charge of both Marketing and Sales at Prestige for nearly four years, and was in charge of Marketing for two years before that...ideal experience for the ISC job. On the phone and in his subsequent interview, Dan freely admits he was fired, as Will had guessed. But he stresses that it was due to a policy conflict: he wanted to be much more aggressive than he was allowed to be... wanted to investment-spend on the introduction of some new products, right after making a product line acquisition that was taking longer to pay out than originally projected to the Board of Directors last year. So he's out. And...yes, Andrea Applewhite did move up to his job.

Will hears Dan out and pitches the ISC proprietary drug division presidency. Dan is delighted to have a shot at running his own show as President, even though the $840 million business is less than a quarter of the size of corporate Prestige, for which Dan controlled both Marketing & Sales. Moreover, Dan is happy to hear about a job that doesn't require relocation, because his wife has a lucrative law practice in New York. *Dan's lucky, too, that Gloria grabbed those files*, thinks Will.

Of course Will immediately does some preliminary reference checking to confirm Dawson's story. After all, he *was* fired. Among Will's reference calls is one to Andrea Applewhite...ostensibly just to congratulate Andrea on her promotion and ask the circumstances surrounding it since, despite the promotion, Andrea would probably give her right arm for the ISC job.

From Andrea and two other sources Will gets the straight story on Dawson, and it's not really damaging. The acquisition is substantially underperforming the projections Dawson and the President made to the Board, but not so badly that, in the long run, it won't prove a sound diversification. But right now Prestige has got itself into a cash crisis. There have also been some foreign currency losses. And the President just put up a very costly new factory...another good long-range investment...but underutilized now, and raising cost-of-goods. So Dawson's heavy investment spending proposals for new marketing programs...and his blunt outspokenness in support of them... couldn't have come at a worse time. Sensing the Board's frustration, the President seems to have "thrown Dan Dawson to the wolves," says Andrea Applewhite, "maybe partly to save his own skin."

Will is satisfied that Dawson is basically a competent executive, has no relevant personal faults, and seems to be someone who could be guided and groomed by Bill Beane and Sherm Summit into a successful marketing-oriented company President. His personality, however, won't appeal to them nearly as much as Andrea Applewhite's would. But Dawson is a solid citizen. In fact, Will will be very pleased if every other prospective candidate for the ISC job stands up to preliminary referencing as well as Dawson has.

So at this point, Will has put together a fairly sketchy slate of candidates... not perfect, but at least it's a start:

1. **Charlie Comstock:** Even though he's at Adam Labs, a small company, his track record looks good on paper, and he has a stint with a top-ten firm (Parker Labs) on his resume. He may be a promising find.

2. **Ethan Evans:** Another candidate who looks great on paper and, according to Doris who spoke to him briefly in person, is very polished with an air of success about him. As someone from BioDynamics, he should impress ISC.

3. **Dan Dawson:** Although he's just been let go by Prestige Panacea, he has a very good background and seems to be able to handle himself well. Also, his story checks out.

Not bad. Not bad at all, thinks Will. At least he has a few possibilities. Jn fact, he's beginning to think the ISC search may turn out to be the least of his current problems. He winces as he thinks about the troubles on some of his other searches.

Moreover, Will still has a few more places to look. He and Gloria's researchers have done their homework on the executives at Maxi-Medi-Marketing and Cosa Nostrums, plus some more of the smaller companies, and

Will is ready to get in touch with the most likely prospects gleaned from online information services, corporate Websites, and from researchers' phone calls. Of course the whole process began when one of Gloria's assistants checked the well-organized computer listings of the many thousands of files Gordon, Rossi & Boodles maintains on all the U.S. executives it has had any sort of contact with in recent years...from being a client or a candidate, to merely having submitted a resume.

Fortunately, three of the eight new prospects Will wants to call are people who haven't previously gotten into GR&B's central computer. Wilma has already flagged those three "no-prior-record" people on the computer as Will's property; now no other GR&B recruiter can communicate with them until Will gives them up. Meanwhile, he can contact them or not, as he sees fit. Moreover, a fourth new prospect Will hears about is also available to Will, even though he's been tracked in GR&B's system for years. It seems that he was returned to "available" status in GR&B's central system just a few days after Gloria in New York and Randy in San Francisco scoured the files for Will's and Doris DeWitt's respective searches. Unfortunately, the remaining four new prospects are on file at GR&B and out of Will's reach; three files are assigned to Doris DeWitt, and one is assigned to another GR&B recruiter.

The first name on Will's list of prospects to call is Gerry Glib at Maxi-Medi-Marketing. He's corporate Senior VP in charge of Sales and Marketing, and is apparently a heavy hitter. His name appears in several on-line directories, and Will is surprised and delighted to find that he's not yet in Gordon, Rossi & Boodles' files, and hence not yet off-limits to Will or any other GR&B recruiter. *Eat your heart out, Doris DeWitt, out there in sunny California. Better get to work!*

Gerry turns out to be quite enthusiastic about the idea of a job change... so much so that it does make Will wonder just a bit what Gerry's situation at Maxi-Medi-Marketing might actually be. But Gerry sounds like an outstanding candidate, and a brief breakfast meeting confirms Will's initial impression. Gerry seems to have a lot of ideas for aggressive marketing campaigns for ISC's proprietary drug lines. Without revealing Summit's *MaturiTeen* plans, Will probes Dawson's familiarity with e-commerce. He hasn't actually done anything in that area. Indeed, most *proprietary* drug companies have not. But he seems incredibly well informed on the subject. Dawson looks like he may be exactly the person Will is looking for.

Another candidate from the same company, Phyllis Finley, isn't quite so strong. She's one of two Marketing VPs splitting product line responsibility in their Consumer Division and therefore is actually a whole level below Gerry. She's probably a *little* junior for ISC's position. But she seems very intelligent, creative, and hardworking. And of course, she'd also offer ISC something of a price advantage compared to most of the other candidates. Will decides to put Phyllis on the "B" list; she's not a top candidate, but she can be introduced to Summit if the "A" list turns out to be too short.

Another candidate is Donna Powers, EVP - Marketing of the Proprietary Drugs Division at Cosa Nostrums. She seems to have accomplished miracles in getting distribution for her firm's new products, with extremely aggressive trade promotions...fighting for shelf space chain by chain, and almost store by store. "Cosa's field sales force is the hardest-hitting in the business," Will is told by a prospect in another company, who turns Will down and recommends Powers. Powers, compensation is unusually high for a top marketing executive, and the ISC job would be a lateral move financially. However, Powers says she's interested in making a move for personal reasons. She claims to be happy at Cosa Nostrums and, as far as Will has been able to discover, the firm is also happy with her performance. But Powers, a single parent, wants to move back to the New York area because her daughter has been accepted at the New York City Ballet School. Unfortunately her present employer has nothing to offer her there. So it might turn out that Cosa Nostrum's loss will be ISC's gain.

The combination of Powers' experience and her forceful and enthusiastic handling of Will's phone call makes Will add her to the "A" team. The list now looks like this:

A

Charlie Comstock — Adam Labs

Ethan Evans — Bio-Dynamics

Dan Dawson — formerly Prestige Panacea

Gerry Glib — Maxi-Medi-Marketing

Donna Powers — Cosa Nostrums

B

Phyllis Finley — Maxi-Medi-Marketing

The very next day brings one of those near-misses that makes Will grind his teeth. He gets a call from Kathryn Keane, the Marketing VP at Parker Laboratories...which is off-limits to GR&B recruiters. Kathryn is an ideal candidate for the ISC job. Will, who has called her for suggestions in the past, thought of her when the search began. But, with Parker off-limits, approaching Kathryn was out of the question. Now here's Kathryn on the phone, announcing that she's eager to leave Parker Labs!

"I want to get out of here, Will. They've appointed a new Group Executive, a guy I've known and disliked for years. When I was just starting out as an Assistant Product Manager, he was Group Product Manager, and he wanted to get a little more familiar than I thought was appropriate, so I put him in his place. Unfortunately, he's been knifing me every chance he's gotten ever since. We've become a lot bigger company since then, and I've been able to stay out of his way. But now the carousel has swung around again. He's not my *direct* boss, but he's *his* boss; and he's already starting to make my life miserable. This turkey doesn't pass up any chance to knock me, or make me look bad. By now, I've done so well that maybe he thinks I'm a threat to him... even though I'm two layers down. Of course, I'd have been promoted to just one layer down, if he hadn't got his promotion. I just know if I don't get out of here soon, he's gonna cause me real trouble. Will, have you got anything for me?"

Will thinks sadly of the ISC job, a perfect match for the experience and capabilities of Kathryn Keane. But of course it would be as much as Will's job is worth to try to bring them together.

"Kathryn," he replies, "you know I think you're an outstanding executive. But we have a client relationship with your employer...and quite specifically with your division, where we put in a head of R&D three months ago. You know the rules. I couldn't possibly show you anything."

"Isn't there some way to make an exception? It's not like you're raiding the place or anything. I've already made up my mind to leave Parker Labs."

"The only time I can make an exception to the rule is when an executive has already told someone in the supervisory line directly above them...their boss, or their boss's boss...that he or she is looking around and wants to leave."

Will begins to feel a surge of excitement. Maybe he *can* get a really outstanding candidate for ISC. Absent-mindedly, he sweeps a pile of pink telephone slips—unanswered, but marked "Not Urgent"—into the wastebasket.

"Could you go to your boss and tell him how you feel about this guy? Explain that you think he's out to ruin your career, and that you intend to start looking around."

"I don't think I can do that, Will," says Kathryn. "My boss and I get along okay, but we're just not close enough on a personal level for me to trust him. And now *he's* also feeling pressure from this guy. If he thought I was going to leave soon, he'd probably run right upstairs and suggest they get me out immediately, just to prove he's beginning to think on his new boss's wave length."

"How about going up another level, to Charley Phipps, your CEO?" asks Will. "One time when Mr. Rossi and I were in talking to Phipps about my possibly doing a search that never materialized, Phipps mentioned you to us among three or four younger people he thought were 'comers' in his organization, but not quite ready yet for what he had in mind."

"I can't do that either," answers Kathryn matter-of-factly. "After all, he's the one who promoted this guy...and you can bet the guy is really in solid with him at this point. There's really no way. I'm stymied. There are only two people to tell, and I can't talk to either one of them."

"I'm sorry to hear that, Kathryn," says Will sympathetically. *Sorrier than you'll ever know, since I have the perfect job for you right here in my hand, and I'm straining to find decent candidates.* "But I have to play by the rules over here if I want to keep my job. Listen, keep in touch, and let me know if anything changes over there."

Will hangs up with a bang. *What a total downer! Here's a great candidate, who's begging for the job, and she'd be excellent and it would be ideal timing for her, and in the long run it wouldn't hurt the company either because they'll eventually lose her; yet I can't get at her for ISC.* Will questions...and not for the first time...the wisdom of his decision to earn a living as a retainer recruiter.

Will's bad mood is soon to grow even worse. Putting on his suit coat and straightening his tie, he strolls down the hall to share a cup of stomach-destroying coffee with Buddy and commiserate about the day-to-day struggles of their work. In the course of telling Buddy how many things have gone wrong with the ISC search, he eventually breaks down and admits he does have a few promising candidates, among them a guy named Gerry Glib.

"Gerry Glib? Gerry Glib! Gerry Glib!! Hahahahaha!!!" Buddy begins to laugh so uncontrollably that he spills coffee on the stack of resumes on his desk.

"Why are you laughing? What's so funny? What do you know about Gerry Glib?" demands Will.

Buddy finally calms down and wipes his eyes.

"So you got taken by Gerry Glib, huh? Don't let it worry you. It's happened to the best of us."

"What do you mean?" Will finds he's talking through clenched teeth.

"Gerry's one of those guys who's all talk and no action. In interviews, he sounds wonderful. He can sell himself, no doubt about it. But once he gets the job, that's the end of it. One of the big foreign drug companies made the mistake of letting him open up a marketing subsidiary on the Coast to try to penetrate the U.S. market with some of their proprietary items that they got FDA approval to sell over here. They had to give him a lot of rope, and two years later all they had to show for it was a huge stack of bills and an exquisitely decorated office. As far as I know, he never brought in a single dollar's worth of business. Didn't you see the entry I made on Gerry in the computer? It's all in there."

"Well, I thought Gloria must have checked. She's always extremely careful about procedure."

"Maybe she missed him because he's filed under Gaspar G. Glib, his actual name... did you know that?...but he always goes by Gerry. Also, I made his file when he was still at Messerschmidt, and they're known for their industrial products...most people here don't realize they're in drugs, too. She probably assumed that Gaspar at Messerschmidt and Gerry at Maxi-Medi-Marketing were two different people."

Will's heart sinks as he recalls the glowing description Gerry gave him of that episode in his career...somehow he managed to make it sound like a smashing success.

"I can't believe it," he says crossly. "You mean he's no good at all?"

"No good at all," says Buddy. "I'm surprised you didn't hear that from the people you asked about him. The guy's a laughingstock of the industry."

Will admits that he didn't bother to check Gerry out very thoroughly...he'd seemed so impressive. And Will was in such need of a good candidate, he just jumped at Gerry when he saw him on the corporate Website page that Gloria printed out. Will was in a hurry, got careless, and made a mistake. He's grateful that he found out *before* he presented Gerry to Mr. Summit...although he wishes he hadn't let Buddy get one up on him. He knows it will be weeks before Buddy lets him forget his gullibility. *What the hell, it happens to all of us every now and then.* Will crumples his styrofoam cup and heads back to his own office. He has calls to make for another search assignment before the day is over.

First Report to Sherm Summit

The next week, Summit...scheduled to be in the city for a meeting with ISC's investment bankers...has drinks with Will after work. They settle down comfortably at a table in the bar of the New York Yacht Club, and Summit gets right down to the business at hand.

"What have you got for me?," he queries.

"In covering the top companies in the drug field," responds Will smoothly, "I've come up with several people I think you'll find interesting."

"Tell me about them," commands Summit.

"I looked into BioDynamics, one of the companies on your list, and I've got you a real heavyweight. His name is Ethan Evans, and he was just recently promoted from Marketing VP to a job on corporate staff."

"Sounds like coming to ISC as division head would be a lateral move for him," says Summit, shrewdly putting his finger on a weakness in the situation at once.

"That's true. But he's interested anyway because it would get him back into the action."

"What about money?" asks Summit shrewdly.

"I think he's making about $760,000 at BioDynamics, with everything included."

"Well, I don't want to pay more than that unless I absolutely have to. Would this guy leave California and come to our area, without some additional monetary incentive?"

"I think so," Will replies, rather tentatively. "I'll talk to him about it. But I have a hunch that if he could be heading a division as President, with a corporation that intends to really back his unit, he'd go for it." *Damned right he'd go for it. It's a lot better than sitting around waiting to be fired.*

"Another company I've already been into is Maxi-Medi-Marketing. There's only one genuine possibility there: Phyllis Finley, one of two Marketing VPs in one of their divisions. She's a relatively young woman, moving rapidly up the ladder, and I've heard some good things about her from other people in the industry."

"Sounds interesting. What's she making?"

"Her taxable income is about $365,000, but they have an excellent deferred bonus program at Maxi-Medi, and at her level she might be getting as much as $120,000 or so additional."

"So she's about ready to step up to our range...maybe a bit low." Summit takes another belt of his Chivas and water. "What else have you got for me?"

Tough old bastard, thinks Will.

"I've also looked into Prestige Panacea. I find that their top marketing guy...Senior VP of both Marketing and Sales...left a few weeks ago, and his replacement has only been in the job for that short time. She's supposed to be a good marketing executive, but has never before had any experience with sales...never even served any time in the sales force. But I did locate the guy who left, Dan Dawson. He's a seasoned pro in the proprietary drug field, and he might be just the one to step into your job and start running."

"Why did he leave Prestige?"

"I've checked that out, and he comes up pretty clean. It's a bit of a story, which I can discuss with you now if you..."

"No, we'll get to that later, if he's still around when you present your finalists," says Summit. "Anyone else?"

"One of the most interesting possibilities is a woman from Cosa Nostrums who has personal reasons for wanting to move back to the New York area. I'm still checking her references, but she looks very promising."

"And is that all?" presses Summit.

"There's also a man from a small company, Adam Laboratories, out in Phoenix. He's got a background with Parker Labs, and I hear the company he's with is doing very well now."

"Never heard of the place, but if he seems to be big enough..."

"I'm seeing him this weekend. If I'm satisfied after an interview, I'll pass him on. Sometimes there's real talent in those smaller companies. People are attracted by the autonomy and the chance to build up an equity stake."

"Well, it sounds like you've come up with a few possibilities," says Summit with a small note of satisfaction in his voice.

And you'll never know how hard I worked to do it! Will pauses to consider the companies he's just discussed, and the gap between the way this interim report has impressed Summit and the daunting circumstances Will has dealt with:

"Top Ten" Companies That Appear Searched	***"Top Ten" Companies That Have Been Searched***
BioDynamics	
Maxi-Medi-Marketing	**Maxi-Medi-Marketing**
Prestige Panacea	
Cosa Nostrums	**Cosa Nostrums**

"By the way, what did you find out about that resume I passed along to you?" Summit impales Will with his piercing blue eyes.

Curse the man's memory! Why couldn't he have forgotten?

"I'm checking him out," assures Will. He meets Summit's gaze without the slightest appearance of flinching...but he does call the waiter over to order another glass of Chablis.

"I'll be interested to know what the story is on him," says Summit. Obviously, he's not going to let the subject of Sam Sage die from neglect. Will realizes that he's probably going to have to show Sam the ISC job. *Too bad, Buddy. Stand by for a ram!*

"Now I hope I'm not throwing you a curve," continues Summit with just a hint of malice gleaming in his eye, "but I've got another candidate I'd like you to check out. His name's Jim Johnson, and he's currently a division head at Daisy Foods."

Will looks up with a surprised expression. Summit has been quite specific about wanting nothing other than a drug background...and now here he is proposing someone from the food industry.

"I know I said I wanted someone with a drug background," says Summit, just as if he'd read Will's thoughts. "I was afraid that someone without plenty of drug experience might take too long to get up to speed, and our situation definitely calls for fast action. But Johnson was recommended very strongly to me by someone I respect, someone who's been on my Board for a number of years. He happened to learn that Johnson has just been passed over for the presidency at Daisy Foods. Apparently, there were several good candidates inside the firm, and another guy just happened to win out.

"I understand that the situation is all very friendly...and in fact Daisy wants to keep Johnson if they can," Summit continues. "But he's quietly looking around to see if he can find something with a more open future. I checked Johnson out with Bill Beane, and Bill was delighted to hear he might be available. He told me, 'He's one of the best guys in the industry...why, he may be the only guy who knows more about marketing food than I do!' So with such good recommendations, I think we owe it to ourselves to take a look at Johnson, even though he does come from the food industry."

Will is relieved to hear that Summit's latest enthusiasm comes from Daisy, a company he happens to know is open to Gordon, Rossi & Boodles. This time he can move quickly, and show Summit that he's perfectly willing to act on client-suggested candidates.

"I'll be happy to check him out," answers Will with real warmth. "With any luck, I can get to him tomorrow." *I wish I'd known Summit would take a food person. It might have made my life a lot easier these last few weeks.*

But in fact Will is perfectly aware that if *he* had approached Summit with this Jim Johnson, or someone like him, Summit would have bridled and reminded Will that he asked for drug background only. When clients are paying, they want their preferences respected. Only they can decide to change the parameters of their search.

But all in all, Will leaves the Yacht Club happy. His five preliminary candidates passed muster, and on top of that, he now has a sixth who comes straight from the client. Four weeks ago, it seemed virtually impossible that Will would be able to find even one decent candidate. Now he has a half-dozen that Summit considers appropriate. And the marvel is that four of them come from top firms in the field, the very ones where Summit wanted him to look...a feat Will never thought he'd achieve.

A Recruiter's Work Is Never Done

Wilma locates Al Umans, ISC's Senior VP - Human Resources, in Seattle at the main plant and warehouse of SomeThinThweet, a $90 million subsidiary that produces low-calorie candy, and gets him on the phone for Will. "Would you believe," says Al, "that this whole big union drive got started in this little shop? How's the Drug Division search coming?" Will gives Al the same optimistic report over the phone that he gave to Mr. Summit.

But Will knows that he still needs to look further for ISC. Although the slate he just presented to Summit is plausible, Will is painfully aware that it's not really quite as good as it looks. Ethan Evans, let's face it, does have a problem making decisions...even though not enough to get him fired during 18 years at BioDynamics. Sherm Summit will almost certainly decide against him during interviews. And if by slim chance he doesn't, Will's final referencing will discourage hiring Evans. *I don't want my long-term relationship with ISC riding on how well they like Ethan Evans three years from now*, thinks Will. Dan Dawson was fired, and Will has seen other clients just as decisive as Summit begin to waver when it comes time to sign up someone a competitor has discarded. Phyllis Finley is a little junior for the position. Only Donna Powers and Charlie Comstock seem problem-free.

Too bad, Will! Charlie Comstock's clay feet are immediately obvious, when he comes in from Phoenix for his interview at GR&B. Charlie talks too much and listens too little. He gives long, rambling answers to Will's carefully phrased questions. And, worse yet, he never includes any facts and figures that might let Will objectively assess Charlie's performance. By the time their hour-long interview is concluded, Will finds himself in real doubt as to whether Charlie actually has contributed anything to Adam Labs' fine growth in sales and profitability. But whatever Charlie might or might not have done at Adam, he's simply too poor a personal communicator to present to a sharp Fortune 1000 CEO like Summit. Not only would Charlie be shredded during the interview, but Will would surely feel the repercussions as well. Sadly, Will strikes Charlie's name from his list of candidates.

While Will is looking for new candidates, other executives are looking for Will. Lanny Lawrence, a marketing executive at CompuMedic, whom Will placed about seven years ago at a different company, phones Will. Since he now works at CompuMedic, he is of course off-limits. Lanny, an extremely ambitious careerist, speaks with a note of petulance in his voice.

"Will, Lanny Lawrence here. I hear you've been calling around for someone to go to ISC as President of their proprietary drug division. Why the hell didn't you call me?"

I hate this kind of conversation. "Lanny, I certainly *did* think of you. But you know that CompuMedic is one of our best clients. I can't take you out."

"But surely you can make an exception for a good friend. I mean, I'm not desperate to leave or anything, but that ISC job is an outstanding opportunity that comes at the perfect point in my career. I could be here another three or four years before I get a shot at a job at that level. Come on...it'll be okay. I'll tell them I was the one who approached you, not vice versa."

Will spends a couple seconds imagining what Mr. Rossi would say if he heard GR&B had gone into CompuMedic, and winces. He's going to have to think fast to head Lanny off. Unfortunately, Lanny's just the aggressive sort of person who would go straight to ISC himself, with or without Will's cooperation.

"Lanny, you know that for you I might try to find a way to get around the rules...if I thought the job was really...well..." He lets his voice trail off.

Lanny is obligingly quick to read a meaning into Will's vague remark. "The only thing that might be wrong with that ISC job is that I've heard through the grapevine that in the last few years they've really cut back the advertising budget for their proprietary drug division. It could be a great job. But if the parent company isn't going to back up the marketing effort, well, that's another story."

"What can I tell you?" answers Will thoughtfully. He pauses to let his lack of reassurance sink in. As the silence grows, Will deliberately represses his memory of Summit's crystal clear explanation of how the problem came about and how it's going to be corrected.

Finally Lanny says decisively, "Well, I wouldn't want to be put out on a limb like that. I mean, to make that division grow and become truly profitable, you've got to have lots of advertising support. Without it, you just can't make things happen. And I can't afford to let a no-win situation like that louse up my career."

Will sighs as he hangs up the phone. His strategy, unhelpful as it may have been to Lanny, has obviously succeeded. He didn't lie. And yet there's little chance that Lanny will try to go directly after the ISC job.

But Will still needs to find one or two more really good people who are not off-limits for the ISC search. He goes back to his printouts, back to his notes, back to his sources. And, wonder of wonders, a new name *does* crop up. Roy Ricardo is a highly regarded U.S. marketing executive who's been working for a South American drug firm, heading their proprietary division. Obviously he took the foreign assignment as a stepping-stone career move. Now he's ready to leave Buenos Aires and return to the States, so he's begun getting in touch with his contacts to see what might be available. One of them...the VP - Manufacturing at Better & Best, whom Roy has kept in touch with since they worked together ten years ago...mentioned Roy to Will.

Will is humming to himself as he checks Roy out. His background is comprehensive and his track record is extraordinary. Bilingual, although born, raised, and Princeton-educated in the U.S., Roy had a meteoric rise to Group

Product Manager for all pain-relievers, a $760 million business, at Prestige Panacea here in the U.S. by the time he was 30 years old. Then in the hope of getting strong general management experience before age 35, Roy accepted a very lucrative offer to join the Argentinian company as President of a division which he's doubled in size (to $147 million) in just three years. *Wow*, thinks Will, *he'll be gangbusters for ISC!* Optimistically, Will checks out Roy's present employer to see if it's a client company that's off-limits at Gordon, Rossi & Boodles. Just as he has surmised, Los Medicamentos is not recognized by the computer. GR&B has never done business with this South American firm, even though it has a tiny U.S. subsidiary, so it's perfectly okay for Will to recruit its executives.

It's almost as an afterthought that Will asks Wilma to check whether Roy Ricardo belongs to any other GR&B recruiter. So he's stunned by the bad news. It turns out that Roy *is* in the computer, and is currently assigned to Doug Abel, one of Will's colleagues down the long corridor at GR&B. Will is concerned, but he doesn't give up hope. He knows that Doug has no assignment that involves anything in the consumer goods industry, much less proprietary drugs, so he assumes Doug is merely using Roy as a source on something involving South America. He hopes a stroll down the hall will enable him to talk Doug into relinquishing Roy, who's tailor-made for the ISC job.

But Will soon discovers that Doug isn't taking so cooperative a view of the situation. He tells Will that Roy is a prospect for his most urgent search...a corporate Marketing VP for Brute Force, one of America's leading manufacturers of heavy-duty industrial motors.

"Industrial motors! That's insane. Roy Ricardo is a *consumer* marketing guy, who just incidentally happens to be exactly what ISC is looking for. His proprietary drug experience is going to be wasted in industrial motors."

"You know that, Will, and I know that. But the people at Brute Force don't know that. And they're the ones who are paying their money to get their choice. They want someone with a consumer products background to jazz up their marketing approach."

"But surely the poor guy doesn't want to go into industrial motors...and move to Anthracite Valley to do it!"

"You're probably right that he doesn't especially want to go into industrial motors. But he does want to come back to the States, now that his twins will be entering junior high school in the fall. And he'll probably take the first offer he gets, because he can't run a very efficient campaign from Buenos Aires. Brute Force will pay well. And after all, it's probably the only job he's going to know about...at least the only one from GR&B. Will, I'm absolutely going to keep Ricardo. Do you think it's easy to find anyone in any sort of consumer marketing who wants to go into industrial motors? I searched for weeks before I found this guy. And so far he's my only acceptable candidate. I don't want him to know about any other job in the entire universe, and certainly not a presidency in proprietary drugs. No, Roy Ricardo is going to work for Brute Force in Anthracite Valley."

Will can recognize an immovable object when he sees one. Obviously, Doug is not going to give up Roy Ricardo. And to be fair, Will admits that, in Doug's shoes, he'd behave exactly the same way.

Ironically, Will's final candidate for the ISC job comes to him almost effortlessly. He and Buddy are again having a relaxing drink at the Four Seasons when Will begins to recount the Herculean effort of getting together a credible group of candidates on his ISC search.

"The last time we were here," says Buddy, "we talked about Bill and Allan, and you brought up *RITE*Site.com. I told you I got a couple really good candidates just by visiting the site and checking out the databases. Now my total's up to eight or ten...about one extra person we didn't know about for each of my searches. It doesn't cost us anything to see who's posted. That's totally different from Monster.com and all those other commercial sites. They all charge...and firms like GR&B never pay. Also, sorting on *RITE*Site is extremely easy...easier, actually, than on our GR&B computer, because *RITE*Site sorts by 47 industries, by the jobs in each, by salary ranges, and by geography. If nobody fits, you'll know *fast!* But if there *is* someone, you've hit the jackpot... especially if we don't already have them in our database.

"If the executive has chosen the R*ites*-Honored Option to post an identity-*revealed* resume that only retainer recruiters like us can see, we immediately know who the executive is. In fact, it's probably the very same resume they'd send us in a direct mail campaign. Then you just call 'em or e-mail 'em...same as if they were in our own database. If they're only posting an identity-*concealed* resume the whole world can see, it's still quite easy to deal with them. Click, e-mail 'em your job description, and if they like it, they respond. Of course if they aren't interested, they don't respond...and you can't reach them to try to persuade them. Confidentiality is one of the main points of *RITE*Site.

"So, hard up as you are, didn't you find even one person on *RITE*Site?"

"Buddy, I'm ashamed to say I didn't look. Maybe I was just lazy and was thinking I'd just work off the leads Gloria rounded up from inside the company. But I'll look as soon as I get home tonight. When you click the e-mail to contact someone who's posted an identity-concealed resume that interests you, do you say you're from GR&B?"

"Of course, Will. And I point out that we are one of the *RITES*-Honored search firms. The person I contact can check a pulldown list to see if we are. Also, for a phone number, I always give our switchboard, because that's a number they can also check from the pulldown. Then, when they call and get our receptionist, followed by my assistant or me, they've already built up plenty of reassurance that I'm authentic."

"But remember, Will, we're a *RITES*-Honored firm. Most people choose to use the *RITES*-Honored Option to let us—but not the outside world—know as much about them as possible. They show *RITES*-Honored recruiters the very same identity-*revealed* resume they'd visit our site and input into our computer...or that they'd send us in a direct mail campaign. If they do, there's no need for us to monkey around e-mailing and waiting to see if they respond. For us and other *RITES*-Honored recruiters, their name, street and e-mail addresses, and phone numbers are right out in plain sight. Just phone 'em... same as if they were in our own database."

Will and Buddy go their separate ways...Will to a leisurely dinner with Karen at a new bistro in their swank upper East Side Manhattan neighborhood. When they get home, Will signs onto the Internet and begins searching *RITE*Site's resumes. One marked *Identity-Concealed* looks especially interesting, because the person who indicates he or she is "Chief of Marketing," describes having "more than doubled dollar volume, market share and profits" in "just the past three years"...for an unidentified current employer and discusses very specifically some excellent accomplishments earlier at Prestige and National Anodyne.

"Well, whoever it is, he or she is not making it easy for me. But if they're as good as they look, I'll do whatever it takes to reach 'em," muses Will. *"I wonder why they didn't use the RITES-Honored Option and post an **identity-revealed** resume?"*

Will identifies himself and GR&B—but not ISC—and includes the position description he supplies to prospective candidates and sources. *Okay,* he thinks. *Let's see if I have the same kind of luck Buddy's been having.*

And he does! Will signs on and checks his personal e-mail first thing in the morning and finds he already has an answer. Hooray! The person, Mark Matthews, has sent Will an outstanding "Sales Representative" resume. Clearly he's qualified. And, equally important, Will checks and finds he's ***not*** on GR&B's central computer. Mark's cover note says, "Please call me at home, not at work."

There's a three-hour time difference, so Will doesn't make his call until after he and Karen have had a lovely evening...dinner out, followed by a wonderful performance at the Metropolitan Opera, where one of the children on stage is a girl who's been Karen's patient since she was an infant. As Will slips the key in the apartment door, he apologetically reveals a familiar agenda. "Not very romantic...being married to a headhunter," says Karen, softly. "Try to keep it brief!" Which Will, being a very focused individual, is easily able to do.

Mark Matthews answers on the first ring. Obviously he's been waiting for Will's call. Mark apologizes for not putting an identity-*revealed* resume on *RITE*Site via the *RITES*-Honored Option, so that respected recruiters like Will can call him directly without going through the secretive identity-concealed-resume-plus-e-mail screening process the rest of the world is subjected to on *RITE*Site.

"I don't want to seem paranoid," says Mark. "But I'm with a third-generation family-owned business, with family members scattered throughout the company. They're nice people and I love working with them. But some of the younger ones are nearly my age and wouldn't mind having my job. So that's why I'm doing only the concealed-identity resume part of *RITE*Site. I respect your profession—especially the top end of it—but you see where I'm coming from."

Will does understand. Moreover, he's delighted to learn that Mark Matthews is the top marketing executive in the relatively small but rapidly growing proprietary drug division of the family-owned West Coast conglomerate, and that Mark's achievements are very similar to what ISC hopes to accomplish. Data Drugs is one of the original businesses of this diversified corporation, which is run today by the grandson of its founder. A little over three years ago, Mark Matthews was recruited as Data's VP - Marketing & Sales. Data Drugs had nothing but a couple of old-time small-volume products: a dentifrice for heat- and cold-sensitive teeth recommended by dentists, and an ancient but effective hemorrhoid remedy.

Mark moved decisively into Data's stodgy operation and made some big changes. At his urging, the company took immediate advantage of the newly relaxed FDA regulations to bring out a cough remedy containing a very effective ingredient previously sold by prescription only. He also took the firm's old-fashioned hemorrhoid medication, at the time selling only to a few elderly consumers of longstanding loyalty, and gave it new life with an aggressive advertising campaign that managed to capitalize on the product's long history in a series of television commercials that poked fun at the product, while also selling persuasively and remaining in good taste.

With Mark's help, Data Drugs has tripled sales and quadrupled profits in less than four years. But the company has not rewarded his efforts with commensurate recognition and increased compensation. So he's ready to make a move, and ISC seems like the perfect next step. It would be an astonishing advance in his career, and it would bring him the additional money he's looking for.

Will wonders why, if Mark is as good as he seems to be and if Data Drugs is growing so rapidly, he and Data escaped notice when Gloria's team combed on-line information sources. The answer is that Data Drugs is not only privately owned, it cloaks itself in privacy as a company. Data does not belong to any industry associations, Mark is not allowed to attend or speak at industry meetings, and no financial analysts are following this non-public company. So Mark, being a talented—although an incredibly busy—marketing executive, took a very logical step to market himself by joining *RITE*Site.com and posting his Identity-Concealed Resume.

Mark is also an exceedingly energetic and highly motivated person. Will explains that there is some urgency, if Mark wants to be considered, because Will soon has to report to his client on the best people he has found. Immediately Mark offers to fly to New York on Saturday (the very next day) to see Will—getting away during the week would be almost impossible anyway—and gives Will the home phone numbers of three potential references he's sure would be willing to talk to Will on the weekend. Will needs preliminary references, because Mark drew attention to himself...he was not recommended by one of Will's respected industry contacts. Now Will is just as delighted with Mark's enthusiasm, drive, flexibility, and efficiency as he is with his excellent track record.

And Mark in person—although quite young for the success he's achieved—is impressively mature...a logical thinker, a clear and succinct communicator, well dressed, well groomed, and warmly down-to-earth, with an engaging sense of humor.

Mark is an exceptionally attractive candidate. As far as Will is concerned, his slate is now complete.

Will had already done preliminary referencing on all his other candidates. He knows they have the recent job titles, experience, and college degrees they're claiming, and also that current observers consider them competent and morally upright. Moreover, all candidates know they must submit to Will's intensive final referencing prior to actual hiring by Mr. Summit...if and when both he and they are inclined to take that step.

The Final Slate

By the end of his search, Will is very pleased. He has seven attractive candidates for Summit. The finalists are:

1. **Ethan Evans**: a senior executive with BioDynamics, a top-tier firm. Evans merits consideration, no matter what his decision-making problems might be.

2. **Phyllis Finley**: an impressive young woman on the way up at Maxi-Medi-Marketing, also a top firm. She's definitely a contender, even though her experience is a bit light.

3. **Dan Dawson**: until recently with Prestige Panacea, a top-tier firm that's one of Mr. Summit's favorites. Even though he's been fired, Dawson definitely gives a good account of himself.

4. **Sam Sage**: his experience has been mainly with ethical pharmaceuticals rather than proprietary drugs, and he's a leading candidate on Buddy Young's Expodex search. Nonetheless he's become a candidate in whom Summit is interested.

5. **Jim Johnson**: highly recommended by a Director of ISC and a favorite of Bill Beane, although his background at Daisy Foods is certainly not what Summit originally asked for.

6. **Donna Powers**: the person at Cosa Nostrums most appropriate for ISC, although more oriented toward field sales management and sales promotion than toward advertising- and image-oriented consumer products marketing.

7. **Mark Matthews**: last, but not least...Will's latest find and—along with Sage, Powers, and Johnson—one of the most

> attractive candidates. He's a rapidly rising young marketing superstar who despite being from Data Drugs, a still-small but (thanks to him) explosively growing proprietary drug division, has a brief but proven track record in doing just what Mr. Summit wants accomplished. Sales and earnings of the operation Mark joined three and a half years ago had been flat for seven prior years under the leadership of the family member who's still CEO today. Clearly, it's Mark who's made the difference.

Will allows himself a twinge of pride, as he watches Wilma staple his slightly edited version of each person's resume into its own beige steel-engraved GR&B folio. *Beautiful!*, thinks Will. *Some good people, too. Summit's paying $250,000 ...nearly $36,000 each. He deserves quality and he's getting it.*

The phone rings. Wilma answers, looks up, and announces that Kathryn Keane is calling.

How ironic!, thinks Will. *There's nobody I'd rather show Summit than Kathryn. And with that jerk giving her grief over at Parker Labs, she'd surely love to meet Summit. It could be her once-in-a-lifetime chance not only to get out of Parker, but also to wind up running a proprietary drug company as President...her career goal for all these years. And now she calls!* But Will's delighted with his candidates. So he sinks comfortably into his interviewing chair, instead of returning to his desk, as he picks up the phone.

"We've known each other a long time. May I ask you a favor?" says Kathryn.

"Of course. You've always helped me. I really appreciate your suggestions. Tell me what I can do."

"If I email you my resume, would you look it over? I updated it in a hurry, and I'd love to have your thoughts, because I'm having dinner tonight with Carl and Cynthia Cato. She's my dearest friend since high school. Her career is in hotel management, and she was running a fabulous place in Singapore, when Carl bought it out. You've heard of him...his father founded Cato-Colossus in Las Vegas, and now Carl's built that into an international chain of resorts and casinos. Well, one thing led to another and now they're married. They have year-old twins and they work together in running the business. Forgive the trivia, Will, but it's why I need the resume.

"Since I called you to say I wanted out of Parker Labs, I've been networking...but only with you and with friends I can trust to keep quiet. Because if the guy I told you about ever found out, he might try to use my looking outside as a reason to get rid of me and not even pay the severance I should get after 17 years over here.

"Well, my first call was to Cynthia, and I used John Lucht's 'ask-for-a-reference-rather-than-a-job' technique. I said 'I'm thinking about leaving Parker Labs ...and maybe even getting into hospitality, as you've suggested so many times. You know me, Cynthia, and what it takes to succeed in the marketing and general management of hotel chains and real estate developments. Would you be a reference for me, if and when there's interest from folks in your field?'

"She said, 'Absolutely! I've always said you'd be a genius at what I do.' You see, Will, I've vacationed—usually at almost no cost—at some of those resorts she's been running all over the world. Every time I left, I handed her my suggestions...on brochures, check-in, decor, menus, room service, special events, tie-ins with local attractions and so on. And always she's said, 'Your bill would have been $10,000 or whatever. But I got more than that in consulting...and for free, because your suite would have been empty.' Well, bottom line, Will, she and Carl are in town, and they want to see me tonight. 'I'm *not* going to be a reference for you,' she said; 'Carl and I are going to offer you a job.'

"Now what they're talking about, as I gather, is for me to head an entirely new venture. It's out near Aspen, where I'd dearly love to be, because I love skiing, horseback riding, and everything about the outdoors. It seems they signed the papers last week to take over an enormous resort being built on an empty mountainside. The place is two-thirds completed, but it ran way over in construction costs, and lost its funding from the banks and insurance companies.

"Carl and Cynthia got it for twelve cents on the dollar. And the main reason is that it's got a terrible marketing problem. That's why they want me. The location is far, far away from any other resort, and nobody's ever heard of where it is at all. They say the skiing will be fabulous. But Aspen is 130 miles away, and the nearest little town is 45.

"Have you got time for all this, Will? I know you're busy."

"Sure Kathryn. I was taking a little break. My next interview is 10 minutes away; I'll relax 'til then."

"Now here's something you don't know about me, Will. My hobby, which I love, is real estate. I've been buying houses, fixing, and reselling them, and I've built up maybe $900,000 in equity that way. So even though I've thoroughly enjoyed raising Parker Labs to #1 in colds and flu brands and almost #1 in headache remedies, I could happily switch to a career in real estate.

"But here's the problem, and why the resume has really got to explain me to Cynthia and Carl. First, I make a lot more money than they may be planning to offer...$590,000, plus options and a car. Cynthia, I know, was only making about $210,000 when she ran that huge hotel in Singapore, although she got a fabulous suite and every conceivable living expense as a freebee within the hotel. The resume has got to show them that I rescued dying brands and built new ones, and made millions and millions of dollars for Parker Labs. My marketing and sales people and I have been eating our competitors' lunch!"

Yes, and I know one you've made very hungry!, thinks Will.

"The second problem is that Carl and Cynthia are probably thinking of me for *VP - Marketing*. I suspect they're *not* thinking of me for President of the whole thing. And that's the only way I'd ever go there. That's the challenge I'd love. Because *everything* needs to be done. Construction has to be finished, and interior design, decorating and landscaping. And what about transportation? Planes, helicopters, buses? Even getting a decent road in there. And should there be a community? Supermarkets, stores, gas stations?

"And the umbrella over everything is *marketing*. What to name it. How to position it. How to target and bring in customers...for vacations, for conferences, for sales of condos and time-shares and on and on. You can see why maybe they wouldn't be willing to bet on a proprietary drug person to do all that. So you see, Will, my resume's got a big job to do. They like me, they respect me, and they want to hire me. But the question is *for what?"*

"Well, Kathryn, fire away. I'll read your resume as soon as it's here." Will phones his stockbroker. When he looks up, Wilma hands him Kathryn's resume.

Wow! She's even better than I realized. Fabulous accomplishments. And all in proprietary drugs...exactly what Summit wants. I only wish I could show her to him. And look at this resume. She's got *to be smart! It's so clear and brief. Four concise pages, based mainly on numbers, not self-praising adjectives. Easy to scan. Inviting use of white space. Nothing stated that's obvious. And no jargon. No need to know proprietary drugs, or even consumer products, to see that she's* made money *for Parker Labs. In fact,* thinks Will, *this paperwork is just as strong as Sam Sage's* (pp. 220-27). *And that's saying a lot, because Sam's resume got action from Summit...and it's one of the best* I've *ever read.*

So Will phones Kathryn and tells her the resume is exceptional. Her friends can't fail to see that her work at Parker Labs—although different—is fully equivalent to what a President will have to do to finish building their resort and make it successful. Sadly, Will still can't tell her that he's filling a job she might like even better.

Will quickly forgets Kathryn, as he devours tomato soup and a tuna-melt at his desk, while perusing a stack of retyped resumes Wilma has put there for his approval before stapling them into GR&B's chic folders. Will handles about six searches simultaneously, so he can't waste time on lunch dates. Only when an important client or potential candidate is involved does Will go out.

At four o'clock Will is sorting through resume printouts allocated to him for a CFO search, when Wilma taps him on the shoulder. Kathryn's on the phone.

"Hi Kathryn. How'd it go?"

"So well, Will, that it's almost scary. They both read the resume right at the table. We had a great talk. And just as we were about to leave Carl pulled out an envelope, scribbled something on the paper and passed it to Cynthia. She nodded and passed it to me. It was an offer letter. And best of all, VP of Marketing was crossed out; President was written over it. Unfortunately, money was only $240,000. But they said they want to know exactly what I'm making, so they can try to create something I'll find financially attractive. Oh, and one more thing. With the letter was a floor plan of the former owner's intended penthouse apartment, with acres of space, walls of glass, fireplaces, and a huge terrace with a heated pool. I'll be *required* to live there if I take the job.

"So I'm flying out this weekend to look the place over. If it's anything like they've presented it, and if I can push up the money, I may be off to Colorado and an exciting new challenge. But Will, could I trouble you for another favor? If I email it, would you take a look at the letter? See whether you think it would give me adequate protection, if they up the money and I go ahead?"

"Sure Kathryn. Send it. I'll let you know what I think."

Even before he hangs up the phone, a plan is forming in Will's mind. *I'll take that letter over to Hamilton Rossi. Sure he's tight with Charley Phipps, the Chairman of Parker Labs. And ordinarily he'd have a fit if I pitched Kathryn on Summit's job. But* now *if we recruited her, there'd be written proof that she was leaving anyway. It wouldn't just be our word and hers that she was determined to go. Don't know if he'll buy it. But it's worth a try.*

Moments later, email in hand, Will is in Hamilton Rossi's corner suite. "You young turks think you can bend the rules whenever it suits your purpose," says Rossi. "That's why Red" [Tapecutter] "and I are always keeping our eyes peeled. Because every time GR&B gets caught raiding one of our clients, there are always plenty of other firms that have been begging for their business for months—maybe years—who'll say, ***'We would never do that!'*** Whether they would or not doesn't matter. They've never *had* any business from our client. So at that moment they're saintly pure, and we're prostitutes. I don't want anyone in this firm *ever* to put me in that position!

"But with that said, Will, I think in this instance I *can* be a little flexible. Ordinarily, for us to be in the clear, you'd have had to get this woman to inform someone above her that she was actively looking. She could have lied. And, we could have accepted her word. We wouldn't have had to challenge her honesty by calling the person...although sometimes I've done that when I was suspicious and the client was important.

"But here's this offer letter in black-and-white on Cato World Corp. stationery. Leave this copy with me. I'll deal with Charley Phipps, if your woman winds up getting the job and he finds out we were involved. Have you got other candidates? She may *not* be the one they hire. Anyway, go ahead. Show Summit there's no other search firm even half as good as GR&B!"

Will's elated. He immediately calls Kathryn and asks if she'd like to have a shot at becoming President of a $840 million proprietary drug company with a strong commitment to fund aggressive marketing programs and maybe even to make acquisitions...a company determined to move rapidly into the top ten in the field.

"Would I! Is the Pope Catholic? You have my resume. Get it over there right away!"

Will explains that he'll be presenting several candidates to Summit on Friday ...Kathryn among them. And she reconfirms her intent to fly out to Colorado over the weekend. "Frankly, Will, I have no idea which I'd choose, if I had tempting offers from both. My whole career has been aimed at running my own company in proprietary drugs, toiletries, cosmetics, or some other consumer product. And yet I love real estate, the outdoors, and the mountains. For months I've been down in the dumps. Now I'm on a 'Rocky Mountain High!' Will, you're a good friend. Thank you for your help."

Will *is* a good friend. But notice that throughout all this, he's had to follow his interests, the firm's interests, his client's interests and—except for commenting on her resume and offer letter—*not* Kathryn's. Nice as he is, Will's in business, not social work.

Are Eight Enough?

Will's absolutely thrilled to be headed out to see Mr. Summit with presentations on no less than eight attractive candidates in his sleek Dunhill attache. The last time he was in Summit's office Will wondered how he could ever fulfill the Chairman's high expectations. Now he's introducing not one but eight attractive candidates. Three are from companies strictly off-limits to Will. And he's done this without breaking any of GR&B's ethical client-protection rules. Notice again the first seven beginning on page 495. And now...

8. **Kathryn Keane**: Frosting on the cake. Will already had several candidates of the exceptional calibre a demanding client like Summit pays $250,000 to meet, plus lesser but still impressive ones. Now he can also present the #1 most appropriate candidate from Parker Labs, one of Summit's preferred "source" companies. Two days ago Will could only have muttered vague excuses if asked whether he succeeded in penetrating this "prime-target" company. Today, despite Parker's being off-limits, Will can answer, "Yes; we've got the very best person in their organization for your needs."

"Client meetings *always* go well, when you're superbly prepared," jokes Will in response to Buddy's "How'd it go?" as they both step into the elevator at 8:15 the next morning. Indeed, Will's fine work *was* favorably received by Mr. Summit. "Interesting people," he told Will. I'm going to interview every one of them. I can see why Bill Beane felt we should go back and use you again."

A modest "Thank you" was Will's only reply. But he was moved by the warmth and respect in the Chairman's voice. *Demanding, but appreciative! No wonder Bill Beane enjoys working for him.*

Bill Beane wasn't present, so Will left Bill's set of presentations with Summit's assistant, who promised to pass them along. And while Will was in Lustretown with Summit, Wilma tracked down Al Umans, ISC's Senior VP - Human Resources, at ISC's huge distribution center in Denver. He'll get an identical set by FedEx.

Will *was* surprised—and also delighted—by Summit's decision to meet all eight. The wily Chairman likes to interview outsiders as a "due diligence" check on the quality and thinking of his own people. Having spent $250,000 to have Will identify and evaluate outsiders, Summit opens his door to them. Afterward, he'll be sure he's chosen the best Will could find. And he'll have learned a lot more from these outsiders than if he'd spent equal time with his own employees.

Actually, Will's eight candidates are a very large slate. Four to six would have been Will's usual number. However, Johnson *came* from Summit. Retainer recruiters welcome client-supplied candidates and treat them impartially, but never want them to be the only—or almost the only—attractive choice. So recruiters don't reduce the number of their candidates merely to include client ones.

Kathryn Keane is the second "extra" within the eight. She was a lucky last-minute accident. Will had assumed her to be hopelessly off-limits.

Winding up with *six rather than just four*, however, *wasn't* an accident. Will had never submitted candidates to Summit before. And from experience he knew that people as strong—and therefore as potentially opinionated—as Summit may habitually reject most of anything presented to them. They think, "Whatever anyone brings me can't possibly be as good as if I send them back to look for more."

Having observed Will's struggle to develop his slate, we know how damaging it would have been if Will had presented only his top three or four candidates and Summit had thrown out some of those rarities. That's why smart retainer recruiters like Will never present just their top few. With his slate of six (expanded by accident to eight), Will was prepared to lose two or three, while still keeping his favorites alive for final interviewing and selection.

You caught the word! Will does have *favorites*. His criteria: (1) Who can do the job so well that the client will return to Will for more people. (2) Whose personality and behavior will fit the organization so well that the client will return to Will for more people, and (3) Who seems to *like* Will enough to come back to him and not go to a different recruiter for more people. The factors are ranked in order of importance. None is unimportant.

Notice, too, that Will has chosen to do "Slate" type recruiting. He's looking over an entire industry and helping his client pick the *one best person* (certainly that's been Summit's goal). When a search is for president, general manager, or a head-of-function, such as marketing or R&D, then recruiting the industry's very best person can often move the business from "also ran" to #1. After all, *some* company has to be #1...and that's what leaders are hired to accomplish! Notice too, that there's a twofold change in the industry's balance-of-power when you grab its #1 best person away from your competitor: (1) You're strengthened. (2) The previously-strongest company is weakened.

Whenever a company wants to move ahead competitively by getting the best players at every position, "Slate" type recruiting is the only choice: Examine *all* the key people in the field; interview the top few; and hire #1 among those.

There is, however, a prevalent alternative to "Slate" recruiting. It has several names: "Sequential," "Process," and "Beauty Parade" are all apt. But I prefer to call it "Dope-a-Week" recruiting. The goal is *not* to get the very best person and change the competitive balance-of-power. But rather, to assure the client that continual activity is going on and he or she is shaping it.

Under "Sequential" or "Dope-a-Week" recruiting, the client is sent one plausible candidate after another—ideally about one per week—until he or she has "looked at enough people to make a decision" or at least has become sufficiently bored or fatigued to allow the Wheel of Fortune to...COME......TO......... A............STOP (read decision). Which is not to say a fine result is never obtained that way. But merely to point out that the method is designed to manipulate the client and smooth out time-demands on the recruiter, who conducts lots of searches simultaneously and can feed most of them from the long-grey-line of candidates in the firm's 200,000- to 400,000-person computerized database. Indeed one of America's largest and finest firms used to (and perhaps still does) tout the superiority of its services by telling potential clients, *"We guarantee that you'll see your first candidate within a week."* And presumably another the week after that. You can, of course, stop whenever you wish.

While Will certainly didn't anticipate the Chairman's decision to interview all eight candidates, he's not in the least unnerved by it. Each is appropriate and several are outstanding. Ordinarily Bill Beane, as Group Executive to whom the new Drug Division President will report, would screen the slate and present one or two to Summit for final endorsement. But Will's just as happy with the opposite scenario. Probably, as Summit has implied, Beane is the busier of the two. And, as Summit told Will, "This way we don't waste Bill's time on anyone we're not really interested in." *Nor mine,* thinks Will, since Beane is unlikely to want to resurrect anyone Summit rejects, nor to reject *all* the people Summit likes.

Will's presentations contain candidate phone numbers, and only Summit's assistant knows his availability. So it's agreed that she'll set up the interview appointments. Will phones the candidates to alert them to her call, and to remind them to let him know in advance the date of their interview and to phone him immediately afterward to debrief.

Down to the Wire

Summit's first decision is to rule out Ethan Evans.

"You know," he says to Will in a follow-up phone call, "I suspect this guy was kicked upstairs. He definitely lacks the fire in the belly you want to see in a division head. Corporate staff seems like the best place for him. He's the kind of guy who can tell you the pros and cons of every situation, but I don't think he can go on and make a decision about which risk to take."

"That's very perceptive," responds Will tactfully. "I've heard some things along those same lines, which I would have wanted you to consider if you were interested in going forward with him."

"No, I don't think he's right for us. I liked him personally, and I could see him as a staff analyst or a consultant; certainly he knows the industry. But I don't think he'll deliver in the crunch."

Summit signs off, letting Will know that he's seeing Sam Sage tomorrow afternoon. Twenty minutes later, however, Mr. S calls back.

"Sage just called and canceled his appointment! Seems he just this morning signed the papers to do a leveraged buyout of the Accura Flavors & Fragrances Division of Medica Suisse. Accura is an 80-year-old company...$96 million...in New Jersey. They'd fallen way behind their competitors by the time the Swiss bought them four years ago, and things haven't improved since. Just scraping along...not losing money, but not making anything much either.

"Sage says he's always wanted to own a company," Summit continues, "and this may be the only chance he'll ever get. Sounds like a very fine fellow. If I were his age again, and had a chance to go it alone, I'd do the same damn thing. Anyway, I wanted you to know. I've re-read your paperwork on all these people and Sage looked like one of the very best. I'm sorry to lose him."

Wow! I knew Sam was working on some deals, thinks Will, *but I never imagined he'd get one to happen. This is bad news for me. But it'll hit Buddy like a ton of bricks. Sam was his front-runner on Expodex. Hope Buddy's finally got some depth on that search...*

Three days later, Summit calls with another status report. Phyllis Finley has also fallen by the wayside. Just as Will suspected, Summit finds her experience a bit too light. "In a few more years, she'd be right for us...or we'd take her today in another position. But for the presidency right now I have to pass.

"Actually, Will, I intend to tell a few folks over here about her. She's just our type... energetic, optimistic, creative...very intelligent and analytical. Also, I suspect, *very* strong and assertive. And with the nicest possible way about her. Somebody, I suspect, who'd get things done without ruffling too many feathers. She's exactly the sort of person we should be grooming for the future.

"Which gives me one idea how we might eventually bring her over here. Bill Beane and Graham Rusk are thinking of splitting off some of their Foods Division product managers and field sales people into a separate unit to handle just their spices, condiments, and herbal teas...giving those products a separate image as high quality almost gourmet items, and raising their prices and margins. I don't know if they have anyone in mind to head that, but I think someone like Phyllis would be superb. And I'm sure she'd like them and they'd like her."

Wow! thinks Will. *Could be a by-product! And the fee'd be over $100,000, maybe as much as $140,000. Am I glad I presented her even though I knew she was light, just so she could be shot down instead of one of my top candidates...if Summit had been in a shooting mood. And now I might make an extra bundle!* There's nothing a retainer recruiter likes better than placing two people from a single search. The second fee is pure profit. And yet it's perfectly proper. Contingency recruiters get paid for each placement; so do retainer recruiters.

Will makes suitable noises, and Summit continues without responding.

"I especially like Kathryn Keane and Mark Matthews. Her personality is as fine as Phyllis's. She's from Parker Labs, a company we prefer. And she's done it all. Every bit of experience we could possibly want she's had. Also, I love the entrepreneurial spirit she's shown in her private life. Did you know that she's already made several hundred thousand dollars buying, remodeling and selling houses?

"Now young Matthews isn't as advanced as Kathryn Keane and, until he got there, who'd ever heard of Data Drugs? But he has done *exactly* what we want. You had to turn over a stone to find him,Will," says Summit approvingly. "And I think he's pretty interesting. I'm having Lucy" [Summit's assistant] "bring back Dawson, Powers, Johnson, Keane, and Matthews. This time they'll talk to Bill Beane. If it were my call, I'd have cut two or three more. But I want Bill to feel he's fully in on this decision."

You've got the makings of an executive recruiter, Mr. Chairman, thinks Will; *How'd you like less pay and harder work?* Happily, Will turns to the other five searches he's conducting. *Tough as it was to begin with, the ISC search is now a piece of cake!*

A week passes. All of the candidates contact Will or he calls them. All enjoyed meeting Summit and wish to go further. The one unnerving call is from Kathryn Keane. "I really like Mr. Summit," she says. "He was so charming and informal...and so genuinely interested in what I've done. It was almost more him selling me than me selling him. However, I must tell you, Will, my trip to Denver was even better than I expected. They've got the most beautiful mountainside...easily a match for Aspen or Vail. And we—I should say they—own 30,000 acres, dominating the slopes *and* the access road for nearly 25 miles. We can do whatever we want! And the physical plant is awesome...500 hotel rooms, plus 150 one- and two-bedroom condos."

I don't like that 'we' pronoun one bit, thinks Will, as Kathryn drones on enthusiastically. *If she might drop out, I wish she'd do it now, before Summit and Beane get to thinking that she's the best.* Will has had other clients initially praise his entire slate and later send him out for a whole new group, after their clear-cut favorite has slipped away. He considers steering Kathryn into a frank discussion. *But there's danger in that too*, he decides, so he merely exchanges pleasantries and signs off.

On a happier note, Will also hears from Al Umans, ISC's Senior VP of HR, who's now at ISC's West Coast headquarters in L.A. Al reports that "Summit is very pleased with the search so far. He's enjoying meeting those attractive people you've sent him. Of course, you'd have been mud, Will, if any of them had been a dope. As it is, you're riding high. You may even place that Finley woman, in addition to the person we're searching for. The Chairman liked her a lot."

Will's call to Bill Beane offering to discuss the candidates prior to Bill's meeting them goes very well indeed. Beane has read Will's presentations and, of course, already knows and feels enthusiastic about Jim Johnson. "The others sound good too, especially Keane and Matthews."

Within a week, Will hears from Summit again. "At this point we've eliminated Dan Dawson, although he seems competent. We found him a little rigid...perhaps a bit too insistent on doing things precisely his way. He might not be the team player we need. Frankly, Bill and I could have warmed more to Dawson, if there weren't others we like especially well in terms of personal characteristics. Maybe I shouldn't say *we*, because they haven't yet been in to see Bill. It's just that he and I—quite fortunately—tend to like the same types. And, I guess the converse is true; we tend not to like the same traits in people.

"And on that basis, there's another person that just isn't quite on our wavelength, even though she's also a very fine person. That's Donna Powers. She seems a bit like Dawson, a little rigid, maybe a little autocratic—I have no way of knowing that; I just suspect it. But what really turned me off in her interview was that she seemed very territorial. She clearly didn't like other people encroaching on her turf. I can't imagine her cheerfully letting me carry the ball on this search for someone reporting to her, as Bill's been perfectly happy to do.

"I'm proud to say that we're a very collegial organization over here. I like to walk into any office and ask any question of anyone at any time. There's no standing on ceremony. Donna mentioned a couple times that she wasn't happy when their CEO happened to walk into one of her regional sales offices and start asking questions and making suggestions without clearing them with her first. Well, she certainly has a point. And in theory, at least, she's absolutely right. But the behavior she described is what, unfortunately, I often do. So I suspect she wouldn't be happy here and we wouldn't be happy with her.

And with three people remaining who're the sort we like so well, why bother with her?

"Which brings us to our best three finalists in my opinion. Jim Johnson, whom Bill has known a long time and likes a lot. I do too. His personality would definitely fit in. However, if we have people just as good to work with, who come straight out of proprietary drugs and have equally impressive track records, I'll go with them over Johnson.

"And Will, my boy, we do." *Now it's **my boy**,* thinks Will. *You can't beat that!* "We've got Kathryn Keane and Mark Matthews. I think they're clearly ahead of the others. Frankly, Will, my money's on Kathryn. As I told you, ISC has eight divisions and not one has a woman President. And she's far more experienced than Mark is.

Well maybe, thinks Will, *but Kathryn may be slipping away. Everything may hinge on what's in the offer letter that will arrive by FedEx tomorrow morning. I sure as hell hope it's nothing amazing!*

Summit winds up jovially. *That's a mood I've never seen before, although Bill Beane has described it.* "Bill and Al Umans are seeing Kathryn tomorrow morning and Mark tomorrow afternoon. Then Bill and I are having dinner tomorrow night. Who knows, we may have our new Division President by the time we get to coffee and dessert."

Will's cheerful goodbye matches the Chairman's buoyant humor. But Will's visibly shaken. Wilma asks what's wrong?

"Five minutes ago I had five great candidates on the ISC search. Now I've got no more than two. Summit has dumped Powers and Dawson, thinking he can have his choice of Keane or Matthews. Johnson he says he also likes on a personal basis, but he prefers Kathryn's and Mark's proprietary drug backgrounds. Actually he as much as said Keane is his choice.

"But *I* know that Kathryn's waiting for an offer letter from that real estate thing out in Denver. Ironically, it will arrive at her apartment tomorrow by FedEx, precisely while she's out at ISC with Bill Beane and Al Umans. So she may be convincing Bill to want her—Summit already does—at the same time she's getting another offer she can't and won't refuse. Damn it, Wilma, I've known I might lose her ever since our last phone conversation. Whenever she mentioned that blasted resort it was ***our*** 30,000 acres and ***our*** 500 rooms. That's not a good sign!

"Fortunately Summit also likes Matthews. But it's one thing to like him as a runner-up, and entirely different to accept him as #1, after losing the #1 he really wants. Besides, Bill has never met either Kathryn or Mark. It would be just my luck for him to fall for Kathryn, hate Mark, and then not be able to convince Summit to hire Johnson, whom Bill likes a lot. Then I can just hear them both coming back to me and saying, 'Look, we can't agree on either Mark Matthews or Jim Johnson. So why don't you just go back into the marketplace and see if there's anyone we can both get excited about.'"

"Oh come on," says Wilma. "You're figuring everything that can go wrong will go wrong. Don't torture yourself. It probably won't go that way at all."

By 5:30 Will's so concerned that he grabs his coat, goes down in the elevator, whooshes through the revolving door, and *walks* the 36 blocks up Park Avenue to his condo and the one person who'll help him ignore his black thoughts. The apartment is dark. Not a good sign. There's a note for Will on the demilune in the foyer. "Will, don't wait up. The Shelby child has been transferred to intensive care, and what I'm hearing doesn't sound at all good. I'll do my best. Love you!"

"Damn!" says Will out loud, as he scrounges through an empty fridge and finally grabs a can of Campbell's bean soup from the shelf over the broom closet. Without bothering to "add water and heat," he devours the cold, solid mass. When Karen comes in at 2:00 a.m. Will's asleep in a chair. "Happy dreams, Mr. Headhunter," she says as she wearily covers him with an afghan and proceeds to the master bedroom suite alone.

The next morning in the office Will tries to concentrate on his other searches, but time moves slowly. His mind keeps returning to ISC. *I'll bet Kathryn is wowing Bill Beane. Of course she* should *if she wants the job. But* does *she?* And later: *Kathryn's probably on her way back to Manhattan. Probably Bill, Al, or even the Chairman took her to lunch, trying to sell her on ISC. Now it's Mark Matthews' turn. I hope he gives the performance of his life. He'll have to, to replace Kathryn, if she's persuaded them and then she walks away.*

Will's nervous reverie is interrupted by a flurry of call-backs on messages he's left with various "sources" (people who might identify others) and "prospects" (potential candidates). At 4 o'clock the receptionist buzzes. Kathryn Keane doesn't want to interrupt...but would like to see Will, if he happens to be free. Otherwise she'll drop off an envelope for him. Wilma suggests coffee as she ushers Kathryn in, and is soon back with two steaming cups.

"Look at this," says Kathryn, handing Will a FedEx envelope. He reaches inside and pulls out a letter just like the one Kathryn emailed him earlier, except that the salary figure has been raised from $240,000 to $450,000.

Fantastic! thinks Will. *Summit's expecting to pay $590,000. And with ISC's Stock Option and Stock Grant Plans, he's figuring the job at $750,000 total first year's comp. Also, ISC has a great comp expert, who'll chart out how all the parts of their program kick in at various times in the next few years to produce terrific progress in money. The Denver outfit probably doesn't have anyone like that. We'll not only* pay *more, but it's going to be very* evident *that we're offering a lot more.*

But there's something else deeper down in the cardboard envelope. "What's this?" asks Will.

"What does it say on the front?"

"Deed."

"Well, Will, that's what it is. A deed for the condo I'll be *required* to occupy if I go there. Remember? It's the place the original developer planned to live in himself. Here's the floor plan. Living room thirty by forty, formal dining room, library, three bedrooms, two more bedrooms and a bath for the help, a huge slate terrace with a small heated pool maybe twenty-by-twenty—and *three* fireplaces. Will, when we make the resort successful, that condo is worth at least seven million dollars...maybe more. And after five years, I'll own it free and clear. I get 20% ownership at the end of each year with the company...even if I should go to work in another of their resorts. And while I'm there, they pay all the expenses of the condo. Of course I'll be using it to entertain celebrities. In fact that's part of my marketing strategy...to get big names and trendsetters to leave Aspen and Vail and come with us."

"What about the career in consumer products you've worked so hard to build?" asks Will. "I want to hear about your interviews today. But even before we discuss them, let me say that I'm almost positive you're about to get the opportunity you've always dreamed about. If you play your cards right, you can be President of ISC's Proprietary Drug Division. But your mind's made up, isn't it?"

"It is, Will. I wish it weren't. And Will, I so hate to let down Bill Beane and Sherm Summit. They're brilliant business people. And so nice...both of them. If I were already with them, I'd never have started working my personal contacts and asked Cynthia and Carl for a reference rather than a job."

"What did you tell them?"

"Carl and Cynthia?"

"No Sherm Summit and Bill Beane."

"Nothing, really. We just had a great meeting. Further steps were left up in the air. Bill Beane said he had another person to see this afternoon. So they still haven't made up *their* minds. But I must say, Bill asked me to come back and see him after my meeting with Al Umans, and he then took me in to see Sherm again, and the three of us had lunch in Sherm's dining room."

Will Pickham is too professional—and indeed too decent and sensible—to try high-pressuring Kathryn at this point. Instead, he says, "Why not just sleep on it tonight. I'll find out how things went for you and the other candidate, and get an idea of what they're about to offer you. Then you can make a final decision with a clear head...and with all the facts on the table."

"Thanks, Will. I really feel you want the best for me. And that's amazing, from a headhunter. Most are like used car salesmen. You're *so* different."

Will walks Kathryn to the elevator. He stops in the men's room on the way back to his office. Alone, he slams his fist on the red granite sink-counter and lets out a four-letter word...passionately enough to vent his feelings, but quietly enough not to be heard beyond the double mahogany doors.

"You look awful," says Wilma, when Will returns.

"Of course. Everything's going just as I told you yesterday. She's turning the job down, after they've decided she's perfect and nobody else will do. Now they'll throw out Mark Matthews—whom Summit *loved* only yesterday—and ask me to start all over again!"

"What do they think of Matthews?" asks Wilma, practical as always.

"Oh you're right, Wilma. Things could still be okay if they like him better than her," says Will. *Fat chance! It's easy for you to stay cool. You go home at 5:30. You don't give a thought to this craziness 'til morning...and never on weekends. Meanwhile I'm working lots of evenings and Saturdays and Sundays, on the phone or travelling...* Abruptly Will pulls out of his self-indulgent mood. *So what's the worst that can happen? I have to start over. Big deal! I wonder if the Shelby boy lived or died. Other folks have problems bigger than yours, Will Pickham!*

From Will's introspection comes a plan of action: *I'll call Bill Beane at home tonight. I'll never influence what he and the Chairman decide if I don't act fast.* So after Will and Karen enjoy a dinner of Chinese take-out Will brings home, he's on the phone.

"Bill Beane," says Bill, picking up in his den, where he's peering at his computer screen, manipulating models of his businesses according to various acquisition, divestiture, and investment scenarios.

"Bill, it's Will Pickham. How did things go with Kathryn Keane and Mark Matthews today?"

"Great. I hadn't met either of them, although the Chairman had told me about them. I liked them both. As you probably know, Sherm prefers Kathryn. Certainly she's the more advanced of the two. She's headed all marketing and sales for a much larger company, Parker Labs. And she's done a great job. Also her personality is terrific. She has real leadership ability. I happen to know their Southeastern Regional Sales Manager, who worked for me years ago. And he says she met a lot of resistance and prejudice among the old timers in the field and she overcame it beautifully. Now she's firmly in charge all up and down their marketing and sales organization, and she's very well respected.

"Will, Kathryn's the Chairman's choice walking away. But I'll tell you something, absolutely in confidence. I don't like her as well as Mark for our purposes. For this reason..."

Thank God! Who cares why you don't like her as well. What I desperately need right now is just for you ***not*** *to. With you favoring Mark, I may have a shot at holding this search together!*

"...and this reason only," continues Bill: "Kathryn has always worked in large companies with exceptionally fine resources. First at Pan-Global Advertising agency...one of the world's largest and richest, where she was on the Parker Labs account. Then she was invited over to Parker, America's third-largest proprietary drug company. They've got more budget, and more people than just about any other company in the field. So whenever Kathryn wants something done, she's got hordes of good people to carry out her directions.

"But our situation is nothing like that. We have *very few* people and limited resources. And the crew we have isn't particularly good, because nobody like Kathryn has been picking and pruning them over the years.

"Our situation, on the other hand, is precisely what Mark has had to deal with his whole career. He started out in his dad's local direct mail agency, just a letter shop really, which closed up while Mark was still in Business School. Then he worked for that little ad agency in Detroit. And now he's burning up product category after product category at Data Drugs, that small family-owned outfit on the West Coast. At Data he's only had shoestring money, a local ad agency, and a staff chosen mainly by nepotism; I gather every aunt, uncle, and cousin's on the payroll. Besides—and I feel this is *also* major—he's been selling strictly through brokers. That's how we sell. He doesn't have the huge direct sales force Parker Labs has. So the way I see it, Mark has personally had to be the creative dynamo powering his businesses, whereas Kathryn has merely been doing a very good job in very professional organizations. They're both very good. But, I'd pick Mark."

"That's very insightful," says Will. *Of course Kathryn has loads of independent creativity,* thinks Will. *I know that and the Catos know that. That's why they're so eager to get her. And brokers / schmokers, she can cope with any selling force. But there's no point in contradicting Bill, just to set the record straight. The objective isn't to make ISC appreciate someone they can't get, but rather to make them* want *the person they* can *get.* Will winds up the call by further complimenting Bill Beane's analysis.

Will's at his desk at GR&B by 8:15 in the morning. No one else answers, so he picks up when his direct line buzzes. It's Sherm Summit. "Will, a quick word on yesterday, when we had our two favorites back here, Kathryn Keane and Mark Matthews. Things went very well. Kathryn is *such* an exciting talent. You've done a fine job in bringing us the head of all sales and marketing for Parker Labs, one of the top three companies. And that Matthews is a promising lad. Bill and I had a great lunch with Kathryn yesterday. We'd have offered her the job then, but Bill hadn't yet met young Matthews. He came in the afternoon."

"What did Bill think of Matthews?" asks Will offhandedly, trying to focus Summit on what he'll hear from Bill Beane.

"Actually, Will, I haven't had a chance to compare notes with Bill. He had a dental appointment at 5:30."

"Bill and I spoke on the phone last night," says Will. "I think he shares your liking for both candidates. And he has some very interesting further observations. But you should hear them from him."

"Fine. I'll be seeing Bill in a little while on another matter. We'll talk then. I mostly called you, Will, just to thank you for your good work and the fine way this search is turning out."

"Thank you Sherm. It's a pleasure to be working for you." *Well, aren't we getting chummy! That's the first time I've felt I could call him Sherm, as Bill does. Hope Bill can swing the Chairman over to Mark. That'll be a lot easier, if Summit stays in this mood and still thinks he's got a choice. We can always get down to Mark as the last-fish-in-the-barrel. That's more scary. Let's see if I can play out this hand with finesse!*

It's 9:00 on the nose, when Wilma, taking off her coat, sticks her head in Will's office and announces that Donna Powers is on the phone. "Just a quick 'What's-going-on?' call, Will. Haven't heard anything from you since our talk the day after I was over to see Summit at ISC. He said they'd be having second-round interviews in a couple weeks. Anything further on that?"

"Donna, I'm sorry, I probably should have called you to say 'Not yet' for the second round. Sherm Summit liked you—and about four other candidates—very much. The only problem has been to get on Bill Beane's calendar. We nailed a couple appointments...and that was it. And at least one of those <u>people</u>..." *I can't say 'her' or 'him' and maintain secrecy in such a small industry,* thinks Will "...will probably turn down the ISC job. So really we've got a long way to go. I hope to have more to report by the end of next week, or at least the following week. So I'll be calling you soon. How's business? Some of my clients in other fields are seeing an upsurge. But I suppose pain relievers and deodorants aren't as much affected by the ups-and-downs of the general economy."

"No, Will. People get headaches and sweat in good times and bad," says Donna, "I'll look forward to your call. Thanks. Bye now." *Well I got through that one all right,* thinks Will. *I knew that little shot of banal at the end would cut off the conversation before we got into the specifics I didn't want to talk about.*

There's no point in killing her enthusiasm; we may have to come back to her, muses Will. When he looks up, Wilma's handing him printouts on another of his searches. It's their first encounter of the day, and Will begins by sincerely complimenting her on having stressed a far more optimistic scenario for the ISC search than the sour one he blurted out yesterday afternoon.

"Will, I've known you now nearly three years. Things seldom turn out as badly as you foresee them. So lots of times you torture yourself needlessly. But that same ability to see disaster a mile off enables you to take steps to prevent it. And no matter what goes wrong, or how depressed or disgusted you get, you hang in there looking for new solutions. In my opinion, that's what makes you so successful."

"Wilma, *you're* one of the reasons I'm successful. Thank you." *Amazing how close we are*, thinks Will.

"Now, Wilma, let's cut this mutual admiration. If you can, please get Dan Dawson on the phone. I don't think I've got a prayer of shoehorning him into ISC. But if Summit gets frustrated by Kathryn's turn-down and hesitates to fall back on Mark, he may at least be willing to bring Donna and Dan in to meet Bill. Which may be enough to remind him he's had a tremendous search and let him settle on Mark. Thank heaven, Bill *prefers* Mark! In any event, I don't think I can possibly go back into the marketplace and get anyone better than Mark, Donna, or Dan...at least not without tearing up our off-limits rules. Remember, I've still got Doris DeWitt going full blast out there on the Coast. I have to keep everyone I've got as interested as possible.

The morning passes. So does the afternoon. *So far so good,* thinks Will. *Maybe I'll luck out. Right about now Bill should be talking to Sherm, telling him why he prefers Mark to Kathryn. Bill's got a reasonable argument. And besides the job reports to Bill. He ought to be able to have whomever he wants!*

It's 6:15 and Will is just outside his office door when his direct line buzzes. Wilma's gone. He answers. "Hi Will, this is Mark Matthews. Sorry to be late getting back to you, but I've been tied up all day. In a small family-owned firm like this, being mysteriously gone as I was yesterday is noticed. So I plunged in busy as hell today, showing myself to absolutely everyone. But luckily I've got you before you leave the office. Just wanted you to know that things went fabulously well yesterday with Bill Beane and Sherm Summit. Bill especially. And Bill'd be my boss. He and I see eye to eye on everything. Believe it or not we even have daughters with the same first name. How's that for being on the same wavelength?

"Sherm was friendly, but I had very little time with him. I spent nearly four hours with Bill. He even drove me to the airport, where I caught my plane with just minutes to spare. I never saw anyone so warm and open as Bill. He flat out said that unless Summit objects—which I see no indication of—I'm his choice for the job. We even talked money. Bill said he was sure he could get me at least $520,000, plus options and benefits, maybe more.

Smart! Bill, thinks Will. *You remembered what I taught you when we recruited Graham. Say "X-minus-10%...**maybe-more**." Test 'em with something just a little under where you intend to wind up. That launches a trial balloon, and still keeps room to maneuver. If disappointment is written all over their face, you can immediately go to your full amount. And having said "maybe more," you can deal with a counteroffer if there is one without seeming to knuckle under, merely by presenting your "actual offer." If there's no further hitch, you can throw in the last bit of money at the end without being pushed for it. That delights the employee, and sparks immediate personal loyalty to you as their new boss. Good work, Bill!*

All in all, Will leaves his office feeling almost as optimistic tonight as he was apprehensive last night. *I just may pull this one through,* he muses, as he pulls out his cell phone, calls Karen, and suggests they meet at a neighborhood bistro. "Let's not even turn on the kitchen light, much less go in there."

Morning dawns especially fresh and bright, and Will's at his desk by 8:00 sharp. Lucky too, because the phone rings, and it's Sherm Summit. "Will, Bill wants Mark Matthews, and not Kathryn Keane! I would *never* have picked him over Kathryn. However, he *is* a promising lad and Bill has his reasons, which make some sense to me. Tell me, you don't have any *other* folks we should be looking at, do you?"

Will's heart skips a beat. But instead of answering he pauses strategically, prompting Summit to continue. "Anyway," says Summit, "I'm not going to overrule him."

Whooopeeeeee! is the silent scream in Will's head, momentarily drowning out Summit's voice on the phone. *No need to start over. Besides, there was nowhere to start anyway!*

"...and that's why I feel kind of sheepish and embarrassed, Will," continues Summit. *Now what did I miss?* "Which is why I'd really appreciate it if you'd call and kind of let her down gracefully. When I implied she was going to be my choice, she really was. So would you take care of that for me, Will? And of course I'm also going to write Kathryn a note. I want to keep in touch.

"She's exactly the kind of person we need over here...and who knows what the future may bring?"

"Absolutely, I'll take care of it. I'll make sure she understands." *Little do you know how* ***well*** *she understands!*

Moments later Bill Beane's on the line announcing that Mark Matthews will be the new President of ISC's Proprietary Drug Division. "But Will," says Beane, "you had a couple absolutely outstanding finalists. And Sherm is right. We really should have more women at the Division President level. As soon as Mark gets up and running, I'd like to see a New Vice President of Marketing in that Division...and I'd love someone from a big company like Parker Labs. That would provide a counterpoint to Mark's mainly small-company/entrepreneurial experience.

"Now Will, Kathryn mentioned her Director of Product Management, who's got a strong market research background. She's a woman, and we'd love to have more women in higher jobs over here. And if she can cut it with Kathryn, she's probably very, very good. It would be too hopelessly tacky for me to go after her right after Kathryn's just told me about her. But keep her in mind. We may soon be confirming a VP Marketing search. And you may feel that you can go after her, even if I can't."

No way!, thinks Will. *I'm blocked and can't touch her. But I'm glad to hear there's another search on the way...another $120,000 to maybe $150,000 fee in the pipeline!*

"Well, Bill, I'm excited," says Will. "I think you've made a brilliant choice. Sherm called me just a few minutes ago to say he was letting you have your way on Mark. So in his mind, it's clearly your call. If Mark doesn't turn out exactly right, that could be an embarrassment to you. Which brings us to references. I've already done preliminary checks on both Mark and Kathryn, so there won't be any big surprises. But let me call Mark for still more names. That way, we'll have an in-depth reading, which may even help you in managing him. And if by some long shot there *is* something negative, we'd better know now, not later. Also, I'll write a report that will protect us *both* with Summit as having done plenty of 'due diligence.'

"When I'm through—and I'll make it a point to finish within the next 24 hours—you can call Mark and, unless there's something neither of us expects, you can tell him he's hired, and welcome him aboard. You can also tell him you've got him some extra bucks. Put him exactly where you want him on the salary chart. He'll feel he's joining a company and a boss that really appreciate him. Considering the importance of this upward move to his career, I don't think there's any counteroffer a family outfit like Data Drugs can possibly make to keep him. But let's get him jumping out of his skin with enthusiasm for ISC and for you."

"Right on, Will. You know what you're doing. That's why I like working with you."

Will immediately places a call to Mark Matthews. "Things look really great," says Will. You're right about Bill Beane. He does favor you, although he also likes the other candidate a lot. And the Chairman, too, thinks you're terrific. But he's *just* as enthusiastic about another person, who has lots more experience with much bigger companies than you do. At the wire, references become very important. Have you given any thought to additional people I can call?"

"Yes, I'm all ready for that. You know we're a small privately-held company with family members and in-laws all over the place, so I have to be unbelievably careful. But I read this book called *Rites of Passage at $100,000 to $1 Million+* and it said you wouldn't let me off the hook without in-depth referencing just because I have to maintain confidentiality. So I've identified quite a list. Folks from every one of my former jobs...a few people here that I'd trust with my life...also people I've worked with here who've since left...plus outside suppliers, customers, and others who can give you a clear reading on how I'm regarded here. And to make it easy for you to check, I've put down home as well as office numbers for the folks who don't mind being called about me at home. Want me to email you the list?"

"How many people?"

"I don't know, maybe fourteen, fifteen...something like that."

"And they're all *business?* I don't want anybody from your church or club, or your doctor or lawyer, or old school friends you've known for 20 years."

"No problem. I'm well aware of that. You'll be talking to former bosses, subordinates, coworkers, and other people who really know how well I do my work."

Wow, here's a guy with nothing to hide, thinks Will. That's even more proof we've got the right person. With almost no effort I'll look like I did a heroic job of referencing, and my report will be one more shot of hard sell to reassure Sherm that they were right to turn down Kathryn and choose Mark.

Will completes plenty of calls in just a couple afternoon hours, plus the evening.

At 9:00 the next morning Will calls Bill Beane and enthusiastically relays in detail Mark's outstanding references. "Bill, why don't you call Mark around noon our time, when he's just getting into the office, tell him about his new, higher salary, and welcome him enthusiastically to ISC. I'll wait to call and congratulate him until after he gets home this evening. That way I can find out what happened when he went in to resign, and make sure there's no counter-offer and nothing brewing at home that could cause us a problem."

Reports listing the references Will has spoken to, plus a summary of what the overall group said, go out to Beane, Summit, and Al Umans by FedEx. "When you've got it, flaunt it!," says Will, as he maps follow-up with Wilma.

Will sighs with relief that it's all over...and that both Summit and Bill Beane feel they've had an outstanding search. It will soon be 9:00 a.m. in L.A., so Will tries a long distance call to Al Umans and reaches another very happy man. The 2,400-person facility in Denver...Al's biggest worry... voted "No" on Friday, and that outcome is almost certain to be echoed in the remaining five West Coast locations, which vote tomorrow.

Everything proceeds smoothly. In a couple days, with both Mark and ISC unequivocally committed, Will promptly calls the unsuccessful candidates to tell them the outcome and thank them for their participation. He also calls GR&B's billing department to tell them Mark Matthews' estimated first year's compensation, so that a final bill bringing Gordon, Rossi & Boodles' fee to one-third of that amount can be mailed out. Then he calls Doris DeWitt in GR&B's L.A. office to tell her that Wilma will be transferring to Doris everyone tagged on the computer for the ISC search.

And finally, Will calls Karen to propose a really special celebratory dinner at the restaurant of her choice (she opts for the main dining room at Caneel Bay on the next long weekend). And then he turns his attention back to the real problem of his existence at the moment: the troublesome search for a chief financial officer for a struggling apparel company just 39 blocks down Fifth Avenue from GR&B.

Victory...and an unending challenge. They're all in a day's work for Super Recruiter Will Pickham.

The Box Score

Now that it's all over, let's take a look at how each of the principals in our little drama has fared. Who are the winners? Who are the losers? Could any of them have done things differently?

Sherm Summit

Our wily CEO is delighted with the outcome, especially after Will's reference report renews and expands his initial enthusiasm for Mark Matthews. Ever the fine leader, Mr. Summit is also pleased with his decision to let Bill Beane select his own key subordinate.

Moreover, Mr. S is enjoying the good feeling that comes from knowing he got a very professional search and that, as a result, ISC has been strengthened. He heard about a range of appropriate possibilities and interviewed eight attractive candidates...at least three of whom he viewed very positively.

Of course, what the Chairman doesn't know is that Will knew of other outstanding people he couldn't approach, because they worked for other GR&B clients, or were allocated to other GR&B recruiters.

But bear this in mind: although GR&B's traditional —and these days generous—two-year off-limits rule worked against Mr. Summit on this search, it operated to his benefit during the two years following GR&B's search to bring in Graham Rusk. And now it'll protect ISC for two more years. Moreover, the rule that kept Will's hands off other GR&B recruiters' candidates also kept theirs off Sherm Summit's candidates.

The most important thing is that Summit justifiably feels Will's services have been worth the $250,000 he paid for them. He'll almost certainly return to Will at Gordon, Rossi & Boodles the next time he's unable to fill a key position on his own.

Will Pickham

On this assignment, as on most others, Will's had his ups and downs.

At the outset, the situation looked bleak. Undaunted, Will threw himself into solving the problem. He had to work hard to come up with his slate of candidates. But after all, that's what he's handsomely paid to do. Will prides himself on his resourcefulness, and not without reason. Now he has brought in a sizable fee for Gordon, Rossi & Boodles, and he'll be getting more business from Integrated Standard Corporation in the future.

Above all, Will has done his very best to serve both his client and his firm. He's happy that he was able to complete the assignment to the eminent satisfaction of Sherm Summit and Bill Beane; glad he was patient about waiting for more work from ISC instead of beginning to take people out; and pleased to have extended a great opportunity to Mark Matthews.

Will has also expanded his circle of well-deserved professional and personal relationships. Mr. Summit—now "Sherm"—has Will clearly in mind for future searches, as do Bill Beane, Mark Matthews and Graham Rusk. Kathryn Keane will use Will to fill three positions in Colorado and will introduce him to Cynthia and Carl, who'll not only use Will to fill several posts in their global organization, but will also recommend him and GR&B to other potential clients in various places around the world.

With respect to the overseas search opportunities that come Will's way, he will either (1) handle them himself, if they're high-paying (hence high-fee) and in locations he'd enjoy visiting or (2) "hand them off" to people in local GR&B offices, meanwhile pocketing substantial income merely for having "brought in the business."

Bill Beane

Bill made the right choice. Right because Mark Matthews will do an exceptionally fine job. And right too, because merely echoing the Chairman's preference for Kathryn Keane would not only have failed to hire her, but might—and we'll never know for sure—have sent Will off on additional weeks or months of searching. For reasons we know, but Bill doesn't, further work would have been unlikely to yield candidates any better than, or even as good as, the original ones.

Decisiveness is a hallmark of a fine executive. So is instinct...the inexplicable ability to often come up with a correct decision without having an entirely correct or complete basis for it. So too are the self-confidence and integrity that lead to independent thought and action. Bill Beane clearly has all those fine traits. They're why the Chairman is grooming Bill to be his successor...COO in 6 months and CEO in 3 years. And why, backed by fine executives like Graham Rusk and Mark Matthews, Bill will help make Summit's final years at ISC resoundingly successful. Moreover, Bill's success after the

Chairman leaves will be the culmination of Sherm Summit's success.

Bill's loyalty is another positive trait. Will did fine work for Bill in recruiting Graham Rusk. Therefore Bill recommended Will for the current search. As Will continually re-earns Bill's trust, he'll receive it again and again. Their business relationship will grow into a lasting personal friendship.

Al Umans

Too bad that the labor emergency has kept ISC's Senior VP - Human Resources from being more accessible to Mr. Summit at this time and more directly involved in the search...particularly at the outset. But Al too is properly pleased with the outcome, and with the diligence and speed Will has demonstrated.

Busy as he is, Al needs outside professionals he can depend on. Will's now on Al's short list of preferred recruiters. Al will warmly recommend Will to other ISC executives who need recruiting services and, when the subject of executive search comes up, to Chief HR Officers of other companies, as well.

Andrea Applewhite

Andrea has no idea she was ever involved in the ISC search. And in a sense, she wasn't, since she was never told about the job, and ISC was never told about her. In Will's mind, however, Andrea was...and still is...the prototype of the person Summit wanted.

True, as Will told Summit in presenting Andrea's unemployed ex-boss Dan Dawson as the logical candidate from off-limits Prestige Panacea, Andrea has never supervised a field sales force. But Summit had not stipulated that criterion. And Summit didn't know—as Will does—how ideally Andrea's superior personal characteristics (like Kathryn Keane's and Phyllis Finley's) would have fitted into an ISC team that already includes Bill Beane and Graham Rusk. Indeed, mildly negative personal characteristics were what caused Summit to drop Dan Dawson, the executive he *did* see from Prestige Panacea.

So it's pretty clear that Andrea Applewhite could have been a leading contender for the Proprietary Drug Division presidency...and very likely the winner. But Will's hands were tied.

Nonetheless, Andrea's weren't.

Right now, as she savors her new promotion to Dan Dawson's job, Andrea is making excellent career progress...and without giving any thought to the "Rites of Passage," which should be learned early and well by all high-potential executives. We congratulate Andrea and wish her well.

However, it will be ironic if tomorrow morning as she scans the "Who's News" section of *The Wall Street Journal*, Andrea notes wistfully that someone almost exactly her age is stepping up to the presidency of a sizable proprietary drug operation from a far lesser position than Andrea held even before her recent promotion, and thinks: *What a career-making opportunity...I wish I were in his shoes!* You probably could have been, Andrea, if you'd made up your mind a while ago that you were ready for a presidency, and if you'd joined us in studying how to precipitate opportunity, rather than just waiting for it to happen.

Karol Klasner

As VP - Marketing at National Anodyne, a company high on Mr. Summit's "hit list," Karol is another potentially ideal candidate, who doesn't know what she may have missed. Since she worked for an off-limits firm, Will ruled her out immediately. So Karol continues where she is, without ever realizing she had an excellent shot at becoming president of a sizable proprietary drug company.

That's ironic, because Karol is an unusually able, assertive, and career-centered person. Weeks before Will was phoned by Sherm Summit, Karol had noted in the Trade papers (1) that the previous President of ISC's Proprietary Drug division had been forced out, and (2) that no successor was announced. She could have:

(1) Identified a mutual acquaintance [see "Targeted Networking," [p. 57] who could have introduced her to Mr. Summit.

(2) Or if she were afraid to expose her willingness to leave National Anodyne for even the most exceptional opportunity, she could have used "Sponsored Direct Mail" [see pp. 277-87] to get her identity-disguised resume directly into Summit's hands. He *does* take note of a superb and timely letter-and-resume, as Sam Sage's experience proves [pages 479-80, 482, 492-93,and 504].

(3) Or she could have taken the straightforward approach of

merely writing to Summit herself. Obviously there'd have been some danger of exposure. But maybe not too much. Even if Summit "spilled the beans"—which we know he's too gentlemanly to do—National Anodyne probably *wouldn't* fire someone as good as Karol, even if they did find out that she attempted to grasp a once-in-a-lifetime opportunity. Indeed, if she trusts her boss and is friends with him or her (which should be but isn't always so), she might even have defused the risk in advance with words like these:

> "There may not be two other people in America with enough boss/subordinate friendship and trust to have this conversation. But I got a hare brained idea last night after reading about the President of ISC's Proprietary Drug Division being tossed out. Now of course my ideal way to move up to a presidency would be for you become COO, and hopefully move me into your job; because I ***love this company***. In fact, I often get calls from headhunters and ***always turn them down***. But here's a long-shot that perhaps I should play. There are only about a dozen major presidencies in the entire industry and maybe only four or five of them will be filled from the outside in this decade. So what do you think? Would you mind if I sent him a letter? I won't do it if you say No."

Now more than ever before, business loyalties tend to be to *people* we know and trust, rather than to the corporation which, in the hands of other people or in the same hands under changed circumstances, has a proven tendency to do surprising and unpleasant things to us. Twenty years ago such a conversation would have been unthinkable. Today it may not be.

Charlie Comstock

For Charlie, from Adam Labs, the ISC search has been a learning experience. He was thrilled to be contacted by Will and flown to New York for an interview. He correctly assumed that Will's call meant he was beginning to make a name for himself. But since he was never introduced to the client, Charlie, no dummy, concluded that he must have fouled up the interview... which was indeed true.

Therefore, Charlie has decided that if he wants to get ahead, he'll have to learn to do better. So he's signed up for a workshop that videotapes executives in mock presentations and interviews. Now he's perfecting the art of crisp, succinct, factual answers, a relaxed presence, and the ability to really listen to his interviewer. When opportunity knocks again, Charlie will be ready.

Dan Dawson

When he got tossed out of Prestige Panacea, Dan took a very logical step. He dispatched his cover letter and resume by e-mail to a large number of highly respected retainer recruiting firms, including GR&B. His reward there was an interview at ISC, where he was one of five top finalists. He lost out only because others with superior credentials or attributes...and (in Jim Johnson's case) personal recommendations...became his competition.

If Dan had mailed elegant on-paper letters and resumes to his most likely *employers*, he'd have reached Mr. Summit *before* the Chairman paid Will $250,000 to provide a slate of candidates. Dan comes from one of the top-three companies on Mr. Summit's "wish list." Who knows? Dan might have won, if he'd reached Summit directly *and* early.

As an experienced executive, Dan can accept his failure to get the ISC job philosophically. But what he can't understand is why he doesn't hear from anyone at GR&B for nearly a year after Will phoned to report that Mark Matthews was selected. Obviously GR&B thought Dan was good enough to introduce to ISC. But long afterward, GR&B seems to have totally dropped him from consideration.

GR&B notwithstanding, Dan will soon get several attractive offers through introductions by other top search firms that received his resume through the same instant nearly effortless email transmission by which Dan sent it to GR&B...the EMAIL MY RESUME function on *RITE*Site.com. Still other *RITES*-Honored recruiters will find Dan's *identity-revealed* resume when searching *RITE*Site's database for candidates (as Will would have found it too, if he'd originally looked). In addition, a couple very intriguing offers will come from entrepreneurs who find Dan's *identity-concealed* resume on *RITE*Site, send him their identity and proposition through *RITE*Site's computer, and get a response from him that opens a dialog.

Dan Dawson may not understand what went wrong at GR&B, but we do. Immediately after Will's ISC search ended, Wilma reassigned Dan on GR&B's computer to Doris DeWitt. Ironically this ideal hand-off *sidelined* Dan. Doris got him just as her search was "put on hold," pending the outcome of a sudden unfriendly tender offer for BioDynamics. Negotiations dragged on. Ten months later the merger went through, and the search was terminated. Only then did Doris's assistant clear Doris's holds on prospects for the BioDynamics search and make them—Dan included—available to other GR&B recruiters.

Ethan Evans

It was a stroke of good luck for Ethan Evans at BioDynamics that Doris DeWitt and Will made their deal. Doris got a chance at the people who turned Will down, in return for clearing Ethan Evans for the ISC search. Everybody won: Doris got more prospects. Will got a candidate who represented an off-limits company. And Ethan got an interview. True, he didn't get the job, but Ethan made two very valuable contacts in Sherm Summit and Bill Beane.

Obviously, Ethan is living on borrowed time at Biodynamics. Soon he'll be forced out. Then, packaging his job search within a search for consulting assignments [see pp. 401-02], Ethan will recontact Sherm Summit. Having been impressed with Evans' broad knowledge, even though doubtful of his decisiveness, the Chairman will assign Ethan a comprehensive review of the proprietary drug industry and ISC's current and future opportunities. "Who cares if he's not decisive," Summit will say to Bill Beane and Mark Matthews. "He certainly knows the industry, and he impresses me as someone who can identify all the options. Let him gather the information. *We'll* know what to do about it!"

Ethan will find—much to his surprise—that he enjoys consulting and is good at it. He's personable and knows most of the industry's top executives. His work will be based more on chatty phone calls than on Internet and/or library research. But he'll bring a wealth of practical information to his clients. Ultimately, Ethan will develop "Crandall's Way" monthly retainers [see pp. 403-06] with six companies. As an outgrowth of his consulting, he'll also publish a successful industry newsletter.

Phyllis Finley

Phyllis was lucky to be working at Maxi-Medi-Marketing, a company open to Will, and she was pleased to be considered for such a high-level position. She realized that she was probably a bit too junior, so she wasn't unduly disappointed when Will tactfully explained that ISC had chosen someone with more experience. And since Phyllis wasn't actively looking for another job, she didn't notice that nobody at GR&B called her for nearly a year.

But when Doris' assistant eventually cancels Phyllis' allocation to Doris within GR&B, Phyllis will soon be called by another GR&B recruiter who'll have an opening that's just right for Phyllis.

But that's not all she'll get from the episode we've witnessed. Remember how taken Sherm Summit was with Phyllis' personality? One of her great strengths is that she *listens*. She's *interested* in what others say. She *remembers*. And she *stays in touch*.

Phyllis's pleasant hour-and-a-half with Mr. Summit was obviously a contact worth nurturing. Rather than sit awkwardly eavesdropping when Summit took an urgent phone call, Phyllis walked to a window and gazed out. Afterward, she mentioned seeing purple grackles and a scarlet tanager. Birds, it turned out, are also a fascination of Sherm and Joyce Summit.

So, on *appropriately rare* occasions over the next couple years, Phyllis will send Mr. Summit a few relevant clippings from U.S. and foreign periodicals [see p. 454]. He'll reciprocate with Joyce's article on setting up neighborhood wildlife preserves. And Phyllis' phone call complimenting Mrs. S on her activities will lead to knowing the Summits socially in the narrow context of a shared interest. Five years from now, Phyllis Finley will be invited by Joyce Summit to join the Board of the National Audubon Society. Contacts Phyllis makes there will greatly enrich her business *and* personal life. But that's another story.

Wynot Showitdahl

Wynot did an excellent job with his resume and cover letter. And he must have had a great record to report. We know all that because his mailing influenced Mr. Summit sufficiently to choose him along with Sam Sage out of the large number of resumes Summit routinely receives.

But what good did Wynot's hard work and proven skill do him?

None at all, because he failed to clean up social networking debris from nine years ago. Worse yet, he republished his old naked party pic quite recently. Will he ever grow up?.

Takishia had every reason and right to pick up the refuse Wynot left abandoned in the public domain. On the other hand. she had no right to hack his current social networking accounts. In the legal realm, she played with fire. Fortunately, both she and Will were discrete. Their confirming Wynot's current adventurousness will go unnoticed...and it may save Mr. S and ISC the possibility of big time future embarrassment.

Wynot will never know what hit him. In fact, it was a bullet from his own gun...and he pulled the trigger.

What about Takishia? Is she a highly unusual resource that only Will is fortunate enough to have? No. These days there are social networking wizards at the disposal of many high-level executive search professionals...either on-payroll with other primary duties, or operating as outside consultants.

Wise up Wynot!

You're your own worst enemy!

Gerry Glib

Gerry has serious problems. His brief involvement with the ISC search merely highlighted them. Gloria's thoroughness (and Will's desperation) led them both to find Gerry on Maxi-Medi-Marketing's corporate Website and in the various online directories. Luckily, however, Will's talk with Buddy revealed Gerry's shortcomings as, in the end, referencing would also have done. Had Gerry been a truly competent executive, the result might have been very different. But, given Gerry's poor track record, nothing came of his meeting with Will. In fact, Gerry is now on thin ice at Maxi-Medi-Marketing and is quietly beginning to look for something else.

Gerry was neither helped nor harmed.

He'll never recognize or admit it, but his best bet is to abandon the executive suite and get into one-on-one selling of costly items, such as real estate. That doesn't match Gerry's self image, but it does fit his talents. Too bad he will insist on continuing to be a rotten executive, when he could become a superb salesman.

Kathryn Keane

Kathryn seems mighty lucky these days...especially in view of her predicament a few weeks ago. Then, her outstanding success at Parker Labs was in jeopardy. Indeed, it looked as if we might witness a downward spiral...conceivably even to dismissal followed by justified but hard-to-win litigation.

Since then, Kathryn's had her choice of two extremely appealing situations. The ISC job wasn't actually offered to her. But that was only because Will knew she wouldn't accept it. Therefore, he encouraged rather than rebutted Bill Beane's notion that she is less creative than we know she really is.

Is Kathryn's good fortune just luck?

Not at all. She's a lovely person. A true friend, who keeps up relationships that have no obvious business angle. Staying in touch with her dearest high school friend led to free rooms at places Cynthia was running all over the world. But Kathryn didn't merely "eat-and-run." Instead, she wrote those helpful lists of suggestions after each visit. Kathryn didn't expect they'd lead to a pay-off. She just wanted to help. And in the end, her generous spirit was richly rewarded.

Was it luck that led Kathryn to "ask for a reference rather than a job"? [see p. 25]. No, she read that in a book. This book. And I'm delighted to report that that concept was a gift to me from someone I helped 25 years ago. Like Kathryn, he came to take...but didn't leave without giving.

Was it luck that built Kathryn's friendship with Will long before she needed it? No. She went out of her way to provide good suggestions when he asked for them. Again, it was her *basic nature*, not mere self-interest, that motivated her kindness.

Do nice people always finish first? No. Witness Kathryn's problem at Parker Labs. But nice people tend to know people. In times of need, they have more contacts to approach, as Kathryn did.

Needless to say, Kathryn stays in touch. She'll write "thank you" notes to Sherm Summit and Bill Beane, and add them to her holiday card list [p. 453]. And—yes, you guessed it—she'll wind up selling both of them condos... merely by clipping little hand-written "here's-how-it-turned-out" notes to the lavish brochures she'll produce for the resort.

Need I say it? The resort will be a huge success, and Kathryn will revel in her new career. The future holds other pleasant surprises too. Who do you think will become the junior U.S. Senator from Colorado nine years from now?

Jim Johnson

Jim has handled himself very well in his secretive search for a more exciting future since being passed over for the presidency at Daisy Foods. By approaching ISC through networking, he got past the executive recruiter. Will would never have presented him to Summit, because Jim lacked the proprietary drug background Summit demanded. By going directly to ISC, Jim got considered...and became a strong finalist.

Today Jim's future looks rosy. Summit, much impressed, will keep him in mind for future openings and will mention him to the CEO of a soft goods conglomerate, which is putting Summit on its Board.

Will was happy to have one of his "finds," rather than Jim, get the ISC job. But he's highly impressed with Jim, and will present him as his own discovery just as soon as he (1) gets an appropriate search, and (2) simultaneously has the right to "use" Jim within GR&B.

Meanwhile, of course, Jim continues his low-profile program of quiet personal contact and very discreet networking. Lately he's also been concentrating on the investment and commercial banking community...quietly seeking leads on companies that may be available for purchase. No deal is in the works yet. But Jim's meeting and impressing many highly knowledgeable and widely-connected people. Indeed, one of them is the ISC Board member who brought Jim to Sherm Summit's attention.

However, having lost out on the ISC opportunity, Jim wants to speed up the unavoidably slow pace of his cautious networking. So he's now lining up a "sponsor" for a secretive direct mail campaign [see pp. 277-84]. Within the next four weeks Jim will get his message to virtually every CEO in America who might control an appropriate opportunity. And he'll do that without ever letting Daisy Foods know he's determined to get out as soon as possible. We'll be reading exciting news about Jim in *The Wall Street Journal* very soon.

Lanny Lawrence

Lanny is perhaps the only executive in the entire group who really got shafted. He knew about the opening at ISC, and wanted the job. Moreover, he would have been an extremely strong candidate. But because Will did what he absolutely had to do to protect GR&B's client relationship with CompuMedic, Lanny drew the wrong conclusion about the open position at ISC.

The moral of Lanny's story is that he should have investigated the ISC job far more thoroughly. His casual call to Will was not enough. Lanny would have been a lot better off if he'd fully understood how the executive recruiting business works and what Will's needs and problems were. Clearly Lanny needs an initiation into the "Rites of Passage."

Mark Matthews

Mark is the obvious winner. He had fine credentials for the ISC job; he was able to alert and impress Will; he worked for a company that had no client relationship with Gordon, Rossi & Boodles; and when Will needed him he was not allocated to any other recruiter at GR&B. So Mark was introduced and, in the end, got the job.

A series of happy accidents?

Hardly. Crushingly busy accomplishing his remarkable record for Data Drugs, an obscure private company, this young marketing superstar spent a few minutes marketing himself. He joined *Rite*Site.com and used some of its features. One hit the jack pot. He posted a single version of his resume (he could have posted more), displaying his achievements but keeping his name, the name of his company, and other identifying facts ***concealed***.

Will Pickham visited *Rite*Site, found it easy to search, and found that—unlike all of the commercial sites and 2 of the "Big 4" executive paid membership sites—it did not charge a fee to view its resumes. Being affiliated with the prestigious GR&B, Will would never even consider paying a fee to view an outside database. But he followed Buddy to *Rite*Site and found the visit well worthwhile. Will was intrigued by Mark's resume, and emailed Mark via *Rite*Site's computer. Mark answered promptly, turned out to be as impressive as his identity-concealed resume implied, was eagerly interested in Will's position, followed up with speed and enthusiasm...and the rest is history!

Mark was smart to put his background with the identity of his current company safely concealed out in the open where not just Will Pickham, but every recruiter, every employer, and indeed every human on the planet seeking an executive could easily find it. It's a good thing he did. Privately owned, Data Drugs receives almost no coverage in the trade press, belongs to no trade associations, does not allow its executives to make speeches at industry events and probably would not have allowed Mark to publish an article in any trade association publication. Mark, on the other hand didn't want to be overlooked, so he took a relatively easy step to prevent that happening.

The only thing Mark could have done better would have been to choose the *Rites*-Honored Option and make his identity-*revealed* resume available to recruiters from the nearly 600 *Rites*-Honored retainer search firms. Then Will would have been able to contact Mark without having to email him via

*RITE*Site's computer and wait for a reply. If Will had not been so hard pressed to find candidates and/or if there had been several enticing resumes identity-*revealed* using the *RITES*-Honored Option, Will probably would not have bothered to email Mark, who would have missed out on his chance-of-a-lifetime opportunity.

Luckily, that's not what happened

Mark wins.

Will wins.

We congratulate them both.

Donna Powers

Donna just wasn't destined to join ISC.

Her marketing slant is toward sales promotion and hard-hitting field sales force activity at the grass roots retailer level, in contrast to big-budget TV campaigns aimed at the consumer. In that, she reflects the philosophy and successful operating methods of the company in which she's gained all of her experience. Unfortunately, her orientation...and her personality...weren't quite what Summit and Beane were buying this time around.

Donna's a very fine person. Other employers, with other needs and other personality preferences will have an entirely different reaction. Very soon she'll achieve her desired move to New York. And her daughter's emerging ballet talent will more than justify the job change. Both Donna and her daughter will enter exciting new periods of growth and success.

Donna will never know it, but she owes Will Pickham a debt of gratitude. His appeal to Red Tapecutter has cleared the internal client-protection blockage at GR&B. And now that Cosa Nostrums is no longer off-limits, she'll soon hear about another GR&B search. Wilma will immediately transfer Donna from Will to Doris DeWitt. When Doris calls, Donna will *decisively* turn down Doris's proposal, frankly explaining that she wants to relocate to New York City and nowhere else. Because Donna also makes some helpful suggestions, Doris will make a point of immediately returning Donna to the system...not wanting to delay any further opportunities for Donna through

GR&B. By sheer luck, the next job that GR&B shows her will be in New York—not California—and Donna will be the winning candidate.

In a sense, Donna doesn't deserve the success she's about to have. Wanting a quick move to a particular place, she should have mounted an all-out campaign, rather than just waiting for the accidental actions of retainer search firms to solve her problem. Personal contact activity [Chapter 3]; taking fullest advantage of a *RITE*Site.com membership; perhaps some cautious networking among strangers [Chapter 4]; plus a secretive direct mail campaign targeted on the New York area [Chapter 13] would have maximized her likelihood of success. In job hunting terms, she hasn't really worked hard enough for the success she's going to have. She's about to win the lottery. On rare occasions long shots *do* come in.

Roy Ricardo

To some extent, Roy's a victim of the way retainer search firms do business...meeting the needs of clients, not candidates. Roy was highly-qualified for the ISC job. And certainly he'd have preferred to stay in the drug industry and live near New York, rather than go into the industrial motor business and wind up in Anthracite Valley. But, "owned" by Doug Abel for the Brute Force search, Roy couldn't be shown the ISC job or any other within GR&B. He'll never know that a far better alternative existed. Eventually Roy will join Brute Force, just to get back to the States. However, he'd have been a lot happier at ISC.

Obviously, Roy should have written directly to the chief executives of all the companies that interested him, just as Sam Sage did. Roy's list would surely have included Sherm Summit, just as Sam's did. Roy could readily have been exposed to both ISC and Brute Force, just as Sam Sage got a shot at both ISC and Expodex. Roy's credentials are superior to Mark Matthews' and Roy's similarly enthusiastic personality is equally engaging. Moreover, there is every reason to believe that if Roy had taken advantage of *RITE*Site, as Mark did, Roy and not Mark would be entering the exciting new presidency at ISC.

Roy went all the way to Argentina to acquire his impressive experience and track record in general management which, added to his proprietary drug marketing experience in the U.S., would have made him an ideal candidate at ISC. Now, however, he goes back to a marketing-only position, and enters a field he would never have chosen voluntarily. Out-of-the-country executives need the most comprehensive and aggressive job-hunting campaigns they can possibly mount. Sadly, Roy's fell short.

Rita Rosen

We've never met Rita. But she's the Director of Product Management Kathryn mentioned so glowingly to Bill Beane. Bill will forget her. But Will won't. He'll ask Kathryn about Rita, hear the same enthusiastic comments Bill heard, and enter her into GR&B's central computer with a few hastily worded —but absolutely glowing—comments. Will won't, however, get in touch with Rita to ask for a resume because Parker Labs, as we well know, is off-limits to GR&B.

Moreover, when Will later undertakes the search Bill Beane alluded to in originally mentioning Rita to Will, Will won't be able to go after Rita. He'll fill his very good slate with candidates from non-off-limits companies.

But from now on, Will and other GR&B recruiters *will* be calling Rita for her suggestions on searches where she would *not* be a logical candidate. Indeed, the help she graciously gives to another GR&B recruiter will mature into the same sort of mutually supportive friendship Kathryn and Will have enjoyed. The details needn't concern us. But one day history will repeat itself...to Rita's considerable benefit.

Sam Sage

Sam's an extremely savvy executive. He bypassed the allocated-to-another-recruiter-in-the-firm obstacle that kept Roy Ricardo from learning about the ISC position. And all it took was a direct mail campaign that included Sherm Summit, CEO of a company that obviously belonged on Sam's list.

Sam's mailing got action from Mr. S for two reasons:

1. It was very impressive, and
2. Summit had an immediate need.

Because of Sherm Summit's insistence, Sam was finally shown the ISC opportunity, in a *rare* exception to the rule that retainer recruiting firms will never show candidates more than one job at a time. Sam got "***parallel processing***" in the easiest, surest way...not because he demanded it, but because he stimulated the recruiter's *client* to demand it.

In the end, of course, Sam walked away from the ISC opportunity. He didn't even go to his interview. That was another lucky break for Mark Matthews, because both Sherm Summit and Bill Beane would have chosen Sam over Mark on the basis of Sam's far greater experience...all of it impressively successful.

Fortunately for Sam—and for Mark—Sam has mastered all the "Rites of Passage." Career-long cultivation of executive recruiter relationships led to Sam's exploration, with Buddy, of the Expodex opportunity. A classic direct mail campaign with superb paperwork [see pp. 220-27 & p. 258] broke through to the ISC opportunity. And creative use of personal contacts and networking...coupled with an "underutilized asset" discussion [see p. 436-37] with his old friends at Medica Suisse...led Sam to a "buyable" company and financing for the deal.

A few weeks ago, Sam suffered a severe setback. Today he's happier and more challenged than he ever dreamed of being. Sam's got a once-in-a-lifetime entrepreneurial opportunity. And you can be sure he'll make the most of it.

Let's bring you to the attention of

You're informed.

Having read Rites of Passage, you know the advantages to executives of 100% retainer-compensated search firms. Their payment method virtually forces good behavior—for example, no wide unpaid circulation of resumes.

You know, too, that firms doing a mixture of contingency and retainer work are under no such economic restraint.

You've just read a fictionalized look inside a sizeable retainer search firm. Turn the page to see the roughly 600 retainer-only firms in the U.S. and Canada. They range in size from the giants, to prestigious boutiques, to a few notably prominent independent practitioners.

All fill different jobs. And all do not supply candidates without being paid to do so.

With respect to these leading firms, are you interested

Outstanding Search Firms

Ever since RITES OF PASSAGE *first appeared, it has provided a listing of outstanding exclusively retainer-compensated executive recruiting firms, commencing with 91 fine U.S. firms in its first edition.*

In every subsequent printing, this listing has been refined and expanded along with the rest of RITES *until, at present, nearly 600 outstanding search firms throughout the United States & Canada are recognized.*

Today, the RITES OF PASSAGE *listing is widely-known as a unique and valuable service to both individuals and employers.*

APPENDIX II

Outstanding Retainer Executive Recruiters

Have you decided to cultivate prominent retainer search firms?

Here is a carefully selected list of nearly 600 leading U.S. and Canadian firms. Included are North America's largest, plus the highly important medium-sized and "boutique" firms you might otherwise overlook. Chosen from many thousands of firms, these are the "creme de la creme."

Because these firms work only "on retainer," ***each is filling a completely different list of jobs***. You'll have entirely non-overlapping exposure, even if you contact ***all*** of these firms. Note that a vast majority are generalists and likely to undertake searches that interest you. Some (clearly marked) are specialists. Don't bother contacting any who are not in your field.

Most of these firms accept resumes by email. To (1) almost effortlessly choose and email the hundreds of firms that fit your needs and also (2) completely bypass your Internet vendor's restrictions on sending multiple emails, use Email My Resume on RiteSite.com.

Transmission details: When you email, apply a "Dear Recruiters" email cover letter not addressed to any specific person in the firm. A growing number of these firms request that you visit their Web sites to input your information, even though they continue to accept email submissions. A very rare few accept only on-paper mailings. RiteSite.com assists you with all transmission methods.

If you decide to submit by postal mail, send to the firm's home office and ***do*** address your cover letter to a specific person. If a firm has multiple offices, their first address here in *Rites of Passage* is their home office.

Cities having branch offices are also listed, each with phone number and the name of a local manager. Locally and nationally you can, if you wish, phone and ask who specializes in your field. However, unless you're trying to target a personal appointment, there's virtually no advantage. Inside-the-firm procedures will normally redistribute your inquiry appropriately.

Although *not essential*, you may decide to send an on-paper letter and resume to one person in each of a large firm's offices. But also email the ***firm!*** If only an electronic file is kept, in a few weeks the papers will have served their purpose and be discarded. If papers ***are*** kept, extras will be discarded. Redundancy will not cause any negative reaction.

Firms marked by * belong to the Association of Executive Search Consultants (AESC), a retainer search firm trade association.

Note: Addresses, key staff, and preferred ways to receive resumes are constantly changing. For a continual updating of this list plus expansion to include branch office addresses and the ability to do "mail merge" word-processing of cover letters and easy emailing of your resume to your selection of dozens—or preferably hundreds—of these firms, please visit:

RiteSite.com

A La Carte International
(SPECIALIZE IN Food Industry)
1609 Bohnhoff Drive, Suite A
P.O. Box 4506
Virginia Beach, VA 23454
(757) 425-6111
fax (757) 481-2071
alacarte@wedofood.com
www.wedofood.com
Michael J. Romaniw, President

ABACO International/ TranSearch International*
2 Riverway, Suite 1710
Houston, TX 77056
(713) 965-0876
fax (713) 965-0189
info@abaco-intl.com
www.abaco-intl.com
Marie Guillot, Chairman

Adam Smith Consulting, LLC
2434 South Walter Reed Drive, Suite D
Arlington, VA 22206
(703) 998-8118
fax (571) 275-0969
adam@adamsmithconsulting.net
www.adamsmithconsulting.net
Adam Smith, Chief Executive Officer

Adams Douglas
(SPECIALIZE IN Diversity)
2200 NW 159th Street, Suite 400
Clive, IA 50325
(515) 334-0090
fax (515) 334-5023
desmund@adamsdouglas.com
adamsdouglas.com
Desmund Adams, Principal

Advantage Partners, Inc.*
29225 Chagrin Boulevard, Suite 300
Cleveland, OH 44122
(216) 514-1212
fax (216) 514-1213
resume@advantagepartnersinc.com
www.advantagepartnersinc.com
James B. McPolin, Partner
Nikki C. Bondi, Managing Partner
Also:
Henderson, NV (216) 514-1212
Tiona M. Thompson, Partner

Aegis Consulting
(SPECIALIZE IN High Tech, Internet Commerce, and Consumer Industries)
420 Lexington Avenue, Suite 3781
New York, NY 10163
(212) 687-2200
fax (212) 687-0079
www.aegisnet.com
Nancy Caudill, Director
Dante Sucgang, Director
Also:
Prairie Village, KS
(913) 648-2714
Gary D. Brown, Director

Aegis Group Search Consultants, LLC
(SPECIALIZE IN Health Care)
1358 Village Drive
Detroit, MI 48207
(248) 344-1450
fax (248) 347-2231
resume@aegis-group.com
www.aegis-group.com
Timothy J. Ignash, Founder & Partner
John E. Green, President & Partner

Agora Consulting
8310 Lauralwood Lane
Colorado Springs, CO 80919
(719) 219-0360
fax (719) 272-8361
resume@agoraconsulting.com
www.agoraconsulting.com
Rob Lauer, Director

Albertini Group
5550 LBJ Freeway, Suite 700
Dallas, TX 75240
(972) 726-5550
fax (214) 889-5570
info@albertinigroup.com
www.albertinigroup.com
Libba Sapitsky, Vice President
Nancy Albertini, Chairman

Alder Koten
9595 Six Pines, Suite 8210
The Woodlands, TX 77380
(713) 893-1630
candidates@alderkoten.com
www.alderkoten.com
Silva Flores, Partner
Also:
Dallas, TX (214) 556-3860
Clement Wigger, Managing Partner
The Woodlands, TX
(713) 893-1630
Jorge Davalos, Managing Partner
Jose J. Ruiz, Chief Executive Officer

Allegis Partners
7312 Parkway Drive
Hanover, MD 21076
(877) 247-4426
careers@insearchworldwide.com
www.allegis-partners.com
James Perry, Managing Director
Art Davidson, Managing Director
John Davidson, Managing Director
Christine Rae DeYoung, Managing Director
Edwin Felice, Managing Director
Doug G. Hanslip, Managing Director
John Markey, Global Managing Director
Mille Mashel, Managing Director
Ang Onorato, Managing Director

Allen & Associates Executive Search
4555 Lake Forest Drive, Suite 650
Cincinnati, OH 45242
(513) 563-3040
resumes@allensearch.com
www.allensearch.com
Michael Allen, President

Allen Austin Executive Search*
4543 Post Oak Place, Suite 217
Houston, TX 77027
(713) 355-1900
fax (713) 355-1901
resumes@allenaustinsearch.com
www.allenaustinsearch.com
Rob L. Andrews, Chairman & Chief Executive Officer
Elizabeth Andrews, Partner
Mary Campagnano, Partner
Jim Davenport, Partner
David Deaton, Partner
Kevin Ford, Partner
Tom Fritsch, Partner
Wendy Johnstone-Burt, Partner
Gary Payne, Partner
Enrique Saavedra, Partner
Mark Spillard, Head of Technology Practice
Heather Stone, Director of Research
Peggy Tate, Partner
Kathleen Williams, Partner
Also:
Fredericksburg, VA
(540) 373-7828
Frank DiPasquale, Partner
Madison, WI (608) 225-6804
Michael Noack, Partner
Ridgefield, CT (203) 894-8315
Pat Carlucci, Senior Partner
San Antonio, TX (210) 648-2743
Jackie Gorman, Senior Partner

Allen Evans Klein International
305 Madison Avenue
New York, NY 10165
(212) 983-9300
fax (212) 983-9272
info@allenevans.com
allenevans.com
Robert Klein, Managing Partner

Allerton Heneghan & O'Neill
1415 West 22nd Street, Tower Floor
Oak Brook, IL 60523
(630) 645-2294
fax (630) 645-2298
resume@ahosearch.com
www.ahosearch.com
Donald A. Heneghan, Managing Partner
Jennifer A. Cushing, Partner
Terrence J. McSherry, Partner
Bruce R. Ralph, Partner

Alliance Search Management, Inc.
(Specialize in Healthcare)
594 Sawdust Road, Suite 194
The Woodlands, TX 77380
(281) 419-5111
kathy@alliancesearch.com
www.alliancesearch.com
Kathy Powell-Florip, President

American Executive Management, Inc.
30 Federal Street
Salem, MA 01970
(978) 744-5923
execsearch@americanexecutive.us
www.americanexecutive.us/
Edward J. Cloutier, President

Anderson & Associates*
(Specialize in Non-Profit, Healthcare, Finance & Manufacturing)
112 South Tryon Street, Suite 800
Charlotte, NC 28284
(704) 347-0090
fax (704) 347-0064
info@andersonexecsearch.com
www.andersonexecsearch.com
Douglas K. Anderson, President
Paul F. Betzold, Leader of Healthcare
Also:
Overland Park, KS
(913) 649-5238
Richard S. Jarman, Consultant

Anderson & McGinley
(Specialize in IT, Technology, BioTech, Pharmaceuticals, Finance)
660 Harvard Avenue, Suite 56
Santa Clara, CA 95051
(415) 378-1955
andersonmcginleysearch@gmail.com
www.andersonmcginley.com
Ronald H. Anderson, Managing Director

Anderson Partners
6860 North Dallas Parkway, Suite 200
Plano, TX 75024
(214) 267-9787
fax (972) 371-5330
admin@anderson-partners.com
www.anderson-partners.com
David C. Anderson, Founder & Managing Partner
Kevin S. Anderson, Partner

The Andre Group Inc.
(Specialize in Human Resources Executives)
1220 Valley Forge Road, Suite 19
Phoenixville, PA 19460
(610) 917-2212
info@theandregroup.com
www.theandregroup.com
Kevin Mulcrone, Senior Vice President
Kevin Fitzpatrick, Senior Vice President
Mike Mayer, Director

Annie Gray Associates, Inc.
12120 Sixth Street East
St. **Petersburg, FL** 33706
(314) 973-7890

ag@anniegray.com
Annie Gray, President & Chief Executive Officer

Anthony Andrew, LLC

(Specialize in Information Technology)
16775 Addison Road, Suite 405
Addison, TX 75001
(214) 377-1763
resume@anthonyandrew.com
www.anthonyandrew.com
Anthony A. Cinello, President

David Aplin Group

2150 Scarth Street, Suite 200
Regina, SK S4P 2H7
(306) 359-2550
fax (306) 359-2555
search@executivesource.ca
www.aplin.com
Holly Hetherington, Partner
Shelley Lipon, Partner
Also:
Calgary, AB (403) 261-9000
Chris Fong, Vice President
Edmonton, AB (780) 428-6663
Greg Penney, Vice President
Halifax, NS (902) 461-1616
Amy Reid, Vice President
Mississauga, ON (905) 566-9700
Janet Chappell, National Practice Leader
Paul Farkas, National Practice Leader
Ottawa, ON (613) 288-2211
James Baker, Vice President
Saskatoon, SK (306) 933-2428
Jacqueline Gallagher, Managing Consultant
Toronto, ON (647) 776-5000
Grant Robinson, Vice President
Vancouver, BC (604) 648-2799
Anna Montesano, Branch Manager
Winnipeg, MB (204) 235-0000
Mark Shayna, Vice President

Ariail & Associates

(Specialize in Furniture and Furnishings Manufacturing)
7800 Airport Center Drive, Suite 401
Greensboro, NC 27409
(336) 275-2906
fax (336) 644-1990
rariail@ariailassoc.com
www.ariailassoc.com
Randolph C. Ariail, President
Also:
Summerfield, NC (336) 275-2906
Randolph C. Ariail, President

Ashford Management Group, Inc.

(Specialize in Retailing Industry)
2295 Parklake Drive, Suite 425
Atlanta, GA 30345
(770) 938-6260
fax (770) 621-9529
info@ashfordsearch.com
www.ashfordsearch.com
Janis E. Martinez, President

Steven Ast & Partners

(Specialize in Non-profit)
Two Stamford Landing
150 Southfield Avenue, Suite 1302
Stamford, CT 06902
(203) 559-8390
fax (203) 921-0304
info@stevenast.com
www.stevenast.com
Steven T. Ast, Founder

Austin McGregor

3500 Oak Lawn Avenue, Suite 550
Dallas, TX 75219
(972) 488-0500
fax (972) 488-0535
info@austinmcgregor.com
www.austinmcgregor.com
Stephen Sterrett, Managing Partner
Also:
Mattoon, IL (217) 235-1051
Paul Bailey, Partner

Austin-Michael, LP

(Specialize in Retail & Wholesale)
1746 Cole Boulevard, Suite 225
Lakewood, Co 80401
(303) 271-1558
info@austin-michael.com
www.austin-michael.com
Jose L. Tamez, Managing Partner
Norm Wills, Senior Partner

Avery James, Inc.*

(Specialize in Engineering, Aerospace/Defense & Information Technology)
6601 Center Drive West, Suite 500
Los Angeles, CA 90045
(310) 342-8224
fax (310) 348-8150
resume@averyjames.com
www.averyjames.com
Michele James, President & Founder

B.E. Smith, Inc.

(Specialize in Healthcare)
8801 Renner Avenue
Lenexa, KS 66219
(800) 467-9117
cburch@besmith.com
www.besmith.com
John Doug Smith, President & Chief Executive Officer
Mark Madden, Vice President Executive Search

Baker & Associates LLC

(Specialize in Academic, Health Sciences & Not-for-Profit)
4799 Olde Towne Parkway, Suite 202
Marietta, GA 30068
(770) 395-2760
jbaker@baasearch.com
www.baasearch.com
Jerry H. Baker, President
Martin M. Baker, Vice President
Anya Gray, Principal

Ballein Search Partners

(Specialize in Health Care)
Post Office Box 5204
Oak Brook, IL 60522
(630) 322-9220
fax (630) 322-9221
kathy@balleinsp.com
Kathleen M. Ballein, President

Barnes Development Group, LLC

11425 North Shorecliff Lane
Mequon, WI 53092
(262) 241-1016
fax (262) 241-8438
resume@barnesdevelopment.com
Richard E. Barnes, President & Co-Owner

Barrack Hill Partners

6423 Northwest 30th Avenue
Boca Raton, FL 33496
(561) 716-1119
resumes@bhp-us.com
Debra Caplan, Managing Partner

Bartholdi Partners, Inc.

(Specialize in High Technology, Communication, Healthcare Technology, Government Services)
2465 Freetown Drive
Reston, VA 20191
(703) 476-5519
info@bartholdisearch.com
www.bartholdisearch.com

Theodore G. Bartholdi, Founding Partner
Jacques DeLabry, Partner
Carol Holt, Partner
Susan Mills, Partner
Walter Wilowaty, Partner

Barton Associates, Inc.
4314 Yoakum Boulevard
Houston, TX 77006
(713) 961-9111
fax (713) 993-9399
research@bartona.com
www.bartona.com
Beth A. Barton, Partner
Sean E. Barton, Partner

Battalia Winston International*
555 Madison Avenue, 19th Floor
New York, NY 10022
(212) 308-8080
fax (212) 308-1309
jbennett@amropbw.com
www.amropbw.com
Dale Winston, Chairwoman & Chief Executive Officer
Jo A. Bennett, Partner
Joseph J. Carideo, Partner
Walter J. McGuigan, Partner
Debra Pollick, Partner
Also:
Boston, MA (617) 345-5505
Ryan Mahady, Partner
Bruce H. Walton, Partner
Chicago, IL (312) 704-0050
Richard W. Folts, Partner
Peter M. Gomez, Partner
Susan Medina, Partner
Rob Miller, Partner
Edison, NJ (732) 549-8200
Gilbert J. Carrara, Partner
John A. Ebeling, Partner
Terence M. Gallagher, President & COO
Adam J. Millinger, Partnerr
Los Angeles, CA (310) 284-8080
Michael D. McClain, Partner
Washington, DC (202) 626-8080
Kathryn Griffin, Partner

Martin H. Bauman Associates, LLC
150 East 58th Street, 37th Floor
New York, NY 10155
(212) 752-6580
resume@baumanassociates.com
Martin H. Bauman, President

The Beam Group
414 Mill Creek Road
Gladwyne, PA 19035
(215) 988-2100
info@beamgroup.com
www.beamgroup.com
Russell A. Glicksman, President and Chief Executive Officer
Also:
New York, NY (212) 476-4150
Richard M. Coffina, Executive Vice President
Ponte Vedre Beach, FL
(904) 864-6295
Thomas W. Kelly, Executive Vice President

Beaudine & Associates, Inc.
9925 Haynes Bridge Road, Suite 200-122
Alpharetta, GA 30022
(770) 685-5500
fax (770) 865-1552
info@beaudine.com
www.beaudine.com
Frank R. Beaudine, President

The Bedford Consulting Group Inc.*
145 Adelaide Street West, Suite 400
Toronto, ON M5H 4E5
(416) 963-9000
fax (416) 963-9998
search@bedfordgroup.com
www.bedfordgroup.com
Steven Pezim, Founding Partner & Co-Managing Director
Hart Hillman, Partner
Howard J. Pezim, Founding Partner & Co-Managing Director
Also:
Oakville, ON (905) 338-7008
Russ Buckland, Partner
Frank Galati, Managing Partner
Lisa Heidman, Partner

Martin D. Behan & Associates
123 East 39th Street
New York, NY 10016
(800) 526-8279
mbehanassociates@gmail.com
Martin D. Behan

Joy Reed Belt Search Consultants, Inc.
5804 North Grand Boulevard
Post Office Box 54410
Oklahoma City, OK 73154
(405) 842-5155
fax (405) 842-6357
executiverecruiter@joyreedbelt.com
www.joyreedbeltsearch.com
Joy Reed Belt, President

Bench International Search Inc.
(Specialize in Pharmaceutical & Biotechnology)
12121 Wilshire Boulevard, Suite 750
Los Angeles, CA 90025
(310) 854-9900
fax (310) 854-9000
resumes@benchinternational.com
www.benchinternational.com
Denise DeMan, President and Chief Executive Officer
Also:
New York, NY (212) 372-8900
Janet Foulkes, Global Senior Vice President
San Francisco, CA
(415) 362-1770
Karen Fulmer, Senior Vice President

Bender Executive Search
(Specialize in Marketing and Sales)
100 South Middle Neck Road
Great Neck, NY 11021
(516) 650-8545
benderexec@aol.com
www.benderexecutivesearch.com
Alan S. Bender, President

Berkhemer Clayton Inc.
(Specialize in Communications, Marketing, Finance & Diversity)
241 South Figueroa Street, Suite 300
Los Angeles, CA 90012
(213) 621-2300
fax (213) 621-2309
resumes@berkhemerclayton.com
berkhemerclayton.com
Betsy Berkhemer-Credaire, President
Fred J. Clayton, Chief Executive Officer

Bialla & Associates Inc.*
4000 Bridgeway, Suite 201
Sausalito, CA 94965
(415) 332-7111
fax (415) 332-3964
vitob@bialla.com
www.bialla.com
Vito Bialla, Partner & Founder
David Archambault, Partner
Richard Henley, Partner
John McCrea, Partner

Chip Novick, Partner

Paul J. Biestek Associates, Inc.

800 East Northwest Highway, Suite 700
Post Office Box 101
Palatine, IL 60074
(847) 825-5131
search@biestek-associates.com
Paul J. Biestek, President

Bio Human Capital

(Specialize in Life Sciences)
100 Overlook Center, 2nd Floor
Princeton, NJ 08540
(609) 844-7597
ra@biohumancapital.com
www.biohumancapital.com
Richard J. Alexander, Managing Partner
Monica Hill, Partner

BioQuest LLC

(Specialize in Biotechnology & Pharmaceutical)
100 Spear Street, Suite 1125
San Francisco, CA 94105
(415) 777-2422
fax (415) 777-4363
resumes@bioquestinc.com
www.bioquestinc.com
Roger J. Anderson, Managing Partner
Karen Bertrand, Senior Vice President
Kim Ennis, Partner
Gale Richards, Partner
H. Jurgen Weber, Founding Managing Partner
Also:
Newport Beach, CA
(949) 488-8018
Dave Mildrew, Senior Vice President

Bishop Partners

(Specialize in Entertainment, Media & Communications)
28 West 44th Street, Suite 1120
New York, NY 10036
(212) 986-3419
info@bishoppartners.com
www.bishoppartners.com
Susan K. Bishop, President & Chief Executive Officer

Blackshaw Partners, LLC

4401 Northside Parkway, Suite 510
Atlanta, GA 30327
(404) 949-3060
fax (404) 949-3061
resumes@blackshawpartners.com
www.blackshawpartners.com
Brian M. Blackshaw, Founding Partner
Greg Embry, Partner
Mark Weinstein, Partner
Also:
Woodland Hills, CA
(818) 996-5323
William Tsai, Partner

Blair & Company, LLC

(Specialize in Pharmaceutical & Biotechnology Clinical Develoment)
2 Greenwich Office Park, Suite 300
Greenwich, CT 06831
(203) 532-4411
fax (203) 622-0321
gblair@blairandcompany.com
www.blairandcompany.com
Gail Blair, President

Blake Hansen & Schmidt, Limited

5514 Ridgeway Court
Westlake Village, CA 91362
(818) 879-1192
fax (818) 879-0282
contact@blakehansenschmidt.com
www.blakehansenschmidt.com
Jeri Schmidt, President

J: Blakslee International

(Specialize in Pharmaceuticals, Biotechnology & Medical)
336 Bon Air Center, # 369
Greenbrae, CA 94904
(805) 794-0701
fax (415) 389-7302
resumes@jblakslee.com
Jan H. Blakslee, President

Blaney Executive Search

(Specialize in High Tech)
Damonmill Square
9 Pond Lane, Suite 2E
Concord, MA 01742
(978) 371-2192
jblaney@blaneyinc.com
www.blaneyinc.com
John A. Blaney, President

Paula Blank International

(Specialize in Life Sciences, Biotech, Healthcare)
520 South El Camino Real, Suite 342
San Mateo, CA 94402-1726
(650) 685-6855
fax (650) 685-0671
bios@paulablankinternational.com
www.paulablankinternational.com
Paula Ellen Blank, Principal

Barry Blostein Executive Search

(Specialize in Canadian Searches Only)
Toronto
Toronto, ON L4J 3E7
(905) 763-0728
barry.blostein@sympatico.ca
Barry Blostein, President

Blu Era*

(Specialize in Canada Searches)
116-8 Avenue SW, Suite 200
Calgary, AB T2P 1B3
(403) 532-7959
fax (403) 532-7974
info@bluera.ca
www.bluera.ca/
Rick Lancaster, Partner
Sarah Hawitt, Partner

Blue Diamond Management Group, Inc.

(Specialize in Biotech, Pharmaceutical, & Medical Devices)
Building #204
366 5 East Bay Drive, Suite 138
Largo, FL 33771
(727) 524-1335
fax (727) 538-9587
Sue Almy, President

BlueStar Search Partners, LLC

(Specialize in Financial Services)
30 Old Kings Highway
Darien, CT 06820
(203) 202-2100
fax (203) 972-3474
evan@bluestarsearch.com
www.bluestarsearch.com
Evan Clark, Partner
Brendan O'Brien, Partner
Liz Richardson, Partner

Bluestone* Leadership Services

Bankers Hall-West Tower
888 Third Street S.W., Suite 4430
Calgary, AB T2P 5C5
(587) 353-9800
www.altopartners.com
William Basarsky, Managing Director
Kevin Hall, Managing Director
Shauna Louie, Managing Director

BMF Reynolds, Inc.
(SPECIALIZE IN Health Care, Nuclear Energy)
366 Nassau Street
Post Office Box 157
Princeton, NJ 08540
(609) 688-8700
inquiry@bmfr.com
John H. Reynolds, President

Boardwalk Consulting LLC
(SPECIALIZE IN Non-Profit)
The Candler Building
127 Peachtree Street NE, Suite 200
Atlanta, GA 30303
(404) 262-7392
fax (404) 795-0855
info@boardwalkconsulting.com
www.boardwalkconsulting.com
Kathy Bremer, Senior Director
Michelle Bufkin, Director
Sam Pettway, Director

Bobbie Stone International, LLC
(SPECIALIZE IN Healthcare Industry)
66 Witherspoon Street, Suite #314
Princeton, NJ 08542
(866) 750-1500
fax (866) 760-1500
bsiinfo@bobbiestoneexecutive-search.com
www.bobbiestoneexecutivesearch.com
Bobbie Stone, President

Bohan & Bradstreet, Inc.
Concept Park
741 Boston Post Road, Suite 101
Gilford, CT 06437
(203) 453-5535
fax (203) 453-5545
info@bohan-bradstreet.com
www.bohan-bradstreet.com
Edward B. Bradstreet, President

Bonell Ryan Inc.
415 Madison Avenue, 15th Floor
New York, NY 10022
(646) 673-8620
fax (646) 673-8401
info@bonellryan.com
www.bonellryan.com
Debra Ryan, President

Bonnell Associates
40 Richards Avenue, Third Floor
Norwalk, CT 06854
(203) 319-7214
fax (203) 319-7219
info@bonnellassociates.com
www.bonnellassociates.com
William R. Bonnell, President

Bosch & Associates LLC
Post Office Box 1030
Greens Farms, CT 06838
(203) 255-8700
fax (203) 259-4959
human.resources@boschllc.com
www.boschllc.com
Eric E. Bosch, President

Boston Search Group, Inc.
(SPECIALIZE IN Technology, On-line education, Life Sciences, Biotech)
224 Clarendon Street, Suite 41
Boston, MA 02116
(617) 266-4333
fax (781) 735-0562
rprotsik@bsgweb.com
www.bsgweb.com
Ralph Protsik, Co-Founder and Managing Director
Clark Waterfall, Co-Founder and Managing Director

Bowman & Associates
(SPECIALIZE IN Medical Devices)
Post Office Box 450149
Atlanta, GA 31145
(404) 329-9314
fax (404) 320-3114
Mary Bowman, President

Boyden*
50 Broadway
Hawthorne, NY 10532
(914) 747-0093
fax (914) 747-0108
inquiry@boyden.com
www.boyden.com
Christopher Clarke, President
Also:
Atlanta, GA (678) 441-9600
Brian Clark, Managing Director
Daniel C. Grassi, Managing Director
Robert S. Travis, Managing Director
Baltimore, MD (410) 625-3800
Timothy C. McNamara, Managing Director
Calgary, AB (403) 237-6603
Lachlin McKinnon, Managing Director
Andy Sharman, Managing Director
Brent C. Shervey, Managing Director
Alan Travis, Principal
Robert S. Travis, Managing Director
Chicago, IL (312) 565-1300
Trina D. Gordon, Chairman
Catherine Gray, Managing Director
John S. Gude, Managing Director
Richard Kolpasky, Managing Director
Richard A. McCallister, Managing Director
Paul Schmidt, Managing Director
Houston, TX (713) 655-0123
Doug Ehrenkranz, Managing Director
Alicia Russell Hasell, Managing Director
James N. J. Hertlein, Managing Director
Thomas C. Zay, Managing Director
Miami, FL (786) 552-3460
Thomas Connelly, Managing Director
New York, NY (212) 949-9400
Lisa Amore, Managing Director
Jeanne E. Branthover, Managing Director
J. Gregory Coleman, Managing Director
Andrei Costache, Managing Director
Howard J. Gross, Managing Director
Kate Quinn, Managing Director
Andrew Reese, Managing Director
Ken Rich, Managing Director
Pittsburgh, PA (412) 756-1000
Thomas T. Flannery, Managing Director
Andrew Gardner, Managing Director
Stacey Holland, Managing Director
John R. Howard, Managing Director
Sarah Stewart, Managing Director
San Francisco, CA (415) 874-3700
Ross L. Blanchard, Managing Director
Martie Bond, Managing Director
Lori Christiansen, Managing Director
John Holland, Managing Director
Meredith Morre, Managing Director
Seiki Murono, Managing Director
Trevor Pritchard, Managing Director
Neil Sims, Managing Director
Summit, NJ (908) 598-0400
Gary J. Kastenbaum, Managing Director
Carlyle R. Newell, Managing Director
Toronto, ON (416) 862-1273
Janice Detta Colli, Managing Director
Doug Weir, Managing Director

Washington, DC (202) 536-5168
Bill Hanbury, Principal
Kimmo Kartano, Principal
N. Derek Wilkinson, Managing Director

THE BRADBURY GROUP, INC.

(SPECIALIZE IN PREFER WEST COAST CANDIDATES, HIGH TECH, BIOTECH, ENGINEERING CONSULTING)
2112 Vizcaya Way
Campbell, CA 95008
(408) 377-5400
fax (408) 377-4644
paul@ifindem.com
www.ifindem.com
Paul Bradbury, Managing Principal

BRADY PARTNERS EXECUTIVE SEARCH

4069 Yellow Ginger Glen, Suite 200
Norcross, GA 30092
(770) 734-0303
bradysearch@aol.com
Rick W. Brady, Partner

THE BRAND COMPANY, INC.

181 Shores Drive
Vero Beach, FL 32963
(772) 231-1807
J. Brand Spangenberg, Chairman

THE BRENTWOOD GROUP, LTD.

(SPECIALIZE IN HIGH TECH)
1980 Willamette Falls Drive, Suite 260
West Linn, OR 97068
(503) 697-8136
fax (503) 697-8161
contact@brentwoodgroup.com
www.brentwoodgroup.com
Frank Moscow, Founder & President
Also:
Eagle, ID (208) 333-2570
Tom Haley, Manager Director

BRIANT ASSOCIATES, INC.

(SPECIALIZE IN MANUFACTURING POSITIONS)
18 - 2 East Dundee Road, Suite 202
Barrington, IL 60010
(847) 382-5725
fax (847) 382-7265
resume@briantassociates.com
www.briantassociates.com
Rick Bingham, Partner
Larissa Klavins, Partner

BRIDGE ASSOCIATES

1209 North Fourth Street, Suite 103
Manchester, IA 52057
(563) 927-6301
bridgeassoc@yahoo.com
Amanda Hawker, Managing Director

BRIDGEGATE LLC

(SPECIALIZE IN INFORMATION TECHNOLOGY)
17701 Cowan Avenue, Suite 240
Irvine, CA 92614
(949) 553-9200
fax (949) 660-1810
info@bridgegate.com
www.bridgegate.com
Kevin M. Rosenberg, Managing Partner
Joshua Goodman, Partner
Joel May, Partner
Also:
Manhattan Beach, CA
(310) 546-8147
Kevin M. Rosenberg, Managing Partner

THE BRIDGESPAN GROUP

(SPECIALIZE IN NON-PROFIT)
465 California Street, 11th Street
San Francisco, CA 94104
(415) 627-1100
donna.davidson@bridgespan.org
www.bridgespan.org
Julie King, Director of Executive Search
Also:
Boston, MA (617) 572-2833
Paul L. Rosenberg, Head of Boston Office, Partner
New York, NY (646) 562-8900
Richard Steele, Head of Office, Partner

BRIGHAM HILL CONSULTANCY

(SPECIALIZE IN NOT-FOR-PROFIT)
2909 Cole Avenue, Suite 220
Dallas, TX 75204
(214) 871-8700
fax (214) 871-6004
brigham@brighamhill.com
www.brighamhill.com
L. Lincoln Eldredge, President

BROOKE CHASE ASSOCIATES, INC.

(SPECIALIZE IN KITCHEN/BATH, HARDWARE, BUILDING MATERIALS, PLUMBING, METALS, LAWN/GARDEN, HVAC)
1543 Second Street, Suite 201
Sarasota, FL 34236
(877) 374-0039
fax (941) 358-3311
info@brookechase.com
www.brookechase.com
Joseph J. McElmeel, Chairman/CEO
Rich Miller, Managing Director
Also:
Chicago, IL (312) 744-0033
Joseph J. McElmeel, Chairman/CEO

DF BROWN & ASSOCIATES

197 Crogan Street, Suite 203
Lawrenceville, GA 30046
(770) 979-1253
fax (404) 393-9704
info@dfbrownatlanta.com
www.dfbrownatlanta.com
David F. Brown, President & CEO

BROWN SCHROEDER & ASSOCIATES, INC.

(SPECIALIZE IN NON-PROFIT)
100 East Walton Street, Suite 600E
Chicago, IL 60611
(312) 343-5593
resumes@brownschroeder.com
www.brownschroeder.com
Frank C. Schroeder, Principal & Co-Founder
Also:
San Francisco, CA
(415) 244-5901
James Armstrong, Senior Consultant

B. BROWNSON & ASSOCIATES LP

2825 Wilcrest Drive, Suite 530
Houston, TX 77042
(713) 626-4790
fax (713) 877-1745
brownsonassoc@brownson.com
www.brownson.com
Bruce F. E. Brownson, President & CEO

BUFFKIN & ASSOCIATES, LLC*

10 Cadillac Drive, Suite 190
Brentwood, TN 37027
(615) 988-2582
fax (615) 771-0099
info@thebuffingroup.com
www.thebuffkingroup.com
Craig Buffkin, Managing Director
Roland Lundy, Partner
Also:
Alexandria, VA (703) 629-9789
Brenda Doherty, Partner
Greenwich, CT (203) 769-1302
Brian Kelley, Partner

New **York City, NY**
(646) 354-6507
Tom Rosenwald, Partner

The Burling Group Ltd.
600 North Kingsbury Street, Suite 1507
Chicago, IL 60654
(312) 397-0888
web@burlinggroup.com
www.burlinggroup.com
Ronald Deitch, President

Joseph R. Burns and Associates, Inc.
8 Stafford Drive
Madison, NJ 07940-2727
(973) 377-1350
fax (973) 377-9350
Joseph R. Burns, President

Busch International
(SPECIALIZE IN SEMICONDUCTOR INDUSTRY & HIGH TECH AT VP/CEO LEVEL ONLY)
477 South San Antonio Road
Los Altos, CA 94022
(650) 949-6500
jack@buschint.com
www.buschint.com
Jack Busch, Managing Partner

Butterfass, Pepe & MacCallan, Inc.
(SPECIALIZE IN FINANCIAL SERVICES)
Post Office Box 179
Franklin Lakes, NJ 07417
(201) 560-9500
fax (201) 560-9506
staff@bpmi.com
www.bpmi.com
Stanley W. Butterfass, Principal
Angelo Pamieri, Principal
Leonida R. Pepe, Principal

BuysideResources, Inc.
15 Cypress Branch Way, Suite 207-C
Palm Coast, FL 32137
(386) 586-6265
info@buysideresources.com
www.buysideresources.com
Christopher B. Cann, Managing Director

The Caldwell Partners* International
165 Avenue Road
Toronto, ON M5R 3S4
(416) 920-7702
fax (416) 922-8646
leaders@caldwell.ca
www.caldwell.ca/
Ron Charles, Partner
Kelly Blair, Partner
Anne Fawcett, Partner
Jeff Freeborough, Partner
Mike Gooley, Partner
Avo Oudabachian, Partner
Elan Pratzer, Partner
Heather Ring, Partner
Denise Tobin, Managing Partner
Also:
Atlanta, GA (404) 946-4199
Jeff Lemming, Partner
Calgary, AB (403) 265-8780
Les Gombik, Partner
Sean McLean, Partner
Drew Railton, Partner
Encino, CA (818) 995-7800
Darin A. DeWitt, Partner
Neal Maslan, Managing Partner
Smooch Repovich Reynolds, Partner
John Wasley, Managing Partner
Irving, TX (214) 748-3200
Jim Bethmann, Partner
Mike T. Kelly, Partner
John Siggins, Partner
Dave Winston, Managing Partner
New York, NY (212) 953-3220
Elizabeth Bernich, Partner
Scott Bilby, Partner
Gerry Cameron, Partner
Paul Heller, Partner
Constance Kassouf, Partner
Michael Martinolich, Partner
Jerry McGrath, Partner
Paul Medagia, Partner
Sean Scanlon, Partner
Richard Stein, Partner
San Francisco, CA
(415) 983-7700
Michael Ballenger, Partner
Mercedes Chatfield-Taylor, Partner
Kristin Hebert, Partner
Stamford, CT (203) 324-6400
Michael DeCosta, Partner
Jodie Emery, Partner
Peter Reed, Partner
Eric Roeloffs, Partner
Vancouver, BC (604) 669-3550
Harry Parslow, Partner
Drew Railton, Partner

Lee Calhoon & Company, Inc.
(SPECIALIZE IN HEALTHCARE & LIFE SCIENCES)
1621 Birchrun Road
P.O. Box 201
Birchrunville, PA 19421
(610) 469-9000
fax (610) 469-0398
resume@leecalhoon.com
www.leecalhoon.com
Bill Fedora, Principal
Christopher Calhoon, Principal
Lee Calhoon, President and Chief Executive Officer
Patricia Calhoon, Principal

Caliber Associates
(SPECIALIZE IN LIFE SCIENCES)
6336 Greenwich Drive, Suite C
San Diego, CA 92122
(858) 551-7880
fax (858) 551-7887
info@caliberassociates.com
www.caliberassociates.com
Steven P. Hochberg, President & Founder
Also:
North Wales, PA (610) 222-2206
Steve P. Hochberg, President

Callan Associates, Ltd.
1211 West 22nd Street, Suite 821
Oak Brook, IL 60523
(630) 574-9300
fax (630) 574-3099
info@callanassociates.com
www.callanassociates.com
Robert M. Callan, Managing Partner
Elizabeth C. Beaudin, Partner
Robert M. Callan, Partner
Marianne C. Ray, Partner

Cambridge Management Planning, Inc.
2323 Yonge Street, Suite 203
Toronto, ON M4P 2C9
(416) 484-8408
fax (416) 484-0151
mail@cambridgemgmt.com
www.cambridgemgmt.com
Graham Carver, Founding Partner & President

Cannellos - Smartt Associates, LLC
(SPECIALIZE IN FINANCE, BIOTECHNOLOGY & PHARMACEUTICAL)
30 Wagner Lane
Hillsborough, NJ 08844
(908) 369-0041
fax (908) 369-0042
rcannellos@csa-search.com
www.csa-search.com
Rick Cannellos, Partner
Rudy Smartt, Partner

Canny, Bowen Inc.*
400 Madison Avenue, Suite 11D
New York, NY 10017
(212) 949-6611
fax (212) 949-5191
resumes@cannybowen.com
cannybowen.com
Greg Gabel, Managing Director
David R. Peasback, Chief Executive Officer & President
Adam Shavulsky, Managing Director
Jeff Wilkens, Principal

The Caplan-Taylor Group
(Specialize in Pharmaceuticals & Biotechnology)
897 Oak Park Boulevard, PMB 308
Pismo Beach, CA 93449
(805) 489-7590
info@caplantaylorgroup.com
John Caplan, Partner

Capodice & Associates
(Specialize in Franchise, Restaurant, Hospitality)
Midtown Plaza
1243 South Tamiami Trail
Sarasota, FL 34239
(941) 906-1990
fax (941) 906-1991
peter@capodice.com
www.capodice.com
Peter Capodice, President

The Capstone Partnership*
(Specialize in Investment Banking, Corporate Finance,Legal, & Human Resources)
100 Park Avenue, 34th Floor
New York, NY 10017
(212) 843-0200
fax (212) 843-3411
info@capstonepartnership.com
www.capstonepartnership.com
Rolfe I. Kopelan, Managing Partner

Cardinal Mark
(Specialize in Information Technology, Medical Technology, Industrial)
17113 Minnetonka Boulevard, Suite 112
Minnetonka, MN 55345
(952) 314-4636
fax (610) 228-7390
jimz@cardinalmark.com
www.cardinalmark.com
James J. Zuehlke, Principal
Also:
Greensboro, NC (336) 691-0626
Charles G. Roer, Principal

CareerMaker, Inc.
555 Bryant Street, Suite 251
Palo Alto, CA 94301
(408) 369-1100
info@careermaker.com
www.careermaker.com
Kenneth Downey, Founder & CEO
Also:
New York, NY (212) 362-2222
Kenneth Downey, Founder & CEO

CareerSMITH*
(Specialize in Engineering and Construction Management)
220 Newport Center Drive, Suite 11-364
Newport Beach, CA 92660
(949) 481-3058
fax (949) 640-5751
Careers@careersmith.com
www.careersmith.com
E. Brian Smith, President and Chief Executive Officer

Carrington & Carrington Ltd.*
(Specialize in African-American, Hispanic and other diverse professionals)
39 South LaSalle Street, Suite 400
Chicago, IL 60603-1557
(312) 606-0015
fax (312) 606-0501
resume@carringtonandcarrington.com
www.carringtonandcarrington.com
Marian H. Carrington, Principal
Willie E. Carrington, Principal

Carter Baldwin Executive Search
200 Mansell Court East, Suite 450
Roswell, GA 30076
(678) 448-0000
connect@carterbaldwin.com
www.carterbaldwin.com
Price Harding, Managing Partner
David Clapp, Managing Partner
Roslyn Dickerson, Partner
David Sobocinski, Partner
Jennifer Poole Sobocinski, Partner

The Carter Group, L.L.C.
(Specialize in Hi Tech, Manufacturing & Financial Services)
1621 University Boulevard South, Suite B2
Mobile, AL 36609
(251) 342-0999
fax (251) 342-7999
info@thecartergroup.com
www.thecartergroup.com
Guy W. Carter, President
Also:
Naperville, IL (224) 383-4483
Richard Burgess, Vice President & Partner

Caruthers & Company, LLC
(Specialize in Corporate Communications/Public Affairs)
980 Post Road East, Suite 104
Westport, CT 06880
(203) 221-3234
Robert D. Caruthers, Principal

Catalyst Search Group
(Specialize in Technology & IT)
655 Deerfield Road, Suite 100-170
Deerfield, IL 60015
(888) 598-4440
ritesite@cooltechjobs.com
www.cooltechjobs.com
Greg Ambrose, Managing Director

Cejka Search*
(Specialize in Health Care)
4 City Place Drive, Suite 300
Saint Louis, MO 63141
(800) 296-2698
fax (314) 726-0026
cst@cejkasearch.com
www.Cejkasearch.com
Lois Dister, Executive Vice President
Ben H. Brouhard, Senior Vice President
Paul Esselman, Executive Vice President
Deedra Hartung, Senior Executive Vice President
Rebecca Kapphahn, Vice President
Mark Prosperi, Vice President
Michael Tucker, Vice President
Michael S. Dunford, Executive Vice President

Centennial, Inc.
(Specialize in Focusing on placements in KY, OH, and IN.)
Towers of Kenwood
8044 Montgomery Road, Suite 260
Cincinnati, OH 45236
(513) 366-3760
fax (513) 366-3761
3943-MH1543@emailagent.max-hire.net
www.centennialinc.com
Mike A. Sipple, Vice President

Centerstone Executive Search, Inc.
(Specialize in Retailing, Food

& E-Commerce)
U.S. Bank Centre
1420 Fifth Avenue, 22nd Floor
Seattle, WA 98101
(425) 836-8445
resumes@centerstonesearch.com
www.centerstonesearch.com
Kim Villeneuve, President and Chief Executive Officer
Liz Etkin, Senior Vice President
Cindy Fratarcangeli, Senior Vice President
Stephen Wood, Executive Vice President

CFO Selections, LLC

(Specialize in Finance Positions in all Industries)
14432 SE Eastgate Way, Suite 400
Bellevue, WA 98007
(206) 686-4480
fax (425) 455-6727
info@cfoselections.com
www.cfoselections.com
Tom Varga, Managing Partner
Mark Tranter, Partner

Chadick Ellig, Inc.*

300 Park Avenue
New York, NY 10022
(212) 688-8671
fax (212) 308-4510
resume@chadickellig.com
www.chadickellig.com
Susan L. Chadick, Chief Executive Officer
Janice Ellig, Chief Executive Officer
Stacy Lauren Musi, Managing Director
Lan Nguyen, Managing Director

Chandler Group Executive Search, Inc.

4165 Shoreline Drive, Suite 220
Spring Park, MN 55384
(952) 471-3000
fax (952) 471-3021
resumes@chandgroup.com
www.chandgroup.com
Brad J. Chandler, Principal
Cynthia A. Chandler, Principal
Nancy L. Hanna, Vice President
Thom B. Telfer, Partner

Change Management Associates, Inc.

50 Harrison Street, Suite 202D
Hoboken, NJ 07030
(201) 795-2900
resumes@chgmgmt.com
www.chgmgmt.com
Edward J. McBride, Chief Executive Officer

Chanko Ward, Ltd.

2 West 45th Street, Suite 1201
New York, NY 10036
(212) 869-4040
info@chankoward.com
www.chankoward.com
Jim Chanko, President

Chicago Research Group, Inc.

2245- C Ashley Crossing Drive
Charleston, SC 29414
(919) 968-0120
dmarshall@chicagoresearch.com
www.chicagoresearch.com
Deborah Marshall, President

CHM Partners International, LLC

(Specialize in Life Sciences, Financial Services, Manufacturing)
P.O. Box 9006
Morristown, NJ 07963
(973) 459-9699
fax (973) 966-6933
smcdowell@chm-partners.com
www.chm-partners.com
Robert N. McDowell, Managing Partner
Scott McDowell, Managing Partner

Choi & Burns LLC

(Specialize in Investment Banking, Equity Research, Venture Capital, Private Equity)
156 West 56th Street, 18th Floor
New York, NY 10019
(212) 755-7051
fax (212) 355-2610
info@choiburns.com
www.choiburns.com
Julie A. Choi, President and Chief Executive Officer
Bethany E. Burns, Managing Director
Gau Junnarkar, Managing Director
Sumi W. Kang, Managing Director
Jill Niemczyk, Managing Director
Susan Yie, Managing Director

Chrisman & Company, Inc.

(Specialize in Financial Services)
350 South Figueroa St., Suite 550
Los Angeles, CA 90071
(213) 620-1192
fax (213) 620-1693
info@chrismansearch.com
www.chrismansearch.com
Timothy R. Chrisman, President

Cizek Associates, Inc.

2415 East Camelback Road, Suite 700
Phoenix, AZ 85016
(602) 553-1066
fax (602) 553-1166
jobseeker@cizekassociates.com
www.cizekassociates.com
Marti J. Cizek, President
Also:
Oak Brook, IL (708) 534-7860
John T. Cizek, Principal
Paso Robles, CA (650) 343-2600
Edward G. Linskey, Senior Vice President

Clarey Andrews & Klein, Inc.

1347 Hillside Road
Northbrook, IL 60062
(847) 498-2870
resumes@clarey-a-klein.com
www.clarey-a-klein.com
Jack R. Clarey, Principal

Clarey/Napier International

(Specialize in Energy, Oil, Gas, Finance)
1221 McKinney Street, Suite 3112
Houston, TX 77010
(713) 238-6705
fax (713) 236-4778
cni@cnintl.com
www.cnintl.com
William A. Clarey, Partner
Ginger L. Napier, Partner

The Coelyn Group

(Specialize in Healthcare and Life Sciences)
1 Park Plaza, Suite 600
Irvine, CA 92614
(949) 553-8855
fax (866) 436-2171
contact@coelyngroup.com
www.coelyngroup.com
Ronald H. Coelyn, Partner
Lynn S. Nishimoto, Partner

Coffou Partners, Inc.

880 North Lake Shore Drive, Suite #13C
Chicago, IL 60611
(312) 867-1920
info@coffou.com
www.coffou.com
Sara Coffou, President

Cole, Warren and Long, Inc.

Two Penn Center Plaza, Suite 312
Philadelphia, PA 19102-1703
(215) 563-0701
fax (215) 563-2907
rcole@cwl-inc.com
www.cwl-inc.com
Ronald J. Cole, President

Coleman Lew & Associates, Inc.

Post Office Box 36489
Charlotte, NC 28236
(704) 377-0362
fax (704) 377-0424
research@colemanlew.com
www.colemanlew.com
Charles E. Lew, Chairman
James E. Bostic, Partner & Managing Director
Kenneth D. Carrick, President

Columbia Consulting Group, Inc.

Twin Knolls Professional Center
5525 Twin Knolls Road, Suite 331
Columbia, MD 21045
(443) 276-2525
fax (443) 276-2536
info@ccgsearch.com
www.ccgsearch.com
Lawrence J. Holmes, President
Robert C. Gauthier, Managing Director
Heinz-Otto Georg, Managing Director
Matthew C. Kostmayer, Managing Director
Thomas J. McMahon, Managing Director
Also:
New York, NY (212) 832-2525
James Cornehlsen, Managing Director
Gregory L. Ohman, Managing Director

Compass Group Ltd.

Birmingham Place Building
401 South Old Woodward Avenue, Suite 310
Birmingham, MI 48009
(248) 540-9110
fax (248) 647-8288
Paul W. Czamanske, President & Chief Executive Officer
James W. Sturtz, Vice President

Conard Associates, Inc.

74 Northeastern Blvd., Unit 22A
Nashua, NH 03062
(603) 886-0600
fax (603) 804-0421
rod@conard.com
www.conardassociates.com
Rod Conard, Chief Executive Officer

Conboy Sur & Morice Associates Inc.

15 Churchville Road, Suite 170
Bel Air, MD 21014
(410) 925-4122
resumes@csma-cons.com
www.conboysur.com
William K. Sur, President
Also:
Essex, CT (410) 925-4122
Jim Morice, Managing Partner

Conex, Inc.

950 Third Avenue, 9th Floor
New York, NY 10022
(212) 371-3737
fax (212) 371-3897
mail@conex-usa.com
Fred Siegel, President-USA

Robert Connelly & Associates, Inc.

(Specialize in Commercial Real Estate, Architecture, Engineering, Construction, Agribusiness)
5200 Willson Road, Suite 150
Minneapolis, MN 55424
(952) 925-3039
fax (952) 922-5762
info@robertconnelly.com
www.robertconnelly.com
Robert F. Olsen, President

Conroy Ross Partners Ltd.

3800 Bow Valley Square 2
205 Fifth Avenue SW
Calgary, AB T2P 3G6
(403) 261-8080
fax (403) 261-8085
mail@conroyross.com
www.conroyross.com
M. James Conroy, Founder
Dustin Anderson, Partner
Lorraine Chan, Partner
S. Scott Doupe, Partner
Greg Pocherewny, Partner
Darcy Verhun, Office Managing Partner
Also:
Edmonton, AB (780) 432-5490
Mike Bacchus, Chief Executive Officer
Antara Gabinet, Partner
Terri Davis Nobert, Office Managing Partner
Michael Ross, Founder
Halifax, NS (902) 429-0728
Craig Coady, Partner
Regina, SK (306) 949-8875
Gregory Fieger, Office Managing Partner
Toronto, ON (416) 800-5550
Jim Botrie, Partner
Randy De Piero, Partner

Convergence Recruiting Solutions

3370 New Heritage Drive
Alpharetta, GA 30022
(678) 879-7980
info@convergencerecruiting.com
www.convergencerecruiting.com
Scott K. Kaufman, President

Conway and Greenwood, Inc.

815 Holt Drive
Raleigh, NC 27608
(919) 833-9000
fax (919) 833-6613
candidateinquiry@conwaygreen-wood.com
www.conwaygreenwood.com
Paul Conway, President

Conyngham Partners LLC

(Specialize in Healthcare & Pharmaceutical)
P.O. Box 94
Ridgewood, NJ 07451
(201) 652-3444
resume@conynghampartners.com
www.conynghampartners.com
Beth Conyngham, President

Cook & Company

12 Masterton Road
Bronxville, NY 10708
(914) 779-4838
fax (914) 773-1885
search@cook-co.com
www.cook-co.com
Patricia S. Cook, Chairman & Chief Executive Officer

Corporate Search International

980 Hammond Drive, Suite 650
Atlanta, GA 30328
(770) 399-8489
fax (770) 740-0939
submit@corpsearchintl.com
William Chambers, Executive Vice President

Keith Collins, Executive Vice President

The Corporate Source Group, Inc.
5420 Bay Center Drive, Suite 105
Tampa, FL 33609
(813) 286-4422
fax (978) 475-6800
inquiry@csg-search.com
www.csg-search.com
Mark Hausherr, Senior Vice President
Also:
Andover, MA (978) 475-6400
Dana Willis, President
North Potomac, MD (301) 294-8866
Tara Stotz, Senior Vice President

Corporate Strategies Search
10900 NE Fourth Street, Suite 2300
Bellevue, WA 98004
(425) 274-7834
fax (425) 274-7835
craig@corporatestrategiessearch.com
www.corporatestrategiessearch.com
Craig McDonald, President

Corso, Mould & Associates
2 St. Clair Avenue East, Suite 800
Toronto, ON M4T 4T5
(416) 488-4111
resumes@cmaexecutivesearch.com
www.cmaexecutivesearch.com
John J. Corso, Partner
J. Steven Mould, Partner

Crist Kolder Associates
21 West Second Street, 3rd Floor
Hinsdale, IL 60521
(630) 321-1110
fax (630) 321-1112
www.cristkolder.com
Peter D. Crist, Chairman
Jackie Boyd, Vice President
Josh Crist, Managing Director
Clement Johnson, Managing Director
Thomas Kolder, President
Phil McCall, Managing Director
Scott W. Simmons, Managing Director

Crowder & Company
(Specialize in Automotive)
40950 Woodward Ave., Suite 335
Bloomfield Hills, MI 48304
(248) 645-0909
fax (248) 645-2366
ewc@crowdercompany.com
www.crowdercompany.com
Edward W. Crowder, President

Crowe-Innes & Associates, LLC*
1120 Mar West, Suite D
Tiburon, CA 94920
(415) 789-1422
fax (415) 435-6867
resumes@croweinnes.com
www.croweinnes.com
Jenny Crowe-Innes, President and Chief Executive Officer
Beth Gerken Logan, Vice President
Gaye Varney, Research Director
Also:
Santa Clara, CA (408) 850-7179
Arthur J. Pedroza, Vice President & Managing Director

cStone & Associates
12707 High Bluff Drive, 2nd Floor
San Diego, CA 92130
(858) 350-4331
fax (858) 794-1450
resumes@deliveringleadership.com
www.deliveringleadership.com
Carrie Stone, President

CT Partners*
1166 Avenue of the Americas, 3rd Floor
New York, NY 10036
(212) 588-3500
fax (212) 688-5754
www.ctnet.com
Brian Sullivan, Chief Executive Officer
Tim Boerkoel, Managing Partner
Barry Bregman, Vice Chairman
James DiFilippo, Managing Partner
Marc Gasperino, Managing Partner
Paul Groce, Managing Partner
John Hawkins, Vice Chairman
Daniel Kaplan, Managing Partner
John J. Keller, Vice Chairman
Charles King, Vice Chairman
Helga Long, Managing Partner
Peter Metzger, Vice Chairman
Ronald Porter, Vice Chairman
Adam Prager, Managing Partner
Burke St. John, Vice Chairman
Also:
Boston, MA (617) 316-5500
Debra Germaine, Managing Partner
Robert Gorog, Partner
Joseph McCabe, Vice Chairman
David Merwin, Partner
Chicago, IL (312) 253-6610
Keith Meyer, Vice Chairman
Laurie A. O'Shea, Vice Chairman
David Rossi, Partner
Les Stern, Partner
Jeremy Zeman, Partner
Cleveland, OH (216) 682-3200
Adam Kohn, Vice Chairman
Morten Nielsen, Managing Partner
Umesh Ramakrishnan, Vice Chairman
Kip Schmidt, Partner
Robert Voth, Managing Partner
Columbia, MD (443) 393-0001
Ernest Brittingham, Partner
Buster Houchins, Vice Chairman
Redwood Shores, CA (650) 801-0980
Loran Kaminsky, Partner
Tom Koch, Partner
Dayton Ogden, Partner
Rick Sklarin, Partner
Washington, DC (202) 730-7910
Michael DeSimone, Managing Partner
Martin Mendelsohn, Partner
Peter Metzger, Vice Chairman

M. J. Curran & Associates, Inc.
(Specialize in Biotechnology, Investment Management, Real Estate, Healthcare, Manufacturing, So)
304 Newberry Street, Suite 509
Boston, MA 02115
(617) 247-7700
mjcsearch@aol.com
Martin J. Curran, President

Curran Partners, Inc.*
Six Landmark Square, 5th Floor
Suite 400
Stamford, CT 06901
(203) 359-5737
fax (203) 363-5353
research@curranpartners.com
www.curranpartners.com
Michael N. Curran, Partner
Valerie Riddle, Partner
Thomas J. Vos, Partner

Curry Company
25 Eastfield Road
Mount Vernon, NY 10552
(914) 667-5735
curryco@nyc.rr.com
William E. Halpin, Managing Director
Joan Gagan, Managing Director

Judith Cushman & Associates, Inc.
(Specialize in Public Relations,

Marketing, Communications, Investor Relations)
15600 NE Eighth Street, Suite B1, PMB 128
Bellevue, WA 98008
(425) 392-8660
fax (425) 644-9043
jcushman@jc-a.com
www.jc-a.com
Judith Cushman, President

D. Hilton Associates, Inc.

(Specialize in Credit Union, Finance, Banking)
9450 Grogan's Mill Road, Suite 200
The Woodlands, TX 77380
(800) 367-0433
fax (281) 292-8893
resumes@dhilton.com
www.dhilton.com
David Hilton, President
Janice Shisler, Senior Vice President of Executive Recruiting

Dahl Morrow International

(Specialize in IT, Defense, Intelligence)
1821 Michael Faraday Drive, Suite 202
Reston, VA 20190
(703) 787-8117
fax (703) 787-8114
resumes@dahl-morrowintl.com
www.dahl-morrowintl.com
Andy Steinem, Chief Executive Officer
Barbara Steinem, President

DAK Associates, Inc.

(Specialize in Financial Services)
555 North Lane, Suite 5020
Conshohocken, PA 19428
(610) 834-1100
fax (610) 834-7722
clientservices@dakassociates.com
www.dakassociates.com
Daniel A. Kreuter, President
Steven Clark, Managing Director

The Dalley Hewitt Company

P. O. Box 19973
Atlanta, GA 30325
(404) 992-5065
fax (404) 355-6136
resumes@dalleyhewitt.com
www.DalleyHewitt.com
Rives D. Hewitt, Principal

Dalton Group, LLC

15954 Jackson Creek Parkway, Suite B-323
Monument, CO 80132
(719) 495-7898
fax (719) 344-2309
resume@daltongroupllc.com
Bret Dalton, President

Daly & Company Inc.

175 Federal Street
Boston, MA 02110
(617) 262-2800
fax (617) 728-4477
contact@dalyco.com
www.dalyco.com
Dan Daly, President

D'Antoni Partners, Inc.

(Specialize in Health Care Services & Life Sciences)
122 West John Carpenter Freeway, Suite 525
Irving, TX 75039
(972) 719-4400
fax (972) 719-4401
info@dantonipartners.com
www.dantonipartners.com
Richard R. D'Antoni, Managing Partner
Donna M. Rodio, Partner

Alan Darling Consulting

374 South Dover Road
South Newfane, VT 05351
(802) 348-6365
fax (802) 348-7826
alandarling@alandarling.com
www.alandarling.com
Alan Darling, President

Daubenspeck & Associates, Ltd.*

Two Prudential Plaza
180 N. Stetson Avenue, Suite 1935
Chicago, IL 60601
(312) 297-4100
fax (312) 828-0696
rd@daubenspeck.com
www.daubenspeck.com
Ken Daubenspeck, Managing Director

Davenport Major Executive Search*

(Specialize in Life Sciences and Technology)
12770 High Bluff Drive, Suite 320
San Diego, CA 92130
(858) 847-0700
fax (858) 847-0701
www.davenportmajor.com
Stacey Davenport, Partner
Susan Major, Partner

Daversa Partners

(Specialize in Technology & Media)
177 Broad Street, 11th Floor
Stamford, CT 06901
(203) 961-7000
fax (203) 961-7001
carol.bell@daversapartners.com
www.daversapartners.com
Carol B. Bell, Partner
Paul Daversa, Chief Executive Officer
Also:
Austin, TX (203) 517-1170
Michelle Garland, Managing Partner
New York, NY (646) 669-7869
Carol B. Bell, Partner
Orlando, FL (203) 517-1141
Jason Slattery, Partner
San Francisco, CA (415) 986-7800
Bruce Brown, Managing Partner
Washington, DC (415) 986-7802
Jack Dunn, Office Manager

Davies Park*

(Specialize in Canada Searches)
300 5th Avenue SW, Suite 1810
Calgary, AB T2P 3C4
(403) 263-0600
fax (403) 269-1080
consult@daviespark.com
www.daviespark.com
Allan Nelson, Principal
Mike Kerr, Principal
Also:
Edmonton, AB (780) 420-9980
Elizabeth Hurley, Principal
Anurag Shourie, Principal
Rick Vogel, Principal
Toronto, ON (647) 497-5376
Rob O'Brien, Managing Partner
Vancouver, BC (604) 688-8422
Greg Longster, Principal

John J. Davis & Associates, Inc.

(Specialize in Information Technology)
30 Chatham Road
P.O. Box G
Short Hills, NJ 07078
(973) 467-8339
fax (973) 467-3706
john.davis@jdavisassoc.com
www.johnjdavisandassoc.com
John J. Davis, Managing Partner

Day & Associates*
(Specialize in Health Care)
577 Airport Boulevard, Suite 130
Burlingame, CA 94010
(650) 343-2660
fax (650) 344-8460
info@dayassociates.net
www.dayassociates.net
J. Kevin Day, Principal

Rick Deckelbaum & Associates, LLC
(Specialize in Consumer Goods & Manufacturing)
7474 Creedmoor Road, Suite 270
Raleigh, NC 27613
(919) 247-5887
resumes@rdrecruiters.com
www.rdrecruiters.com
Rick Deckelbaum, President

Patrick Delaney & Associates, Inc.
70 West Madison, Suite 1400 #14038A
Chicago, IL 60602
(888) 797-0070
www.pdelaney.us/
Patrick J. Delaney, Principal

Development Resources, Inc.*
1601 North Kent Street, Suite 1200
Arlington, VA 22209
(703) 294-6684
fax (703) 522-6741
search@driconsulting.com
www.driconsulting.com
Jennifer M. Dunlap, President
Also:
New York, NY (212) 209-1042
Carmel G. Napolitano, Partner

DHI Partners
33 Chandler Road
Andover, MA 01810
(978) 470-3979
chris_dona@dhipartners.com
www.dhipartners.com
Christopher Dona, Managing Partner

DHR International, Inc.
10 South Riverside Plaza, Suite 2220
Chicago, IL 60606
(312) 782-1581
fax (312) 782-2096
resumes@dhrinternational.com
www.dhrinternational.com
David H. Hoffmann, Chairman & Chief Executive Officer
Douglas Black, Chief Financial Officer
Dwain Celistan, Executive Vice President
Sal DiFranco, Executive Vice President
April Drury, Senior Vice President
Robert Godfrey, Executive Vice President
Tom Goodrich, Executive Vice President
Justin Hirsch, President-JobPlex, Inc.
Geoffrey Hoffman, Chief Executive Officer
Aneil Luhan, Vice President
Marissa Martin, Vice President
Mary Lee Montague, Executive Vice President
Brad Newpoff, Executive Vice President
Craig Randall, Office Managing Partner
James L. Schroeder, Executive Vice President
Nick Slee, Executive Vice President
Michelle Smead, Executive Vice President
Marcey Rubin Stamas, Senior Client Partner
Glenn Sugiyama, Executive Vice President
Also:
Ann Arbor, MI (734) 761-2630
Boyd Falconer, Managing Director
Atlanta, GA (678) 385-5000
Robert Baker, Executive Vice President
John Blank, Executive Vice President
Mona Bopanna, Executive Vice President
Robert C. Chandler, Executive Vice President
Brian McGowan, Managing Director
Donna Pratt, Executive Vice President
Robin Singleton, Executive Vice President
Clyde Stutts, Executive Vice President
Austin, TX (512) 328-6363
Lance Winn, Executive Vice President
Birmingham, MI (248) 258-0616
Douglas R. Allen, Executive Vice President
Patricia Watters Binkley, Executive Vice President
Jeffrey A. Evans, Executive Vice President
Boyd Falconer, Managing Director
Cyd F. Kinney, Executive Vice President
Calgary, AB (403) 262-7476
Jill Schofield, Executive Vice President
Carmel, CA (831) 620-6550
Adam Charlson, Vice President
Michael Kotelec, Executive Vice President
Pravesh Mehra, Vice President
Carmel, IN (317) 924-3712
Rick Brown, Executive Vice President & Managing Director
Charleston, SC (843) 579-1800
Jay Millen, Managing Director
Chevy Chase, MD (202) 362-2700
Julia Eakes, Executive Vice President
Stephen A. Hayes, Vice Chairman/President
Linda Madrid, Vice President
James Martin, Vice President
Cincinnati, OH (513) 762-7690
Ted Plattenburg, Executive Vice President
Denver, CO (303) 629-0730
Kristi LeBlanc, Executive Vice President
Martin M. Pocs, Vice Chairman & Managing Director
Franklin, TN (615) 732-6298
John Blank, Vice President
Houston, TX (713) 626-9494
Jeffery L. Smith, Executive Vice President
Rick Walker, Executive Vice President
Lansing, MI (517) 886-9010
Boyd Falconer, Managing Director
Merritt J. Norvell, Executive Vice President & Managing Director
Pat Richter, Executive Vice President & Managing Director
Gordon S. White, Executive Vice President & Managing Director
Los Angeles, CA (310) 789-7333
Adam D. Charlson, Executive Vice President
Julia Eakes, Executive Vice President
Bob Marchant, Executive Vice President
Miami, FL (786) 866-5400
Manuel Corsino, Executive Vice President & Managing Director
Milwaukee, WI (414) 456-0850
Dennis C. Hood, Vice Chairman & Managing Director
Minneapolis, MN (612) 343-0306
Clare Cizek, Executive Vice President
Laura Fries, Executive Vice President
Ronald Woessner, Vice President
Shawn P. Woessner, Executive Vice President
New York, NY (212) 883-6800
James Abruzzo, Executive Vice President
Keith Giarman, Global Leader of Venture Capital

Jeffrey Golove, Executive Vice President
Deborah Graf, Executive Vice President
Louis M. Hipp, Executive Vice President
Joseph C. Huddle, Executive Vice President
Donald M. Kilinski, Executive Vice President
Betrand Kimper, Vice President
Gayle Mattson, Executive Vice President
Pravesh Mehra, Vice President
Lawrence R. Noble, Executive Vice President
James L. Schroeder, Executive Vice President
Frank T. Spencer, Managing Director
Suzy Stewart, Executive Vice President
David Treussard, Executive Vice President
Palm Beach, FL (561) 429-8700
Victor Kleinman, Executive Vice President & Managing Director
Phoenix, AZ (602) 992-7810
David A. Bruno, Vice Chairman & Managing Director
Stuart Fiordalis, Executive Vice President
William R. Franquemont, Executive Vice President
Pittsburgh, PA (412) 261-1492
Joseph G. Christman, Executive Vice President & Managing Director
David P. Smith, Executive Vice President
Plano, TX (214) 347-8083
Sayres Dudley, Executive Vice President
Kirk Durossette, Vice President
Stacey Holland, Vice President
Princeton, NJ (609) 275-5900
Dan Carney, Executive Vice President & Managing Director
Jeffrey Golove, Executive Vice President & Managing Director
Bertrand Kimper, Vice President
Bonnie Sharps, Executive Vice President & Managing Director
Saint Louis, MO (314) 727-2000
Andy Cornwell, Executive Vice President & Managing Director
Philip DeFord, Executive Vice President & Managing Director
Steve Elias, Executive Vice President & Managing Director
Robert Godfrey, Executive Vice President & Managing Director
Scott Harris, Executive Vice President & Managing Director
David Hoffmann, Chairman
Nick Slee, Executive Vice President
Derrick Stewart, Vice President
San Francisco, CA (415) 617-6230
Adam Charlson, Executive Vice President
Sal DiFranco, Executive Vice President
Keith Giarman, Executive Vice President
Michael Kotelec, Executive Vice President
David Madden, Executive Vice President
Pravesh Mehra, Executive Vice President
John Spencer, Executive Vice President
Stamford, CT (203) 316-9004
Gayle Mattson, Executive Vice President
Tara McKernan, Executive Vice President
Toronto, ON (416) 941-8974
Robert Armstrong, Executive Vice President
Rives Dalley Hewitt, Executive Vice President
Sussannah Kelly, Executive Vice President
Rod Malcolm, Executive Vice President
Waltham, MA (781) 839-7055
John Baker, Executive Vice President & Managing Director
Diane Coletti, Executive Vice President & Managing Director

Dieck Executive Search

(Specialize in Midwestern Companies Generalist Firm)
30 Rough Lee Court
Madison, WI 53705
(608) 238-1000
dan@dieckexecutivesearch.com
www.dieckexecutivesearch.com
Dan Dieck, President & Chief Executive Officer

DiMarchi Partners, Inc.

P.O. Box 1147
Niwot, CO 80544
(303) 415-9300
paul@dimarchi.com
www.dimarchi.com
Paul M. DiMarchi, President

The Dinerstein Group

45 Rockerfeller Plaza, Suite 2000
New York, NY 10111
(212) 332-3224
jd@dinersteingroup.com
www.dinersteingroup.com
Jan Dinerstein, President
Also:
Stamford, CT (203) 222-7766
Jan Dinerstein, President

The Dingman Company, Inc.

650 Hampshire Road, Suite 116
Westlake Village, CA 91361-4211
(805) 778-1777
fax (805) 778-9288
resumes@dingman.com
www.dingman.com
H. Bruce Dingman, President

Dinte Resources, Inc.

8300 Greensboro Drive, Suite 750
McLean, VA 22102
(703) 448-3300
fax (703) 448-0215
dri@dinte.com
www.dinte.com
Paul Dinte, Chief Executive Officer

Diversified Search*

2005 Market Street, 33rd Floor
Philadelphia, PA 19103
(215) 732-6666
fax (215) 568-8399
resume@divsearch.com
www.divsearch.com
Judith M. von Seldeneck, Founder & Chairman
Mackie MacLean, Managing Partner
Also:
Atlanta, GA (404) 814-2330
J. Veronica Biggins, Managing Director
Kevin B. Kelly, Managing Director
Edward H. Shartar, Managing Director
Chicago, IL (312) 235-1996
Donald Clark, Managing Director
Julie Kanak, Managing Director
James D.S. Pruett, Managing Director
Henry J. Scherck, Managing Director
Miami, FL (305) 577-0046
Frederic Comins, Managing Director
Marjorie Kean, Managing Director
Lorena Keough, Managing Director
John Mestepey, Managing Director
Lauren E. Smith, Managing Director
New York, NY (212) 542-2575
Gerald F. Cattie, Managing Director
Hugo Fueglein, Managing Director
Tracy V. McMillan, Managing Director
Cheryl O'Cruz Young, Managing Director

Tracy O'Such, Managing Director
Harvey Schiller, Managing Director
Pasadena, CA (626) 535-0809
Kevin Chase, Managing Director
Stephen S. Morreale, Chief Operating Officer
San Francisco, CA (415) 445-9300
Betty Hasler, Managing Director
Tony Leng, Managing Director
Bart Penfold, Managing Director
Washington, DC (202) 540-8860
Jan Molino, Managing Director
Lonnie P. Taylor, Managing Director

The Domann Organization Inc.

(Specialize in Biotech & Life Sciences)
18270 Via De Santa Fe, Suite 100
Rancho **Santa Fe, CA** 92067
(858) 756-2127
cv@Domann.net
www.domann.net
William A. Domann, Founder & Cheif Executive Officer
Also:
Columbia, MD (410) 964-0236
William A. Domann, Founder & Cheif Executive Officer
Madison, WI (608) 441-8000
William A. Domann, Founder & Cheif Executive Officer
Palo Alto, CA (415) 726-9704
William A. Domann, Founder & Cheif Executive Officer

Donahue/Patterson Associates, Inc.

8833 Elm Valley Road
Union Pier, MI 49129
(312) 732-0999
info@donahuepatterson.com
www.donahuepatterson.com
Mick E.M. Donahue, Partner
Buzz Patterson, Partner
Also:
Chicago, MI (312) 622-8585
Eric Douglas Keene, Partner

Dougan & Associates

(Specialize in Petroleum Industry)
1400 Woodloch Forest Drive, Suite 425
Woodlands, TX 77380
(281) 999-7209
fax (281) 405-5580
dougansearch@comcast.net
www.dougansearch.com
David W Dougan, President

Steven Douglas Associates

1301 International Parkway, Suite 510
Fort Lauderdale, FL 33323
(954) 385-8595
fax (954) 385-1414
mshore@stevendouglas.com
www.stevendouglas.com
Matt Shore, President
Also:
Los Angeles, CA (213) 261-0785
Linda Harper, Managing Director
Minneapolis, MN (952) 913-2235
Karen Melby, Managing Director
New York, NY (646) 926-0220
Jon Bolton, Managing Director
Omaha, NE (954) 385-8595
Jonathon Duncan, Managing Director
Orlando, FL (954) 540-3777
Tammy Curtis, Partner
Tampa, FL (813) 909-4200
Tammy Curtis, Partner

Dowd Associates*

(Specialize in Finance & Treasury)
777 Westchester Avenue, Suite 120
White Plains, NY 10604
(914) 251-1515
fax (914) 251-1321
mail@dowdassociates.com
www.dowdassociates.com
Richard Dowd, President

James Drury Partners

The John Hancock Center
875 N. Michigan Avenue, Suite 3805
Chicago, IL 60611
(312) 654-6708
fax (312) 654-6710
resume@jdrurypartners.com
www.jdrurypartners.com
James J. Drury, Chairman & Chief Executive Officer

J. H. Dugan & Company

(Specialize in Plastics Industry)
225 The Crossroads Boulevard, Suite 415
Carmel, CA 93923
(800) 254-3396
fax (888) 530-5670
plastic-recruiter@jhdugan.com
www.jhdugan.com
John H. Dugan, Chairman

Dunlap & Sullivan Associates

(Specialize in Sales & Marketing Positions)
29 Pearl Street Northwest, Suite 125
Grand Rapids, MI 49503
(616) 458-4142
fax (616) 458-4203
dunsul@aol.com
www.dunsul.com
John P. Sullivan, President

Marci Dwyer Executive Search

935 Harmony Hill Road
West Chester, PA 19380
(610) 873-4734
mdexs@comcast.net
www.marcidwyerexecutivesearch.com
Marci Dwyer, Principal

Dynamic Synergy Corporation

600 Entrada Drive, Building B
Santa Monica, CA 90402
(650) 493-2000
info@dynamicsynergy.com
www.dynamicsynergy.com
Mark J. Landay, Managing Director

Early Cochran & Olson, LLC

(Specialize in Lawyers)
One East Wacker Drive, Suite 2510
Chicago, IL 60601
(312) 595-4200
fax (312) 595-4209
cc@ecollc.com
www.ecollc.com
Corinne Cochran, Principal
B. Tucker Olson, Principal

Eastman & Beaudine, Inc.

(Specialize in Sports & Entertainment)
7201 Bishop Road, Suite 220
Plano, TX 75024
(972) 312-1012
fax (972) 312-1020
ceo@eastman-beaudine.com
www.eastman-beaudine.com
Robert E. Beaudine, President & CEO

Education Search Services

(Specialize in Higher Education)
1740 Oxmoor Road, Suite A
Birmingham, AL 35209

(800) 448-0926
fax (205) 870-1553
inquire@whelesspartners.com
Michael Wheless, Practice Leader
Kevin Arvin, Academic Administrator
Mabry Smith, Senior Partner

Edwards Consulting Firm, Inc.

2871-D North Decatur Road, Suite 171
Decatur, GA 30033
(404) 288-8824
resumes@edwardsconsultingfirm.com
www.edwardsconsultingfirm.com
Damali Edwards, President

Edwards Executive Search, LLC

(SPECIALIZE IN Manufacturing, Construction, Distribution, Utilities & Energy)
111 East Chestnut, Suite 25DE
Chicago, IL 60611
(800) 453-2570
contact@edwards-search.com
www.edwards-search.com
W. Lynton Edwards, Founding Partner

EFL Associates

11440 Tomahawk Creek Parkway
Leawood, KS 66211
(913) 234-1560
eflinfo@eflassociates.com
www.eflassociates.com
Jason M. Meschke, President
Also:
Denver, CO (720) 200-7000
Mary Hobson, Executive Vice President & Managing Director

The Elliot Company

439 Church Street
Mt. **Pleasant, SC** 29464
(843) 388-0900
suppt.staff@elliottco.net
www.elliottco.net
Roger S. Elliot, President

The Elliot Group LLC

(SPECIALIZE IN Hospitality, Food Service & Manufacturing)
Tarrytown Corporate Center
505 White Plains Road, Suite 228
Tarrytown, NY 10591
(914) 631-4904
fax (914) 631-6481
www.theelliotgroup.com
Alice Elliot, Chief Executive Officer

Also:
Alpharetta, GA (770) 664-5354
Joan Ray, Executive Vice President
Austin, TX (512) 454-0477
Troy Erb, Vice President

Elwell & Associates

3100 West Liberty Street, Suite E
Ann Arbor, MI 48103
(248) 488-9750
fax (248) 488-9751
elwellas@elwellassociates.com
Steve Elwell, President

Empire International

1147 Lancaster Avenue
Berwyn, PA 19312
(610) 647-7976
fax (610) 647-8488
info@empire-internl.com
www.empire-internl.com
Victor Combe, President

Epsen, Fuller / IMD International Search Group*

(SPECIALIZE IN Consumer Products, Retail, Technology/ Telecom, Life Sciences, Finance)
Jockey Hollow Park
5 Cold Hill Road, Suite 20
Mendham, NJ 07945
(973) 387-4900
fax (973) 359-9928
info@epsenfuller.com
www.epsenfuller.com
Thomas J. Fuller, General Managing Partner
Also:
New York, NY (212) 619-0089
Thomas J. Fuller, General Managing Partner
San Francisco, CA (415) 773-2819
Thomas J. Fuller, General Managing Partner

ESGI Executive Search Consultants

(SPECIALIZE IN Technology)
445 Shady Lane
Huntingdon Valley, PA 19006
(610) 834-0277
fax (610) 834-9845
resumes@esgisearch.com
esgisearch.com
Evan Scott, President
Donald H. Janssen, Managing Director
Also:
Washington, DC (202) 842-0441
Robert M. Russell, Managing Partner

ET Search, Inc.

(SPECIALIZE IN Tax Specialists)
1250 Prospect Street
P.O. Box 2389
La Jolla, CA 92038
(858) 459-3443
fax (858) 459-4147
ets@etsearch.com
www.etsearch.com
Kathleen Jennings, President

Ethos Consulting Inc.

3219 East Camelback Road, Suite 515
Phoenix, AZ 85018
(480) 296-3801
fax (480) 664-7270
conrad@ethosconsulting.com
www.ethosconsulting.com
Conrad E. Prusak, President

EWK International

2839 Paces Ferry Road, Suite 1165
Atlanta, GA 30339
(770) 405-8333
atlanta@ewki.com
www.ewki.com
Charles Chalk, Managing Partner

Executive Resources International, LLC

63 Atlantic Avenue
Boston, MA 02110
(617) 742-8970
resumes@erisearch.net
www.erisearch.net
John C. Jay, Managing Director
John C. Mechem, Partner

Executive Search International

1525 Centre Street
Newton, MA 02461
(617) 527-8787
info@execsearchintl.com
www.execsearchintl.com
Les Gore, Managing Partner

The Executive Source, Inc.

(SPECIALIZE IN Human Resources)
55 Fifth Avenue
New York, NY 10003
(212) 691-5505
fax (212) 691-9839
tes1@executivesource.com
www.executivesource.com
Sarah J. Marks, Principal
Michael A. Brown, Managing

Director
Richard C. Plazza, Principal

EXI, Inc.

(Specialize in Technology, Financial Services, Diversity, Marketing, HR)
3340 Peachtree Road North East
Post Office Box 191468
Atlanta, GA 31119
(404) 262-2952
fax (404) 262-0932
resumes@exicareers.com
www.exicareers.com
Lance Coachman, Principal

The Ferneborg Group*

1700 South El Camino Real, Suite 410
San Mateo, CA 94402
(650) 577-0100
fax (650) 577-0122
resume@execsearch.com
www.execsearch.com
John R. Ferneborg, Senior Partner
John W. Ferneborg, Managing Partner

Fiderion Financial Services Group

(Specialize in Financial Services)
3280 Peachtree Road NW, Suite 2625
Atlanta, GA 30305
(404) 995-4700
fax (404) 995-4701
resumes@fiderion.com
www.fiderion.com
James B. Norton, President &Chief Executive Officer
Todd A. Stratton, Partner
Also:
Cleveland, OH (216) 241-0158
Glenn Anderson, Managing Director
Glenn G. Anderson, Partner
New York, NY (646) 502-7170
Jennifer Powell, Partner
San Francisco, CA (415) 293-8577
Jeff Campbell, Managing Director

Filcro Media Staffing

(Specialize in Broadcasting & Media)
521 Fifth Avenue
New York, NY 10175
(212) 599-0909
fax (212) 599-1023
mail@executivesearch.tv
www.executivesearch.tv/
Tony Filson, President and Chief Executive Officer

Eileen Finn & Associates

230 Park Avenue, 10th Floor
New York, NY 10169
(212) 687-1260
fax (212) 551-1473
eileen@eileenfinn.com
www.eileenfinn.com
Eileen Finn, President

Howard Fischer Associates International

(Specialize in Information Technology)
1800 Kennedy Boulevard, Suite 700
Philadelphia, PA 19103
(215) 568-8363
fax (215) 568-4815
search@hfischer.com
www.hfischer.com
Howard M. Fischer, President and Chief Executive Officer
Adam J. Fischer, Managing Partner
John Kuper, Partner
Also:
Boston, MA (617) 956-6805
Jeff Disandro, Partner
Campbell, CA (408) 374-0580
Drew Hoffman, Partner

Fischer Group International, Inc.

Building A
296 Country Club Road, Second Floor
Avon, CT 06001
(860) 404-7700
fax (860) 404-7799
info@fischergroupintl.com
www.fischergroupintl.com
John C. Fischer, President

Fisher Personnel Management Services

2351 N. Filbert Road
Exeter, CA 93221
(559) 594-5774
fax (559) 594-5777
HookMe@Fisheads.net
www.fisheads.net
Neal Fisher, Principal
Judy Gibson, Principal

FitzDrake Search, Inc.

47293 Middle Bluff Place,Suite201
Sterling, VA 20165
(703) 433-0220
www.fitzdrakesearch.com
Michael Drake, Partner
Bill Fitzgerald, Partner

Fitzgerald Associates Executive Search

(Specialize in Healthcare)
24 Beaman Lane
North Falmouth, MA 02556
(508) 563-2732
info@fitzsearch.com
www.fitzsearch.com
Geoffrey Fitzgerald, President

Fleming Associates of New Orleans

3850 North Causeway Boulevard, Suite 630
Metairie, LA 70002
(504) 836-7090
David W. McClung, Managing Partner

Foley Proctor Yoskowitz LLC

(Specialize in Health Care)
One Cattano Avenue
Morristown, NJ 07960
(973) 605-1000
fax (973) 605-1020
resume@fpysearch.com
www.fpysearch.com
Thomas J. Foley, Senior Partner
Reggie Yoskowitz, Senior Partner

L. W. Foote Company

301 116th Avenue SE, Suite 105
P.O. Box 52762
Bellevue, WA 98015
(425) 451-1660
fax (425) 451-1535
email@lwfoote.com
www.lwfoote.com
Leland W. Foote, Founder
Dwayne S. Foote, President

Francis & Associates*

6923 Vista Drive
West **Des Moines, IA** 50266
(515) 221-9800
fax (515) 221-9806
knovak@fa-search.com
www.fa-search.com
Dwaine Francis, Managing Partner
Karen Novak Swalwell, Executive Vice President

KS Frary & Associates, Inc.
16 Schooner Ridge
Marblehead, MA 01945
(781) 631-2464
fax (617) 710-9039
ksfrary@comcast.net
www.ksfrary.com
Kevin S. Frary, President

Furst Group/MPI
(SPECIALIZE IN Health Care)
2902 McFarland Road, Suite 100
Rockford, IL 61107
(800) 642-9940
fax (877) 642-9930
furstgroup@furstgroup.com
www.furstgroup.com
Dennis L. Pankratz, Principal
Sherrie L. Barch, President
Also:
Chicago, IL (800) 642-9940
Kevin Reddy, Vice President
Minneapolis, MN (800) 642-9940
Pete Eisenbarth, Vice President
Phoenix, AZ (800) 642-9940
Dan Ford, Vice President
San Francisco, CA (800) 642-9940
Dan Ford, Vice President
Washington, DC (800) 642-9940
Deanna L. Banks, Principal

Gaffney Management Consultants, Inc.
(SPECIALIZE IN Manufacturing & Industrial)
6 Woodshole Court
Henderson, NV 89052
(847) 592-3220
fax (702) 614-5198
info@gaffneyinc.com
www.gaffneyinc.com
Bill Gaffney, President

Jay Gaines & Company, Inc.*
(SPECIALIZE IN Finance & MIS)
767 Third Avenue, 27th Floor
New York, NY 10017
(212) 308-9222
fax (212) 308-5146
jgandco@jaygaines.com
www.jaygaines.com
Jay Gaines, President

D Gallagher, LLC
1281 Gulf of Mexico Drive, Suite 606
Longboat Key, FL 34228
(941) 387-0755
dgallagher@dgallagherllc.com
www.dgallagherllc.com
David W. Gallagher, Partner

Gans, Gans & Associates, Inc.
7445 Quail Meadow Road
Plant City, FL 33565
(813) 986-4441
fax (813) 986-4775
resumes@gansgans.com
www.gansgans.com
Simone Gans Barefield, President & CEO

The Garms Group, Inc.
(SPECIALIZE IN High Tech)
830 West Route 22, Suite 250
Lake Zurich, IL 60047
(847) 382-7200
dangarms@garms.com
www.garms.com
Daniel S. Garms, Managing Director

Garrett Associates, Inc.
(SPECIALIZE IN Healthcare)
3685 Peachtree Road, Suite 13
Atlanta, GA 30319
(404) 364-0001
fax (404) 231-9884
ABingham@GarrettAssociatesInc.com
www.garrettassociatesinc.com
Linda Garrett, Principal

Garrett Search Partners, LLC
(SPECIALIZE IN Manufacturing & Professional Services)
200 South Wacker Drive, Suite 3100
Chicago, IL 60606
(312) 224-8417
fax (312) 224-8033
resumes@garrettsearch.com
www.garrettsearch.com
Chelsea A. Garrett, President & CEO

Genesis Executive*
(SPECIALIZE IN Energy Industry)
5th Avenue Southwest, Suite 1800
Calgary, AB T2P 3R7
(403) 237-8622
fax (403) 233-7622
info@genesisexecutive.ca
www.genesisexecutive.ca/
Trish Hines, President

Gilbert Tweed International
415 Madison Avenue, 20th Floor
New York, NY 10017-1111
(212) 758-3000
fax (212) 832-1040
www.gilberttweed.com
Stephanie L. Pinson, President
Karen L. DelPrete, Managing Partner
Janet Tweed, Chief Executive Officer & Co-Founder
Also:
Alexandria, VA (703) 763-4216
David Beed, Managing Director
East Lansing, MI (517) 339-9009
Ken Glickman, Managing Director
Houston, TX (713) 517-8314
Matthew Hiller, Managing Director
Laguna Beach, CA (949) 281-7339
Theresa Bastedo, Managing Director
Wellesley, MA (617) 784-4958
Neil Greco, Managing Director

Global Sage*
(SPECIALIZE IN Finance, Investment Banking, Asset Management)
2 Rector Street, Suite 408
New York, NY 10006
(646) 557-3000
fax (646) 557-3099
americas@globalsage.com
www.globalsage.com
Ann Knight, President

Susan Goldberg Executive Search Consulting*
(SPECIALIZE IN Mktg, Sales, B.D, Prog., Production in Entertainment)
360 East 88th Street, Suite 12C
New York, NY 10128
(212) 876-7100
susan@susangoldbergsearch.com
www.susangoldbergsearch.com
Susan Goldberg, President

Goodrich & Sherwood Executive Search*
52 Vanderbilt Avenue, Suite 501
New York, NY 10017
(212) 808-0400
resume@goodsher.com
www.goodsher.com
Charles D. Wright, Managing Partner
Andrew Sherwood, Managing Partner

Goodwin & Company
P.O. Box 33036
Washington, DC 20033
(202) 785-9292
fax (202) 785-9297
tom@goodwinco.com
www.goodwinco.com
Tom L. Goodwin, President

Goodwin Executive Search
766 Whitaker Mill Road
Raleigh, NC 27608
(919) 424-7902
info@goodwinsearch.com
www.goodwinsearch.com
Bill Goodwin, Principal

The Goodwin Group
5555 Glenridge Connector, Suite 200
Atlanta, GA 30342
(770) 436-3410
fax (770) 436-3722
contact@goodwin-group.com
www.goodwin-group.com
Joe D. Goodwin, President & Chief Executive Officer

The Governance Group, Inc.
33 Union Place, 3rd Floor
Summit, NJ 07901
(908) 277-1800
fax (908) 277-4445
resumes@governancegroup.com
www.governancegroup.com
Gary Kastenbaum, Managing Director
Steven N. Schrenzel, Managing Director

Gow & Partners
570 Lexington Avenue, 18th Floor
New York, NY 10022
(212) 753-7568
fax (212) 753-0204
roddy.gow@gowpartners.com
www.gowpartners.com
Roddy Gow, Chairman

A. Davis Grant & Company
(SPECIALIZE IN MIS & INFORMATION TECHNOLOGY)
13 Lake Park Drive
Piscataway, NJ 08854
(732) 463-1414
fax (732) 463-1824
info@adg.net
www.adg.net
Allan D. Grossman, Senior Partner

Grant Cooper & Associates
One North Brentwood, Suite 610
Saint Louis, MO 63105
(314) 726-5291
fax (314) 726-5294
resume@grantcooper.com
www.grantcooper.com
Carrie Hackett, Managing Partner
Susan Cejka, Managing Partner
Ronald J. Chod, Managing Partner
J. Dale Meier, Managing Partner

Grantham & Co. Inc.
2465 Foxwood Drive
Chapel Hill, NC 27514-6801
(919) 932-5650
fax (919) 942-1624
grantham@granthamco.com
www.searchforintegrity.com
John D. Grantham, President

Greenwich Harbor Partners*
(SPECIALIZE IN MEDIA AND ENTERTAINMENT)
330 Madison Avenue, 6th Floor
New York, NY 10017
(212) 572-8353
info@greenwichharborpartners.com
www.greenwichharborpartners.com
Carrie Pryor, Managing Partner

Jack Groban & Associates
445 South Figueroa Street, Suite 2600
P.O. Box 480555
Los Angeles, CA 90048
(213) 627-6818
fax (213) 612-7797
jack@jackgroban.com
www.jackgroban.com
Jack Groban, President

Grossberg & Associates
(SPECIALIZE IN MANUFACTURING & DISTRIBUTION)
805 West Fitzhenry Court
Glenwood, IL 60425
(630) 574-0066
bobgsearch@aol.com
Robert M. Grossberg, Managing Partner

Groupe Hebert
Drummond Street, Suite 3431
Montreal, QC H3G 1X6
(514) 876-1076
fax (514) 876-9158
cv@groupehebert.com
Guy Hebert, President

Gundersen Partners, L.L.C.
(SPECIALIZE IN MARKETING & GENERAL MANAGEMENT)
30 Irving Place, 2nd Floor
New York, NY 10003
(212) 677-7660
fax (212) 358-0275
esteffen@gpllc.com
www.gundersenpartners.com
Steven Gundersen, Chief Executive Officer
Also:
San Francisco, CA
(415) 441-3777
Neil Fink, Managing Director

Gustin Partners Ltd.
(SPECIALIZE IN INFORMATION TECHNOLOGY)
The Ware Mill
2276 Washington Street
Newton **Lower Falls, MA** 02462-1452
(617) 332-0800
fax (617) 332-0882
info@gustinpartners.com
www.gustinpartners.com
Charles A. Gustin, Chairman & Chief Executive Officer

Hadley Lockwood, Inc.
(SPECIALIZE IN HEDGE FUNDS)
501 Madison Avenue, 5th Floor
New York, NY 10022
(212) 785-4405
fax (212) 785-4415
resumes@hadleyconsulting.com
www.hadleyconsulting.com
Irwin Brandon, President
George V. McGough, President

Hailes & Associates
(SPECIALIZE IN TECHNOLOGY & GENERAL MANAGEMENT)
257 The Prado
Atlanta, GA 30309
(404) 876-7715
fax (404) 892-7142
info@hailes.com
www.hailes.com
Brian Hailes, President

Halbrecht Lieberman Associates, Inc.
(SPECIALIZE IN SENIOR LEVEL INFORMATION TECHNOLOGY EXECUTIVES ONLY)

32 Surf Road, Suite A
Westport, CT 06880
(203) 222-4890
fax (203) 222-4895
info@hlassoc.com
www.hlassoc.com
Beverly Lieberman, President

Hampton Consulting, LLC

(SPECIALIZE IN Investment Industry)
6080 Center Drive, Suite 600
Los Angeles, CA 90045
(310) 823-1850
fax (310) 822-1216
resumes@hamptonsearch.com
www.hamptonsearch.com
Lynn A. Williams, President

Handler & Associates, Inc.

Building 1500
2255 Cumberland Parkway SE
Atlanta, GA 30339
(770) 805-5000
fax (770) 805-5011
resume@handler.com
www.handler.com
Eric Handler, Founding Partner
William A. Smyth, Senior Partner
Allen Tansil, Founding Partner

Handy Associates Corp.

420 Lexington Avenue, Suite 1644
New York, NY 10170
(212) 697-5600
fax (212) 697-8547
info@handypartners.com
Gaffney J. Feskoe, Partner
Patrick J. Brennan, Managing Partner

Bente Hansen Executive Search

12707 High Bluff Drive, 2nd Floor
San Diego, CA 92130
(858) 350-4330
fax (760) 634-1533
www.bentehansen.com
Bente Hansen, Managing Director

Harris Search Associates

4236 Tuller Road, Suite 2 South
Dublin, OH 43017
(614) 798-8500
fax (614) 798-8588
info@harrisandassociates.com
www.harrisandassociates.com
Jeffrey G. Harris, Managing Partner

Harvard Aimes Group

(SPECIALIZE IN Corporate Risk Management & Safety Claims Management)
6 Holcomb Street
P. O. Box 16006
West Haven, CT 06516
(203) 933-1976
fax (203) 933-0281
JJG1@riskmanagementsearch.com
www.riskmanagementsearch.com
James J. Gunther, Principal

Haskell & Stern Associates Inc.

380 Madison Avenue, 7th Floor
New York, NY 10017
(212) 856-4451
Allan D. R. Stern, Managing Director

Healthcare Management Group, Inc.

(SPECIALIZE IN Healthcare)
10320 Howe Lane
Leawood, KS 66206
(913) 207-0022
fax (913) 648-6936
www.hmg.jobs/
Rita Johnson, Principal

Heath/Norton Associates, Inc.

301 Crocus Court, Suite 7L
Datyon, NJ 08810
(732) 329-4663
hnsearch@aol.com
Richard S. Stoller, Managing Partner

Hechkoff Executive Search Inc.

(SPECIALIZE IN Professional Services, IT, Public & Investor Relations)
51 East 42nd Street, Suite 500
New York, NY 10017
(212) 935-2100
fax (212) 935-2199
search@hechkoff.com
www.hechkoff.com
Robert B. Hechkoff, President & Founder

Heidrick & Struggles International, Inc.*

Sears Tower
233 South Wacker Drive, Suite 7000
Chicago, IL 60606-6402
(312) 496-1000
fax (312) 496-1048
chicago@heidrick.com
www.heidrick.com
Patricia J. Coleman, Partner
Chicago, IL (312) 496-1000
John Abele, Managing Partner
Stephen W. Beard, Executive Vice President
Brad S. Berke, Managing Partner
Carlos F. Cata, Partner
Shannon Marie Connors, Partner
Billy Dexter, Partner
Theodore L. Dysart, Vice Chairman
Torrey N. Foster, Partner
John T. Gardner, Vice Chairman
Jonathan M. Graham, Partner
Katherine M. Graham, Managing Partner
Bo Herbst, Partner
Catherine A. Lepard, Partner
Michael J. Loiacano, Partner
Tom Moran, Practice Leader Insurance
Mark Nadler, Partner
Richard Pehlke, Chief Financial Officer
Dale M. Visokey, Partner
Charles E. Wallace, Partner
Also:
Atlanta, GA (404) 682-7400
Charles E. Commander, Partner
M. Evan Lindsay, Vice Chairman
William A. Matthews, Partner
George F. Norton, Partner and Practice Leader Technology
Clifford F. Wright, Managing Partner
Boston, MA (617) 737-6300
Darren C. Cinti, Partner
Michael M. Cullen, Regional Managing Partner
Rebecca Foreman Janjec, Partner
Stuart H. Sadick, Partner
Dallas, TX (214) 706-7700
Matrice Ellis-Kirk, Partner
Kay M. Fuhrman, Partner
Greg Konstans, Partner
Madelaine Pfau, Partner
Denver, CO (720) 932-3839
Ronald J. Brown, Regional Managing Partner
Houston, TX (713) 237-9000
Les T. Csorba, Partner
Mark H. Livingston, Partner
David A. Morris, Partner
Los Angeles, CA (213) 625-8811
Michelle Bonoan, Partner
Richard N. Eidinger, Partner
Jeannie Finkel, Partner
Stephanie Mica Goldsmith, Partner
Jim Hart, President
David L. Vied, Regional Managing Partner
Kathy Vrabeck, Partner

Menlo Park, CA (650) 234-1500
Keith Deussing, Partner
Rebecca Foreman Janic, Partner
Jason A. Kranz, Partner
Michael Nieset, Partner
Tim O'Shea, Partner
John P. Strackhouse, Partner
John T. Thompson, Vice Chairman
Miami, FL (305) 262-9246
Shannon Marie Connors, Partner
Guy M. Cote, Partner
Gerald R. Roche, Senior Chairman
Minneapolis, MN (612) 215-6900
Jeremy C. Hanson, Managing Partner
Jason L. Waterman, Partner
New York, NY (212) 867-9876
Jean Allen, Partner
Jean-Louis Alpeyrie, Partner
Chad Astmann, Partner
Paul W. Benson, Partner
David Boehmer, Regional Managing Partner
Lyn Brennan, Partner
Jeffrey Cohn, Partner
Scott Estill, Partner
Elizabeth R. Ewing, Partner
Valerie E. Germain, Managing Partner
Paul Gibson, Partner
Jonathan Goldstein, Partner
Bonnie W. Gwin, Vice Chairman
Lorraine Hack, Partner
Lee Hanson, Vice Chairman
John Hewins, Partner
Timothy L. Holt, Managing Partner
Theodore Jadick, Vice Chairman
David S. Joys, Partner
John Kim, Partner
John E. Lee, Practice Leader Financial Services
Jory J. Marino, Regional Managing Partner
Todd R. Monti, Managing Partner
Michael Nieset, Partner
Anne Lim O'Brien, Vice Chairman
Rusty O'Kelley, Regional Managing Partner
Jim Penny, Partner
Chris Pierce-Cooke, Partner
Vicotria Reese, Managing Partner
Gerard R. Roche, Senior Chairman
Rich Rosen, Partner
Daniel T. Ryan, Partner
Jeffrey S. Sanders, Vice Chairman
Phil Schneidermeyer, Partner
Lynne Seid, Partner
Michael J. Speck, Partner
John Strackhouse, Partner
Nathaniel J. Sutton, Vice Chairman
Todd Taylor, Partner
John T. Thompson, Vice Chairman
John S. Wood, Vice Chairman
Philadelphia, PA (215) 988-1000
Robert J. Atkins, Partner
Keith E. Deussing, Partner
Michele C. Heid, Partner
Guy Sava, Partner
John P. Strackhouse, Partner
San Francisco, CA (415) 981-2854
Ron Brown, Partner
Lauren M. Doliva, Managing Partner
Lee Hanson, Vice Chairman
John Hewins, Partner
John M. Hewins, Partner
Kelly O. Kay, Partner
Eric Olson, Managing Partner
Mary Saxon, Partner
Carolyn Vavrek, Partner
Toronto, ON (416) 361-4700
Rose N. Baker, Managing Partner
Catherine A. Lepard, Partner
Andrea Waines, Partner
Washington, DC (202) 331-4900
Matthew C. Aiello, Parter
Donald S. Biskin, Partner
Daniel Edwards, Managing Partner
Michael J. Flagg, Partner
Julien Ha, Practice Leader Legal Practice
Joseph C. Haberman, Managing Partner
Randy Jayne, Partner
Dale E. Jones, Vice Chairman
Eric Joseph, Partner
Krishnan Rajagopalan, Managing Partner

J. Brad Herbeck, Inc.

1860 West Winchester Road, Suite 109
Libertyville, IL 60048
(847) 247-1400
brad@jbradherbeck.com
www.jbradherbeck.com
J. Brad Herbeck, President

Herbert Mines Associates, Inc.*

(SPECIALIZE IN BEAUTY, FASHION, RETAIL, CONSUMER GOODS)
600 Lexington Avenue, Second Floor
New York, NY 10022
(212) 355-0909
hma@herbertmines.com
www.herbertmines.com
Harold D. Reiter, Chairman & Chief Executive Officer

HFC Executive Search

Building III
919 Conestroga Road, Suite 214
Rosemont, PA 19010
(610) 527-3100
fax (610) 527-3184
execsearch@hfcsearch.com
www.hfcsearch.com
I. H. Chip Clothier, Managing Partner
John R. Fell, Managing Partner
Edward R. Walsh, Managing Partner

Higdon Partners*

(SPECIALIZE IN INVESTMENT MANAGEMENT)
230 Park Avenue, Suite 951
New York, NY 10169
(212) 986-4662
fax (212) 986-5002
info@hbm-llc.com
www.hbm-llc.com
Henry G. Higdon, Managing Partner
Jane Bierwirth, Managing Partner
Maryann Bovich, Partner
Edward Fowler, Managing Partner
Also:
Charlottesville, VA (434) 977-0061
Edward Fowler, Managing Partner

Hire Consulting Services

2647 Gateway Road, #105-305
Carlsbad, CA 92009
(760) 230-4301
info@hireconsultant.com
www.hireconsultant.com
Mark James, President & CEO

Hobbs & Towne, Inc.

(SPECIALIZE IN ENERGY & CLEAN TECH, IT, LIFE SCIENCES, MANUFACTURING)
PMB 269
P.O. Box 987
Valley Forge, PA 19482
(610) 783-4600
fax (610) 783-4511
info@hobbstowne.com
www.hobbstowne.com
Robert B. Hobbs, Managing Partner & Executive Vice President
Kevin Brown, Senior Partner
Steve Kyryk, Partner
Roland Olsen, Senior Partner
Marc Salamone, Partner
Andrew F. Towne, President
Also:
Menlo Park, CA (650) 461-4576
Dan Cremins, Partner
Teague Splaine, Partner
New York, NY (646) 624-9772
Stephen Bishop, Vice President
San Francisco, CA (415) 963-3838
Wes Goldstein, Senior Partner

Toronto, ON (416) 975-9187
Bart Tichelman, Partner

Hodges Partners

(SPECIALIZE IN Healthcare)
100 Highland Park Village, Suite 200
Dallas, TX 75205
(214) 902-7900
jannah@hodgespartners.com
www.hodgespartners.com
Jannah Hodges, Managing Director

Harvey Hohauser & Associates, LLC

5600 New King Street, Suite 355
Troy, MI 48098
(248) 641-1400
fax (248) 641-1929
information@hohauser.com
www.hohauser.com
Harvey R. Hohauser, Chief Executive Officer
Todd Hohauser, President

The Holman Group, Inc.*

(SPECIALIZE IN CEOs, Venture Capital Partners, Information Technology)
1592 Union Street
San Francisco, CA 94123
(415) 441-6500
fax (415) 358-9000
jsh@holmangroup.net
www.holmangroup.net
Jonathan S. Holman, President

J. B. Homer Associates Inc.

(SPECIALIZE IN Information Technology)
708 Third Avenue, Floor 22
New York, NY 10017
(212) 697-3300
fax (212) 986-5086
info@JBHomer.com
www.JBHomer.com
Judy B. Homer, President

Horgan Splaine Partners

111 West Saint John Street, Suite 910
San Jose, CA 95113
(408) 971-4000
www.horgansplaine.com
Bryan McDougall, Partner

Hornberger Management Company

(SPECIALIZE IN Construction & Real Estate Development)
One Commerce Center, 7th Floor
Wilmington, DE 19801
(302) 573-2541
fax (302) 371-5771
hmc@hmc.com
www.hmc.com
Frederick C. Hornberger, President

Horton International, LLC

Town Center
29 South Main Street, Suite 327
West Hartford, CT 06107
(860) 521-0101
fax (860) 521-0140
www.horton-usa.com
Larry C. Brown, Managing Partner
Also:
New York, NY (860) 521-0101
Larry C. Brown, Managing Director
Robert J. Gilchrist, Managing Director
West Hartford, CT
(860) 521-0101
Robert J. Gilchrist, Managing Partner
Westtown, PA (484) 467-1658
Andy Foy, Principal Consultant
Wilmette, IL (224) 216-9295
Deborah Snow Walsh, Managing Director

Howe-Lewis International

(SPECIALIZE IN Health Care)
450 Seventh Avenue, Suite 2009
New York, NY 10123
(212) 697-5000
fax (212) 697-6600
howelewis@howe-lewis.com
www.howe-lewis.com
Patricia Anne Greco, Co-Managing Director
Ester Rosenberg, Co-Managing Director

HRD Consultants, Inc.*

(SPECIALIZE IN Human Resources)
1812 Front Street
Scotch Plains, NJ 07076
(908) 228-5500
fax (908) 322-8961
hrd@aol.com
www.hrdconsultants.com
Marcia Glatman, President

E. A. Hughes & Company

(SPECIALIZE IN Apparel & Home Fashion)
200 Park Avenue South, Suite 1608
New York, NY 10003
(212) 689-4600
fax (212) 689-4975
hr@eahughes.com
www.eahughes.com
Elaine A. Hughes, President & Founder

Hunt Howe Partners LLC*

170 Mason Street
Greenwich, CT 06830
(203) 661-1600
fax (203) 340-2738
whowe@hunthowe.com
www.hunthowe.com
James E. Hunt, Partner
William S. Howe, Partner
Jeff G. Neuberth, Partner
Sandra K. Rupp, Partner

Michael Hunter & Associates

(SPECIALIZE IN Technology)
1999 South Bascom Avenue, Suite 700
Campbell, CA 95008
(925) 249-0900
fax (925) 249-0700
admin@michaelhunterassociates.com
www.michaelhunterassociates.com
Michael Hunter, President

Hutchinson Group Inc.

260 Adelaide Street East, Suite 100
Toronto, ON M5A 1N1
(416) 499-6621
search@hutchgroup.com
www.hutchgroup.com
H. David Hutchinson, President

HVS International*

(SPECIALIZE IN Hospitality Industry)
369 Willis Avenue
Mineola, NY 11501
(516) 248-8828
fax (516) 742-3059
kkefgen@hvsinternational.com
www.hvs.com
Keith Kefgen, President HVS Executive Search

I.S.T. Company

(SPECIALIZE IN Healthcare, Biotech, Pharma)
900 Springwood Drive
Conroe, TX 77385
(281) 292-8188
jim@biotechsearch.net
www.biotechsearch.net

Jim Giammatteo, President & COO

IDEALWAVE SOLUTIONS*
(SPECIALIZE IN WIRELESS INDUSTRY)
580 Putnam Avenue
Cambridge, MA 02139
(603) 512-4944
www.idealwave.com
Mark Newhall, Managing Director

INGENIUM PARTNERS, INC.
10880 Baur Boulevard
St. **Louis, MO** 63132
(314) 991-8007
fax (314) 991-8710
jiffrig@ingeniumpartners.com
www.ingeniumpartners.com
Susan Goldenberg, President
Linda Bearman, Partner

INTEGRE PARTNERS, LTD.
500 North Michigan, Suite 300
Chicago, IL 60611
(312) 488-4848
fax (312) 819-5924
info@integrepartners.com
www.integrepartners.com
Ralph E. Dieckmann, Managing Director

ISAACSON, MILLER
263 Summer Street
Boston, MA 02210
(617) 262-6500
fax (617) 986-7101
info@imsearch.com
www.imsearch.com
John M. Isaacson, Managing Director
Arnie Miller, Partner & Founder
Also:
San Francisco, CA
(415) 655-4900
David Bellshaw, Vice President & Director
Washington, DC (202) 682-1504
Jane Gruenebaum, Vice President
Barbara R. Stevens, Vice President & Director

JBK ASSOCIATES, INC.
(SPECIALIZE IN PHARMACEUTICAL & CONSUMER PRODUCTS)
607 East Palisade Avenue
Englewood, NJ 07632
(201) 567-9070
fax (201) 567-9078
info@jbkassociates.net
www.jbkassociates.net
Julie Kampf, President
Also:
West **Palm Beach, FL**
(561) 515-6026
Julie Kampf, President

JL CORNERSTONE
(SPECIALIZE IN REAL ESTATE, RETAIL & HOSPITALITY)
401 Bay Street, Suite 1600
Toronto, ON M5H 2Y4
(416) 646-6600
lglazin@jlcornerstone.com
www.jlcornerstone.com
Lynne Glazin, Partner
Jill MacLeod, Partner

JM SEARCH
(SPECIALIZE IN PAPER, PLASTICS, CHEMICALS & PACKAGING INDUSTRIES)
1045 First Avenue, Suite 110
King **of Prussia, PA** 19406
(610) 964-0200
fax (610) 964-8596
jmcompany@jmsearch.com
www.jmsearch.com
John C. Marshall, Chief Executive Officer & Founding Partner
John D. Hildebrand, Founding Partner
Robert A. Sargent, Founding Partner
Also:
New York, NY (212) 868-9600
Steven Baumruk, Vice President

JONAS, WALTERS & ASSOCIATES, INC.
3872 South Lake Drive, Suite 401
Milwaukee, WI 53235
(414) 291-2828
fax (414) 378-0033
info@jonaswalters.com
www.jonaswalters.com
William F. Walters, President
Donald S. Hucko, Senior Vice President

JONES & EGAN, INC.
(SPECIALIZE IN FINANCIAL SERVICES)
521 Fifth Avenue, Suite 1700
New York, NY 10175
(212) 292-5070
fax (212) 292-5071
info@jonesegan.com
Jonathan C. Jones, Principal
John F. Egan, Principal

JANET JONES-PARKER & ASSOCIATES
(SPECIALIZE IN HUMAN RESOURCES)
Chatham Crossing
11312 US 15 - 501 North, Suite 107
Post Office Box 307
Chapel Hill, NC 27517
(919) 696-4485
jonespark1@aol.com
www.janetjonesparker.com
Janet Jones-Parker, Managing Director

JR BECHTLE & COMPANY
(SPECIALIZE IN INTERNATIONAL AND EUROPEAN COMPANIES)
2000 Glades Road, Suite 410
Boca Raton, FL 33431
(561) 955-0012
fax (561) 955-0091
jrb.resume@jrbechtle.com
www.jrbechtle.com
Egon L. Lacher, Managing Partner
Also:
Oak Brook, IL (630) 203-2120
Herb Hassig, Managing Partner
West Burlington, MA
(781) 229-5804
Egon L. Lacher, Managing Partner

JSG GROUP
179 Main Street North, Suite 400
Markham, ON L3P 1Y2
(905) 477-3625
info@jsggroup.com
www.jsggroup.com
Richard W. Birarda, Managing Partner

KANEKO & ASSOCIATES*
4041 MacArthur Boulevard, Suite 222
Newport Beach, CA 92660
(949) 860-7200
fax (949) 860-7208
www.kanekoassociates.com
Nobi Kaneko, President

KANZER ASSOCIATES, INC.
500 North Michigan Avenue, Suite 2035
Chicago, IL 60611
(312) 464-0831
fax (312) 464-3719
info@kanzer.com
www.kanzer.com
William F. Kanzer, President

GARY KAPLAN & ASSOCIATES
201 South Lake Avenue, Suite 804
Pasadena, CA 91101
(626) 796-8100
fax (626) 796-1003
garykaplan@charter.net

www.gkasearch.com
Gary Kaplan, President
Also:
Wynnewood, PA (610) 642-5644
Alan J. Kaplan, President

Kaplan & Associates, Inc.*

1220 Medford Road
Wynnewood, PA 19096
(610) 642-5644
fax (610) 642-5645
search@kasearch.com
www.kasearch.com
Alan J. Kaplan, President

KarrScheffelSullinger, LLC

(SPECIALIZE IN Finance)
505 Montgomery Street, Suite 600
San Francisco, CA 94111
(925) 930-2312
fax (603) 699-4771
Cliff@karrscheffel.com
www.karrscheffel.com
Clifford Scheffel, Managing Partner
Liz Karr-Pola, Partner
Gayle Rydinski, Partner
Scott Sullinger, Partner
Kristi Walters, Partner

Martin Kartin & Company, Inc.

211 East 70th Street, Suite 34E
New York, NY 10021
(212) 628-7676
fax (212) 628-8838
mkartin@martinkartin.com
www.martinkartin.com
Martin Kartin, President

Kaye/Bassman International Corp.

19111 North Dallas Parkway, Suite 200
Dallas, TX 75287
(972) 931-5242
fax (972) 931-9683
careers@kbic.com
www.kbic.com
Jeff Kaye, President & CEO

Kazan International, Inc.

(SPECIALIZE IN Healthcare)
190 Main Street, Suite 101
P.O. Box 571
Gladstone, NJ 07934
(908) 901-0900
fax (908) 901-0990
resume@kazansearch.com
www.kazansearch.com
J. Neil Kazan, Managing Director
Brian N. Kazan, Managing Director
Also:
Bellevue, WA (425) 943-7709
J. Robert Tassone, Managing Partner

Michael Kelly Associates

(SPECIALIZE IN Healthcare & Financial)
230 Park Avenue, Suite 1000
New York, NY 10169
(212) 808-6599
mkelly@michaelkellyassociates.com
www.michaelkellyassociates.com
Michael P. Kelly, President
Also:
Red Bank, NJ (732) 924-4799
Michael P. Kelly, President

Kennedy & Company

225 West Washington Street, Suite 2200
Chicago, IL 60606
(312) 372-0099
fax (312) 372-0629
info@kennedycompanyinc.com
www.kennedycompanyinc.com
Lenore Meyer, Vice President

Kenniff & Racine*

Place Sherbrooke
1010 Sherbrooke Street West, Suite 818
Montreal, QC H3A 2R7
(514) 282-9798
fax (514) 282-9899
www.kenniffracine.com
Patrick Kenniff, Partner
Also:
Toronto, ON (416) 572-2333
Robert Racine, Partner

Kensington International

1515 West 22nd Street, Suite 500
Oak Brook, IL 60523
(630) 571-0123
fax (603) 571-3139
info@kionline.com
www.kionline.com
Brian Clarke, Managing Partner
Richard George, Managing Partner
Also:
Chicago, IL (312) 658-1088
Mary Jane Schermer, Executive Vice President
Deerfield, IL (847) 964-5651
Catherine Sutherland, Executive Vice President
Houston, TX (832) 564-1617
Brian Clarke, Managing Partner
Red Bank, NJ (732) 933-2651
Brian Clarke, Managing Partner

Kenzer Group, LLC

One Penn Plaza, Suite 6300
New York, NY 10119
(212) 308-4300
fax (917) 534-6280
ny@kenzer.com
www.kenzergroup.com
Kitty Keane, Vice President
Robert D. Kenzer, Chairman
Marc N. Moskowitz, President

KFA Search

(SPECIALIZE IN Life Sciences - Biotech, Healthcare, Pharm, Medical Devices)
337 Saint Augustine Boulevard
Jacksonville Beach, FL 32250
(877) 280-0030
resumes@KFAsearch.com
www.KFAsearch.com
Kathleen H. Fehling, President & Founder
Also:
Raleigh, NC (877) 280-0030
Jake Fehling, Vice President
San Francisco, CA (877) 280-0030
Carrie I. Steffes, Research Associate

Kincannon & Reed*

(SPECIALIZE IN Food, Agribusiness, Life Sciences)
40 Stoneridge Drive, Suite 101
Waynesboro, VA 22980
(540) 941-3460
fax (540) 301-6320
krcontact@krsearch.net
www.krsearch.com
Kelly Kincannon, Chairman
J. Suzanne Cox, Managing Director
Gregory J. Duerksen, President
Ellen Von Fange, Managing Director
Also:
Scottsdale, AZ (480) 553-6330
Michael L. Cooper, Managing Partner

Kinkead Partners

(SPECIALIZE IN Industrial Sales & Marketing)
106 Quarry Road
Glastonbury, CT 06033
(860) 659-4664
fax (860) 760-6043
info@kinkeadsearch.com
www.kinkeadsearch.com
David N. Kinkead, President

KINSER & BAILLOU, LLC.
590 Madison Avenue, 21st Floor
New York, NY 10022
(212) 588-8801
fax (212) 588-8802
search@kinserbaillou.com
www.kinserbaillou.com
Astrid Von Baillou, President

KIRADJIEFF & GOODE EXECUTIVE SEARCH, INC.
River Place
57 River Street, Suite 202
Wellesley, MA 02481
(781) 489-6777
fax (781) 489-6767
cgoode@kg-inc.com
www.kg-inc.com
Richard W. Goode, Chief Executive Officer & Managing Director
Laura K. Goode, Managing Director

KITTLEMAN & ASSOCIATES, LLC
(SPECIALIZE IN NON-PROFIT)
233 South Wacker Drive, 84th Floor
Chicago, IL 60606
(312) 986-1166
fax (312) 986-0895
search@kittleman.net
www.kittleman.net
Richard M. King, President & CEO

KNAPP CONSULTANTS
(SPECIALIZE IN AEROSPACE, HIGH TECH)
Post Office Box 505
Westport Point, MA 02791
(508) 636-8882
fax (508) 636-7253
consultantknapp@aol.com
Ronald A. Knapp, President

KNIGHTSBRIDGE EXECUTIVE SEARCH*
250 Yonge Street, Suite 2800
P.O. Box 20
Toronto, ON M5B 2L7
(416) 923-5555
fax (416) 923-6175
executivesearch@knightsbridge.ca
www.knightsbridge.ca/
Brad P. Beveridge, Managing Director
Malcolm Bernstein, Partner
Judi Bradette, Partner
Angela Eckford, Partner
Rita Eskudt, Partner
Tim Hewat, Partner
Lisa Knight, Partner
Janice Kussner, Partner
Jock McGregor, Partner
Sharon Neelin, Partner
Jack Penaligon, Partner
Ed Perkovic, Director of Research
Larry Ross, Partner
Also:
Burlington, ON (289) 288-5360
Ann Brudette, Principal
Calgary, AB (403) 410-7149
Mark Hopkins, Managing Partner
Charlottetown, PI (902) 940-2181
Mark Surrette, President
Chicago, IL (312) 988-9350
Virginia Clarke, Principal
Halifax, NS (902) 421-1330
Mark Surrette, President
London, ON (519) 772-1139
Catherine Copp, Principal
Markham, ON (647) 777-3105
Kim Spurgeon, Principal
Mississauga, ON (905) 277-7340
Ann Burdette, Partner
Moncton, NB (506) 854-8169
Jennifer Murray, Principal
Montreal, QC (514) 954-9549
Charles Belle Isle, Partner
Guy Djandji, Partner
Ottawa, ON (613) 569-4910
Margo Hoyt, Principal
Saint John, NB (506) 847-0359
Jennifer Murray, Principal
St John's, **NL** (709) 722-6890
Lloyd Powell, Partner
Sudbury, ON (705) 662-1314
Colleen Gordon-Boyce, Partner
Vancouver, BC (604) 678-9344
Richard Whaley, Managing Director
Waterloo, ON (519) 772-1139
Catherine Copp, Principal

KOENIG & ASSOCIATES, LLC
(SPECIALIZE IN LIFE SCIENCES)
P. O. Box 535
Chatham, NJ 07928
(973) 701-9699
fax (973) 701-9165
inquire@koenig-associates.com
www.koenig-associates.com
Mary C. Koening, President

KORN/FERRY INTERNATIONAL*
1900 Avenue of the Stars, Suite 2600
Los Angeles, CA 90067
(310) 552-1834
fax (310) 553-6452
www.ekornferry.com
Caroline Nahas, Managing Director-Southern California
Gary D. Burnison, Chief Executive Officer
Robert Damon, President North America
Also:
Atlanta, GA (404) 577-7542
Bob Baxter, Office Managing Partner
Boston, MA (617) 345-0200
Robert K. Sullivan, Office Managing Director
Calgary, AB (403) 269-3277
Bob Sutton, Managing Director
Chicago, IL (312) 466-1834
Mark Pierce, Senior Client Partner
Cincinnati, OH (513) 366-8344
Rosaleena Marcellus, Office Managing Director
Dallas, TX (214) 954-1834
Ronald J. Zera, Managing Director
Durango, CO (970) 385-4955
Kathy Woods, Office Managing Director
Houston, TX (713) 651-1834
Eric Nielsen, Office Managing Director
Irvine, CA (949) 851-1834
Peter Santora, Managing Director & Practice Leader
McLean, VA (703) 547-0500
Bernadine Karunaratne, Office Manager
Miami, FL (305) 377-4121
Bonnie Crabtree, Managing Director
Minneapolis, MN (612) 339-0927
Karin Lucas, Office Managing Director
Montreal, QC (514) 397-9655
Brigitte Simard, Office Managing Director
New York, NY (212) 687-1834
Anthony J. LoPinto, Regional Managing Director
Philadelphia, PA (215) 496-6666
David Shabot, Managing Director
Princeton, NJ (609) 452-8848
Richard Arons, Managing Director
Reston, VA (703) 761-7020
Kim Shanahan, Office Manager
San Francisco, CA (415) 956-1834
Robert Ferguson, Office Managing Director
Stamford, CT (203) 359-3350
Julie Goldberg, Office Managing Director
Toronto, ON (416) 365-1841
Dov Zevy, Managing Director
Vancouver, BC (604) 684-1834
Kevin McBurney, Managing Director
Waltham, MA (888) 652-9975
Oris Stuart, Office Managing Director

Washington, DC (202) 822-9444
Nels Olson, Office Managing Director

Kors Montgomery International
(Specialize in High Tech & Energy)
14306 Heatherfield, Suite 200
Houston, TX 77079
(713) 840-7101
fax (281) 493-2446
pkors@korsmontgomery.com
R. Paul Kors, Partner

Krauthamer & Associates, Inc.
5530 Wisconsin Avenue, Suite 1202
Chevy Chase, MD 20815
(301) 654-7533
fax (301) 654-0136
tdorfman@krauthamerinc.com
www.krauthamerinc.com
Gary L. Krauthamer, Principal
Todd A. Dorfman, Principal
Ellen S. Dorfman, Principal

Krecklo International
(Specialize in MIS & Technology)
1250 Boulevard Rene-Levesque Ouest, Suite 2200
Montreal, QC H3B 4W8
(514) 281-9999
montreal@krecklo.com
www.krecklo.com
Brian D. Krecklo, Managing Director
Also:
Cornwell, ON (613) 363-8883
Brian D. Krecklo, Senior Consultant

Kremple Consulting Group
222 Reward Street
Nevada City, CA 95959
(530) 265-5688
fax (530) 265-4648
jkremple@krempleconsulting.com
www.krempleconsulting.com
Jeffrey Kremple, Managing Partner

Kristan International Executive Search Inc.
12 Greenway Plaza, Suite 1100
Houston, TX 77046
(713) 961-3040
fax (713) 961-3626
executivesearch@kristan.com
www.kristan.com
Robert Kristan, President

Kristophers Consultants
(Specialize in Architectural, Civil/Infrastructure Engineering, Consumer Products)
5551 North Osceola
Chicago, IL 60656
(773) 594-1301
kcabai@aol.com
Kevin Cabai, President

Lambert Group International, LLC
191 Post Road West
Westport, CT 06880
(203) 221-2899
jerry.lambert@lambert-group.com
Gerald M. Lambert, President

Lancor Group*
One Montgomery Street, Floor 25
San Francisco, CA 94104
(415) 263-9168
fax (800) 936-7260
www.lancorgroup.com
Jamie Carter, Partner
Also:
Chagrin, OH (440) 337-4147
Chris Conti, Partner
San Francisco, CA (415) 263-9168
Simon Francis, Partner

The Landstone Group
(Specialize in Technology, Life Sciences & Consumer)
15 East 40th Street, Room 700
New York, NY 10016
(212) 972-7300
fax (212) 972-7309
mail@landstonegroup.com
www.landstonegroup.com
Jeffrey Heath, Managing Principal

Lantern Partners
(Specialize in Supply Chain, Financial, Technology, Consumer Goods)
250 South Wacker Drive, Suite 600
Chicago, IL 60606
(312) 962-4740
fax (312) 258-0260
resumes@lanternpartners.com
www.lanternpartners.com
Christopher A. Morgan, Founding Partner
Richard G. Hypes, Partner
Paul C. Maranville, Partner
Paul C. Maranville, Partner
Collin L. Sprau, Partner
Michael B. Wyman, Partner

The Lapham Group, Inc.
80 Park Avenue, Third Floor
New York, NY 10016-2533
(212) 599-0644
fax (212) 697-2688
info@thelaphamgroup.com
www.thelaphamgroup.com
Lawrence L. Lapham, Chairman
Craig L. Lapham, President

Lasher Associates
1276 Manor Drive South
Weston, FL 33326
(954) 217-5081
resume@lasherassociates.com
www.lasherassociates.com
Charles Mick Lasher, President
Also:
Parker, CO (720) 488-8678
Daniel B. Bronson, Senior Vice President

Lauer, Sbarbaro Associates
2 Westbrook Corporate Center, Suite 100
Westchester, IL 60154
(708) 531-0100
fax (708) 947-9075
SBARBS@AOL.com
www.ema-partners.com
Richard D. Sbarbaro, Chairman
William J. Yacullo, President

Leadership Group Executive Search LLC
(Specialize in Internet, E-Commerce & Telecommunications)
2603 Camino Ramon
San Ramon, CA 94583
(925) 360-8000
resume@lges.com
www.lges.com
Bob Currie, Partner
Also:
Charleston, SC (415) 235-6217
Michael Lee, Partner
Kirsten Smith, Partner
Palo Alto, CA (925) 253-1424
Lindsay Lautz, Partner
San Ramon, CA (925) 683-3312
Ray Fortney, Partner
Westhampton, NY (631) 998-3465
John Calamia, Partner

Leadership Search Partners
2205 K Oak Ridge Road, Suite 102
Oak Ridge, NC 27310
(336) 210-8430
lsp@usa.net
www.golsp.com
A. Dave McCuaig, Principal
Also:
Toronto, ON (647) 668-1229
A. Dave McCuaig, Principal

Lee Heagy & Company
(SPECIALIZE IN LIFE SCIENCES AND AGRIBUSINESS)
779 Follin Farm Lane
Great Falls, VA 22066
(703) 879-6792
dlee@leeheagy.com
www.leeheagy.com
Donna N. Lee, President

Legacy Bowes
(SPECIALIZE IN CANADA SEARCHES)
Kensington Building
275 Portage Avenue, Suite 1400
Winnipeg, MB R3B 2B3
(204) 947-5525
fax (204) 957-5384
www.legacybowes.com
Barbara Bowes, President
Paul Croteau, Managing Partner

Legacy Executive Search Partners, Inc.
67 Yonge Street, Suite 808
Toronto, ON M5E 1J8
(416) 814-5809
fax (416) 814-5733
toronto@lesp.ca
www.lesp.ca/
Keith McLean, Partner
Also:
Calgary, AB (403) 269-7767
Ron Prokosch, Managing Partner
Toronto, ON (416) 814-5809
Paul F. Crath, Partner

Leland Partners, Inc.
1115 Loyola Drive
Libertyville, IL 60048
(847) 362-0363
fax (847) 362-0282
contact@lelandpartnersinc.com
www.lelandpartnersinc.com
Richard W. Steel, President

Levin & Company, Inc.
(SPECIALIZE IN PHARMACEUTICALS, BIOMED & LIFE SCIENCES)
470 Atlantic Avenue, 4th Floor
Boston, MA 02210
(617) 573-5258
fax (617) 573-5259
www.levinandcompany.com
Becky Ruhmann Levin, Chief Executive Officer
Also:
Berwyn, PA (610) 727-4000
Margaret O'Rourke, Managing Director
Los Angeles, CA (310) 229-5915
Christos Richards, President
San Francisco, CA (415) 912-2860
Evan Fishel, Vice President

Lindsey & Company
484 Boston Post Road
P.O. Box 1273
Darien, CT 06820
(203) 655-1590
info@lindseycompany.com
www.lindseycompany.com
Thomas K. McInerney, Managing Partner
Paul J. Bova, Managing Partner
Charles J.G. Brown, Managing Partner
Michael V. Garcia, Managing Partner
Lary L. Lindsey, Chief Executive Officer
Peter G. Newsham, Managing Partner
Frank Thayer, Managing Partner
David N. Verner, Managing Partner

Lipson & Company
(SPECIALIZE IN ENTERTAINMENT AND MEDIA POSITIONS)
10350 Santa Monica Boulevard, Suite 205
Los Angeles, CA 90025
(310) 277-4646
fax (310) 277-8585
inquiries@lipsonco.com
www.lipsonco.com
Howard R. Lipson, Principal

Livingston, Runquist & Company
209 Bruce Park Avenue
Greenwich, CT 06830
(203) 618-8400
Peter R. Livingston, President

Locke and Key Executive Search
P.O. Box 6746
Oakland, CA 94603
(510) 533-2005
fax (510) 533-2055
lklocke@lockeandkey.com
www.lockeandkey.com
Lisa K. Locke, Founder

Logistics Management Resources, Inc.
(SPECIALIZE IN SUPPLY CHAIN AND PURCHASING)
81 Third Avenue
Nyack, NY 10960
(845) 353-6194
fax (845) 638-4621
mslater@logisticsresources.com
Marjorie Slater, President

The Lovell Company
(SPECIALIZE IN CONSUMER PRODUCTS & PACKAGED GOODS)
55 Madison Avenue, 4th Floor
Morristown, NJ 07960
(973) 285-3286
lovell@thelovellcompany.com
Rebecka Lovell, President

Lovett and Lovett Executive Search
National City Center Building
6 North Main Street, Suite 130
Dayton, OH 45402
(937) 512-6999
fax (937) 512-6990
tom@lovetts.com
www.lovettandlovett.com
Tom Lovett, President

The John Lucht Consultancy Inc.
301 Fayetteville Street, Suite 3106
Raleigh, NC 27601
(919) 301-0339
resumes@luchtconsultancy.com
www.luchtconsultancy.com
John Lucht, President

Charles Luntz & Associates, Inc.
(SPECIALIZE IN SUITE 223)
1734 Clarkson Road
Chesterfield, MO 63017
(314) 374-2949
contact@charlesluntz.com
www.charlesluntz.com
Charles Luntz, President

M & A Executive Search
The Sathe Building

5821 Cedar Lake Road South
St. **Louis Park, MN** 55416
(952) 545-6980
fax (952) 525-1088
cmccoy@maexecsearch.com
www.maexecsearch.com
Chandler McCoy, Partner & President
Also:
Minneapolis, MN (952) 545-6980
Greg Albrecht, Partner

The Macdonald Group, Inc.

P.O. Box 11
Monchs Corner, SC 29461
(873) 761-3368
G. William Macdonald, President

The Madison Group

25 Rockledge Avenue, Suite 309
White Plains, NY 10601
(914) 649-1275
inquiries@themadisongroup.net
www.themadisongroup.net
David Soloway, Managing Director

Magellan International, L.P.

(SPECIALIZE IN Professional Services)
3200 Southwest Freeway, Suite 3300
Houston, TX 77027
(713) 439-7485
fax (713) 439-7489
milp@milp.com
www.milp.com
Jonathan H. Phillips, President
Bryan Vaughn, Senior Managing Director

Mainstay Partners, Inc.

(SPECIALIZE IN Technology, Financial Services, Clean Technology, Medical Devices)
281 Winter Street, Suite 305
Waltham, MA 02451
(781) 425-5265
fax (781) 425-5272
malosco@mainstaypartners.com
www.mainstaypartners.com
Mario Alosco, Partner
John Hoagland, Partner
Jim von der Linden, Partner

T. Malouf & Company

(SPECIALIZE IN Sports, Fitness & Active Recreation, Commericail & Non-Profit Industries)
4845 Pearl East Circle, Suite 101
Boulder, CO 80301
(303) 295-9599
info@tmalouf.com
www.tmalouf.com
Terry Malouf, President and Chief Executive Officer

Management Resource Group, Ltd.

2805 Eastern Avenue
Davenport, IA 52803
(563) 323-3333
fax (563) 326-0682
dportes@mrgpeople.com
www.mrgpeople.com
Daniel H. Portes, Chairman
Also:
Hiawatha, IA (319) 294-9499
Andrea Wagner, Sr. Consultant

Mancino Burfield Edgerton

(SPECIALIZE IN Life Sciences Industry)
111 West Street
Belle Mead, NJ 08502
(609) 520-8400
fax (908) 431-7544
gene@mbels.com
www.mbels.com
Gene Mancino, Partner
Also:
Doylestown, PA (215) 230-8999
Paul Edgerton, Partner
Westfield, NJ (908) 232-3274
Elaine Burfield, Partner

Mandrake

(SPECIALIZE IN Mainly Canadian Placements)
55 St. Clair Avenue West, Suite 401
Toronto, ON M4V 2Y7
(416) 922-5400
fax (416) 922-1356
info@mandrake.ca
www.mandrake.ca/
Stafan Danis, Chief Executive Officer
Also:
Montreal, QC (514) 878-4224
Normand Lebeau, President--Montreal

Michael E. Marion & Associates, Inc.

Murray Hill Square
98 Floral Avenue
Murry Hill, NJ 07974
(908) 771-9330
fax (908) 665-9380
info@marionsearch.com
www.marionsearch.com
Michael E. Marion, Senior Partner
Andrew J. Marion, Senior Partner

Marra Peters & Partners

99 Morris Avenue
Springfield, NJ 07081
(877) 966-1960
info@marrapeters.com
www.marrapeters.com
John V. Marra, President
Charles J. Pelisson, Vice President

Marshall Consultants, LLC

(SPECIALIZE IN Public Relations, Corporate Communications, Investor and Marketing Communication)
660 Pracht Street
Ashland, OR 97520
(541) 488-3121
marshcons@gmail.com
www.marshallconsultants.com
Larry Marshall, Managing Partner
Joy Marshall, Managing Partner

J. Martin & Associates

(SPECIALIZE IN California Based Searches Only)
10820 Holman Avenue, Suite 103
Los Angeles, CA 90024
(310) 475-5380
jmexecsrch@aol.com
Judy R. Martin, Principal

Martin Partners, LLC

(SPECIALIZE IN Consulting, Financial Services, Healthcare, Biotechnology)
224 South Michigan Avenue, Suite 620
Chicago, IL 60604
(312) 922-1800
fax (312) 922-1813
resume@martinpartners.com
www.martinpartners.com
Theodore B. Martin, Managing Partner
Sherry Brickman, Partner
Thomas Jagielo, Partner

Matte Consulting Group

3501 Peel Street
Montreal, QC H3A 1W7
(514) 848-1008
fax (514) 848-9157
admin@matteiic.com
www.matteiic.com
Richard Matte, Managing Partner
Michel St. Louis, Partner

Maxwell Drummond International*

10375 Richmond Avenue, Suite 1830
Houston, TX 77042
(713) 316-4480
fax (713) 316-4483
houston@maxwelldrummond.com
www.maxwell-drummond.com
Jamie Ferguson, Vice President
Also:
Calgary, AB (403) 538-4722
Graeme Edge, General Manager-Canada
Houston, TX (713) 316-4480
Brian Coffman, Vice President

The McAulay Firm

Bank of America Corporate Center
100 North Tryon Street, Suite 5220
Charlotte, NC 28202
(704) 342-1880
fax (704) 342-0825
info@mcaulay.com
www.mcaulay.com
Albert L. McAulay, President
Steven B. Smith, President

McCarthy Bertschy & Associates, Inc.

10 South Riverside Plaza, Suite 1800
Chicago, IL 60606
(312) 474-9255
fax (312) 474-6099
info@mccarthybertschy.com
www.mccarthybertschy.com
Christopher T. Bertschy, Managing Partner

McCormack & Farrow

949 South Coast Drive, Suite 620
Costa Mesa, CA 92626
(714) 549-7222
fax (714) 549-7227
resumes@mfsearch.com
www.mfsearch.com
Jerry M. Farrow, Managing Partner
Helen E. Friedman, Partner
Gene Phelps, Senior Partner
Alex Sanchez, Senior Partner
Kenneth L. Thompson, Senior Partner

McCormack & Warren

(SPECIALIZE IN NONPROFIT & DIVERSITY EXECUTIVE SEARCH, HIGHER EDUCATION, HEALTHCARE)
1775 East Palm Canyon Drive, Suite 110-202
Palm Springs, CA 92264
(323) 549-9200
fax (323) 549-9222
search@mccormackandwarren.com
www.mccormackandwarren.com
Joseph A. McCormack, Managing Partner
Justin Warren, Managing Partner

McCracken & Partners Executive Search, Inc.*

120 Adelaide Street West, Suite 2210
Toronto, ON M5H 1T1
(416) 363-8900
fax (866) 809-8900
info@mccracken-partners.com
www.mccracken-partners.com
Diane Armstrong, Partner

McDermott & Bull Executive Search

2 Venture, Suite 100
Irvine, CA 92618
(949) 753-1700
fax (949) 753-7438
resume@mbsearch.net
www.mbsearch.net
Rod McDermott, Managing Partner
Chris Bull, Managing Partner
Also:
Century City, CA (424) 202-3663
Meiko Takayama, Consultant

G.E. McFarland & Company

535 Colonial Park Drive
Roswell, GA 30075
(770) 992-0900
fax (770) 640-0067
gemcfarland@mindspring.com
Charles P. Beall, Managing Partner

The McIntyre Company*

(SPECIALIZE IN RETAIL, GROCERY, CONSUMER PRODUCTS, MANUFACTURING)
375 North Front Street, Suite 222
Columbus, OH 43215
(614) 318-8000
cahmed@mcintyreco.com
www.mcintyreco.com
Cookie McIntyre, President

McKinley Arend International

3200 Southwest Freeway, Suite 3300
Houston, TX 77027-7526
(713) 623-6400
fax (281) 741-7184
careertalk@mckinleyarend.com
www.mckinleyarend.com
Lewis W. Arend, Co-Managing Director

MDR Associates

(SPECIALIZE IN HEALTH CARE)
231 Altara Avenue
Coral Gables, FL 33146
(800) 327-1585
fax (305) 567-0843
info@mdrsearch.com
www.mdrsearch.com
Judith Berger, President
Stephen G. Schoen, Executive Director

James Mead & Company

(SPECIALIZE IN CONSUMER PACKAGED GOODS)
15 Old Danbury Road, Suite 202
Wilton, CT 06897-2524
(203) 834-6300
fax (203) 834-6301
mailbox@jmeadco.com
James D. Mead, President
Arthur S. Brown, Executive Vice President & Partner

Peter Meder & Company

1420 Lake Shore Drive
Chicago, IL 60610
(312) 867-7149
pmeder@pmedercompany.com
www.pmedercompany.com
Peter F. Meder, Managing Partner

Meng, Finseth, Peeps & Associates

Del Amo Executive Plaza
3858 Carson Street, Suite 202
Torrance, CA 90503
(310) 316-0706
info@mengfinseth.com
www.perfectweb.biz/
Charles M. Meng, Founder & Managing Partner
Also:
Palo Alto, CA (650) 325-5959
Stephen Peeps, Partner
Torrance, CA (310) 316-0706
Cameron Wisowaty, Partner

Merritt Hawkins & Associates

(SPECIALIZE IN PHYSICIANS & HEALTHCARE)
5001 Statesman Drive
Irving, TX 75063
(469) 524-1400
fax (469) 524-1421

info@merritthawkins.com
www.merritthawkins.com
Jim Merritt, President
Also:
Atlanta, GA (770) 396-4800
Mark Smith, Managing Director
Irvine, CA (949) 477-8017
Kevin Perpetua, Managing Director
Irving, TX (800) 685-2272
Joseph Caldwell, Managing Director
Joseph Hawkins, Chief Executive Officer

Messett Associates, Inc.

7700 North Kendall Drive, Suite 502
Miami, FL 33156
(305) 275-1000
fax (305) 274-4462
messett@messett.com
www.messett.com
William J. Messett, President

Anthony Michael & Company

(SPECIALIZE IN FINANCIAL SERVICES)
266 Main Street, Suite 31B
Medfield, MA 02052
(800) 565-5578
fax (508) 242-9550
mjk@anthonymichaelco.com
Michael J. Kulesza, Senior Managing Director

Michael Shirley Associates, Inc.

5350 West 94th Terrace, Suite 102
Prairie Village, KS 66207
(913) 341-7655
fax (913) 341-7657
michael@mshirleyassociates.com
www.mshirleyassociates.com
Michael R. Shirley, President

Gregory Michaels & Associates, Inc.

155 North Wacker Drive, 42nd Floor
Chicago, IL 60606
(312) 377-2100
gcrecos@gregorymichaels.com
www.gregorymichaels.com
Gregory P. Crecos, Managing Partner

Millbrook Partners, LLC

160 Church Street
P.O. Box 66
Millbrook, NY 12545
(845) 677-2500
fax (845) 677-3315
research@millbrooksearch.com
www.millbrooksearch.com
Robert Whaley, Founder & Managing Partner

Miller Black Associates*

10 Bradley Lane
Mystic, CT 06355
(860) 536-2340
jm@millerblackllc.com
www.millerblackllc.com
Joanna Black, Managing Director

Millican Solutions, Inc.

(SPECIALIZE IN PEDIATRIC LEADERSHIP SPECIALISTS)
546 Silicon Drive, Suite 100
Southlake, TX 76092
(847) 421-5800
info@millicansolutions.com
millicansolutions.com
Wesley D. Millican, President & Founder

MIXTEC Group*

(SPECIALIZE IN AGRIBUSINESS)
3786 La Crescenta Avenue, Suite 104
Glendale, CA 91208
(818) 541-0124
mixtec@mixtec.net
www.mixtec.net
Christopher C. Nelson, President
Jerry Butt, Vice President
Also:
Monterey, CA (831) 373-7077
Leonard Batti, Managing Director

MJS Executive Search

52 Main Street
Hastings-on-**Hudson, NY** 10706
(914) 631-1774
fax (914) 220-8380
info@mjsearch.com
www.mjsearch.com
Matthew J. Schwartz, President
Laurie Rosenfield, Principal

The Montana Group

10125 Crosstown Circle, Suite 300
Eden Prairie, MN 55344
(952) 941-0966
fax (952) 941-4462
Fred A. Montana, President

Morgan Samuels Company*

6420 Wilshire Boulevard, Suite 1100
Los Angeles, CA 90048
(310) 205-2200
fax (310) 205-2201
info@morgansamuels.com
www.morgansamuels.com
Bert C. Hensley, Chairman & Chief Executive Officer
Janice DiPietro, President
Martin J. Hewett, Senior Client Partner
Lewis J. Samuels, Founder
Also:
Bloomfield, MI (248) 509-4100
Martin J. Hewett, Partner
Boston, MA (617) 219-9800
Todd Wyles, Partner
Chicago, IL (312) 489-8288
Bert C. Hensley, Chairman & Chief Executive Officer
Kansas City, MO (816) 533-4370
John R. Copeland, Partner
John R. Copeland, Partner
New York, NY (646) 837-7682
Marilyn Draper, Partner
Newport Beach, CA (949) 566-8055
Monica L. Bua, Senior Client Partner

Morice Consulting, LLC

18 Navy Lane
Essex, CT 06426
(203) 249-1020
fax (860) 767-3928
James L. Morice, President & CEO

Morris & Berger, Inc.

(SPECIALIZE IN NONPROFIT)
500 North Brand Boulevard, Suite 2150
Glendale, CA 91203-1923
(818) 507-1234
fax (818) 507-4770
mb@morrisberger.com
www.morrisberger.com
Karin Berger-Stellar, Partner
Jay V. Berger, Partner

Moyer, Sherwood Associates*

(SPECIALIZE IN COMMUNICATIONS, PUBLIC RELATIONS & INVESTMENT RELATIONS)
28 West 44th Street, Suite 1120
New York, NY 10036
(212) 554-4008
fax (212) 554-4188
research@moyersherwood.com
www.moyersherwood.com
David S. Moyer, President
Also:

Stamford, CT (203) 622-1074
David S. Moyer, President

Mruk & Partners
230 Park Avenue, Suite 1000
New York, NY 10169
(212) 808-3076
fax (212) 983-8047
Edwin S. Mruk, Senior Partner

MSA Executive Search*
(SPECIALIZE IN HEALTHCARE)
700 West 47th Street, Suite 400
Kansas City, MO 64112
(888) 513-0158
fax (888) 513-6208
resumes@msasearch.com
www.msasearch.com
Jane Groves, Executive Vice President
Robert Erra, President

MTA Partners
(SPECIALIZE IN HEALTH CARE)
5068 West Plano Parkway
Plano, TX 75093
(972) 335-1882
Michael Tucker, Managing Partner
Brooke Myers, Partner

P. J. Murphy & Associates, Inc.
735 North Water Street, Suite 720
Milwaukee, WI 53202
(414) 277-9777
fax (414) 277-7626
pjmurphy@pjmurphy.com
www.pjmurphy.com
Patrick J. Murphy, Chairman

Mycoff Fry & Prouse, LLC
(SPECIALIZE IN UTILITY INDUSTRY)
12935 US Highway 285
Conifer, CO 80433
(303) 607-5372
fax (303) 607-5463
mail@mfpllc.us
www.mycoffassociates.com
Carl A. Mycoff, Principal
Scott A. Fry, Principal
Lanie L. Prouse, Principal

Myers McRae, Inc.
(SPECIALIZE IN HIGHER EDUCATION)
515 Mullberry Street, Suite 200
Macon, GA 31201
(478) 330-6222
fax (478) 330-5611
myersmcrae@myersmcrae.com
www.myersmcrae.com
Kenny Daugherty, Executive Vice President
R. Kirby Godsey, Chairman
Emily P. Myers, President

Nagler Robins Partners, Inc.
61 Prentice Road, Suite 100
Newton, MA 02459-1325
(617) 969-0405
info@nrpinc.com
www.nrpinc.com
Jeri N. Robins, Managing Director
Lee G. Nagler, Managing Director

New Directions Search, Inc.
1127 Wheaton Oaks Court
Post Office Box 88
Wheaton, IL 60189
(630) 462-1840
fax (630) 462-1862
info@ndsearch.com
www.ndsearch.com
Dale A. Frank, Chief Executive Officer
Nate A. Frank, President
John M. Morton, Managing Director
Rick L. Santarelli, Senior Vice President

New World Healthcare Solutions, Inc.
(SPECIALIZE IN HEALTHCARE)
116 West 23rd Street
New York, NY 10011
(845) 429-2034
irashapiro@newworldhealthcare.com
Ira E. Shapiro, Chief Executive Officer

Newman Tucker Group, Inc.
2800 North Central Avenue, Suite 1740
Phoenix, AZ 85004
(602) 595-8600
customerservice@newmantucker-group.com
Charles Newman, Partner

Nordeman Grimm, Inc.
65 East 55th Street, 33rd Floor
New York, NY 10022
(212) 935-1000
fax (212) 980-1443
resume@nordemangrimm.com
www.nordemangrimm.com
Jacques C. Nordeman, Chairman

Norman Broadbent*
1800 Century Park East, Suite 645
Los Angeles, CA 90069
(310) 229-5741
losangeles@normanbroadbent.com
www.normanbroadbent.com
Sally Drexler, Managing Director

Northeast Consulting Group
35 Consulting Drive, Suite 1135
Trumbull, CT 06611
(203) 880-5011
fax (203) 762-8403
Charles G. Roy, Managing Director

Northpoint Partners LLC
(SPECIALIZE IN MEDICAL DEVICES, BIOTECH, PHARMA, & HEALTHCARE)
13652 Duluth Drive
Apple Valley, MN 55124
(612) 584-0394
executive@northpoint-partners.com
www.northpoint-partners.com
Mark Klingsheim, Managing Partner
Bill Goodman, Partner
Shawn Severson, Partner

Nosal Partners, LLC
(SPECIALIZE IN HIGH TECH, COMMUNICATIONS, SOFTWARE, AND E-COMMERCE)
100 First Street, Suite 2200
San Francisco, CA 94105
(415) 369-2200
fax (415) 369-2202
info@nosalpartners.com
nosalpartners.com
David Nosal, Chairman & Cheif Executive Officer
Also:
Atlanta, GA (404) 446-3650
Susan Oliver, Senior Partner
Chardon, OH (440) 940-6315
Caryn Avante, Client Partner
La Jolla, CA (858) 456-3585
Donald E. Parker, Senior Partner
Milwaukee, WI (414) 716-6160
Mike Magurany, Partner
Minneapolis, MN (612) 746-8200
Terri Naughtin, Managing Partner
New York, NY (917) 639-4048
Robert Kobayashi, Managing Partner
Santa Monica, CA (310) 471-1555
Robert W. Bellano, Senior Partner

Nuessle Kurdziel & Weiss, Inc.
1601 Market Street, Suite 390
Philadelphia, PA 19103
(215) 561-3700
fax (215) 561-3745
srpositions@aol.com
www.nkwsearch.com
John Kurdziel, Managing Partner
Gerald Weiss, Partner

Ober & Company
11777 San Vicente Boulevard, Suite 860
Los Angeles, CA 90049
(310) 207-1127
Lynn W. Ober, President

O'Connor, O'Connor, Lordi Ltd.
Gulf Tower
707 Grant Street, Suite 2727
Pittsburgh, PA 15219-1908
(412) 261-4020
fax (412) 261-4480
info@oolltd.com
www.oolltd.com
Thomas F. O'Connor, President
Rick Brown, Executive Vice President
Tim Tetrick, Senior Vice President

Odgers Berndtson*
280 Park Avenue, 27th Floor West
New York, NY 10017
(212) 972-7287
fax (212) 572-6499
info@odgersberndtson.com
www.odgersberndtson.com
Steve Potter, Managing Partner
Also:
Boston, MA (617) 208-4542
Alex Thomson, Partner
Calgary, AB (403) 410-6700
Kevin J. Gregor, Managing Partner
Timothy J. Hamilton, Managing Partner
Janet E. Soles, Managing Partner
Chicago, IL (224) 353-4226
Pat Corey, Partner
Paul Hanson, Partner
Dallas, TX (214) 363-5200
David Gabriel, Partner
Halifax, NS (902) 491-7788
Eric Beaudan, Managing Partner
Los Altos, CA (408) 569-3565
Andy Dolich, Partner
Montreal, QC (514) 937-1000
Genevieve Falconetto, Managing Partner
Ottawa, ON (613) 749-9909
Ronald Robertson, Managing Partner
Toronto, ON (416) 366-1990
W. Carl Lovas, Managing Partner
Paul R. A. Stanley, Managing Partner
Vancouver, BC (604) 685-0261
Kenneth Werker, Managing Partner

The Ogdon Partnership
375 Park Avenue, Suite 2409
New York, NY 10152-0175
(212) 308-1600
fax (212) 755-3819
info@ogdon.com
Thomas H. Ogdon, President

O'Keefe & Partners Executive Search
(Specialize in Consumer Products)
4 Corporate Drive, Suite 490
Shelton, CT 06484
(203) 929-4222
fax (203) 926-9073
smoore@okeefepartners.com
www.okeefepartners.com
John V. O'Keefe, Founder, Chairman & CEO
Also:
Costa Mesa, CA (714) 852-3178
Jay O'Keefe, Partner
Plymouth, MA (508) 746-0022
Kevin B. Murphy, Senior Partner
Shelton, CT (203) 929-4222
Kathy J. O'Keefe, Co-Founder

The Onstott Group*
55 William Street, Suite 210
Wellesley, MA 02481
(781) 235-3050
fax (781) 235-8653
info@onstott.com
www.onstott.com
Joseph E. Onstott, Managing Director
Pat Campbell, Co-Founder

Oppedisano & Company, LLC
(Specialize in Investment Management and Wealth Management)
733 Summer Street, Suite 205
Stamford, CT 06901
(203) 324-0144
fax (203) 324-8964
eo@oppedisanoco.com
www.oppedisanoco.com
Edward A. Oppedisano, Managing Principal & Founder

Opportunity Resources, Inc.
(Specialize in Nonprofit & Cultural Organizations)
196 East 75th Street, Suite 14H
New York, NY 10021
(212) 744-4409
fax (212) 744-5004
search@opportunityresources.net
www.opportunityresources.net
Freda Mindlin, President

Optimum Talent*
(Specialize in Canada Searches)
25 York Street, Suite 1802
Toronto, ON M5J 2V5
(416) 364-2605
fax (416) 364-2519
toronto@optimumtalent.com
www.optimumtalent.com
Virginia Murray, Managing Partner
Also:
London, ON (519) 913-8029
Virginia Murray, Managing Partner
Markham, ON (905) 513-8578
Virginia Murray, Managing Partner
Mississauga, ON (905) 755-0630
Virginia Murray, Managing Partner
Montreal, QC (514) 932-0159
Michel Lizotte, Senior Vice President
Quebec, QC (418) 650-6200
Pierre Martineau, Vice President
Waterloo, ON (519) 746-2616
Virginia Murray, Managing Partner

O'Shea, Divine & Company, Inc.
5000 Birch Street, Suite 3000
Newport Beach, CA 92660
(949) 720-9070
fax (912) 673-8427
bob@divinesearch.com
www.divinesearch.com
Robert S. Divine, Founder
Also:
St. Mary'**s, GA** (949) 500-5203
Robert S. Divine, Founder

Dennis P. O'Toole & Associates, Inc.*
(Specialize in Hospitality & Leisure)
102 Laurel Avenue
Larchmont, NY 10538
(914) 833-3712
dpotooleassoc@aol.com
Dennis P. O'Toole, President

Ovca Associates, Inc.
410 Upper Lake Road
Lake Sherwood, CA 91361
(805) 370-1028
fax (805) 370-1027
contact@ovcaassociates.com
www.ovcaassociates.com
William J. Ovca, President

Overlook Group, LLC
338 Commerce Drive
P.O. Box 5146
Westport, CT 06881
(203) 341-9190
JTucci@overlookgroupllc.com
Joseph Tucci, Principal

Page-Wheatcroft & Company, Ltd.
(Specialize in High Tech, Law & Consulting)
Campbell Center
8150 North Central Expressway, Tower 2 Suite 1625
Dallas, TX 75206
(214) 393-4662
spage@p-wco.com
www.p-wco.com
Stephen J. L. Page, Chairman & Chief Executive Officer

Kirk Palmer & Associates, Inc.
(Specialize in Retailing & Fashion)
500 Fifth Avenue, Suite 1500
New York, NY 10110
(212) 983-6477
fax (212) 599-2597
resume@kirkpalmer.com
www.kirkpalmer.com
Kirk Palmer, Chief Executive Officer

Park Square Executive Search
101 Main Street, 14th Floor
Cambridge, MA 02142
(617) 401-2990
www.parksquaresearch.com
Bruce Rychlik, Managing Partner
Jonathan Fortescue, Managing Partner
Aaron Lapat, Managing Partner
Also:
Menlo Park, CA (650) 308-8140
Erik R. Lundh, Managing Partner

D. P. Parker & Associates Inc.
(Specialize in High Tech)
One Hollis Street, Suite 233
Wellesley, MA 02482
(781) 237-1220
fax (781) 237-4702
info@dpparker.com
www.dpparker.com
David P. Parker, President

Parker Executive Search
5 Concourse Parkway, Suite 2900
Atlanta, GA 30328
(770) 804-1996
fax (770) 804-1917
support@parkersearch.com
www.parkersearch.com
Daniel F. Parker, President

Pauze Group
(Specialize in Marketing, Communications, Business Development)
1470 rue Peel Tower A, Suite 1000
Montreal, QC H3A 1T1
(514) 845-2128
fax (514) 845-8687
info@groupepauze.com
www.groupepauze.com
Michel Pauze, President

Pawlik/Dorman Partners
(Specialize in Manufacturing, Technology, Professional Services)
2639 North Southport
Chicago, IL 60614
(773) 296-0950
info@pawlikdorman.com
www.pawlikdorman.com
Bernadette M. Pawlik, Senior Partner

Pearson Partners International, Inc.
8080 North Central Expressway, Suite 1200
Dallas, TX 75206
(214) 292-4130
fax (214) 292-4140
Response@PearsonPartnersIntl.com
www.pearsonpartnersintl.com
William D. Rowe, Vice President
Keith D. Pearson, Vice Chairman
Robert L. Pearson, Chief Executive Officer
Also:
Fort Lauderdale, FL (954) 463-2290
Jill C. Pearson, Principal
Fort Worth, TX (817) 886-4425
Renee Arrington, Principal
Honolulu, HI (214) 675-2141
Robert L. Pearson, Chief Executive

R.H. Perry & Associates, Inc.
(Specialize in Higher Education)
2607 31st Street NW
Washington, DC 20008
(202) 965-6464
fax (202) 338-3953
info@rhperry.com
www.rhperry.com
Robert Hastings Perry, President

Phillips Oppenheim*
(Specialize in Non-Profits)
521 Fifth Avenue, Floor 29
New York, NY 10175
(212) 953-1770
fax (212) 953-1775
info@phillipsoppenheim.com
www.phillipsoppenheim.com
Debra Oppenheim, Principal
Jane Phillips Donaldson, Principal
Also:
Washington, DC (202) 434-8774
Leslie Maddin, Managing Director

Pinnacle Associates, LLC
383 Diablo Road, Suite 109
Danville, CA 94526
(925) 241-7666
info@pinnaclea.com
www.pinnaclea.com
I. Solomon Aqua, Managing Partner
Robert Hurd, Partner
Peter Hwang, Partner Melanie Patterson, Partner

Pinton Forrest & Madden*
Guinness Tower
1055 West Hastings Street, Suite 2020
Vancouver, BC V6E 2E9
(604) 689-9970
fax (604) 689-9943
pfm@pfmsearch.com
www.pfmsearch.com
Casey Forrest, Partner
George Madden, Partner

Rene Plessner Associates Inc.
(Specialize in Cosmetics & Fragrances)
200 East 74th Street, Penthouse A
New York, NY 10021
(212) 421-3490
fax (212) 421-3999
www.plessner.com
Rene Plessner, President

Plummer & Associates, Inc.

(Specialize in Retail, Direct Marketing, Food Service & E-Commerce)
P.O. Box 607
New Canaan, CT 06840
(800) 603-9981
resume@plummersearch.com
www.plummersearch.com
John Plummer, President

Poirier, Hoevel & Company

3021 Calle de Marejada
Camarillo, CA 93010
(800) 207-3427
fax (805) 604-1285
info@phandco.com
www.phandco.com
Michael J. Hoevel, President

David Powell, Inc.

(Specialize in High Tech & Biotechnology)
3190 Clearview Way, Suite 100
San Mateo, CA 94402
(650) 357-6000
fax (650) 357-6001
dpi@davidpowell.com
www.davidpowell.com
David L. Powell, Chairman
David L. Powell, President
Also:
San Ramon, CA (650) 357-6000
David L. Powell, President

T. Pratt & Associates, Ltd.

(Specialize in Healthcare)
3821 East State, Suite 121
Rockford, IL 61108
(815) 397-2899
tyler@prattassoc.com
www.tylerprattassociates.com
Tyler P. Pratt, President

Preng & Associates, Inc.

(Specialize in Energy and Natural Resources)
2925 Briarpark, Suite 1111
Houston, TX 77042
(713) 266-2600
fax (713) 266-3070
houston@preng.com
www.preng.com
David E. Preng, President & Founder
Charles L. Carpenter, Research Director

Preston Human Capital Group

2 St. Clair Avenue West, Suite 605
Toronto, ON M4V 1L5
(416) 597-3301
fax (416) 640-0927
resume@phcap.ca
www.phcap.ca/
Cathy Preston, President

Preston-Reffett, LLC

74 East State Street, 1st Floor
Doylestown, PA 18901
(215) 489-9055
fax (215) 489-9059
gpreston@prestonreffett.com
www.prestonreffett.com
Gary Preston, Managing Partner
Also:
Arlington, VA (703) 351-5062
Ronald Flom, Managing Director
Bellevue, WA (425) 637-2993
Bill Reffett, Managing Partner
Fairfax, VA (703) 261-6010
Marshall Reffett, Managing Director
Morristown, NJ (973) 993-3131
Hayes Reilly, Managing Director
New York, NY (212) 835-1543
Elaine Erickson, Senior Managing Director
Washington, DC (703) 537-0877
Margaret Gottlieb, Managing Director
Williamsville, NY (716) 639-7629
David Whipple, Managing Director
Winter Park, FL (407) 637-2207
Jennifer McCorey, Managing Director

The Prince Houston Group

420 Lexington Avenue, Suite 2048
New York, NY 10170
(212) 313-9891
fax (212) 313-9892
recruit@princehouston.com
www.princehouston.com
Marylin L. Prince, Partner
James Houston, Partner

ProSearch, Inc.*

(Specialize in Information Technology & Finance)
1160 Limekiln Pike, Suite 100
Ambler, PA 19002
(215) 659-9005
resume@prosearch.com
www.prosearch.com
Suzanne F. Fairlie, President

The Prout Group*

1111 Superior Avenue, Suite 1120
Cleveland, OH 44114
(216) 771-5530
fax (216) 771-2260
resumes@proutgroup.com
www.proutgroup.com
Patrick M. Prout, President & Chief Executive Officer
Betsy Bruening, Vice President
Also:
New York, NY (212) 593-8240
Patrick M. Prout, Managing Director

Quick Leonard Kieffer International

(Specialize in Healthcare)
555 West Jackson Boulevard, Floor 2
Chicago, IL 60661
(312) 876-9800
fax (312) 876-9264
resume@qlksearch.com
www.qlksearch.com
Roger A. Quick, Chief Executive Officer
Michael C. Kieffer, Chairman

Quorum Associates, LLC

(Specialize in Finance & Multi-National Companies)
1005 Chapman Street
Yorktown Heights, NY 10598
(914) 320-6251
fax (212) 231-8121
info@quorumassociates.com
www.quorumassociates.com
Francis S.H. Goldwyn, Chief Operations Officer

Raines International Inc.*

75 Rockefeller Plaza, 27th Floor
New York, NY 10019
(212) 997-1100
fax (212) 997-0196
research@rainesinternational.com
www.rainesinternational.com
Bruce R. Raines, President
Also:
Boston, MA (617) 878-2022
Bruce R. Raines, President
Morristown, NJ (973) 539-0988
Bruce R. Raines, President

The Ransford Group

Neil Esperson Building
808 Travis Street, Suite 1200
Houston, TX 77002
(713) 722-7281

Dean E. McMann, Chief Executive Officer & Co-Chairman

Ratliff & Taylor
6450 Rockside Woods Boulevard S
Independence, OH 44131
(216) 901-6000
fax (216) 447-1559
SFrammartino@rtcpi.com
www.ratliffandtaylor.com
Frederick E. Taylor, President
Mike Milby, Chief Executive Officer
Jim Ratliff, Founder & Chairman

Red Arrow Recruiters, LLC
4840 Amber Valley Parkway
Fargo, ND 58104
(701) 364-5411
ttaylor@redarrowrecruiters.com
Roger Nelson, President

Redwood Partners, Ltd.
(SPECIALIZE IN INTERNATIONAL ADVISORY)
1410 Broadway, Suite 1507
New York, NY 10018
(212) 843-8585
fax (212) 843-9093
resume@redwoodpartners.com
www.redwoodpartners.com
Michael Flannery, Senior Managing Partner
Kailah Matyas, Managing Partner

Reed Shay & Company, LLC
(SPECIALIZE IN HIGH TECHNOLOGY)
775 East Blithedale, Suite 503
Mill Valley, CA 94941
(781) 674-2539
fax (415) 354-3399
robin@reedshay.com
www.reedshay.com
Robin Reed, Principal

Reeder & Associates, Ltd.
(SPECIALIZE IN HEALTH CARE)
1095 Old Roswell Road, Suite F
Roswell, GA 30076
(770) 649-7523
fax (770) 649-7543
research@reederassoc.com
www.reederassoc.com
Michael S. Reeder, President

Renaud Foster*
(SPECIALIZE IN CANADA SEARCHES)
100 Sparks Street, Suite 550
Ottawa, ON K1P 5B7
(613) 231-6666
fax (613) 231-6663
ottawa@renaudfoster.com
www.renaudfoster.com
Lili-Ann Foster, President
Also:
Montreal, QC (800) 513-8117
Lili-Ann Foster, President
Toronto, ON (800) 513-8117
Robert M. Yalden, Senior Associate

Retail IQ, LLC
(SPECIALIZE IN RETAIL AND HOSPITALITY INDUSTRIES)
350 South Main Street, Suite 216
Doylestown, PA 18901
(215) 489-9055
gpreston@retail-iq.com
www.retail-iq.com
Gary Preston, Managing Partner
Also:
Bellevue, WA (425) 637-2993
Bill Reffett, Managing Partner
Fairfax, VA (703) 537-0877
Tom Smith, Managing Partner

Reyman Associates
20 North Michigan Avenue, Suite 520
Chicago, IL 60602
(312) 580-0808
fax (312) 580-1181
sreyman@reymanassoc.com
www.reymanassoc.com
Susan Reyman, President

Russell Reynolds Associates, Inc.*
200 Park Avenue, Suite 2300
New York, NY 10166-0002
(212) 351-2000
fax (212) 370-0896
www.russellreynolds.com
James M. Bagley, Managing Director
Ron Lumbra, Managing Director & Area Manager
Also:
Atlanta, GA (404) 577-3000
Lawrence Kenney, Managing Director
Boston, MA (617) 523-1111
Mark Adams, Managing Director-Area Manager
Calgary, AB (403) 776-4174
Andy Macrae, Office Manager
Chicago, IL (312) 993-9696
Jeremy Rickman, Area Manager
Dallas, TX (214) 220-2033
Stuart Guthrie, Area Manager
Houston, TX (713) 754-5995
Stephen Newton, Managing Director
Los Angeles, CA (310) 775-8960
Jeffrey M. Warren, Managing Director-Area Manager
Minneapolis, MN (612) 332-6966
Robert W. Macdonald, Managing Director-Area Manager
Palo Alto, CA (650) 233-2400
Charley Geoly, Managing Director-Area Manager
San Francisco, CA (415) 352-3300
Tuck Rickards, Managing Director-Area Manager
Stamford, CT (203) 905-3341
William Henderson, Managing Director
Toronto, ON (416) 364-3355
Shawn Cooper, Managing Director-Country Manager
Washington, DC (202) 654-7800
Eric L. Vautour, Managing Director-Area Manager

Rhodes Associates
(SPECIALIZE IN REAL ESTATE AND FINANCIAL SERVICES)
555 Fifth Avenue, Floor 6
New York, NY 10017
(212) 983-2000
fax (212) 983-8333
infony@rhodesassociates.com
www.rhodesassociates.com
Steven Littman, Managing Partner
Jane Lyons, Partner

Ridenour & Associates
(SPECIALIZE IN DIRECT INTERACTIVE & INTEGRATED MARKETING)
1555 North Sandburg Terrace, Suite 602
Chicago, IL 60610
(312) 787-8228
fax (312) 787-8528
ssridenour@aol.com
www.ridenourassociates.com
Suzanne Swenson Ridenour, President

Riotto-Jones & Company, LLC
(SPECIALIZE IN WEALTH MANAGEMENT)
630 Mercer Avenue
Hartsdale, NY 10530
(212) 697-4575
fax (914) 683-3633
rjc@riottojones.com
www.riottojones.com
Anthony R. Riotto, President

Robinson Consulting Group
Harmon Cove Towers

Secaucus, NJ 07094
(201) 617-9595
fax (201) 617-1434
rcgsearch@yahoo.com
Bruce Robinson, President
Eric B. Robinson, Vice President & Partner
Also:
Peoria, AZ (602) 502-6392
John C. Robinson, Vice President & Partner

Rogers-McManamon Executive Search
(SPECIALIZE IN Med-Tech, Pharmaceutical, Biomedical)
33781 Via Cascada
San **Juan Capistrano, CA** 92675
(949) 496-1614
fax (949) 496-2305
Rogers@mcmanamon.com
Gay Rogers, Partner

ROI International Inc.
(SPECIALIZE IN Telecommunications & Managed Healthcare)
336 Park Avenue North
Renton, WA 98055
(425) 264-2100
fax (425) 264-2101
hr@roi-intl.com
www.roi-intl.com
Marc Goyette, President

Ropes Associates, Inc.
(SPECIALIZE IN Real Estate)
333 North New River Drive East, Suite 3000
Fort Lauderdale, FL 33301
(954) 525-6600
fax (954) 779-7279
sharon@ropesassociates.com
www.ropesassociates.com
John N. Ropes, President & Founder

Alexander Ross & Company
(SPECIALIZE IN Change Management and Learning)
100 Park Avenue, 34th Floor
New York, NY 10017
(212) 889-9333
fax (212) 864-5111
resumes@alexanderross.com
www.alexanderross.com
Ben Lichtenstein, Founder

RSM McGladrey
801 Nicollet Avenue, 11th Floor
West Tower
Minneapolis, MN 55402
(612) 376-9541
linda.rosso@rsmi.com
www.rsmmcgladrey.com
Linda Rosso, Search Consultant

RSMR*
308 West Erie Street
Chicago, IL 60654
(312) 957-0337
info@rsmr.com
www.rsmr.com
Christopher Swan, Managing Director

RSR Partners
600 Steamboat Road
Greenwich, CT 06830
(203) 618-7000
fax (203) 618-7011
resumes@rsrpartners.com
www.rsrpartners.com
Russell S. Reynolds, Chairman & Chief Executive Officer
Joseph A. Bailey, Managing Director
Carter L. Burgress, Managing Director
Nona K. Footz, Managing Director
Colin S. Graham, Managing Director
Thomas L. McLane, Managing Director
Wendelyne C. H. Murphy, Managing Director
Timothy W. O'Brien, Managing Director
Russell Trey Reynolds, Managing Director
Bruce J. Robertson, Managing Director
Barrett J. Stephens, Managing Director
P. Jason Ward, Managing Director
Also:
Los Angeles, CA (213) 986-4840
Gary J. Matus, Managing Director
New York, NY (212) 661-5725
John K. Keitt, Managing Director
Graham E. Michener, Managing Director
Charles G.T. Stonehill, Managing Director
Northfield, IL (312) 981-8860
Bradford L. McLane, Managing Director

RTP and Associates
1042 Willow Creek Road, Suite A101-479
Prescott, AZ 86301
(928) 713-6265
fax (928) 443-3083
resume@rtpassociates.com
www.rtpassociates.com
Bob Pike, Principal
Also:
Phoenix, AZ (602) 476-7288
Steve Batisto, Principal

Rurak & Associates, Inc.
1875 Eye Street NW, Suite 500
Washington, DC 20006
(202) 857-5218
fax (202) 429-9574
resumes@rurakassociates.com
Zbigniew T. Rurak, President

Rusher Loscavio Executive Search
(SPECIALIZE IN High Tech, Insurance, Financial Services, Non Profit)
369 Pine Street, Suite 221
San Francisco, CA 94104
(415) 765-6600
fax (415) 765-6601
resumes@rll.com
www.rll.com
J. Michael Loscavio, President
Robert Fisher, President -Non Profit
William H. Rusher, Chairman & Chief Executive Officer

Rust & Associates, Inc.
P.O. Box 3829
Suwanee, GA 30024
(678) 388-9895
fax (678) 921-0597
john@rustassociates.com
www.rustassociates.com
John R. Rust, President

The Sagacity Group
7 Sherman Court
Plainsboro, NJ 08536
(609) 799-7944
fax (609) 275-1755
info@sagacitygroup.com
Randall Brett, Managing Director

Salveson Stetson Group, Inc.*
Radnor Financial Center
150 North Radnor Chester Road, Suite F100
Radnor, PA 19087
(610) 341-9020
fax (610) 341-9025
wolf@ssgsearch.com
www.ssgsearch.com
John F. Salveson, Partner
Sally W. Stetson, Partner

Norm Sanders Associates

(SPECIALIZE IN INFORMATION TECHNOLOGY)
4 Bellevue Avenue
Rumson, NJ 07760
(732) 264-3700
mail@normsanders.com
www.normsanders.com
Walter J. McGuigan, Managing Director

The Sandhurst Group

5332 Seacape Lane, Suite 200
Plano, TX 75093
(972) 769-5227
fax (413) 480-5227
resumes@sandhurstgroup.com
www.sandhurstgroup.com
Phil Resch, Managing Director
Also:
Dallas, TX (214) 676-7774
Harvey Letcher, Managing Director
Herb Wise, Managing Director
Englewood, CO (303) 660-4185
Katherine Evans Blakley, Managing Director
Jim Demchak, Managing Director

Satterfield Renzenbrink Associates

7875 Annesdale Drive
Cincinnati, OH 45243
(513) 561-3679
resumes@satterfield3.com
www.satterfield3.com
Richard W. Satterfield, Managing Partner & Founder
Thomas A. Cruz, Senior Partner
Paul W. Renzenbrink, Managing Partner
Sheryl S. Wengel, Senior Partner
Also:
Carmel, IN (317) 844-8295
John P. Kuklinski, Senior Partner

Savoy Partners Ltd.

(SPECIALIZE IN CONSULTING SERVICES, GOVERNMENT CONTRACTING, SECURITY & DEFENSE, SALES & MARKETI)
1133 20th Street NW, Suite 200
Washington, DC 20036
(202) 887-0666
researchdirector@savoypartners.com
www.savoypartners.com
Robert J. Brudno, Managing Director & Founder

Schweichler Price Mullarkey & Barry

(SPECIALIZE IN HIGH TECH)
Building C
1 Letterman Drive, Suite M900
San Francisco, CA 94129
(415) 924-7200
fax (415) 924-9152
search@schweichler.com
www.schweichler.com
Andrew Price, Managing Partner
Kevin Barry, Managing Partner
Dave Mullarkey, Managing Partner
Lee J. Schweichler, Managing Partner

The Search Alliance

(SPECIALIZE IN HEALTH CARE, BANKING, MANUFACTURING & TECHNOLOGY)
31 South Fourth Street
Amelia Island, FL 32034
(904) 277-2535
fax (904) 277-7924
cgoodman@tsainc.net
www.tsainc.net
Tom Byrnes, Managing Partner

Search America

(SPECIALIZE IN PRIVATE CLUB MANAGEMENT. & HOSPITALITY)
5908 Meadowcreek Drive
Dallas, TX 75248-5451
(972) 233-3302
fax (775) 368-0040
info@searchamericanow.com
www.searchamericanow.com
Harvey M. Weiner, President
Also:
Boca Raton, FL (561) 479-4787
Mark Julian Weiner, Vice President

SeBA International, LLC*

(SPECIALIZE IN FINANCIAL, IT, BIOTECH & MANUFACTURING)
The Lincoln Building
305 Madison Avenue, Suite 2130
New York, NY 10165
(212) 370-7000
fax (212) 370-7011
sebateam@sebasearch.com
www.sebasearch.com
Robert Iommazzo, Managing Partner
Kate Bullis, Managing Partner
Also:
Santa Clara, CA (650) 388-3264
Robert Iommazzo, Managing Partner

Secura Burnett Company LLC

(SPECIALIZE IN FINANCE MANAGEMENT)
599 Bridgeway
Sausalito, CA 94965
(415) 332-8777
fax (415) 331-4404
resume@securaburnettco.com
Louis C. Burnett, Managing Partner
Also:
Indianapolis, IN (317) 241-2400
Lee D. Ashton, Chief Operating Officer

Security & Investigative Placement Consultants, LLC

(SPECIALIZE IN FINANCIAL INVESTIGATION & CORPORATE SECURITY MANAGEMENT)
7710 Woodmont Avenue, #209
Bethesda, MD 20814
(301) 229-6360
fax (301) 263-0907
info@siplacement.com
www.siplacement.com
Kathy L. Lavinder, Executive Director

Seeliger y Conde International LLC

(SPECIALIZE IN SPAIN AND LATIN AMERICAN COMPANY PLACEMENTS)
1111 Brickell Avenue, Suite 2645
Miami, FL 33131
(305) 577-8558
eduardo.rabassa@syc-amrop.com
en.syc-amrop.es/
Eduardo Rabassa, Managing Partner
Also:
Houston, TX (713) 360-4878
Carla Arimont, Partner

Seiden Krieger Associates, Inc.*

445 Park Avenue
New York, NY 10022
(212) 688-8383
fax (212) 688-5289
steven@seidenkrieger.com
www.seidenkrieger.com
Steven A. Seiden, President

Seitchik Corwin and Seitchik

(SPECIALIZE IN APPAREL, FOOTWEAR HOME FURNISHINGS & ACCESSORIES)
67 Milland Drive
Mill Valley, CA 94941
(800) 438-0279

fax (415) 928-8075
blade@seitchikcorwin.com
www.seitchikcorwin.com
J. Blade Corwin, Partner
Also:
New York, NY (212) 370-3592
William Seitchik, Partner

Robert Sellery Associates, Ltd.
(SPECIALIZE IN Not-for-Profit)
4701 Willard Avenue, Suite 1034
Chevy Chase, MD 20815
(301) 312-8727
sellery@sellery.com
www.sellery.com
Robert Sellery, Managing Director

Setren, Smallberg & Associates, Inc.
(SPECIALIZE IN Biotechnology & High Tech)
1330 Broadway, Suite 1830
Oakland, CA 94612
(510) 208-0310
fax (510) 208-0321
larry@setrensmallberg.com
setrensmallberg.com
Larry Setren, Partner
Victor Smallberg, Partner

Sharpstream Life Sciences
(SPECIALIZE IN Pharmaceuticals, Biotech, Medical Devices, Healthcare)
111 Presidential Boulevard, Suite 240
Bala Cynwud, PA 19004
(484) 567-2900
fax (610) 941-9288
info@sharpstream.com
www.sharpstream.com
Craig Natale, Managing Director, US

Shepherd Bueschel & Provus, Inc.
4146 North Harding Avenue, Suite 3230
Chicago, IL 60618
(773) 588-3230
fax (773) 588-3227
sbp@sbpsearch.com
David A. Bueschel, Principal
Barbara L. Provus, Principal
Daniel M. Shepherd, Principal

Shoemaker & Associates
1862 Independence Square, Suite A
Atlanta, GA 30338
(770) 395-7225
fax (770) 395-1090
lshoemaker@shoemakersearch.com
www.shoemakersearch.com
Larry C. Shoemaker, President

M. Shulman, Inc.
563 Vermont Street
San Francisco, CA 94107
(415) 437-6756
shulmaninc@comcast.net
Melvin Shulman, President

John Sibbald & Associates, Inc.
(SPECIALIZE IN Hospitality)
221 East Commercial Boulevard
Lauderdale by **the Sea, FL** 33308
(954) 493-9091
fax (954) 493-9911
jsibbald@sibbaldassociates.com
www.sibbaldassociates.com
John R. Sibbald, President

Siegel & Associates, Inc.
Two Union Square
601 Union Street, Suite 4200
Seattle, WA 98101
(206) 622-4282
fax (206) 622-4058
admin@siegel-associates.com
www.siegel-associates.com
Larry Siegel, Principal

Signature Search
4650 West Spencer Street, Suite 22
Appleton, WI 54914
(920) 749-9300
fax (920) 968-4650
mmueller@signaturesearch.com
www.signaturesearch.com
Michael S. Mueller, President & Chief Executive Officer
Also:
Green Bay, WI (920) 884-2550
Nancy Thompson, Partner
Raleigh, NC (919) 341-3032
Chip Magee, Vice President

Daniel A. Silverstein Associates, Inc.
(SPECIALIZE IN Health Care, Pharmaceuticals, Biotech, Medical Devices)
777 Yamato Road, Suite 100
Boca Raton, FL 33431
(561) 981-1801
fax (561) 998-7073
rpaul@dassearch.com
www.dassearch.com
Daniel A. Silverstein, President

SIMA International
(SPECIALIZE IN Not for Profit, Faith Based)
450 North Main Street
Stillwater, MN 55082-5060
(651) 351-7214
fax (651) 351-7216
info@peoplemanagementnc.com
www.simainternational.com
Mark K. Stevenson, Chairman & Senior Partner
Robert J. Stevenson, Chairman & Senior Partner
Also:
Cheshire, CT (203) 271-2846
Steven M. Darter, President
Franklin, TN (615) 261-4623
Tommy W. Thomas, Managing Director
Monument, CO (719) 488-4433
Robert W. Peters, Managing Director

Skott/Edwards Consultants
7 Royal Drive
Cherry Quay, NJ 08723
(732) 920-1883
fax (732) 477-1541
search@skottedwards.com
www.skottedwards.com
Skott B. Burkland, President

Slayton Search Partners, Inc.*
311 South Wacker, Suite 3200
Chicago, IL 60606
(312) 456-0080
fax (312) 456-0089
resume@slaytonsearchpartners.com
www.slaytonsearchpartners.com
Richard S. Slayton, President

Smith&Syberg,Inc.*
505 Washington Street, Suite 2A
Columbus, IN 47201
(812) 372-7254
fax (812) 372-7275
mail@smithandsyberg.com
www.smithandsyberg.com
Joseph E. Smith, Partner
Keith A. Syberg, Partner

H.C. Smith, Ltd.
24000 Mercantile Road, Unit 7
Beachwood, OH 44122
(216) 752-9966
fax (216) 752-9970
info@hcsmith.com
www.hcsmith.com
Herb Smith, Chairman

Smith, Scott & Associates

P.O. Box 38475
Colorado Springs, CO 80937
(719) 538-4404
fax (866) 334-0643
gary.smith@smithscott.com
www.smithscott.com
Gary J. Smith, Managing Partner

Snowden Associates

(Specialize in Manufacturing, Banking, Finance)
1 New Hampshire Avenue, Suite 125
Portsmouth, NH 03801
(603) 431-1553
fax (603) 431-3809
portsmouth@snowdenassociates.com
www.snowdenassociates.com
Len Rishkofski, President & CEO
Also:
Bedford, NH (877) 603-5678
Len Rishkofski, President & CEO
Boston, MA (877) 603-5678
Len Rishkofski, President & CEO
Nashua, NH (877) 603-5678
Len Rishkofski, President & CEO
Portland, ME (877) 603-5678
Len Rishkofski, President & CEO

Sockwell Partners

800 East Boulevard, Suite 200
Charlotte, NC 28203
(704) 372-1865
fax (704) 372-8960
lhorton@sockwell.com
www.sockwell.com
Robert Sherrill, Managing Director
Susan Jernigan, Managing Director
Lyttleton Rich, Managing Director
Steve Sellers, Managing Partner
Also:
Chapel Hill, NC (919) 929-6260
Elizabeth Denton, Managing Director

Solomon-Page Group LLC

(Specialize in Life Sciences and Healthcare)
260 Madison Avenue
New York, NY 10016
(212) 403-6166
fax (212) 824-1505
www.spghealthcare.com
Marc Gouran, President - Healthcare
Also:
Conshohocken, PA (610) 941-2782
Marc Gouran, President
San Diego, CA (619) 291-2300
Thomas M. Murphy, Senior Vice President Biotechnology

Solutions Group

Post Office Box 360805
Birmingham, AL 35236
(205) 663-1301
fax (205) 663-1306
sgsearch@aol.com
Hinky Verchot, President

Spano Pratt

625 North Broadway, Suite 200
Milwaukee, WI 53202
(414) 283-9533
fax (414) 291-8957
info@spanopratt.com
www.spanopratt.com
Jamie Pratt, Partner
Rose Spano Iannelli, Partner

Spence Associates International Inc.

530 Bufflehead Drive
Kiawah Island, SC 29455
(843) 768-6706
fax (843) 768-6706
web@spenceassociates.com
Gene L. Spence, President

Spencer Stuart*

353 North Clark, Suite 2500
Chicago, IL 60654
(312) 822-0080
fax (312) 822-0116
contact@spencerstuart.com
www.spencerstuart.com
Kevin M. Connelly, Chairman
Matthew D. Belda, Consultant
Rich Brennen, Consultant
Suzanne M. Burns, Consultant
Lynn K. Cherney, Consultant
Mark G. Ciolek, Consultant
Susan Coffin, Consultant
Charles M. Falcone, Office Manager
Amanda C. Fox, Consultant
Kathleen S. Lennon, Consultant
Stewart Lumsden, Consultant
Kim S. McKesson, Consultant
John Milman, Consultant
Christopher C. Nadherny, Managing Director
Sheila M. O'Grady, Consultant
Stephen G. Patscot, Consultant
Thomas G. Putrim, Consultant
Thomas J. Snyder, Office Manager
Melanie L. Steinbach, Consultant
Gilbert R. Stenholm, Consultant
Francois P. Truc, Consultant
Alvan Turner, Consultant
Greg Welch, Consultant
Also:
Atlanta, GA (404) 504-4400
Nicolas J. Albizzatti, Consultant
James M. Carty, Consultant
Lee Esler, Office Manager
Graham W. Galloway, Consultant
Carl Gilchrist, Consultant
Sharon S. Hall, Consultant
Timothy J. Henn, Consultant
Charles L. Jordan, Consultant
John T. Mitchell, Consultant
William B. Reeves, Consultant
Katie Mitchell Tucker, Consultant
Boston, MA (617) 531-5731
Michael J. Anderson, Consultant
George M. Anderson, Consultant
Thomas D. Carey, Consultant
Mark I. Furman, Consultant
Mary B. Gorman, Consultant
Jason C.W. Hancock, Office Manager
Stephen P. Kelner, Consultant
Mary F. Moriarty, Consultant
Jerry Noonan, Consultant
Emmelyn M. O'Meara, Consultant
Deborah Prothrow-Stith, Consultant
Fleur Segal, Consultant
Calgary, AB (403) 538-8658
Cliff W. Howe, Office Manager
John McKay, Search Consultant
Coral Gables, FL (305) 443-9911
Michael J. Bell, Consultant
Robert S. DeVries, Office Manager
Joseph M. Kopsick, Consultant
David MacEachern, Consultant
Dallas, TX (214) 672-5200
Randall D. Kelley, Consultant
David M. Love, Consultant
Isvaldo B. Perez, Consultant
Terry W. Price, Consultant
Steven A. Rivard, Office Manager
Houston, TX (713) 225-1621
Mary D. Bass, Consultant
Chadwick D. Covey, Consultant
Brad A. Farnsworth, Consultant
Jeffrey E. Hyler, Consultant
Tom M. Simmons, Consultant
Irvine, CA (949) 930-8000
Brigette Frankel, Director
Fran Helms, Consultant
Tarun R. Inuganti, Office Manager
Kristine M. Johnson, Consultant
Bruce J. Lachenauer, Consultant
Los Angeles, CA (310) 209-0610
Kelley L. Brack, Consultant
Stephanie A. Davis, Consultant
Felicia K. Gorcyca, Consultant
Judy Havas, Consultant
Jennifer P. Heenan, Consultant
Soo J. Hong, Consultant
Tarun R. Inuganti, Office Manager
Todd D. Labeaune, Consultant
Jack R. Schlosser, Managing

Director
Minneapolis, MN (612) 313-2000
Susan S. Boren, Partner
Simon J. Foster, Consultant
Patrick B. Walsh, Office Manager
Erik J. Wordelman, Consultant
Montreal, QC (514) 288-3377
Louis Daniel Desjardins, Search Consultant
Jerome Piche, Office Manager
New York, NY (212) 336-0200
Stephen R. Blackman, Consultant
Joseph H. Boccuzi, Leader Life Sciences Practice
Jennifer Bol, Consultant
Arthur S. Brown, Consultant
Jordan L. Brugg, Consultant
Sarah Burley Reid, Consultant
Lloyd E. Campbell, Consultant
John R. Collett, Consultant
David S. Daniel, Chief Executive Officer
Thomas T. Daniels, Consultant
Julie Hembrock Daum, Consultant
Peter K. Gonye, Consultant
Susan S. Hart, Consultant
Bernhard Kickenweiz, Consultant
Richard Lannamann, Consultant
Filomena Leonardi, Consultant
Eric Leventhal, Office Manager
Sandy McLane, Consultant
Justin Menkes, Consultant
Catherine R. Nathan, Consultant
Thomas J. Neff, Partner
Tom Scanlon, Partner
Robin Soren, Partner
Kathryn S. Sugerman, Partner
Joel Von Ranson, Partner
Kristin Wait, Partner
Ben Williams, Partner
Nicholas S. Young, Partner
Philadelphia, PA (215) 814-1600
Jeffrey T. Constable, Office Manager
Marie Ford, Consultant
Jennifer Herrmann, Consultant
Frank Marsteller, Consultant
Connie McCann, Consultant
Philip M. Murphy, Consultant
Alexis H. Stiles, Consultant
San Francisco, CA (415) 495-4141
Elizabeth J. Fisher, Consultant
Kimberly Fullerton, Consultant
Mimi Hancock, Consultant
Phil Johnston, Consultant
Lisa W. Maibach, Consultant
Karen D. Quint, Consultant
William R. Schutte, Office Manager
Thomas Seclow, Consultant
Robert Stark, Consultant
Mark K. Yowe, Consultant
San Mateo, CA (650) 356-5500
Cathy Anterasian, Consultant
Jason Baumgarten, Consultant
Jason Baumgarten, Consultant
James J. Buckley, Consultant
T. Christopher Butler, Consultant
Albert Climent, Manager
Michael E. Dickstein, Consultant
Ben J. Holzemer, Office Manager
Ben J. Holzemer, Office Manager
Edgardo G. Montoya, Consultant
Kristin H. Richards, Consultant
Nayla Rizk, Consultant
Jonathan R. Vibal, Consultant
Ryan Weber, Consultant
Seattle, WA (206) 224-5660
Michael E. Dickstein, Consultant
Stamford, CT (203) 324-6333
Janine C. Ames, Consultant
Peter Bogin, Consultant
Arthur S. Brown, Office Manager
James M. Citrin, Consultant
William B. Clemens, Office Manager
Michele E. Haertel, Consultant
Valerie R. Harper, Office Manager
George H. Jamison, Managing Director
Claudia Lacy Kelly, Consultant
Adam J. Kovach, Consultant
Anthony T. Laudico, Consultant
Dayton Ogden, Consultant
Michael Partington, Consultant
Richard M. Routhier, Consultant
Lambert A. Rugani, Consultant
Greg Sedlock, Consultant
Toronto, ON (416) 361-0311
Patrick J.L. Bliley, Consultant
John Koopman, Office Manager
Andrew J. MacDougall, Consultant
Carter Powis, Consultant
Sharon Rudy, Consultant
Peter R. Simon, Consultant
Tanya Van Biesen, Consultant
Washington, DC (202) 639-8111
Jacqueline Arends, Partner
Leslie Hortum, Office Manager
Sally M. Sterling, Partner

Spilman & Associates, Inc.

5956 Sherry Lane, Suite 1000
Dallas, TX 75219
(972) 788-4044
info@spilmanassociates.com
www.spilmanassociates.com
Mary Spilman, Managing Partner

Stanton Chase International*

400 Galleria Parkway, Suite 1500
Atlanta, GA 30339
(404) 252-3677
fax (678) 385-6717
atlanta@stantonchase.com
www.stantonchase.com
Dean Bare, Regional Vice President, North America
Also:
Austin, TX (512) 502-9833
David Harap, Director
Baltimore, MD (410) 528-8400
Ted Muendel, Managing Director & International Chairman
Boca Raton, FL (561) 997-0011
William E. Frank, Managing Director
Juan D. Morales, Managing Director
Boston, MA (617) 988-2887
Thomas W. Barao, Managing Director
Brentwood, TN (615) 371-6113
Daniel Casteel, Managing Director
Calgary, AB (403) 262-6780
Christine Fisher, Managing Director
Ward Garven, Managing Director
Dallas, TX (972) 455-9211
Steve B. Watson, Managing Director
Lake Forest, IL (847) 722-4180
Bernard Layton, Managing Director
Montreal, QC (514) 935-3468
Emerson Hughes, Managing Director
New York, NY (212) 808-0040
Charles D. Wright, Managing Director
San Francisco, CA (415) 398-1001
Paul K. Herrerias, Managing Director
Santa Monica, CA (310) 474-1029
Edward J. Savage, Managing Director

Staub Warmbold Associates Inc.

575 Madison Avenue, 10th Floor
New York, NY 10022
(212) 605-0554
fax (212) 759-7304
resumes@staubwarmbold.com
www.staubwarmbold.com
Robert A. Staub, President

Adam Steele & Associates

1209 North Fourth Street
Manchester, IA 52057
(563) 927-6401
asteeleassoc@yahoo.com
A. R. Hawkes, Managing Director

Steinbrun Hughes and Associates
(Specialize in Financial Services, CFO's, Strategy & Investment Banking)
2444 Wilshire Boulevard, Suite 414
Santa Monica, CA 90403
(310) 857-1257
fax (310) 857-1264
resumes@steinbrunhughes.com
www.steinbrunhughes.com
Lisa A. Hughes, Partner

Stephens Associates, Ltd., Inc.
(Specialize in High Tech)
5186 Blazer Parkway
Post Office Box 151114
Dublin, OH 43017
(614) 766-7900
fax (614) 766-7990
saltd@stephensassoc.com
www.stephensassoc.com
Stephen A. Martinez, President

Michael Stern Associates, Inc.
20 Bay Street, 11th Floor
Toronto, ON M5J 2N8
(416) 593-0100
fax (416) 214-2043
admin@michaelstern.com
www.michaelstern.com
Michael Stern, President

The Stevens Group
110 Stone Canyon, Suite 101
New Braunfels, TX 78132
(830) 964-5701
fax (817) 887-5946
info@thestevensgroup.com
www.thestevensgroup.com
Ken G. Stevens, Managing Director

Stevens, Valentine & McKeever
162 West Collins Court
Blackwood, NJ 08012
(856) 228-1216
fax (856) 228-0410
svm@execusearchresources.com
www.execusearchresources.com
Leonard W. Stevens, Principal

Stewart, Stein & Scott, Ltd.
1301 Cambridge Street, Suite 109
Minneapolis, MN 55343
(952) 545-8151
fax (952) 545-8464
research@stewartstein.net
www.stewartstein.net
Jeffrey O. Stewart, President, Founding Partner
Terry Stein, Founding Partner

Stewart/Laurence Associates, LLC
(Specialize in High Technology & Life Sciences)
P.O. Box 81146
Boca Raton, FL 33481
(561) 961-4739
fax (561) 807-2557
mel@stewartlaurence.com
www.stewartlaurence.com
Mel Stewart Klein, President

Stiles Associates, LLC
(Specialize in Manufacturing Companies, All Functions)
276 Newport Road, Suite 208
New London, NH 03257
(603) 526-6566
fax (603) 526-6185
tberio@leanexecs.com
www.leanexecs.com
Linford E. Stiles, Chairman
Jason S. Stiles, President

Stone Murphy
5500 Wayzata Boulevard, Suite 1020
Minneapolis, MN 55416
(763) 591-2300
fax (763) 591-2301
sm@stonemurphy.com
www.stonemurphy.com
Toni M. Barnum, Partner
Bob Cowan, Managing Director
Al Giesen, Managing Director

Stranberg Resource Group
10 South Riverside Plaza, #1800
Chicago, IL 60606
(312) 626-2770
info@stranberg.com
www.stranberg.com
James R. Stranberg, Managing Partner
Anne L. Joosep, Partner
Kate Stranberg, Partner

Straube Associates
853 Turnpike Street
North Andover, MA 01845
(978) 687-1993
fax (978) 687-1886
sstraube@straubeassociates.com
www.straubeassociates.com
Stanley H. Straube, President

Strawn Arnold & Associates, Ltd.
(Specialize in Health Care)
2508 Ashley Worth Boulevard, Suite 150
Austin, TX 78738
(512) 263-1131
fax (512) 263-4149
genmail@salainc.com
www.salainc.com
Connie Pate, Partner
Jeff P. Ashpitz, Managing Partners
John L. Groover, Managing Partner
David M. Leech, Executive Vice President
Chris Schneider, Executive Vice President
Also:
Madison, NJ (973) 520-8928
Mark Durham, Executive Vice President
Mountain Lakes, NJ
(973) 335-3125
Oliver Esman, Partner

The Stuart Compton Group
400 Colony Square
1201 Peachtree, Suite 200
Atlanta, GA 30361
(404) 872-7600
fax (404) 420-2402
info@stuartcompton.com
www.stuartcompton.com
Richard L. Gallo, Vice President

C.W. Sweet, Inc.
950 North Michigan Avenue, Suite 4202
Chicago, IL 60611
(312) 649-9328
Charles Sweet, President

Tandy, Morrison & LaTour LLC
113 West Montgomery Street
Baltimore, MD 21230
(717) 371-7153
ctandy@tmlsearch.com
www.tmlsearch.com
Charles W. Tandy, Principal
Catherine Morrison, Principal
Also:
Evanston, IL (847) 864-4200
Stephen LaTour, Principal

Tarnow Associates
551 Park Avenue, Suite 4
Scotch Plains, NJ 07076
(908) 288-7700
fax (908) 288-7634
info@tarnow.com
www.tarnow.com

Emil Vogel, Managing Partner

Taylor Winfield*

(Specialize in High Tech & Venture Capital)
One Lincoln Centre
5400 LBJ Freeway, Suite 810
Dallas, TX 75240
(972) 392-1400
fax (972) 392-1455
candidates@taylorwinfield.com
www.taylorwinfield.com
Ann Zeichner, Managing Director
Connie J. Adair, Chief Executive Officer
Kirk Harrell, Managing Director
Also:
Menlo Park, CA (650) 779-4611
Gerri Kies, Managing Director
Amy Vernetti, Managing Director
New York, NY (972) 392-1400
Lynn Durant, Managing Director

Telford, Adams & Alexander

402 West Broadway, Suite 900
San Diego, CA 92101
(619) 464-0848
fax (619) 464-1077
taasandiego@aol.com
John T. Alexander, Managing Principal

Tessera Executive Search

Waterpark Place
20 Bay Street, Suite 1100
Toronto, ON M5J 2N8
(416) 862-9987
growthleaders@tesserasearch.ca
www.tesserasearch.ca/
Peter Grech, Managing Partner

Thacher Executive Search*

(Specialize in Consumer Products & Services, Technology, and Business Services)
126 Monticello Avenue
Piedmont, CA 94611
(510) 596-9011
adam@thachersearch.com
www.thachersearch.com
Adam Thacher, Managing Director

Thomas Resource Group, Inc.

(Specialize in Life Sciences)
550 Tenaya Drive, Suite 100
Tiburon, CA 94920
(415) 999-5609
terry@thomasresource.com
www.thomasresource.com
Terry Thomas, President

TillmanCarlson

311 South Wacker Drive, Suite 5250
Chicago, IL 60606
(312) 922-8200
fax (312) 922-1590
resumes@TillmanCarlson.com
www.TillmanCarlson.com
J. Robert Tillman, Partner
Kelly A. Carlson, Partner

TKJ Associates

606 Post Road East, Suite 568
Westport, CT 06880
(203) 454-3838
fax (203) 454-9868
resumes@tkjassociates.com
www.tkjassociates.com
Tammy K. Jersey, President

TNS Partners, Inc.

3600 Shire Boulevard, Suite 208
Richardson, TX 75082
(214) 369-3565
fax (214) 369-9865
info@tnspartners.com
www.tnspartners.com
Craig C. Neidhart, Partner
Kathy Carter, Partner
John K. Semyan, Partner

Skip Tolette Executive Search

(Specialize in Information Technology)
577 West Saddle River Road
Saddle River, NJ 07458
(201) 818-0970
fax (201) 818-0970
skiptol@aol.com
Skip Tolette, Partner

Toombs Inc.

(Specialize in Only Canadian Searches)
Vantage Pointe
1053 10 Street SW, Suite 206
Calgary, AB T2R 1S6
(403) 777-2360
calgary@toombsinc.com
www.toombsinc.com
Mark Toombs, President
Kathleen Wollenbert, Senior Vice President & General Manager
Also:
Edmonton, AB (780) 424-4700
Tracey Lillis, Senior Vice President
Vancouver, BC (604) 899-2095
Peter Saulnier, Vice President & General Manager

Transearch

308 West Erie Street, 3rd Floor
Chicago, IL 60654
(312) 957-0337
fax (312) 957-0335
chicago@transearch.com
www.transearch.com
John Ryan, Partner
Also:
Miami, FL (305) 358-8822
Luisa Guzman, Managing Partner

Transearch-Latin America

1111 Brickell Avenue, Suite 8102125
Miami, FL 33131
(305) 358-8822
fax (305) 358-8780
miami@transearch.com
www.transearch.com
Luisa Guzman, Managing Partner

Travis & Company

(Specialize in Medical Devices, Biotechnology & Pharmaceuticals)
P.O. Box 590356
Newton Center, MA 02459
(978) 878-3232
resumes@travisandco.com
www.travisandco.com
Michael J. Travis, President

Trendl Associates, Ltd.

941 West Winona, Suite 1W
Chicago, IL 60640
(773) 728-6973
fax (773) 728-6976
resumes@trendl.net
www.trendl.net
Joseph R. Trendl, President
Barbara Kauffman, Managing Principal

Tyler & Company

(Specialize in Healthcare & Life Sciences)
400 Northridge Road, Suite 1250
Atlanta, GA 30350
(770) 396-3939
fax (770) 396-6693
resumesub@tylerandco.com
www.tylerandco.com
J. Larry Tyler, Chairman & Chief Executive Officer
Elizabeth B. Hanckel, Senior Vice President
Also:
Austin, TX (512) 329-2785
Nelson A. Mann, Senior Vice President
Chadds Ford, PA (610) 558-6100
Patricia A. Hoffmeir, Senior Vice

President
Dennis J. Kain, President
Stephanie J. Underwood, Senior Vice President
Charlotte, NC (704) 845-2227
George E. Linney, Vice President

The Vanderbloemen Search Group
(Specialize in Religion)
5504 Morningside Drive
Houston, TX 77005
(713) 300-9665
support@vanderbloemen.com
www.vanderbloemen.com
William Vanderbloemen, Chief Executive Officer & Founder

VerKamp-Joyce Associates, Inc.
(Specialize in Manufacturing)
4320 Winfield Road, Suite 200
Warrenville, IL 60555
(630) 836-8030
sheilajoyce@att.net
Sheila M. Joyce, Managing Partner
J. Frank VerKamp, Partner

The Verriez Group Inc.
One London Place
255 Queens Avenue, Suite 1000
London, ON N6A 5R8
(519) 673-3463
fax (519) 673-4748
verriez@verriez.com
www.verriez.com
Paul M. Verriez, President
Also:
Toronto, ON (416) 847-0036
Paul M. Verriez, President

Vetted Solutions*
(Specialize in Non-Profits and Associations)
888 16th Street NW, Suite 800
Washington, DC 20006
(202) 544-4749
jim.zaniello@vettedsolutions.com
www.vettedsolutions.com
Jim Zaniello, President

Vlcek & Company, Inc.
620 Newport Center Drive, Suite 1100
Newport Beach, CA 92660
(949) 752-0661
mail@vlcekco.com
www.vlcekco.com
Thomas J. Vlcek, President

Vogrinc & Short, Inc.
429 South Phelps Avenue, Suite 708
Rockford, IL 61108
(815) 394-1001
fax (815) 394-1046
brianv@vogshort.com
www.vogshort.com
Brian Vogrinc, Partner
Thomas Short, Partner

Wakefield Talabisco International
11 East 44th Street, Suite 1206
New York, NY 10017
(212) 661-8600
fax (212) 661-8832
contact@wtali.com
www.wtali.com
Barbara Talabisco, Partner/President/CEO

Waldthausen & Associates, Inc.
(Specialize in German Companies placements)
1910 Abbott Street, Suite 201
Charlotte, NC 28203
(704) 372-2172
fax (704) 372-2039
research@waldthauseninc.com
www.waldthauseninc.com
Kurt G. Waldthausen, Partner

Walling, June & Associates
(Specialize in Health Care & Financial Services)
P.O. Box 116
Davidsonville, MD 21035
(301) 261-7132
www.wallingjune.com
Gregory J. Walling, Senior Partner

Deborah Snow Walsh, Inc.
1000 Skokie Boulevard, Suite 400
Wilmette, IL 60091
(847) 920-0089
fax (847) 920-0884
srexec@dswalsh.com
www.dswalsh.com
Deborah Snow Walsh, President
Hilary Dexter, Executive Vice President

Warren & Morris, Ltd.
(Specialize in Communications, Hi Tech & Entertainment)
15102 Sun Valley Lane
P.O. Box 1090
Del Mar, CA 92014
(858) 461-0040
fax (858) 481-6221
cmorris@warrenmorrisltd.com
www.warrenmorrisltd.com
Charles C. Morris, Senior Partner

Waterhouse Executive Search
(Specialize in Canada Searches Only)
402 Queen Street
Saskatoon, SK S7K 0M3
(306) 934-1743
fax (306) 934-1630
peggiekoenig@waterhousesearch.com
www.waterhousesearch.com
Peggie Koenig, Vice President
Also:
Vancouver, BC (604) 806-7715
Grant C. Smith, Senior Partner

R. J. Watkins & Company, Ltd.
750 B Street, Suite 3300
San Diego, CA 92101
(619) 299-3094
fax (619) 725-4950
bwatkins@rjwatkins.com
www.rjwatkins.com
Robert J. Watkins, Chairman

Watson Group LLC
4 Sharp Hill Lane
Ridgefield, CT 06877
(203) 894-1978
maggie@watsongroupllc.com
Maggie Watson, Managing Partner

Waveland International Inc.
Two Prudential Plaza
180 North Stetson Avenue, Suite 1440
Chicago, IL 60601
(312) 739-9600
fax (312) 228-9600
info@wavelandsearch.com
www.wavelandsearch.com
Phillip D. Greenspan, Partner
Philip J. Nicholson, Partner
Nelson Rodriquez, Managing Partner
Also:
Dallas, TX (972) 851-7200
Tim Feaster, Partner
Ho-Ho-**Kus, NJ** (914) 391-3056
Michael J. Koeller, Managing Director

D. L. Weiss and Associates

18201 Von Karman Avenue, Suite 310
Irvine, CA 92612-1005
(949) 833-5001
fax (949) 833-5073
mail@dlweiss.com
David L. Weiss, President

Wellington Management Group

(SPECIALIZE IN CONSUMER PRODUCTS, RETAIL, INDUSTRIAL PRODUCTS, MANUFACTURING, COMMUNICATIONS, S)
300 Delaware Avenue, Suite 1380
Wilmington, DE 19801
(215) 569-8900
fax (302) 651-0126
resumes@wellingtonmg.com
www.wellingtonmg.com
Robert Scott Campbell, Managing Partner
Walter R. Romanchek, Co-Founder

Wells, Inc.

(SPECIALIZE IN FINANCIAL SERVICES AND TECHNOLOGY)
4200 Dublin Road
Columbus, OH 43221
(614) 876-0651
info@wellsinc.com
www.wellsinc.com
Mark D. Wells, President

Jude M. Werra & Associates, LLC

205 Bishop's Way, Suite 226
Brookfield, WI 53005
(262) 797-9166
fax (262) 797-9540
jmwa@judewerra.com
judewerra.com
Jude M. Werra, President

Westcott Thomas & Associates Ltd.

(SPECIALIZE IN CONCENTRATION IN GOVERNMENT, ASSOCIATIONS, HUMAN RESOURCES, SALES & MARKETING)
92 Caplan Avenue, Suite 308
Barrie, ON L4N 0Z7
(705) 733-2477
fax (705) 719-9235
westcott@vianet.ca
Michael J. Thomas, President & Chief Executive Officer

The Westminster Group, Inc.

(SPECIALIZE IN FINANCIAL SERVICES, MANUFACTURING, PACKAGING)
121 Gadsden Street
Chester, SC 29706
(800) 436-2101
fax (803) 385-2735
candidates@wgpeople.com
www.wgpeople.com
Gloria Kellerhals, Managing Partner
Tom Kellerhals, Senior President

S. J. Wexler Associates, Inc.

(SPECIALIZE IN HUMAN RESOURCES & COMMUNICATIONS)
1120 Avenue of the Americas, Floor 4
New York, NY 10036
(212) 626-6599
fax (212) 626-6598
sjwexler@earthlink.net
Suzanne J. Wexler, President

Wheless Partners

Founders Trust Center
1740 Oxmoor Road, Suite A
Birmingham, AL 35209
(800) 448-0926
fax (205) 870-1553
inquire@whelesspartners.com
www.whelesspartners.com
Mike Wheless, Chairman & CEO
Kevin Arvin, Senior Partner & Chief Marketing Officer
Brian Aston, Senior Partner
Michael Ballew, Senior Partner
Beth Butler, Senior Partner
Gene Head, Senior Partner
Ed McCracken, President - Healthcare Division
Mabry Smith, President & Managing Partner
Barry Vines, Senior Partner
Chris Vines, Senior Partner
Scott Watson, Senior Partner
Michael Wheless, President - Houston

The WhiteRock Group, LLC

(SPECIALIZE IN FINANCIAL SERVICES)
145 West 57th Street, 9th Floor
New York, NY 10019
(212) 258-2780
fax (212) 258-2784
mb90901@hotmail.com
www.whiterockgroup.com
Gustavo G. Dolfino, President

Whitney Group

(SPECIALIZE IN FINANCIAL SERVICES)
747 Third Avenue, 17th Floor
New York, NY 10017
(212) 508-3500
fax (212) 508-3540
recruiter@whitneygroup.com
www.whitneygroup.com
Gary S. Goldstein, Chief Executive Officer & Chairman
Alicia Lazaro, Managing Director
Michael D. Zinn, Chief Operating Officer

The Whittaker Group

(SPECIALIZE IN HEALTHCARE)
2232 South Main Street, Suite 437
Ann Arbor, MI 48103
(734) 475-9300
fax (866) 740-1395
mwhittaker@wgsearch.com
www.whittakergroup.org
Michelle Whittaker-McCracken, Managing Partner & Founder

Robert J. Williams & Associates

1621 Garden Street
Palatine, IL 60067
(847) 397-9205
fax (847) 397-9204
rjwa@comcast.net
Robert J. Williams, President

Williams Executive Search, Inc.

8500 Normandale Lake Boulevard, Suite 610
Minneapolis, MN 55437
(952) 767-7900
fax (952) 767-7905
resumes@williams-exec.com
www.williams-exec.com
William P. Dubbs, President
Diane Fewer, Executive Search Consultant

Williams, Roth & Hanley, Inc.

7 South Lincoln Street
Hinsdale, IL 60521-3464
(630) 887-7771
fax (630) 850-4682
wrkinc@aol.com
Alan P. Hanley, Partner
Robert J. Roth, Partner

Winguth, Grant & Company

1726 Solano Avenue
Berkeley, CA 94707
(415) 377-8592
fax (510) 524-4092
sgrant@winguthgrant.com
www.winguthgrant.com
Susan G. Grant, President & Partner

Winston Ventures, LLC

P.O. Box 336652
Greeley, CO 80634
(970) 573-6664
fax (970) 494-0102
resumes@winstonventuresllc.com
www.winstonventuresllc.com
Thomas Winston, President
Also:
Williamsburg, VA (757) 876-5222
Mark Hofmeister, President, East Coast

Winthrop Partners Inc.

108 Corporate Park Drive, Suite 220
White Plains, NY 10604
(914) 253-8282
fax (914) 253-6440
winthrop@winthroppartners.com
Steven Goldshore, President

Witt/Kieffer*

(SPECIALIZE IN HEALTH CARE, HIGHER EDUCATION, NON-PROFIT, INSURANCE, E-COMMERCE)
2015 Spring Road, Suite 510
Oak Brook, IL 60523
(630) 990-1370
fax (630) 990-1382
info@wittkieffer.com
www.wittkieffer.com
Michael F. Doody, Senior Vice President
Dennis M. Barden, Senior Vice President
Kathleen M. Gillespie, Senior Vice President
Jordan M. Hadelman, Chairman
Linda B. Hodges, Senior Vice President
Karen E. Otto, Senior Vice President
Charles W.B. Wardell, President
Anne Zenzer, Senior Vice President

Also:
Atlanta, GA (404) 233-1370
Jena E. Abernathy, Vice President
Andrew P. Chastain, Senior Vice President
Stephen J. Kratz, Vice President
Bethesda, MD (301) 654-5070
Anna Wharton Phillips, Senior Vice President & Board Chair
Burlington, MA (781) 272-8899
Emanuel D. Berger, Senior Vice President
Paul W. H. Bohne, Senior Vice President
Kimberly A. Smith, Senior Vice President & Regional Director
Emeryville, CA (510) 420-1370
Stephen N. Kirnon, Vice President
Elaina Spitaels-Genser, Senior Vice President
Houston, TX (713) 266-6779
Marvene M. Eastham, Senior Vice President
Irvine, CA (949) 851-5070
Mark J. Andrew, Senior Vice President
James W. Gauss, Chairman
Richard A. Swan, Vice President
Louisville, KY (502) 228-4030
David Boggs, Practice Leader
New York, NY (212) 686-2676
Gregory R. Santore, Vice President
Saint Louis, MO (314) 862-1370
Christine Mackey-Ross, Senior Vice President

Wojdula & Associates, Ltd.

N7645 East Lakeshore Drive, Suite 200
Whitewater, WI 53190
(608) 271-2000
fax (262) 473-4933
search@wojdula.com
Andrew G. Wojdula, President

D. S. Wolf Group International, LLC

(SPECIALIZE IN INVESTMENT BANKING & CORPORATE FINANCE)
330 Madison Avenue, 20th Floor
New York, NY 10017
(212) 692-9400
fax (212) 692-9221
search_specialist@dswolf.com
www.dswolf.com
David A. Wolf, President

M. Wood Company

(SPECIALIZE IN TECHNOLOGY)
135 South LaSalle Street, Suite 1935
Chicago, IL 60603
(312) 368-0633
fax (312) 368-5052
resume@mwoodco.com
www.mwoodco.com
Milton M. Wood, President

Work & Partners LLC

(SPECIALIZE IN MANAGEMENT CONSULTING, TECHNOLOGY AND CORPORATIONS)
701 Westchester Avenue, Suite 212W
White Plains, NY 10604
(914) 328-2100
fax (914) 328-1693
results@workandpartners.com
www.workandpartners.com
Alan J. Work, President

Dick Wray Executive Search

(SPECIALIZE IN RESTAURANTS, FOOD SERVICE & HOSPITALITY)
3123 Hannan Lane
Soquel, CA 95073
(888) 875-9993
fax (831) 515-5603
dick.wray@dickwray.com
dickwray.com
Dick Wray, Chairman & CEO
Rebecca Patt, Vice President
Also:
Palm Harbor, FL (888) 875-9993
Robert Gershberg, Managing Partner

Janet Wright & Associates, Inc.

(SPECIALIZE IN PUBLIC & NON-PROFIT)
174 Bedford Road, Suite 200
Toronto, ON M5R 2K9
(416) 923-3008
fax (416) 923-8311
admin@jwasearch.com
www.jwasearch.com
Janet Wright, President

WTW Associates, Inc./IIC Partners*

(SPECIALIZE IN ENTERTAINMENT, MEDIA, INTERNET, LAW SERVICES, FINANCIAL SERVICES)
675 Third Avenue, Suite 2808
New York, NY 10017
(212) 972-6990
fax (212) 297-0546
wtwassoc@wtwassociates.com
www.wtwassociates.com
Warren T. Wasp, President

Wyatt & Jaffe

4999 France Avenue South, Suite 260
Minneapolis, MN 55410-1759
(612) 285-2858
fax (612) 285-2786
resumes@wyattjaffe.com
www.wyattjaffe.com
Mark Jaffe, President

Yaekle & Company

Post Office Box 615
Granville, OH 43023
(740) 587-7366
fax (740) 587-1973
info@yaekleco.com
www.yaekleco.com
Gary W. Yaekle, Partner

Zay & Company International/IIC Partners

Atlanta Financial Center
3353 Peachtree Road NE, Suite M30
Post Office Box 52599
Atlanta, GA 30355
(404) 876-9986
fax (404) 876-0277
www.zaycointl.com
Thomas C. Zay, Chairman & President

Egon Zehnder International Inc.

350 Park Avenue, 8th Floor
New York, NY 10022
(212) 519-6000
fax (212) 519-6060
newyork@egonzehnder.com
www.zehnder.com
Alan D. Hilliker, Office Leader
Also:
Atlanta, GA (404) 836-2800
Sean McClenaghan, Office Leader
Boston, MA (617) 535-3500
James D. Satterthwaite, Office Leader
Calgary, AB (403) 718-3700
Brian E. Harry, Office Leader
Chicago, IL (312) 260-8800
Karl W. Alleman, Managing Partner
Coral Gables, FL (305) 569-1000
German Herrera, Office Leader
Dallas, TX (972) 728-5910
Christopher J. Pfeiffer, Office Leader
Houston, TX (713) 331-6700
Trent S. Aulbaugh, Office Leader
Los Angeles, CA (213) 337-1500
Todd Hutchings, Office Leader
Montreal, QC (514) 876-4249
Marc Normandin, Managing Director-Canada
Palo Alto, CA (650) 847-3000
Todd Hutchings, Office Leader
San Francisco, CA (415) 963-8500
Joanne W. Yun, Office Leader
Toronto, ON (416) 364-0222
Jan J. Stewart, Managing Partner

Zingaro & Company

(SPECIALIZE IN HEALTH CARE)
6601 Carrington Drive
Austin, TX 78749
(512) 327-7277
fax (512) 327-1774
search@zingaro.com
www.zingaro.com
Ronald J. Zingaro, President

INDEX

About the Author, John Lucht and This Book, *Rites of Passage at $100,000 to $1 Million+*

John Lucht is one of America's top executive recruiters. Since 1971, he has brought senior executives into major corporations in the U.S. and overseas...as head of The John Lucht Consultancy Inc. in New York City since 1977, and for six prior years at Heidrick and Struggles, NY, where he was an officer. Earlier he was in general management or marketing with Bristol-Myers, J. Walter Thompson, and Tetley Tea. His B.S. and J.D. are from the University of Wisconsin.

Rites of Passage was critically acclaimed and immediately achieved its continuing status as the #1 bestselling book of job-changing and lifetime career advice for executives when it first appeared three decades ago. Since then it has been continually updated by John Lucht, who vows to "keep ***Rites*** the most frank, fresh and authoritative source of insider's career information for executives." This new 2014 edition is the latest and most comprehensive in the series.

Revised, expanded and updated with each new printing, ***Rites*** becomes more widely read and influential year after year.* With over 300,000 copies in print, it has already helped hundreds of thousands of executives find new and more rewarding and satisfying jobs or, alternatively, to move up in their current company.

Focusing further on executive upward mobility, John Lucht has also written ***Insights for the Journey...Navigating to Thrive, Enjoy, and Prosper in Senior Management*** for those who want to achieve the full advancement and rewards they deserve in their current companies.

Recently, ***Rites*** has become widely used among new segments of readers. It's the text for career courses in many business and professional schools and undergraduate programs as well, and has become a favorite handbook to help officers retiring from the armed forces find high-level civilian jobs.

John Lucht has also written the **EXECUTIVE JOB-CHANGING WORKBOOK**, which further helps users implement his ***Rites of Passage*** principles. The **WORKBOOK** combined with ***Rites*** constitutes what John Drake, founder of D B M Inc., has called "the strongest, most comprehensive total program available in print."

**Rites* has been in scores of publications (several times in many), including: Business Week, Wall Street Journal, Forbes, USA Today, New York Times, Working Woman, Self, Boston Globe, Denver Post, Chicago Tribune, The Philadelphia Inquirer, Los Angeles Times, Chief Executive, Seattle Times, American Way, Financial World, Portland Telegram, Dallas Morning News, Omaha World-Herald, New York Daily News, Savvy, Salt Lake City Tribune, American Banker, Women's Wear Daily, Psychology Today, Minneapolis Star & Tribune, Industry Week, Newsday, Success, Investor's Business Daily, St. Louis Post-Dispatch, Training, Publishers Weekly, San Antonio Express News, National Business Employment Weekly, Harper's Bazaar, Chicago Sun-Times, Board Room Reports, Newark Star-Ledger, Cleveland Plain Dealer, Baltimore Sun, El Paso Times, Wichita Eagle, Across the Board (The Conference Board), Men's Health, Personnel Executive, Training & Development Journal, Atlanta Journal/Constitution, Indianapolis Star & News, Executive Female, Manchester Union Leader, Personnel Administrator, Worcester Telegram, Akron Beacon Journal, Brandweek, Human Resource Executive, Madison State Journal & Capitol Times, Albany Times Union, Career News (Harvard Business School Alumni Career Services), Corpus Christi Caller-Times, The Bricker Bulletin, Canadian Industrial Relations & Personnel Development, World Executive's Digest (serving Asia from Singapore), China Technology Market News (mainland China), and many more.

WRITING SAMPLES

Writing samples in this book show you representative types of writing about literature—from initial notes to a revised, final research paper. Reading these samples along with their commentary should help you understand what is expected when your instructor asks you to write about the literature you are reading.

CRITICAL APPROACHES

This short guide to important critical approaches briefly explains the tools that professional critics and theorists employ when they write about literature.

THE NORTON INTRODUCTION TO LITERATURE

SHORTER TWELFTH EDITION

KELLY J. MAYS

UNIVERSITY OF NEVADA, LAS VEGAS

W. W. NORTON & COMPANY New York, London

W. W. Norton & Company has been independent since its founding in 1923, when William Warder Norton and Mary D. Herter Norton first published lectures delivered at the People's Institute, the adult education division of New York City's Cooper Union. The firm soon expanded its program beyond the Institute, publishing books by celebrated academics from America and abroad. By mid-century, the two major pillars of Norton's publishing program—trade books and college texts—were firmly established. In the 1950s, the Norton family transferred control of the company to its employees, and today—with a staff of four hundred and a comparable number of trade, college, and professional titles published each year—W. W. Norton & Company stands as the largest and oldest publishing house owned wholly by its employees.

Editor: Spencer Richardson-Jones
Project Editor: Christine D'Antonio
Associate Editor: Emily Stuart
Editorial Assistant: Rachel Taylor
Manuscript Editor: Jude Grant
Managing Editor, College: Marian Johnson
Managing Editor, College Digital Media: Kim Yi
Production Manager: Ashley Horna
Media Editor: Carly Fraser Doria
Assistant Media Editor: Cara Folkman
Media Editorial Assistant: Ava Bramson
Marketing Manager, Literature: Kimberly Bowers
Design Director: Rubina Yeh
Book Designer: Jo Anne Metsch
Photo Editor: Evan Luberger
Photo Research: Julie Tesser
Permissions Manager: Megan Schindel
Permissions Clearer: Margaret Gorenstein
Composition: Westchester Book Group
Manufacturing: LSC Communications

Printed in the United States of America

The Library of Congress has cataloged an earlier edition as follows:
Library of Congress Cataloging-in-Publication Data
The Norton Introduction to Literature / [edited by] Kelly J. Mays,
University Of Nevada, Las Vegas. — Shorter Twelfth Edition.
pages cm
Includes bibliographical references and index.
ISBN 978-0-393-93892-0 (pbk. : alk. paper) 1. Literature—Collections.
I. Mays, Kelly J., editor.
PN6014.N67 2016
808.8—dc23

2015034604

This edition: **ISBN 978-0-393-62357-4**

W. W. Norton & Company, Inc., 500 Fifth Avenue, New York, NY 10110

www.wwnorton.com

W. W. Norton & Company Ltd., 15 Carlisle Street, London W1D 3BS

6 7 8 9 0

Contents

Fiction

Drama